PEARSON CUSTOM BUSINESS RESOURCES

Dr. Joseph Rottman
Information Systems, Concepts and
Applications: Using Applications to
Create Business Solutions

PEARSON

ISBN 10: 1-269-28836-9
ISBN 13: 978-1-269-28836-1

PEARSON

Table of Contents

Chapter 2

Global E-business and Collaboration

From Chapter 2 of *Management Information Systems: Managing the Digital Firm*, 12/e. Kenneth C. Laudon, Jane P. Laudon. Copyright © 2012 by Pearson Education. Published by Prentice Hall.

Global E-business and Collaboration

Interactive Sessions:

Domino's Sizzles with Pizza Tracker

Virtual Meetings: Smart Management

AMERICA'S CUP 2010: USA WINS WITH INFORMATION TECHNOLOGY

The BMW Oracle Racing organization won the 33rd America's Cup yacht race in Valencia, Spain on February 18, 2010. The BMW Oracle boat USA, backed by software billionaire Larry Ellison, beat Alinghi, the Swiss boat backed by Ernesto Bertarelli, a Swiss billionaire. It's always a spectacle when two billionaires go head to head for the prize. Lots and lots of money, world-class talent, and in this case, the best technologies and information systems in the world. In the end, the 114-foot USA won handily the first two races of a best-of-three series, reaching speeds over 35 miles an hour, three times faster than the wind. As far as experts can figure, USA is the fastest sailboat in history.

So what kind of technology can you get for a $300 million sailboat? Start with the physical structure: a three hulled trimaran, 114 feet long, fashioned from carbon fiber shaped into a form descended from Polynesian outrigger boats over a thousand years old. The hull is so light it only extends six inches into the water. Forget about a traditional mast (that's the pole that holds up the sails) and forget about sails too. Think about a 233-foot airplane wing also made from carbon fiber that sticks up from the boat deck 20 stories high. Instead of cloth sails, think about a stretchy aeronautical fabric over a carbon fiber frame that is hydraulically controlled to assume any shape you want, sort of like a stretchy garment hugs the body's bones. The result is a wing, not a sail, whose shape can be changed from pretty near flat to quite curved just like an aircraft wing.

Controlling this wickedly sleek sailboat requires a lightning-fast collection of massive amounts of data, powerful data management, rapid real-time data analysis, quick decision making, and immediate measurement of the results. In short, all the information technologies needed by a modern business firm. When you can perform all these tasks thousands of times in an hour, you can incrementally improve your performance and have an overwhelming advantage over less IT-savvy opponents on race day.

For USA, this meant using 250 sensors on the wing, hull, and rudder to gather real-time data on pressure, angles, loads, and strains to monitor the effectiveness of each adjustment. The sensors track 4,000 variables, 10 times a second, producing 90 million data points an hour.

Managing all these data is Oracle Database 11g data management software. The data are wirelessly transferred to a tender ship running Oracle 11g for near real-time analysis using a family of formulas (called velocity prediction formulas) geared to understanding what makes the boat go fast. Oracle's Application Express presentation graphics summarize the millions of data points and present the boat managers with charts that make sense of the information. The data are also sent to Oracle's Austin data center for more in- depth analysis. Using powerful data analysis tools, USA managers were able to find relationships they had never thought about before. Over several years of practice, from day one to the day before the race, the crew of USA could chart a steady improvement in performance.

All this meant "sailing" had changed, perhaps been trans-

Gilles Martin-Raget/BMW ORACLE Racing

formed by IT. Each crew member wore a small mobile handheld computer on his wrist to display data on the key performance variables customized for that person's responsibilities, such as the load balance on a specific rope or the current aerodynamic performance of the wing sail. Rather than stare at the sails or the sea, the crew had to be trained to sail like pilots looking at instruments. The helmsman turned into a pilot looking at data displayed on his sunglasses with an occasional glance at the deck crew, sea state, and competitors.

Professional and amateur sailors across the world wondered if the technology had transformed sailing into something else. The billionaire winner Larry Ellison sets the rules for the next race, and the blogs are speculating that he will seek a return to simpler more traditional boats that need to be sailed, not flown like airplanes. Yet few really believe Ellison will give up a key IT advantage in data collection, analysis, presentation, and performance-based decision making.

Sources: Jeff Erickson, "Sailing Home with the Prize," *Oracle Magazine*, May/June 2010; www.america's cup.com, accessed May 21,2010; and www.bmworacleracing.com, accessed May 21, 2010.

The experience of BMW Oracle's USA in the 2010 America's Cup competition illustrates how much organizations today, even those in traditional sports such as sailing, rely on information systems to improve their performance and remain competitive. It also shows how much information systems make a difference in an organization's ability to innovate, execute, and in the case of business firms, grow profits.

The chapter-opening diagram calls attention to important points raised by this case and this chapter. The America's Cup contenders were confronted with both a challenge and opportunity. Both were locked in the world's most competitive sailing race. They staffed their crews with the best sailors in the world. But sailing ability was not enough. There were opportunities for improving sailing performance by changing and refining the design of the competing vessels using information systems intensively for this purpose.

Because Oracle is one of the world's leading information technology providers, the company was a natural for using the most advanced information technology to continually improve USA's design and performance. But information technology alone would not have produced a winning boat. The Oracle team had to revise many of the processes and procedures used in sailing to take advantage of the technology, including training experienced sailors to work more like pilots with high-tech instruments and sensors. Oracle won the America's Cup because it had learned how to apply new technology to improve the processes of designing and sailing a competitive sailboat.

1 BUSINESS PROCESSES AND INFORMATION SYSTEMS

In order to operate, businesses must deal with many different pieces of information about suppliers, customers, employees, invoices and payments, and of course their products and services. They must organize work activities that use this information to operate efficiently and enhance the overall performance of the firm. Information systems make it possible for firms to manage all their information, make better decisions, and improve the execution of their business processes.

BUSINESS PROCESSES

Business processes refer to the manner in which work is organized, coordinated, and focused to produce a valuable product or service. Business processes are the collection of activities required to produce a product or service. These activities are supported by flows of material, information, and knowledge among the participants in business processes. Business processes also refer to the unique ways in which organizations coordinate work, information, and knowledge, and the ways in which management chooses to coordinate work.

To a large extent, the performance of a business firm depends on how well its business processes are designed and coordinated. A company's business processes can be a source of competitive strength if they enable the company to innovate or to execute better than its rivals. Business processes can also be liabilities if they are based on outdated ways of working that impede organizational responsiveness and efficiency. The chapter-opening case describing the processes used to sail the 2010 winning America's Cup boat clearly illustrates these points, as do many of the other cases in this text.

Every business can be seen as a collection of business processes, some of which are part of larger encompassing processes. For instance, designing a new sailboat model, manufacturing components, assembling the finished boat, and revising the design and construction are all part of the overall production process. Many business processes are tied to a specific functional area. For example, the sales and marketing function is responsible for identifying customers, and the human resources function is responsible for hiring employees. Table 1 describes some typical business processes for each of the functional areas of business.

TABLE 1   EXAMPLES OF FUNCTIONAL BUSINESS PROCESSES

FUNCTIONAL AREA	BUSINESS PROCESS
Manufacturing and production	Assembling the product
	Checking for quality
	Producing bills of materials
Sales and marketing	Identifying customers
	Making customers aware of the product
	Selling the product
Finance and accounting	Paying creditors
	Creating financial statements
	Managing cash accounts
Human resources	Hiring employees
	Evaluating employees' job performance
	Enrolling employees in benefits plans

Other business processes cross many different functional areas and require coordination across departments. For instance, consider the seemingly simple business process of fulfilling a customer order (see Figure 1). Initially, the sales department receives a sales order. The order passes first to accounting to ensure the customer can pay for the order either by a credit verification or request for immediate payment prior to shipping. Once the customer credit is established, the production department pulls the product from inventory or produces the product. Then the product is shipped (and this may require working with a logistics firm, such as UPS or FedEx). A bill or invoice is generated by the accounting department, and a notice is sent to the customer indicating that the product has shipped. The sales department is notified of the shipment and prepares to support the customer by answering calls or fulfilling warranty claims.

What at first appears to be a simple process, fulfilling an order, turns out to be a very complicated series of business processes that require the close coordination of major functional groups in a firm. Moreover, to efficiently perform all these steps in the order fulfillment process requires a great deal of information. The required information must flow rapidly both within the firm from one decision maker to another; with business partners, such as delivery firms; and with the customer. Computer-based information systems make this possible.

HOW INFORMATION TECHNOLOGY IMPROVES BUSINESS PROCESSES

Exactly how do information systems improve business processes? Information systems automate many steps in business processes that were formerly performed manually, such as checking a client's credit, or generating an invoice and shipping order. But today, information technology can do much more. New technology can actually change the flow of information, making it possible for many more people to access and share information, replacing sequential steps

FIGURE 1   THE ORDER FULFILLMENT PROCESS

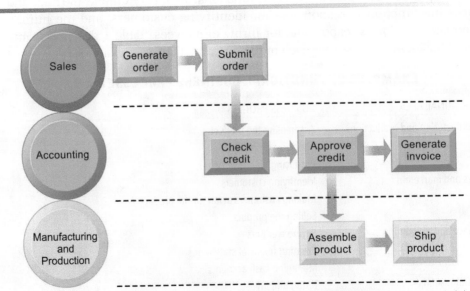

Fulfilling a customer order involves a complex set of steps that requires the close coordination of the sales, accounting, and manufacturing functions.

with tasks that can be performed simultaneously, and eliminating delays in decision making. New information technology frequently changes the way a business works and supports entirely new business models. Downloading a Kindle e-book from Amazon, buying a computer online at Best Buy, and downloading a music track from iTunes are entirely new business processes based on new business models that would be inconceivable without today's information technology.

That's why it's so important to pay close attention to business processes, both in your information systems course and in your future career. By analyzing business processes, you can achieve a very clear understanding of how a business actually works. Moreover, by conducting a business process analysis, you will also begin to understand how to change the business by improving its processes to make it more efficient or effective. We examine business processes with a view to understanding how they might be improved by using information technology to achieve greater efficiency, innovation, and customer service.

2   TYPES OF INFORMATION SYSTEMS

Now that you understand business processes, it is time to look more closely at how information systems support the business processes of a firm. Because there are different interests, specialties, and levels in an organization, there are different kinds of systems. No single system can provide all the information an organization needs.

A typical business organization has systems supporting processes for each of the major business functions—systems for sales and marketing, manufacturing and production, finance and accounting, and human resources. You can find examples of systems for each of these business functions in the Learning Tracks for this chapter. Functional systems that operate independently of each other are becoming a thing of the past because they cannot easily share information to support cross-functional business processes. Many have been replaced with large-scale cross-functional systems that integrate the activities of related business processes and organizational units. We describe these integrated cross-functional applications later in this section.

A typical firm also has different systems supporting the decision-making needs of each of the main management groups. Operational management, middle management, and senior management each use systems to support the decisions they must make to run the company. Let's look at these systems and the types of decisions they support.

SYSTEMS FOR DIFFERENT MANAGEMENT GROUPS

A business firm has systems to support different groups or levels of management. These systems include transaction processing systems, management information systems, decision-support systems, and systems for business intelligence.

Transaction Processing Systems

Operational managers need systems that keep track of the elementary activities and transactions of the organization, such as sales, receipts, cash deposits, payroll, credit decisions, and the flow of materials in a factory. **Transaction**

processing systems (TPS) provide this kind of information. A transaction processing system is a computerized system that performs and records the daily routine transactions necessary to conduct business, such as sales order entry, hotel reservations, payroll, employee record keeping, and shipping.

The principal purpose of systems at this level is to answer routine questions and to track the flow of transactions through the organization. How many parts are in inventory? What happened to Mr. Smith's payment? To answer these kinds of questions, information generally must be easily available, current, and accurate.

At the operational level, tasks, resources, and goals are predefined and highly structured. The decision to grant credit to a customer, for instance, is made by a lower-level supervisor according to predefined criteria. All that must be determined is whether the customer meets the criteria.

Figure 2 illustrates a TPS for payroll processing. A payroll system keeps track of money paid to employees. An employee time sheet with the employee's name, social security number, and number of hours worked per week represents a single transaction for this system. Once this transaction is input into the system, it updates the system's master file (or database) that permanently maintains employee information for the organization. The data in the system are combined in different ways to create reports of interest to management and government agencies and to send paychecks to employees.

Managers need TPS to monitor the status of internal operations and the firm's relations with the external environment. TPS are also major producers of information for the other systems and business functions. For example, the payroll system illustrated in Figure 2, along with other accounting TPS,

FIGURE 2   A PAYROLL TPS

A TPS for payroll processing captures employee payment transaction data (such as a time card). System outputs include online and hard-copy reports for management and employee paychecks.

supplies data to the company's general ledger system, which is responsible for maintaining records of the firm's income and expenses and for producing reports such as income statements and balance sheets. It also supplies employee payment history data for insurance, pension, and other benefits calculations to the firm's human resources function and employee payment data to government agencies such as the U.S. Internal Revenue Service and Social Security Administration.

Transaction processing systems are often so central to a business that TPS failure for a few hours can lead to a firm's demise and perhaps that of other firms linked to it. Imagine what would happen to UPS if its package tracking system were not working! What would the airlines do without their computerized reservation systems?

Business Intelligence Systems for Decision Support

Middle management needs systems to help with monitoring, controlling, decision-making, and administrative activities. The principal question addressed by such systems is this: Are things working well?

We define management information systems as the study of information systems in business and management. The term **management information systems (MIS)** also designates a specific category of information systems serving middle management. MIS provide middle managers with reports on the organization's current performance. This information is used to monitor and control the business and predict future performance.

MIS summarize and report on the company's basic operations using data supplied by transaction processing systems. The basic transaction data from TPS are compressed and usually presented in reports that are produced on a regular schedule. Today, many of these reports are delivered online. Figure 3 shows how a typical MIS transforms transaction-level data from order process-

FIGURE 3   HOW MANAGEMENT INFORMATION SYSTEMS OBTAIN THEIR DATA FROM THE ORGANIZATION'S TPS

In the system illustrated by this diagram, three TPS supply summarized transaction data to the MIS reporting system at the end of the time period. Managers gain access to the organizational data through the MIS, which provides them with the appropriate reports.

ing, production, and accounting into MIS files that are used to provide managers with reports. Figure 4 shows a sample report from this system.

MIS serve managers primarily interested in weekly, monthly, and yearly results. These systems typically provide answers to routine questions that have been specified in advance and have a predefined procedure for answering them. For instance, MIS reports might list the total pounds of lettuce used this quarter by a fast-food chain or, as illustrated in Figure 4, compare total annual sales figures for specific products to planned targets. These systems generally are not flexible and have little analytical capability. Most MIS use simple routines, such as summaries and comparisons, as opposed to sophisticated mathematical models or statistical techniques.

In contrast, **decision-support systems (DSS)** support more non-routine decision making. They focus on problems that are unique and rapidly changing, for which the procedure for arriving at a solution may not be fully predefined in advance. They try to answer questions such as these: What would be the impact on production schedules if we were to double sales in the month of December? What would happen to our return on investment if a factory schedule were delayed for six months?

Although DSS use internal information from TPS and MIS, they often bring in information from external sources, such as current stock prices or product prices of competitors. These systems use a variety of models to analyze the data and are designed so that users can work with them directly.

An interesting, small, but powerful, DSS is the voyage-estimating system of a subsidiary of a large American metals company that exists primarily to carry bulk cargoes of coal, oil, ores, and finished products for its parent company. The firm owns some vessels, charters others, and bids for shipping contracts in the open market to carry general cargo. A voyage-estimating system calculates financial and technical voyage details. Financial calculations include ship/time costs (fuel, labor, capital), freight rates for various types of cargo, and port expenses. Technical details include a myriad of factors, such as ship cargo capacity, speed, port distances, fuel and water consumption, and loading patterns (location of cargo for different ports).

FIGURE 4   **SAMPLE MIS REPORT**

Consolidated Consumer Products Corporation Sales by Product and Sales Region: 2011

PRODUCT CODE	PRODUCT DESCRIPTION	SALES REGION	ACTUAL SALES	PLANNED	ACTUAL versus PLANNED
4469	Carpet Cleaner	Northeast	4,066,700	4,800,000	0.85
		South	3,778,112	3,750,000	1.01
		Midwest	4,867,001	4,600,000	1.06
		West	4,003,440	4,400,000	0.91
	TOTAL		16,715,253	17,550,000	0.95
5674	Room Freshener	Northeast	3,676,700	3,900,000	0.94
		South	5,608,112	4,700,000	1.19
		Midwest	4,711,001	4,200,000	1.12
		West	4,563,440	4,900,000	0.93
	TOTAL		18,559,253	17,700,000	1.05

This report, showing summarized annual sales data, was produced by the MIS in Figure 3.

The system can answer questions such as the following: Given a customer delivery schedule and an offered freight rate, which vessel should be assigned at what rate to maximize profits? What is the optimal speed at which a particular vessel can maximize its profit and still meet its delivery schedule? What is the optimal loading pattern for a ship bound for the U.S. West Coast from Malaysia? Figure 5 illustrates the DSS built for this company. The system operates on a desktop personal computer, providing a system of menus that makes it easy for users to enter data or obtain information.

The voyage-estimating DSS we have just described draws heavily on models. Other systems supporting non-routine decision making are more data-driven, focusing instead on extracting useful information from large quantities of data. For example, Intrawest—the largest ski operator in North America—collects and stores large amounts of customer data from its Web site, call center, lodging reservations, ski schools, and ski equipment rental stores. It uses special software to analyze these data to determine the value, revenue potential, and loyalty of each customer so managers can make better decisions on how to target their marketing programs. The system segments customers into seven categories based on needs, attitudes, and behaviors, ranging from "passionate experts" to "value-minded family vacationers." The company then e-mails video clips that would appeal to each segment to encourage more visits to its resorts.

All of the management systems we have just described are systems for business intelligence. **Business intelligence** is a contemporary term for data and software tools for organizing, analyzing, and providing access to data to help managers and other enterprise users make more informed decisions.

Business intelligence applications are not limited to middle managers, and can be found at all levels of the organization, including systems for senior management. Senior managers need systems that address strategic issues and long-term trends, both in the firm and in the external environment. They are

FIGURE 5　VOYAGE-ESTIMATING DECISION-SUPPORT SYSTEM

This DSS operates on a powerful PC. It is used daily by managers who must develop bids on shipping contracts.

concerned with questions such as these: What will employment levels be in five years? What are the long-term industry cost trends, and where does our firm fit in? What products should we be making in five years? What new acquisitions would protect us from cyclical business swings?

Executive support systems (ESS) help senior management make these decisions. They address non-routine decisions requiring judgment, evaluation, and insight because there is no agreed-on procedure for arriving at a solution. ESS present graphs and data from many sources through an interface that is easy for senior managers to use. Often the information is delivered to senior executives through a **portal**, which uses a Web interface to present integrated personalized business content.

ESS are designed to incorporate data about external events, such as new tax laws or competitors, but they also draw summarized information from internal MIS and DSS. They filter, compress, and track critical data, displaying the data of greatest importance to senior managers. Increasingly, such systems include business intelligence analytics for analyzing trends, forecasting, and "drilling down" to data at greater levels of detail.

For example, the CEO of Leiner Health Products, one of the largest manufacturers of private-label vitamins and supplements in the United States, has an ESS that provides on his desktop a minute-to-minute view of the firm's financial performance as measured by working capital, accounts receivable, accounts payable, cash flow, and inventory. The information is presented in the form of a **digital dashboard**, which displays on a single screen graphs and charts of key performance indicators for managing a company. Digital dashboards are becoming an increasingly popular tool for management decision makers.

Dundas Data Visualization's digital dashboard delivers comprehensive and accurate information for decision making. The graphical overview of key performance indicators helps managers quickly spot areas that need attention.

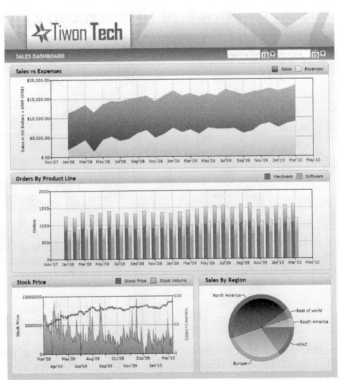

Dundas Data Visualization, Inc.

The Interactive Session on Organizations describes real-world examples of several types of systems we have just described that are used by a successful fast-food chain. Note the types of systems illustrated in this case and the role they play in improving business performance and competitiveness.

SYSTEMS FOR LINKING THE ENTERPRISE

Reviewing all the different types of systems we have just described, you might wonder how a business can manage all the information in these different systems. You might also wonder how costly it is to maintain so many different systems. And you might wonder how all these different systems can share information and how managers and employees are able to coordinate their work. In fact, these are all important questions for businesses today.

Enterprise Applications

Getting all the different kinds of systems in a company to work together has proven a major challenge. Typically, corporations are put together both through normal "organic" growth and through acquisition of smaller firms. Over a period of time, corporations end up with a collection of systems, most of them older, and face the challenge of getting them all to "talk" with one another and work together as one corporate system. There are several solutions to this problem.

One solution is to implement **enterprise applications**, which are systems that span functional areas, focus on executing business processes across the business firm, and include all levels of management. Enterprise applications help businesses become more flexible and productive by coordinating their business processes more closely and integrating groups of processes so they focus on efficient management of resources and customer service.

There are four major enterprise applications: enterprise systems, supply chain management systems, customer relationship management systems, and knowledge management systems. Each of these enterprise applications integrates a related set of functions and business processes to enhance the performance of the organization as a whole. Figure 6 shows that the architecture for these enterprise applications encompasses processes spanning the entire organization and, in some cases, extending beyond the organization to customers, suppliers, and other key business partners.

Enterprise Systems Firms use **enterprise systems**, also known as enterprise resource planning (ERP) systems, to integrate business processes in manufacturing and production, finance and accounting, sales and marketing, and human resources into a single software system. Information that was previously fragmented in many different systems is stored in a single comprehensive data repository where it can be used by many different parts of the business.

For example, when a customer places an order, the order data flow automatically to other parts of the company that are affected by them. The order transaction triggers the warehouse to pick the ordered products and schedule shipment. The warehouse informs the factory to replenish whatever has been depleted. The accounting department is notified to send the customer an invoice. Customer service representatives track the progress of the order through every step to inform customers about the status of their orders. Managers are able to use firm-wide information to make more precise and timely decisions about daily operations and longer-term planning.

INTERACTIVE SESSION: ORGANIZATIONS

DOMINO'S SIZZLES WITH PIZZA TRACKER

When it comes to pizza, everyone has an opinion. Some of us think that our current pizza is just fine the way it is. Others have a favorite pizza joint that makes it like no one else. And many pizza lovers in America agreed up until recently that Domino's home-delivered pizza was among the worst. The home-delivery market for pizza chains in the United States is approximately $15 billion per year. Domino's, which owns the largest home-delivery market share of any U.S. pizza chain, is finding ways to innovate by overhauling its in-store transaction processing systems and by providing other useful services to customers, such as its Pizza Tracker. And more important, Domino's is trying very hard to overcome its reputation for poor quality by radically improving ingredients and freshness. Critics believe the company significantly improved the quality of its pizza and customer service in 2010.

Domino's was founded in 1960 by Tom Monaghan and his brother James when they purchased a single pizza store in Ypsilanti, Michigan. The company slowly began to grow, and by 1978, Domino's had 200 stores. Today, the company is headquartered in Ann Arbor, Michigan, and operates almost 9,000 stores located in all 50 U.S. states and across the world in 60 international markets. In 2009, Domino's had $1.5 billion in sales and earned $80 million in profit.

Domino's is part of a heated battle among prominent pizza chains, including Pizza Hut, Papa John's, and Little Caesar. Pizza Hut is the only chain larger than Domino's in the U.S., but each of the four has significant market share. Domino's also competes with local pizza stores throughout the U.S. To gain a competitive advantage Domino's needs to deliver excellent customer service, and most importantly, good pizza. But it also benefits from highly effective information systems.

Domino's proprietary point-of-sale system, Pulse, is an important asset in maintaining consistent and efficient management functions in each of its restaurants. A point-of-sale system captures purchase and payment data at a physical location where goods or services are bought and sold using computers, automated cash registers, scanners, or other digital devices.

In 2003, Domino's implemented Pulse in a large portion of its stores, and those stores reported improved customer service, reduced mistakes, and shorter training times. Since then, Pulse has become a staple of all Domino's franchises. Some of the functions Pulse performs at Domino's franchises are taking and customizing orders using a touch-screen interface, maintaining sales figures, and compiling customer information. Domino's prefers not to disclose the specific dollar amounts that it has saved from Pulse, but it's clear from industry analysts that the technology is working to cut costs and increase customer satisfaction.

More recently, Domino's released a new hardware and software platform called Pulse Evolution, which is now in use in a majority of Domino's more than 5,000 U.S. branches. Pulse Evolution improves on the older technology in several ways. First, the older software used a 'thick-client' model, which required all machines using the software to be fully equipped personal computers running Windows. Pulse Evolution, on the other hand, uses 'thin-client' architecture in which networked workstations with little independent processing power collect data and send them over the Internet to powerful Lenovo PCs for processing. These workstations lack hard drives, fans, and other moving parts, making them less expensive and easier to maintain. Also, Pulse Evolution is easier to update and more secure, since there's only one machine in the store which needs to be updated.

Along with Pulse Evolution, Domino's rolled out its state-of-the-art online ordering system, which includes Pizza Tracker. The system allows customers to watch a simulated photographic version of their pizza as they customize its size, sauces, and toppings. The image changes with each change a customer makes. Then, once customers place an order, they are able to view its progress online with Pizza Tracker. Pizza Tracker displays a horizontal bar that tracks an order's progress graphically. As a Domino's store completes each step of the order fulfillment process, a section of the bar becomes red. Even customers that place their orders via telephone can monitor their progress on the Web using Pizza Tracker at stores using Pulse Evolution. In 2010, Domino's introduced an online polling system to continuously upload information from local stores.

As with most instances of organizational change of this magnitude, Domino's experienced some resistance. Domino's originally wanted its franchises to select Pulse to comply with its requirements for data security, but some franchises have resisted switching to Pulse and sought alternative systems. After Domino's tried to compel those franchises to use Pulse, the U.S. District Court for Minnesota sided with franchisees who claimed that Domino's could not force them to use this system. Now, Domino's continues to make improvements to Pulse in an effort to make it overwhelmingly appealing to all franchisees.

Pizza Hut and Papa John's also have online ordering capability, but lack the Pizza Tracker and the simulated pizza features that Domino's has successfully implemented. Today, online orders account for almost 20 percent of all of Domino's orders, which is up from less than 15 percent in 2008. But the battle

to sell pizza with technology rages on. Pizza Hut customers can now use their iPhones to place orders, and Papa John's customers can place orders by texting. With many billions of dollars at stake, all the large national pizza chains will be developing innovative new ways of ordering pizza and participating in its creation.

Sources: PRN Newswire, "Servant Systems Releases Domino's Store Polling Software," PRN Newswire, April 14, 2010; Julie Jargon, "Domino's IT Staff Delivers Slick Site, Ordering System," *The Wall Street Journal*, November 24, 2009; www.dominosbiz.com, accessed May 17, 2010; Paul McDougall, "Interop: Domino's Eyes Microsoft Cloud," *Information Week*, April 26, 2010; "Domino's Builds New Foundation Under Proprietary Store Tech," *Nation's Restaurant News*, February 25, 2009; "and "Inside Domino's 'Pizza Tracker.' What It Does, Why, and How," *Nation's Restaurant News*, February 27, 2008.

CASE STUDY QUESTIONS

1. What kinds of systems are described in this case? Identify and describe the business processes each supports. Describe the inputs, processes, and outputs of these systems.

2. How do these systems help Domino's improve its business performance?

3. How did the online pizza ordering system improve the process of ordering a Domino's pizza?

4. How effective are these systems in giving Domino's a competitive edge? Explain your answer.

MIS IN ACTION

Visit Domino's Web site and examine the order placement and Pizza Tracker features. Then answer the following questions:

1. What steps does Pizza Tracker display for the user? How does the Pizza Tracker improve the customer experience?

2. Would the Pizza Tracker service influence you to order pizza from Domino's instead of a competing chain? Why or why not?

3. What improvements would you make to the order placement feature?

Supply Chain Management Systems Firms use **supply chain management (SCM) systems** to help manage relationships with their suppliers. These systems help suppliers, purchasing firms, distributors, and logistics companies share information about orders, production, inventory levels, and delivery of products and services so that they can source, produce, and deliver goods and services efficiently. The ultimate objective is to get the right amount of their products from their source to their point of consumption in the least amount of time and at the lowest cost. These systems increase firm profitability by lowering the costs of moving and making products and by enabling managers to make better decisions about how to organize and schedule sourcing, production, and distribution.

Supply chain management systems are one type of **interorganizational system** because they automate the flow of information across organizational boundaries. You will find examples of other types of interorganizational information systems throughout this text because such systems make it possible for firms to link electronically to customers and to outsource their work to other companies.

Customer Relationship Management Systems Firms use **customer relationship management (CRM) systems** to help manage their relationships with their customers. CRM systems provide information to coordinate all of the business processes that deal with customers in sales, marketing, and service to optimize revenue, customer satisfaction, and customer retention. This information helps firms identify, attract, and retain the most profitable customers; provide better service to existing customers; and increase sales.

FIGURE 6 **ENTERPRISE APPLICATION ARCHITECTURE**

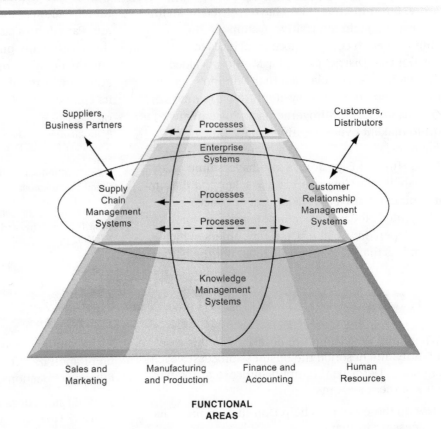

Suppliers,
Business Partners

Customers,
Distributors

Processes

Enterprise
Systems

Supply
Chain
Management
Systems

Processes

Customer
Relationship
Management
Systems

Processes

Knowledge
Management
Systems

Sales and
Marketing

Manufacturing
and Production

Finance and
Accounting

Human
Resources

**FUNCTIONAL
AREAS**

Enterprise applications automate processes that span multiple business functions and organizational levels and may extend outside the organization.

Knowledge Management Systems Some firms perform better than others because they have better knowledge about how to create, produce, and deliver products and services. This firm knowledge is difficult to imitate, unique, and can be leveraged into long-term strategic benefits. **Knowledge management systems (KMS)** enable organizations to better manage processes for capturing and applying knowledge and expertise. These systems collect all relevant knowledge and experience in the firm, and make it available wherever and whenever it is needed to improve business processes and management decisions. They also link the firm to external sources of knowledge.

Intranets and Extranets

Enterprise applications create deep-seated changes in the way the firm conducts its business, offering many opportunities to integrate important business data into a single system. They are often costly and difficult to implement. Intranets and extranets deserve mention here as alternative tools for increasing integration and expediting the flow of information within the firm, and with customers ad suppliers.

Intranets are simply internal company Web sites that are accessible only by employees. The term "intranet" refers to the fact that it is an internal network, in contrast to the Internet, which is a public network linking organizations and other external networks. Intranets use the same technologies and techniques as the larger Internet, and they often are simply a private access area in a larger company Web site. Likewise with extranets. Extranets are company Web sites that are accessible to authorized vendors and suppliers, and often used to coordinate the movement of supplies to the firm's production apparatus.

For example, Six Flags, which operates 19 theme parks throughout North America, maintains an intranet for its 2,500 full-time employees that provides company-related news and information on each park's day-to-day operations, including weather forecasts, performance schedules, and details about groups and celebrities visiting the parks. The company also uses an extranet to broadcast information about schedule changes and park events to its 30,000 seasonal employees.

E-BUSINESS, E-COMMERCE, AND E-GOVERNMENT

The systems and technologies we have just described are transforming firms' relationships with customers, employees, suppliers, and logistic partners into digital relationships using networks and the Internet. So much business is now enabled by or based upon digital networks that we use the terms "electronic business" and "electronic commerce" frequently.

Electronic business, or **e-business**, refers to the use of digital technology and the Internet to execute the major business processes in the enterprise. E-business includes activities for the internal management of the firm and for coordination with suppliers and other business partners. It also includes **electronic commerce**, or **e-commerce**.

E-commerce is the part of e-business that deals with the buying and selling of goods and services over the Internet. It also encompasses activities supporting those market transactions, such as advertising, marketing, customer support, security, delivery, and payment.

The technologies associated with e-business have also brought about similar changes in the public sector. Governments on all levels are using Internet technology to deliver information and services to citizens, employees, and businesses with which they work. **E-government** refers to the application of the Internet and networking technologies to digitally enable government and public sector agencies' relationships with citizens, businesses, and other arms of government.

In addition to improving delivery of government services, e-government makes government operations more efficient and also empowers citizens by giving them easier access to information and the ability to network electronically with other citizens. For example, citizens in some states can renew their driver's licenses or apply for unemployment benefits online, and the Internet has become a powerful tool for instantly mobilizing interest groups for political action and fund-raising.

3 SYSTEMS FOR COLLABORATION AND TEAMWORK

With all these systems and information, you might wonder how is it possible to make sense out of them? How do people working in firms pull it all together, work towards common goals, and coordinate plans and actions? Information systems can't make decisions, hire or fire people, sign contracts, agree on deals, or adjust the price of goods to the marketplace. In addition to the types of systems we have just described, businesses need special systems to support collaboration and teamwork.

WHAT IS COLLABORATION?

Collaboration is working with others to achieve shared and explicit goals. Collaboration focuses on task or mission accomplishment and usually takes place in a business, or other organization, and between businesses. You collaborate with a colleague in Tokyo having expertise on a topic about which you know nothing. You collaborate with many colleagues in publishing a company blog. If you're in a law firm, you collaborate with accountants in an accounting firm in servicing the needs of a client with tax problems.

Collaboration can be short-lived, lasting a few minutes, or longer term, depending on the nature of the task and the relationship among participants. Collaboration can be one-to-one or many-to-many.

Employees may collaborate in informal groups that are not a formal part of the business firm's organizational structure or they may be organized into formal teams. Teams are part of the organization's business structure for getting things done. **Teams** have a specific mission that someone in the business assigned to them. They have a job to complete. The members of the team need to collaborate on the accomplishment of specific tasks and collectively achieve the team mission. The team mission might be to "win the game," or "increase online sales by 10%," or "prevent insulating foam from falling off a space shuttle." Teams are often short-lived, depending on the problems they tackle and the length of time needed to find a solution and accomplish the mission.

Collaboration and teamwork are more important today than ever for a variety of reasons.

- *Changing nature of work.* The nature of work has changed from factory manufacturing and pre-computer office work where each stage in the production process occurred independently of one another, and was coordinated by supervisors. Work was organized into silos. Within a silo, work passed from one machine tool station to another, from one desktop to another, until the finished product was completed. Today, the kinds of jobs we have require much closer coordination and interaction among the parties involved in producing the service or product. A recent report from the consulting firm McKinsey and Company argued that 41 percent of the U.S. labor force is now composed of jobs where interaction (talking, e-mailing, presenting, and persuading) is the primary value-adding activity. Even in factories, workers today often work in production groups, or pods.

- *Growth of professional work.* "Interaction" jobs tend to be professional jobs in the service sector that require close coordination, and collaboration. Professional jobs require substantial education, and the sharing of information and opinions to get work done. Each actor on the job brings specialized expertise to the problem, and all the actors need to take one another into account in order to accomplish the job.

- *Changing organization of the firm.* For most of the industrial age, managers organized work in a hierarchical fashion. Orders came down the hierarchy, and responses moved back up the hierarchy. Today, work is organized into groups and teams, who are expected to develop their own methods for accomplishing the task. Senior managers observe and measure results, but are much less likely to issue detailed orders or operating procedures. In part this is because expertise has been pushed down in the organization, as have decision-making powers.

- *Changing scope of the firm.* The work of the firm has changed from a single location to multiple locations—offices or factories throughout a region, a nation, or even around the globe. For instance, Henry Ford developed the first mass-production automobile plant at a single Dearborn, Michigan factory. In 2010, Ford expected to produce about 3 million automobiles and employ over 200,000 employees at 90 plants and facilities worldwide. With this kind of global presence, the need for close coordination of design, production, marketing, distribution, and service obviously takes on new importance and scale. Large global companies need to have teams working on a global basis.

- *Emphasis on innovation.* Although we tend to attribute innovations in business and science to great individuals, these great individuals are most likely working with a team of brilliant colleagues, and all have been preceded by a long line of earlier innovators and innovations. Think of Bill Gates and Steve Jobs (founders of Microsoft and Apple), both of whom are highly regarded innovators, and both of whom built strong collaborative teams to nurture and support innovation in their firms. Their initial innovations derived from close collaboration with colleagues and partners. Innovation, in other words, is a group and social process, and most innovations derive from collaboration among individuals in a lab, a business, or government agencies. Strong collaborative practices and technologies are believed to increase the rate and quality of innovation.

- *Changing culture of work and business.* Most research on collaboration supports the notion that diverse teams produce better outputs, faster, than individuals working on their own. Popular notions of the crowd ("crowdsourcing," and the "wisdom of crowds") also provide cultural support for collaboration and teamwork.

BUSINESS BENEFITS OF COLLABORATION AND TEAMWORK

There are many articles and books that have been written about collaboration, some of them by business executives and consultants, and a great many by academic researchers in a variety of businesses. Nearly all of this research is anecdotal. Nevertheless, among both business and academic communities there is a general belief that the more a business firm is "collaborative," the more successful it will be, and that collaboration within and among firms is more essential than in the past.

A recent global survey of business and information systems managers found that investments in collaboration technology produced organizational improvements that returned over four times the amount of the investment, with the greatest benefits for sales, marketing, and research and development functions (Frost and White, 2009). Another study of the value of collaboration also found that the overall economic benefit of collaboration was significant: for every word seen by an employee in e-mails from others, $70 of additional revenue was generated (Aral, Brynjolfsson, and Van Alstyne, 2007).

Table 2 summarizes some of the benefits of collaboration identified by previous writers and scholars. Figure 7 graphically illustrates how collaboration is believed to impact business performance.

While there are many presumed benefits to collaboration, you really need a supportive business firm culture and the right business processes before you can achieve meaningful collaboration. You also need a healthy investment in collaborative technologies. We now examine these requirements.

TABLE 2 BUSINESS BENEFITS OF COLLABORATION

BENEFIT	RATIONALE
Productivity	People working together can complete a complex task faster than the same number of people working in isolation from one another. There will be fewer errors.
Quality	People working collaboratively can communicate errors, and correct actions faster, when they work together than if they work in isolation. Can lead to a reduction in buffers and time delay among production units.
Innovation	People working collaboratively in groups can come up with more innovative ideas for products, services, and administration than the same number working in isolation from one another.
Customer service	People working together in teams can solve customer complaints and issues faster and more effectively than if they were working in isolation from one another.
Financial performance (profitability, sales, and sales growth)	As a result of all of the above, collaborative firms have superior sales growth and financial performance.

FIGURE 7 REQUIREMENTS FOR COLLABORATION

Successful collaboration requires an appropriate organizational structure and culture, along with appropriate collaboration technology.

BUILDING A COLLABORATIVE CULTURE AND BUSINESS PROCESSES

Collaboration won't take place spontaneously in a business firm, especially if there is no supportive culture or business processes. Business firms, especially large firms, had in the past a reputation for being "command and control" organizations where the top leaders thought up all the really important matters, and then ordered lower-level employees to execute senior management plans. The job of middle management supposedly was to pass messages back and forth, up and down the hierarchy.

Command and control firms required lower-level employees to carry out orders without asking too many questions, with no responsibility to improve processes, and with no rewards for teamwork or team performance. If your workgroup needed help from another work group, that was something for the bosses to figure out. You never communicated horizontally, always vertically, so management could control the process. As long as employees showed up for work, and performed the job satisfactorily, that's all that was required. Together, the expectations of management and employees formed a culture, a set of assumptions about common goals and how people should behave. Many business firms still operate this way.

A collaborative business culture and business processes are very different. Senior managers are responsible for achieving results but rely on teams of employees to achieve and implement the results. Policies, products, designs, processes, and systems are much more dependent on teams at all levels of the organization to devise, to create, and to build products and services. Teams are rewarded for their performance, and individuals are rewarded for their performance in a team. The function of middle managers is to build the teams, coordinate their work, and monitor their performance. In a collaborative culture, senior management establishes collaboration and teamwork as vital to the organization, and it actually implements collaboration for the senior ranks of the business as well.

TOOLS AND TECHNOLOGIES FOR COLLABORATION AND TEAMWORK

A collaborative, team-oriented culture won't produce benefits if there are no information systems in place to enable collaboration. Currently there are hundreds of tools designed to deal with the fact that, in order to succeed in our jobs, we are all dependent on one another, our fellow employees, customers, suppliers, and managers. Table 3 lists the most important types of collaboration software tools. Some high-end tools like IBM Lotus Notes are expensive, but powerful enough for global firms. Others are available online for free (or with premium versions for a modest fee) and are suitable for small businesses. Let's look more closely at some of these tools.

TABLE 3   FIFTEEN CATEGORIES OF COLLABORATIVE SOFTWARE TOOLS

E-mail and instant messaging	White boarding
Collaborative writing	Web presenting
Collaborative reviewing/editing	Work scheduling
Event scheduling	Document sharing (including wikis)
File sharing	Mind mapping
Screen sharing	Large audience Webinars
Audio conferencing	Co-browsing
Video conferencing	

Source: mindmeister.com, 2009.

E-mail and Instant Messaging (IM)

E-mail and instant messaging have been embraced by corporations as a major communication and collaboration tool supporting interaction jobs. Their software operates on computers, cell phones, and other wireless handheld devices and includes features for sharing files as well as transmitting messages. Many instant messaging systems allow users to engage in real-time conversations with multiple participants simultaneously. Gartner technology consultants predict that within a few years, instant messaging will be the "de facto tool" for voice, video, and text chat for 95 percent of employees in big companies.

Social Networking

We've all visited social networking sites such as MySpace and Facebook, which feature tools to help people share their interests and interact. Social networking tools are quickly becoming a corporate tool for sharing ideas and collaborating among interaction-based jobs in the firm. Social networking sites such as Linkedin.com provide networking services to business professionals, while other niche sites have sprung up to serve lawyers, doctors, engineers, and even dentists. IBM built a Community Tools component into its Lotus Notes collaboration software to add social networking features. Users are able to submit questions to others in the company and receive answers via instant messaging.

Wikis

Wikis are a type of Web site that makes it easy for users to contribute and edit text content and graphics without any knowledge of Web page development or programming techniques. The most well-known wiki is Wikipedia, the largest collaboratively edited reference project in the world. It relies on volunteers, makes no money, and accepts no advertising. Wikis are ideal tools for storing and sharing company knowledge and insights. Enterprise software vendor SAP AG has a wiki that acts as a base of information for people outside the company, such as customers and software developers who build programs that interact with SAP software. In the past, those people asked and sometimes answered questions in an informal way on SAP online forums, but that was an inefficient system, with people asking and answering the same questions over and over.

At Intel Corporation, employees built their own internal wiki, and it has been edited over 100,000 times and viewed more than 27 million times by Intel employees. The most common search is for the meaning of Intel acronyms such as EASE for "employee access support environment" and POR for "plan of record." Other popular resources include a page about software engineering processes at the company. Wikis are destined to become the major repository for unstructured corporate knowledge in the next five years in part because they are so much less costly than formal knowledge management systems and they can be much more dynamic and current.

Virtual Worlds

Virtual worlds, such as Second Life, are online 3-D environments populated by "residents" who have built graphical representations of themselves known as avatars. Organizations such as IBM and INSEAD, an international business school with campuses in France and Singapore, are using this virtual world to house online meetings, training sessions, and "lounges." Real-world people represented by avatars meet, interact, and exchange ideas at these virtual locations. Communication takes place in the form of text messages similar to instant messages.

Internet-Based Collaboration Environments

There are now suites of software products providing multi-function platforms for workgroup collaboration among teams of employees who work together from many different locations. Numerous collaboration tools are available, but the most widely used are Internet-based audio conferencing and video conferencing systems, online software services such as Google Apps/Google Sites, and corporate collaboration systems such as Lotus Notes and Microsoft SharePoint.

Virtual Meeting Systems For many businesses, including investment banking, accounting, law, technology services, and management consulting, extensive travel is a fact of life. The expenses incurred by business travel have been steadily rising in recent years, primarily due to increasing energy costs. In an effort to reduce travel expenses, many companies, both large and small, are adopting videoconferencing and Web conferencing technologies.

Companies such as Heinz, General Electric, Pepsico, and Wachovia are using virtual meeting systems for product briefings, training courses, strategy sessions, and even inspirational chats.

An important feature of leading-edge high-end videoconferencing systems is **telepresence** technology, an integrated audio and visual environment that allows a person to give the appearance of being present at a location other than his or her true physical location. The Interactive Session on Management describes telepresence and other technologies for hosting these "virtual" meetings. You can also find video cases on this topic.

Google Apps/Google Sites One of the most widely used "free" online services for collaboration is Google Apps/Google Sites. Google Sites allows users to quickly create online, group-editable Web sites. Google Sites is one part of the larger Google Apps suite of tools. Google Sites users can design and populate Web sites in minutes and, without any advanced technical skills, post a variety of files including calendars, text, spreadsheets, and videos for private, group, or public viewing and editing.

Google Apps works with Google Sites and includes the typical desktop productivity office software tools (word processing, spreadsheets, presentation, contact management, messaging, and mail). A Premier edition charging businesses $50 per year for each user offers 25 gigabytes of mail storage, a 99.9-percent uptime guarantee for e-mail, tools to integrate with the firm's existing infrastructure, and 24/7 phone support. Table 4 describes some of the capabilities of Google Apps/Google Sites.

TABLE 4 GOOGLE APPS/GOOGLE SITES COLLABORATION FEATURES

GOOGLE APPS/GOOGLE SITES CAPABILITY	DESCRIPTION
Google Calendar	Private and shared calendars; multiple calendars
Google Gmail	Google's free online e-mail service, with mobile access capabilities
Google Talk	Instant messaging, text and voice chat
Google Docs	Online word processing, presentation, spreadsheet, and drawing software; online editing and sharing
Google Sites	Team collaboration sites for sharing documents, schedules, calendars; searching documents and creating group wikis
Google Video	Private hosted video sharing
Google Groups	User-created groups with mailing lists, shared calendars, documents, sites, and video; searchable archives

INTERACTIVE SESSION: MANAGEMENT

VIRTUAL MEETINGS: SMART MANAGEMENT

Instead of taking that 6:30 A.M. plane to make a round of meetings in Dallas, wouldn't it be great if you could attend these events without leaving your desktop? Today you can, thanks to technologies for videoconferencing and for hosting online meetings over the Web. A June 2008 report issued by the Global e-Sustainability Initiative and the Climate Group estimated that up to 20 percent of business travel could be replaced by virtual meeting technology.

A videoconference allows individuals at two or more locations to communicate simultaneously through two-way video and audio transmissions. The critical feature of videoconferencing is the digital compression of audio and video streams by a device called a codec. Those streams are then divided into packets and transmitted over a network or the Internet. Until recently, the technology was plagued by poor audio and video performance, and its cost was prohibitively high for all but the largest and most powerful corporations. Most companies deemed videoconferencing a poor substitute for face-to-face meetings.

However, vast improvements in videoconferencing and associated technologies have renewed interest in this way of working. Videoconferencing is now growing at an annual rate of 30 percent. Proponents of the technology claim that it does more than simply reduce costs. It allows for "better" meetings as well: it's easier to meet with partners, suppliers, subsidiaries, and colleagues from within the office or around the world on a more frequent basis, which in most cases simply cannot be reasonably accomplished through travel. You can also meet with contacts that you wouldn't be able to meet at all without videoconferencing technology.

For example, Rip Curl, a Costa Mesa, California, producer of surfing equipment, uses videoconferencing to help its designers, marketers, and manufacturers collaborate on new products. Executive recruiting firm Korn/Ferry International uses video interviews to screen potential candidates before presenting them to clients.

Today's state-of-the-art videoconferencing systems display sharp high-definition TV images. The top-of-the-line videoconferencing technology is known as telepresence. Telepresence strives to make users feel as if they are actually present in a location different from their own. You can sit across a table from a large screen showing someone who looks quite real and life-size, but may be in Brussels or Hong Kong. Only the handshake and exchange of business cards are missing. Telepresence products provide the highest-quality videoconferencing available on the market to date. Cisco Systems has installed telepresence systems in more than 500 organizations around the world. Prices for fully equipped telepresence rooms can run to $500,000.

Companies able to afford this technology report large savings. For example, technology consulting firm Accenture reports that it eliminated expenditures for 240 international trips and 120 domestic flights in a single month. The ability to reach customers and partners is also dramatically increased. Other business travelers report tenfold increases in the number of customers and partners they are able to reach for a fraction of the previous price per person. MetLife, which installed Cisco Telepresence in three dedicated conference rooms in Chicago, New York, and New Jersey, claims that the technology not only saved time and expense but also helped the company meet its "green" environmental goals of reducing carbon emissions by 20 percent in 2010.

Videoconferencing products have not traditionally been feasible for small businesses, but another company, LifeSize, has introduced an affordable line of products as low as $5,000. Overall, the product is easy to use and will allow many smaller companies to use a high-quality videoconferencing product.

There are even some free Internet-based options like Skype videoconferencing and ooVoo. These products are of lower quality than traditional videoconferencing products, and they are proprietary, meaning they can only talk to others using that very same system. Most videoconferencing and telepresence products are able to interact with a variety of other devices. Higher-end systems include features like multi-party conferencing, video mail with unlimited storage, no long-distance fees, and a detailed call history.

Companies of all sizes are finding Web-based online meeting tools such as WebEx, Microsoft Office Live Meeting, and Adobe Acrobat Connect especially helpful for training and sales presentations. These products enable participants to share documents and presentations in conjunction with audioconferencing and live video via Webcam. Cornerstone Information Systems, a Bloomington, Indiana, business software company with 60 employees, cut its travel costs by 60 percent and the average time to close a new sale by 30 percent by performing many product demonstrations online.

Before setting up videoconferencing or telepresence, it's important for a company to make sure it really needs the technology to ensure that it will be a profitable venture. Companies should determine how their employees conduct meetings, how they communicate and with what technologies, how much travel they do, and their network's capabilities. There are still plenty of times when face-to-face interaction is more desirable, and often traveling to meet a client is essential for cultivating clients and closing sales.

Videoconferencing figures to have an impact on the business world in other ways, as well. More employees may be able to work closer to home and balance their work and personal lives more efficiently; traditional office environments and corporate headquarters may shrink or disappear; and freelancers, contractors, and workers from other countries will become a larger portion of the global economy.

Sources: Joe Sharkey, "Setbacks in the Air Add to Lure of Virtual Meetings, *The New York Times*, April 26, 2010; Bob Evans, "Pepsi Picks Cisco for Huge TelePresence Deal," February 2, 2010; Esther Schein, "Telepresence Catching On, But Hold On to Your Wallet," *Computerworld*, January 22, 2010; Christopher Musico, "Web Conferencing: Calling Your Conference to Order," *Customer Relationship Management*, February 2009; and Brian Nadel, "3 Videoconferencing Services Pick Up Where Your Travel Budget Leaves Off," *Computerworld*, January 6, 2009; Johna Till Johnson, "Videoconferencing Hits the Big Times.... For Real," *Computerworld*, May 28, 2009.

CASE STUDY QUESTIONS

1. One consulting firm has predicted that video and Web conferencing will make business travel extinct. Do you agree? Why or why not?

2. What is the distinction between videoconferencing and telepresence?

3. What are the ways in which videoconferencing provides value to a business? Would you consider it smart management? Explain your answer.

4. If you were in charge of a small business, would you choose to implement videoconferencing? What factors would you consider in your decision?

MIS IN ACTION

Explore the WebEx Web site (www.webex.com) and answer the following questions:

1. List and describe its capabilities for small-medium and large businesses. How useful is WebEx? How can it help companies save time and money?

2. Compare WebEx video capabilities with the videoconferencing capabilities described in this case.

3. Describe the steps you would take to prepare for a Web conference as opposed to a face-to-face conference.

Google has developed an additional Web-based platform for real-time collaboration and communication called Google Wave. "Waves" are "equal parts conversation and document," in which any participant of a wave can reply anywhere in the message, edit the content, and add or remove participants at any point in the process. Users are able to see responses from other participants on their "wave" while typing occurs, accelerating the pace of discussion.

For example, Clear Channel Radio in Greensboro, North Carolina, used Google Wave for an on air and online promotion that required input from sales people, the sales manager, the station program director, the station promotions director, the online content coordinator, and the Web manager. Without Google Wave, these people would have used numerous back and forth e-mails, sent graphics files to each other for approval, and spent large amounts of time tracking people down by phone. Wave helped them complete the entire project in just a fraction of time it would normally have taken (Boulton, 2010).

Microsoft SharePoint Microsoft SharePoint is the most widely adopted collaboration system for small and medium-sized firms that use Microsoft server and networking products. Some larger firms have adopted it as well. SharePoint is a browser-based collaboration and document management platform, combined with a powerful search engine that is installed on corporate servers.

SharePoint has a Web-based interface and close integration with everyday tools such as Microsoft Office desktop software products. Microsoft's strategy is to take advantage of its "ownership" of the desktop through its Microsoft Office and Windows products. For Microsoft, the path towards enterprise-wide collaboration starts with the Office desktop and Microsoft network servers. SharePoint software makes it possible for employees to share their Office documents and collaborate on projects using Office documents as the foundation.

SharePoint products and technologies provide a platform for Web-based collaboration at the enterprise level. SharePoint can be used to host Web sites that organize and store information in one central location to enable teams to coordinate work activities, collaborate on and publish documents, maintain task lists, implement workflows, and share information via wikis, blogs, and Twitter-style status updates. Because SharePoint stores and organizes information in one place, users can find relevant information quickly and efficiently while working together closely on tasks, projects, and documents.

Here is a list of SharePoint's major capabilities:

- Provides a single workspace for teams to coordinate schedules, organize documents, and participate in discussions, within the organization or over an extranet.
- Facilitates creation and management of documents with the ability to control versions, view past revisions, enforce document-specific security, and maintain document libraries.
- Provides announcements, alerts, and discussion boards to inform users when actions are required or changes are made to existing documentation or information.
- Supports personalized content and both personal and public views of documents and applications.
- Provides templates for blogs and wikis to help teams share information and brainstorm.
- Provides tools to manage document libraries, lists, calendars, tasks, and discussion boards offline, and to synchronize changes when reconnected to the network.
- Provides enterprise search tools for locating people, expertise, and content.

Sony Electronics, a leading provider of consumer and professional electronics products with more 170,000 employees around the world, uses Microsoft Office SharePoint Server 2010 to improve information access, enhance collaboration, and make better use of experts inside the company. Sony uses SharePoint's wiki tools to capture and organize employees' insights and comments into a company-wide body of knowledge, and its people search feature to identify employees with expertise about specific projects and research areas. The company also used SharePoint to create a central file-sharing repository. This helps employees collaboratively write, edit, and exchange documents and eliminates the need to e-mail documents back and forth. All of these improvements have cut development time on key projects from three to six months to three to six weeks. (Microsoft, 2010).

Lotus Notes For very large firms (Fortune 1000 and Russell 2000 firms), the most widely used collaboration tool is IBM's Lotus Notes. Lotus Notes was an early example of groupware, a collaborative software system with capabilities for sharing calendars, collective writing and editing, shared database access, and electronic meetings, with each participant able to see and display information from others and other activities. Notes is now Web-enabled with enhancements for social networking (Lotus Connections) and a scripting and application development environment so that users can build custom applications to suit their unique needs.

IBM Software Group defines Lotus Notes as an "integrated desktop client option for accessing business e-mail, calendars, and applications on an IBM Lotus Domino server." The Notes software installed on the user's client computer allows the machine to be used as a platform for e-mail, instant messaging (working with Lotus Sametime), Web browsing, and calendar/resource reservation work, as well as for interacting with collaborative applications. Today, Notes also provides blogs, wikis, RSS aggregators, CRM, and help desk systems.

Thousands of employees at hundreds of large firms such as Toshiba, Air France, and Global Hyatt Corporation use IBM Lotus Notes as their primary collaboration and teamwork tools. Firmwide installations of Lotus Notes at a large Fortune 1000 firm may cost millions of dollars a year and require extensive support from the corporate information systems department. Although online tools like the Google collaboration services described earlier do not require installation on corporate servers or much support from the corporate IS staff, they are not as powerful as those found in Lotus Notes. It is unclear whether they could scale to the size of a global firm (at least for now). Very large firms adopt IBM Lotus Notes because Notes promises higher levels of security and reliability, and the ability to retain control over sensitive corporate information.

For example, EuroChem, the largest agrochemical company in Russia and one of Europe's top three fertilizer producers, used Lotus Notes to create a single standard platform for collaboration and document management. The software facilitates cooperation and collaboration among geographically dispersed regional production centers and provides a secure automated platform for document exchange. With Lotus Notes, EuroChem is able to register and control all documents, to establish routing paths for document approval, and to maintain a full history of all movements and changes. Security features allow the company to create a personalized work environment for each user and to prevent unauthorized users from accessing sensitive information (IBM, 2009).

Large firms in general do not feel secure using popular online software services for "strategic" applications because of the implicit security concerns. However, most experts believe that these concerns will diminish as experience with online tools grows, and the sophistication of online software service suppliers increases to protect security and reduce vulnerability. Table 5 describes additional online collaboration tools.

Checklist for Managers: Evaluating and Selecting Collaboration Software Tools

With so many collaboration tools and services available, how do you choose the right collaboration technology for your firm? To answer this question, you need a framework for understanding just what problems these tools are designed to solve. One framework that has been helpful for us to talk about collaboration tools is the time/space collaboration matrix developed in the early 1990s by a number of collaborative work scholars (Figure 8).

TABLE 5   OTHER POPULAR ONLINE COLLABORATION TOOLS

TOOL	DESCRIPTION
Socialtext	An enterprise server-based collaboration environment which provides social networking, Twitter-like micro-blogging , wiki workspaces, with integrated weblogs, distributed spreadsheets, and a personal home page for every user. Delivered in a variety of hosted cloud services, as well as on-site appliances to provide enterprise customers with flexible deployment options that meet their security requirements.
Zoho	Collecting and collaborating on text, line drawings, images, Web pages, video, RSS feeds. Project management (includes task management, work flow, reports, time tracking, forums, and file sharing). Free or monthly charge for premium service.
BlueTie	Online collaboration with e-mail, scheduling, to-do lists, contact management, file sharing. $4.99 per user per month.
Basecamp	Sharing to-do lists, files, message boards, milestone tracking. Free for a single project, $24/month for 15 projects with 5 gigabytes of storage.
Onehub	Sharing documents, calendars, Web bookmarks; e-mail integration and IM. Manage hub resources; bulletin board.
WorkZone	Collaboration with file sharing; project management; customization; security.

Socialtext's enterprise social networking products-including microblogging, blogs, wikis, profiles and social spreadsheets-enable employees to share vital information and work together in real-time. Built on a flexible, Web-oriented architecture, Socialtext integrates with virtually any traditional system of record, such as CRM and ERP, enabling companies to discuss, collaborate, and take action on key business processes.

FIGURE 8   THE TIME/SPACE COLLABORATION TOOL MATRIX

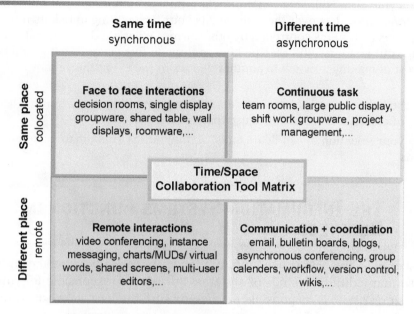

Collaboration technologies can be classified in terms of whether they support interactions at the same or different time or place, and whether these interactions are remote or co-located.

The time/space matrix focuses on two dimensions of the collaboration problem: time and space. For instance, you need to collaborate with people in different time zones and you cannot all meet at the same time. Midnight in New York is noon in Bombay, so this makes it difficult to have a video-conference (the people in New York are too tired). Time is clearly an obstacle to collaboration on a global scale.

Place (location) also inhibits collaboration in large global or even national and regional firms. Assembling people for a physical meeting is made difficult by the physical dispersion of distributed firms (firms with more than one location), the cost of travel, and the time limitations of managers.

The collaboration technologies we have just described are ways of overcoming the limitations of time and space. Using this time/space framework will help you to choose the most appropriate collaboration and teamwork tools for your firm. Note that some tools are applicable in more than one time/place scenario. For example, Internet collaboration suites such as Lotus Notes have capabilities for both synchronous (instant messaging, electronic meeting tools) and asynchronous (e-mail, wikis, document editing) interactions.

Here's a "to-do" list to get started. If you follow these six steps, you should be led to investing in the correct collaboration software for your firm at a price you can afford, and within your risk tolerance.

1. What are the collaboration challenges facing the firm in terms of time and space? Locate your firm in the time/space matrix. Your firm can occupy more than one cell in the matrix. Different collaboration tools will be needed for each situation.

2. Within each cell of the matrix where your firm faces challenges, exactly what kinds of solutions are available? Make a list of vendor products.

3. Analyze each of the products in terms of their cost and benefits to your firm. Be sure to include the costs of training in your cost estimates, and the costs of involving the information systems department if needed.

4. Identify the risks to security and vulnerability involved with each of the products. Is your firm willing to put proprietary information into the hands of external service providers over the Internet? Is your firm willing to risk its important operations to systems controlled by other firms? What are the financial risks facing your vendors? Will they be here in three to five years? What would be the cost of making a switch to another vendor in the event the vendor firm fails?

5. Seek the help of potential users to identify implementation and training issues. Some of these tools are easier to use than others.

6. Make your selection of candidate tools, and invite the vendors to make presentations.

4 THE INFORMATION SYSTEMS FUNCTION IN BUSINESS

We've seen that businesses need information systems to operate today and that they use many different kinds of systems. But who is responsible for running these systems? Who is responsible for making sure the hardware, software, and other technologies used by these systems are running properly and are up to date? End users manage their systems from a business standpoint, but managing the technology requires a special information systems function.

In all but the smallest of firms, the **information systems department** is the formal organizational unit responsible for information technology services. The information systems department is responsible for maintaining the hardware, software, data storage, and networks that comprise the firm's IT infrastructure.

THE INFORMATION SYSTEMS DEPARTMENT

The information systems department consists of specialists, such as programmers, systems analysts, project leaders, and information systems managers. **Programmers** are highly trained technical specialists who write the software instructions for computers. **Systems analysts** constitute the principal liaisons between the information systems groups and the rest of the organization. It is the systems analyst's job to translate business problems and requirements into information requirements and systems. **Information systems managers** are leaders of teams of programmers and analysts, project managers, physical facility managers, telecommunications managers, or database specialists. They are also managers of computer operations and data entry staff. Also, external specialists, such as hardware vendors and manufacturers, software firms, and consultants, frequently participate in the day-to-day operations and long-term planning of information systems.

In many companies, the **information systems department** is headed by a **chief information officer (CIO)**. The CIO is a senior manager who oversees the use of information technology in the firm. Today's CIOs are expected to have a strong business background as well as information systems expertise and to play a leadership role in integrating technology into the firm's business strategy. Large firms today also have positions for a chief security officer, chief knowledge officer, and chief privacy officer, all of whom work closely with the CIO.

The **chief security officer (CSO)** is in charge of information systems security for the firm and is responsible for enforcing the firm's information security policy. (Sometimes this position is called the chief information security officer [CISO] where information systems security is separated from physical security.) The CSO is responsible for educating and training users and information systems specialists about security, keeping management aware of security threats and breakdowns, and maintaining the tools and policies chosen to implement security.

Information systems security and the need to safeguard personal data have become so important that corporations collecting vast quantities of personal data have established positions for a **chief privacy officer (CPO)**. The CPO is responsible for ensuring that the company complies with existing data privacy laws.

The **chief knowledge officer (CKO)** is responsible for the firm's knowledge management program. The CKO helps design programs and systems to find new sources of knowledge or to make better use of existing knowledge in organizational and management processes.

End users are representatives of departments outside of the information systems group for whom applications are developed. These users are playing an increasingly large role in the design and development of information systems.

In the early years of computing, the information systems group was composed mostly of programmers who performed highly specialized but limited technical functions. Today, a growing proportion of staff members are systems analysts and network specialists, with the information systems department acting as a powerful change agent in the organization. The information systems department suggests new business strategies and new information-based products and services, and coordinates both the development of the technology and the planned changes in the organization.

ORGANIZING THE INFORMATION SYSTEMS FUNCTION

There are many types of business firms, and there are many ways in which the IT function is organized within the firm. A very small company will not have a formal information systems group. It might have one employee who is responsible for keeping its networks and applications running, or it might use consultants for these services. Larger companies will have a separate information systems department, which may be organized along several different lines, depending on the nature and interests of the firm. Our Learning Track describes alternative ways of organizing the information systems function within the business.

The question of how the information systems department should be organized is part of the larger issue of IT governance. **IT governance** includes the strategy and policies for using information technology within an organization. It specifies the decision rights and framework for accountability to ensure that the use of information technology supports the organization's strategies and objectives. How much should the information systems function be centralized? What decisions must be made to ensure effective management and use of information technology, including the return on IT investments? Who should make these decisions? How will these decisions be made and monitored? Firms with superior IT governance will have clearly thought out the answers (Weill and Ross, 2004).

5   HANDS-ON MIS PROJECTS

The projects in this section give you hands-on experience analyzing opportunities to improve business processes with new information system applications, using a spreadsheet to improve decision making about suppliers, and using Internet software to plan efficient transportation routes.

Management Decision Problems

1. Don's Lumber Company on the Hudson River is one of the oldest retail lumberyards in New York State. It features a large selection of materials for flooring, decks, moldings, windows, siding, and roofing. The prices of lumber and other building materials are constantly changing. When a customer inquires about the price on pre-finished wood flooring, sales representatives consult a manual price sheet and then call the supplier for the most recent price. The supplier in turn uses a manual price sheet, which has been updated each day. Often the supplier must call back Don's sales reps because the company does not have the newest pricing information immediately on hand. Assess the business impact of this situation, describe how this process could be improved with information technology, and identify the decisions that would have to be made to implement a solution. Who would make those decisions?

2. Henry's Hardware is a small family business in Sacramento, California. The owners must use every square foot of store space as profitably as possible. They have never kept detailed inventory or sales records. As soon as a shipment of goods arrives, the items are immediately placed on store shelves. Invoices from suppliers are only kept for tax purposes. When an item is sold, the item number and price are rung up at the cash register. The owners use their own judgment in identifying items that need to be reordered. What is the business impact of this situation? How could information systems help the owners run their business? What data should these systems capture? What decisions could the systems improve?

Improving Decision Making: Using a Spreadsheet to Select Suppliers

Software skills: Spreadsheet date functions, data filtering, DAVERAGE function
Business skills: Analyzing supplier performance and pricing

In this exercise, you will learn how to use spreadsheet software to improve management decisions about selecting suppliers. You will start with raw transactional data about suppliers organized as a large spreadsheet list. You will use the spreadsheet software to filter the data based on several different criteria to select the best suppliers for your company.

You run a company that manufactures aircraft components. You have many competitors who are trying to offer lower prices and better service to customers, and you are trying to determine whether you can benefit from better supply chain management. In myMISlab, you will find a spreadsheet file that contains a list of all of the items that your firm has ordered from its suppliers during the past three months. A sample is shown below, but the Web site may have a more recent version of this spreadsheet for this exercise. The fields in the spreadsheet file include vendor name, vendor identification number, purchaser's order number, item identification number and item description (for each item ordered from the vendor), cost per item, number of units of the item ordered (quantity), total cost of each

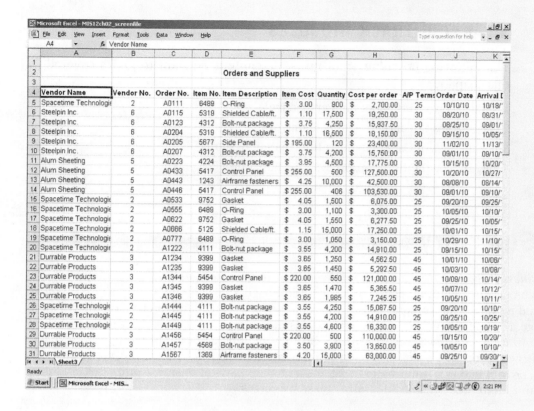

order, vendor's accounts payable terms, order date, and actual arrival date for each order.

Prepare a recommendation of how you can use the data in this spreadsheet database to improve your decisions about selecting suppliers. Some criteria to consider for identifying preferred suppliers include the supplier's track record for on-time deliveries, suppliers offering the best accounts payable terms, and suppliers offering lower pricing when the same item can be provided by multiple suppliers. Use your spreadsheet software to prepare reports to support your recommendations.

Achieving Operational Excellence: Using Internet Software to Plan Efficient Transportation Routes

In this exercise, you will use the same online software tool that businesses use to map out their transportation routes and select the most efficient route. The MapQuest (www.mapquest.com) Web site includes interactive capabilities for planning a trip. The software on this Web site can calculate the distance between two points and provide itemized driving directions to any location.

You have just started working as a dispatcher for Cross-Country Transport, a new trucking and delivery service based in Cleveland, Ohio. Your first assignment is to plan a delivery of office equipment and furniture from Elkhart, Indiana (at the corner of E. Indiana Ave. and Prairie Street) to Hagerstown, Maryland (corner of Eastern Blvd. N. and Potomac Ave.). To guide your trucker, you need to know the most efficient route between the two cities. Use MapQuest to find the route that is the shortest distance between the two cities. Use MapQuest again to find the route that takes the least time. Compare the results. Which route should Cross-Country use?

LEARNING TRACK MODULES

The following Learning Tracks provide content relevant to topics covered in this chapter:

1. Systems from a Functional Perspective
2. IT Enables Collaboration and Teamwork
3. Challenges of Using Business Information Systems
4. Organizing the Information Systems Function

Review Summary

1. **What are business processes? How are they related to information systems?**

   A business process is a logically related set of activities that defines how specific business tasks are performed, and it represents a unique way in which an organization coordinates work, information, and knowledge. Managers need to pay attention to business processes because they determine how well the organization can execute its business, and they may be a source of strategic advantage. There are business processes specific to each of the major business functions, but many business processes are cross-functional. Information systems automate parts of business processes, and they can help organizations redesign and streamline these processes.

2. **How do systems serve the different management groups in a business?**

   Systems serving operational management are transaction processing systems (TPS), such as payroll or order processing, that track the flow of the daily routine transactions necessary to conduct business. Management information systems (MIS) produce reports serving middle management by condensing information from TPS, and these are not highly analytical. Decision-support systems (DSS) support management decisions that are unique and rapidly changing using advanced analytical models. All of these types of systems provide business intelligence that helps managers and enterprise employees make more informed decisions. These systems for business intelligence serve multiple levels of management, and include executive support systems (ESS) for senior management that provide data in the form of graphs, charts, and dashboards delivered via portals using many sources of internal and external information.

3. **How do systems that link the enterprise improve organizational performance?**

   Enterprise applications are designed to coordinate multiple functions and business processes. Enterprise systems integrate the key internal business processes of a firm into a single software system to improve coordination and decision making. Supply chain management systems help the firm manage its relationship with suppliers to optimize the planning, sourcing, manufacturing, and delivery of products and services. Customer relationship management (CRM) systems coordinate the business processes surrounding the firm's customers. Knowledge management systems enable firms to optimize the creation, sharing, and distribution of knowledge. Intranets and extranets are private corporate networks based on Internet technology that assemble information from disparate systems. Extranets make portions of private corporate intranets available to outsiders.

4. **Why are systems for collaboration and teamwork so important and what technologies do they use?**

   Collaboration is working with others to achieve shared and explicit goals. Collaboration and teamwork have become increasingly important in business because of globalization, the decentralization of decision making, and growth in jobs where interaction is the primary value-adding activity. Collaboration is believed to enhance innovation, productivity, quality, and customer service. Effective collaboration today requires a supportive organizational culture as well as information systems and tools for collaborative work. Collaboration tools include e-mail and instant messaging, wikis, videoconferencing systems, virtual worlds, social networking systems, cell phones, and Internet collaboration platforms such as Google Apps/Sites, Microsoft SharePoint, and Lotus Notes.

5. *What is the role of the information systems function in a business?*

The information systems department is the formal organizational unit responsible for information technology services. It is responsible for maintaining the hardware, software, data storage, and networks that comprise the firm's IT infrastructure. The department consists of specialists, such as programmers, systems analysts, project leaders, and information systems managers, and is often headed by a CIO.

Key Terms

Business intelligence
Chief information officer (CIO)
Chief knowledge officer (CKO)
Chief privacy officer (CPO)
Chief security officer (CSO)
Collaboration
Customer relationship management (CRM) systems
Decision-support systems (DSS)
Digital dashboard
Electronic business (e-business)
Electronic commerce (e-commerce)
E-government
End users
Enterprise applications

Enterprise systems
Executive support systems (ESS)
Information systems department
Information systems managers
Interorganizational system
IT governance
Knowledge management systems (KMS)
Management information systems (MIS)
Portal
Programmers
Supply chain management (SCM) systems
Systems analysts
Teams
Telepresence
Transaction processing systems (TPS)

Review Questions

1. What are business processes? How are they related to information systems?

- Define business processes and describe the role they play in organizations.
- Describe the relationship between information systems and business processes.

2. How do systems serve the various levels of management in a business?

- Describe the characteristics of transaction processing systems (TPS) and the roles they play in a business.
- Describe the characteristics of management information systems (MIS) and explain how MIS differ from TPS and from DSS.
- Describe the characteristics of decision-support systems (DSS) and how they benefit businesses.

- Describe the characteristics of executive support systems (ESS) and explain how these systems differ from DSS.

3. How do systems that link the enterprise improve organizational performance?

- Explain how enterprise applications improve organizational performance.
- Define enterprise systems, supply chain management systems, customer relationship management systems, and knowledge management systems and describe their business benefits.
- Explain how intranets and extranets help firms integrate information and business processes.

4. Why are systems for collaboration and teamwork so important and what technologies do they use?

- Define collaboration and teamwork and explain why they have become so important in business today.
- List and describe the business benefits of collaboration.
- Describe a supportive organizational culture and business processes for collaboration.
- List and describe the various types of collaboration and communication systems.

5. What is the role of the information systems function in a business?
   - Describe how the information systems function supports a business.
   - Compare the roles played by programmers, systems analysts, information systems managers, the chief information officer (CIO), chief security officer (CSO), and chief knowledge officer (CKO).

Discussion Questions

1. How could information systems be used to support the order fulfillment process illustrated in Figure 1? What are the most important pieces of information these systems should capture? Explain your answer.

2. Identify the steps that are performed in the process of selecting and checking out a book from your college library and the information that flows among these activities. Diagram the process. Are there any ways this process could be improved to improve the performance of your library or your school? Diagram the improved process.

3. How might the BMW Oracle team have used collaboration systems to improve the design and performance of the America's Cup sailboat USA? Which system features would be the most important for these tasks?

Video Cases

Video Cases and Instructional Videos illustrating some of the concepts in this chapter are available. Contact your instructor to access these videos.

Collaboration and Teamwork: Describing Management Decisions and Systems

With a team of three or four other students, find a description of a manager in a corporation in *BusinessWeek*, *Fortune*, *The Wall Street Journal*, or another business publication or do your research on the Web. Gather information about what the manager's company does and the role he or she plays in the company. Identify the organizational level and business function where this manager works. Make a list of the kinds of decisions this manager has to make and the kind of information the manager would need for those decisions. Suggest how information systems could supply this information. If possible, use Google Sites to post links to Web pages, team communication announcements, and work assignments. Try to use Google Docs to develop a presentation of your findings for the class.

Collaboration and Innovation at Procter & Gamble
CASE STUDY

Look in your medicine cabinet. No matter where you live in the world, odds are that you'll find many Procter & Gamble products that you use every day. P&G is the largest manufacturer of consumer products in the world, and one of the top 10 largest companies in the world by market capitalization. The company is known for its successful brands, as well as its ability to develop new brands and maintain its brands' popularity with unique business innovations. Popular P&G brands include Pampers, Tide, Bounty, Folgers, Pringles, Charmin, Swiffer, Crest, and many more. The company has approximately 140,000 employees in more than 80 countries, and its leading competitor is Britain-based Unilever. Founded in 1837 and headquartered in Cincinnati, Ohio, P&G has been a mainstay in the American business landscape for well over 150 years. In 2009, it had $79 billion in revenue and earned a $13.2 billion profit.

P&G's business operations are divided into three main units: Beauty Care, Household Care, and Health and Well-Being, each of which are further subdivided into more specific units. In each of these divisions, P&G has three main focuses as a business. It needs to maintain the popularity of its existing brands, via advertising and marketing; it must extend its brands to related products by developing new products under those brands; and it must innovate and create new brands entirely from scratch. Because so much of P&G's business is built around brand creation and management, it's critical that the company facilitate collaboration between researchers, marketers, and managers. And because P&G is such a big company, and makes such a wide array of products, achieving these goals is a daunting task.

P&G spends 3.4 percent of revenue on innovation, which is more than twice the industry average of 1.6 percent. Its research and development teams consist of 8,000 scientists spread across 30 sites globally. Though the company has an 80 percent "hit" rate on ideas that lead to products, making truly innovative and groundbreaking new products is very difficult in an extremely competitive field like consumer products. What's more, the creativity of bigger companies like P&G has been on the decline, with the top consumer goods companies accounting for only 5 per-cent of patents filed on home care products in the early 2000s.

Finding better ways to innovate and develop new ideas is critical in a marketplace like consumer goods, and for any company as large as P&G, finding methods of collaboration that are effective across the enterprise can be difficult. That's why P&G has been active in implementing information systems that foster effective collaboration and innovation. The social networking and collaborative tools popularized by Web 2.0 have been especially attractive to P&G management, starting at the top with former CEO A.G. Lafley. Lafley was succeeded by Robert McDonald in 2010, but has been a major force in revitalizing the company.

When Lafley became P&G's CEO in 2000, he immediately asserted that by the end of the decade, the company would generate half of its new product ideas using sources from outside the company, both as a way to develop groundbreaking innovations more quickly and to reduce research and development costs. At the time, Lafley's proclamation was considered to be visionary, but in the past 10 years, P&G has made good on his promise.

The first order of business for P&G was to develop alternatives to business practices that were not sufficiently collaborative. The biggest culprit, says Joe Schueller, Innovation Manager for P&G's Global Business Services division, was perhaps an unlikely one: e-mail. Though it's ostensibly a tool for communication, e-mail is not a sufficiently collaborative way to share information; senders control the flow of information, but may fail to send mail to colleagues who most need to see it, and colleagues that don't need to see certain e-mails will receive mailings long after they've lost interest. Blogs and other collaborative tools, on the other hand, are open to anyone interested in their content, and attract comments from interested users.

However, getting P&G employees to actually use these newer products in place of e-mail has been a struggle for Schueller. Employees have resisted the changes, insisting that newer collaborative tools represent more work on top of e-mail, as opposed to a better alternative. People are accustomed to e-mail, and there's significant organizational inertia against switching to a new way of doing things. Some P&G

processes for sharing knowledge were notoriously inefficient. For instance, some researchers used to write up their experiments using Microsoft Office applications, then print them out and glue them page by page into notebooks. P&G was determined to implement more efficient and collaborative methods of communication to supplant some of these outdated processes.

To that end, P&G launched a total overhaul of its collaboration systems, led by a suite of Microsoft products. The services provided include unified communications (which integrates services for voice transmission, data transmission, instant messaging, e-mail, and electronic conferencing), Microsoft Live Communications Server functionality, Web conferencing with Live Meeting, and content management with SharePoint. According to P&G, over 80,000 employees use instant messaging, and 20,000 use Microsoft Outlook, which provides tools for e-mail, calendaring, task management, contact management, note taking, and Web browsing. Outlook works with Microsoft Office SharePoint Server to support multiple users with shared mailboxes and calendars, SharePoint lists, and meeting schedules.

The presence of these tools suggests more collaborative approaches are taking hold. Researchers use the tools to share the data they've collected on various brands; marketers can more effectively access the data they need to create more highly targeted ad campaigns; and managers are more easily able to find the people and data they need to make critical business decisions.

Companies like P&G are finding that one vendor simply isn't enough to satisfy their diverse needs. That introduces a new challenges: managing information and applications across multiple platforms. For example, P&G found that Google search was inadequate because it doesn't always link information from within the company, and its reliance on keywords for its searches isn't ideal for all of the topics for which employees might search. P&G decided to implement a new search product from start-up Connectbeam, which allows employees to share bookmarks and tag content with descriptive words that appear in future searches, and facilitates social networks of coworkers to help them find and share information more effectively.

The results of the initiative have been immediate. For example, when P&G executives traveled to meet with regional managers, there was no way to integrate all the reports and discussions into a single document. One executive glued the results of experiments into Word documents and passed them out at a conference. Another executive manually entered his data and speech into PowerPoint slides, and then e-mailed the file to his colleagues. One result was that the same file ended up in countless individual mailboxes. Now, P&G's IT department can create a Microsoft SharePoint page where that executive can post all of his presentations. Using SharePoint, the presentations are stored in a single location, but are still accessible to employees and colleagues in other parts of the company. Another collaborative tool, InnovationNet, contains over 5 million research-related documents in digital format accessible via a browser-based portal. That's a far cry from experiments glued in notebooks.

One concern P&G had when implementing these collaborative tools was that if enough employees didn't use them, the tools would be much less useful for those that did use them. Collaboration tools are like business and social networks–the more people connect to the network, the greater the value to all participants. Collaborative tools grow in usefulness as more and more workers contribute their information and insights. They also allow employees quicker access to the experts within the company that have needed information and knowledge. But these benefits are contingent on the lion's share of company employees using the tools.

Another major innovation for P&G was its large-scale adoption of Cisco TelePresence conference rooms at many locations across the globe. For a company as large as P&G, telepresence is an excellent way to foster collaboration between employees across not just countries, but continents. In the past, telepresence technologies were prohibitively expensive and overly prone to malfunction. Today, the technology makes it possible to hold high-definition meetings over long distances. P&G boasts the world's largest rollout of Cisco TelePresence technology.

P&G's biggest challenge in adopting the technology was to ensure that the studios were built to particular specifications in each of the geographically diverse locations where they were installed. Cisco accomplished this, and now P&G's estimates that 35 percent of its employees use telepresence regularly. In some locations, usage is as high as 70 percent. Benefits of telepresence include significant travel savings, more efficient flow of ideas, and quicker decision making. Decisions that once took days now take minutes.

Laurie Heltsley, P&G's director of global business services, noted that the company has saved $4 for every $1 invested in the 70 high-end telepresence systems it has installed over the past few years.

These high-definition systems are used four times as often as the company's earlier versions of videoconferencing systems.

Sources: Joe Sharkey, "Setbacks in the Air Add to Lure of Virtual Meetings," *The New York Times*, April 26, 2010; Matt Hamblen, "Firms Use Collaboration Tools to Tap the Ultimate IP-Worker Ideas," *Computerworld*, September 2, 2009; "Computerworld Honors Program: P&G", 2008; www.pg.com, accessed May 18, 2010; "Procter & Gamble Revolutionizes Collaboration with Cisco TelePresence," www.cisco.com, accessed May 18, 2010; "IT's Role in Collaboration at Procter &Gamble," *Information Week*, February 1, 2007.

CASE STUDY QUESTIONS

1. What is Procter & Gamble's business strategy? What is the relationship of collaboration and innovation to that business strategy?

2. How is P&G using collaboration systems to execute its business model and business strategy? List and describe the collaboration systems and technologies it is using and the benefits of each.

3. Why were some collaborative technologies slow to catch on at P&G?

4. Compare P&G's old and new processes for writing up and distributing the results of a research experiment.

5. Why is telepresence such a useful collaborative tool for a company like P&G?

6. Can you think of other ways P&G could use collaboration to foster innovation?

References

"The Radicati Group Releases 'Instant Messaging Market, 2008-2012.'" Reuters.com (January 7, 2009).

Alter, Allan. "Unlocking the Power of Teams." CIO Insight (March 2008).

Aral, Sinan; Erik Brynjolfsson; and Marshall Van Alstyne, "Productivity Effects of Information Diffusion in Networks," MIT Center for Digital Business (July 2007).

Berlind, David. "Google Apps Refresh Sets up Death Match with Microsoft," Information Week, April 12, 2010;

Bernoff, Josh and Charlene Li."Harnessing the Power of Social Applications." MIT Sloan Management Review (Spring 2008).

Boulton, Clint. "Google Wave Used for Disparate Collaboration Cases." eWeek (February 22, 2010).

Broadbent, Marianne and Ellen Kitzis. The New CIO Leader. Boston, MA: Harvard Business Press (2004).

Cash, James I. Jr., Michael J. Earl, and Robert Morison. "Teaming Up to Crack Innovation and Enterprise Integration." Harvard Business Review (November 2008).

Chen, Daniel Q., David S. Preston, and Weidong Xia. "Antecedents and Effects of CIO Supply-Side and Demand-Side Leadership: A Staged Maturity Model."Journal of Management Information Systems 27, No. 1 (Summer 2010).

Easley, Robert F., Sarv Devaraj, and J. Michael Crant."Relating Collaborative Technology Use to Teamwork Quality and Performance: An Empirical Analysis." Journal of Management Information Systems 19, no. 4 (Spring 2003)

Frost & White. "Meetings Around the World II: Charting the Course of Advanced Collaboration." (October 14, 2009).

IBM. "EuroChem Finds the Right Chemistry for Collaboration with IBM." (June 30, 2009).

Johnson, Bradfor, James Manyika, and Lareina Yee. "The Next Revolution in Interactions," McKinsey Quarterly No. 4 (2005).

Johnston, Russell, and Michael J. Vitale. "Creating Competitive Advantage with Interorganizational Information Systems." MIS Quarterly 12, no. 2 (June 1988).

Lardi-Nadarajan, Kamales. "Doing Business in Virtual Worlds." CIO Insight (March 2008).

Malone, Thomas M., Kevin Crowston, Jintae Lee, and Brian Pentland. "Tools for Inventing Organizations: Toward a Handbook of Organizational Processes." Management Science 45, no. 3 (March 1999).

McAfee, Andrew P. "Shattering the Myths About Enterprise 2.0." Harvard Business Review (November 2009).

Microsoft Corporation. "Sony Electronics Improves Collaboration, Information Access, and Productivity." (May 12, 2010).

Nolan, Richard, and F. Warren McFarland. "Information Technology and the Board of Directors." Harvard Business Review (October 1, 2005).

Oracle Corporation. "Alcoa Implements Oracle Solution 20% below Projected Cost, Eliminates 43 Legacy Systems." www.oracle.com, accessed August 21, 2005.

Perez, Dan. "The New Data-Driven U.S. Government." SIPA News (January 2010).

Picarelle, Lisa. Planes, Trains, and Automobiles." Customer Relationship Management (February 2004).

Poltrock, Steven and Mark Handel. "Models of Collaboration as the Foundation for Collaboration Technologies. Journal of Management Information Systems 27, No. 1 (Summer 2010).

Premier Global Services. "Evaluating Shift to Online Communication Tools."(2010).

Raghupathi, W. "RP". "Corporate Governance of IT: A Framework for Development." Communications of the ACM 50, No. 8 (August 2007).

Rapoza, Jim. "SharePoint Moves into the Modern Web Age." eWeek (January 18, 2010).

Reinig, Bruce A. "Toward an Understanding of Satisfaction with the Process and Outcomes of Teamwork." Journal of Management Information Systems 19, no. 4 (Spring 2003)

SAP. "Alcan Packaging Implements mySAP SCM to Increase Shareholder Value." www.mysap.com, accessed August 20, 2005.

Siebdrat, Frank, Martin Hoegl, and Holger Ernst. "How to Manage Virtual Teams." MIT Sloan Management Review 50, No. 4 (Summer 2009).

Soat, John. "Tomorrow's CIO." Information Week (June 16, 2008).

Vance, Ashlee. "Microsoft's SharePoint Thrives in the Recession." The New York Times (August 7, 2009).

Weill, Peter and Jeanne W. Ross. IT Governance. Boston: Harvard Business School Press (2004).

Weill, Peter, and Jeanne Ross. "A Matrixed Approach to Designing IT Governance." MIT Sloan Management Review 46, no. 2 (Winter 2005).

Chapter 4

Ethical and Social Issues in Information Systems

From Chapter 4 of *Management Information Systems: Managing the Digital Firm*, 12/e. Kenneth C. Laudon, Jane P. Laudon. Copyright © 2012 by Pearson Education. Published by Prentice Hall. All rights reserved.

Ethical and Social Issues in Information Systems

BEHAVIORAL TARGETING AND YOUR PRIVACY: YOU'RE THE TARGET

Ever get the feeling somebody is trailing you on the Web, watching your every click? Wonder why you start seeing display ads and pop-ups just after you've been scouring the Web for a car, a dress, or cosmetic product? Well, you're right: your behavior is being tracked, and you are being targeted on the Web so that you are exposed to certain ads and not others. The Web sites you visit track the search engine queries you enter, pages visited, Web content viewed, ads clicked, videos watched, content shared, and the products you purchase. Google is the largest Web tracker, monitoring thousands of Web sites. As one wag noted, Google knows more about you than your mother does. In March 2009, Google began displaying ads on thousands of Google-related Web sites based on their previous online activities. To parry a growing public resentment of behavioral targeting, Google said it would give users the ability to see and edit the information that it has compiled about their interests for the purposes of behavioral targeting.

Behavioral targeting seeks to increase the efficiency of online ads by using information that Web visitors reveal about themselves online, and if possible, combine this with offline identity and consumption information gathered by companies such as Acxiom. One of the original promises of the Web was that it can deliver a marketing message tailored to each consumer based on this data, and then measure the results in terms of click-throughs and purchases. The technology used to implement online tracking is a combination of cookies, Flash cookies, and Web beacons (also called Web bugs). Web beacons are small programs placed on your computer when you visit any of thousands of Web sites. They report back to servers operated by the beacon owners the domains and Web pages you visited, what ads you clicked on, and other online behaviors. A recent study of 20 million Web pages published by 2 million domains found Google, Yahoo, Amazon, YouTube, Photobucket, and Flickr among the top 10 Web-bugging sites. Google alone accounts for 20% of all Web bugs. The average home landing page at the top 100 Web domains has over 50 tracking cookies and bugs. And you thought you were surfing alone?

Firms are experimenting with more precise targeting methods. Snapple used behavioral targeting methods (with the help of an online ad firm Tacoda) to identify the types of people attracted to Snapple Green Tea. Answer: people who like the arts and literature, travel internationally, and visit health sites. Microsoft offers MSN advertisers access to personal data derived from 270 million worldwide Windows Live users. The goal of Web beacons and bugs is even more granular: these tools can be used to identify your personal interests and behaviors so precisely targeted ads can be shown to you.

The growth in the power, reach, and scope of behavioral targeting has drawn the attention of privacy groups and the Federal Trade Commission (FTC). Currently, Web tracking is unregulated. In November 2007, the FTC opened hearings to consider proposals from privacy advocates to develop a "do not track list," to develop visual online cues to alert people to tracking, and to allow people to opt out. In the Senate, hearings on behavioral targeting were held throughout 2009 and the first half of 2010 with attention shifting to the privacy of personal location information. While Google, Microsoft, and Yahoo pleaded for legislation to protect them

iStockphoto.com 2010

from consumer lawsuits, the FTC refused to consider new legislation to protect the privacy of Internet users. Instead, the FTC proposed industry self-regulation. In 2009, a consortium of advertising firms (the Network Advertising Initiative) responded positively to FTC-proposed principles to regulate online behavioral advertising. In 2010, Congressional committees pressed leading Internet firms to allow users more opportunities to turn off tracking tools, and to make users aware on entry to a page that they are being tracked. In June 2010, the FTC announced it is examining Facebook Inc.'s efforts to protect user privacy.

All of these regulatory efforts emphasize transparency, user control over their information, security, and the temporal stability of privacy promises (unannounced and sudden changes in information privacy may not be allowed).

Perhaps the central ethical and moral question is understanding what rights individuals have in their own personally identifiable Internet profiles. Are these "ownership" rights, or merely an "interest" in an underlying asset? How much privacy are we willing to give up in order to receive more relevant ads? Surveys suggest that over 70 percent of Americans do not want to receive targeted ads.

Sources: "Web Bug Report," SecuritySpace, July, 2010; Miguel Helft, "Technology Coalition Seeks Stronger Privacy Laws," *New York Times*, March 30, 2010; "Study Finds Behaviorally-Targeted Ads More Than Twice As Valuable, Twice as Effective As Non-targerted Online Ads," Network Advertising Initiative, March 24, 2010; Steve Lohr, "Redrawing the Route to Online Privacy," New York Times, February 28, 2010; "The Collection and Use of Location Information for Commercial Purposes Hearings," U.S. House of Representatives, Committee on Energy and Commerce, Subcommittee on Commerce, Trade and Consumer Protection, February 24, 2010; Tom Krazit, "Groups Call for New Checks on Behavioral Ad Data," CNET News, September 1, 2009; Robert Mitchell, "What Google Knows About You," *Computerworld*, May 11, 2009; Stephanie Clifford, "Many See Privacy on Web as Big Issue, Survey Says," *The New York Times*, March 16, 2009; Miguel Helft, "Google to Offer Ads Based on Interests," *The New York Times*, March 11, 2009; and David Hallerman, "Behavioral Targeting: Marketing Trends," *eMarketer*, June 2008.

The growing use of behavioral targeting techniques described in the chapter-opening case shows that technology can be a double-edged sword. It can be the source of many benefits (by showing you ads relevant to your interests) but it can also create new opportunities for invading your privacy, and enabling the reckless use of that information in a variety of decisions about you.

The chapter-opening diagram calls attention to important points raised by this case and this chapter. Online advertising titans like Google, Microsoft, and Yahoo are all looking for ways to monetize their huge collections of online behavioral data. While search engine marketing is arguably the most effective form of advertising in history, banner display ad marketing is highly inefficient because it displays ads to everyone regardless of their interests. Hence the search engine marketers cannot charge much for display ad space. However, by tracking the online movements of 200 million U.S. Internet users, they can develop a very clear picture of who you are, and use that information to show you ads that might be of interest to you. This would make the marketing process more efficient, and more profitable for all the parties involved.

But this solution also creates an ethical dilemma, pitting the monetary interests of the online advertisers and search engines against the interests of individuals to maintain a sense of control over their personal information and their privacy. Two closely held values are in conflict here. As a manager, you will need to be sensitive to both the negative and positive impacts of information systems for your firm, employees, and customers. You will need to learn how to resolve ethical dilemmas involving information systems.

- Purchase ad network firms for tracking
- Develop information policies
- Combine search engine firms with advertising networking firms
- Develop strategies to fend off privacy critics and federal government legislation
- Coordinate industry-wide responses to claims of privacy invasion
- Develop huge databases to track individual behavior online
- Develop software to profile individuals

Business Challenges
- Displays decline in utility and price
- Desire to monetize huge collections of Web behavioral data

Management

Organization → **Information System**

Technology
- Develop digital profiles on millions of Web users and target "relevant" ads to them

Business Solutions
- Advertising networks track and profile individuals online
- Display ads become more relevant, effective, and valuable
- Invades the privacy of 200 million individuals

1 UNDERSTANDING ETHICAL AND SOCIAL ISSUES RELATED TO SYSTEMS

I n the past 10 years, we have witnessed, arguably, one of the most ethically challenging periods for U.S. and global business. Table 1 provides a small sample of recent cases demonstrating failed ethical judgment by senior and middle managers. These lapses in management ethical and business judgment occurred across a broad spectrum of industries.

In today's new legal environment, managers who violate the law and are convicted will most likely spend time in prison. U.S. federal sentencing guidelines adopted in 1987 mandate that federal judges impose stiff sentences on business

TABLE 1 RECENT EXAMPLES OF FAILED ETHICAL JUDGMENT BY SENIOR MANAGERS

Lehman Brothers (2008–2010)	One of the oldest American investment banks collapses in 2008. Lehman used information systems and accounting sleight of hand to conceal its bad investments. Lehman also engaged in deceptive tactics to shift investments off its books.
WG Trading Co. (2010)	Paul Greenwood, hedge fund manager and general partner at WG Trading, pled guilty to defrauding investors of $554 million over 13 years; Greenwood has forfeited $331 million to the government and faces up to 85 years in prison.
Minerals Management Service (U.S. Department of the Interior) (2010)	Managers accused of accepting gifts and other favors from oil companies, letting oil company rig employees write up inspection reports, and failing to enforce existing regulations on offshore Gulf drilling rigs. Employees systematically falsified information record systems.
Pfizer, Eli Lilly, and AstraZeneca (2009)	Major pharmaceutical firms paid billions of dollars to settle U.S. federal charges that executives fixed clinical trials for antipsychotic and pain killer drugs, marketed them inappropriately to children, and claimed unsubstantiated benefits while covering up negative outcomes. Firms falsified information in reports and systems.
Galleon Group (2009)	Founder of the Galleon Group criminally charged with trading on insider information, paying $250 million to Wall Street banks, and in return received market information that other investors did not get.
Siemens (2009)	The world's largest engineering firm paid over $4 billion to German and U.S. authorities for a decades-long, world-wide bribery scheme approved by corporate executives to influence potential customers and governments. Payments concealed from normal reporting accounting systems.

executives based on the monetary value of the crime, the presence of a conspiracy to prevent discovery of the crime, the use of structured financial transactions to hide the crime, and failure to cooperate with prosecutors (U.S. Sentencing Commission, 2004).

Although in the past business firms would often pay for the legal defense of their employees enmeshed in civil charges and criminal investigations, now firms are encouraged to cooperate with prosecutors to reduce charges against the entire firm for obstructing investigations. These developments mean that, more than ever, as a manager or an employee, you will have to decide for yourself what constitutes proper legal and ethical conduct.

Although these major instances of failed ethical and legal judgment were not masterminded by information systems departments, information systems were instrumental in many of these frauds. In many cases, the perpetrators of these crimes artfully used financial reporting information systems to bury their decisions from public scrutiny in the vain hope they would never be caught. In this chapter, we talk about the ethical dimensions of these and other actions based on the use of information systems.

Ethics refers to the principles of right and wrong that individuals, acting as free moral agents, use to make choices to guide their behaviors. Information systems raise new ethical questions for both individuals and societies because they create opportunities for intense social change, and thus threaten existing distributions of power, money, rights, and obligations. Like other technologies, such as steam engines, electricity, the telephone, and the radio, information technology can be used to achieve social progress, but it can also be used to commit crimes and threaten cherished social values. The development of information technology will produce benefits for many and costs for others.

Ethical issues in information systems have been given new urgency by the rise of the Internet and electronic commerce. Internet and digital firm technologies make it easier than ever to assemble, integrate, and distribute information, unleashing new concerns about the appropriate use of customer information, the protection of personal privacy, and the protection of intellectual property.

Other pressing ethical issues raised by information systems include establishing accountability for the consequences of information systems, setting standards to safeguard system quality that protects the safety of the individual and society, and preserving values and institutions considered essential to the quality of life in an information society. When using information systems, it is essential to ask, "What is the ethical and socially responsible course of action?"

A MODEL FOR THINKING ABOUT ETHICAL, SOCIAL, AND POLITICAL ISSUES

Ethical, social, and political issues are closely linked. The ethical dilemma you may face as a manager of information systems typically is reflected in social and political debate. One way to think about these relationships is given in Figure 1. Imagine society as a more or less calm pond on a summer day, a delicate ecosystem in partial equilibrium with individuals and with social and political institutions. Individuals know how to act in this pond because social institutions (family, education, organizations) have developed well-honed rules of behavior, and these are supported by laws developed in the political sector that prescribe behavior and promise sanctions for violations. Now toss a rock into the center of the pond. What happens? Ripples, of course.

FIGURE 1 **THE RELATIONSHIP BETWEEN ETHICAL, SOCIAL, AND POLITICAL ISSUES IN AN INFORMATION SOCIETY**

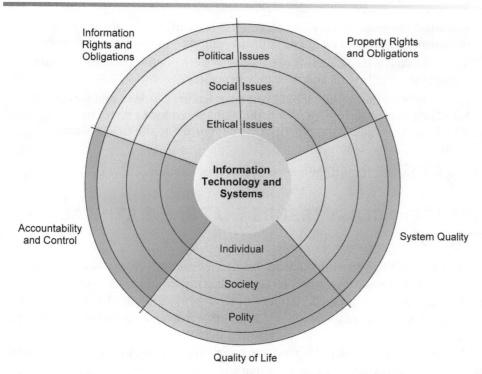

The introduction of new information technology has a ripple effect, raising new ethical, social, and political issues that must be dealt with on the individual, social, and political levels. These issues have five moral dimensions: information rights and obligations, property rights and obligations, system quality, quality of life, and accountability and control.

Imagine instead that the disturbing force is a powerful shock of new information technology and systems hitting a society more or less at rest. Suddenly, individual actors are confronted with new situations often not covered by the old rules. Social institutions cannot respond overnight to these ripples—it may take years to develop etiquette, expectations, social responsibility, politically correct attitudes, or approved rules. Political institutions also require time before developing new laws and often require the demonstration of real harm before they act. In the meantime, you may have to act. You may be forced to act in a legal gray area.

We can use this model to illustrate the dynamics that connect ethical, social, and political issues. This model is also useful for identifying the main moral dimensions of the information society, which cut across various levels of action—individual, social, and political.

FIVE MORAL DIMENSIONS OF THE INFORMATION AGE

The major ethical, social, and political issues raised by information systems include the following moral dimensions:

Information rights and obligations. What **information rights** do individuals and organizations possess with respect to themselves? What can they protect?

Property rights and obligations. How will traditional intellectual property rights be protected in a digital society in which tracing and accounting for ownership are difficult and ignoring such property rights is so easy?

Accountability and control. Who can and will be held accountable and liable for the harm done to individual and collective information and property rights?

System quality. What standards of data and system quality should we demand to protect individual rights and the safety of society?

Quality of life. What values should be preserved in an information- and knowledge-based society? Which institutions should we protect from violation? Which cultural values and practices are supported by the new information technology?

We explore these moral dimensions in detail in Section 3.

KEY TECHNOLOGY TRENDS THAT RAISE ETHICAL ISSUES

Ethical issues long preceded information technology. Nevertheless, information technology has heightened ethical concerns, taxed existing social arrangements, and made some laws obsolete or severely crippled. There are four key technological trends responsible for these ethical stresses and they are summarized in Table 2.

The doubling of computing power every 18 months has made it possible for most organizations to use information systems for their core production processes. As a result, our dependence on systems and our vulnerability to system errors and poor data quality have increased. Social rules and laws have not yet adjusted to this dependence. Standards for ensuring the accuracy and reliability of information systems are not universally accepted or enforced.

Advances in data storage techniques and rapidly declining storage costs have been responsible for the multiplying databases on individuals—employees, customers, and potential customers—maintained by private and public organizations. These advances in data storage have made the routine violation of individual privacy both cheap and effective. Massive data storage systems are inexpensive enough for regional and even local retailing firms to use in identifying customers.

Advances in data analysis techniques for large pools of data are another technological trend that heightens ethical concerns because companies and government agencies are able to find out highly detailed personal information

TABLE 2 TECHNOLOGY TRENDS THAT RAISE ETHICAL ISSUES

TREND	IMPACT
Computing power doubles every 18 months	More organizations depend on computer systems for critical operations.
Data storage costs rapidly declining	Organizations can easily maintain detailed databases on individuals.
Data analysis advances	Companies can analyze vast quantities of data gathered on individuals to develop detailed profiles of individual behavior.
Networking advances	Copying data from one location to another and accessing personal data from remote locations are much easier.

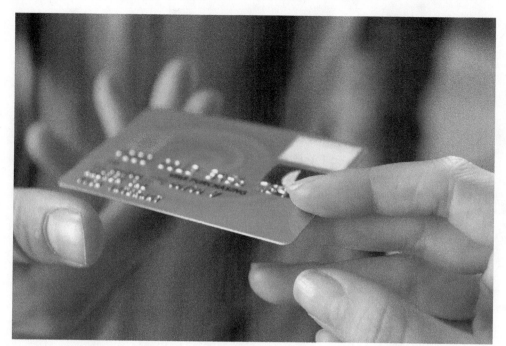

Credit card purchases can make personal information available to market researchers, telemarketers, and direct-mail companies. Advances in information technology facilitate the invasion of privacy.

iStockphoto.com 2010

about individuals. With contemporary data management tools, companies can assemble and combine the myriad pieces of information about you stored on computers much more easily than in the past.

Think of all the ways you generate computer information about yourself—credit card purchases, telephone calls, magazine subscriptions, video rentals, mail-order purchases, banking records, local, state, and federal government records (including court and police records), and visits to Web sites. Put together and mined properly, this information could reveal not only your credit information but also your driving habits, your tastes, your associations, and your political interests.

Companies with products to sell purchase relevant information from these sources to help them more finely target their marketing campaigns. The use of computers to combine data from multiple sources and create electronic dossiers of detailed information on individuals is called **profiling**.

For example, several thousand of the most popular Web sites allow DoubleClick (owned by Google), an Internet advertising broker, to track the activities of their visitors in exchange for revenue from advertisements based on visitor information DoubleClick gathers. DoubleClick uses this information to create a profile of each online visitor, adding more detail to the profile as the visitor accesses an associated DoubleClick site. Over time, DoubleClick can create a detailed dossier of a person's spending and computing habits on the Web that is sold to companies to help them target their Web ads more precisely.

ChoicePoint gathers data from police, criminal, and motor vehicle records; credit and employment histories; current and previous addresses; professional licenses; and insurance claims to assemble and maintain electronic dossiers on almost every adult in the United States. The company sells this personal information to businesses and government agencies. Demand for personal data is so enormous that data broker businesses such as ChoicePoint are flourishing.

A new data analysis technology called **nonobvious relationship awareness (NORA)** has given both the government and the private sector even more powerful profiling capabilities. NORA can take information about people from many disparate sources, such as employment applications, telephone records, customer listings, and "wanted" lists, and correlate relationships to find obscure hidden connections that might help identify criminals or terrorists (see Figure 2).

NORA technology scans data and extracts information as the data are being generated so that it could, for example, instantly discover a man at an airline ticket counter who shares a phone number with a known terrorist before that person boards an airplane. The technology is considered a valuable tool for homeland security but does have privacy implications because it can provide such a detailed picture of the activities and associations of a single individual.

Finally, advances in networking, including the Internet, promise to greatly reduce the costs of moving and accessing large quantities of data and open the possibility of mining large pools of data remotely using small desktop machines, permitting an invasion of privacy on a scale and with a precision heretofore unimaginable.

FIGURE 2   NONOBVIOUS RELATIONSHIP AWARENESS (NORA)

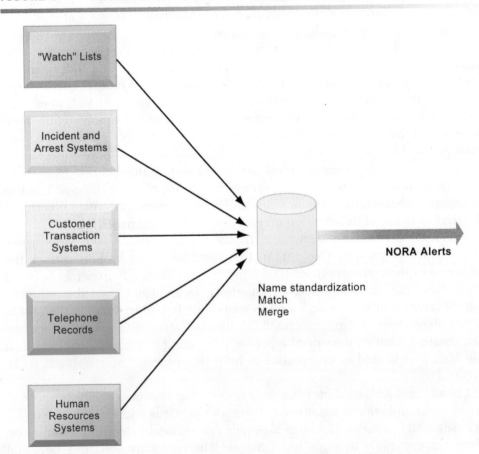

NORA technology can take information about people from disparate sources and find obscure, nonobvious relationships. It might discover, for example, that an applicant for a job at a casino shares a telephone number with a known criminal and issue an alert to the hiring manager.

2 ETHICS IN AN INFORMATION SOCIETY

Ethics is a concern of humans who have freedom of choice. Ethics is about individual choice: When faced with alternative courses of action, what is the correct moral choice? What are the main features of ethical choice?

BASIC CONCEPTS: RESPONSIBILITY, ACCOUNTABILITY, AND LIABILITY

Ethical choices are decisions made by individuals who are responsible for the consequences of their actions. **Responsibility** is a key element of ethical action. Responsibility means that you accept the potential costs, duties, and obligations for the decisions you make. **Accountability** is a feature of systems and social institutions: It means that mechanisms are in place to determine who took responsible action, and who is responsible. Systems and institutions in which it is impossible to find out who took what action are inherently incapable of ethical analysis or ethical action. **Liability** extends the concept of responsibility further to the area of laws. Liability is a feature of political systems in which a body of laws is in place that permits individuals to recover the damages done to them by other actors, systems, or organizations. **Due process** is a related feature of law-governed societies and is a process in which laws are known and understood, and there is an ability to appeal to higher authorities to ensure that the laws are applied correctly.

These basic concepts form the underpinning of an ethical analysis of information systems and those who manage them. First, information technologies are filtered through social institutions, organizations, and individuals. Systems do not have impacts by themselves. Whatever information system impacts exist are products of institutional, organizational, and individual actions and behaviors. Second, responsibility for the consequences of technology falls clearly on the institutions, organizations, and individual managers who choose to use the technology. Using information technology in a socially responsible manner means that you can and will be held accountable for the consequences of your actions. Third, in an ethical, political society, individuals and others can recover damages done to them through a set of laws characterized by due process.

ETHICAL ANALYSIS

When confronted with a situation that seems to present ethical issues, how should you analyze it? The following five-step process should help:

1. *Identify and describe clearly the facts.* Find out who did what to whom, and where, when, and how. In many instances, you will be surprised at the errors in the initially reported facts, and often you will find that simply getting the facts straight helps define the solution. It also helps to get the opposing parties involved in an ethical dilemma to agree on the facts.

2. *Define the conflict or dilemma and identify the higher-order values involved.* Ethical, social, and political issues always reference higher values. The parties to a dispute all claim to be pursuing higher values (e.g., freedom, privacy, protection of property, and the free enterprise system). Typically, an ethical issue involves a dilemma: two diametrically opposed courses of action that support worthwhile values. For example, the chapter-ending case study illustrates two competing values: the need to improve health care record keeping and the need to protect individual privacy.

3. *Identify the stakeholders.* Every ethical, social, and political issue has stakeholders: players in the game who have an interest in the outcome, who have invested in the situation, and usually who have vocal opinions. Find out the identity of these groups and what they want. This will be useful later when designing a solution.

4. *Identify the options that you can reasonably take.* You may find that none of the options satisfy all the interests involved, but that some options do a better job than others. Sometimes arriving at a good or ethical solution may not always be a balancing of consequences to stakeholders.

5. *Identify the potential consequences of your options.* Some options may be ethically correct but disastrous from other points of view. Other options may work in one instance but not in other similar instances. Always ask yourself, "What if I choose this option consistently over time?"

CANDIDATE ETHICAL PRINCIPLES

Once your analysis is complete, what ethical principles or rules should you use to make a decision? What higher-order values should inform your judgment? Although you are the only one who can decide which among many ethical principles you will follow, and how you will prioritize them, it is helpful to consider some ethical principles with deep roots in many cultures that have survived throughout recorded history:

1. Do unto others as you would have them do unto you (the **Golden Rule**). Putting yourself into the place of others, and thinking of yourself as the object of the decision, can help you think about fairness in decision making.

2. If an action is not right for everyone to take, it is not right for anyone **(Immanuel Kant's Categorical Imperative)**. Ask yourself, "If everyone did this, could the organization, or society, survive?"

3. If an action cannot be taken repeatedly, it is not right to take at all **(Descartes' rule of change)**. This is the slippery-slope rule: An action may bring about a small change now that is acceptable, but if it is repeated, it would bring unacceptable changes in the long run. In the vernacular, it might be stated as "once started down a slippery path, you may not be able to stop."

4. Take the action that achieves the higher or greater value **(Utilitarian Principle)**. This rule assumes you can prioritize values in a rank order and understand the consequences of various courses of action.

5. Take the action that produces the least harm or the least potential cost **(Risk Aversion Principle)**. Some actions have extremely high failure costs of very low probability (e.g., building a nuclear generating facility in an urban area) or extremely high failure costs of moderate probability (speeding and automobile accidents). Avoid these high-failure-cost actions, paying greater attention to high-failure-cost potential of moderate to high probability.

6. Assume that virtually all tangible and intangible objects are owned by someone else unless there is a specific declaration otherwise. (This is the **ethical "no free lunch" rule.**) If something someone else has created is useful to you, it has value, and you should assume the creator wants compensation for this work.

Actions that do not easily pass these rules deserve close attention and a great deal of caution. The appearance of unethical behavior may do as much harm to you and your company as actual unethical behavior.

PROFESSIONAL CODES OF CONDUCT

When groups of people claim to be professionals, they take on special rights and obligations because of their special claims to knowledge, wisdom, and respect. Professional codes of conduct are promulgated by associations of professionals, such as the American Medical Association (AMA), the American Bar Association (ABA), the Association of Information Technology Professionals (AITP), and the Association for Computing Machinery (ACM). These professional groups take responsibility for the partial regulation of their professions by determining entrance qualifications and competence. Codes of ethics are promises by professions to regulate themselves in the general interest of society. For example, avoiding harm to others, honoring property rights (including intellectual property), and respecting privacy are among the General Moral Imperatives of the ACM's Code of Ethics and Professional Conduct.

SOME REAL-WORLD ETHICAL DILEMMAS

Information systems have created new ethical dilemmas in which one set of interests is pitted against another. For example, many of the large telephone companies in the United States are using information technology to reduce the sizes of their workforces. Voice recognition software reduces the need for human operators by enabling computers to recognize a customer's responses to a series of computerized questions. Many companies monitor what their employees are doing on the Internet to prevent them from wasting company resources on non-business activities.

In each instance, you can find competing values at work, with groups lined up on either side of a debate. A company may argue, for example, that it has a right to use information systems to increase productivity and reduce the size of its workforce to lower costs and stay in business. Employees displaced by information systems may argue that employers have some responsibility for their welfare. Business owners might feel obligated to monitor employee e-mail and Internet use to minimize drains on productivity. Employees might believe they should be able to use the Internet for short personal tasks in place of the telephone. A close analysis of the facts can sometimes produce compromised solutions that give each side "half a loaf." Try to apply some of the principles of ethical analysis described to each of these cases. What is the right thing to do?

3 | THE MORAL DIMENSIONS OF INFORMATION SYSTEMS

In this section, we take a closer look at the five moral dimensions of information systems first described in Figure 1. In each dimension, we identify the ethical, social, and political levels of analysis and use real-world examples to illustrate the values involved, the stakeholders, and the options chosen.

INFORMATION RIGHTS: PRIVACY AND FREEDOM IN THE INTERNET AGE

Privacy is the claim of individuals to be left alone, free from surveillance or interference from other individuals or organizations, including the state. Claims to privacy are also involved at the workplace: Millions of employees are subject to electronic and other forms of high-tech surveillance (Ball, 2001). Information technology and systems threaten individual claims to privacy by making the invasion of privacy cheap, profitable, and effective.

The claim to privacy is protected in the U.S., Canadian, and German constitutions in a variety of different ways and in other countries through various statutes. In the United States, the claim to privacy is protected primarily by the First Amendment guarantees of freedom of speech and association, the Fourth Amendment protections against unreasonable search and seizure of one's personal documents or home, and the guarantee of due process.

Table 3 describes the major U.S. federal statutes that set forth the conditions for handling information about individuals in such areas as credit reporting, education, financial records, newspaper records, and electronic communications. The Privacy Act of 1974 has been the most important of these laws, regulating the federal government's collection, use, and disclosure of information. At present, most U.S. federal privacy laws apply only to the federal government and regulate very few areas of the private sector.

Most American and European privacy law is based on a regime called **Fair Information Practices (FIP)** first set forth in a report written in 1973 by a federal government advisory committee (U.S. Department of Health, Education, and Welfare, 1973). FIP is a set of principles governing the collection and use of information about individuals. FIP principles are based on the notion of a mutuality of interest between the record holder and the individual. The individual has an interest in engaging in a transaction, and the record keeper—usually a business or government agency-requires information about the individual to support the transaction. Once information is gathered, the individual maintains an interest in the record, and the record may not be used to support other activities without the individual's consent. In 1998, the FTC restated and extended the original FIP to provide guidelines for protecting online privacy. Table 4 describes the FTC's Fair Information Practice principles.

The FTC's FIP principles are being used as guidelines to drive changes in privacy legislation. In July 1998, the U.S. Congress passed the Children's Online Privacy Protection Act (COPPA), requiring Web sites to obtain parental permission before collecting information on children under the age of 13. (This law is

TABLE 3 FEDERAL PRIVACY LAWS IN THE UNITED STATES

GENERAL FEDERAL PRIVACY LAWS	PRIVACY LAWS AFFECTING PRIVATE INSTITUTIONS
Freedom of Information Act of 1966 as Amended (5 USC 552)	Fair Credit Reporting Act of 1970
Privacy Act of 1974 as Amended (5 USC 552a)	Family Educational Rights and Privacy Act of 1974
Electronic Communications Privacy Act of 1986	Right to Financial Privacy Act of 1978
Computer Matching and Privacy Protection Act of 1988	Privacy Protection Act of 1980
Computer Security Act of 1987	Cable Communications Policy Act of 1984
Federal Managers Financial Integrity Act of 1982	Electronic Communications Privacy Act of 1986
Driver's Privacy Protection Act of 1994	Video Privacy Protection Act of 1988
E-Government Act of 2002	The Health Insurance Portability and Accountability Act of 1996 (HIPAA)
	Children's Online Privacy Protection Act (COPPA) of 1998
	Financial Modernization Act (Gramm-Leach-Bliley Act) of 1999

TABLE 4   FEDERAL TRADE COMMISSION FAIR INFORMATION PRACTICE PRINCIPLES

1. Notice/awareness (core principle). Web sites must disclose their information practices before collecting data. Includes identification of collector; uses of data; other recipients of data; nature of collection (active/inactive); voluntary or required status; consequences of refusal; and steps taken to protect confidentiality, integrity, and quality of the data.

2. Choice/consent (core principle). There must be a choice regime in place allowing consumers to choose how their information will be used for secondary purposes other than supporting the transaction, including internal use and transfer to third parties.

3. Access/participation. Consumers should be able to review and contest the accuracy and completeness of data collected about them in a timely, inexpensive process.

4. Security. Data collectors must take responsible steps to assure that consumer information is accurate and secure from unauthorized use.

5. Enforcement. There must be in place a mechanism to enforce FIP principles. This can involve self-regulation, legislation giving consumers legal remedies for violations, or federal statutes and regulations.

in danger of being overturned.) The FTC has recommended additional legislation to protect online consumer privacy in advertising networks that collect records of consumer Web activity to develop detailed profiles, which are then used by other companies to target online ads. Other proposed Internet privacy legislation focuses on protecting the online use of personal identification numbers, such as social security numbers; protecting personal information collected on the Internet that deals with individuals not covered by COPPA; and limiting the use of data mining for homeland security.

In February 2009, the FTC began the process of extending its fair information practices doctrine to behavioral targeting. The FTC held hearings to discuss its program for voluntary industry principles for regulating behavioral targeting. The online advertising trade group Network Advertising Initiative (discussed later in this section), published its own self-regulatory principles that largely agreed with the FTC. Nevertheless, the government, privacy groups, and the online ad industry are still at loggerheads over two issues. Privacy advocates want both an opt-in policy at all sites and a national Do Not Track list. The industry opposes these moves and continues to insist on an opt-out capability being the only way to avoid tracking (Federal Trade Commission, 2009). Nevertheless, there is an emerging consensus among all parties that greater transparency and user control (especially making opt-out of tracking the default option) is required to deal with behavioral tracking.

Privacy protections have also been added to recent laws deregulating financial services and safeguarding the maintenance and transmission of health information about individuals. The Gramm-Leach-Bliley Act of 1999, which repeals earlier restrictions on affiliations among banks, securities firms, and insurance companies, includes some privacy protection for consumers of financial services. All financial institutions are required to disclose their policies and practices for protecting the privacy of nonpublic personal information and to allow customers to opt out of information-sharing arrangements with nonaffiliated third parties.

The Health Insurance Portability and Accountability Act (HIPAA) of 1996, which took effect on April 14, 2003, includes privacy protection for medical records. The law gives patients access to their personal medical records maintained by health care providers, hospitals, and health insurers, and the right to authorize how protected information about themselves can be used or disclosed. Doctors, hospitals, and other health care providers must limit the disclosure of personal information about patients to the minimum amount necessary to achieve a given purpose.

The European Directive on Data Protection

In Europe, privacy protection is much more stringent than in the United States. Unlike the United States, European countries do not allow businesses to use personally identifiable information without consumers' prior consent. On October 25, 1998, the European Commission's Directive on Data Protection went into effect, broadening privacy protection in the European Union (EU) nations. The directive requires companies to inform people when they collect information about them and disclose how it will be stored and used. Customers must provide their informed consent before any company can legally use data about them, and they have the right to access that information, correct it, and request that no further data be collected. **Informed consent** can be defined as consent given with knowledge of all the facts needed to make a rational decision. EU member nations must translate these principles into their own laws and cannot transfer personal data to countries, such as the United States, that do not have similar privacy protection regulations.

Working with the European Commission, the U.S. Department of Commerce developed a safe harbor framework for U.S. firms. A **safe harbor** is a private, self-regulating policy and enforcement mechanism that meets the objectives of government regulators and legislation but does not involve government regulation or enforcement. U.S. businesses would be allowed to use personal data from EU countries if they develop privacy protection policies that meet EU standards. Enforcement would occur in the United States using self-policing, regulation, and government enforcement of fair trade statutes.

Internet Challenges to Privacy

Internet technology has posed new challenges for the protection of individual privacy. Information sent over this vast network of networks may pass through many different computer systems before it reaches its final destination. Each of these systems is capable of monitoring, capturing, and storing communications that pass through it.

It is possible to record many online activities, including what searches have been conducted, which Web sites and Web pages have been visited, the online content a person has accessed, and what items that person has inspected or purchased over the Web. Much of this monitoring and tracking of Web site visitors occurs in the background without the visitor's knowledge. It is conducted not just by individual Web sites but by advertising networks such as Microsoft Advertising, Yahoo, and DoubleClick that are capable of tracking all browsing behavior at thousands of Web sites. Tools to monitor visits to the World Wide Web have become popular because they help businesses determine who is visiting their Web sites and how to better target their offerings. (Some firms also monitor the Internet usage of their employees to see how they are using company network resources.) The commercial demand for this personal information is virtually insatiable.

Web sites can learn the identities of their visitors if the visitors voluntarily register at the site to purchase a product or service or to obtain a free service, such as information. Web sites can also capture information about visitors without their knowledge using cookie technology.

Cookies are small text files deposited on a computer hard drive when a user visits Web sites. Cookies identify the visitor's Web browser software and track visits to the Web site. When the visitor returns to a site that has stored a cookie, the Web site software will search the visitor's computer, find the cookie, and know what that person has done in the past. It may also update the cookie, depending on the activity during the visit. In this way, the site can customize its contents for each visitor's interests. For example, if you purchase a book on Amazon.com and return later from the same browser, the site will welcome you by name and recommend other books of interest based on your past purchases. DoubleClick, described earlier in this chapter, uses cookies to build its dossiers with details of online purchases and to examine the behavior of Web site visitors. Figure 3 illustrates how cookies work.

Web sites using cookie technology cannot directly obtain visitors' names and addresses. However, if a person has registered at a site, that information can be combined with cookie data to identify the visitor. Web site owners can also combine the data they have gathered from cookies and other Web site monitoring tools with personal data from other sources, such as offline data collected from surveys or paper catalog purchases, to develop very detailed profiles of their visitors.

There are now even more subtle and surreptitious tools for surveillance of Internet users. Marketers use Web beacons as another tool to monitor online behavior. **Web beacons**, also called *Web bugs,* are tiny objects invisibly embedded in e-mail messages and Web pages that are designed to monitor the behavior of the user visiting a Web site or sending e-mail. The Web beacon captures and transmits information such as the IP address of the user's computer, the time a Web page was viewed and for how long, the type of Web browser that retrieved the beacon, and previously set cookie values. Web beacons are placed on popular Web sites by "third party" firms who pay the Web sites a fee for access to their audience. Typical popular Web sites contain 25–35 Web beacons.

Other **spyware** can secretly install itself on an Internet user's computer by piggybacking on larger applications. Once installed, the spyware calls out to Web sites to send banner ads and other unsolicited material to the user, and it can also report the user's movements on the Internet to other computers.

About 75 percent of global Internet users use Google search and other services, making Google the world's largest collector of online user data. Whatever Google does with its data has an enormous impact on online privacy. Most experts

FIGURE 3   **HOW COOKIES IDENTIFY WEB VISITORS**

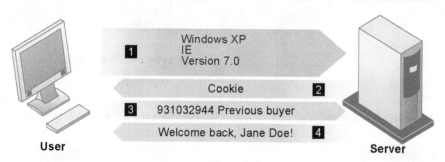

1. The Web server reads the user's Web browser and determines the operating system, browser name, version number, Internet address, and other information.
2. The server transmits a tiny text file with user identification information called a cookie, which the user's browser receives and stores on the user's computer hard drive.
3. When the user returns to the Web site, the server requests the contents of any cookie it deposited previously in the user's computer.
4. The Web server reads the cookie, identifies the visitor, and calls up data on the user.

Cookies are written by a Web site on a visitor's hard drive. When the visitor returns to that Web site, the Web server requests the ID number from the cookie and uses it to access the data stored by that server on that visitor. The Web site can then use these data to display personalized information.

believe that Google possesses the largest collection of personal information in the world—more data on more people than any government agency. Table 5 lists the major Google services that collect user data and how Google uses these data.

For a number of years, Google has been using behavioral targeting to help it display more relevant ads based on users' search activities. One of its programs enables advertisers to target ads based on the search histories of Google users, along with any other information the user submits to Google that Google can obtain, such as age, demographics, region, and other Web activities (such as blogging). An additional program allows Google to help advertisers select keywords and design ads for various market segments based on search histories, such as helping a clothing Web site create and test ads targeted at teenage females.

Google has also been scanning the contents of messages received by users of its free Web-based e-mail service called Gmail. Ads that users see when they read their e-mail are related to the subjects of these messages. Profiles are developed on individual users based on the content in their e-mail. Google now displays targeted ads on YouTube and on Google mobile applications, and its DoubleClick ad network serves up targeted banner ads.

In the past, Google refrained from capitalizing too much on the data it collected, considered the best source of data about user interests on the Internet. But with the emergence of rivals such as Facebook who are aggressively tracking and selling online user data, Google has decided to do more to profit from its user data.

The United States has allowed businesses to gather transaction information generated in the marketplace and then use that information for other marketing purposes without obtaining the informed consent of the individual whose information is being used. U.S. e-commerce sites are largely content to publish statements on their Web sites informing visitors about how their information will be used. Some have added opt-out selection boxes to these information policy statements. An **opt-out** model of informed consent permits the collection of personal information until the consumer specifically requests that the

TABLE 5 HOW GOOGLE USES THE DATA IT COLLECTS

GOOGLE FEATURE	DATA COLLECTED	USE
Google Search	Google search topics Users' Internet addresses	Targeting text ads placed in search results
Gmail	Contents of e-mail messages	Targeting text ads placed next to the e-mail messages
DoubleClick	Data about Web sites visited on Google's ad network	Targeting banner ads
YouTube	Data about videos uploaded and downloaded; some profile data	Targeting ads for Google display-ad network
Mobile Maps with My Location	User's actual or approximate location	Targeting mobile ads based on user's ZIP code
Google Toolbar	Web-browsing data and search history	No ad use at present
Google Buzz	Users' Google profile data and connections	No ad use at present
Google Chrome	Sample of address-bar entries when Google is the default search engine	No ad use at present
Google Checkout	User's name, address, transaction details	No ad use at present
Google Analytics	Traffic data from Web sites using Google's Analytics service	No ad use at present

data not be collected. Privacy advocates would like to see wider use of an **opt-in** model of informed consent in which a business is prohibited from collecting any personal information unless the consumer specifically takes action to approve information collection and use.

The online industry has preferred self-regulation to privacy legislation for protecting consumers. In 1998, the online industry formed the Online Privacy Alliance to encourage self-regulation to develop a set of privacy guidelines for its members. The group promotes the use of online seals, such as that of TRUSTe, certifying Web sites adhering to certain privacy principles. Members of the advertising network industry, including Google's DoubleClick, have created an additional industry association called the Network Advertising Initiative (NAI) to develop its own privacy policies to help consumers opt out of advertising network programs and provide consumers redress from abuses.

Individual firms like AOL, Yahoo!, and Google have recently adopted policies on their own in an effort to address public concern about tracking people online. AOL established an opt-out policy that allows users of its site to not be tracked. Yahoo follows NAI guidelines and also allows opt-out for tracking and Web beacons (Web bugs). Google has reduced retention time for tracking data.

In general, most Internet businesses do little to protect the privacy of their customers, and consumers do not do as much as they should to protect themselves. Many companies with Web sites do not have privacy policies. Of the companies that do post privacy polices on their Web sites, about half do not monitor their sites to ensure they adhere to these policies. The vast majority of online customers claim they are concerned about online privacy, but less than half read the privacy statements on Web sites (Laudon and Traver, 2010).

In one of the more insightful studies of consumer attitudes towards Internet privacy, a group of Berkeley students conducted surveys of online users, and of complaints filed with the Federal Trade Commission involving privacy issues. Here are some of their results. User concerns: people feel they have no control over the information collected about them, and they don't know who to complain to. Web site practices: Web sites collect all this information, but do not let users have access; the policies are unclear; they share data with "affiliates" but never identify who the affiliates are and how many there are. (MySpace, owned by NewsCorp, has over 1,500 affiliates with whom it shares online information.) Web bug trackers: they are ubiquitous and we are not informed they are on the pages we visit. The results of this study and others suggest that consumers are not saying "Take my privacy, I don't care, send me the service for free." They are saying "We want access to the information, we want some controls on what can be collected, what is done with the information, the ability to opt out of the entire tracking enterprise, and some clarity on what the policies really are, and we don't want those policies changed without our participation and permission." (The full report is available at knowprivacy.org.)

Technical Solutions

In addition to legislation, new technologies are available to protect user privacy during interactions with Web sites. Many of these tools are used for encrypting e-mail, for making e-mail or surfing activities appear anonymous, for preventing client computers from accepting cookies, or for detecting and eliminating spyware.

There are now tools to help users determine the kind of personal data that can be extracted by Web sites. The Platform for Privacy Preferences, known as P3P, enables automatic communication of privacy policies between an e-commerce site and its visitors. **P3P** provides a standard for communicating a Web site's

Web sites are posting their privacy policies for visitors to review. The TRUSTe seal designates Web sites that have agreed to adhere to TRUSTe's established privacy principles of disclosure, choice, access, and security.

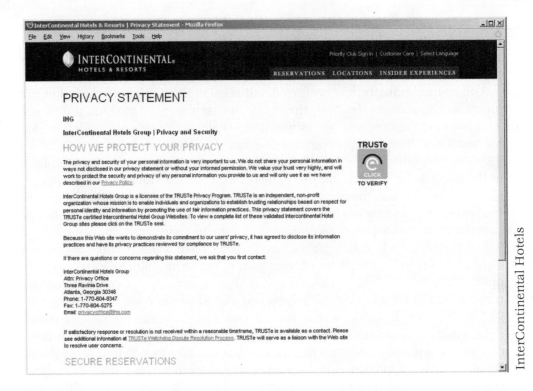

InterContinental Hotels

privacy policy to Internet users and for comparing that policy to the user's preferences or to other standards, such as the FTC's FIP guidelines or the European Directive on Data Protection. Users can use P3P to select the level of privacy they wish to maintain when interacting with the Web site.

The P3P standard allows Web sites to publish privacy policies in a form that computers can understand. Once it is codified according to P3P rules, the privacy policy becomes part of the software for individual Web pages (see Figure 4). Users of Microsoft Internet Explorer Web browsing software can access and read the P3P site's privacy policy and a list of all cookies coming from the site. Internet Explorer enables users to adjust their computers to screen out all cookies or let in selected cookies based on specific levels of privacy. For example, the "Medium" level accepts cookies from first-party host sites that have opt-in or opt-out policies but rejects third-party cookies that use personally identifiable information without an opt-in policy.

However, P3P only works with Web sites of members of the World Wide Web Consortium who have translated their Web site privacy policies into P3P format. The technology will display cookies from Web sites that are not part of the consortium, but users will not be able to obtain sender information or privacy statements. Many users may also need to be educated about interpreting company privacy statements and P3P levels of privacy. Critics point out that only a small percentage of the most popular Web sites use P3P, most users do not understand their browser's privacy settings, and there is no enforcement of P3P standards—companies can claim anything about their privacy policies.

PROPERTY RIGHTS: INTELLECTUAL PROPERTY

Contemporary information systems have severely challenged existing laws and social practices that protect private intellectual property. **Intellectual property** is considered to be intangible property created by individuals or

FIGURE 4   THE P3P STANDARD

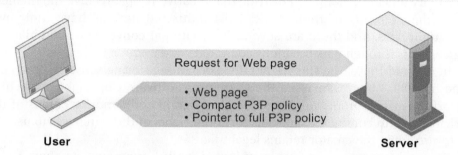

1. The user with P3P Web browsing software requests a Web page.
2. The Web server returns the Web page along with a compact version of the Web site's policy and a pointer to the full P3P policy. If the Web site is not P3P compliant, no P3P data are returned.
3. The user's Web browsing software compares the response from the Web site with the user's privacy preferences. If the Web site does not have a P3P policy or the policy does not match the privacy levels established by the user, it warns the user or rejects the cookies from the Web site. Otherwise, the Web page loads normally.

P3P enables Web sites to translate their privacy policies into a standard format that can be read by the user's Web browser software. The browser software evaluates the Web site's privacy policy to determine whether it is compatible with the user's privacy preferences.

corporations. Information technology has made it difficult to protect intellectual property because computerized information can be so easily copied or distributed on networks. Intellectual property is subject to a variety of protections under three different legal traditions: trade secrets, copyright, and patent law.

Trade Secrets

Any intellectual work product—a formula, device, pattern, or compilation of data—used for a business purpose can be classified as a **trade secret**, provided it is not based on information in the public domain. Protections for trade secrets vary from state to state. In general, trade secret laws grant a monopoly on the ideas behind a work product, but it can be a very tenuous monopoly.

Software that contains novel or unique elements, procedures, or compilations can be included as a trade secret. Trade secret law protects the actual ideas in a work product, not only their manifestation. To make this claim, the creator or owner must take care to bind employees and customers with nondisclosure agreements and to prevent the secret from falling into the public domain.

The limitation of trade secret protection is that, although virtually all software programs of any complexity contain unique elements of some sort, it is difficult to prevent the ideas in the work from falling into the public domain when the software is widely distributed.

Copyright

Copyright is a statutory grant that protects creators of intellectual property from having their work copied by others for any purpose during the life of the author plus an additional 70 years after the author's death. For corporate-owned works, copyright protection lasts for 95 years after their initial creation. Congress has extended copyright protection to books, periodicals, lectures, dramas, musical compositions, maps, drawings, artwork of any kind, and motion pictures. The intent behind copyright laws has been to encourage creativity and authorship by ensuring that creative people receive the financial and other benefits of their work. Most industrial nations have their own copyright laws, and there are several international conventions and bilateral agreements through which nations coordinate and enforce their laws.

In the mid-1960s, the Copyright Office began registering software programs, and in 1980, Congress passed the Computer Software Copyright Act, which clearly provides protection for software program code and for copies of the original sold in commerce, and sets forth the rights of the purchaser to use the software while the creator retains legal title.

Copyright protects against copying of entire programs or their parts. Damages and relief are readily obtained for infringement. The drawback to copyright protection is that the underlying ideas behind a work are not protected, only their manifestation in a work. A competitor can use your software, understand how it works, and build new software that follows the same concepts without infringing on a copyright.

"Look and feel" copyright infringement lawsuits are precisely about the distinction between an idea and its expression. For instance, in the early 1990s, Apple Computer sued Microsoft Corporation and Hewlett-Packard for infringement of the expression of Apple's Macintosh interface, claiming that the defendants copied the expression of overlapping windows. The defendants countered that the idea of overlapping windows can be expressed only in a single way and, therefore, was not protectable under the merger doctrine of copyright law. When ideas and their expression merge, the expression cannot be copyrighted.

In general, courts appear to be following the reasoning of a 1989 case—*Brown Bag Software vs. Symantec Corp.*—in which the court dissected the elements of software alleged to be infringing. The court found that similar concept, function, general functional features (e.g., drop-down menus), and colors are not protectable by copyright law (*Brown Bag Software vs. Symantec Corp.*, 1992).

Patents

A **patent** grants the owner an exclusive monopoly on the ideas behind an invention for 20 years. The congressional intent behind patent law was to ensure that inventors of new machines, devices, or methods receive the full financial and other rewards of their labor and yet make widespread use of the invention possible by providing detailed diagrams for those wishing to use the idea under license from the patent's owner. The granting of a patent is determined by the United States Patent and Trademark Office and relies on court rulings.

The key concepts in patent law are originality, novelty, and invention. The Patent Office did not accept applications for software patents routinely until a 1981 Supreme Court decision that held that computer programs could be a part of a patentable process. Since that time, hundreds of patents have been granted and thousands await consideration.

The strength of patent protection is that it grants a monopoly on the underlying concepts and ideas of software. The difficulty is passing stringent criteria of nonobviousness (e.g., the work must reflect some special understanding and contribution), originality, and novelty, as well as years of waiting to receive protection.

Challenges to Intellectual Property Rights

Contemporary information technologies, especially software, pose severe challenges to existing intellectual property regimes and, therefore, create significant ethical, social, and political issues. Digital media differ from books, periodicals, and other media in terms of ease of replication; ease of transmission; ease of alteration; difficulty in classifying a software work as a program, book, or even music; compactness—making theft easy; and difficulties in establishing uniqueness.

The proliferation of electronic networks, including the Internet, has made it even more difficult to protect intellectual property. Before widespread use of networks, copies of software, books, magazine articles, or films had to be stored on physical media, such as paper, computer disks, or videotape, creating some hurdles to distribution. Using networks, information can be more widely reproduced and distributed. The Seventh Annual Global Software Piracy Study conducted by the International Data Corporation and the Business Software Alliance reported that the rate of global software piracy climbed to 43 percent in 2009, representing $51 billion in global losses from software piracy. Worldwide, for every $100 worth of legitimate software sold that year, an additional $75 worth was obtained illegally (Business Software Alliance, 2010).

The Internet was designed to transmit information freely around the world, including copyrighted information. With the World Wide Web in particular, you can easily copy and distribute virtually anything to thousands and even millions of people around the world, even if they are using different types of computer systems. Information can be illicitly copied from one place and distributed through other systems and networks even though these parties do not willingly participate in the infringement.

Individuals have been illegally copying and distributing digitized MP3 music files on the Internet for a number of years. File-sharing services such as Napster, and later Grokster, Kazaa, and Morpheus, sprung up to help users locate and swap digital music files, including those protected by copyright. Illegal file sharing became so widespread that it threatened the viability of the music recording industry. The recording industry won some legal battles for shutting these services down, but has not been able to halt illegal file sharing entirely. As more and more homes adopt high-speed Internet access, illegal file sharing of videos will pose similar threats to the motion picture industry.

Mechanisms are being developed to sell and distribute books, articles, and other intellectual property legally on the Internet, and the **Digital Millennium Copyright Act (DMCA)** of 1998 is providing some copyright protection. The DMCA implemented a World Intellectual Property Organization Treaty that makes it illegal to circumvent technology-based protections of copyrighted materials. Internet service providers (ISPs) are required to take down sites of copyright infringers that they are hosting once they are notified of the problem.

Microsoft and other major software and information content firms are represented by the Software and Information Industry Association (SIIA), which lobbies for new laws and enforcement of existing laws to protect intellectual property around the world. The SIIA runs an antipiracy hotline for individuals to report piracy activities, offers educational programs to help organizations combat software piracy, and has published guidelines for employee use of software.

ACCOUNTABILITY, LIABILITY, AND CONTROL

Along with privacy and property laws, new information technologies are challenging existing liability laws and social practices for holding individuals and institutions accountable. If a person is injured by a machine controlled, in part, by software, who should be held accountable and, therefore, held liable? Should a public bulletin board or an electronic service, such as America Online, permit the transmission of pornographic or offensive material (as broadcasters), or should they be held harmless against any liability for what users transmit (as is true of common carriers, such as the telephone system)? What about the Internet? If you outsource your information processing, can you hold the external vendor liable for injuries done to your customers? Some real-world examples may shed light on these questions.

Computer-Related Liability Problems

During the last week of September 2009, thousands of customers of TD Bank, one of the largest banks in North America, scrambled to find their payroll checks, social security checks, and savings and checking account balances. The bank's 6.5 million customers were temporarily out of funds because of a computer glitch. The problems were caused by a failed effort to integrate systems of TD Bank and Commerce Bank. A spokesperson for TD Bank, said that "while the overall integration of the systems went well, there have been some speed-bumps in the final stages, as you might expect with a project of this size and complexity." (Vijayan, 2009). Who is liable for any economic harm caused to individuals or businesses that could not access their full account balances in this period?

This case reveals the difficulties faced by information systems executives who ultimately are responsible for any harm done by systems developed by their staffs. In general, insofar as computer software is part of a machine, and the machine injures someone physically or economically, the producer of the software and the operator can be held liable for damages. Insofar as the software acts like a book, storing and displaying information, courts have been reluctant to hold authors, publishers, and booksellers liable for contents (the exception being instances of fraud or defamation), and hence courts have been wary of holding software authors liable for booklike software.

In general, it is very difficult (if not impossible) to hold software producers liable for their software products that are considered to be like books, regardless of the physical or economic harm that results. Historically, print publishers, books, and periodicals have not been held liable because of fears that liability claims would interfere with First Amendment rights guaranteeing freedom of expression.

What about software as a service? ATM machines are a service provided to bank customers. Should this service fail, customers will be inconvenienced and perhaps harmed economically if they cannot access their funds in a timely manner. Should liability protections be extended to software publishers and operators of defective financial, accounting, simulation, or marketing systems?

Software is very different from books. Software users may develop expectations of infallibility about software; software is less easily inspected than a book, and it is more difficult to compare with other software products for quality; software claims actually to perform a task rather than describe a task, as a book does; and people come to depend on services essentially based on software. Given the centrality of software to everyday life, the chances are excellent that liability law will extend its reach to include software even when the software merely provides an information service.

Telephone systems have not been held liable for the messages transmitted because they are regulated common carriers. In return for their right to provide telephone service, they must provide access to all, at reasonable rates, and achieve acceptable reliability. But broadcasters and cable television stations are subject to a wide variety of federal and local constraints on content and facilities. Organizations can be held liable for offensive content on their Web sites, and online services, such as America Online, might be held liable for postings by their users. Although U.S. courts have increasingly exonerated Web sites and ISPs for posting material by third parties, the threat of legal action still has a chilling effect on small companies or individuals who cannot afford to take their cases to trial.

SYSTEM QUALITY: DATA QUALITY AND SYSTEM ERRORS

The debate over liability and accountability for unintentional consequences of system use raises a related but independent moral dimension: What is an acceptable, technologically feasible level of system quality? At what point should system managers say, "Stop testing, we've done all we can to perfect this software. Ship it!" Individuals and organizations may be held responsible for avoidable and foreseeable consequences, which they have a duty to perceive and correct. And the gray area is that some system errors are foreseeable and correctable only at very great expense, an expense so great that pursuing this level of perfection is not feasible economically—no one could afford the product.

For example, although software companies try to debug their products before releasing them to the marketplace, they knowingly ship buggy products because the time and cost of fixing all minor errors would prevent these products from ever being released. What if the product was not offered on the marketplace, would social welfare as a whole not advance and perhaps even decline? Carrying this further, just what is the responsibility of a producer of computer services—should it withdraw the product that can never be perfect, warn the user, or forget about the risk (let the buyer beware)?

Three principal sources of poor system performance are (1) software bugs and errors, (2) hardware or facility failures caused by natural or other causes, and (3) poor input data quality. There is a technological barrier to perfect software, and users must be aware of the potential for catastrophic failure. The software industry has not yet arrived at testing standards for producing software of acceptable but not perfect performance.

Although software bugs and facility catastrophes are likely to be widely reported in the press, by far the most common source of business system failure is data quality. Few companies routinely measure the quality of their data, but individual organizations report data error rates ranging from 0.5 to 30 percent.

QUALITY OF LIFE: EQUITY, ACCESS, AND BOUNDARIES

The negative social costs of introducing information technologies and systems are beginning to mount along with the power of the technology. Many of these negative social consequences are not violations of individual rights or property crimes. Nevertheless, these negative consequences can be extremely harmful to individuals, societies, and political institutions. Computers and information technologies potentially can destroy valuable elements of our culture and society even while they bring us benefits. If there is a balance of good and bad consequences of using information systems, who do we hold responsible for the bad consequences? Next, we briefly examine some of the negative social consequences of systems, considering individual, social, and political responses.

Balancing Power: Center Versus Periphery

An early fear of the computer age was that huge, centralized mainframe computers would centralize power at corporate headquarters and in the nation's capital, resulting in a Big Brother society, as was suggested in George Orwell's novel *1984*. The shift toward highly decentralized computing, coupled with an ideology of empowerment of thousands of workers, and the decentralization of decision making to lower organizational levels, have reduced the fears of power centralization in institutions. Yet much of the empowerment described in popular business magazines is trivial. Lower-level employees may be empowered to make minor decisions, but the key policy decisions may be as centralized as in the past.

Rapidity of Change: Reduced Response Time to Competition

Information systems have helped to create much more efficient national and international markets. The now-more-efficient global marketplace has reduced the normal social buffers that permitted businesses many years to adjust to competition. Time-based competition has an ugly side: The business you work for may not have enough time to respond to global competitors and may be wiped out in a year, along with your job. We stand the risk of developing a "just-in-time society" with "just-in-time jobs" and "just-in-time" workplaces, families, and vacations.

Maintaining Boundaries: Family, Work, and Leisure

Parts of this text were produced on trains and planes, as well as on vacations and during what otherwise might have been "family" time. The danger to ubiquitous computing, telecommuting, nomad computing, and the "do anything anywhere" computing environment is that it is actually coming true. The traditional boundaries that separate work from family and just plain leisure have been weakened.

Although authors have traditionally worked just about anywhere (typewriters have been portable for nearly a century), the advent of information

Although some people enjoy the convenience of working at home, the "do anything anywhere" computing environment can blur the traditional boundaries between work and family time.

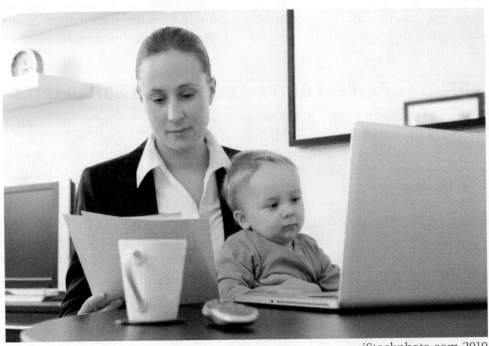

iStockphoto.com 2010

systems, coupled with the growth of knowledge-work occupations, means that more and more people are working when traditionally they would have been playing or communicating with family and friends. The work umbrella now extends far beyond the eight-hour day.

Even leisure time spent on the computer threatens these close social relationships. Extensive Internet use, even for entertainment or recreational purposes, takes people away from their family and friends. Among middle school and teenage children, it can lead to harmful anti-social behavior, such as the recent upsurge in cyberbullying.

Weakening these institutions poses clear-cut risks. Family and friends historically have provided powerful support mechanisms for individuals, and they act as balance points in a society by preserving private life, providing a place for people to collect their thoughts, allowing people to think in ways contrary to their employer, and dream.

Dependence and Vulnerability

Today, our businesses, governments, schools, and private associations, such as churches, are incredibly dependent on information systems and are, therefore, highly vulnerable if these systems fail. With systems now as ubiquitous as the telephone system, it is startling to remember that there are no regulatory or standard-setting forces in place that are similar to telephone, electrical, radio, television, or other public utility technologies. The absence of standards and the criticality of some system applications will probably call forth demands for national standards and perhaps regulatory oversight.

Computer Crime and Abuse

New technologies, including computers, create new opportunities for committing crime by creating new valuable items to steal, new ways to steal them, and new ways to harm others. **Computer crime** is the commission of illegal acts through the use of a computer or against a computer system. Computers or computer systems can be the object of the crime (destroying a company's computer center or a company's computer files), as well as the instrument of a crime (stealing computer lists by illegally gaining access to a computer system using a home computer). Simply accessing a computer system without authorization or with intent to do harm, even by accident, is now a federal crime.

Computer abuse is the commission of acts involving a computer that may not be illegal but that are considered unethical. The popularity of the Internet and e-mail has turned one form of computer abuse—spamming—into a serious problem for both individuals and businesses. **Spam** is junk e-mail sent by an organization or individual to a mass audience of Internet users who have expressed no interest in the product or service being marketed. Spammers tend to market pornography, fraudulent deals and services, outright scams, and other products not widely approved in most civilized societies. Some countries have passed laws to outlaw spamming or to restrict its use. In the United States, it is still legal if it does not involve fraud and the sender and subject of the e-mail are properly identified.

Spamming has mushroomed because it only costs a few cents to send thousands of messages advertising wares to Internet users. According to Sophos, a leading vendor of security software, spam accounted for 97 percent of all business e-mail during the second quarter of 2010 (Schwartz, 2010). Spam costs for businesses are very high (estimated at over $50 billion per year) because of the computing and network resources consumed by billions of unwanted e-mail messages and the time required to deal with them.

Internet service providers and individuals can combat spam by using spam filtering software to block suspicious e-mail before it enters a recipient's e-mail inbox. However, spam filters may block legitimate messages. Spammers know how to skirt around filters by continually changing their e-mail accounts, by incorporating spam messages in images, by embedding spam in e-mail attachments and electronic greeting cards, and by using other people's computers that have been hijacked by botnets. Many spam messages are sent from one country while another country hosts the spam Web site.

Spamming is more tightly regulated in Europe than in the United States. On May 30, 2002, the European Parliament passed a ban on unsolicited commercial messaging. Electronic marketing can be targeted only to people who have given prior consent.

The U.S. CAN-SPAM Act of 2003, which went into effect on January 1, 2004, does not outlaw spamming but does ban deceptive e-mail practices by requiring commercial e-mail messages to display accurate subject lines, identify the true senders, and offer recipients an easy way to remove their names from e-mail lists. It also prohibits the use of fake return addresses. A few people have been prosecuted under the law, but it has had a negligible impact on spamming. Although Facebook and MySpace have won judgments against spammers, most critics argue the law has too many loopholes and is not effectively enforced (Associated Press, 2009).

Another negative impact of computer technology is the rising danger from people using cell phones to send text messages while driving. Many states have outlawed this behavior, but it has been difficult to eradicate. The Interactive Session on Organizations explores this topic.

Employment: Trickle-Down Technology and Reengineering Job Loss

Reengineering work is typically hailed in the information systems community as a major benefit of new information technology. It is much less frequently noted that redesigning business processes could potentially cause millions of mid-level managers and clerical workers to lose their jobs. One economist has raised the possibility that we will create a society run by a small "high tech elite of corporate professionals . . . in a nation of the permanently unemployed" (Rifkin, 1993).

Other economists are much more sanguine about the potential job losses. They believe relieving bright, educated workers from reengineered jobs will result in these workers moving to better jobs in fast-growth industries. Missing from this equation are unskilled, blue-collar workers and older, less well-educated middle managers. It is not clear that these groups can be retrained easily for high-quality (high-paying) jobs. Careful planning and sensitivity to employee needs can help companies redesign work to minimize job losses.

Equity and Access: Increasing Racial and Social Class Cleavages

Does everyone have an equal opportunity to participate in the digital age? Will the social, economic, and cultural gaps that exist in the United States and other societies be reduced by information systems technology? Or will the cleavages be increased, permitting the better off to become even more better off relative to others?

These questions have not yet been fully answered because the impact of systems technology on various groups in society has not been thoroughly studied. What is known is that information, knowledge, computers, and access

INTERACTIVE SESSION: ORGANIZATIONS

THE PERILS OF TEXTING

Cell phones have become a staple of modern society. Nearly everyone has them, and people carry and use them at all hours of the day. For the most part, this is a good thing: the benefits of staying connected at any time and at any location are considerable. But if you're like most Americans, you may regularly talk on the phone or even text while at the wheel of a car. This dangerous behavior has resulted in increasing numbers of accidents and fatalities caused by cell phone usage. The trend shows no sign of slowing down.

In 2003, a federal study of 10,000 drivers by the National Highway Traffic Safety Administration (NHTSA) set out to determine the effects of using cell phones behind the wheel. The results were conclusive: talking on the phone is equivalent to a 10-point reduction in IQ and a .08 blood alcohol level, which law enforcement considers intoxicated. Hands-free sets were ineffective in eliminating risk, the study found, because the conversation itself is what distracts drivers, not holding the phone. Cell phone use caused 955 fatalities and 240,000 accidents in 2002. Related studies indicated that drivers that talked on the phone while driving increased their crash risk fourfold, and drivers that texted while driving increased their crash risk by a whopping 23 times.

Since that study, mobile device usage has grown by an order of magnitude, worsening this already dangerous situation. The number of wireless subscribers in America has increased by around 1,000 percent since 1995 to nearly 300 million overall in 2010, and Americans' usage of wireless minutes increased by approximately 6,000 percent. This increase in cell phone usage has been accompanied by an upsurge in phone-related fatalities and accidents: In 2010, it's estimated that texting caused 5,870 fatalities and 515,000 accidents, up considerably from prior years. These figures are roughly half of equivalent statistics for drunk driving. Studies show that drivers know that using the phone while driving is one of the most dangerous things you can do on the road, but refuse to admit that it's dangerous when they themselves do it.

Of users that text while driving, the more youthful demographic groups, such as the 18–29 age group, are by far the most frequent texters. About three quarters of Americans in this age group regularly text, compared to just 22 percent of the 35–44 age group. Correspondingly, the majority of accidents involving mobile device use behind the wheel involve young adults. Among this age group, texting behind the wheel is just one of a litany of problems raised by frequent texting: anxiety, distraction, failing grades, repetitive stress injuries, and sleep deprivation are just some of the other problems brought about by excessive use of mobile devices. Teenagers are particularly prone to using cell phones to text because they want to know what's happening to their friends and are anxious about being socially isolated.

Analysts predict that over 800 billion text messages will be sent in 2010. Texting is clearly here to stay, and in fact has supplanted phone calls as the most commonly used method of mobile communication. People are unwilling to give up their mobile devices because of the pressures of staying connected. Neurologists have found that the neural response to multitasking by texting while driving suggests that people develop addictions to the digital devices they use most, getting quick bursts of adrenaline, without which driving becomes boring.

There are interests opposed to legislation prohibiting cell phone use in cars. A number of legislators believe that it's not state or federal government's role to prohibit poor decision making. Auto makers, and some safety researchers, are arguing that with the proper technology and under appropriate conditions, communicating from a moving vehicle is a manageable risk. Louis Tijerina, a veteran of the NHTSA and Ford Motor Co. researcher, notes that even as mobile phone subscriptions have surged to over 250 million during the past decade, the death rate from accidents on the highways has fallen.

Nevertheless, lawmakers are increasingly recognizing the need for more powerful legislation barring drivers from texting behind the wheel. Many states have made inroads with laws prohibiting texting while operating vehicles. In Utah, drivers crashing while texting can receive 15 years in prison, by far the toughest sentence for texting while driving in the nation when the legislation was enacted. Utah's law assumes that drivers understand the risks of texting while driving, whereas in other states, prosecutors must prove that the driver knew about the risks of texting while driving before doing so.

Utah's tough law was the result of a horrifying accident in which a speeding college student, texting at the wheel, rear-ended a car in front. The car lost control, entered the opposite side of the road, and was hit head-on by a pickup truck hauling a trailer, killing the driver instantly. In September 2008, a train engineer in California was texting within a minute prior to the most fatal train accident in almost two decades. Californian authorities responded by banning the use of cell phones by train workers while on duty.

In total, 31 states have banned texting while driving in some form, and most of those states have a full ban for phone users of all ages. The remaining states are likely to follow suit in coming years as well. President Obama also banned texting while driving for all federal government employees in October 2009. Still, there's more work to be done to combat this dangerous and life-threatening practice.

Sources: Paulo Salazar, "Banning Texting While Driving," WCBI.com, August 7, 2010; Jerry Hirsch, "Teen Drivers Dangerously Divide Their Attention," *Los Angeles Times*, August 3, 2010; www.drivinglaws.org, accessed July 2010; www.drivinglaws.org, accessed July 7, 2010; Matt Richtel, "Driver Texting Now an Issue in the Back Seat," *The New York Times*, September 9, 2009; Matt Richtel, "Utah Gets Tough With Texting Drivers," *The New York Times*, August 29, 2009; Matt Richtel, "In Study, Texting Lifts Crash Risk by Large Margin," *The New York Times*, July 28, 2009; Matt Richtel, "Drivers and Legislators Dismiss Cellphone Risks," *The New York Times*, July 19, 2009; Tom Regan, "Some Sobering Stats on Texting While Driving," *The Christian Science Monitor*, May 28, 2009; Katie Hafner, "Texting May be Taking a Toll on Teenagers," *The New York Times*, May 26, 2009; and Tara Parker-Pope, "Texting Until Their Thumbs Hurt," The *New York Times*, May 26, 2009.

CASE STUDY QUESTIONS

1. Which of the five moral dimensions of information systems identified in this text is involved in this case?

2. What are the ethical, social, and political issues raised by this case?

3. Which of the ethical principles described in the text are useful for decision making about texting while driving?

MIS IN ACTION

1. Many people at state and local levels are calling for a federal law against texting while driving. Use a search engine to explore what steps the federal government has taken to discourage texting while driving.

2. Most people are not aware of the widespread impact of texting while driving across the United States. Do a search on "texting while driving." Examine all the search results for the first two pages. Enter the information into a two-column table. In the left column put the locality of the report and year. In the right column give a brief description of the search result, e.g., accident, report, court judgment, etc. What can you conclude from these search results and table?

to these resources through educational institutions and public libraries are inequitably distributed along ethnic and social class lines, as are many other information resources. Several studies have found that certain ethnic and income groups in the United States are less likely to have computers or online Internet access even though computer ownership and Internet access have soared in the past five years. Although the gap is narrowing, higher-income families in each ethnic group are still more likely to have home computers and Internet access than lower-income families in the same group.

A similar **digital divide** exists in U.S. schools, with schools in high-poverty areas less likely to have computers, high-quality educational technology programs, or Internet access availability for their students. Left uncorrected, the digital divide could lead to a society of information haves, computer literate and skilled, versus a large group of information have-nots, computer illiterate and unskilled. Public interest groups want to narrow this digital divide by making digital information services—including the Internet—available to virtually everyone, just as basic telephone service is now.

Health Risks: RSI, CVS, and Technostress

The most common occupational disease today is **repetitive stress injury (RSI)**. RSI occurs when muscle groups are forced through repetitive actions often with high-impact loads (such as tennis) or tens of thousands of repetitions under low-impact loads (such as working at a computer keyboard).

The single largest source of RSI is computer keyboards. The most common kind of computer-related RSI is **carpal tunnel syndrome (CTS)**, in which pressure on the median nerve through the wrist's bony structure, called a carpal tunnel, produces pain. The pressure is caused by constant repetition of keystrokes: in a single shift, a word processor may perform 23,000 keystrokes. Symptoms of carpal tunnel syndrome include numbness, shooting pain, inability to grasp objects, and tingling. Millions of workers have been diagnosed with carpal tunnel syndrome.

RSI is avoidable. Designing workstations for a neutral wrist position (using a wrist rest to support the wrist), proper monitor stands, and footrests all contribute to proper posture and reduced RSI. Ergonomically correct keyboards are also an option. These measures should be supported by frequent rest breaks and rotation of employees to different jobs.

RSI is not the only occupational illness computers cause. Back and neck pain, leg stress, and foot pain also result from poor ergonomic designs of workstations. **Computer vision syndrome (CVS)** refers to any eyestrain condition related to display screen use in desktop computers, laptops, e-readers, smartphones, and hand-held video games. CVS affects about 90 percent of people who spend three hours or more per day at a computer (Beck, 2010). Its symptoms, which are usually temporary, include headaches, blurred vision, and dry and irritated eyes.

The newest computer-related malady is **technostress**, which is stress induced by computer use. Its symptoms include aggravation, hostility toward humans, impatience, and fatigue. According to experts, humans working continuously with computers come to expect other humans and human institutions to behave like computers, providing instant responses, attentiveness, and

iStockphoto.com 2010

Repetitive stress injury (RSI) is the leading occupational disease today. The single largest cause of RSI is computer keyboard work.

an absence of emotion. Technostress is thought to be related to high levels of job turnover in the computer industry, high levels of early retirement from computer-intense occupations, and elevated levels of drug and alcohol abuse.

The incidence of technostress is not known but is thought to be in the millions and growing rapidly in the United States. Computer-related jobs now top the list of stressful occupations based on health statistics in several industrialized countries.

To date, the role of radiation from computer display screens in occupational disease has not been proved. Video display terminals (VDTs) emit nonionizing electric and magnetic fields at low frequencies. These rays enter the body and have unknown effects on enzymes, molecules, chromosomes, and cell membranes. Long-term studies are investigating low-level electromagnetic fields and birth defects, stress, low birth weight, and other diseases. All manufacturers have reduced display screen emissions since the early 1980s, and European countries, such as Sweden, have adopted stiff radiation emission standards.

In addition to these maladies, computer technology may be harming our cognitive functions. Although the Internet has made it much easier for people to access, create, and use information, some experts believe that it is also preventing people from focusing and thinking clearly. The Interactive Session on Technology highlights the debate that has emerged about this problem.

The computer has become a part of our lives—personally as well as socially, culturally, and politically. It is unlikely that the issues and our choices will become easier as information technology continues to transform our world. The growth of the Internet and the information economy suggests that all the ethical and social issues we have described will be heightened further as we move into the first digital century.

INTERACTIVE SESSION: TECHNOLOGY

TOO MUCH TECHNOLOGY?

Do you think that the more information managers receive, the better their decisions? Well, think again. Most of us can no longer imagine the world without the Internet and without our favorite gadgets, whether they're iPads, smartphones, laptops, or cell phones. However, although these devices have brought about a new era of collaboration and communication, they also have introduced new concerns about our relationship with technology. Some researchers suggest that the Internet and other digital technologies are fundamentally changing the way we think—and not for the better. Is the Internet actually making us "dumber," and have we reached a point where we have too much technology? Or does the Internet offer so many new opportunities to discover information that it's actually making us "smarter." And, by the way, how do we define "dumber" and "smarter" in an Internet age?

Wait a second, you're saying. How could this be? The Internet is an unprecedented source for acquiring and sharing all types of information. Creating and disseminating media has never been easier. Resources like Wikipedia and Google have helped to organize knowledge and make that knowledge accessible to the world, and they would not have been possible without the Internet. And other digital media technologies have become indispensable parts of our lives. At first glance, it's not clear how such advancements could do anything but make us smarter.

In response to this argument, several authorities claim that making it possible for millions of people to create media—written blogs, photos, videos—has understandably lowered the quality of media. Bloggers very rarely do original reporting or research but instead copy it from professional resources. YouTube videos contributed by newbies to video come nowhere near the quality of professional videos. Newspapers struggle to stay in business while bloggers provide free content of inconsistent quality.

But similar warnings were issued in response to the development of the printing press. As Gutenberg's invention spread throughout Europe, contemporary literature exploded in popularity, and much of it was considered mediocre by intellectuals of the era. But rather than being destroyed, it was simply in the early stages of fundamental change. As people came to grips with the new technology and

the new norms governing it, literature, newspapers, scientific journals, fiction, and non-fiction all began to contribute to the intellectual climate instead of detracting from it. Today, we can't imagine a world without print media.

Advocates of digital media argue that history is bound to repeat itself as we gain familiarity with the Internet and other newer technologies. The scientific revolution was galvanized by peer review and collaboration enabled by the printing press. According to many digital media supporters, the Internet will usher in a similar revolution in publishing capability and collaboration, and it will be a resounding success for society as a whole.

This may all be true, but from a cognitive standpoint, the effects of the Internet and other digital devices might not be so positive. New studies suggest that digital technologies are damaging our ability to think clearly and focus. Digital technology users develop an inevitable desire to multitask, doing several things at once while using their devices.

Although TV, the Internet, and video games are effective at developing our visual processing ability, research suggests that they detract from our ability to think deeply and retain information. It's true that the Internet grants users easy access to the world's information, but the medium through which that information is delivered is hurting our ability to think deeply and critically about what we read and hear. You'd be "smarter" (in the sense of being able to give an account of the content) by reading a book rather than viewing a video on the same topic while texting with your friends.

Using the Internet lends itself to multitasking. Pages are littered with hyperlinks to other sites; tabbed browsing allows us to switch rapidly between two windows; and we can surf the Web while watching TV, instant messaging friends, or talking on the phone. But the constant distractions and disruptions that are central to online experiences prevent our brains from creating the neural connections that constitute full understanding of a topic. Traditional print media, by contrast, makes it easier to fully concentrate on the content with fewer interruptions.

A recent study conducted by a team of researchers at Stanford found that multitaskers are not only more easily distracted, but were also surprisingly poor at multitasking compared to people who rarely do so themselves. The team also found that multitaskers receive a jolt of excitement when confronted with a new piece of information or a new call, message, or e-mail.

The cellular structure of the brain is highly adaptable and adjusts to the tools we use, so multitaskers quickly become dependent on the excitement they experience when confronted with something new. This means that multitaskers continue to be easily distracted, even if they're totally unplugged from the devices they most often use.

Eyal Ophir, a cognitive scientist on the research team at Stanford, devised a test to measure this phenomenon. Subjects self-identifying as multitaskers were asked to keep track of red rectangles in series of images. When blue rectangles were introduced, multitaskers struggled to recognize whether or not the red rectangles had changed position from image to image. Normal testers significantly outperformed the multitaskers. Less than three percent of multitaskers (called "supertaskers") are able to manage multiple information streams at once; for the vast majority of us, multitasking does not result in greater productivity.

Neuroscientist Michael Merzenich argues that our brains are being 'massively remodeled' by our constant and ever-growing usage of the Web. And it's not just the Web that's contributing to this trend. Our ability to focus is also being undermined by the constant distractions provided by smart phones and other digital technology. Television and video games are no exception. Another study showed that when presented with two identical TV shows, one of which had a news crawl at the bottom, viewers retained much more information about the show without the news crawl. The impact of these technologies on children may be even greater than the impact on adults, because their brains are still developing, and they already struggle to set proper priorities and resist impulses.

The implications of recent research on the impact of Web 2.0 "social" technologies for management decision making are significant. As it turns out, the "always-connected" harried executive scurrying through airports and train stations, holding multiple voice and text conversations with clients and co-workers on sometimes several mobile devices, might not be a very good decision maker. In fact, the quality of decision making most likely falls as the quantity of digital information increases through multiple channels, and managers lose their critical thinking capabilities. Likewise, in terms of management productivity, studies of Internet use in the workplace suggest that Web 2.0 social technologies offer managers new opportunities to waste time rather than focus on their responsibilities. Checked your Facebook page today? Clearly we need to find out more about the impacts of mobile and social technologies on management work.

Sources: Randall Stross, "Computers at Home: Educational Hope vs. Teenage Reality," *The New York Times*, July 9, 2010; Matt Richtel, "Hooked on Gadgets, and Paying a Mental Price," *The New York Times*, June 6, 2010; Clay Shirky, "Does the Internet Make you Smarter?" *The Wall Street Journal*, June 4, 2010; Nicholas Carr, "Does the Internet Make you Dumber?" *The Wall Street Journal*, June 5, 2010; Ofer Malamud and Christian Pop-Echeles, "Home Computer Use and the Development of Human Capital," January 2010; and "Is Technology Producing a Decline in Critical Thinking and Analysis?" Science Daily, January 29, 2009.

CASE STUDY QUESTIONS

1. What are some of the arguments for and against the use of digital media?

2. How might the brain affected by constant digital media usage?

3. Do you think these arguments outweigh the positives of digital media usage? Why or why not?

4. What additional concerns are there for children using digital media? Should children under 8 use computers and cellphones? Why or why not?

MIS IN ACTION

1. Make a daily log for 1 week of all the activities you perform each day using digital technology (such as cell phones, computers, television, etc.) and the amount of time you spend on each. Note the occasions when you are multitasking. On average, how much time each day do you spend using digital technology? How much of this time do you spend multitasking? Do you think your life is too technology-intense? Justify your response.

4   HANDS-ON MIS PROJECTS

The projects in this section give you hands-on experience in analyzing the privacy implications of using online data brokers, developing a corporate policy for employee Web usage, using blog creation tools to create a simple blog, and using Internet newsgroups for market research.

Management Decision Problems

1. USAData's Web site is linked to massive databases that consolidate personal data on millions of people. Anyone with a credit card can purchase marketing lists of consumers broken down by location, age, income level, and interests. If you click on Consumer Leads to order a consumer mailing list, you can find the names, addresses, and sometimes phone numbers of potential sales leads residing in a specific location and purchase the list of those names. One could use this capability to obtain a list, for example, of everyone in Peekskill, New York, making $150,000 or more per year. Do data brokers such as USAData raise privacy issues? Why or why not? If your name and other personal information were in this database, what limitations on access would you want in order to preserve your privacy? Consider the following data users: government agencies, your employer, private business firms, other individuals.

2. As the head of a small insurance company with six employees, you are concerned about how effectively your company is using its networking and human resources. Budgets are tight, and you are struggling to meet payrolls because employees are reporting many overtime hours. You do not believe that the employees have a sufficiently heavy work load to warrant working longer hours and are looking into the amount of time they spend on the Internet.

WEB USAGE REPORT FOR THE WEEK ENDING JANUARY 9, 2010.

USER NAME	MINUTES ONLINE	WEB SITE VISITED
Kelleher, Claire	45	www.doubleclick.net
Kelleher, Claire	107	www.yahoo.com
Kelleher, Claire	96	www.insweb.com
McMahon, Patricia	83	www.itunes.com
McMahon, Patricia	44	www.insweb.com
Milligan, Robert	112	www.youtube.com
Milligan, Robert	43	www.travelocity.com
Olivera, Ernesto	40	www.CNN.com
Talbot, Helen	125	www.etrade.com
Talbot, Helen	27	www.nordstrom.com
Talbot, Helen	35	www.yahoo.com
Talbot, Helen	73	www.ebay.com
Wright, Steven	23	www.facebook.com
Wright, Steven	15	www.autobytel.com

Each employee uses a computer with Internet access on the job. You requested the preceding weekly report of employee Web usage from your information systems department.

- Calculate the total amount of time each employee spent on the Web for the week and the total amount of time that company computers were used for this purpose. Rank the employees in the order of the amount of time each spent online.

- Do your findings and the contents of the report indicate any ethical problems employees are creating? Is the company creating an ethical problem by monitoring its employees' use of the Internet?
- Use the guidelines for ethical analysis presented in this chapter to develop a solution to the problems you have identified.

Achieving Operational Excellence: Creating a Simple Blog

Software skills: Blog creation
Business skills: Blog and Web page design

In this project, you'll learn how to build a simple blog of your own design using the online blog creation software available at Blogger.com. Pick a sport, hobby, or topic of interest as the theme for your blog. Name the blog, give it a title, and choose a template for the blog. Post at least four entries to the blog, adding a label for each posting. Edit your posts, if necessary. Upload an image, such as a photo from your hard drive or the Web to your blog. (Google recommends Open Photo, Flickr: Creative Commons, or Creative Commons Search as sources for photos. Be sure to credit the source for your image.) Add capabilities for other registered users, such as team members, to comment on your blog. Briefly describe how your blog could be useful to a company selling products or services related to the theme of your blog. List the tools available to Blogger (including Gadgets) that would make your blog more useful for business and describe the business uses of each. Save your blog and show it to your instructor.

Improving Decision Making: Using Internet Newsgroups for Online Market Research

Software Skills: Web browser software and Internet newsgroups
Business Skills: Using Internet newsgroups to identify potential customers

This project will help develop your Internet skills in using newsgroups for marketing. It will also ask you to think about the ethical implications of using information in online discussion groups for business purposes.

You are producing hiking boots that you sell through a few stores at this time. You think your boots are more comfortable than those of your competition. You believe you can undersell many of your competitors if you can significantly increase your production and sales. You would like to use Internet discussion groups interested in hiking, climbing, and camping both to sell your boots and to make them well known. Visit groups.google.com, which stores discussion postings from many thousands of newsgroups. Through this site you can locate all relevant newsgroups and search them by keyword, author's name, forum, date, and subject. Choose a message and examine it carefully, noting all the information you can obtain, including information about the author.

- How could you use these newsgroups to market your boots?
- What ethical principles might you be violating if you use these messages to sell your boots? Do you think there are ethical problems in using newsgroups this way? Explain your answer.
- Next use Google or Yahoo.com to search the hiking boots industry and locate sites that will help you develop other new ideas for contacting potential customers.
- Given what you have learned in this chapter, prepare a plan to use newsgroups and other alternative methods to begin attracting visitors to your site.

LEARNING TRACK MODULES

The following Learning Tracks provide content relevant to the topics covered in this chapter:

1. Developing a Corporate Code of Ethics for Information Systems
2. Creating a Web Page

Review Summary

1. *What ethical, social, and political issues are raised by information systems?*

    Information technology is introducing changes for which laws and rules of acceptable conduct have not yet been developed. Increasing computing power, storage, and networking capabilities—including the Internet—expand the reach of individual and organizational actions and magnify their impacts. The ease and anonymity with which information is now communicated, copied, and manipulated in online environments pose new challenges to the protection of privacy and intellectual property. The main ethical, social, and political issues raised by information systems center around information rights and obligations, property rights and obligations, accountability and control, system quality, and quality of life.

2. *What specific principles for conduct can be used to guide ethical decisions?*

    Six ethical principles for judging conduct include the Golden Rule, Immanuel Kant's Categorical Imperative, Descartes' rule of change, the Utilitarian Principle, the Risk Aversion Principle, and the ethical "no free lunch" rule. These principles should be used in conjunction with an ethical analysis.

3. *Why do contemporary information systems technology and the Internet pose challenges to the protection of individual privacy and intellectual property?*

    Contemporary data storage and data analysis technology enables companies to easily gather personal data about individuals from many different sources and analyze these data to create detailed electronic profiles about individuals and their behaviors. Data flowing over the Internet can be monitored at many points. Cookies and other Web monitoring tools closely track the activities of Web site visitors. Not all Web sites have strong privacy protection policies, and they do not always allow for informed consent regarding the use of personal information. Traditional copyright laws are insufficient to protect against software piracy because digital material can be copied so easily and transmitted to many different locations simultaneously over the Internet.

4. *How have information systems affected everyday life?*

    Although computer systems have been sources of efficiency and wealth, they have some negative impacts. Computer errors can cause serious harm to individuals and organizations. Poor data quality is also responsible for disruptions and losses for businesses. Jobs can be lost when computers replace workers or tasks become unnecessary in reengineered business processes. The ability to own and use a computer may be exacerbating socioeconomic disparities among different racial groups and social classes. Widespread use of computers increases opportunities for computer crime and computer abuse. Computers can also create health problems, such as RSI, computer vision syndrome, and technostress.

Key Terms

Accountability
Carpal tunnel syndrome (CTS)
Computer abuse
Computer crime
Computer vision syndrome (CVS)
Cookies
Copyright
Descartes' rule of change
Digital divide
Digital Millennium Copyright Act (DMCA)
Due process

Ethical "no free lunch" rule
Ethics
Fair Information Practices (FIP)
Golden Rule
Immanuel Kant's Categorical Imperative
Information rights
Informed consent
Intellectual property
Liability
Nonobvious relationship awareness (NORA)
Opt-in
Opt-out

P3P
Patent
Privacy
Profiling
Repetitive stress injury (RSI)
Responsibility
Risk Aversion Principle

Safe harbor
Spam
Spyware
Technostress
Trade secret
Utilitarian Principle
Web beacons

Review Questions

1. What ethical, social, and political issues are raised by information systems?

   - Explain how ethical, social, and political issues are connected and give some examples.

   - List and describe the key technological trends that heighten ethical concerns.

   - Differentiate between responsibility, accountability, and liability.

2. What specific principles for conduct can be used to guide ethical decisions?

   - List and describe the five steps in an ethical analysis.

   - Identify and describe six ethical principles.

3. Why do contemporary information systems technology and the Internet pose challenges to the protection of individual privacy and intellectual property?

- Define privacy and fair information practices.

- Explain how the Internet challenges the protection of individual privacy and intellectual property.

- Explain how informed consent, legislation, industry self-regulation, and technology tools help protect the individual privacy of Internet users.

- List and define the three different regimes that protect intellectual property rights.

4. How have information systems affected everyday life?

   - Explain why it is so difficult to hold software services liable for failure or injury.

   - List and describe the principal causes of system quality problems.

   - Name and describe four quality-of-life impacts of computers and information systems.

   - Define and describe technostress and RSI and explain their relationship to information technology.

Discussion Questions

1. Should producers of software-based services, such as ATMs, be held liable for economic injuries suffered when their systems fail?

2. Should companies be responsible for unemployment caused by their information systems? Why or why not?

3. Discuss the pros and cons of allowing companies to amass personal data for behavioral targeting.

Video Cases

Video Cases and Instructional Videos illustrating some of the concepts in this chapter are available. Contact your instructor to access these videos.

Collaboration and Teamwork: Developing a Corporate Ethics Code

With three or four of your classmates, develop a corporate ethics code that addresses both employee privacy and the privacy of customers and users of the corporate Web site. Be sure to consider e-mail privacy and employer monitoring of worksites, as well as corporate use of information about employees concerning their off-the-job behavior (e.g.,

lifestyle, marital arrangements, and so forth). If possible, use Google Sites to post links to Web pages, team communication announcements, and work assignments; to brainstorm; and to work collaboratively on project documents. Try to use Google Docs to develop your solution and presentation for the class.

When Radiation Therapy Kills
CASE STUDY

When new expensive medical therapies come along, promising to cure people of illness, one would think that the manufacturers, doctors, and technicians, along with the hospitals and state oversight agencies, would take extreme caution in their application and use. Often this is not the case. Contemporary radiation therapy offers a good example of society failing to anticipate and control the negative impacts of a technology powerful enough to kill people.

For individuals and their families suffering through a battle with cancer, technical advancements in radiation treatment represent hope and a chance for a healthy, cancer-free life. But when these highly complex machines used to treat cancers go awry or when medical technicians and doctors fail to follow proper safety procedures, it results in suffering worse than the ailments radiation aims to cure. A litany of horror stories underscores the consequences when hospitals fail to provide safe radiation treatment to cancer patients. In many of these horror stories, poor software design, poor human-machine interfaces, and lack of proper training are root causes of the problems.

The deaths of Scott Jerome-Parks and Alexandra Jn-Charles, both patients of New York City hospitals, are prime examples of radiation treatments going awry. Jerome-Parks worked in southern Manhattan near the site of the World Trade Center attacks, and suspected that the tongue cancer he developed later was related to toxic dust that he came in contact with after the attacks. His prognosis was uncertain at first, but he had some reason to be optimistic, given the quality of the treatment provided by state-of-the-art linear accelerators at St. Vincent's Hospital, which he selected for his treatment. But after receiving erroneous dosages of radiation several times, his condition drastically worsened.

For the most part, state-of-the-art linear accelerators do in fact provide effective and safe care for cancer patients, and Americans safely receive an increasing amount of medical radiation each year. Radiation helps to diagnose and treat all sorts of cancers, saving many patients' lives in the process, and is administered safely to over half of all cancer patients. Whereas older machines were only capable of imaging a tumor in two dimensions and projecting straight beams of radiation, newer linear accelerators are capable of modeling cancerous tumors in three dimensions and shaping beams of radiation to conform to those shapes.

One of the most common issues with radiation therapy is finding ways to destroy cancerous cells while preserving healthy cells. Using this beam-shaping technique, radiation doesn't pass through as much healthy tissue to reach the cancerous areas. Hospitals advertised their new accelerators as being able to treat previously untreatable cancers because of the precision of the beam-shaping method. Using older machinery, cancers that were too close to important bodily structures were considered too dangerous to treat with radiation due to the imprecision of the equipment.

How, then, are radiation-related accidents increasing in frequency, given the advances in linear acceleration technology? In the cases of Jerome-Parks and Jn-Charles, a combination of machine malfunctions and user error led to these frightening mistakes. Jerome-Parks's brain stem and neck were exposed to excessive dosages of radiation on three separate occasions because of a computer error. The linear accelerator used to treat Jerome-Parks is known as a multi-leaf collimator, a newer, more powerful model that uses over a hundred metal "leaves" to adjust the shape and strength of the beam. The St. Vincent's hospital collimator was made by Varian Medical Systems, a leading supplier of radiation equipment.

Dr. Anthony M. Berson, St. Vincent's chief radiation oncologist, reworked Mr. Jerome Parks's radiation treatment plan to give more protection to his teeth. Nina Kalach, the medical physicist in charge of implementing Jerome-Parks's radiation treatment plan, used Varian software to revise the plan. State records show that as Ms. Kalach was trying to save her work, the computer began seizing up, displaying an error message. The error message asked if Ms. Kalach wanted to save her changes before the program aborted and she responded that she did. Dr. Berson approved the plan.

Six minutes after another computer crash, the first of several radioactive beams was turned on, followed by several additional rounds of radiation the next few days. After the third treatment, Ms. Kalach ran a test to verify that the treatment plan was carried out as prescribed, and found that the multileaf collimator, which was supposed to focus the beam precisely on Mr. Jerome Parks's tumor, was wide open. The patient's entire neck had been exposed and Mr. Jerome-Parks had seven times the prescribed dose of radiation.

As a result of the radiation overdose, Mr. Jerome-Parks's experienced deafness and near-blindness, ulcers in his mouth and throat, persistent nausea, and severe pain. His teeth were falling out, he couldn't swallow, and he was eventually unable to breathe. He died soon after, at the age of 43.

Jn-Charles's case was similarly tragic. A 32-year old mother of two from Brooklyn, she was diagnosed with an aggressive form of breast cancer, but her outlook seemed good after breast surgery and chemotherapy, with only 28 days of radiation treatments left to perform. However, the linear accelerator used at the Brooklyn hospital where Jn-Charles was treated was not a multi-leaf collimator, but instead a slightly older model, which uses a device known as a "wedge" to prevent radiation from reaching unintended areas of the body.

On the day of her 28th and final session, technicians realized that something had gone wrong. Jn-Charles's skin had slowly begun to peel and seemed to resist healing. When the hospital looked into the treatment to see why this could have happened, they discovered that the linear accelerator lacked the crucial command to insert the wedge, which must be programmed by the user. Technicians had failed to notice error messages on their screens indicating the missing wedge during each of the 27 sessions. This meant that Jn-Charles had been exposed to almost quadruple the normal amount of radiation during each of those 27 visits.

Ms. Jn-Charles's radiation overdose created a wound that would not heal despite numerous sessions in a hyperbaric chamber and multiple surgeries. Although the wound closed up over a year later, she died shortly afterwards.

It might seem that the carelessness or laziness of the medical technicians who administered treatment is primarily to blame in these cases, but other factors have contributed just as much. The complexity of new linear accelerator technology has not been accompanied with appropriate updates in software, training, safety procedures, and staffing. St. Vincent's hospital stated that system crashes similar to those involved in the improper therapy for Mr. Jerome-Parks "are not uncommon with the Varian software, and these issues have been communicated to Varian on numerous occasions."

Manufacturers of these machines boast that they can safely administer radiation treatment to more and more patients each day, but hospitals are rarely able to adjust their staffing to handle those workloads or increase the amount of training technicians receive before using newer machines. Medical technicians incorrectly assume that the new systems and software are going to work correctly, but in reality they have not been tested over long periods of time.

Many of these errors could have been detected if the machine operators were paying attention. In fact, many of the reported errors involve mistakes as simple and as egregious as treating patients for the wrong cancers; in one example, a brain cancer patient received radiation intended for breast cancer. Today's linear accelerators also lack some of the necessary safeguards given the amounts of radiation that they can deliver. For example, many linear accelerators are unable to alert users when a dosage of radiation far exceeds the necessary amount to effectively damage a cancerous tumor. Though responsibility ultimately rests with the technician, software programmers may not have designed their product with the technician's needs in mind.

Though the complexity of newer machines has exposed the inadequacy of the safety procedures hospitals employ for radiation treatments, the increasing number of patients receiving radiation due to the speed and increased capability of these machines has created other problems. Technicians at many of the hospitals reporting radiation-related errors reported being chronically overworked, often dealing with over a hundred patients per day. These already swamped medical technicians are not forced to check over the settings of the linear accelerators that they are handling, and errors that are introduced to the computer systems early on are difficult to detect. As a result, the same erroneous treatment may be administered repeatedly, until the technicians and doctors have a reason to check it. Often, the reason is a seriously injured patient.

Further complicating the issue is the fact that the total number of radiation-related accidents each year is essentially unknown. No single agency exists to collect data across the country on these accidents, and many states don't even require that accidents be reported. Even in states that do, hospitals are often reluctant to report errors that they've made, fearful that it will scare potential patients away, affecting their bottom lines. Some instances of hospital error are difficult to detect, since radiation-related cancer may appear a long while after the faulty treatment, and under-radiation doesn't result in any observable injury. Even in New York, which has one of the strictest accident reporting requirements in place and keeps reporting hospitals anonymous to encourage them to share their data, a significant portion of errors go unreported—perhaps even a majority of errors.

The problem is certainly not unique to New York. In New Jersey, 36 patients were over-radiated at a single hospital by an inexperienced team of technicians, and the mistakes continued for months in the absence of a system that detected treatment errors. Patients in Louisiana, Texas, and California repeatedly received incorrect dosages that led to other crippling ailments. Nor is the issue unique to the United States. In Panama, 28 patients at the National Cancer Institute received overdoses of radiation for various types of cancers. Doctors had ordered medical physicists to add a fifth "block," or metal sheet similar to the "leaves" in a multi-leaf collimator, to their linear accelerators, which were only designed to support four blocks. When the staff attempted to get the machine software to work with the extra block, the results were miscalculated dosages and over-radiated patients.

The lack of a central U.S. reporting and regulatory agency for radiation therapy means that in the event of a radiation-related mistake, all of the groups involved are able to avoid ultimate responsibility. Medical machinery and software manufacturers claim that it's the doctors and medical technicians' responsibility to properly use the machines, and the hospitals' responsibility to properly budget time and resources for training. Technicians claim that they are understaffed and overworked, and that there are no procedures in place to check their work and no time to do so even if there were. Hospitals claim that the newer machinery lacks the proper fail-safe mechanisms and that there is no room on already limited budgets for the training that equipment manufacturers claim is required.

Currently, the responsibility for regulating these incidents falls upon the states, which vary widely in their enforcement of reporting. Many states require no reporting at all, but even in a state like Ohio,

which requires reporting of medical mistakes within 15 days of the incident, these rules are routinely broken. Moreover, radiation technicians do not require a license in Ohio, as they do in many other states.

Dr. Fred A. Mettler, Jr., a radiation expert who has investigated radiation accidents worldwide, notes that "while there are accidents, you wouldn't want to scare people to death where they don't get needed radiation therapy." And it bears repeating that the vast majority of the time, radiation works, and saves some people from terminal cancer. But technicians, hospitals, equipment and software manufacturers, and regulators all need to collaborate to create a common set of safety procedures, software features, reporting standards, and certification requirements for technicians in order to reduce the number of radiation accidents.

Sources: Walt Bogdanich, "Medical Group Urges New Rules on Radiation," *The New York Times*, February 4, 2010; "As Technology Surges, Radiation Safeguards Lag," *The New York Times*, January 27, 2010; "Radiation Offers New Cures, and Ways to Do Harm," *The New York Times*, January 24, 2010; and "Case Studies: When Medical Radiation Goes Awry," *The New York Times*, January 21, 2010.

CASE STUDY QUESTIONS

1. What concepts in the chapter are illustrated in this case? What ethical issues are raised by radiation technology?

2. What management, organization, and technology factors were responsible for the problems detailed in this case? Explain the role of each.

3. Do you feel that any of the groups involved with this issue (hospital administrators, technicians, medical equipment and software manufacturers) should accept the majority of the blame for these incidents? Why or why not?

4. How would a central reporting agency that gathered data on radiation-related accidents help reduce the number of radiation therapy errors in the future?

5. If you were in charge of designing electronic software for a linear accelerator, what are some features you would include? Are there any features you would avoid?

References

Angst, Corey M. and Ritu Agarwal. "Adoption of Electronic Health Records in the Presence of Privacy Concerns: The Elaboration Likelihood Model and Individual Persuasion." MIS Quarterly 33, No. 2 (June 2009).

Baumstein, Avi. "New Tools Close Holes in Cam-Spam." Information Week (February 23, 2009).

Beck, Melinda. "Becoming a Squinter Nation." The Wall Street Journal (August 17, 2010).

Bhattacharjee, Sudip, Ram D. Gopal, and G. Lawrence Sanders. "Digital Music and Online Sharing: Software Piracy 2.0?" Communications of the ACM 46, no.7 (July 2003).

Bowen, Jonathan. "The Ethics of Safety-Critical Systems."Communications of the ACM 43, no. 3 (April 2000).

Brown Bag Software vs. Symantec Corp. 960 F2D 1465 (Ninth Circuit, 1992).

Carr, Nicholas. "Tracking Is an Assault on Liberty, with Real Dangers." The Wall Street Journal (August 7, 2010).

Chellappa, Ramnath K. and Shivendu Shivendu. "An Economic Model of Privacy: A Property Rights Approach to Regulatory Choices for Online Personalization." Journal of Management Information Systems 24, no. 3 (Winter 2008).

Clifford, Stephanie. "Web Coupons Know Lots About You, and They Tell." The New York Times (April 16, 2010)

Culnan, Mary J. and Cynthia Clark Williams. "How Ethics Can Enhance Organizational Privacy." MIS Quarterly 33, No. 4 (December 2009).

Farmer, Dan and Charles C. Mann. "Surveillance Nation." Part I Technology Review (April 2003) and Part II (Technology Review (May 2003)..

Goodman, Joshua, Gordon V. Cormack, and David Heckerman. "Spam and the Ongoing Battle for the Inbox." Communications of the ACM 50, No. 2 (February 2007).

Grimes, Galen A. "Compliance with the CAN-SPAM Act of 2003." Communications of the ACM 50, No. 2 (February 2007).

Harper, Jim. "It's Modern Trade: Web Users Get as Much as They Give." The Wall Street Journal (August 7, 2010).

Hsieh, J.J. Po-An, Arun Rai, and Mark Keil. "Understanding Digital Inequality: Comparing Continued Use Behavioral Models of the Socio-Economically Advantaged and Disadvantaged." MIS Quarterly 32, no. 1 (March 2008).

Jackson, Linda A., Alexander von Eye, Gretchen Barbatsis, Frank Biocca, Hiram E. Fitzgerald, and Yong Zhao. "The Impact of Internet Use on the Other Side of the Digital Divide." Communications of the ACM 47, no. 7 (July 2004).

Jackson, Thomas W., Ray Dawson, and Darren Wilson. "Understanding Email Interaction Increases Organizational Productivity." Communications of the ACM 46, no. 8 (August 2003).

Laudon, Kenneth C. and Carol Guercio Traver. E-Commerce: Business, Technology, Society 7th Edition. Upper Saddle River, NJ: Prentice-Hall (2011).

Laudon, Kenneth C. Dossier Society: Value Choices in the Design of National Information Systems. New York: Columbia University Press (1986b).

Lohr, Steve. "How Privacy Vanishes Online." The New York Times (March 16, 2010.)

Matt Richtel, "Hooked on Gadgets,and Paying a Mental Price," The New York Times, June 7, 2010.

Nord, G. Daryl, Tipton F. McCubbins, and Jeretta Horn Nord. "E-Monitoring in the Workplace: Privacy, Legislation, and Surveillance Software. Communications of the ACM 49, No. 8 (August 2006).

Okerson, Ann. "Who Owns Digital Works?" Scientific American (July 1996).

Payton, Fay Cobb."Rethinking the Digital Divide." Communications of the ACM 46, no. 6 (June 2003)

Rapoza, Jim. "Web Bug Alert." EWeek (June 15, 2009).

Rifkin, Jeremy. "Watch Out for Trickle-Down Technology." The New York Times (March 16, 1993).

Rigdon, Joan E. "Frequent Glitches in New Software Bug Users." The Wall Street Journal (January 18, 1995).

Risen, James and Eric Lichtblau. "E-Mail Surveillance Renews Concerns in Congress." The New York Times (June 17, 2009).

Schwartz, Matthew J. "Sophos: U.S. Leads List of Spam Originators." Information Week (July 15, 2010).

Singer, Natasha. "Shoppers Who Can't Have Secrets." The New York Times (April 30, 2010).

Smith, H. Jeff, and John Hasnas. "Ethics and Information Systems: The Corporate Domain." MIS Quarterly 23, no. 1 (March 1999).

Smith, H. Jeff. "The Shareholders vs. Stakeholders Debate." MIS Sloan Management Review 44, no. 4 (Summer 2003).

Steel, Emily and Jessica E. Vascellaro. "Facebook, MySpace Confront Privacy Loophole." The Wall Street Journal (May 21, 2010).

Steel, Emily and Julia Angwin,"On the Web's Cutting Edge, Anonymity in Name Only." The Wall Street Journal (August 4, 2010).

Steel, Emily. "Marketers Watch Friends Interact Online." The Wall Street Journal (April 15, 2010)

_____"Exploring Ways to Build a Better Consumer Profile," The Wall Street Journal (March 15, 2010)

Story, Louise. "To Aim Ads, Web Is Keeping Closer Eye on You." The New York Times (March 10, 2008).

Stout, Hilary. "Antisocial Networking?" The New York Times (May 2, 2010).

United States Department of Health, Education, and Welfare. Records, Computers, and the Rights of Citizens. Cambridge: MIT Press (1973).

Urbaczewski, Andrew and Leonard M. Jessup. "Does Electronic Monitoring of Employee Internet Usage Work?" Communications of the ACM 45, no. 1 (January 2002).

Valentino-Devries, Jennifer and Emily Steel. "'Cookies' Cause Bitter Backlash." The Wall Street Journal (September 19, 2010).

Vascellaro, Jessica E. "Google Agonizes on Privacy as Ad World Vaults Ahead." The Wall Street Journal (August 10, 2010).

Xu, Heng, Hock-Hai Teo, Bernard C.Y. Tan, and Ritu Agarwal. "The Role of Push-Pull Technology in Privacy Calculus: The Case of Location-Based Services." Journal of Management Information Systems 26, No. 3 (Winter 2010).

Chapter 6

Foundations of Business Intelligence: Databases and Information Management

From Chapter 6 of *Management Information Systems: Managing the Digital Firm*, 12/e. Kenneth C. Laudon, Jane P. Laudon. Copyright © 2012 by Pearson Education. Published by Prentice Hall. All rights reserved.

Foundations of Business Intelligence: Databases and Information Management

RR DONNELLEY TRIES TO MASTER ITS DATA

Right now you are most likely using an RR Donnelley product. Chicago-based RR Donnelley is a giant commercial printing and service company providing printing services, forms and labels, direct mail, and other services. The company's recent expansion has been fueled by a series of acquisitions, including commercial printer Moore Wallace in 2005 and printing and supply chain management company Banta in January 2007. RR Donnelley's revenue has jumped from $2.4 billion in 2003 to over $9.8 billion today.

However, all that growth created information management challenges. Each acquired company had its own systems and its own set of customer, vendor, and product data. Coming from so many different sources, the data were often inconsistent, duplicated, or incomplete. For example, different units of the business might each have a different meaning for the entity "customer." One might define "customer" as a specific billing location, while another might define "customer" as the legal parent entity of a company. Donnelley had to use time-consuming manual processes to reconcile the data stored in multiple systems in order to get a clear enterprise-wide picture of each of its customers, since they might be doing business with several different units of the company. These conditions heightened inefficiencies and costs.

RR Donnelley had become so big that it was impractical to store the information from all of its units in a single system. But Donnelley still needed a clear single set of data that was accurate and consistent for the entire enterprise. To solve this problem, RR Donnelley turned to master data management (MDM). MDM seeks to ensure that an organization does not use multiple versions of the same piece of data in different parts of its operations by merging disparate records into a single authenticated master file. Once the master file is in place, employees and applications access a single consolidated view of the company's data. It is especially useful for companies such as Donnelley that have data integration problems as a result of mergers and acquisitions.

Implementing MDM is a multi-step process that includes business process analysis, data cleansing, data consolidation and reconciliation, and data migration into a master file of all the company's data. Companies must identify what group in the company "owns" each piece of data and is responsible for resolving inconsistent definitions of data and other discrepancies. Donnelley launched its MDM program in late 2005 and began creating a single set of identifiers for its customer and vendor data. The company opted for a registry model using Purisma's Data Hub in which customer data continue to reside in the system where they originate but are registered in a master "hub" and cross-referenced so applications can find the data. The data in their source system are not touched.

Nearly a year later, Donnelley brought up its

Customer Master Data Store, which integrates the data from numerous systems from Donnelley acquisitions. Data that are outdated, incomplete, or incorrectly formatted are corrected or eliminated. A registry points to where the source data are stored. By having a single consistent enterprise-wide set of data with common definitions and standards, management is able to easily find out what kind of business and how much business it has with a particular customer to identify top customers and sales opportunities. And when Donelley acquires a company, it can quickly see a list of overlapping customers.

Sources: John McCormick, "Mastering Data at R.R. Donnelley," *Information Management Magazine*, March 2009; www.rrdonnelley.com, accessed June 10, 2010; and www.purisma.com, accessed June 10, 2010.

RR Donnelley's experience illustrates the importance of data management for businesses. Donnelley has experienced phenomenal growth, primarily through acquisitions. But its business performance depends on what it can or cannot do with its data. How businesses store, organize, and manage their data has a tremendous impact on organizational effectiveness.

The chapter-opening diagram calls attention to important points raised by this case and this chapter. Management decided that the company needed to centralize the management of the company's data. Data about customers, vendors, products, and other important entities had been stored in a number of different systems and files where they could not be easily retrieved and analyzed. They were often redundant and inconsistent, limiting their usefulness. Management was unable to obtain an enterprise-wide view of all of its customers at all of its acquisitions to market its products and services and provide better service and support.

In the past, RR Donnelley had used heavily manual paper processes to reconcile its inconsistent and redundant data and manage its information from an enterprise-wide perspective. This solution was no longer viable as the organization grew larger. A more appropriate solution was to identify, consolidate, cleanse, and standardize customer and other data in a single master data management registry. In addition to using appropriate technology, Donnelley had to correct and reorganize the data into a standard format and establish rules, responsibilities, and procedures for updating and using the data.

A master data management system helps RR Donnelley boost profitability by making it easier to identify customers and sales opportunities. It also improves operational efficiency and decision making by having more accurate and complete customer data available and reducing the time required to reconcile redundant and inconsistent data.

1 ORGANIZING DATA IN A TRADITIONAL FILE ENVIRONMENT

An effective information system provides users with accurate, timely, and relevant information. Accurate information is free of errors. Information is timely when it is available to decision makers when it is needed. Information is relevant when it is useful and appropriate for the types of work and decisions that require it.

You might be surprised to learn that many businesses don't have timely, accurate, or relevant information because the data in their information systems have been poorly organized and maintained. That's why data management is so essential. To understand the problem, let's look at how information systems arrange data in computer files and traditional methods of file management.

FILE ORGANIZATION TERMS AND CONCEPTS

A computer system organizes data in a hierarchy that starts with bits and bytes and progresses to fields, records, files, and databases (see Figure 1). A bit represents the smallest unit of data a computer can handle. A group of bits, called a byte, represents a single character, which can be a letter, a

FIGURE 1   THE DATA HIERARCHY

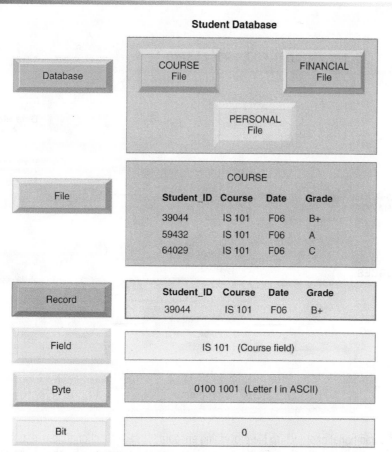

A computer system organizes data in a hierarchy that starts with the bit, which represents either a 0 or a 1. Bits can be grouped to form a byte to represent one character, number, or symbol. Bytes can be grouped to form a field, and related fields can be grouped to form a record. Related records can be collected to form a file, and related files can be organized into a database.

number, or another symbol. A grouping of characters into a word, a group of words, or a complete number (such as a person's name or age) is called a **field**. A group of related fields, such as the student's name, the course taken, the date, and the grade, comprises a **record**; a group of records of the same type is called a **file**.

For example, the records in Figure 1 could constitute a student course file. A group of related files makes up a **database**. The student course file illustrated in Figure 1 could be grouped with files on students' personal histories and financial backgrounds to create a student database.

A record describes an entity. An **entity** is a person, place, thing, or event on which we store and maintain information. Each characteristic or quality describing a particular entity is called an **attribute**. For example, Student_ID, Course, Date, and Grade are attributes of the entity COURSE. The specific values that these attributes can have are found in the fields of the record describing the entity COURSE.

PROBLEMS WITH THE TRADITIONAL FILE ENVIRONMENT

In most organizations, systems tended to grow independently without a company-wide plan. Accounting, finance, manufacturing, human resources, and sales and marketing all developed their own systems and data files. Figure 2 illustrates the traditional approach to information processing.

FIGURE 2   TRADITIONAL FILE PROCESSING

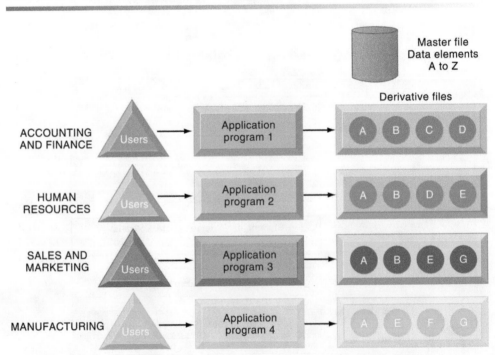

The use of a traditional approach to file processing encourages each functional area in a corporation to develop specialized applications. Each application requires a unique data file that is likely to be a subset of the master file. These subsets of the master file lead to data redundancy and inconsistency, processing inflexibility, and wasted storage resources.

Each application, of course, required its own files and its own computer program to operate. For example, the human resources functional area might have a personnel master file, a payroll file, a medical insurance file, a pension file, a mailing list file, and so forth until tens, perhaps hundreds, of files and programs existed. In the company as a whole, this process led to multiple master files created, maintained, and operated by separate divisions or departments. As this process goes on for 5 or 10 years, the organization is saddled with hundreds of programs and applications that are very difficult to maintain and manage. The resulting problems are data redundancy and inconsistency, program-data dependence, inflexibility, poor data security, and an inability to share data among applications.

Data Redundancy and Inconsistency

Data redundancy is the presence of duplicate data in multiple data files so that the same data are stored in more than place or location. Data redundancy occurs when different groups in an organization independently collect the same piece of data and store it independently of each other. Data redundancy wastes storage resources and also leads to **data inconsistency**, where the same attribute may have different values. For example, in instances of the entity COURSE illustrated in Figure 1, the Date may be updated in some systems but not in others. The same attribute, Student_ID, may also have different names in different systems throughout the organization. Some systems might use Student_ID and others might use ID, for example.

Additional confusion might result from using different coding systems to represent values for an attribute. For instance, the sales, inventory, and manufacturing systems of a clothing retailer might use different codes to represent clothing size. One system might represent clothing size as "extra large," whereas another might use the code "XL" for the same purpose. The resulting confusion would make it difficult for companies to create customer relationship management, supply chain management, or enterprise systems that integrate data from different sources.

Program-Data Dependence

Program-data dependence refers to the coupling of data stored in files and the specific programs required to update and maintain those files such that changes in programs require changes to the data. Every traditional computer program has to describe the location and nature of the data with which it works. In a traditional file environment, any change in a software program could require a change in the data accessed by that program. One program might be modified from a five-digit to a nine-digit ZIP code. If the original data file were changed from five-digit to nine-digit ZIP codes, then other programs that required the five-digit ZIP code would no longer work properly. Such changes could cost millions of dollars to implement properly.

Lack of Flexibility

A traditional file system can deliver routine scheduled reports after extensive programming efforts, but it cannot deliver ad hoc reports or respond to unanticipated information requirements in a timely fashion. The information required by ad hoc requests is somewhere in the system but may be too expensive to retrieve. Several programmers might have to work for weeks to put together the required data items in a new file.

Poor Security

Because there is little control or management of data, access to and dissemination of information may be out of control. Management may have no way of knowing who is accessing or even making changes to the organization's data.

Lack of Data Sharing and Availability

Because pieces of information in different files and different parts of the organization cannot be related to one another, it is virtually impossible for information to be shared or accessed in a timely manner. Information cannot flow freely across different functional areas or different parts of the organization. If users find different values of the same piece of information in two different systems, they may not want to use these systems because they cannot trust the accuracy of their data.

2   THE DATABASE APPROACH TO DATA MANAGEMENT

Database technology cuts through many of the problems of traditional file organization. A more rigorous definition of a **database** is a collection of data organized to serve many applications efficiently by centralizing the data and controlling redundant data. Rather than storing data in separate files for each application, data are stored so as to appear to users as being stored in only one location. A single database services multiple applications. For example, instead of a corporation storing employee data in separate information systems and separate files for personnel, payroll, and benefits, the corporation could create a single common human resources database.

DATABASE MANAGEMENT SYSTEMS

A **database management system (DBMS)** is software that permits an organization to centralize data, manage them efficiently, and provide access to the stored data by application programs. The DBMS acts as an interface between application programs and the physical data files. When the application program calls for a data item, such as gross pay, the DBMS finds this item in the database and presents it to the application program. Using traditional data files, the programmer would have to specify the size and format of each data element used in the program and then tell the computer where they were located.

The DBMS relieves the programmer or end user from the task of understanding where and how the data are actually stored by separating the logical and physical views of the data. The *logical view* presents data as they would be perceived by end users or business specialists, whereas the *physical view* shows how data are actually organized and structured on physical storage media.

The database management software makes the physical database available for different logical views required by users. For example, for the human resources database illustrated in Figure 3, a benefits specialist might require a view consisting of the employee's name, social security number, and health insurance coverage. A payroll department member might need data such as the employee's name, social security number, gross pay, and net pay. The data for

FIGURE 3   HUMAN RESOURCES DATABASE WITH MULTIPLE VIEWS

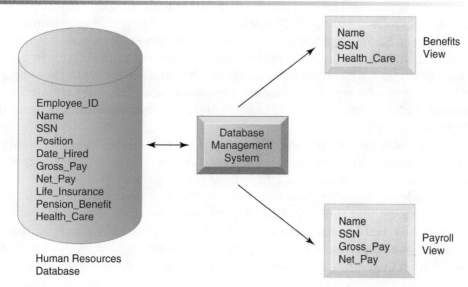

A single human resources database provides many different views of data, depending on the information requirements of the user. Illustrated here are two possible views, one of interest to a benefits specialist and one of interest to a member of the company's payroll department.

all these views are stored in a single database, where they can be more easily managed by the organization.

How a DBMS Solves the Problems of the Traditional File Environment

A DBMS reduces data redundancy and inconsistency by minimizing isolated files in which the same data are repeated. The DBMS may not enable the organization to eliminate data redundancy entirely, but it can help control redundancy. Even if the organization maintains some redundant data, using a DBMS eliminates data inconsistency because the DBMS can help the organization ensure that every occurrence of redundant data has the same values. The DBMS uncouples programs and data, enabling data to stand on their own. Access and availability of information will be increased and program development and maintenance costs reduced because users and programmers can perform ad hoc queries of data in the database. The DBMS enables the organization to centrally manage data, their use, and security.

Relational DBMS

Contemporary DBMS use different database models to keep track of entities, attributes, and relationships. The most popular type of DBMS today for PCs as well as for larger computers and mainframes is the **relational DBMS**. Relational databases represent data as two-dimensional tables (called relations). Tables may be referred to as files. Each table contains data on an entity and its attributes. Microsoft Access is a relational DBMS for desktop systems, whereas DB2, Oracle Database, and Microsoft SQL Server are relational DBMS for large mainframes and midrange computers. MySQL is a popular open-source DBMS, and Oracle Database Lite is a DBMS for small handheld computing devices.

Let's look at how a relational database organizes data about suppliers and parts (see Figure 4). The database has a separate table for the entity SUPPLIER and a table for the entity PART. Each table consists of a grid of columns and rows of data. Each individual element of data for each entity is stored as a separate field, and each field represents an attribute for that entity. Fields in a relational database are also called columns. For the entity SUPPLIER, the supplier identification number, name, street, city, state, and ZIP code are stored as separate fields within the SUPPLIER table and each field represents an attribute for the entity SUPPLIER.

The actual information about a single supplier that resides in a table is called a row. Rows are commonly referred to as records, or in very technical terms, as **tuples**. Data for the entity PART have their own separate table.

The field for Supplier_Number in the SUPPLIER table uniquely identifies each record so that the record can be retrieved, updated, or sorted and it is called a **key field**. Each table in a relational database has one field that is designated as its **primary key**. This key field is the unique identifier for all the information in any row of the table and this primary key cannot be duplicated.

FIGURE 4   RELATIONAL DATABASE TABLES

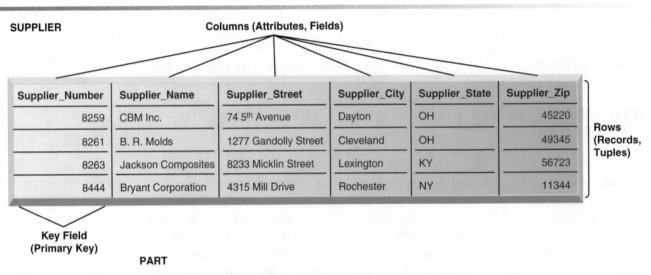

A relational database organizes data in the form of two-dimensional tables. Illustrated here are tables for the entities SUPPLIER and PART showing how they represent each entity and its attributes. Supplier_Number is a primary key for the SUPPLIER table and a foreign key for the PART table.

Supplier_Number is the primary key for the SUPPLIER table and Part_Number is the primary key for the PART table. Note that Supplier_Number appears in both the SUPPLIER and PART tables. In the SUPPLIER table, Supplier_Number is the primary key. When the field Supplier_Number appears in the PART table it is called a **foreign key** and is essentially a lookup field to look up data about the supplier of a specific part.

Operations of a Relational DBMS

Relational database tables can be combined easily to deliver data required by users, provided that any two tables share a common data element. Suppose we wanted to find in this database the names of suppliers who could provide us with part number 137 or part number 150. We would need information from two tables: the SUPPLIER table and the PART table. Note that these two files have a shared data element: Supplier_Number.

In a relational database, three basic operations, as shown in Figure 5, are used to develop useful sets of data: select, join, and project. The *select* operation creates a subset consisting of all records in the file that meet stated criteria. Select creates, in other words, a subset of rows that meet certain criteria. In our example, we want to select records (rows) from the PART table where the Part_Number equals 137 or 150. The *join* operation combines relational tables to provide the user with more information than is available in individual tables. In our example, we want to join the now-shortened PART table (only parts 137 or 150 will be presented) and the SUPPLIER table into a single new table.

The *project* operation creates a subset consisting of columns in a table, permitting the user to create new tables that contain only the information required. In our example, we want to extract from the new table only the following columns: Part_Number, Part_Name, Supplier_Number, and Supplier_Name.

Object-Oriented DBMS

Many applications today and in the future require databases that can store and retrieve not only structured numbers and characters but also drawings, images, photographs, voice, and full-motion video. DBMS designed for organizing structured data into rows and columns are not well suited to handling graphics-based or multimedia applications. Object-oriented databases are better suited for this purpose.

An **object-oriented DBMS** stores the data and procedures that act on those data as objects that can be automatically retrieved and shared. Object-oriented database management systems (OODBMS) are becoming popular because they can be used to manage the various multimedia components or Java applets used in Web applications, which typically integrate pieces of information from a variety of sources.

Although object-oriented databases can store more complex types of information than relational DBMS, they are relatively slow compared with relational DBMS for processing large numbers of transactions. Hybrid **object-relational DBMS** systems are now available to provide capabilities of both object-oriented and relational DBMS.

Databases in the Cloud

Suppose your company wants to use cloud computing services. Is there a way to manage data in the cloud? The answer is a qualified "Yes." Cloud computing providers offer database management services, but these services typically have less functionality than their on-premises counterparts. At the moment,

FIGURE 5   THE THREE BASIC OPERATIONS OF A RELATIONAL DBMS

PART

Part_Number	Part_Name	Unit_Price	Supplier_Number
137	Door latch	22.00	8259
145	Side mirror	12.00	8444
150	Door molding	6.00	8263
152	Door lock	31.00	8259
155	Compressor	54.00	8261
178	Door handle	10.00	8259

Select Part_Number = 137 or 150

SUPPLIER

Supplier_Number	Supplier_Name	Supplier_Street	Supplier_City	Supplier_State	Supplier_Zip
8259	CBM Inc.	74 5th Avenue	Dayton	OH	45220
8261	B. R. Molds	1277 Gandolly Street	Cleveland	OH	49345
8263	Jackson Components	8233 Micklin Street	Lexington	KY	56723
8444	Bryant Corporation	4315 Mill Drive	Rochester	NY	11344

Join by Supplier_Number

Part_Number	Part_Name	Supplier_Number	Supplier_Name
137	Door latch	8259	CBM Inc.
150	Door molding	8263	Jackson Components

Project selected columns

The select, join, and project operations enable data from two different tables to be combined and only selected attributes to be displayed.

the primary customer base for cloud-based data management consists of Web-focused start-ups or small to medium-sized businesses looking for database capabilities at a lower price than a standard relational DBMS.

Amazon Web Services has both a simple non-relational database called SimpleDB and a Relational Database Service, which is based on an online implementation of the MySQL open source DBMS. Amazon Relational Database Service (Amazon RDS) offers the full range of capabilities of MySQL. Pricing is based on usage. (Charges run from 11 cents per hour for a small database using 1.7 GB of server memory to $3.10 per hour for a large database using 68 GB of server memory.) There are also charges for the volume of data stored, the number of input-output requests, the amount of data written to the database, and the amount of data read from the database.

Amazon Web Services additionally offers Oracle customers the option to license Oracle Database 11g, Oracle Enterprise Manager, and Oracle Fusion Middleware to run on the Amazon EC2 (Elastic Cloud Compute) platform.

Microsoft SQL Azure Database is a cloud-based relational database service based on Microsoft's SQL Server DBMS. It provides a highly available, scalable database service hosted by Microsoft in the cloud. SQL Azure Database helps reduce costs by integrating with existing software tools and providing symmetry with on-premises and cloud databases.

TicketDirect, which sells tickets to concerts, sporting events, theater performances, and movies in Australia and New Zealand, adopted the SQL Azure Database cloud platform in order to improve management of peak system loads during major ticket sales. It migrated its data to the SQL Azure database. By moving to a cloud solution, TicketDirect is able to scale its computing resources in response to real-time demand while keeping costs low.

CAPABILITIES OF DATABASE MANAGEMENT SYSTEMS

A DBMS includes capabilities and tools for organizing, managing, and accessing the data in the database. The most important are its data definition language, data dictionary, and data manipulation language.

DBMS have a **data definition** capability to specify the structure of the content of the database. It would be used to create database tables and to define the characteristics of the fields in each table. This information about the database would be documented in a data dictionary. A **data dictionary** is an automated or manual file that stores definitions of data elements and their characteristics.

Microsoft Access has a rudimentary data dictionary capability that displays information about the name, description, size, type, format, and other properties of each field in a table (see Figure 6). Data dictionaries for large corporate databases may capture additional information, such as usage, ownership (who in the organization is responsible for maintaining the data), authorization; security, and the individuals, business functions, programs, and reports that use each data element.

Querying and Reporting

DBMS includes tools for accessing and manipulating information in databases. Most DBMS have a specialized language called a **data manipulation language** that is used to add, change, delete, and retrieve the data in the database. This language contains commands that permit end users and programming specialists to extract data from the database to satisfy information requests and develop applications. The most prominent data manipulation language today is **Structured Query Language**, or **SQL**. Figure 7 illustrates the SQL query that

FIGURE 6   MICROSOFT ACCESS DATA DICTIONARY FEATURES

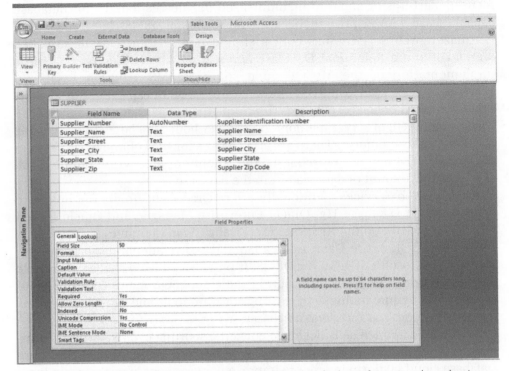

Microsoft Access has a rudimentary data dictionary capability that displays information about the size, format, and other characteristics of each field in a database. Displayed here is the information maintained in the SUPPLIER table. The small key icon to the left of Supplier_Number indicates that it is a key field.

would produce the new resultant table in Figure 5. You can find out more about how to perform SQL queries in our Learning Tracks for this chapter.

Users of DBMS for large and midrange computers, such as DB2, Oracle, or SQL Server, would employ SQL to retrieve information they needed from the database. Microsoft Access also uses SQL, but it provides its own set of user-friendly tools for querying databases and for organizing data from databases into more polished reports.

In Microsoft Access, you will find features that enable users to create queries by identifying the tables and fields they want and the results, and then selecting the rows from the database that meet particular criteria. These actions in turn are translated into SQL commands. Figure 8 illustrates how

FIGURE 7   EXAMPLE OF AN SQL QUERY

```
SELECT PART.Part_Number, PART.Part_Name, SUPPLIER.Supplier_Number,
SUPPLIER.Supplier_Name
FROM PART, SUPPLIER
WHERE PART.Supplier_Number = SUPPLIER.Supplier_Number AND
Part_Number = 137 OR Part_Number = 150;
```

Illustrated here are the SQL statements for a query to select suppliers for parts 137 or 150. They produce a list with the same results as Figure 5.

FIGURE 8   AN ACCESS QUERY

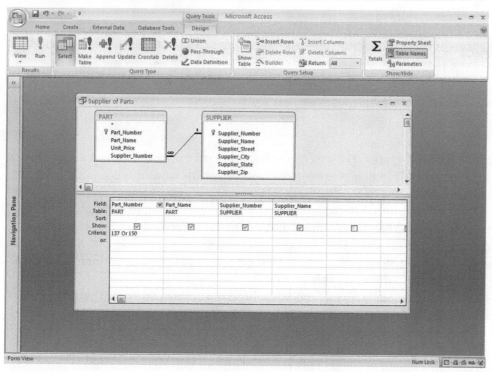

Illustrated here is how the query in Figure 7 would be constructed using Microsoft Access query-building tools. It shows the tables, fields, and selection criteria used for the query.

the same query as the SQL query to select parts and suppliers would be constructed using the Microsoft query-building tools.

Microsoft Access and other DBMS include capabilities for report generation so that the data of interest can be displayed in a more structured and polished format than would be possible just by querying. Crystal Reports is a popular report generator for large corporate DBMS, although it can also be used with Access. Access also has capabilities for developing desktop system applications. These include tools for creating data entry screens, reports, and developing the logic for processing transactions.

DESIGNING DATABASES

To create a database, you must understand the relationships among the data, the type of data that will be maintained in the database, how the data will be used, and how the organization will need to change to manage data from a company-wide perspective. The database requires both a conceptual design and a physical design. The conceptual, or logical, design of a database is an abstract model of the database from a business perspective, whereas the physical design shows how the database is actually arranged on direct-access storage devices.

Normalization and Entity-Relationship Diagrams

The conceptual database design describes how the data elements in the database are to be grouped. The design process identifies relationships among data elements and the most efficient way of grouping data elements together to meet business information requirements. The process also identifies redundant data elements and the groupings of data elements required for specific

FIGURE 9   AN UNNORMALIZED RELATION FOR ORDER

ORDER (Before Normalization)

| Order_
Number | Order_
Date | Part_
Number | Part_
Name | Unit_
Price | Part_
Quantity | Supplier_
Number | Supplier_
Name | Supplier_
Street | Supplier_
City | Supplier_
State | Supplier_
Zip |

An unnormalized relation contains repeating groups. For example, there can be many parts and suppliers for each order. There is only a one-to-one correspondence between Order_Number and Order_Date.

application programs. Groups of data are organized, refined, and streamlined until an overall logical view of the relationships among all the data in the database emerges.

To use a relational database model effectively, complex groupings of data must be streamlined to minimize redundant data elements and awkward many-to-many relationships. The process of creating small, stable, yet flexible and adaptive data structures from complex groups of data is called **normalization**. Figures 9 and 10 illustrate this process.

In the particular business modeled here, an order can have more than one part but each part is provided by only one supplier. If we build a relation called ORDER with all the fields included here, we would have to repeat the name and address of the supplier for every part on the order, even though the order is for parts from a single supplier. This relationship contains what are called repeating data groups because there can be many parts on a single order to a given supplier. A more efficient way to arrange the data is to break down ORDER into smaller relations, each of which describes a single entity. If we go step by step and normalize the relation ORDER, we emerge with the relations illustrated in Figure 10. You can find out more about normalization, entity-relationship diagramming, and database design in the Learning Tracks for this chapter.

Relational database systems try to enforce **referential integrity** rules to ensure that relationships between coupled tables remain consistent. When one table has a foreign key that points to another table, you may not add a record to the table with the foreign key unless there is a corresponding record in the linked table. In the database we examined earlier in this chapter, the foreign key

FIGURE 10   NORMALIZED TABLES CREATED FROM ORDER

PART

| Part_
Number | Part_
Name | Unit_
Price | Supplier_
Number |
| Key | | | |

LINE_ITEM

| Order_
Number | Part_
Number | Part_
Quantity |
| Key | | |

SUPPLIER

| Supplier_
Number | Supplier_
Name | Supplier_
Street | Supplier_
City | Supplier_
State | Supplier_
Zip |
| Key | | | | | |

ORDER

| Order_
Number | Order_
Date |
| Key | |

After normalization, the original relation ORDER has been broken down into four smaller relations. The relation ORDER is left with only two attributes and the relation LINE_ITEM has a combined, or concatenated, key consisting of Order_Number and Part_Number.

Supplier_Number links the PART table to the SUPPLIER table. We may not add a new record to the PART table for a part with Supplier_Number 8266 unless there is a corresponding record in the SUPPLIER table for Supplier_Number 8266. We must also delete the corresponding record in the PART table if we delete the record in the SUPPLIER table for Supplier_Number 8266. In other words, we shouldn't have parts from nonexistent suppliers!

Database designers document their data model with an **entity-relationship diagram**, illustrated in Figure 11. This diagram illustrates the relationship between the entities SUPPLIER, PART, LINE_ITEM, and ORDER. The boxes represent entities. The lines connecting the boxes represent relationships. A line connecting two entities that ends in two short marks designates a one-to-one relationship. A line connecting two entities that ends with a crow's foot topped by a short mark indicates a one-to-many relationship. Figure 11 shows that one ORDER can contain many LINE_ITEMs. (A PART can be ordered many times and appear many times as a line item in a single order.) Each PART can have only one SUPPLIER, but many PARTs can be provided by the same SUPPLIER.

It can't be emphasized enough: If the business doesn't get its data model right, the system won't be able to serve the business well. The company's systems will not be as effective as they could be because they'll have to work with data that may be inaccurate, incomplete, or difficult to retrieve. Understanding the organization's data and how they should be represented in a database is perhaps the most important lesson you can learn from this course.

For example, Famous Footwear, a shoe store chain with more than 800 locations in 49 states, could not achieve its goal of having "the right style of shoe in the right store for sale at the right price" because its database was not properly designed for rapidly adjusting store inventory. The company had an Oracle relational database running on an IBM AS/400 midrange computer, but the database was designed primarily for producing standard reports for management rather than for reacting to marketplace changes. Management could not obtain precise data on specific items in inventory in each of its stores. The company had to work around this problem by building a new database where the sales and inventory data could be better organized for analysis and inventory management.

3 USING DATABASES TO IMPROVE BUSINESS PERFORMANCE AND DECISION MAKING

Businesses use their databases to keep track of basic transactions, such as paying suppliers, processing orders, keeping track of customers, and paying employees. But they also need databases to provide information that will help the company

FIGURE 11   AN ENTITY-RELATIONSHIP DIAGRAM

This diagram shows the relationships between the entities SUPPLIER, PART, LINE_ITEM, and ORDER that might be used to model the database in Figure 10.

run the business more efficiently, and help managers and employees make better decisions. If a company wants to know which product is the most popular or who is its most profitable customer, the answer lies in the data.

For example, by analyzing data from customer credit card purchases, Louise's Trattoria, a Los Angeles restaurant chain, learned that quality was more important than price for most of its customers, who were college-educated and liked fine wine. Acting on this information, the chain introduced vegetarian dishes, more seafood selections, and more expensive wines, raising sales by more than 10 percent.

In a large company, with large databases or large systems for separate functions, such as manufacturing, sales, and accounting, special capabilities and tools are required for analyzing vast quantities of data and for accessing data from multiple systems. These capabilities include data warehousing, data mining, and tools for accessing internal databases through the Web.

DATA WAREHOUSES

Suppose you want concise, reliable information about current operations, trends, and changes across the entire company If you worked in a large company, obtaining this might be difficult because data are often maintained in separate systems, such as sales, manufacturing, or accounting. Some of the data you need might be found in the sales system, and other pieces in the manufacturing system. Many of these systems are older legacy systems that use outdated data management technologies or file systems where information is difficult for users to access.

You might have to spend an inordinate amount of time locating and gathering the data you need, or you would be forced to make your decision based on incomplete knowledge. If you want information about trends, you might also have trouble finding data about past events because most firms only make their current data immediately available. Data warehousing addresses these problems.

What Is a Data Warehouse?

A **data warehouse** is a database that stores current and historical data of potential interest to decision makers throughout the company. The data originate in many core operational transaction systems, such as systems for sales, customer accounts, and manufacturing, and may include data from Web site transactions. The data warehouse consolidates and standardizes information from different operational databases so that the information can be used across the enterprise for management analysis and decision making.

Figure 12 illustrates how a data warehouse works. The data warehouse makes the data available for anyone to access as needed, but it cannot be altered. A data warehouse system also provides a range of ad hoc and standardized query tools, analytical tools, and graphical reporting facilities. Many firms use intranet portals to make the data warehouse information widely available throughout the firm.

Catalina Marketing, a global marketing firm for major consumer packaged goods companies and retailers, operates a gigantic data warehouse that includes three years of purchase history for 195 million U.S. customer loyalty program members at supermarkets, pharmacies, and other retailers. It is the largest loyalty database in the world. Catalina's retail store customers analyze this database of customer purchase histories to determine individual customers' buying preferences. When a shopper checks out at the cash register of one of

FIGURE 12   COMPONENTS OF A DATA WAREHOUSE

The data warehouse extracts current and historical data from multiple operational systems inside the organization. These data are combined with data from external sources and reorganized into a central database designed for management reporting and analysis. The information directory provides users with information about the data available in the warehouse.

Catalina's retail customers, the purchase is instantly analyzed along with that customer's buying history in the data warehouse to determine what coupons that customer will receive at checkout along with a receipt.

The U.S. Internal Revenue Service (IRS) maintains a Compliance Data Warehouse that consolidates taxpayer data that had been fragmented among many different legacy systems, including personal information about taxpayers and archived tax returns. These systems had been designed to process tax return forms efficiently but their data were very difficult to query and analyze. The Compliance Data Warehouse integrates taxpayer data from many disparate sources into a relational structure, which makes querying and analysis much easier. With a complete and comprehensive picture of taxpayers, the warehouse helps IRS analysts and staff identify people who are most likely to cheat on their income tax payments and respond rapidly to taxpayer queries.

Data Marts

Companies often build enterprise-wide data warehouses, where a central data warehouse serves the entire organization, or they create smaller, decentralized warehouses called data marts. A **data mart** is a subset of a data warehouse in which a summarized or highly focused portion of the organization's data is placed in a separate database for a specific population of users. For example, a company might develop marketing and sales data marts to deal with customer information. Before implementing an enterprise-wide data warehouse, bookseller Barnes & Noble maintained a series of data marts—one for point-of-sale data in retail stores, another for college bookstore sales, and a third for online sales. A data mart typically focuses on a single subject area or line of business, so it usually can be constructed more rapidly and at lower cost than an enterprise-wide data warehouse.

TOOLS FOR BUSINESS INTELLIGENCE: MULTIDIMENSIONAL DATA ANALYSIS AND DATA MINING

Once data have been captured and organized in data warehouses and data marts, they are available for further analysis using tools for business intelligence. Business intelligence tools enable users to analyze data to see new patterns, relationships, and insights that are useful for guiding decision making.

Principal tools for business intelligence include software for database querying and reporting, tools for multidimensional data analysis (online analytical processing), and tools for data mining. This section will introduce you to these tools.

Online Analytical Processing (OLAP)

Suppose your company sells four different products—nuts, bolts, washers, and screws—in the East, West, and Central regions. If you wanted to ask a fairly straightforward question, such as how many washers were sold during the past quarter, you could easily find the answer by querying your sales database. But what if you wanted to know how many washers sold in each of your sales regions and compare actual results with projected sales?

To obtain the answer, you would need **online analytical processing (OLAP)**. OLAP supports multidimensional data analysis, enabling users to view the same data in different ways using multiple dimensions. Each aspect of information—product, pricing, cost, region, or time period—represents a different dimension. So, a product manager could use a multidimensional data analysis tool to learn how many washers were sold in the East in June, how that compares with the previous month and the previous June, and how it compares with the sales forecast. OLAP enables users to obtain online answers to ad hoc questions such as these in a fairly rapid amount of time, even when the data are stored in very large databases, such as sales figures for multiple years.

Figure 13 shows a multidimensional model that could be created to represent products, regions, actual sales, and projected sales. A matrix of actual sales can be stacked on top of a matrix of projected sales to form a cube with six faces. If you rotate the cube 90 degrees one way, the face showing will be product versus actual and projected sales. If you rotate the cube 90 degrees again, you will see region versus actual and projected sales. If you rotate 180 degrees from the original view, you will see projected sales and product versus region. Cubes can be nested within cubes to build complex views of data. A company would use either a specialized multidimensional database or a tool that creates multidimensional views of data in relational databases.

Data Mining

Traditional database queries answer such questions as, "How many units of product number 403 were shipped in February 2010?" OLAP, or multidimensional analysis, supports much more complex requests for information, such as "Compare sales of product 403 relative to plan by quarter and sales region for the past two years." With OLAP and query-oriented data analysis, users need to have a good idea about the information for which they are looking.

Data mining is more discovery-driven. Data mining provides insights into corporate data that cannot be obtained with OLAP by finding hidden patterns and

FIGURE 13   MULTIDIMENSIONAL DATA MODEL

The view that is showing is product versus region. If you rotate the cube 90 degrees, the face will show product versus actual and projected sales. If you rotate the cube 90 degrees again, you will see region versus actual and projected sales. Other views are possible.

relationships in large databases and inferring rules from them to predict future behavior. The patterns and rules are used to guide decision making and forecast the effect of those decisions. The types of information obtainable from data mining include associations, sequences, classifications, clusters, and forecasts.

- *Associations* are occurrences linked to a single event. For instance, a study of supermarket purchasing patterns might reveal that, when corn chips are purchased, a cola drink is purchased 65 percent of the time, but when there is a promotion, cola is purchased 85 percent of the time. This information helps managers make better decisions because they have learned the profitability of a promotion.

- In *sequences*, events are linked over time. We might find, for example, that if a house is purchased, a new refrigerator will be purchased within two weeks 65 percent of the time, and an oven will be bought within one month of the home purchase 45 percent of the time.

- *Classification* recognizes patterns that describe the group to which an item belongs by examining existing items that have been classified and by inferring a set of rules. For example, businesses such as credit card or telephone companies worry about the loss of steady customers. Classification helps discover the characteristics of customers who are likely to leave and can provide a model to help managers predict who those customers are so that the managers can devise special campaigns to retain such customers.

- *Clustering* works in a manner similar to classification when no groups have yet been defined. A data mining tool can discover different groupings within data, such as finding affinity groups for bank cards or partitioning a database into groups of customers based on demographics and types of personal investments.

- Although these applications involve predictions, *forecasting* uses predictions in a different way. It uses a series of existing values to forecast what other values will be. For example, forecasting might find patterns in data to help managers estimate the future value of continuous variables, such as sales figures.

These systems perform high-level analyses of patterns or trends, but they can also drill down to provide more detail when needed. There are data mining applications for all the functional areas of business, and for government and scientific work. One popular use for data mining is to provide detailed analyses of patterns in customer data for one-to-one marketing campaigns or for identifying profitable customers.

For example, Harrah's Entertainment, the second-largest gambling company in its industry, uses data mining to identify its most profitable customers and generate more revenue from them. The company continually analyzes data about its customers gathered when people play its slot machines or use Harrah's casinos and hotels. Harrah's marketing department uses this information to build a detailed gambling profile, based on a particular customer's ongoing value to the company. For instance, data mining lets Harrah's know the favorite gaming experience of a regular customer at one of its Midwest riverboat casinos, along with that person's preferences for room accomodations, restaurants, and entertainment. This information guides management decisions about how to cultivate the most profitable customers, encourage those customers to spend more, and attract more customers with high revenue-generating potential. Business intelligence has improved Harrah's profits so much that it has become the centerpiece of the firm's business strategy.

Predictive analytics use data mining techniques, historical data, and assumptions about future conditions to predict outcomes of events, such as the probability a customer will respond to an offer or purchase a specific product. For example, the U.S. division of The Body Shop International plc used predictive analytics with its database of catalog, Web, and retail store customers to identify customers who were more likely to make catalog purchases. That information helped the company build a more precise and targeted mailing list for its catalogs, improving the response rate for catalog mailings and catalog revenues.

Text Mining and Web Mining

Business intelligence tools deal primarily with data that have been structured in databases and files. However, unstructured data, most in the form of text files, is believed to account for over 80 percent of an organization's useful information. E-mail, memos, call center transcripts, survey responses, legal cases, patent descriptions, and service reports are all valuable for finding patterns and trends that will help employees make better business decisions. **Text mining** tools are now available to help businesses analyze these data. These tools are able to extract key elements from large unstructured data sets, discover patterns and relationships, and summarize the information. Businesses might turn to text mining to analyze transcripts of calls to customer service centers to identify major service and repair issues.

Text mining is a relatively new technology, but what's really new are the myriad ways in which unstructured data are being generated by consumers and the business uses for these data. The Interactive Session on Technology explores some of these business applications of text mining.

The Web is another rich source of valuable information, some of which can now be mined for patterns, trends, and insights into customer behavior. The discovery and analysis of useful patterns and information from the World Wide Web is called **Web mining**. Businesses might turn to Web mining to help them understand customer behavior, evaluate the effectiveness of a particular Web site, or quantify the success of a marketing campaign. For instance, marketers use Google Trends and Google Insights for Search services, which track the popularity of various words and phrases used in Google search queries, to learn what people are interested in and what they are interested in buying.

INTERACTIVE SESSION: TECHNOLOGY

WHAT CAN BUSINESSES LEARN FROM TEXT MINING?

Text mining is the discovery of patterns and relationships from large sets of unstructured data—the kind of data we generate in e-mails, phone conversations, blog postings, online customer surveys, and tweets. The mobile digital platform has amplified the explosion in digital information, with hundreds of millions of people calling, texting, searching, "apping" (using applications), buying goods, and writing billions of e-mails on the go.

Consumers today are more than just consumers: they have more ways to collaborate, share information, and influence the opinions of their friends and peers, and the data they create in doing so have significant value to businesses. Unlike structured data, which are generated from events such as completing a purchase transaction, unstructured data have no distinct form. Nevertheless, managers believe such data may offer unique insights into customer behavior and attitudes that were much more difficult to determine years ago.

For example, in 2007, JetBlue experienced unprecedented levels of customer discontent in the wake of a February ice storm that resulted in widespread flight cancellations and planes stranded on Kennedy Airport runways. The airline received 15,000 e-mails per day from customers during the storm and immediately afterwards, up from its usual daily volume of 400. The volume was so much larger than usual that JetBlue had no simple way to read everything its customers were saying.

Fortunately, the company had recently contracted with Attensity, a leading vendor of text analytics software, and was able to use the software to analyze all of the e-mail it had received within two days. According to JetBlue research analyst Bryan Jeppsen, Attensity Analyze for Voice of the Customer (VoC) enabled JetBlue to rapidly extract customer sentiments, preferences, and requests it couldn't find any other way. This tool uses a proprietary technology to automatically identify facts, opinions, requests, trends, and trouble spots from the unstructured text of survey responses, service notes, e-mail messages, Web forums, blog entries, news articles, and other customer communications. The technology is able to accurately and automatically identify the many different "voices" customers use to express their feedback (such as a negative voice, positive voice, or conditional voice), which helps organiza-

tions pinpoint key events and relationships, such as intent to buy, intent to leave, or customer "wish" events. It can reveal specific product and service issues, reactions to marketing and public relations efforts, and even buying signals.

Attensity's software integrated with JetBlue's other customer analysis tools, such as Satmetrix's Net Promoter metrics, which classifies customers into groups that are generating positive, negative, or no feedback about the company. Using Attensity's text analytics in tandem with these tools, JetBlue developed a customer bill of rights that addressed the major issues customers had with the company.

Hotel chains like Gaylord Hotels and Choice Hotels are using text mining software to glean insights from thousands of customer satisfaction surveys provided by their guests. Gaylord Hotels is using Clarabridge's text analytics solution delivered via the Internet as a hosted software service to gather and analyze customer feedback from surveys, e-mail, chat messaging, staffed call centers, and online forums associated with guests' and meeting planners' experiences at the company's convention resorts. The Clarabridge software sorts through the hotel chain's customer surveys and gathers positive and negative comments, organizing them into a variety of categories to reveal less obvious insights. For example, guests complained about many things more frequently than noisy rooms, but complaints of noisy rooms were most frequently correlated with surveys indicating an unwillingness to return to the hotel for another stay.

Analyzing customer surveys used to take weeks, but now takes only days, thanks to the Clarabridge software. Location managers and corporate executives have also used findings from text mining to influence decisions on building improvements.

Wendy's International adopted Clarabridge software to analyze nearly 500,000 messages it collects each year from its Web-based feedback forum, call center notes, e-mail messages, receipt-based surveys, and social media. The chain's customer satisfaction team had previously used spreadsheets and keyword searches to review customer comments, a very slow manual approach. Wendy's management was looking for a better tool to speed analysis, detect emerging issues, and pinpoint troubled areas of the business at the store, regional, or corporate level.

The Clarabridge technology enables Wendy's to track customer experiences down to the store level within minutes. This timely information helps store, regional, and corporate managers spot and address problems related to meal quality, cleanliness, and speed of service.

Text analytics software caught on first with government agencies and larger companies with information systems departments that had the means to properly use the complicated software, but Clarabridge is now offering a version of its product geared towards small businesses. The technology has already caught on with law enforcement, search tool interfaces, and "listening platforms" like Nielsen Online. Listening platforms are text mining tools that focus on brand management, allowing companies to determine how consumers feel about their brand and take steps to respond to negative sentiment.

Structured data analysis won't be rendered obsolete by text analytics, but companies that are able to use both methods to develop a clearer picture of their customers' attitudes will have an easier time establishing and building their brand and gleaning insights that will enhance profitability.

Sources: Doug Henschen, "Wendy's Taps Text Analytics to Mine Customer Feedback," *Information Week*, March 23, 2010; David Stodder," How Text Analytics Drive Customer Insight" *Information Week*, February 1, 2010; Nancy David Kho, "Customer Experience and Sentiment Analysis," *KMWorld*, February 1, 2010; Siobhan Gorman, "Details of Einstein Cyber-Shield Disclosed by White House," *The Wall Street Journal*, March 2, 2010; www.attensity.com, accessed June 16, 2010; and www.clarabridge.com, accessed June 17, 2010.

CASE STUDY QUESTIONS

1. What challenges does the increase in unstructured data present for businesses?

2. How does text-mining improve decision-making?

3. What kinds of companies are most likely to benefit from text mining software? Explain your answer.

4. In what ways could text mining potentially lead to the erosion of personal information privacy? Explain.

MIS IN ACTION

Visit a Web site such as QVC.com or TripAdvisor.com detailing products or services that have customer reviews. Pick a product, hotel, or other service with at least 15 customer reviews and read those reviews, both positive and negative. How could Web content mining help the offering company improve or better market this product or service? What pieces of information should highlighted?

Web mining looks for patterns in data through content mining, structure mining, and usage mining. Web content mining is the process of extracting knowledge from the content of Web pages, which may include text, image, audio, and video data. Web structure mining extracts useful information from the links embedded in Web documents. For example, links pointing to a document indicate the popularity of the document, while links coming out of a document indicate the richness or perhaps the variety of topics covered in the document. Web usage mining examines user interaction data recorded by a Web server whenever requests for a Web site's resources are received. The usage data records the user's behavior when the user browses or makes transactions on the Web site and collects the data in a server log. Analyzing such data can help companies determine the value of particular customers, cross marketing strategies across products, and the effectiveness of promotional campaigns.

DATABASES AND THE WEB

Have you ever tried to use the Web to place an order or view a product catalog? If so, you were probably using a Web site linked to an internal corporate database. Many companies now use the Web to make some of the information in their internal databases available to customers and business partners.

Suppose, for example, a customer with a Web browser wants to search an online retailer's database for pricing information. Figure 14 illustrates how that customer might access the retailer's internal database over the Web. The user accesses the retailer's Web site over the Internet using Web browser software on his or her client PC. The user's Web browser software requests data from the organization's database, using HTML commands to communicate with the Web server.

Because many back-end databases cannot interpret commands written in HTML, the Web server passes these requests for data to software that translates HTML commands into SQL so that they can be processed by the DBMS working with the database. In a client/server environment, the DBMS resides on a dedicated computer called a **database server**. The DBMS receives the SQL requests and provides the required data. The middleware transfers information from the organization's internal database back to the Web server for delivery in the form of a Web page to the user.

Figure 14 shows that the middleware working between the Web server and the DBMS is an application server running on its own dedicated computer. The application server software handles all application operations, including transaction processing and data access, between browser-based computers and a company's back-end business applications or databases. The application server takes requests from the Web server, runs the business logic to process transactions based on those requests, and provides connectivity to the organization's back-end systems or databases. Alternatively, the software for handling these operations could be a custom program or a CGI script. A CGI script is a compact program using the *Common Gateway Interface (CGI)* specification for processing data on a Web server.

There are a number of advantages to using the Web to access an organization's internal databases. First, Web browser software is much easier to use than proprietary query tools. Second, the Web interface requires few or no changes to the internal database. It costs much less to add a Web interface in front of a legacy system than to redesign and rebuild the system to improve user access.

Accessing corporate databases through the Web is creating new efficiencies, opportunities, and business models. ThomasNet.com provides an up-to-date online directory of more than 600,000 suppliers of industrial products, such as chemicals, metals, plastics, rubber, and automotive equipment. Formerly called Thomas Register, the company used to send out huge paper catalogs with this information. Now it provides this information to users online via its Web site and has become a smaller, leaner company.

Other companies have created entirely new businesses based on access to large databases through the Web. One is the social networking site MySpace, which helps users stay connected with each other or meet new people.

FIGURE 14   LINKING INTERNAL DATABASES TO THE WEB

Client with
Web browser

Internet

Web
server

Application
server

Database
server

Database

Users access an organization's internal database through the Web using their desktop PCs and Web browser software.

MySpace features music, comedy, videos, and "profiles" with information supplied by 122 million users about their age, hometown, dating preferences, marital status, and interests. It maintains a massive database to house and manage all of this content. Facebook uses a similar database.

4   MANAGING DATA RESOURCES

Setting up a database is only a start. In order to make sure that the data for your business remain accurate, reliable, and readily available to those who need it, your business will need special policies and procedures for data management.

ESTABLISHING AN INFORMATION POLICY

Every business, large and small, needs an information policy. Your firm's data are an important resource, and you don't want people doing whatever they want with them. You need to have rules on how the data are to be organized and maintained, and who is allowed to view the data or change them.

An **information policy** specifies the organization's rules for sharing, disseminating, acquiring, standardizing, classifying, and inventorying information. Information policy lays out specific procedures and accountabilities, identifying which users and organizational units can share information, where information can be distributed, and who is responsible for updating and maintaining the information. For example, a typical information policy would specify that only selected members of the payroll and human resources department would have the right to change and view sensitive employee data, such as an employee's salary or social security number, and that these departments are responsible for making sure that such employee data are accurate.

If you are in a small business, the information policy would be established and implemented by the owners or managers. In a large organization, managing and planning for information as a corporate resource often requires a formal data administration function. **Data administration** is responsible for the specific policies and procedures through which data can be managed as an organizational resource. These responsibilities include developing information policy, planning for data, overseeing logical database design and data dictionary development, and monitoring how information systems specialists and end-user groups use data.

You may hear the term **data governance** used to describe many of these activities. Promoted by IBM, data governance deals with the policies and processes for managing the availability, usability, integrity, and security of the data employed in an enterprise, with special emphasis on promoting privacy, security, data quality, and compliance with government regulations.

A large organization will also have a database design and management group within the corporate information systems division that is responsible for defining and organizing the structure and content of the database, and maintaining the database. In close cooperation with users, the design group establishes the physical database, the logical relations among elements, and the access rules and security procedures. The functions it performs are called **database administration**.

ENSURING DATA QUALITY

A well-designed database and information policy will go a long way toward ensuring that the business has the information it needs. However, additional steps must be taken to ensure that the data in organizational databases are accurate and remain reliable.

What would happen if a customer's telephone number or account balance were incorrect? What would be the impact if the database had the wrong price for the product you sold or your sales system and inventory system showed different prices for the same product? Data that are inaccurate, untimely, or inconsistent with other sources of information lead to incorrect decisions, product recalls, and financial losses. Inaccurate data in criminal justice and national security databases might even subject you to unnecessarily surveillance or detention, as described in the chapter-ending case study.

According to Forrester Research, 20 percent of U.S. mail and commercial package deliveries were returned because of incorrect names or addresses. Gartner Inc. reported that more than 25 percent of the critical data in large Fortune 1000 companies' databases is inaccurate or incomplete, including bad product codes and product descriptions, faulty inventory descriptions, erroneous financial data, incorrect supplier information, and incorrect employee data. (Gartner, 2007).

Think of all the times you've received several pieces of the same direct mail advertising on the same day. This is very likely the result of having your name maintained multiple times in a database. Your name may have been misspelled or you used your middle initial on one occasion and not on another or the information was initially entered onto a paper form and not scanned properly into the system. Because of these inconsistencies, the database would treat you as different people! We often receive redundant mail addressed to Laudon, Lavdon, Lauden, or Landon.

If a database is properly designed and enterprise-wide data standards established, duplicate or inconsistent data elements should be minimal. Most data quality problems, however, such as misspelled names, transposed numbers, or incorrect or missing codes, stem from errors during data input. The incidence of such errors is rising as companies move their businesses to the Web and allow customers and suppliers to enter data into their Web sites that directly update internal systems.

Before a new database is in place, organizations need to identify and correct their faulty data and establish better routines for editing data once their database is in operation. Analysis of data quality often begins with a **data quality audit**, which is a structured survey of the accuracy and level of completeness of the data in an information system. Data quality audits can be performed by surveying entire data files, surveying samples from data files, or surveying end users for their perceptions of data quality.

Data cleansing, also known as *data scrubbing*, consists of activities for detecting and correcting data in a database that are incorrect, incomplete, improperly formatted, or redundant. Data cleansing not only corrects errors but also enforces consistency among different sets of data that originated in separate information systems. Specialized data-cleansing software is available to automatically survey data files, correct errors in the data, and integrate the data in a consistent company-wide format.

Data quality problems are not just business problems. They also pose serious problems for individuals, affecting their financial condition and even their jobs. The Interactive Session on Organizations describes some of these impacts, as it details the data quality problems found in the companies that collect and report consumer credit data. As you read this case, look for the management, organization, and technology factors behind this problem, and whether existing solutions are adequate.

INTERACTIVE SESSION: ORGANIZATIONS

CREDIT BUREAU ERRORS—BIG PEOPLE PROBLEMS

You've found the car of your dreams. You have a good job and enough money for a down payment. All you need is an auto loan for $14,000. You have a few credit card bills, which you diligently pay off each month. But when you apply for the loan you're turned down. When you ask why, you're told you have an overdue loan from a bank you've never heard of. You've just become one of the millions of people who have been victimized by inaccurate or outdated data in credit bureaus' information systems.

Most data on U.S. consumers' credit histories are collected and maintained by three national credit reporting agencies: Experian, Equifax, and TransUnion. These organizations collect data from various sources to create a detailed dossier of an individual's borrowing and bill paying habits. This information helps lenders assess a person's credit worthiness, the ability to pay back a loan, and can affect the interest rate and other terms of a loan, including whether a loan will be granted in the first place. It can even affect the chances of finding or keeping a job: At least one-third of employers check credit reports when making hiring, firing, or promotion decisions.

U.S. credit bureaus collect personal information and financial data from a variety of sources, including creditors, lenders, utilities, debt collection agencies, and the courts. These data are aggregated and stored in massive databases maintained by the credit bureaus. The credit bureaus then sell this information to other companies to use for credit assessment.

The credit bureaus claim they know which credit cards are in each consumer's wallet, how much is due on the mortgage, and whether the electric bill is paid on time. But if the wrong information gets into their systems, whether through identity theft or errors transmitted by creditors, watch out! Untangling the mess can be almost impossible.

The bureaus understand the importance of providing accurate information to both lenders and consumers. But they also recognize that their own systems are responsible for many credit-report errors. Some mistakes occur because of the procedures for matching loans to individual credit reports.

The sheer volume of information being transmitted from creditors to credit bureaus increases the likelihood of mistakes. Experian, for example, updates 30 million credit reports each day and roughly 2 billion credit reports each month. It matches the identifying personal information in a credit application or credit account with the identifying personal information in a consumer credit file. Identifying personal information includes items such as name (first name, last name and middle initial), full current address and ZIP code, full previous address and ZIP code, and social security number. The new credit information goes into the consumer credit file that it best matches.

The credit bureaus rarely receive information that matches in all the fields in credit files, so they have to determine how much variation to allow and still call it a match. Imperfect data lead to imperfect matches. A consumer might provide incomplete or inaccurate information on a credit application. A creditor might submit incomplete or inaccurate information to the credit bureaus. If the wrong person matches better than anyone else, the data could unfortunately go into the wrong account.

Perhaps the consumer didn't write clearly on the account application. Name variations on different credit accounts can also result in less-than-perfect matches. Take the name Edward Jeffrey Johnson. One account may say Edward Johnson. Another may say Ed Johnson. Another might say Edward J. Johnson. Suppose the last two digits of Edward's social security number get transposed—more chance for mismatches.

If the name or social security number on another person's account partially matches the data in your file, the computer might attach that person's data to your record. Your record might likewise be corrupted if workers in companies supplying tax and bankruptcy data from court and government records accidentally transpose a digit or misread a document.

The credit bureaus claim it is impossible for them to monitor the accuracy of the 3.5 billion pieces of credit account information they receive each month. They must continually contend with bogus claims from consumers who falsify lender information or use shady credit-repair companies that challenge all the negative information on a credit report regardless of its validity. To separate the good from the bad, the credit bureaus use an automated e-OSCAR (Electronic Online Solution for Complete and Accurate Reporting) system to forward consumer disputes to lenders for verification.

If your credit report showed an error, the bureaus usually do not contact the lender directly to correct the information. To save money, the bureaus send consumer protests and evidence to a data processing center run by a third-party contractor. These contractors rapidly summarize every complaint with a short comment and 2-digit code from a menu of 26 options. For example, the code A3 designates "belongs to another individual with a similar name." These summaries are often too brief to include the background banks need to understand a complaint.

Although this system fixes large numbers of errors (data are updated or corrected for 72 percent of disputes), consumers have few options if the system fails. Consumers who file a second dispute without providing new information might have their dispute dismissed as "frivolous." If the consumer tries to contact the lender that made the error on their own, banks have no obligation to investigate the dispute—unless it's sent by a credit bureau.

Sources: Dennis McCafferty, "Bad Credit Could Cost You a Job," *Baseline*, June 7, 2010; Kristen McNamara, "Bad Credit Derails Job Seekers," *The Wall Street Journal*, March 16, 2010; Anne Kadet, Lucy Lazarony, "Your Name Can Mess Up Your Credit Report, Bankrate.com, accessed July 1, 2009; "Credit Report Fix a Headache," *Atlanta Journal-Constitution*, June 14, 2009; and "Why Credit Bureaus Can't Get It Right," *Smart Money*, March 2009.

CASE STUDY QUESTIONS

1. Assess the business impact of credit bureaus' data quality problems for the credit bureaus, for lenders, for individuals.

2. Are any ethical issues raised by credit bureaus' data quality problems? Explain your answer.

3. Analyze the management, organization, and technology factors responsible for credit bureaus' data quality problems.

4. What can be done to solve these problems?

MIS IN ACTION

Go to the Experian Web site (www.experian.com) and explore the site, with special attention to its services for businesses and small businesses. Then answer the following questions:

1. List and describe five services for businesses and explain how each uses consumer data. Describe the kinds of businesses that would use these services.

2. Explain how each of these services is affected by inaccurate consumer data.

5   HANDS-ON MIS PROJECTS

The projects in this section give you hands-on experience in analyzing data quality problems, establishing company-wide data standards, creating a database for inventory management, and using the Web to search online databases for overseas business resources.

Management Decision Problems

1. Emerson Process Management, a global supplier of measurement, analytical, and monitoring instruments and services based in Austin, Texas, had a new data warehouse designed for analyzing customer activity to improve service and marketing that was full of inaccurate and redundant data. The data in the warehouse came from numerous transaction processing systems in Europe, Asia, and other locations around the world. The team that designed the warehouse had assumed that sales groups in all these areas would enter customer names and addresses the same way, regardless of their location. In fact, cultural differences combined with complications from absorbing companies that Emerson had acquired led to multiple ways of entering quotes, billing, shipping, and other data. Assess the potential business impact of these data quality problems. What decisions have to be made and steps taken to reach a solution?

2. Your industrial supply company wants to create a data warehouse where management can obtain a single corporate-wide view of critical sales information to identify best-selling products in specific geographic areas, key customers, and sales trends. Your sales and product information are stored in several different systems: a divisional sales system running on a Unix server and a corporate sales system running on an IBM mainframe. You would like to create a single standard format that consolidates these data from both systems. The following format has been proposed.

PRODUCT_ID	PRODUCT_DESCRIPTION	COST_PER_UNIT	UNITS_SOLD	SALES_REGION	DIVISION	CUSTOMER_ID

The following are sample files from the two systems that would supply the data for the data warehouse:

CORPORATE SALES SYSTEM

PRODUCT_ID	PRODUCT_DESCRIPTION	UNIT_COST	UNITS_SOLD	SALES_TERRITORY	DIVISION
60231	Bearing, 4"	5.28	900,245	Northeast	Parts
85773	SS assembly unit	12.45	992,111	Midwest	Parts

MECHANICAL PARTS DIVISION SALES SYSTEM

PROD_NO	PRODUCT_DESCRIPTION	COST_PER_UNIT	UNITS_SOLD	SALES_REGION	CUSTOMER_ID
60231	4" Steel bearing	5.28	900,245	N.E.	Anderson
85773	SS assembly unit	12.45	992,111	M.W.	Kelly Industries

- What business problems are created by not having these data in a single standard format?

- How easy would it be to create a database with a single standard format that could store the data from both systems? Identify the problems that would have to be addressed.

- Should the problems be solved by database specialists or general business managers? Explain.

- Who should have the authority to finalize a single company-wide format for this information in the data warehouse?

Achieving Operational Excellence: Building a Relational Database for Inventory Management

Software skills: Database design, querying, and reporting
Business skills: Inventory management

Businesses today depend on databases to provide reliable information about items in inventory, items that need restocking, and inventory costs. In this exercise, you'll use database software to design a database for managing inventory for a small business.

Sylvester's Bike Shop, located in San Francisco, California, sells road, mountain, hybrid, leisure, and children's bicycles. Currently, Sylvester's purchases bikes from three suppliers but plans to add new suppliers in the near future. This rapidly growing business needs a database system to manage this information.

Initially, the database should house information about suppliers and products. The database will contain two tables: a supplier table and a product table. The reorder level refers to the number of items in inventory that triggers a decision to order more items to prevent a stockout. (In other words, if the number of units of a particular item in inventory falls below the reorder level, the item should be reordered.) The user should be able to perform several queries and produce several managerial reports based on the data contained in the two tables.

Using the information found in the tables in MyMISLab, build a simple relational database for Sylvester's. Once you have built the database, perform the following activities:

- Prepare a report that identifies the five most expensive bicycles. The report should list the bicycles in descending order from most expensive to least expensive, the quantity on hand for each, and the markup percentage for each.

- Prepare a report that lists each supplier, its products, the quantities on hand, and associated reorder levels. The report should be sorted alphabetically by supplier. Within each supplier category, the products should be sorted alphabetically.

- Prepare a report listing only the bicycles that are low in stock and need to be reordered. The report should provide supplier information for the items identified.

- Write a brief description of how the database could be enhanced to further improve management of the business. What tables or fields should be added? What additional reports would be useful?

Improving Decision Making: Searching Online Databases for Overseas Business Resources

Software skills: Online databases
Business skills: Researching services for overseas operations

Internet users have access to many thousands of Web-enabled databases with information on services and products in faraway locations. This project develops skills in searching these online databases.

Your company is located in Greensboro, North Carolina, and manufactures office furniture of various types. You have recently acquired several new customers in Australia, and a study you commissioned indicates that, with a presence there, you could greatly increase your sales. Moreover, your study indicates that you could do even better if you actually manufactured many of your products locally (in Australia). First, you need to set up an office in Melbourne to establish a presence, and then you need to begin importing from the United States. You then can plan to start producing locally.

You will soon be traveling to the area to make plans to actually set up an office, and you want to meet with organizations that can help you with your operation. You will need to engage people or organizations that offer many services necessary for you to open your office, including lawyers, accountants, import-export experts, telecommunications equipment and support, and even trainers who can help you to prepare your future employees to work for you. Start by searching for U.S. Department of Commerce advice on doing business in Australia. Then try the following online databases to locate companies that you would like to meet with during your coming trip: Australian Business Register (abr.business.gov.au/), Australia Trade Now (australiatradenow.com/), and the Nationwide Business Directory of Australia (www.nationwide.com.au). If necessary, you could also try search engines such as Yahoo and Google. Then perform the following activities:

- List the companies you would contact to interview on your trip to determine whether they can help you with these and any other functions you think vital to establishing your office.

- Rate the databases you used for accuracy of name, completeness, ease of use, and general helpfulness.

- What does this exercise tell you about the design of databases?

LEARNING TRACK MODULES

The following Learning Tracks provide content relevant to topics covered in this chapter:

1. Database Design, Normalization, and Entity-Relationship Diagramming

2. Introduction to SQL

3. Hierarchical and Network Data Models

Review Summary

1. **What are the problems of managing data resources in a traditional file environment and how are they solved by a database management system?**

    Traditional file management techniques make it difficult for organizations to keep track of all of the pieces of data they use in a systematic way and to organize these data so that they can be easily accessed. Different functional areas and groups were allowed to develop their own files independently. Over time, this traditional file management environment creates problems such as data redundancy and inconsistency, program-data dependence, inflexibility, poor security, and lack of data sharing and availability. A database management system (DBMS) solves these problems with software that permits centralization of data and data management so that businesses have a single consistent source for all their data needs. Using a DBMS minimizes redundant and inconsistent files.

2. **What are the major capabilities of DBMS and why is a relational DBMS so powerful?**

    The principal capabilities of a DBMS includes a data definition capability, a data dictionary capability, and a data manipulation language. The data definition capability specifies the structure and content of the database. The data dictionary is an automated or manual file that stores information about the data in the database, including names, definitions, formats, and descriptions of data elements. The data manipulation language, such as SQL, is a specialized language for accessing and manipulating the data in the database.

    The relational database is the primary method for organizing and maintaining data today in information systems because it is so flexible and accessible. It organizes data in two-dimensional tables called relations with rows and columns. Each table contains data about an entity and its attributes. Each row represents a record and each column represents an attribute or field. Each table also contains a key field to uniquely identify each record for retrieval or manipulation. Relational database tables can be combined easily to deliver data required by users, provided that any two tables share a common data element.

3. **What are some important database design principles?**

    Designing a database requires both a logical design and a physical design. The logical design models the database from a business perspective. The organization's data model should reflect its key business processes and decision-making requirements. The process of creating small, stable, flexible, and adaptive data structures from complex groups of data when designing a relational database is termed normalization. A well-designed relational database will not have many-to-many relationships, and all attributes for a specific entity will only apply to that entity. It will try to enforce referential integrity rules to ensure that relationships between coupled tables remain consistent. An entity-relationship diagram graphically depicts the relationship between entities (tables) in a relational database.

4. **What are the principal tools and technologies for accessing information from databases to improve business performance and decision making?**

    Powerful tools are available to analyze and access the information in databases. A data warehouse consolidates current and historical data from many different operational systems in a central database designed for reporting and analysis. Data warehouses support multidimensional data analysis, also known as online analytical processing (OLAP). OLAP represents relationships among data as a multidimensional structure, which can be visualized as cubes of data and cubes within cubes of data, enabling more sophisticated data analysis. Data mining analyzes large pools of data, including the contents of data warehouses, to find patterns and rules that can be used to predict future behavior and guide decision making. Text mining tools help businesses analyze large unstructured data sets consisting of text. Web mining tools focus on analysis of useful patterns and information from the World Wide Web, examining the structure of Web sites and activities of Web site users as well as the contents of Web pages. Conventional databases can be linked via middleware to the Web or a Web interface to facilitate user access to an organization's internal data.

5. *Why are information policy, data administration, and data quality assurance essential for managing the firm's data resources?*

   Developing a database environment requires policies and procedures for managing organizational data as well as a good data model and database technology. A formal information policy governs the maintenance, distribution, and use of information in the organization. In large corporations, a formal data administration function is responsible for information policy, as well as for data planning, data dictionary development, and monitoring data usage in the firm.

   Data that are inaccurate, incomplete, or inconsistent create serious operational and financial problems for businesses because they may create inaccuracies in product pricing, customer accounts, and inventory data, and lead to inaccurate decisions about the actions that should be taken by the firm. Firms must take special steps to make sure they have a high level of data quality. These include using enterprise-wide data standards, databases designed to minimize inconsistent and redundant data, data quality audits, and data cleansing software.

Key Terms

Attribute

Data administration

Data cleansing

Data definition

Data dictionary

Data governance

Data inconsistency

Data manipulation language

Data mart

Data mining

Data quality audit

Data redundancy

Data warehouse

Database

Database (rigorous definition)

Database administration

Database management system (DBMS)

Database server

Entity

Entity-relationship diagram

Field

File

Foreign key

Information policy

Key field

Normalization

Object-oriented DBMS

Object-relational DBMS

Online analytical processing (OLAP)

Predictive analytics

Primary key

Program-data dependence

Record

Referential integrity

Relational DBMS

Structured Query Language (SQL)

Text mining

Tuple

Web mining

Review Questions

1. What are the problems of managing data resources in a traditional file environment and how are they solved by a database management system?

   - List and describe each of the components in the data hierarchy.

   - Define and explain the significance of entities, attributes, and key fields.

   - List and describe the problems of the traditional file environment.

   - Define a database and a database management system and describe how it solves the problems of a traditional file environment.

2. What are the major capabilities of DBMS and why is a relational DBMS so powerful?

   - Name and briefly describe the capabilities of a DBMS.

   - Define a relational DBMS and explain how it organizes data.

   - List and describe the three operations of a relational DBMS.

3. What are some important database design principles?

   - Define and describe normalization and referential integrity and explain how they contribute to a well-designed relational database.

   - Define and describe an entity-relationship diagram and explain its role in database design.

4. What are the principal tools and technologies for accessing information from databases to improve business performance and decision making?

   - Define a data warehouse, explaining how it works and how it benefits organizations.

   - Define business intelligence and explain how it is related to database technology.

   - Describe the capabilities of online analytical processing (OLAP).

   - Define data mining, describing how it differs from OLAP and the types of information it provides.

   - Explain how text mining and Web mining differ from conventional data mining.

   - Describe how users can access information from a company's internal databases through the Web.

5. Why are information policy, data administration, and data quality assurance essential for managing the firm's data resources?

   - Describe the roles of information policy and data administration in information management.

   - Explain why data quality audits and data cleansing are essential.

Discussion Questions

1. It has been said that you do not need database management software to create a database environment. Discuss.

2. To what extent should end users be involved in the selection of a database management system and database design?

3. What are the consequences of an organization not having an information policy?

Video Cases

Video Cases and Instructional Videos illustrating some of the concepts in this chapter are available. Contact your instructor to access these videos.

Collaboration and Teamwork: Identifying Entities and Attributes in an Online Database

With your team of three or four students, select an online database to explore, such as AOL Music, iGo.com, or the Internet Movie Database (IMDb). Explore one of these Web sites to see what information it provides. Then list the entities and attributes that the company running the Web site must keep track of in its databases. Diagram the relationship between the entities you have identified. If possible, use Google Sites to post links to Web pages, team communication announcements, and work assignments; to brainstorm; and to work collaboratively on project documents. Try to use Google Docs to develop a presentation of your findings for the class.

The Terror Watch List Database's Troubles Continue
CASE STUDY

In the aftermath of the 9-11 attacks, the FBI's Terrorist Screening Center, or TSC, was established to consolidate information about suspected terrorists from multiple government agencies into a single list to enhance inter-agency communication. A database of suspected terrorists known as the terrorist watch list was created. Multiple U.S. government agencies had been maintaining separate lists and these agencies lacked a consistent process to share relevant information.

Records in the TSC database contain sensitive but unclassified information on terrorist identities, such as name and date of birth, that can be shared with other screening agencies. Classified information about the people in the watch list is maintained in other law enforcement and intelligence agency databases. Records for the watchlist database are provided by two sources: The National Counterterrorism Center (NCTC) managed by the Office of the Director of National Intelligence provides identifying information on individuals with ties to international terrorism. The FBI provides identifying information on individuals with ties to purely domestic terrorism.

These agencies collect and maintain terrorist information and nominate individuals for inclusion in the TSC's consolidated watch list. They are required to follow strict procedures established by the head of the agency concerned and approved by the U.S. Attorney General. TSC staff must review each record submitted before it is added to the database. An individual will remain on the watch list until the respective department or agency that nominated that person to the list determines that the person should be removed from the list and deleted from the database

The TSC watch list database is updated daily with new nominations, modifications to existing records, and deletions. Since its creation, the list has ballooned to 400,000 people, recorded as 1.1 million names and aliases, and is continuing to grow at a rate of 200,000 records each year. Information on the list is distributed to a wide range of government agency systems for use in efforts to deter or detect the movements of known or suspected terrorists.

Recipient agencies include the FBI, CIA, National Security Agency (NSA), Transportation Security Administration (TSA), Department of Homeland Security, State Department, Customs and Border Protection, Secret Service, U.S. Marshals Service, and the White House. Airlines use data supplied by the TSA system in their NoFly and Selectee lists for prescreening passengers, while the U.S. Customs and Border Protection system uses the watchlist data to help screen travelers entering the United States. The State Department system screens applicants for visas to enter the United States and U.S. residents applying for passports, while state and local law enforcement agencies use the FBI system to help with arrests, detentions, and other criminal justice activities. Each of these agencies receives the subset of data in the watch list that pertains to its specific mission.

When an individual makes an airline reservation, arrives at a U.S. port of entry, applies for a U.S. visa, or is stopped by state or local police within the United States, the frontline screening agency or airline conducts a name-based search of the individual against the records from the terrorist watch list database. When the computerized name-matching system generates a "hit" (a potential name match) against a watch list record, the airline or agency will review each potential match. Matches that are clearly positive or exact matches that are inconclusive (uncertain or difficult to verify) are referred to the applicable screening agency's intelligence or operations center and to the TSC for closer examination. In turn, TSC checks its databases and other sources, including classified databases maintained by the NCTC and FBI to confirm whether the individual is a positive, negative, or inconclusive match to the watch list record. TSC creates a daily report summarizing all positive matches to the watch list and distributes them to numerous federal agencies.

The process of consolidating information from disparate agencies has been a slow and painstaking one, requiring the integration of at least 12 different databases. Two years after the process of integration took place, 10 of the 12 databases had been processed. The remaining two databases (the U.S. Immigration and Customs Enforcement's Automatic Biometric Identification System and the FBI's Integrated Automated Fingerprint Identification System) are both fingerprint databases. There is still more work to be done to optimize the list's usefulness.

Reports from both the Government Accountability Office and the Office of the Inspector General assert that the list contains inaccuracies and that government departmental policies for nomination and removal from the lists are not uniform. There has also been public outcry resulting from the size of the list and well-publicized incidents of obvious non-terrorists finding that they are included on the list.

Information about the process for inclusion on the list must necessarily be carefully protected if the list is to be effective against terrorists. The specific criteria for inclusion are not public knowledge. We do know, however, that government agencies populate their watch lists by performing wide sweeps of information gathered on travelers, using many misspellings and alternate variations of the names of suspected terrorists. This often leads to the inclusion of people who do not belong on watch lists, known as "false positives." It also results in some people being listed multiple times under different spellings of their names.

While these selection criteria may be effective for tracking as many potential terrorists as possible, they also lead to many more erroneous entries on the list than if the process required more finely tuned information to add new entries. Notable examples of 'false positives' include Michael Hicks, an 8-year-old New Jersey Cub Scout who is continually stopped at the airport for additional screening and the late senator Ted Kennedy, who had been repeatedly delayed in the past because his name resembles an alias once used by a suspected terrorist. Like Kennedy, Hicks may have been added because his name is the same or similar to a different suspected terrorist.

These incidents call attention to the quality and accuracy of the data in the TSC consolidated terrorist watch list. In June 2005, a report by the Department of Justice's Office of the Inspector General found inconsistent record counts, duplicate records, and records that lacked data fields or had unclear sources for their data. Although TSC subsequently enhanced its efforts to identify and correct incomplete or inaccurate watch list records, the Inspector General noted in September 2007 that TSC management of the watch list still showed some weaknesses.

Given the option between a list that tracks every potential terrorist at the cost of unnecessarily tracking some innocents, and a list that fails to track many terrorists in an effort to avoid tracking innocents, many would choose the list that tracked every terrorist despite the drawbacks. But to make matters worse for those already inconvenienced by wrongful inclusion on the list, there is currently no simple and quick redress process for innocents that hope to remove themselves from it.

The number of requests for removal from the watch list continues to mount, with over 24,000 requests recorded (about 2,000 each month) and only 54 percent of them resolved. The average time to process a request in 2008 was 40 days, which was not (and still is not) fast enough to keep pace with the number of requests for removal coming in. As a result, law-abiding travelers that inexplicably find themselves on the watch list are left with no easy way to remove themselves from it.

In February 2007, the Department of Homeland Security instituted its Traveler Redress Inquiry Program (TRIP) to help people that have been erroneously added to terrorist watch lists remove themselves and avoid extra screening and questioning. John Anderson's mother claimed that despite her best efforts, she was unable to remove her son from the watch lists. Senator Kennedy reportedly was only able to remove himself from the list by personally bringing up the matter to Tom Ridge, then the Director of the Department of Homeland Security.

Security officials say that mistakes such as the one that led to Anderson and Kennedy's inclusion on no-fly and consolidated watch lists occur due to the matching of imperfect data in airline reservation systems with imperfect data on the watch lists. Many airlines don't include gender, middle name, or date of birth in their reservations records, which increases the likelihood of false matches.

One way to improve screening and help reduce the number of people erroneously marked for additional investigation would be to use a more sophisticated system involving more personal data about individuals on the list. The TSA is developing just such a system, called "Secure Flight," but it has been continually delayed due to privacy concerns regarding the sensitivity and safety of the data it would collect. Other similar surveillance programs and watch lists, such as the NSA's attempts to gather information about suspected terrorists, have drawn criticism for potential privacy violations.

Additionally, the watch list has drawn criticism because of its potential to promote racial profiling and discrimination. Some allege that they were included by virtue of their race and ethnic descent, such as David Fathi, an attorney for the ACLU of Iranian descent, and Asif Iqbal, a U.S. citizen of Pakistani decent with the same name as a Guantanamo detainee. Outspoken critics of U.S. foreign policy, such as some elected officials and university professors, have also found themselves on the list.

A report released in May 2009 by Department of Justice Inspector General Glenn A. Fine found that the FBI had incorrectly kept nearly 24,000 people on its own watch list that supplies data to the terrorist watch list on the basis of outdated or irrelevant information. Examining nearly 69,000 referrals to the FBI list, the report found that 35 percent of those people remained on the list despite inadequate justification. Even more worrisome, the list did not contain the names of people who should have been listed because of their terrorist ties.

FBI officials claim that the bureau has made improvements, including better training, faster processing of referrals, and requiring field office supervisors to review watch-list nominations for accuracy and completeness. But this watch list and the others remain imperfect tools. In early 2008, it was revealed that 20 known terrorists were not correctly listed on the consolidated watch list. (Whether these individuals were able to enter the U.S. as a result is unclear.)

Umar Farouk Abdulmutallab, the Nigerian who unsuccessfully tried to detonate plastic explosives on the Northwest Airlines flight from Amsterdam to Detroit on Christmas Day 2009, had not made it onto the no-fly list. Although Abdulmutallab's father had reported concern over his son's radicalization to the U.S. State Department, the Department did not revoke Adbulmutallab's visa because his name was misspelled in the visa database, so he was allowed to enter the United States. Faisal Shahzad, the Times Square car bomber, was apprehended on May 3, 2010, only moments before his Emirates airline flight to Dubai and Pakistan was about to take off. The airline had failed to check a last-minute update to the no-fly list that had added Shahzad's name.

Sources: Scott Shane, "Lapses Allowed Suspect to Board Plane," *The New York Times*, May 4, 2010; Mike McIntire, "Ensnared by Error on Growing U.S. Watch List," *The New York Times*, April 6, 2010; Eric Lipton, Eric Schmitt, and Mark Mazzetti, "Review of Jet Bomb Plot Shows More Missed Clues," *The New York Times*, January 18, 2010; Lizette Alvarez, "Meet Mikey, 8: U.S. Has Him on Watch List," *The New York Times*, January 14, 2010; Eric Lichtblau, "Justice Dept. Finds Flaws in F.B.I. Terror List," *The New York Times*, May 7, 2009; Bob Egelko, "Watch-list Name Confusion Causes Hardship," *San Francisco Chronicle*, March 20, 2008; "Reports Cite Lack of Uniform Policy for Terrorist Watch List," *The Washington Post*, March 18, 2008; Siobhan Gorman, "NSA's Domestic Spying Grows as Agency Sweeps Up Data," *The Wall Street Journal*, March 10, 2008; Ellen Nakashima, and Scott McCartney, "When Your Name is Mud at the Airport," *The Wall Street Journal*, January 29, 2008.

CASE STUDY QUESTIONS

1. What concepts in this chapter are illustrated in this case?

2. Why was the consolidated terror watch list created? What are the benefits of the list?

3. Describe some of the weaknesses of the watch list. What management, organization, and technology factors are responsible for these weaknesses?

4. How effective is the system of watch lists described in this case study? Explain your answer.

5. If you were responsible for the management of the TSC watch list database, what steps would you take to correct some of these weaknesses?

6. Do you believe that the terror watch list represents a significant threat to individuals' privacy or Constitutional rights? Why or why not?

References

Cappiello, Cinzia, Chiara Francalanci, and Barbara Pernici. "Time-Related Factors of Data Quality in Multichannel Information Systems." Journal of Management Information Systems 20, no. 3 (Winter 2004).

Chen, Andrew N. K., Paulo B. Goes, and James R. Marsden. "A Query-Driven Approach to the Design and Management of Flexible Database Systems." Journal of Management Information Systems 19, no. 3 (Winter 2002-2003).

Clifford, James, Albert Croker, and Alex Tuzhilin. "On Data Representation and Use in a Temporal Relational DBMS." Information Systems Research 7, no. 3 (September 1996).

Eckerson, Wayne W. "Data Quality and the Bottom Line." The Data Warehousing Institute (2002).

Fayyad, Usama, Ramasamy Ramakrishnan, and Ramakrisnan Srikant. "Evolving Data Mining into Solutions for Insights." Communications of the ACM 45, no.8 (August 2002).

Foshay, Neil, Avinandan Mukherjee and Andrew Taylor. "Does Data Warehouse End-User Metadata Add Value? Communications of the ACM 50, no. 11 (November 2007).

Gartner Inc. "'Dirty Data' is a Business Problem, not an IT Problem, Says Gartner." Sydney, Australia (March 2, 2007).

Henschen, Doug. "Text Mining for Customer Insight." Information Week (November 30, 2009).

Henschen, Doug. "Big and Fast." Information Week (August 9, 2010).

Henschen, Doug. "The Data Warehouse Revised." Information Week (May 26, 2008).

Henschen, Doug."Wendy's Taps Text Analytics to Mine Customer Feedback," Information Week (March 23, 2010).

Hoffer, Jeffrey A., Mary Prescott, and Heikki Toppi. Modern Database Management, 10th ed. Upper Saddle River, NJ: Prentice-Hall (2011).

Jinesh Radadia. "Breaking the Bad Data Bottlenecks." Information Management (May/June 2010).

Kim, Yong Jin, Rajiv Kishore, and G. Lawrence Sanders. "From DQ to EQ: Understanding Data Quality in the Context of E-Business System"Communications of the ACM 48, no. 10 (October 2005).

Klau, Rick. "Data Quality and CRM." Line56.com, accessed March 4, 2003.

Kroenke, David M. and David Auer. Database Processing 11e. Upper Saddle River, NJ: Prentice-Hall (2010).

Lee, Yang W., and Diane M. Strong. "Knowing-Why about Data Processes and Data Quality." Journal of Management Information Systems 20, no. 3 (Winter 2004).

Loveman, Gary. "Diamonds in the Datamine." Harvard Business Review (May 2003).

McKnight, William. "Seven Sources of Poor Data Quality." Information Management (April 2009).

Pierce, Elizabeth M. "Assessing Data Quality with Control Matrices." Communications of the ACM 47, no. 2 (February 2004).

Redman, Thomas. Data Driven: Profiting from Your Most Important Business Asset. Boston: Harvard Business Press (2008).

Stodder, David."Customer Insights." Information Week (February 1, 2010)

Chapter 8

Securing Information Systems

From Chapter 8 of *Management Information Systems: Managing the Digital Firm*, 12/e. Kenneth C. Laudon, Jane P. Laudon. Copyright © 2012 by Pearson Education. Published by Prentice Hall. All rights reserved.

Securing Information Systems

Interactive Sessions:

When Antivirus Software Cripples Your Computers

How Secure Is the Cloud?

YOU'RE ON FACEBOOK? WATCH OUT!

Facebook is the world's largest online social network, and increasingly, the destination of choice for messaging friends, sharing photos and videos, and collecting "eyeballs" for business advertising and market research. But, watch out! It's also a great place for losing your identity or being attacked by malicious software.

How could that be? Facebook has a security team that works hard to counter threats on that site. It uses up-to-date security technology to protect its Web site. But with 500 million users, it can't police everyone and everything. And Facebook makes an extraordinarily tempting target for both mischief-makers and criminals.

Facebook has a huge worldwide user base, an easy-to-use Web site, and a community of users linked to their friends. Its members are more likely to trust messages they receive from friends, even if this communication is not legitimate. Perhaps for these reasons, research from the Kaspersky Labs security firm shows malicious software on social networking sites such as Facebook and MySpace is 10 times more successful at infecting users than e-mail-based attacks. Moreover, IT security firm Sophos reported on February 1, 2010, that Facebook poses the greatest security risk of all the social networking sites.

Here are some examples of what can go wrong:

According to a February 2010 report from Internet security company NetWitness, Facebook served as the primary delivery method for an 18-month-long hacker attack in which Facebook users were tricked into revealing their passwords and downloading a rogue program that steals financial data. A legitimate-looking Facebook e-mail notice asked users to provide information to help the social network update its login system. When the user clicked the "update" button in the e-mail, that person was directed to a bogus Facebook login screen where the user's name was filled in and that person was prompted to provide his or her password. Once the user supplied that information, an "Update Tool," installed the Zeus "Trojan horse" rogue software program designed to steal financial and personal data by surreptitiously tracking users' keystrokes as they enter information into their computers. The hackers, most likely an Eastern European criminal group, stole as many as 68,000 login credentials from 2,400 companies and government agencies for online banking, social networking sites, and e-mail.

The Koobface worm targets Microsoft Windows users of Facebook, Twitter, and other social networking Web sites in order to gather sensitive information from the victims such as credit card numbers. Koobface was first detected in December 2008. It spreads by delivering bogus Facebook messages to people who are "friends" of a Facebook user whose computer has already been infected. Upon receipt, the message directs the recipients to a third-party Web site, where they are prompted to download what is purported to be an update of the Adobe Flash player. If they download and execute the file, Koobface is able to infect their system and use the computer for more malicious work.

For much of May 2010, Facebook members and their

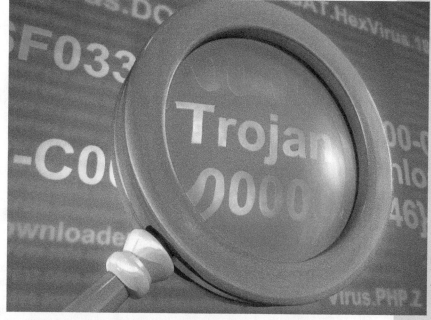

friends were victims of a spam campaign that tries to e-mail unsolicited advertisements and steal Facebook users' login credentials. The attack starts with a message containing a link to a bogus Web page sent by infected users to all of their friends. The message addresses each friend by name and invites that person to click on a link to "the most hilarious video ever." The link transports the user to a rogue Web site mimicking the Facebook login form. When users try to log in, the page redirects back to a Facebook application page that installs illicit adware software, which bombards their computers with all sorts of unwanted ads.

Recovering from these attacks is time-consuming and costly, especially for business firms. A September 2010 study by Panda Security found that one-third of small and medium businesses it surveyed had been hit by malicious software from social networks, and more than a third of these suffered more than $5,000 in losses. Of course, for large businesses, losses from Facebook are much greater.

Sources: Lance Whitney, "Social-Media Malware Hurting Small Businesses," CNET News, September 15, 2010; Raj Dash, "Report: Facebook Served as Primary Distribution Channel for Botnet Army," allfacebook.com, February 18, 2010; Sam Diaz, "Report: Bad Guys Go Social: Facebook Tops Security Risk List," *ZDNet*, February 1, 2010; Lucian Constantin, "Weekend Adware Scam Returns to Facebook," Softpedia, May 29, 2010; Brad Stone, "Viruses that Leave Victims Red in the Facebook," *The New York Times*, December 14, 2009; and Brian Prince, "Social Networks 10 Times as Effective for Hackers, Malware," *eWeek*, May 13, 2009.

The problems created by malicious software on Facebook illustrate some of the reasons why businesses need to pay special attention to information system security. Facebook provides a plethora of benefits to both individuals and businesses. But from a security standpoint, using Facebook is one of the easiest ways to expose a computer system to malicious software—your computer, your friends' computers, and even the computers of Facebook-participating businesses.

The chapter-opening diagram calls attention to important points raised by this case and this chapter. Although Facebook's management has a security policy and security team in place, Facebook has been plagued with many security problems that affect both individuals and businesses. The "social" nature of this site and large number of users make it unusually attractive for criminals and hackers intent on stealing valuable personal and financial information and propagating malicious software. Even though Facebook and its users deploy security technology, they are still vulnerable to new kinds of malicious software attacks and criminal scams. In addition to losses from theft of financial data, the difficulties of eradicating the malicious software or repairing damage caused by identity theft add to operational costs and make both individuals and businesses less effective.

1   SYSTEM VULNERABILITY AND ABUSE

Can you imagine what would happen if you tried to link to the Internet without a firewall or antivirus software? Your computer would be disabled in a few seconds, and it might take you many days to recover. If you used the computer to run your business, you might not be able to sell to your customers or place orders with your suppliers while it was down. And you might find that your computer system had been penetrated by outsiders, who perhaps stole or destroyed valuable data, including confidential payment data from your customers. If too much data were destroyed or divulged, your business might never be able to operate!

In short, if you operate a business today, you need to make security and control a top priority. **Security** refers to the policies, procedures, and technical measures used to prevent unauthorized access, alteration, theft, or physical damage to information systems. **Controls** are methods, policies, and organizational procedures that ensure the safety of the organization's assets; the accuracy and reliability of its records; and operational adherence to management standards.

WHY SYSTEMS ARE VULNERABLE

When large amounts of data are stored in electronic form, they are vulnerable to many more kinds of threats than when they existed in manual form. Through communications networks, information systems in different locations are interconnected. The potential for unauthorized access, abuse, or fraud is not limited to a single location but can occur at any access point in the network. Figure 1 illustrates the most common threats against contemporary information systems. They can stem from technical, organizational, and environmental factors compounded by poor management decisions. In the multi-tier client/server computing environment illustrated here, vulnerabilities exist at each layer and in the communications between the layers. Users at the client layer can cause harm by introducing errors or by accessing systems without

FIGURE 1   **CONTEMPORARY SECURITY CHALLENGES AND VULNERABILITIES**

The architecture of a Web-based application typically includes a Web client, a server, and corporate information systems linked to databases. Each of these components presents security challenges and vulnerabilities. Floods, fires, power failures, and other electrical problems can cause disruptions at any point in the network.

authorization. It is possible to access data flowing over networks, steal valuable data during transmission, or alter messages without authorization. Radiation may disrupt a network at various points as well. Intruders can launch denial-of-service attacks or malicious software to disrupt the operation of Web sites. Those capable of penetrating corporate systems can destroy or alter corporate data stored in databases or files.

Systems malfunction if computer hardware breaks down, is not configured properly, or is damaged by improper use or criminal acts. Errors in programming, improper installation, or unauthorized changes cause computer software to fail. Power failures, floods, fires, or other natural disasters can also disrupt computer systems.

Domestic or offshore partnering with another company adds to system vulnerability if valuable information resides on networks and computers outside the organization's control. Without strong safeguards, valuable data could be lost, destroyed, or could fall into the wrong hands, revealing important trade secrets or information that violates personal privacy.

The popularity of handheld mobile devices for business computing adds to these woes. Portability makes cell phones, smartphones, and tablet computers easy to lose or steal. Smartphones share the same security weaknesses as other Internet devices, and are vulnerable to malicious software and penetration from outsiders. In 2009, security experts identified 30 security flaws in software and operating systems of smartphones made by Apple, Nokia, and BlackBerry maker Research in Motion.

Even the apps that have been custom-developed for mobile devices are capable of turning into rogue software. For example, in December 2009, Google pulled dozens of mobile banking apps from its Android Market because they could have been updated to capture customers' banking credentials. Smartphones used by corporate executives may contain sensitive data such as sales figures, customer names, phone numbers, and e-mail addresses. Intruders may be able to access internal corporate networks through these devices.

Internet Vulnerabilities

Large public networks, such as the Internet, are more vulnerable than internal networks because they are virtually open to anyone. The Internet is so huge that when abuses do occur, they can have an enormously widespread impact. When the Internet becomes part of the corporate network, the organization's information systems are even more vulnerable to actions from outsiders.

Computers that are constantly connected to the Internet by cable modems or digital subscriber line (DSL) lines are more open to penetration by outsiders because they use fixed Internet addresses where they can be easily identified. (With dial-up service, a temporary Internet address is assigned for each session.) A fixed Internet address creates a fixed target for hackers.

Telephone service based on Internet technology is more vulnerable than the switched voice network if it does not run over a secure private network. Most Voice over IP (VoIP) traffic over the public Internet is not encrypted, so anyone with a network can listen in on conversations. Hackers can intercept conversations or shut down voice service by flooding servers supporting VoIP with bogus traffic.

Vulnerability has also increased from widespread use of e-mail, instant messaging (IM), and peer-to-peer file-sharing programs. E-mail may contain attachments that serve as springboards for malicious software or unauthorized access to internal corporate systems. Employees may use e-mail messages to transmit valuable trade secrets, financial data, or confidential customer information to unauthorized recipients. Popular IM applications for consumers do not use a secure layer for text messages, so they can be intercepted and read by outsiders during transmission over the public Internet. Instant messaging activity over the Internet can in some cases be used as a back door to an otherwise secure network. Sharing files over peer-to-peer (P2P) networks, such as those for illegal music sharing, may also transmit malicious software or expose information on either individual or corporate computers to outsiders.

Wireless Security Challenges

Is it safe to log onto a wireless network at an airport, library, or other public location? It depends on how vigilant you are. Even the wireless network in your home is vulnerable because radio frequency bands are easy to scan. Both Bluetooth and Wi-Fi networks are susceptible to hacking by eavesdroppers. Although the range of Wi-Fi networks is only several hundred feet, it can be extended up to one-fourth of a mile using external antennae. Local area networks (LANs) using the 802.11 standard can be easily penetrated by outsiders armed with laptops, wireless cards, external antennae, and hacking software. Hackers use these tools to detect unprotected networks, monitor network traffic, and, in some cases, gain access to the Internet or to corporate networks.

Wi-Fi transmission technology was designed to make it easy for stations to find and hear one another. The *service set identifiers (SSIDs)* identifying the access points in a Wi-Fi network are broadcast multiple times and can be picked up fairly easily by intruders' sniffer programs (see Figure 2). Wireless networks in many locations do not have basic protections against **war driving**,

FIGURE 2   WI-FI SECURITY CHALLENGES

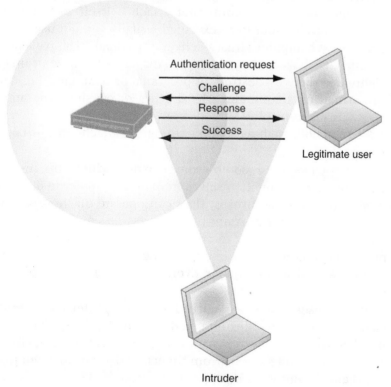

Many Wi-Fi networks can be penetrated easily by intruders using sniffer programs to obtain an address to access the resources of a network without authorization.

in which eavesdroppers drive by buildings or park outside and try to intercept wireless network traffic.

A hacker can employ an 802.11 analysis tool to identify the SSID. (Windows XP, Vista, and 7 have capabilities for detecting the SSID used in a network and automatically configuring the radio NIC within the user's device.) An intruder that has associated with an access point by using the correct SSID is capable of accessing other resources on the network, using the Windows operating system to determine which other users are connected to the network, access their computer hard drives, and open or copy their files.

Intruders also use the information they have gleaned to set up rogue access points on a different radio channel in physical locations close to users to force a user's radio NIC to associate with the rogue access point. Once this association occurs, hackers using the rogue access point can capture the names and passwords of unsuspecting users.

The initial security standard developed for Wi-Fi, called Wired Equivalent Privacy (WEP), is not very effective. WEP is built into all standard 802.11 products, but its use is optional. Many users neglect to use WEP security features, leaving them unprotected. The basic WEP specification calls for an access point and all of its users to share the same 40-bit encrypted password, which can be easily decrypted by hackers from a small amount of traffic. Stronger encryption and authentication systems are now available, such as Wi-Fi Protected Access 2 (WPA2), but users must be willing to install them.

MALICIOUS SOFTWARE: VIRUSES, WORMS, TROJAN HORSES, AND SPYWARE

Malicious software programs are referred to as **malware** and include a variety of threats, such as computer viruses, worms, and Trojan horses. A **computer virus** is a rogue software program that attaches itself to other software programs or data files in order to be executed, usually without user knowledge or permission. Most computer viruses deliver a "payload." The payload may be relatively benign, such as the instructions to display a message or image, or it may be highly destructive—destroying programs or data, clogging computer memory, reformatting a computer's hard drive, or causing programs to run improperly. Viruses typically spread from computer to computer when humans take an action, such as sending an e-mail attachment or copying an infected file.

Most recent attacks have come from **worms**, which are independent computer programs that copy themselves from one computer to other computers over a network. (Unlike viruses, they can operate on their own without attaching to other computer program files and rely less on human behavior in order to spread from computer to computer. This explains why computer worms spread much more rapidly than computer viruses.) Worms destroy data and programs as well as disrupt or even halt the operation of computer networks.

Worms and viruses are often spread over the Internet from files of downloaded software, from files attached to e-mail transmissions, or from compromised e-mail messages or instant messaging. Viruses have also invaded computerized information systems from "infected" disks or infected machines. E-mail worms are currently the most problematic.

Malware targeting mobile devices is not as extensive as that targeting computers, but is spreading nonetheless using e-mail, text messages, Bluetooth, and file downloads from the Web via Wi-Fi or cellular networks. There are now more than 200 viruses and worms targeting mobile phones, such as Cabir, Commwarrior, Frontal.A, and Ikee.B. Frontal.A installs a corrupted file that causes phone failure and prevents the user from rebooting, while Ikee.B turns jailbroken iPhones into botnet-controlled devices. Mobile device viruses pose serious threats to enterprise computing because so many wireless devices are now linked to corporate information systems.

Web 2.0 applications, such as blogs, wikis, and social networking sites such as Facebook and MySpace, have emerged as new conduits for malware or spyware. These applications allow users to post software code as part of the permissible content, and such code can be launched automatically as soon as a Web page is viewed. The chapter-opening case study describes other channels for malware targeting Facebook. In September 2010, hackers exploited a Twitter security flaw to send users to Japanese pornographic sites and automatically generated messages from other accounts (Coopes, 2010).

Table 1 describes the characteristics of some of the most harmful worms and viruses that have appeared to date.

Over the past decade, worms and viruses have caused billions of dollars of damage to corporate networks, e-mail systems, and data. According to Consumer Reports' State of the Net 2010 survey, U.S. consumers lost $3.5 billion

TABLE 1   EXAMPLES OF MALICIOUS CODE

NAME	TYPE	DESCRIPTION
Conficker (aka Downadup, Downup)	Worm	First detected in November 2008. Uses flaws in Windows software to take over machines and link them into a virtual computer that can be commanded remotely. Has more than 5 million computers worldwide under its control. Difficult to eradicate.
Storm	Worm/ Trojan horse	First identified in January 2007. Spreads via e-mail spam with a fake attachment. Infected up to 10 million computers, causing them to join its zombie network of computers engaged in criminal activity.
Sasser.ftp	Worm	First appeared in May 2004. Spread over the Internet by attacking random IP addresses. Causes computers to continually crash and reboot, and infected computers to search for more victims. Affected millions of computers worldwide, disrupting British Airways flight check-ins, operations of British coast guard stations, Hong Kong hospitals, Taiwan post office branches, and Australia's Westpac Bank. Sasser and its variants caused an estimated $14.8 billion to $18.6 billion in damages worldwide.
MyDoom.A	Worm	First appeared on January 26, 2004. Spreads as an e-mail attachment. Sends e-mail to addresses harvested from infected machines, forging the sender's address. At its peak this worm lowered global Internet performance by 10 percent and Web page loading times by as much as 50 percent. Was programmed to stop spreading after February 12, 2004.
Sobig.F	Worm	First detected on August 19, 2003. Spreads via e-mail attachments and sends massive amounts of mail with forged sender information. Deactivated itself on September 10, 2003, after infecting more than 1 million PCs and doing $5 to $10 billion in damage.
ILOVEYOU	Virus	First detected on May 3, 2000. Script virus written in Visual Basic script and transmitted as an attachment to e-mail with the subject line ILOVEYOU. Overwrites music, image, and other files with a copy of itself and did an estimated $10 billion to $15 billion in damage.
Melissa	Macro virus/ worm	First appeared in March 1999. Word macro script mailing infected Word file to first 50 entries in user's Microsoft Outlook address book. Infected 15 to 29 percent of all business PCs, causing $300 million to $600 million in damage.

because of malware and online scams, and the majority of these losses came from malware (Consumer Reports, 2010).

A **Trojan horse** is a software program that appears to be benign but then does something other than expected, such as the Zeus Trojan described in the chapter-opening case. The Trojan horse is not itself a virus because it does not replicate, but it is often a way for viruses or other malicious code to be introduced into a computer system. The term *Trojan horse* is based on the huge wooden horse used by the Greeks to trick the Trojans into opening the gates to their fortified city during the *Trojan War*. Once inside the city walls, Greek soldiers hidden in the horse revealed themselves and captured the city.

At the moment, **SQL injection attacks** are the largest malware threat. SQL injection attacks take advantage of vulnerabilities in poorly coded Web application software to introduce malicious program code into a company's systems and networks. These vulnerabilities occur when a Web application fails to properly validate or filter data entered by a user on a Web page, which might occur when ordering something online. An attacker uses this input validation error to send a rogue SQL query to the underlying database to access the database, plant malicious code, or access other systems on the network. Large Web applications have hundreds of places for inputting user data, each of which creates an opportunity for an SQL injection attack.

A large number of Web-facing applications are believed to have SQL injection vulnerabilities, and tools are available for hackers to check Web applications for these vulnerabilities. Such tools are able to locate a data entry field on a Web page form, enter data into it, and check the response to see if shows vulnerability to a SQL injection.

Some types of spyware also act as malicious software. These small programs install themselves surreptitiously on computers to monitor user Web surfing activity and serve up advertising. Thousands of forms of spyware have been documented.

Many users find such **spyware** annoying and some critics worry about its infringement on computer users' privacy. Some forms of spyware are especially nefarious. **Keyloggers** record every keystroke made on a computer to steal serial numbers for software, to launch Internet attacks, to gain access to e-mail accounts, to obtain passwords to protected computer systems, or to pick up personal information such as credit card numbers. Other spyware programs reset Web browser home pages, redirect search requests, or slow performance by taking up too much memory. The Zeus Trojan described in the chapter-opening case uses keylogging to steal financial information.

HACKERS AND COMPUTER CRIME

A **hacker** is an individual who intends to gain unauthorized access to a computer system. Within the hacking community, the term *cracker* is typically used to denote a hacker with criminal intent, although in the public press, the terms hacker and cracker are used interchangeably. Hackers and crackers gain unauthorized access by finding weaknesses in the security protections employed by Web sites and computer systems, often taking advantage of various features of the Internet that make it an open system that is easy to use.

Hacker activities have broadened beyond mere system intrusion to include theft of goods and information, as well as system damage and **cybervandalism**, the intentional disruption, defacement, or even destruction of a Web site or corporate information system. For example, cybervandals have turned many of the MySpace "group" sites, which are dedicated to interests such as home beer brewing or animal welfare, into cyber-graffiti walls, filled with offensive comments and photographs.

Spoofing and Sniffing

Hackers attempting to hide their true identities often spoof, or misrepresent, themselves by using fake e-mail addresses or masquerading as someone else. **Spoofing** also may involve redirecting a Web link to an address different from the intended one, with the site masquerading as the intended destination. For example, if hackers redirect customers to a fake Web site that looks almost exactly like the true site, they can then collect and process orders, effectively stealing business as well as sensitive customer information from the true site. We provide more detail on other forms of spoofing in our discussion of computer crime.

A **sniffer** is a type of eavesdropping program that monitors information traveling over a network. When used legitimately, sniffers help identify potential network trouble spots or criminal activity on networks, but when used for criminal purposes, they can be damaging and very difficult to detect. Sniffers enable hackers to steal proprietary information from anywhere on a network, including e-mail messages, company files, and confidential reports.

Denial-of-Service Attacks

In a **denial-of-service (DoS) attack**, hackers flood a network server or Web server with many thousands of false communications or requests for services to crash the network. The network receives so many queries that it cannot keep up with them and is thus unavailable to service legitimate requests. A **distributed denial-of-service (DDoS)** attack uses numerous computers to inundate and overwhelm the network from numerous launch points.

For example, during the 2009 Iranian election protests, foreign activists trying to help the opposition engaged in DDoS attacks against Iran's government. The official Web site of the Iranian government (ahmadinejad.ir) was rendered inaccessible on several occasions.

Although DoS attacks do not destroy information or access restricted areas of a company's information systems, they often cause a Web site to shut down, making it impossible for legitimate users to access the site. For busy e-commerce sites, these attacks are costly; while the site is shut down, customers cannot make purchases. Especially vulnerable are small and midsize businesses whose networks tend to be less protected than those of large corporations.

Perpetrators of DoS attacks often use thousands of "zombie" PCs infected with malicious software without their owners' knowledge and organized into a **botnet**. Hackers create these botnets by infecting other people's computers with bot malware that opens a back door through which an attacker can give instructions. The infected computer then becomes a slave, or zombie, serving a master computer belonging to someone else. Once a hacker infects enough computers, her or she can use the amassed resources of the botnet to launch DDos attacks, phishing campaigns, or unsolicited "spam" e-mail.

The number of computers that are part of botnets is variously estimated to be from 6 to 24 million, with thousands of botnets operating worldwide. The largest botnet attack in 2010 was the Mariposa botnet, which started in Spain and spread across the world. Mariposa had infected and controlled about 12.7 million computers in its efforts to steal credit card numbers and online banking passwords. More than half the Fortune 1000 companies, 40 major banks, and numerous government agencies were infected—and did not know it.

The chapter-ending case study describes multiple waves of DDoS attacks targeting a number of Web sites of government agencies and other organizations in South Korea and the United States in July 2009. The attacker used a botnet controlling over 65,000 computers, and was able to cripple some of these sites for several days. Most of the botnet originated from China, and North Korea. Botnet attacks thought to have originated in Russia were responsible for crippling the Web sites of the Estonian government in April 2007 and the Georgian government in July 2008.

Computer Crime

Most hacker activities are criminal offenses, and the vulnerabilities of systems we have just described make them targets for other types of **computer crime** as well. For example, in early July 2009, U.S. federal agents arrested Sergey Aleynikov, a computer programmer at investment banking firm Goldman Sachs, for stealing proprietary computer programs used in making lucrative rapid-fire trades in the financial markets. The software brought Goldman many millions of dollars of profits per year and, in the wrong hands, could have been used to manipulate financial markets in unfair ways. Computer crime is defined by the U.S. Department of Justice as "any violations of criminal law that involve a knowledge of computer technology for their perpetration, investigation, or prosecution." Table 2 provides examples of the computer as a target of crime and as an instrument of crime.

No one knows the magnitude of the computer crime problem—how many systems are invaded, how many people engage in the practice, or the total economic damage. According to the 2009 CSI Computer Crime and Security Survey of 500 companies, participants' average annual loss from computer crime and security attacks was close to $234,000 (Computer Security Institute, 2009). Many companies are reluctant to report computer crimes because the crimes may involve employees, or the company fears that publicizing its vulnerability will hurt its reputation. The most economically damaging kinds of computer crime are

TABLE 2   EXAMPLES OF COMPUTER CRIME

COMPUTERS AS TARGETS OF CRIME

Breaching the confidentiality of protected computerized data

Accessing a computer system without authority

Knowingly accessing a protected computer to commit fraud

Intentionally accessing a protected computer and causing damage, negligently or deliberately

Knowingly transmitting a program, program code, or command that intentionally causes damage to a protected computer

Threatening to cause damage to a protected computer

COMPUTERS AS INSTRUMENTS OF CRIME

Theft of trade secrets

Unauthorized copying of software or copyrighted intellectual property, such as articles, books, music, and video

Schemes to defraud

Using e-mail for threats or harassment

Intentionally attempting to intercept electronic communication

Illegally accessing stored electronic communications, including e-mail and voice mail

Transmitting or possessing child pornography using a computer

DoS attacks, introducing viruses, theft of services, and disruption of computer systems.

Identity Theft

With the growth of the Internet and electronic commerce, identity theft has become especially troubling. **Identity theft** is a crime in which an imposter obtains key pieces of personal information, such as social security identification numbers, driver's license numbers, or credit card numbers, to impersonate someone else. The information may be used to obtain credit, merchandise, or services in the name of the victim or to provide the thief with false credentials. According to Javelin Strategy and Research, losses from identity theft rose to $54 billion in 2009, and over 11 million U.S. adults were victims of identity fraud (Javelin Strategy & Research, 2010).

Identify theft has flourished on the Internet, with credit card files a major target of Web site hackers. Moreover, e-commerce sites are wonderful sources of customer personal information—name, address, and phone number. Armed with this information, criminals are able to assume new identities and establish new credit for their own purposes.

One increasingly popular tactic is a form of spoofing called **phishing**. Phishing involves setting up fake Web sites or sending e-mail or text messages that look like those of legitimate businesses to ask users for confidential personal data. The message instructs recipients to update or confirm records by providing social security numbers, bank and credit card information, and other confidential data either by responding to the e-mail message, by entering the information at a bogus Web site, or by calling a telephone number. EBay, PayPal, Amazon.com, Walmart, and a variety of banks, are among the top spoofed companies.

New phishing techniques called evil twins and pharming are harder to detect. **Evil twins** are wireless networks that pretend to offer trustworthy Wi-Fi connections to the Internet, such as those in airport lounges, hotels, or coffee shops. The bogus network looks identical to a legitimate public network. Fraudsters try to capture passwords or credit card numbers of unwitting users who log on to the network.

Pharming redirects users to a bogus Web page, even when the individual types the correct Web page address into his or her browser. This is possible if pharming perpetrators gain access to the Internet address information stored by Internet service providers to speed up Web browsing and the ISP companies have flawed software on their servers that allows the fraudsters to hack in and change those addresses.

In the largest instance of identity theft to date, Alberto Gonzalez of Miami and two Russian co-conspirators penetrated the corporate systems of TJX Corporation, Hannaford Brothers, 7-Eleven, and other major retailers, stealing over 160 million credit and debit card numbers between 2005 and 2008. The group initially planted "sniffer" programs in these companies' computer networks that captured card data as they were being transmitted between computer systems. They later switched to SQL injection attacks, which we introduced earlier in this chapter, to penetrate corporate databases. In March 2010, Gonzalez was sentenced to 20 years in prison. TJX alone spent over $200 million to deal with its data theft, including legal settlements.

The U.S. Congress addressed the threat of computer crime in 1986 with the Computer Fraud and Abuse Act. This act makes it illegal to access a computer system without authorization. Most states have similar laws, and nations in Europe have comparable legislation. Congress also passed the National Information Infrastructure Protection Act in 1996 to make virus distribution and hacker attacks that disable Web sites federal crimes. U.S. legislation, such as the Wiretap Act, Wire Fraud Act, Economic Espionage Act, Electronic Communications Privacy Act, E-mail Threats and Harassment Act, and Child Pornography Act, covers computer crimes involving intercepting electronic communication, using electronic communication to defraud, stealing trade secrets, illegally accessing stored electronic communications, using e-mail for threats or harassment, and transmitting or possessing child pornography.

Click Fraud

When you click on an ad displayed by a search engine, the advertiser typically pays a fee for each click, which is supposed to direct potential buyers to its products. **Click fraud** occurs when an individual or computer program fraudulently clicks on an online ad without any intention of learning more about the advertiser or making a purchase. Click fraud has become a serious problem at Google and other Web sites that feature pay-per-click online advertising.

Some companies hire third parties (typically from low-wage countries) to fraudulently click on a competitor's ads to weaken them by driving up their marketing costs. Click fraud can also be perpetrated with software programs doing the clicking, and botnets are often used for this purpose. Search engines such as Google attempt to monitor click fraud but have been reluctant to publicize their efforts to deal with the problem.

Global Threats: Cyberterrorism and Cyberwarfare

The cybercriminal activities we have described—launching malware, denial-of-service attacks, and phishing probes—are borderless. Computer security firm Sophos reported that 42 percent of the malware it identified in early 2010 originated in the United States, while 11 percent came from China, and 6 percent from Russia (Sophos, 2010). The global nature of the Internet makes it possible for cybercriminals to operate—and to do harm—anywhere in the world.

Concern is mounting that the vulnerabilities of the Internet or other networks make digital networks easy targets for digital attacks by terrorists, foreign intelligence services, or other groups seeking to create widespread disruption and harm. Such cyberattacks might target the software that runs electrical power grids, air traffic control systems, or networks of major banks and financial institutions. At least 20 countries, including China, are believed to be developing offensive and defensive cyberwarfare capabilities. The chapter-ending case study discusses this problem in greater detail.

INTERNAL THREATS: EMPLOYEES

We tend to think the security threats to a business originate outside the organization. In fact, company insiders pose serious security problems. Employees have access to privileged information, and in the presence of sloppy internal security procedures, they are often able to roam throughout an organization's systems without leaving a trace.

Studies have found that user lack of knowledge is the single greatest cause of network security breaches. Many employees forget their passwords to access computer systems or allow co-workers to use them, which compromises the system. Malicious intruders seeking system access sometimes trick employees into revealing their passwords by pretending to be legitimate members of the company in need of information. This practice is called **social engineering**.

Both end users and information systems specialists are also a major source of errors introduced into information systems. End users introduce errors by entering faulty data or by not following the proper instructions for processing data and using computer equipment. Information systems specialists may create software errors as they design and develop new software or maintain existing programs.

SOFTWARE VULNERABILITY

Software errors pose a constant threat to information systems, causing untold losses in productivity. Growing complexity and size of software programs, coupled with demands for timely delivery to markets, have contributed to an increase in software flaws or vulnerabilities For example, a database-related software error prevented millions of JP Morgan Chase retail and small-business customers from accessing their online bank accounts for two days in September 2010 (Dash, 2010).

A major problem with software is the presence of hidden **bugs** or program code defects. Studies have shown that it is virtually impossible to eliminate all bugs from large programs. The main source of bugs is the complexity of decision-making code. A relatively small program of several hundred lines will contain tens of decisions leading to hundreds or even thousands of different paths. Important programs within most corporations are usually much larger, containing tens of thousands or even millions of lines of code, each with many times the choices and paths of the smaller programs.

Zero defects cannot be achieved in larger programs. Complete testing simply is not possible. Fully testing programs that contain thousands of choices and millions of paths would require thousands of years. Even with rigorous testing, you would not know for sure that a piece of software was dependable until the product proved itself after much operational use.

Flaws in commercial software not only impede performance but also create security vulnerabilities that open networks to intruders. Each year security firms identify thousands of software vulnerabilities in Internet and PC software. For instance, in 2009, Symantec identified 384 browser vulnerabilities: 169 in Firefox, 94 in Safari, 45 in Internet Explorer, 41 in Chrome, and 25 in Opera. Some of these vulnerabilities were critical (Symantec, 2010).

To correct software flaws once they are identified, the software vendor creates small pieces of software called **patches** to repair the flaws without disturbing the proper operation of the software. An example is Microsoft's Windows Vista Service Pack 2, released in April 2009, which includes some security enhancements to counter malware and hackers. It is up to users of the software to track these vulnerabilities, test, and apply all patches. This process is called *patch management*.

Because a company's IT infrastructure is typically laden with multiple business applications, operating system installations, and other system services, maintaining patches on all devices and services used by a company is often time-consuming and costly. Malware is being created so rapidly that companies have very little time to respond between the time a vulnerability and a patch are announced and the time malicious software appears to exploit the vulnerability.

The need to respond so rapidly to the torrent of security vulnerabilities even creates defects in the software meant to combat them, including popular antivirus products. What happened in the spring of 2010 to McAfee, a leading vendor of commercial antivirus software is an example, as discussed in the Interactive Session on Management.

INTERACTIVE SESSION: MANAGEMENT

WHEN ANTIVIRUS SOFTWARE CRIPPLES YOUR COMPUTERS

McAfee is a prominent antivirus software and computer security company based in Santa Clara, California. Its popular VirusScan product (now named AntiVirus Plus) is used by companies and individual consumers across the world, driving its revenues of $1.93 billion in 2009.

A truly global company, McAfee has over 6,000 employees across North America, Europe, and Asia. VirusScan and other McAfee security products address endpoint security, network security, and risk and compliance. The company has worked to compile a long track record of good customer service and strong quality assurance.

At 6 a.m. PDT April 21, 2010, McAfee made a blunder that threatened to destroy that track record and prompted the possible departure of hundreds of valued customers. McAfee released what should have been a routine update for its flagship VirusScan product that was intended to deal with a powerful new virus known as 'W32/wecorl.a". Instead, McAfee's update caused potentially hundreds of thousands of McAfee-equipped machines running Windows XP to crash and fail to reboot. How could McAfee, a company whose focus is saving and preserving computers, commit a gaffe that accomplished the opposite for a significant portion of its client base?

That was the question McAfee's angry clients were asking on the morning of April 21, when their computers were crippled or totally non-functional. The updates mistakenly targeted a critical Windows file, svchost.exe, which hosts other services used by various programs on PCs. Usually, more than one instance of the process is running at any given time, and eliminating them all would cripple any system. Though many viruses, including W32/wecorl.a, disguise themselves using the name svchost.exe to avoid detection, McAfee had never had problems with viruses using that technique before.

To make matters worse, without svchost.exe, Windows computers can't boot properly. VirusScan users applied the update, tried rebooting their systems, and were powerless to act as their systems went haywire, repeatedly rebooting, losing their network capabilities and, worst of all, their ability to detect USB drives, which is the only way of fixing affected computers. Companies using McAfee and

that relied heavily on Windows XP computers struggled to cope with the majority of their machines suddenly failing.

Angry network administrators turned to McAfee for answers, and the company was initially just as confused as its clients regarding how such a monumental slipup could occur. Soon, McAfee determined that the majority of affected machines were using Windows XP Service Pack 3 combined with McAfee VirusScan version 8.7. They also noted that the "Scan Processes on enable" option of VirusScan, off by default in most VirusScan installations, was turned on in the majority of affected computers.

McAfee conducted a more thorough investigation into its mistake and published a FAQ sheet that explained more completely why they had made such a big mistake and which customers were affected. The two most prominent points of failure were as follows: first, users should have received a warning that svchost.exe was going to be quarantined or deleted, instead of automatically disposing of the file. Next, McAfee's automated quality assurance testing failed to detect such a critical error because of what the company called "inadequate coverage of product and operating systems in the test systems used."

The only way tech support staffs working in organizations could fix the problem was to go from computer to computer manually. McAfee released a utility called "SuperDAT Remediation Tool," which had to be downloaded to an unaffected machine, placed on a flash drive, and run in Windows Safe Mode on affected machines. Because affected computers lacked network access, this had to be done one computer at a time until all affected machines were repaired. The total number of machines impacted is not known but it doubtless involved tens of thousands of corporate computers. Needless to say, network administrators and corporate tech support divisions were incensed.

Regarding the flaws in McAfee's quality assurance processes, the company explained in the FAQ that they had not included Windows XP Service Pack 3 with VirusScan version 8.7 in the test configuration of operating systems and McAfee product versions. This explanation flabbergasted many of McAfee's clients and other industry analysts, since XP SP3 is the most widely used desktop PC configuration.

Vista and Windows 7 generally ship with new computers and are rarely installed on functioning XP computers.

Another reason that the problem spread so quickly without detection was the increasing demand for faster antivirus updates. Most companies aggressively deploy their updates to ensure that machines spend as little time exposed to new viruses as possible. McAfee's update reached a large number of machines so quickly without detection because most companies trust their antivirus provider to get it right.

Unfortunately for McAfee, it only takes a single slipup or oversight to cause significant damage to an antivirus company's reputation. McAfee was criticized for its slow response to the crisis and for its initial attempts to downplay the issue's impact on its customers. The company released a

statement claiming that only a small fraction of its customers were affected, but this was soon shown to be false. Two days after the update was released, McAfee executive Barry McPherson finally apologized to customers on the company's blog. Soon after, CEO David DeWalt recorded a video for customers, still available via McAfee's Web site, in which he apologized for and explained the incident.

Sources: Peter Svensson, "McAfee Antivirus Program Goes Berserk, Freezes PCs," Associated Press, April 21, 2010; Gregg Keizer, "McAfee Apologizes for Crippling PCs with Bad Update," *Computerworld*, April 23, 2010 and "McAfee Update Mess Explained," *Computerworld*, April 22, 2010; Ed Bott, "McAfee Admits 'Inadequate' Quality Control Caused PC Meltdown," *ZDNet*, April 22, 2010; and Barry McPherson, "An Update on False Positive Remediation," http://siblog.mcafee.com/support/an-update-on-false-positive-remediation, April 22, 2010.

CASE STUDY QUESTIONS

1. What management, organization, and technology factors were responsible for McAfee's software problem?

2. What was the business impact of this software problem, both for McAfee and for its customers?

3. If you were a McAfee enterprise customer, would you consider McAfee's response to the problem be acceptable? Why or why not?

4. What should McAfee do in the future to avoid similar problems?

MIS IN ACTION

Search online for the apology by Barry McPherson ("Barry McPherson apology") and read the reaction of customers. Do you think McPherson's apology helped or inflamed the situation? What is a "false positive remediation"?

2   BUSINESS VALUE OF SECURITY AND CONTROL

Many firms are reluctant to spend heavily on security because it is not directly related to sales revenue. However, protecting information systems is so critical to the operation of the business that it deserves a second look.

Companies have very valuable information assets to protect. Systems often house confidential information about individuals' taxes, financial assets, medical records, and job performance reviews. They also can contain information on corporate operations, including trade secrets, new product development plans, and marketing strategies. Government systems may store information on weapons systems, intelligence operations, and military targets. These information assets have tremendous value, and the repercussions can be devastating if they are lost, destroyed, or placed in the wrong hands. One study estimated that when the security of a large firm is compromised, the company loses approximately 2.1 percent of its market value within two days of the security breach, which translates into an average loss of $1.65 billion in stock market value per incident (Cavusoglu, Mishra, and Raghunathan, 2004).

Inadequate security and control may result in serious legal liability. Businesses must protect not only their own information assets but also those of customers, employees, and business partners. Failure to do so may open the firm to costly litigation for data exposure or theft. An organization can be held liable for needless risk and harm created if the organization fails to take appropriate protective action to prevent loss of confidential information, data corruption, or breach of privacy. For example, BJ's Wholesale Club was sued by the U.S. Federal Trade Commission for allowing hackers to access its systems and steal credit and debit card data for fraudulent purchases. Banks that issued the cards with the stolen data sought $13 million from BJ's to compensate them for reimbursing card holders for the fraudulent purchases. A sound security and control framework that protects business information assets can thus produce a high return on investment. Strong security and control also increase employee productivity and lower operational costs.

LEGAL AND REGULATORY REQUIREMENTS FOR ELECTRONIC RECORDS MANAGEMENT

Recent U.S. government regulations are forcing companies to take security and control more seriously by mandating the protection of data from abuse, exposure, and unauthorized access. Firms face new legal obligations for the retention and storage of electronic records as well as for privacy protection.

If you work in the health care industry, your firm will need to comply with the Health Insurance Portability and Accountability Act (HIPAA) of 1996. **HIPAA** outlines medical security and privacy rules and procedures for simplifying the administration of health care billing and automating the transfer of health care data between health care providers, payers, and plans. It requires members of the health care industry to retain patient information for six years and ensure the confidentiality of those records. It specifies privacy, security, and electronic transaction standards for health care providers handling patient information, providing penalties for breaches of medical privacy, disclosure of patient records by e-mail, or unauthorized network access.

If you work in a firm providing financial services, your firm will need to comply with the Financial Services Modernization Act of 1999, better known as the **Gramm-Leach-Bliley Act** after its congressional sponsors. This act requires financial institutions to ensure the security and confidentiality of customer data. Data must be stored on a secure medium, and special security measures must be enforced to protect such data on storage media and during transmittal.

If you work in a publicly traded company, your company will need to comply with the Public Company Accounting Reform and Investor Protection Act of 2002, better known as the **Sarbanes-Oxley Act** after its sponsors Senator Paul Sarbanes of Maryland and Representative Michael Oxley of Ohio. This Act was designed to protect investors after the financial scandals at Enron, WorldCom, and other public companies. It imposes responsibility on companies and their management to safeguard the accuracy and integrity of financial information that is used internally and released externally. One of the Learning Tracks for this chapter discusses Sarbanes-Oxley in detail.

Sarbanes-Oxley is fundamentally about ensuring that internal controls are in place to govern the creation and documentation of information in financial statements. Because information systems are used to generate, store, and transport such data, the legislation requires firms to consider information systems security and other controls required to ensure the integrity, confidentiality, and accuracy of their data. Each system application that deals with critical financial reporting data requires controls to make sure the data are accurate. Controls to secure the corporate network, prevent unauthorized access to systems and data, and ensure data integrity and availability in the event of disaster or other disruption of service are essential as well.

ELECTRONIC EVIDENCE AND COMPUTER FORENSICS

Security, control, and electronic records management have become essential for responding to legal actions. Much of the evidence today for stock fraud, embezzlement, theft of company trade secrets, computer crime, and many civil cases is in digital form. In addition to information from printed or typewritten pages, legal cases today increasingly rely on evidence represented as digital data stored on portable floppy disks, CDs, and computer hard disk drives, as well as in e-mail, instant messages, and e-commerce transactions over the Internet. E-mail is currently the most common type of electronic evidence.

In a legal action, a firm is obligated to respond to a discovery request for access to information that may be used as evidence, and the company is required by law to produce those data. The cost of responding to a discovery request can be enormous if the company has trouble assembling the required data or the data have been corrupted or destroyed. Courts now impose severe financial and even criminal penalties for improper destruction of electronic documents.

An effective electronic document retention policy ensures that electronic documents, e-mail, and other records are well organized, accessible, and neither retained too long nor discarded too soon. It also reflects an awareness of how to preserve potential evidence for computer forensics. **Computer forensics** is the scientific collection, examination, authentication, preservation, and analysis of data held on or retrieved from computer storage media in such a way that the information can be used as evidence in a court of law. It deals with the following problems:

- Recovering data from computers while preserving evidential integrity
- Securely storing and handling recovered electronic data
- Finding significant information in a large volume of electronic data
- Presenting the information to a court of law

Electronic evidence may reside on computer storage media in the form of computer files and as *ambient data*, which are not visible to the average user. An example might be a file that has been deleted on a PC hard drive. Data that a computer user may have deleted on computer storage media can be recovered through various techniques. Computer forensics experts try to recover such hidden data for presentation as evidence.

An awareness of computer forensics should be incorporated into a firm's contingency planning process. The CIO, security specialists, information systems staff, and corporate legal counsel should all work together to have a plan in place that can be executed if a legal need arises. You can find out more about computer forensics in the Learning Tracks for this chapter.

3 ESTABLISHING A FRAMEWORK FOR SECURITY AND CONTROL

Even with the best security tools, your information systems won't be reliable and secure unless you know how and where to deploy them. You'll need to know where your company is at risk and what controls you must have in place to protect your information systems. You'll also need to develop a security policy and plans for keeping your business running if your information systems aren't operational.

INFORMATION SYSTEMS CONTROLS

Information systems controls are both manual and automated and consist of both general controls and application controls. **General controls** govern the design, security, and use of computer programs and the security of data files in general throughout the organization's information technology infrastructure. On the whole, general controls apply to all computerized applications and consist of a combination of hardware, software, and manual procedures that create an overall control environment.

General controls include software controls, physical hardware controls, computer operations controls, data security controls, controls over implementation of system processes, and administrative controls. Table 3 describes the functions of each of these controls.

Application controls are specific controls unique to each computerized application, such as payroll or order processing. They include both automated and manual procedures that ensure that only authorized data are completely and accurately processed by that application. Application controls can be classified as (1) input controls, (2) processing controls, and (3) output controls.

Input controls check data for accuracy and completeness when they enter the system. There are specific input controls for input authorization, data conversion, data editing, and error handling. *Processing controls* establish that data are complete and accurate during updating. *Output controls* ensure that

TABLE 3 GENERAL CONTROLS

TYPE OF GENERAL CONTROL	DESCRIPTION
Software controls	Monitor the use of system software and prevent unauthorized access of software programs, system software, and computer programs.
Hardware controls	Ensure that computer hardware is physically secure, and check for equipment malfunction. Organizations that are critically dependent on their computers also must make provisions for backup or continued operation to maintain constant service.
Computer operations controls	Oversee the work of the computer department to ensure that programmed procedures are consistently and correctly applied to the storage and processing of data. They include controls over the setup of computer processing jobs and backup and recovery procedures for processing that ends abnormally.
Data security controls	Ensure that valuable business data files on either disk or tape are not subject to unauthorized access, change, or destruction while they are in use or in storage.
Implementation controls	Audit the systems development process at various points to ensure that the process is properly controlled and managed.
Administrative controls	Formalize standards, rules, procedures, and control disciplines to ensure that the organization's general and application controls are properly executed and enforced.

the results of computer processing are accurate, complete, and properly distributed. You can find more detail about application and general controls in our Learning Tracks.

RISK ASSESSMENT

Before your company commits resources to security and information systems controls, it must know which assets require protection and the extent to which these assets are vulnerable. A risk assessment helps answer these questions and determine the most cost-effective set of controls for protecting assets.

A **risk assessment** determines the level of risk to the firm if a specific activity or process is not properly controlled. Not all risks can be anticipated and measured, but most businesses will be able to acquire some understanding of the risks they face. Business managers working with information systems specialists should try to determine the value of information assets, points of vulnerability, the likely frequency of a problem, and the potential for damage. For example, if an event is likely to occur no more than once a year, with a maximum of a $1,000 loss to the organization, it is not be wise to spend $20,000 on the design and maintenance of a control to protect against that event. However, if that same event could occur at least once a day, with a potential loss of more than $300,000 a year, $100,000 spent on a control might be entirely appropriate.

Table 4 illustrates sample results of a risk assessment for an online order processing system that processes 30,000 orders per day. The likelihood of each exposure occurring over a one-year period is expressed as a percentage. The next column shows the highest and lowest possible loss that could be expected each time the exposure occurred and an average loss calculated by adding the highest and lowest figures together and dividing by two. The expected annual loss for each exposure can be determined by multiplying the average loss by its probability of occurrence.

This risk assessment shows that the probability of a power failure occurring in a one-year period is 30 percent. Loss of order transactions while power is down could range from $5,000 to $200,000 (averaging $102,500) for each occurrence, depending on how long processing is halted. The probability of embezzlement occurring over a yearly period is about 5 percent, with potential losses ranging from $1,000 to $50,000 (and averaging $25,500) for each occurrence. User errors have a 98 percent chance of occurring over a yearly period, with losses ranging from $200 to $40,000 (and averaging $20,100) for each occurrence.

Once the risks have been assessed, system builders will concentrate on the control points with the greatest vulnerability and potential for loss. In this case, controls should focus on ways to minimize the risk of power failures and user errors because anticipated annual losses are highest for these areas.

TABLE 4   ONLINE ORDER PROCESSING RISK ASSESSMENT

EXPOSURE	PROBABILITY OF OCCURRENCE (%)	LOSS RANGE/ AVERAGE ($)	EXPECTED ANNUAL LOSS ($)
Power failure	30%	$5,000–$200,000 ($102,500)	$30,750
Embezzlement	5%	$1,000–$50,000 ($25,500)	$1,275
User error	98%	$200–$40,000 ($20,100)	$19,698

SECURITY POLICY

Once you've identified the main risks to your systems, your company will need to develop a security policy for protecting the company's assets. A **security policy** consists of statements ranking information risks, identifying acceptable security goals, and identifying the mechanisms for achieving these goals. What are the firm's most important information assets? Who generates and controls this information in the firm? What existing security policies are in place to protect the information? What level of risk is management willing to accept for each of these assets? Is it willing, for instance, to lose customer credit data once every 10 years? Or will it build a security system for credit card data that can withstand the once-in-a-hundred-year disaster? Management must estimate how much it will cost to achieve this level of acceptable risk.

The security policy drives policies determining acceptable use of the firm's information resources and which members of the company have access to its information assets. An **acceptable use policy (AUP)** defines acceptable uses of the firm's information resources and computing equipment, including desktop and laptop computers, wireless devices, telephones, and the Internet. The policy should clarify company policy regarding privacy, user responsibility, and personal use of company equipment and networks. A good AUP defines unacceptable and acceptable actions for every user and specifies consequences for noncompliance. For example, security policy at Unilever, the giant multinational consumer goods company, requires every employee equipped with a laptop or mobile handheld device to use a company-specified device and employ a password or other method of identification when logging onto the corporate network.

Security policy also includes provisions for identity management. **Identity management** consists of business processes and software tools for identifying the valid users of a system and controlling their access to system resources. It includes policies for identifying and authorizing different categories of system users, specifying what systems or portions of systems each user is allowed to access, and the processes and technologies for authenticating users and protecting their identities.

Figure 3 is one example of how an identity management system might capture the access rules for different levels of users in the human resources function. It specifies what portions of a human resource database each user is permitted to access, based on the information required to perform that person's job. The database contains sensitive personal information such as employees' salaries, benefits, and medical histories.

The access rules illustrated here are for two sets of users. One set of users consists of all employees who perform clerical functions, such as inputting employee data into the system. All individuals with this type of profile can update the system but can neither read nor update sensitive fields, such as salary, medical history, or earnings data. Another profile applies to a divisional manager, who cannot update the system but who can read all employee data fields for his or her division, including medical history and salary. We provide more detail on the technologies for user authentication later on in this chapter.

DISASTER RECOVERY PLANNING AND BUSINESS CONTINUITY PLANNING

If you run a business, you need to plan for events, such as power outages, floods, earthquakes, or terrorist attacks that will prevent your information systems and your business from operating. **Disaster recovery planning** devises

FIGURE 3   ACCESS RULES FOR A PERSONNEL SYSTEM

SECURITY PROFILE 1

User: Personnel Dept. Clerk

Location: Division 1

Employee Identification
Codes with This Profile: 00753, 27834, 37665, 44116

Data Field Restrictions	Type of Access
All employee data for Division 1 only	Read and Update
• Medical history data	None
• Salary	None
• Pensionable earnings	None

SECURITY PROFILE 2

User: Divisional Personnel Manager

Location: Division 1

Employee Identification
Codes with This Profile: 27321

Data Field Restrictions	Type of Access
All employee data for Division 1 only	Read Only

These two examples represent two security profiles or data security patterns that might be found in a personnel system. Depending on the access rules, a user would have certain restrictions on access to various systems, locations, or data in an organization.

plans for the restoration of computing and communications services after they have been disrupted. Disaster recovery plans focus primarily on the technical issues involved in keeping systems up and running, such as which files to back up and the maintenance of backup computer systems or disaster recovery services.

For example, MasterCard maintains a duplicate computer center in Kansas City, Missouri, to serve as an emergency backup to its primary computer center in St. Louis. Rather than build their own backup facilities, many firms contract with disaster recovery firms, such as Comdisco Disaster Recovery Services in Rosemont, Illinois, and SunGard Availability Services, headquartered in Wayne, Pennsylvania. These disaster recovery firms provide hot sites housing spare computers at locations around the country where subscribing firms can run their critical applications in an emergency. For example, Champion Technologies, which supplies chemicals used in oil and gas operations, is able to switch its enterprise systems from Houston to a SunGard hot site in Scottsdale, Arizona, in two hours.

Business continuity planning focuses on how the company can restore business operations after a disaster strikes. The business continuity plan identifies critical business processes and determines action plans for handling mission-critical functions if systems go down. For example, Deutsche Bank, which provides investment banking and asset management services in 74 different countries, has a well-developed business continuity plan that it continually updates and refines. It maintains full-time teams in Singapore, Hong Kong, Japan, India, and Australia to coordinate plans addressing loss of facilities, personnel, or critical systems so that the company can continue to operate when a catastrophic event occurs. Deutsche Bank's plan distinguishes between processes critical for business survival and those critical to crisis support and is coordinated with the company's disaster recovery planning for its computer centers.

Business managers and information technology specialists need to work together on both types of plans to determine which systems and business processes are most critical to the company. They must conduct a business impact analysis to identify the firm's most critical systems and the impact a systems outage would have on the business. Management must determine the maximum amount of time the business can survive with its systems down and which parts of the business must be restored first.

THE ROLE OF AUDITING

How does management know that information systems security and controls are effective? To answer this question, organizations must conduct comprehensive and systematic audits. An **MIS audit** examines the firm's overall security environment as well as controls governing individual information systems. The auditor should trace the flow of sample transactions through the system and perform tests, using, if appropriate, automated audit software. The MIS audit may also examine data quality.

Security audits review technologies, procedures, documentation, training, and personnel. A thorough audit will even simulate an attack or disaster to test the response of the technology, information systems staff, and business employees.

The audit lists and ranks all control weaknesses and estimates the probability of their occurrence. It then assesses the financial and organizational impact of each threat. Figure 4 is a sample auditor's listing of control weaknesses for a loan system. It includes a section for notifying management of such weaknesses and for management's response. Management is expected to devise a plan for countering significant weaknesses in controls.

4   TECHNOLOGIES AND TOOLS FOR PROTECTING INFORMATION RESOURCES

Businesses have an array of technologies for protecting their information resources. They include tools for managing user identities, preventing unauthorized access to systems and data, ensuring system availability, and ensuring software quality.

IDENTITY MANAGEMENT AND AUTHENTICATION

Large and midsize companies have complex IT infrastructures and many different systems, each with its own set of users. Identity management software automates the process of keeping track of all these users and their system privileges, assigning each user a unique digital identity for accessing each system. It also includes tools for authenticating users, protecting user identities, and controlling access to system resources.

To gain access to a system, a user must be authorized and authenticated. **Authentication** refers to the ability to know that a person is who he or she

FIGURE 4   SAMPLE AUDITOR'S LIST OF CONTROL WEAKNESSES

Function: Loans Location: Peoria, IL	Prepared by: J. Ericson Date: June 16, 2011		Received by: T. Benson Review date: June 28, 2011	
Nature of Weakness and Impact	**Chance for Error/Abuse**		**Notification to Management**	
	Yes/ No	Justification	Report date	Management response
User accounts with missing passwords	Yes	Leaves system open to unauthorized outsiders or attackers	5/10/11	Eliminate accounts without passwords
Network configured to allow some sharing of system files	Yes	Exposes critical system files to hostile parties connected to the network	5/10/11	Ensure only required directories are shared and that they are protected with strong passwords
Software patches can update production programs without final approval from Standards and Controls group	No	All production programs require management approval; Standards and Controls group assigns such cases to a temporary production status		

This chart is a sample page from a list of control weaknesses that an auditor might find in a loan system in a local commercial bank. This form helps auditors record and evaluate control weaknesses and shows the results of discussing those weaknesses with management, as well as any corrective actions taken by management.

claims to be. Authentication is often established by using **passwords** known only to authorized users. An end user uses a password to log on to a computer system and may also use passwords for accessing specific systems and files. However, users often forget passwords, share them, or choose poor passwords that are easy to guess, which compromises security. Password systems that are too rigorous hinder employee productivity. When employees must change complex passwords frequently, they often take shortcuts, such as choosing passwords that are easy to guess or writing down their passwords at their workstations in plain view. Passwords can also be "sniffed" if transmitted over a network or stolen through social engineering.

New authentication technologies, such as tokens, smart cards, and biometric authentication, overcome some of these problems. A **token** is a physical device, similar to an identification card, that is designed to prove the identity of a single user. Tokens are small gadgets that typically fit on key rings and display passcodes that change frequently. A **smart card** is a device about the size of a credit card that contains a chip formatted with access permission and other data. (Smart cards are also used in electronic payment systems.) A reader device interprets the data on the smart card and allows or denies access.

Biometric authentication uses systems that read and interpret individual human traits, such as fingerprints, irises, and voices, in order to grant or deny access. Biometric authentication is based on the measurement of a physical or behavioral trait that makes each individual unique. It compares a person's unique characteristics, such as the fingerprints, face, or retinal image, against a

This PC has a biometric fingerprint reader for fast yet secure access to files and networks. New models of PCs are starting to use biometric identification to authenticate users.

iStockphoto 2010

stored profile of these characteristics to determine whether there are any differences between these characteristics and the stored profile. If the two profiles match, access is granted. Fingerprint and facial recognition technologies are just beginning to be used for security applications, with many PC laptops equipped with fingerprint identification devices and several models with built-in webcams and face recognition software.

FIREWALLS, INTRUSION DETECTION SYSTEMS, AND ANTIVIRUS SOFTWARE

Without protection against malware and intruders, connecting to the Internet would be very dangerous. Firewalls, intrusion detection systems, and antivirus software have become essential business tools.

Firewalls

Firewalls prevent unauthorized users from accessing private networks. A firewall is a combination of hardware and software that controls the flow of incoming and outgoing network traffic. It is generally placed between the organization's private internal networks and distrusted external networks, such as the Internet, although firewalls can also be used to protect one part of a company's network from the rest of the network (see Figure 5).

The firewall acts like a gatekeeper who examines each user's credentials before access is granted to a network. The firewall identifies names, IP addresses, applications, and other characteristics of incoming traffic. It checks this information against the access rules that have been programmed into the system by the network administrator. The firewall prevents unauthorized communication into and out of the network.

In large organizations, the firewall often resides on a specially designated computer separate from the rest of the network, so no incoming request directly accesses private network resources. There are a number of firewall screening technologies, including static packet filtering, stateful inspection, Network Address Translation, and application proxy filtering. They are frequently used in combination to provide firewall protection.

FIGURE 5   A CORPORATE FIREWALL

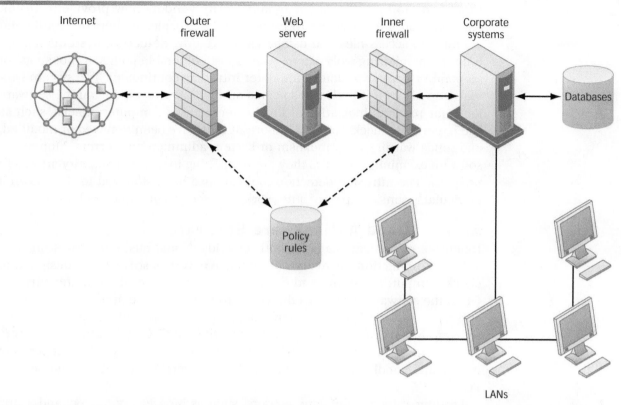

The firewall is placed between the firm's private network and the public Internet or another distrusted network to protect against unauthorized traffic.

Packet filtering examines selected fields in the headers of data packets flowing back and forth between the trusted network and the Internet, examining individual packets in isolation. This filtering technology can miss many types of attacks. *Stateful inspection* provides additional security by determining whether packets are part of an ongoing dialogue between a sender and a receiver. It sets up state tables to track information over multiple packets. Packets are accepted or rejected based on whether they are part of an approved conversation or whether they are attempting to establish a legitimate connection.

Network Address Translation (NAT) can provide another layer of protection when static packet filtering and stateful inspection are employed. NAT conceals the IP addresses of the organization's internal host computer(s) to prevent sniffer programs outside the firewall from ascertaining them and using that information to penetrate internal systems.

Application proxy filtering examines the application content of packets. A proxy server stops data packets originating outside the organization, inspects them, and passes a proxy to the other side of the firewall. If a user outside the company wants to communicate with a user inside the organization, the outside user first "talks" to the proxy application and the proxy application communicates with the firm's internal computer. Likewise, a computer user inside the organization goes through the proxy to talk with computers on the outside.

To create a good firewall, an administrator must maintain detailed internal rules identifying the people, applications, or addresses that are allowed or rejected. Firewalls can deter, but not completely prevent, network penetration by outsiders and should be viewed as one element in an overall security plan.

Intrusion Detection Systems

In addition to firewalls, commercial security vendors now provide intrusion detection tools and services to protect against suspicious network traffic and attempts to access files and databases. **Intrusion detection systems** feature full-time monitoring tools placed at the most vulnerable points or "hot spots" of corporate networks to detect and deter intruders continually. The system generates an alarm if it finds a suspicious or anomalous event. Scanning software looks for patterns indicative of known methods of computer attacks, such as bad passwords, checks to see if important files have been removed or modified, and sends warnings of vandalism or system administration errors. Monitoring software examines events as they are happening to discover security attacks in progress. The intrusion detection tool can also be customized to shut down a particularly sensitive part of a network if it receives unauthorized traffic.

Antivirus and Antispyware Software

Defensive technology plans for both individuals and businesses must include antivirus protection for every computer. **Antivirus software** is designed to check computer systems and drives for the presence of computer viruses. Often the software eliminates the virus from the infected area. However, most antivirus software is effective only against viruses already known when the software was written. To remain effective, the antivirus software must be continually updated. Antivirus products are available for many different types of mobile and handheld devices in addition to servers, workstations, and desktop PCs.

Leading antivirus software vendors, such as McAfee, Symantec, and Trend Micro, have enhanced their products to include protection against spyware. Antispyware software tools such as Ad-Aware, Spybot S&D, and Spyware Doctor are also very helpful.

Unified Threat Management Systems

To help businesses reduce costs and improve manageability, security vendors have combined into a single appliance various security tools, including firewalls, virtual private networks, intrusion detection systems, and Web content filtering and antispam software. These comprehensive security management products are called **unified threat management (UTM)** systems. Although initially aimed at small and medium-sized businesss, UTM products are available for all sizes of networks. Leading UTM vendors include Crossbeam, Fortinent, and Check Point, and networking vendors such as Cisco Systems and Juniper Networks provide some UTM capabilities in their equipment.

SECURING WIRELESS NETWORKS

Despite its flaws, WEP provides some margin of security if Wi-Fi users remember to activate it. A simple first step to thwart hackers is to assign a unique name to your network's SSID and instruct your router not to broadcast it. Corporations can further improve Wi-Fi security by using it in conjunction with virtual private network (VPN) technology when accessing internal corporate data.

In June 2004, the Wi-Fi Alliance industry trade group finalized the 802.11i specification (also referred to as Wi-Fi Protected Access 2 or WPA2) that replaces WEP with stronger security standards. Instead of the static encryption keys used in WEP, the new standard uses much longer keys that continually change, making them harder to crack. It also employs an encrypted authentication system with a central authentication server to ensure that only authorized users access the network.

ENCRYPTION AND PUBLIC KEY INFRASTRUCTURE

Many businesses use encryption to protect digital information that they store, physically transfer, or send over the Internet. **Encryption** is the process of transforming plain text or data into cipher text that cannot be read by anyone other than the sender and the intended receiver. Data are encrypted by using a secret numerical code, called an encryption key, that transforms plain data into cipher text. The message must be decrypted by the receiver.

Two methods for encrypting network traffic on the Web are SSL and S-HTTP. **Secure Sockets Layer (SSL)** and its successor Transport Layer Security (TLS) enable client and server computers to manage encryption and decryption activities as they communicate with each other during a secure Web session. **Secure Hypertext Transfer Protocol (S-HTTP)** is another protocol used for encrypting data flowing over the Internet, but it is limited to individual messages, whereas SSL and TLS are designed to establish a secure connection between two computers.

The capability to generate secure sessions is built into Internet client browser software and servers. The client and the server negotiate what key and what level of security to use. Once a secure session is established between the client and the server, all messages in that session are encrypted.

There are two alternative methods of encryption: symmetric key encryption and public key encryption. In symmetric key encryption, the sender and receiver establish a secure Internet session by creating a single encryption key and sending it to the receiver so both the sender and receiver share the same key. The strength of the encryption key is measured by its bit length. Today, a typical key will be 128 bits long (a string of 128 binary digits).

The problem with all symmetric encryption schemes is that the key itself must be shared somehow among the senders and receivers, which exposes the key to outsiders who might just be able to intercept and decrypt the key. A more secure form of encryption called **public key encryption** uses two keys: one shared (or public) and one totally private as shown in Figure 6. The keys are mathematically related so that data encrypted with one key can be decrypted using only the other key. To send and receive messages, communi-

FIGURE 6 **PUBLIC KEY ENCRYPTION**

A public key encryption system can be viewed as a series of public and private keys that lock data when they are transmitted and unlock the data when they are received. The sender locates the recipient's public key in a directory and uses it to encrypt a message. The message is sent in encrypted form over the Internet or a private network. When the encrypted message arrives, the recipient uses his or her private key to decrypt the data and read the message.

cators first create separate pairs of private and public keys. The public key is kept in a directory and the private key must be kept secret. The sender encrypts a message with the recipient's public key. On receiving the message, the recipient uses his or her private key to decrypt it.

Digital certificates are data files used to establish the identity of users and electronic assets for protection of online transactions (see Figure 7). A digital certificate system uses a trusted third party, known as a certificate authority (CA, or certification authority), to validate a user's identity. There are many CAs in the United States and around the world, including VeriSign, IdenTrust, and Australia's KeyPost.

The CA verifies a digital certificate user's identity offline. This information is put into a CA server, which generates an encrypted digital certificate containing owner identification information and a copy of the owner's public key. The certificate authenticates that the public key belongs to the designated owner. The CA makes its own public key available publicly either in print or perhaps on the Internet. The recipient of an encrypted message uses the CA's public key to decode the digital certificate attached to the message, verifies it was issued by the CA, and then obtains the sender's public key and identification information contained in the certificate. Using this information, the recipient can send an encrypted reply. The digital certificate system would enable, for example, a credit card user and a merchant to validate that their digital certificates were issued by an authorized and trusted third party before they exchange data. **Public key infrastructure (PKI)**, the use of public key cryptography working with a CA, is now widely used in e-commerce.

ENSURING SYSTEM AVAILABILITY

As companies increasingly rely on digital networks for revenue and operations, they need to take additional steps to ensure that their systems and applications

FIGURE 7 DIGITAL CERTIFICATES

Digital certificates help establish the identity of people or electronic assets. They protect online transactions by providing secure, encrypted, online communication.

are always available. Firms such as those in the airline and financial services industries with critical applications requiring online transaction processing have traditionally used fault-tolerant computer systems for many years to ensure 100-percent availability. In **online transaction processing**, transactions entered online are immediately processed by the computer. Multitudinous changes to databases, reporting, and requests for information occur each instant.

Fault-tolerant computer systems contain redundant hardware, software, and power supply components that create an environment that provides continuous, uninterrupted service. Fault-tolerant computers use special software routines or self-checking logic built into their circuitry to detect hardware failures and automatically switch to a backup device. Parts from these computers can be removed and repaired without disruption to the computer system.

Fault tolerance should be distinguished from **high-availability computing**. Both fault tolerance and high-availability computing try to minimize downtime. **Downtime** refers to periods of time in which a system is not operational. However, high-availability computing helps firms recover quickly from a system crash, whereas fault tolerance promises continuous availability and the elimination of recovery time altogether.

High-availability computing environments are a minimum requirement for firms with heavy e-commerce processing or for firms that depend on digital networks for their internal operations. High-availability computing requires backup servers, distribution of processing across multiple servers, high-capacity storage, and good disaster recovery and business continuity plans. The firm's computing platform must be extremely robust with scalable processing power, storage, and bandwidth.

Researchers are exploring ways to make computing systems recover even more rapidly when mishaps occur, an approach called **recovery-oriented computing**. This work includes designing systems that recover quickly, and implementing capabilities and tools to help operators pinpoint the sources of faults in multi-component systems and easily correct their mistakes.

Controlling Network Traffic: Deep Packet Inspection

Have you ever tried to use your campus network and found it was very slow? It may be because your fellow students are using the network to download music or watch YouTube. Bandwith-consuming applications such as file-sharing programs, Internet phone service, and online video are able to clog and slow down corporate networks, degrading performance. For example, Ball Sate University in Muncie, Indiana, found its network had slowed because a small minority of students were using peer-to-peer file-sharing programs to download movies and music.

A technology called **deep packet inspection (DPI)** helps solve this problem. DPI examines data files and sorts out low-priority online material while assigning higher priority to business-critical files. Based on the priorities established by a network's operators, it decides whether a specific data packet can continue to its destination or should be blocked or delayed while more important traffic proceeds. Using a DPI system from Allot Communications, Ball State was able to cap the amount of file-sharing traffic and assign it a much lower priority. Ball State's preferred network traffic speeded up.

Security Outsourcing

Many companies, especially small businesses, lack the resources or expertise to provide a secure high-availability computing environment on their own. They can outsource many security functions to **managed security service**

providers (MSSPs) that monitor network activity and perform vulnerability testing and intrusion detection. SecureWorks, BT Managed Security Solutions Group, and Symantec are leading providers of MSSP services.

SECURITY ISSUES FOR CLOUD COMPUTING AND THE MOBILE DIGITAL PLATFORM

Although cloud computing and the emerging mobile digital platform have the potential to deliver powerful benefits, they pose new challenges to system security and reliability. We now describe some of these challenges and how they should be addressed.

Security in the Cloud

When processing takes place in the cloud, accountability and responsibility for protection of sensitive data still reside with the company owning that data. Understanding how the cloud computing provider organizes its services and manages the data is critical. The Interactive Session on Technology details some of the cloud security issues that should be addressed.

Cloud users need to confirm that regardless of where their data are stored or transferred, they are protected at a level that meets their corporate requirements. They should stipulate that the cloud provider store and process data in specific jurisdictions according to the privacy rules of those jurisdictions. Cloud clients should find how the cloud provider segregates their corporate data from those of other companies and ask for proof that encryption mechanisms are sound. It's also important to know how the cloud provider will respond if a disaster strikes, whether the provider will be able to completely restore your data, and how long this should take. Cloud users should also ask whether cloud providers will submit to external audits and security certifications. These kinds of controls can be written into the service level agreement (SLA) before to signing with a cloud provider.

Securing Mobile Platforms

If mobile devices are performing many of the functions of computers, they need to be secured like desktops and laptops against malware, theft, accidental loss, unauthorized access, and hacking attempts. Mobile devices accessing corporate systems and data require special protection.

Companies should make sure that their corporate security policy includes mobile devices, with additional details on how mobile devices should be supported, protected, and used. They will need tools to authorize all devices in use; to maintain accurate inventory records on all mobile devices, users, and applications; to control updates to applications; and to lock down lost devices so they can't be compromised. Firms should develop guidelines stipulating approved mobile platforms and software applications as well as the required software and procedures for remote access of corporate systems. Companies will need to ensure that all smartphones are up to date with the latest security patches and antivirus/anti-spam software, and they should encrypt communication whenever possible.

ENSURING SOFTWARE QUALITY

In addition to implementing effective security and controls, organizations can improve system quality and reliability by employing software metrics and rigorous software testing. Software metrics are objective assessments of the system in the form of quantified measurements. Ongoing use of metrics allows

INTERACTIVE SESSION: TECHNOLOGY

HOW SECURE IS THE CLOUD?

New York-based investment banking and financial services firm Cowen and Co. has moved its global sales systems to the cloud using Salesforce.com. So far, Cowen's CIO Daniel Flax is pleased. Using cloud services has helped the company lower upfront technology costs, decrease downtime and support additional services. But he's trying to come to grips with cloud security issues.Cloud computing is indeed cloudy, and this lack of transparency is troubling to many.

One of the biggest risks of cloud computing is that it is highly distributed. Cloud applications and application mash-ups reside in virtual libraries in large remote data centers and server farms that supply business services and data management for multiple corporate clients. To save money and keep costs low, cloud computing providers often distribute work to data centers around the globe where work can be accomplished most efficiently. When you use the cloud, you may not know precisely where your data are being hosted, and you might not even know the country where they are being stored.

The dispersed nature of cloud computing makes it difficult to track unauthorized activity. Virtually all cloud providers use encryption, such as Secure Sockets Layer, to secure the data they handle while the data are being transmitted. But if the data are stored on devices that also store other companies' data, it's important to ensure these stored data are encrypted as well.

Indian Harvest Specialtifoods, a Bemidji, Minnesota-based company that distributes rice, grains, and legumes to restaurants worldwide, relies on cloud software provider NetSuite to ensure that its data sent to the cloud are fully protected. Mike Mullin, Indian Harvest's IT director, feels that using SSL (Secure Sockets Layer) to encrypt the data gives him some level of confidence that the data are secure. He also points out that his company and other users of cloud services need to pay attention to their own security practices, especially access controls. "Your side of the infrastructure is just as vulnerable, if not more vulnerable, than the provider's side," he observes.

One way to deal with these problems is to use a cloud vendor that is a public company, which is required by law to disclose how it manages information. Salesforce.com meets this requirement, with strict processes and guidelines for managing its data centers. "We know our data are in the U.S. and we have a report on the very data centers that we're talking about, " says Flax.

Another alternative is to use a cloud provider that give subscribers the option to choose where their cloud computing work takes place. For example, Terremark Worldwide Inc. is giving its subscriber Agora Games the option to choose where its applications run. Terremark has a Miami facility but is adding other locations. In the past, Agora had no say over where Terremark hosted its applications and data.

Even if your data are totally secure in the cloud, you may not be able to prove it. Some cloud providers don't meet current compliance requirements regarding security, and some of those providers, such as Amazon, have asserted that they don't intend to meet those rules and won't allow compliance auditors on-site.

There are laws restricting where companies can send and store some types of information—personally identifiable information in the European Union (EU), government work in the United Sates or applications that employ certain encryption algorithms. Companies required to meet these regulations involving protected data either in the United States or the EU won't be able to use public cloud providers.

Some of these regulations call for proof that systems are securely managed, which may require confirmation from an independent audit. Large providers are unlikely to allow another company's auditors to inspect their data centers. Microsoft found a way to deal with this problem that may be helpful. The company reduced 26 different types of audits to a list of 200 necessary controls for meeting compliance standards that were applied to its data center environments and services. Microsoft does not give every customer or auditor access to its data centers, but its compliance framework allows auditors to order from a menu of tests and receive the results.

Companies expect their systems to be running 24/7, but cloud providers haven't always been able to provide this level of service. Millions of customers of Salesforce.com suffered a 38-minute outage in early January 2009 and others several years earlier. The January 2009 outage locked more than 900,000 subscribers out of crucial applications and data needed to transact business with customers. More than 300,000 customers using Intuit's online network of small business aplications were unable to access these services for two days in June 2010 following a power outage.

Agreements for services such as Amazon EC2 and Microsoft Azure state that these companies are not going to be held liable for data losses or fines or other legal penalties when companies use their services. Both vendors offer guidance on how to use their cloud platforms securely, and they may still be able to protect data better than some companies' home-grown facilities.

Salesforce.com had been building up and redesigning its infrastructure to ensure better service. The company invested $50 million in

Mirrorforce technology, a mirroring system that creates a duplicate database in a separate location and synchronizes the data instantaneously. If one database is disabled, the other takes over. Salesforce.com added two data centers on the East and West coasts in addition to its Silicon Valley facility. The company distributed processing for its larger customers among these centers to balance its database load.

Sources: Seth Fineberg, "A Shadow on the Cloud?" *Information Management*, August, 2010; Ellen Messmer, "Secrecy of Cloud Computing Providers Raises IT Security Risks," *IT World*, July 13, 2010; John Edwards, "Cutting Through the Fog of Cloud Security," *Computerworld*, February 23, 2009; Wayne Rash, "Is Cloud Computing Secure? Prove It," *eWeek*, September 21, 2009; Robert Lemos, "Five Lessons from Microsoft on Cloud Security," *Computerworld*, August 25, 2009; and Mike Fratto, "Cloud Control," *Information Week*, January 26, 2009.

CASE STUDY QUESTIONS

1. What security and control problems are described in this case?

2. What people, organization, and technology factors contribute to these problems?

3. How secure is cloud computing? Explain your answer.

4. If you were in charge of your company's information systems department, what issues would you want to clarify with prospective vendors?

5. Would you entrust your corporate systems to a cloud computing provider? Why or why not?

MIS IN ACTION

Go to www.trust.salesforce.com, then answer the following questions:

1. Click on Security and describe Salesforce.com's security provisions. How helpful are these?

2. Click on Best Practices and describe what subscribing companies can do to tighten security. How helpful are these guidelines?

3. If you ran a business, would you feel confident about using Salesforce.com's on-demand service? Why or why not?

the information systems department and end users to jointly measure the performance of the system and identify problems as they occur. Examples of software metrics include the number of transactions that can be processed in a specified unit of time, online response time, the number of payroll checks printed per hour, and the number of known bugs per hundred lines of program code. For metrics to be successful, they must be carefully designed, formal, objective, and used consistently.

Early, regular, and thorough testing will contribute significantly to system quality. Many view testing as a way to prove the correctness of work they have done. In fact, we know that all sizable software is riddled with errors, and we must test to uncover these errors.

Good testing begins before a software program is even written by using a *walkthrough*—a review of a specification or design document by a small group of people carefully selected based on the skills needed for the particular objectives being tested. Once developers start writing software programs, coding walkthroughs also can be used to review program code. However, code must be tested by computer runs. When errors are discovered, the source is found and eliminated through a process called *debugging*. Our Learning Tracks contain descriptions of methodologies for developing software programs that also contribute to software quality.

5 HANDS-ON MIS PROJECTS

The projects in this section give you hands-on experience analyzing security vulnerabilities, using spreadsheet software for risk analysis, and using Web tools to research security outsourcing services.

Management Decision Problems

1. K2 Network operates online game sites used by about 16 million people in over 100 countries. Players are allowed to enter a game for free, but must buy digital "assets" from K2, such as swords to fight dragons, if they want to be deeply involved. The games can accommodate millions of players at once and are played simultaneously by people all over the world. Prepare a security analysis for this Internet-based business. What kinds of threats should it anticipate? What would be their impact on the business? What steps can it take to prevent damage to its Web sites and continuing operations?

2. A survey of your firm's information technology infrastructure has produced the following security analysis statistics:

SECURITY VULNERABILITIES BY TYPE OF COMPUTING PLATFORM

PLATFORM	NUMBER OF COMPUTERS	HIGH RISK	MEDIUM RISK	LOW RISK	TOTAL VULNERABILITIES
Windows Server (corporate applications)	1	11	37	19	
Windows 7 Enterprise (high-level administrators)	3	56	242	87	
Linux (e-mail and printing services)	1	3	154	98	
Sun Solaris (Unix) (E-commerce and Web servers)	2	12	299	78	
Windows 7 Enterprise user desktops and laptops with office productivity tools that can also be linked to the corporate network running corporate applications and intranet	195	14	16	1,237	

High risk vulnerabilities include non-authorized users accessing applications, guessable passwords, user names matching the password, active user accounts with missing passwords, and the existence of unauthorized programs in application systems.

Medium risk vulnerabilities include the ability of users to shut down the system without being logged on, passwords and screen saver settings that were not established for PCs, and outdated versions of software still being stored on hard drives.

Low risk vulnerabilities include the inability of users to change their passwords, user passwords that have not been changed periodically, and passwords that were smaller than the minimum size specified by the company.

- Calculate the total number of vulnerabilities for each platform. What is the potential impact of the security problems for each computing platform on the organization?
- If you only have one information systems specialist in charge of security, which platforms should you address first in trying to eliminate these vulnerabilities? Second? Third? Last? Why?
- Identify the types of control problems illustrated by these vulnerabilities and explain the measures that should be taken to solve them.
- What does your firm risk by ignoring the security vulnerabilities identified?

Improving Decision Making: Using Spreadsheet Software to Perform a Security Risk Assessment

Software skills: Spreadsheet formulas and charts
Business skills: Risk assessment

This project uses spreadsheet software to calculate anticipated annual losses from various security threats identified for a small company.

Mercer Paints is a small but highly regarded paint manufacturing company located in Alabama. The company has a network in place linking many of its business operations. Although the firm believes that its security is adequate, the recent addition of a Web site has become an open invitation to hackers. Management requested a risk assessment. The risk assessment identified a number of potential exposures. These exposures, their associated probabilities, and average losses are summarized in the following table.

MERCER PAINTS RISK ASSESSMENT

EXPOSURE	PROBABILITY OF OCCURRENCE	AVERAGE LOSS
Malware attack	60%	$75,000
Data loss	12%	$70,000
Embezzlement	3%	$30,000
User errors	95%	$25,000
Threats from hackers	95%	$90,000
Improper use by employees	5%	$5,000
Power failure	15%	$300,000

- In addition to the potential exposures listed, you should identify at least three other potential threats to Mercer Paints, assign probabilities, and estimate a loss range.
- Use spreadsheet software and the risk assessment data to calculate the expected annual loss for each exposure.
- Present your findings in the form of a chart. Which control points have the greatest vulnerability? What recommendations would you make to Mercer Paints? Prepare a written report that summarizes your findings and recommendations.

Improving Decision Making: Evaluating Security Outsourcing Services

Software skills: Web browser and presentation software
Business skills: Evaluating business outsourcing services

Businesses today have a choice of whether to outsource the security function or maintain their own internal staff for this purpose. This project will help develop your Internet skills in using the Web to research and evaluate security outsourcing services.

As an information systems expert in your firm, you have been asked to help management decide whether to outsource security or keep the security function within the firm. Search the Web to find information to help you decide whether to outsource security and to locate security outsourcing services.

- Present a brief summary of the arguments for and against outsourcing computer security for your company.

- Select two firms that offer computer security outsourcing services, and compare them and their services.

- Prepare an electronic presentation for management summarizing your findings. Your presentation should make the case on whether or not your company should outsource computer security. If you believe your company should outsource, the presentation should identify which security outsourcing service should be selected and justify your selection.

LEARNING TRACK MODULES

The following Learning Tracks provide content relevant to topics covered in this chapter:

1. The Booming Job Market in IT Security
2. The Sarbanes-Oxley Act
3. Computer Forensics
4. General and Application Controls for Information Systems
5. Management Challenges of Security and Control
6. Software Vulnerability and Reliability

Review Summary

1. **Why are information systems vulnerable to destruction, error, and abuse?**

   Digital data are vulnerable to destruction, misuse, error, fraud, and hardware or software failures. The Internet is designed to be an open system and makes internal corporate systems more vulnerable to actions from outsiders. Hackers can unleash denial-of-service (DoS) attacks or penetrate corporate networks, causing serious system disruptions. Wi-Fi networks can easily be penetrated by intruders using sniffer programs to obtain an address to access the resources of the network. Computer viruses and worms can disable systems and Web sites. The dispersed nature of cloud computing makes it difficult to track unauthorized activity or to apply controls from afar. Software presents problems because software bugs may be impossible to eliminate and because software vulnerabilities can be exploited by hackers and malicious software. End users often introduce errors.

2. **What is the business value of security and control?**

   Lack of sound security and control can cause firms relying on computer systems for their core business functions to lose sales and productivity. Information assets, such as confidential employee records, trade secrets, or business plans, lose much of their value if they are revealed to outsiders or if they expose the firm to legal liability. New laws, such as HIPAA, the Sarbanes-Oxley Act, and the Gramm-Leach-Bliley Act, require companies to practice stringent electronic records management and adhere to strict standards for security, privacy, and control. Legal actions requiring electronic evidence and computer forensics also require firms to pay more attention to security and electronic records management.

3. **What are the components of an organizational framework for security and control?**

   Firms need to establish a good set of both general and application controls for their information systems. A risk assessment evaluates information assets, identifies control points and control weaknesses, and determines the most cost-effective set of controls. Firms must also develop a coherent corporate security policy and plans for continuing business operations in the event of disaster or disruption. The security policy includes policies for acceptable use and identity management. Comprehensive and systematic MIS auditing helps organizations determine the effectiveness of security and controls for their information systems.

4. **What are the most important tools and technologies for safeguarding information resources?**

   Firewalls prevent unauthorized users from accessing a private network when it is linked to the Internet. Intrusion detection systems monitor private networks from suspicious network traffic and attempts to access corporate systems. Passwords, tokens, smart cards, and biometric authentication are used to authenticate system users. Antivirus software checks computer systems for infections by viruses and worms and often eliminates the malicious software, while antispyware software combats intrusive and harmful spyware programs. Encryption, the coding and scrambling of messages, is a widely used technology for securing electronic transmissions over unprotected networks. Digital certificates combined with public key encryption provide further protection of electronic transactions by authenticating a user's identity. Companies can use fault-tolerant computer systems or create high-availability computing environments to make sure that their information systems are always available. Use of software metrics and rigorous software testing help improve software quality and reliability.

Key Terms

Acceptable use policy (AUP)	Click fraud
Antivirus software	Computer crime
Application controls	Computer forensics
Authentication	Computer virus
Biometric authentication	Controls
Botnet	Cybervandalism
Bugs	Deep packet inspection (DPI)
Business continuity planning	Denial-of-service (DoS) attack

Digital certificates
Disaster recovery planning
Distributed denial-of-service (DDoS) attack
Downtime
Encryption
Evil twin
Fault-tolerant computer systems
Firewall
General controls
Gramm-Leach-Bliley Act
Hacker
High-availability computing
HIPAA
Identity management
Identity theft
Intrusion detection systems
Keyloggers
Malware
Managed security service providers
 (MSSPs)
MIS audit
Online transaction processing
Password
Patches

Pharming
Phishing
Public key encryption
Public key infrastructure (PKI)
Recovery-oriented computing
Risk assessment
Sarbanes-Oxley Act
Secure Hypertext Transfer Protocol
 (S-HTTP)
Secure Sockets Layer (SSL)
Security
Security policy
SQL injection attack
Smart card
Sniffer
Social engineering
Spoofing
Spyware
Token
Trojan horse
Unified threat management (UTM)
War driving
Worms

Review Questions

1. Why are information systems vulnerable to destruction, error, and abuse?

   - List and describe the most common threats against contemporary information systems.
   - Define malware and distinguish among a virus, a worm, and a Trojan horse.
   - Define a hacker and explain how hackers create security problems and damage systems.
   - Define computer crime. Provide two examples of crime in which computers are targets and two examples in which computers are used as instruments of crime.
   - Define identity theft and phishing and explain why identity theft is such a big problem today.
   - Describe the security and system reliability problems created by employees.
   - Explain how software defects affect system reliability and security.

2. What is the business value of security and control?

   - Explain how security and control provide value for businesses.

   - Describe the relationship between security and control and recent U.S. government regulatory requirements and computer forensics.

3. What are the components of an organizational framework for security and control?

   - Define general controls and describe each type of general control.
   - Define application controls and describe each type of application control.
   - Describe the function of risk assessment and explain how it is conducted for information systems.
   - Define and describe the following: security policy, acceptable use policy, and identity management.
   - Explain how MIS auditing promotes security and control.

4. What are the most important tools and technologies for safeguarding information resources?

   - Name and describe three authentication methods.
   - Describe the roles of firewalls, intrusion detection systems, and antivirus software in promoting security.

- Explain how encryption protects information.
- Describe the role of encryption and digital certificates in a public key infrastructure.
- Distinguish between fault-tolerant and high-availability computing, and between disaster recovery planning and business continuity planning.
- Identify and describe the security problems posed by cloud computing.
- Describe measures for improving software quality and reliability.

Discussion Questions

1. Security isn't simply a technology issue, it's a business issue. Discuss.

2. If you were developing a business continuity plan for your company, where would you start? What aspects of the business would the plan address?

3. Suppose your business had an e-commerce Web site where it sold goods and accepted credit card payments. Discuss the major security threats to this Web site and their potential impact. What can be done to minimize these threats?

Video Cases

Video Cases and Instructional Videos illustrating some of the concepts in this chapter are available. Contact your instructor to access these videos.

Collaboration and Teamwork: Evaluating Security Software Tools

With a group of three or four students, use the Web to research and evaluate security products from two competing vendors, such as antivirus software, firewalls, or antispyware software. For each product, describe its capabilities, for what types of businesses it is best suited, and its cost to purchase and install.

Which is the best product? Why? If possible, use Google Sites to post links to Web pages, team communication announcements, and work assignments; to brainstorm; and to work collaboratively on project documents. Try to use Google Docs to develop a presentation of your findings for the class.

Are We Ready for Cyberwarfare?
CASE STUDY

For most of us, the Internet is a tool we use for e-mail, news, entertainment, socializing, and shopping. But for computer security experts affiliated with government agencies and private contractors, as well as their hacker counterparts from across the globe, the Internet has become a battlefield—a war zone where cyberwarfare is becoming more frequent and hacking techniques are becoming more advanced. Cyberwarfare poses a unique and daunting set of challenges for security experts, not only in detecting and preventing intrusions but also in tracking down perpetrators and bringing them to justice.

Cyberwarfare can take many forms. Often, hackers use botnets, massive networks of computers that they control thanks to spyware and other malware, to launch large-scale DDoS attacks on their target's servers. Other methods allow intruders to access secure computers remotely and copy or delete e-mail and files from the machine, or even to remotely monitor users of a machine using more sophisticated software. For cybercriminals, the benefit of cyberwarfare is that they can compete with traditional superpowers for a fraction of the cost of, for example, building up a nuclear arsenal. Because more and more modern technological infrastructure will rely on the Internet to function, cyberwarriors will have no shortage of targets at which to take aim.

Cyberwarfare also involves defending against these types of attacks. That's a major focus of U.S. intelligence agencies. While the U.S. is currently at the forefront of cyberwarfare technologies, it's unlikely to maintain technological dominance because of the relatively low cost of the technologies needed to mount these types of attacks.

In fact, hackers worldwide have already begun doing so in earnest. In July 2009, 27 American and South Korean government agencies and other organizations were hit by a DDoS attack. An estimated 65,000 computers belonging to foreign botnets flooded the Web sites with access requests. Affected sites included those of the White House, the Treasury, the Federal Trade Commission, the Defense Department, the Secret Service, the New York Stock Exchange, and the Washington Post, in addition to the Korean Defense Ministry, National Assembly, the presidential Blue House, and several others.

The attacks were not sophisticated, but were widespread and prolonged, succeeding in slowing down most of the U.S. sites and forcing several South Korean sites to stop operating. North Korea or pro-North Korean groups were suspected to be behind the attacks, but the Pyongyang government denied any involvement.

The lone positive from the attacks was that only the Web sites of these agencies were affected. However, other intrusions suggest that hackers already have the potential for much more damaging acts of cyberwarfare. The Federal Aviation Administration (FAA), which oversees the airline activity of the United States, has already been subject to successful attacks on its systems, including one in 2006 that partially shut down air-traffic data systems in Alaska.

In 2007 and 2008, computer spies broke into the Pentagon's $300 billion Joint Strike Fighter project. Intruders were able to copy and siphon off several terabytes of data related to design and electronics systems, potentially making it easier to defend against the fighter when it's eventually produced. The intruders entered through vulnerabilities of two or three contractors working on the fighter jet project. Fortunately, computers containing the most sensitive data were not connected to the Internet, and were therefore inaccessible to the intruders. Former U.S. officials say that this attack originated in China, and that China had been making steady progress in developing online-warfare techniques. China rebutted these claims, stating that the U.S. media was subscribing to outdated, Cold War-era thinking in blaming them, and that Chinese hackers were not skilled enough to perpetrate an attack of that magnitude.

In December 2009, hackers reportedly stole a classified PowerPoint slide file detailing U.S. and South Korean strategy for fighting a war against North Korea. In Iraq, insurgents intercepted Predator drone feeds using software they had downloaded from the Internet.

Earlier that year, in April, cyberspies infiltrated the U.S. electrical grid, using weak points where computers on the grid are connected to the Internet, and left behind software programs whose purpose is unclear, but which presumably could be used to disrupt the system. Reports indicated that the spies originated in computer networks in China and Russia. Again, both nations denied the charges.

In response to these and other intrusions, the federal government launched a program called "Perfect Citizen" to detect cyberassaults on private companies running critical infrastructure. The U.S. National Security Agency (NSA) plans to install sensors in computer networks for critical infrastructure that would be activated by unusual activity signalling an impending cyberattack. The initial focus will be older large computer control systems that have since been linked to the Internet, making them more vulnerable to cyber attack. NSA will likely start with electric, nuclear, and air-traffic control systems with the greatest impact on national security.

As of this writing, most federal agencies get passing marks for meeting the requirements of the Federal Information Security Management Act, the most recent set of standards passed into law. But as cyberwarfare technologies develop and become more advanced, the standards imposed by this legislation will likely be insufficient to defend against attacks.

In each incident of cyberwarfare, the governments of the countries suspected to be responsible have roundly denied the charges with no repercussions. How could this be possible? The major reason is that tracing identities of specific attackers through cyberspace is next to impossible, making deniability simple.

The real worry for security experts and government officials is an act of cyberwar against a critical resource, such as the electric grid, financial system, or communications systems. First of all, the U.S. has no clear policy about how the country would respond to that level of a cyberattack. Although the electric grid was accessed by hackers, it hasn't yet actually been attacked. A three-year study of U.S. cybersecurity recommended that such a policy be created and made public. It also suggested that the U.S. attempt to find common ground with other nations to join forces in preventing these attacks.

Secondly, the effects of such an attack would likely be devastating. Mike McConnell, the former director of national intelligence, stated that if even a single large American bank were successfully attacked, "it would have an order-of-magnitude greater impact on the global economy" than the World Trade Center attacks, and that "the ability to threaten the U.S. money supply is the equivalent of today's nuclear weapon." Such an attack would have a catastrophic effect on the U.S. financial system, and by extension, the world economy.

Lastly, many industry analysts are concerned that the organization of our cybersecurity is messy, with no clear leader among our intelligence agencies. Several different agencies, including the Pentagon and the NSA, have their sights on being the leading agency in the ongoing efforts to combat cyberwarfare. In June 2009, Secretary of Defense Robert Gates ordered the creation of the first headquarters designed to coordinate government cybersecurity efforts, called Cybercom. Cybercom was activated in May 2010 with the goal of coordinating the operation and protection of military and Pentagon computer networks in the hopes of resolving this organizational tangle.

In confronting this problem, one critical question has arisen: how much control over enforcing cybersecurity should be given to American spy agencies, since they are prohibited from acting on American soil? Cyberattacks know no borders, so distinguishing between American soil and foreign soil means domestic agencies will be unnecessarily inhibited in their ability to fight cybercrime. For example, if the NSA was investigating the source of a cyberattack on government Web sites, and determined that the attack originated from American servers, under our current laws, it would not be able to investigate further.

Some experts believe that there is no effective way for a domestic agency to conduct computer operations without entering prohibited networks within the United States, or even conducting investigations in countries that are American allies. The NSA has already come under heavy fire for its surveillance actions after 9-11, and this has the potential to raise similar privacy concerns. Preventing terrorist or cyberwar attacks may require examining some e-mail messages from other countries or giving intelligence agencies more access to networks or Internet service providers. There is a need for an open debate about what constitutes a violation of privacy and what is acceptable during 'cyber-wartime', which is essentially all the time. The law may need to be changed to accommodate effective cybersecurity techniques, but it's unclear that this can be done without eroding some privacy rights that we consider essential.

As for these offensive measures, it's unclear as to how strong the United States' offensive capabilities for cyberwarfare are. The government closely guards this information, almost all of which is classified. But former military and intelligence officials indicate that our cyberwarfare capabilities have dramatically increased in sophistication in the past year or two.

And because tracking cybercriminals has proven so difficult, it may be that the best defense is a strong offense.

Sources: "Cyber Task Force Passes Mission to Cyber Command,"*Defence Professionals*, September 8, 2010; Siobhan Gorman, "U.S. Plans Cyber Shield for Utilities, Companies," *The Wall Street Journal*, July 8, 2010 and "U.S. Hampered in Fighting Cyber Attacks, Report Says," *The Wall Street Journal*, June, 16, 2010; Siobhan Gorman, Yochi Dreazen and August Cole, "Drone Breach Stirs Calls to Fill Cyber Post," *The Wall Street Journal*, December 21, 2009; Sean Gallagher, "New Threats Compel DOD to Rethink Cyber Strategy," *Defense Knowledge Technologies and Net-Enabled Warfare*, January 22, 2010; Lance Whitney, Cyber Command Chief Details Threat to U.S.," *Military Tech*, August 5, 2010; Hoover, J. Nicholas, "Cybersecurity Balancing Act," *Information Week,* April 27, 2009; David E. Sanger, John Markoff, and Thom Shanker, "U.S. Steps Up Effort on Digital Defenses," *The New York Times*, April 28, 2009; John Markoff and Thom Shanker. "Panel Advises Clarifying U.S. Plans on Cyberwar," *The New York Times*, April 30, 2009; Siobhan Gorman and Evan Ramstad, "Cyber Blitz Hits U.S., Korea," *The Wall Street Journal*, July 9, 2009; Lolita C. Baldor, "White House Among Targets of Sweeping Cyber Attack," Associated Press, July 8, 2009; Choe Sang-Hun, "Cyberattacks Hit U.S. and South Korean Web Sites," *The New York Times*, July 9, 2009; Siobhan Gorman, "FAA's Air-Traffic Networks Breached by Hackers," *The Wall Street Journal*, May 7, 2009; Thom Shanker, "New Military Command for Cyberspace," *The New York Times*, June 24, 2009; David E. Sanger and Thom Shanker, "Pentagon Plans New Arm to Wage Wars in Cyberspace," *The New York Times*, May 29, 2009; Siobhan Gorman, August Cole, and Yochi Dreazen, "Computer Spies Breach Fighter-Jet Project," *The Wall Street Journal*, April 21, 2009; Siobhan Gorman, "Electricity Grid in U.S. Penetrated by Spies," *The Wall Street Journal*, April 8, 2009; "Has Power Grid Been Hacked? U.S. Won't Say," Reuters, April 8, 2009; Markoff, John, "Vast Spy System Loots Computers in 103 Countries." *The New York Times,* March 29, 2009; Markoff, John, "Tracking Cyberspies Through the Web Wilderness," *The New York Times*, May 12, 2009.

CASE STUDY QUESTIONS

1. Is cyberwarfare a serious problem? Why or why not?

2. Assess the management, organization, and technology factors that have created this problem.

3. What solutions have been proposed? Do you think they will be effective? Why or why not?

4. Are there other solutions for this problem that should be pursued? What are they?

References

Ante, Spencer E. "Dark Side Arises for Phone Apps." The Wall Street Journal (June 6, 2010).

-----. "Get Smart: Targeting Phone Security Flaws." The Wall Street Journal (June 15, 2010).

Bernstein, Corinne. "The Cost of Data Breaches." Baseline (April 2009)

Bray, Chad. "Global Cyber Scheme Hits Bank Accounts." The Wall Street Journal (October 1, 2010.)

Brenner, Susan W. "U.S. Cybercrime Law: Defining Offenses." Information Systems Frontiers 6, no. 2 (June 2004).

Cavusoglu, Huseyin, Birendra Mishra, and Srinivasan Raghunathan. "A Model for Evaluating IT Security Investments." Communications of the ACM 47, no. 7 (July 2004).

Chickowski, Ericka. "Is Your Information Really Safe?" Baseline (April 2009).

Choe Sang-Hun, "Cyberattacks Hit U.S. and South Korean Web Sites," The New York Times, July 9, 2009.

Computer Security Institute. "2009 CSI Computer Crime and Security Survey" (2009).

Consumer Reports. "State of the Net 2010." (June 2010).

Coopes, Amy. "Australian 17-Year-Old Takes Blame for Twitter Chaos." AFP (September 22, 2010).

D'Arcy, John and Anat Hovav. "Deterring Internal Information Systems Use." Communications of the ACM 50, no. 10 (October 2007).

Danchev, Dancho."Malware Watch: Rogue Facebook Apps, Fake Amazon Orders, and Bogus Adobe Updates." ZD Net (May 19, 2010).

Dash, Eric. "Online Woes Plague Chase for 2nd Day." The New York Times (September 15, 2010).

Ely, Adam. "Browser as Attack Vector." Information Week (August 9, 2010).

Feretic, Eileen. "Security Lapses More Costly."baselinemag.com, January 26, 2010

Foley, John. "P2P Peril." Information Week (March 17, 2008).

Fratto, Mike. "What's Your Appetite for Risk?" Information Week (June 22, 2009).

Giordano, Scott M. "Electronic Evidence and the Law." Information Systems Frontiers 6, No. 2 (June 2004).

Galbreth, Michael R. and Mikhael Shor. "The Impact of Malicious Agents on the Enterprise Software Industry." MIS Quarterly 34, no. 3 (September 2010).

Gorman, Siobhan. "Broad New Hacking Attack Detected." The Wall Street Journal (February 18, 2010).

Housley, Russ, and William Arbaugh. "Security Problems in 802.11b Networks." Communications of the ACM 46, no. 5 (May 2003).

IBM. "Secure By Design: Building Identity-Based Security into Today's Information Systems." (March 2010).

Ives, Blake, Kenneth R. Walsh, and Helmut Schneider. "The Domino Effect of Password Reuse." Communications of the ACM 47, no.4 (April 2004).

Jagatic Tom, Nathaniel Johnson, Markus Jakobsson, and Filippo Menczer. "Social Phishing." Communications of the ACM 50, no. 10 (October 2007).

Javelin Strategy & Research. "2010 Identity Fraud Survey Report." (2010).

Markoff, John. "Vast Spy System Loots Computers in 103 Countries." The New York Times (March 29, 2009).

McDougall, Paul. "High Cost of Data Loss." Information Week (March 20,2006).

McGraw, Gary. "Real-World Software Security." Information Week (August 9, 2010).

Meckbach, Greg. "MasterCard's Robust Data Centre: Priceless." Computerworld Canada (March 26, 2008).

Mercuri, Rebeca T. "Analyzing Security Costs." Communications of the ACM 46, no. 6 (June 2003).

Mills, Elinor. "Facebook Disables Rogue Data-Stealing, Spamming Apps." CNET News (August 20, 2009).

Mitchell, Dan. "It's Here: It's There; It's Spyware." The New York Times (May 20, 2006).

Null, Christopher. "WPA Cracked in 1 Minute." Yahoo! Tech (August 27, 2009).

Panko, Raymond R. Corporate Computer and Network Security 2e. Upper Saddle River, NJ: Pearson Prentice Hall (2010).

"Plea in Case of Stolen Code from Goldman," Reuters, February 17, 2010

Prince, Brian. "The Growing E-Mail Security Challenge." eWeek (April 21, 2008).

Pug, Ivan P.L. and Qiu-Hong Wang. "Information Security: Facilitating User Precautions Vis a Vis Enforcement Against Attackers. "Journal of Management Information Systems 26, No. 2 (Fall 2009).

Roche, Edward M., and George Van Nostrand. Information Systems, Computer Crime and Criminal Justice. New York: Barraclough Ltd. (2004).

Ryan Naraine, "ActiveX Under Siege," eWeek (February 11, 2008).

Sample, Char and Diana Kelley. "Cloud Computing Security: Infrastructure Issues." Security Curve June 23, 2009).

Sarrel, Matthew. "The Biggest Security Threats Right Now." eWeek (May 6, 2010).

Schwerha, Joseph J., IV. "Cybercrime: Legal Standards Governing the Collection of Digital Evidence." Information Systems Frontiers 6, no. 2 (June 2004).

Sophos. "Security Threat Report: Midyear 2010." (2010).

Spears. Janine L. and Henri Barki. "User Participation in Information Systems Security Risk Management." MIS Quarterly 34, No. 3 (September 2010).

Steel, Emily. "Web Ad Sales Open Door to Viruses." The Wall Street Journal (June 15, 2009).

Symantec. "Symantec Global Internet Security Threat Report: Trends for 2009." (April 2010).

Vance, Ashlee. "If Your Password is 123456, Just Make It HackMe." The New York Times (January 20, 2010).

Volonino, Linda and Stephen R. Robinson. Principles and Practice of Information Security. Upper Saddle River, NJ: Pearson Prentice Hall (2004).

Wang, Huaiqing, and Chen Wang. "Taxonomy of Security Considerations and Software Quality." Communications of the ACM 46, no. 6 (June 2003).

Warkentin, Merrill, Xin Luo, and Gary F. Templeton. "A Framework for Spyware Assessement." Communications of the ACM 48, no. 8 (August 2005).

Westerman, George. IT Risk: Turning Business Threats into Competitive Advantage. Harvard Business School Publishing (2007)

Wright, Ryan T. and Kent Marrett."The Influence of Experiental and Dispositional Factors in Phishing: An Empirical Investigation of the Deceived." Journal of Management Information Systems 27, No. 1 (Summer 2010).

Chapter 9

Achieving Operational Excellence and Customer Intimacy: Enterprise Applications

From Chapter 9 of *Management Information Systems: Managing the Digital Firm*, 12/e. Kenneth C. Laudon, Jane P. Laudon.

Achieving Operational Excellence and Customer Intimacy: Enterprise Applications

CANNONDALE LEARNS TO MANAGE A GLOBAL SUPPLY CHAIN

If you enjoy cycling, you may very well be using a Cannondale bicycle. Cannondale, headquartered in Bethel, Connecticut, is the world-leading manufacturer of high-end bicycles, apparel, footwear, and accessories, with dealers and distributors in more than 66 countries. Cannondale's supply and distribution chains span the globe, and the company must coordinate manufacturing, assembly, and sales/distribution sites in many different countries. Cannondale produces more than 100 different bicycle models each year; 60 percent of these are newly introduced to meet ever-changing customer preferences.

Cannondale offers both make-to-stock and make-to-order models. A typical bicycle requires a 150-day lead time and a four-week manufacturing window, and some models have bills of materials with over 150 parts. (A bill of materials specifies the raw materials, assemblies, components, parts, and quantities of each needed to manufacture a final product.) Cannondale must manage more than 1 million of these bills of materials and more than 200,000 individual parts. Some of these parts come from specialty vendors with even longer lead times and limited production capacity.

Obviously, managing parts availability in a constantly changing product line impacted by volatile customer demand requires a great deal of manufacturing flexibility. Until recently, that flexibility was missing. Cannondale had an antiquated legacy material requirements planning system for planning production, controlling inventory, and managing manufacturing processes that could only produce reports on a weekly basis. By Tuesday afternoon, Monday's reports were already out of date. The company was forced to substitute parts in order to meet demand, and sometimes it lost sales. Cannondale needed a solution that could track the flow of parts more accurately, support its need for flexibility, and work with its existing business systems, all within a restricted budget.

Cannondale selected the Kinaxis RapidResponse on-demand software service as a solution. RapidResponse furnishes accurate and detailed supply chain information via an easy-to-use spreadsheet interface, using data supplied automatically from Cannondale's existing manufacturing systems. Data from operations at multiple sites are assembled in a single place for analysis and decision making. Supply chain participants from different locations are able to model manufacturing and inventory data in "what-if" scenarios to see the impact of alternative actions across the entire supply chain. Old forecasts can be compared to new ones, and the system can evaluate the constraints of a new plan.

Cannondale buyers, planners, master schedulers, sourcers, product managers, customer service, and finance personnel, use RapidResponse for sales reporting, forecasting, monitoring daily inventory availability, and feeding production schedule information to Cannondale's manufacturing and order processing systems. Users are able to see up-to-date information for all sites. Management uses the system daily to examine areas where there are backlogs.

iStockphoto 2010

The improved supply chain information from RapidResponse enables Cannondale to respond to customer orders much more rapidly with lower levels of inventory and safety stock. Cycle times and lead times for producing products have also been reduced. The company's dates for promising deliveries are more reliable and accurate.

Sources: Kinaxis Corp., "Cannondale Improves Customer Response Times While Reducing Inventory Using RapidResponse," 2010; www.kinaxis.com, accessed June 21, 2010; and www.cannondale.com, accessed June 21, 2010.

Cannondale's problems with its supply chain illustrate the critical role of supply chain management (SCM) systems in business. Cannondale's business performance was impeded because it could not coordinate its sourcing, manufacturing, and distribution processes. Costs were unnecessarily high because the company was unable to accurately determine the exact amount of each product it needed to fulfill orders and hold just that amount in inventory. Instead, the company resorted to keeping extra "safety stock" on hand "just in case." When products were not available when the customer wanted them, Cannondale lost sales.

The chapter-opening diagram calls attention to important points raised by this case and this chapter. Like many other firms, Cannondale had a complex supply chain and manufacturing processes to coordinate in many different locations. The company had to deal with hundreds and perhaps thousands of suppliers of parts and raw materials. It was not always possible to have just the right amount of each part or component available when it was needed because the company lacked accurate, up-to-date information about parts in inventory and what manufacturing processes needed those parts.

An on-demand supply chain management software service from Kinaxis helped solve this problem. The Kinaxis RapidResponse software takes in data from Cannondale's existing manufacturing systems and assembles data from multiple sites to furnish a single view of Cannondale's supply chain based on up-to-date information. Cannondale staff are able to see exactly what parts are available or on order as well as the status of bikes in production. With better tools for planning, users are able to see the impact of changes in supply and demand so that they can make better decisions about how to respond to these changes. The system has greatly enhanced operational efficiency and decision making.

1 ENTERPRISE SYSTEMS

Around the globe, companies are increasingly becoming more connected, both internally and with other companies. If you run a business, you'll want to be able to react instantaneously when a customer places a large order or when a shipment from a supplier is delayed. You may also want to know the impact of these events on every part of the business and how the business is performing at any point in time, especially if you're running a large company. Enterprise systems provide the integration to make this possible. Let's look at how they work and what they can do for the firm.

WHAT ARE ENTERPRISE SYSTEMS?

Imagine that you had to run a business based on information from tens or even hundreds of different databases and systems, none of which could speak to one another? Imagine your company had 10 different major product lines, each produced in separate factories, and each with separate and incompatible sets of systems controlling production, warehousing, and distribution.

At the very least, your decision making would often be based on manual hard-copy reports, often out of date, and it would be difficult to really understand what is happening in the business as a whole. Sales personnel might not be able to tell at the time they place an order whether the ordered items are in inventory, and manufacturing could not easily use sales data to plan for new production. You now have a good idea of why firms need a special enterprise system to integrate information.

Enterprise resource planning (ERP) systems are based on a suite of integrated software modules and a common central database. The database collects data from many different divisions and departments in a firm, and from a large number of key business processes in manufacturing and production, finance and accounting, sales and marketing, and human resources, making the data available for applications that support nearly all of an organization's internal business activities. When new information is entered by one process, the information is made immediately available to other business processes (see Figure 1).

If a sales representative places an order for tire rims, for example, the system verifies the customer's credit limit, schedules the shipment, identifies the best shipping route, and reserves the necessary items from inventory. If inventory stock were insufficient to fill the order, the system schedules the manufacture of more rims, ordering the needed materials and components from suppliers. Sales and production forecasts are immediately updated. General ledger and corporate cash levels are automatically updated with the revenue and cost information from the order. Users could tap into the system and find out where that particular order was at any minute. Management could obtain information at any point in time about how the business was operating. The system could also generate enterprise-wide data for management analyses of product cost and profitability.

FIGURE 1   HOW ENTERPRISE SYSTEMS WORK

Enterprise systems feature a set of integrated software modules and a central database that enables data to be shared by many different business processes and functional areas throughout the enterprise.

ENTERPRISE SOFTWARE

Enterprise software is built around thousands of predefined business processes that reflect best practices. Table 1 describes some of the major business processes supported by enterprise software.

Companies implementing this software must first select the functions of the system they wish to use and then map their business processes to the predefined business processes in the software. (One of our Learning Tracks shows how SAP enterprise software handles the procurement process for a new piece of equipment.) Identifying the organization's business processes to be included in the system and then mapping them to the processes in the enterprise software is often a major effort. A firm would use configuration tables provided by the software to tailor a particular aspect of the system to the way it does business. For example, the firm could use these tables to select whether it wants to track revenue by product line, geographical unit, or distribution channel.

TABLE 1   BUSINESS PROCESSES SUPPORTED BY ENTERPRISE SYSTEMS

Financial and accounting processes, including general ledger, accounts payable, accounts receivable, fixed assets, cash management and forecasting, product-cost accounting, cost-center accounting, asset accounting, tax accounting, credit management, and financial reporting.

Human resources processes, including personnel administration, time accounting, payroll, personnel planning and development, benefits accounting, applicant tracking, time management, compensation, workforce planning, performance management, and travel expense reporting.

Manufacturing and production processes, including procurement, inventory management, purchasing, shipping, production planning, production scheduling, material requirements planning, quality control, distribution, transportation execution, and plant and equipment maintenance.

Sales and marketing processes, including order processing, quotations, contracts, product configuration, pricing, billing, credit checking, incentive and commission management, and sales planning.

If the enterprise software does not support the way the organization does business, companies can rewrite some of the software to support the way their business processes work. However, enterprise software is unusually complex, and extensive customization may degrade system performance, compromising the information and process integration that are the main benefits of the system. If companies want to reap the maximum benefits from enterprise software, they must change the way they work to conform to the business processes in the software. To implement a new enterprise system, Tasty Baking Company identified its existing business processes and then translated them into the business processes built into the SAP ERP software it had selected. To ensure it obtained the maximum benefits from the enterprise software, Tasty Baking Company deliberately planned for customizing less than 5 percent of the system and made very few changes to the SAP software itself. It used as many tools and features that were already built into the SAP software as it could. SAP has more than 3,000 configuration tables for its enterprise software.

Leading enterprise software vendors include SAP, Oracle (with its acquisition PeopleSoft) Infor Global Solutions, and Microsoft. There are versions of enterprise software packages designed for small businesses and on-demand versions, including software services delivered over the Web (see the Interactive Session on Technology in Section 4). Although initially designed to automate the firm's internal "back-office" business processes, enterprise systems have become more externally-oriented and capable of communicating with customers, suppliers, and other entities.

BUSINESS VALUE OF ENTERPRISE SYSTEMS

Enterprise systems provide value both by increasing operational efficiency and by providing firm-wide information to help managers make better decisions. Large companies with many operating units in different locations have used enterprise systems to enforce standard practices and data so that everyone does business the same way worldwide.

Coca Cola, for instance, implemented a SAP enterprise system to standardize and coordinate important business processes in 200 countries. Lack of standard, company-wide business processes prevented the company from leveraging its worldwide buying power to obtain lower prices for raw materials and from reacting rapidly to market changes.

Enterprise systems help firms respond rapidly to customer requests for information or products. Because the system integrates order, manufacturing, and delivery data, manufacturing is better informed about producing only what customers have ordered, procuring exactly the right amount of components or raw materials to fill actual orders, staging production, and minimizing the time that components or finished products are in inventory.

Alcoa, the world's leading producer of aluminum and aluminum products with operations spanning 41 countries and 500 locations, had initially been organized around lines of business, each of which had its own set of information systems. Many of these systems were redundant and inefficient. Alcoa's costs for executing requisition-to-pay and financial processes were much higher and its cycle times were longer than those of other companies in its industry. (Cycle time refers to the total elapsed time from the beginning to the end of a process.) The company could not operate as a single worldwide entity.

After implementing enterprise software from Oracle, Alcoa eliminated many redundant processes and systems. The enterprise system helped Alcoa reduce requisition-to-pay cycle time by verifying receipt of goods and automatically generating receipts for payment. Alcoa's accounts payable transaction processing dropped 89 percent. Alcoa was able to centralize financial and procurement activities, which helped the company reduce nearly 20 percent of its worldwide costs.

Enterprise systems provide much valuable information for improving management decision making. Corporate headquarters has access to up-to-the-minute data on sales, inventory, and production and uses this information to create more accurate sales and production forecasts. Enterprise software includes analytical tools for using data captured by the system to evaluate overall organizational performance. Enterprise system data have common standardized definitions and formats that are accepted by the entire organization. Performance figures mean the same thing across the company. Enterprise systems allow senior management to easily find out at any moment how a particular organizational unit is performing, determine which products are most or least profitable, and calculate costs for the company as a whole.

For example, Alcoa's enterprise system includes functionality for global human resources management that shows correlations between investment in employee training and quality, measures the company-wide costs of delivering services to employees, and measures the effectiveness of employee recruitment, compensation, and training.

2   SUPPLY CHAIN MANAGEMENT SYSTEMS

If you manage a small firm that makes a few products or sells a few services, chances are you will have a small number of suppliers. You could coordinate your supplier orders and deliveries using a telephone and fax machine. But if you manage a firm that produces more complex products and services, then you will have hundreds of suppliers, and your suppliers will each have their own set of suppliers. Suddenly, you are in a situation where you will need to coordinate the activities of hundreds or even thousands of other firms in order to produce your products and services. Supply chain management systems are an answer to these problems of supply chain complexity and scale.

THE SUPPLY CHAIN

A firm's **supply chain** is a network of organizations and business processes for procuring raw materials, transforming these materials into intermediate and finished products, and distributing the finished products to customers. It links suppliers, manufacturing plants, distribution centers, retail outlets, and customers to supply goods and services from source through consumption. Materials, information, and payments flow through the supply chain in both directions

Goods start out as raw materials and, as they move through the supply chain, are transformed into intermediate products (also referred to as components or parts), and finally, into finished products. The finished products are shipped to distribution centers and from there to retailers and customers. Returned items flow in the reverse direction from the buyer back to the seller.

Let's look at the supply chain for Nike sneakers as an example. Nike designs, markets, and sells sneakers, socks, athletic clothing, and accessories throughout the world. Its primary suppliers are contract manufacturers with factories in China, Thailand, Indonesia, Brazil, and other countries. These companies fashion Nike's finished products.

Nike's contract suppliers do not manufacture sneakers from scratch. They obtain components for the sneakers—the laces, eyelets, uppers, and soles—from other suppliers and then assemble them into finished sneakers. These suppliers in turn have their own suppliers. For example, the suppliers of soles have suppliers for synthetic rubber, suppliers for chemicals used to melt the rubber for molding, and suppliers for the molds into which to pour the rubber. Suppliers of laces would have suppliers for their thread, for dyes, and for the plastic lace tips.

Figure 2 provides a simplified illustration of Nike's supply chain for sneakers; it shows the flow of information and materials among suppliers, Nike, and Nike's distributors, retailers, and customers. Nike's contract manufacturers are its primary suppliers. The suppliers of soles, eyelets, uppers, and laces are the secondary (Tier 2) suppliers. Suppliers to these suppliers are the tertiary (Tier 3) suppliers.

The *upstream* portion of the supply chain includes the company's suppliers, the suppliers' suppliers, and the processes for managing relationships with them. The *downstream* portion consists of the organizations and processes for distributing and delivering products to the final customers. Companies doing manufacturing, such as Nike's contract suppliers of sneakers, also manage their own *internal supply chain* processes for transforming materials, components, and services furnished by their suppliers into finished products or intermediate products (components or parts) for their customers and for managing materials and inventory.

FIGURE 2   NIKE'S SUPPLY CHAIN

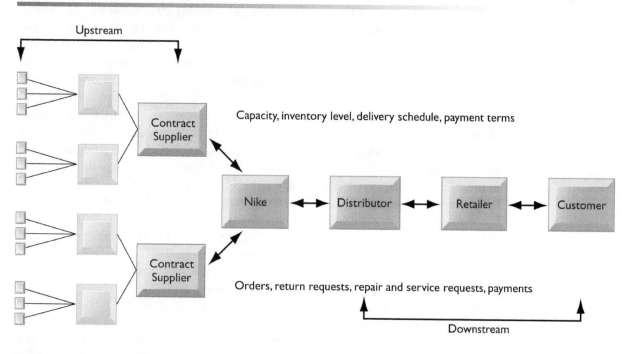

This figure illustrates the major entities in Nike's supply chain and the flow of information upstream and downstream to coordinate the activities involved in buying, making, and moving a product. Shown here is a simplified supply chain, with the upstream portion focusing only on the suppliers for sneakers and sneaker soles.

The supply chain illustrated in Figure 2 only shows two contract manufacturers for sneakers and only the upstream supply chain for sneaker soles. Nike has hundreds of contract manufacturers turning out finished sneakers, socks, and athletic clothing, each with its own set of suppliers. The upstream portion of Nike's supply chain would actually comprise thousands of entities. Nike also has numerous distributors and many thousands of retail stores where its shoes are sold, so the downstream portion of its supply chain is also large and complex.

INFORMATION SYSTEMS AND SUPPLY CHAIN MANAGEMENT

Inefficiencies in the supply chain, such as parts shortages, underutilized plant capacity, excessive finished goods inventory, or high transportation costs, are caused by inaccurate or untimely information. For example, manufacturers may keep too many parts in inventory because they do not know exactly when they will receive their next shipments from their suppliers. Suppliers may order too few raw materials because they do not have precise information on demand. These supply chain inefficiencies waste as much as 25 percent of a company's operating costs.

If a manufacturer had perfect information about exactly how many units of product customers wanted, when they wanted them, and when they could be produced, it would be possible to implement a highly efficient **just-in-time strategy**. Components would arrive exactly at the moment they were needed and finished goods would be shipped as they left the assembly line.

In a supply chain, however, uncertainties arise because many events cannot be foreseen—uncertain product demand, late shipments from suppliers, defective parts or raw materials, or production process breakdowns. To satisfy customers, manufacturers often deal with such uncertainties and unforeseen events by keeping more material or products in inventory than what they think they may actually need. The *safety stock* acts as a buffer for the lack of flexibility in the supply chain. Although excess inventory is expensive, low fill rates are also costly because business may be lost from canceled orders.

One recurring problem in supply chain management is the **bullwhip effect**, in which information about the demand for a product gets distorted as it passes from one entity to the next across the supply chain. A slight rise in demand for an item might cause different members in the supply chain—distributors, manufacturers, suppliers, secondary suppliers (suppliers' suppliers), and tertiary suppliers (suppliers' suppliers' suppliers)—to stockpile inventory so each has enough "just in case." These changes ripple throughout the supply chain, magnifying what started out as a small change from planned orders, creating excess inventory, production, warehousing, and shipping costs (see Figure 3).

For example, Procter & Gamble (P&G) found it had excessively high inventories of its Pampers disposable diapers at various points along its supply chain because of such distorted information. Although customer purchases in stores were fairly stable, orders from distributors would spike when P&G offered aggressive price promotions. Pampers and Pampers' components accumulated in warehouses along the supply chain to meet demand that did not actually exist. To eliminate this problem, P&G revised its marketing, sales, and supply chain processes and used more accurate demand forecasting

The bullwhip is tamed by reducing uncertainties about demand and supply when all members of the supply chain have accurate and up-to-date information. If all supply chain members share dynamic information about inventory

FIGURE 3   **THE BULLWHIP EFFECT**

Inaccurate information can cause minor fluctuations in demand for a product to be amplified as one moves further back in the supply chain. Minor fluctuations in retail sales for a product can create excess inventory for distributors, manufacturers, and suppliers.

levels, schedules, forecasts, and shipments, they have more precise knowledge about how to adjust their sourcing, manufacturing, and distribution plans. Supply chain management systems provide the kind of information that helps members of the supply chain make better purchasing and scheduling decisions. Table 2 describes how firms benefit from these systems.

TABLE 2   HOW INFORMATION SYSTEMS FACILITATE SUPPLY CHAIN MANAGEMENT

INFORMATION FROM SUPPLY CHAIN MANAGEMENT SYSTEMS HELPS FIRMS

Decide when and what to produce, store, and move

Rapidly communicate orders

Track the status of orders

Check inventory availability and monitor inventory levels

Reduce inventory, transportation, and warehousing costs

Track shipments

Plan production based on actual customer demand

Rapidly communicate changes in product design

SUPPLY CHAIN MANAGEMENT SOFTWARE

Supply chain software is classified as either software to help businesses plan their supply chains (supply chain planning) or software to help them execute the supply chain steps (supply chain execution). **Supply chain planning systems** enable the firm to model its existing supply chain, generate demand forecasts for products, and develop optimal sourcing and manufacturing plans. Such systems help companies make better decisions such as determining how much of a specific product to manufacture in a given time period; establishing inventory levels for raw materials, intermediate products, and finished goods; determining where to store finished goods; and identifying the transportation mode to use for product delivery.

For example, if a large customer places a larger order than usual or changes that order on short notice, it can have a widespread impact throughout the supply chain. Additional raw materials or a different mix of raw materials may need to be ordered from suppliers. Manufacturing may have to change job scheduling. A transportation carrier may have to reschedule deliveries. Supply chain planning software makes the necessary adjustments to production and distribution plans. Information about changes is shared among the relevant supply chain members so that their work can be coordinated. One of the most important—and complex—supply chain planning functions is **demand planning**, which determines how much product a business needs to make to satisfy all of its customers' demands. Manugistics and i2 Technologies (both acquired by JDA Software) are major supply chain management software vendors, and enterprise software vendors SAP and Oracle-PeopleSoft offer supply chain management modules.

Whirlpool Corporation, which produces washing; machines, dryers, refrigerators, ovens, and other home appliances, uses supply chain planning systems to make sure what it produces matches customer demand. The company uses supply chain planning software from i2 Technologies, which includes modules for master scheduling, deployment planning, and inventory planning. Whirlpool also installed i2's Web-based tool for Collaborative Planning, Forecasting, and Replenishment (CPFR) for sharing and combining its sales forecasts with those of its major sales partners. Improvements in supply chain planning combined with new state-of-the-art distribution centers helped Whirlpool increase availability of products in stock when customers needed them to 97 percent, while reducing the number of excess finished goods in inventory by 20 percent and forecasting errors by 50 percent (Barrett, 2009).

Supply chain execution systems manage the flow of products through distribution centers and warehouses to ensure that products are delivered to the right locations in the most efficient manner. They track the physical status of goods, the management of materials, warehouse and transportation operations, and financial information involving all parties. Haworth Incorporated's Warehouse Management System (WMS) is an example. Haworth is a world-leading manufacturer and designer of office furniture, with distribution centers in four different states. The WMS tracks and controls the flow of finished goods from Haworth's distribution centers to its customers. Acting on shipping plans for customer orders, the WMS directs the movement of goods based on immediate conditions for space, equipment, inventory, and personnel.

The Interactive Session on Organizations describes how supply chain management software improved decision making and operational performance at Southwest Airlines. This company maintains a competitive edge by combining superb customer service with low costs. Effectively managing its parts inventory is crucial to achieving these goals.

INTERACTIVE SESSION: ORGANIZATIONS

SOUTHWEST AIRLINES TAKES OFF WITH BETTER SUPPLY CHAIN MANAGEMENT

"Weather at our destination is 50 degrees with some broken clouds, but they'll try to have them fixed before we arrive. Thank you, and remember, nobody loves you or your money more than Southwest Airlines."

Crew humor at 30,000 feet? Must be Southwest Airlines. The company is the largest low-fare, high-frequency, point-to-point airline in the world, and largest overall measured by number of passengers per year. Founded in 1971 with four planes serving three cities, the company now operates over 500 air-craft in 68 cities, and has revenues of $10.1 billion. Southwest has the best customer service record among major airlines, the lowest cost structure, and the lowest and simplest fares. The stock symbol is LUV (for Dallas's Love Field where the company is headquartered), but love is the major theme of Southwest's employee and customer relationships. The company has made a profit every year since 1973, one of the few airlines that can make that claim.

Despite a freewheeling, innovative corporate culture, even Southwest needs to get serious about its information systems to maintain profitability. Southwest is just like any other company that needs to manage its supply chain and inventory efficiently. The airline's success has led to continued expansion, and as the company has grown, its legacy informa-tion systems have been unable to keep up with the increasingly large amount of data being generated.

One of the biggest problems with Southwest's legacy systems was lack of information visibility. Often, the data that Southwest's managers needed were safely stored on their systems but weren't "visible", or readily available for viewing or use in other systems. Information about what replacement parts were available at a given time was difficult or impossible to acquire, and that affected response times for everything from mechanical problems to part fulfillment.

For Southwest, which prides itself on its excellent customer service, getting passengers from one location to another with minimal delay is critically important. Repairing aircraft quickly is an important part of accomplishing that goal. The company had $325 million in service parts inventory, so any solution that more efficiently handled that inventory

and reduced aircraft groundings would have a strong impact on the airline's bottom line. Richard Zimmerman, Southwest's manager of inventory management, stated that "there's a significant cost when we have to ground aircraft because we ran out of a part. The long-term, cost-effective way to solve that problem was to increase productivity and to ensure that our maintenance crews were supported with the right spare parts, through the right software application."

Southwest's management started looking for a better inventory management solution, and a ven-dor that was capable of working within the airline's unique corporate culture. After an extensive search, Southwest eventually chose i2 Technologies, a leading supply chain management software and services company that was recently purchased by JDA Software. Southwest implemented the i2 Demand Planner, i2 Service Parts Planner, and i2 Service Budget Optimizer to overhaul its supply chain management and improve data visibility.

I2 Demand Planner improves Southwest's forecasts for all of the part location combinations in its system, and provides better visibility into demand for each part. Planners are able to differen-tiate among individual parts based on criticality and other dimensions such as demand volume, demand variability, and dollar usage. I2 Service Parts Planner helps Southwest replenish its store of parts and ensures that "the right parts are in the right location at the right time." The software can recommend the best mix of parts for each location that will satisfy the customer service requirements of that location at the lowest cost. If excess inventory builds up in certain service locations, the software will recom-mend the most cost-efficient way to transfer that excess inventory to locations with parts deficits. I2 Service Budget Optimizer helps Southwest use its historical data of parts usage to generate forecasts of future parts usage.

Together, these solutions gather data from Southwest's legacy systems and provide useful information to Southwest's managers. Most impor-tantly, Southwest can recognize demand shortages before they become problems, thanks to the visibil-ity provided by i2's solutions. Southwest's managers now have a clear and unobstructed view of all of the data up and down the company's supply chain.

By using what-if analysis, planners can quantify the cost to the company of operating at different levels of service. Zimmerman added that i2 "will help us lower inventory costs and keep our cost per air seat mile down to the lowest in the industry. Also, the solutions will help us ensure that the maintenance team can quickly repair the aircraft so that our customers experience minimal delays." The results of the i2 implementation were

increased availability of parts, increased speed and intelligence of decision making, reduced parts inventory by 15 percent, saving the company over $30 million, and increased service levels from 92 percent prior to the implementation to over 95 percent afterwards.

Sources: Chris Lauer, *Southwest Airlines: Corporations That Changed the World*, Greenwood Press, May 2010; www.i2.com, "Ensuring Optimal Parts Inventory at Southwest Airlines," and "Service Parts Management," accessed April 25, 2010; and www.southwest.com, accessed July 1, 2010.

CASE STUDY QUESTIONS

1. Why is parts inventory management so important at Southwest Airlines? What business processes are affected by the airline's ability or inability to have required parts on hand?

2. Why management, organization, and technology factors were responsible for Southwest's problems with inventory management?

3. How did implementing the i2 software change the way Southwest ran its business?

4. Describe two decisions that were improved by implementing the i2 system.

MIS IN ACTION

Visit i2's site (www.i2.com) and learn more about some of the other companies using its software. Pick one of these companies, then answer the following questions:

1. What problem did the company need to address with i2's software?

2. Why did the company select i2 as its software vendor?

3. What were the gains that the company realized as a result of the software implementation?

GLOBAL SUPPLY CHAINS AND THE INTERNET

Before the Internet, supply chain coordination was hampered by the difficulties of making information flow smoothly among disparate internal supply chain systems for purchasing, materials management, manufacturing, and distribution. It was also difficult to share information with external supply chain partners because the systems of suppliers, distributors, or logistics providers were based on incompatible technology platforms and standards. Enterprise and supply chain management systems enhanced with Internet technology supply some of this integration.

A manager will use a Web interface to tap into suppliers' systems to determine whether inventory and production capabilities match demand for the firm's products. Business partners will use Web-based supply chain management tools to collaborate online on forecasts. Sales representatives will access suppliers' production schedules and logistics information to monitor customers' order status.

Global Supply Chain Issues

More and more companies are entering international markets, outsourcing manufacturing operations, and obtaining supplies from other countries as well as selling abroad. Their supply chains extend across multiple countries and regions. There are additional complexities and challenges to managing a global supply chain.

Global supply chains typically span greater geographic distances and time differences than domestic supply chains and have participants from a number of different countries. Although the purchase price of many goods might be lower abroad, there are often additional costs for transportation, inventory (the need for a larger buffer of safety stock), and local taxes or fees. Performance standards may vary from region to region or from nation to nation. Supply chain management may need to reflect foreign government regulations and cultural differences. All of these factors impact how a company takes orders, plans distribution, sizes warehousing, and manages inbound and outbound logistics throughout the global markets it services.

The Internet helps companies manage many aspects of their global supply chains, including sourcing, transportation, communications, and international finance. Today's apparel industry, for example, relies heavily on outsourcing to contract manufacturers in China and other low-wage countries. Apparel companies are starting to use the Web to manage their global supply chain and production issues.

For example, Koret of California, a subsidiary of apparel maker Kellwood Co., uses e-SPS Web-based software to gain end-to-end visibility into its entire global supply chain. E-SPS features Web-based software for sourcing, work-in-progress tracking, production routing, product-development tracking, problem identification and collaboration, delivery-date projections, and production-related inquiries and reports.

As goods are being sourced, produced, and shipped, communication is required among retailers, manufacturers, contractors, agents, and logistics providers. Many, especially smaller companies, still share product information over the phone, via e-mail, or through faxes. These methods slow down the supply chain and also increase errors and uncertainty. With e-SPS, all supply chain members communicate through a Web-based system. If one of Koret's vendors makes a change in the status of a product, everyone in the supply chain sees the change.

In addition to contract manufacturing, globalization has encouraged outsourcing warehouse management, transportation management, and related operations to third-party logistics providers, such as UPS Supply Chain Solutions and Schneider Logistics Services. These logistics services offer Web-based software to give their customers a better view of their global supply chains. Customers are able to check a secure Web site to monitor inventory and shipments, helping them run their global supply chains more efficiently.

Demand-Driven Supply Chains: From Push to Pull Manufacturing and Efficient Customer Response

In addition to reducing costs, supply chain management systems facilitate efficient customer response, enabling the workings of the business to be driven more by customer demand.

Earlier supply chain management systems were driven by a push-based model (also known as build-to-stock). In a **push-based model**, production master schedules are based on forecasts or best guesses of demand for products, and products are "pushed" to customers. With new flows of information made possible by Web-based tools, supply chain management more easily follows a pull-based model. In a **pull-based model**, also known as a demand-driven model or build-to-order, actual customer orders or purchases trigger events in the supply chain. Transactions to produce and deliver only what customers have ordered move up the supply chain from retailers to distributors to manufacturers and eventually to suppliers. Only products to fulfill these orders move back down the supply chain to the retailer. Manufacturers use only actual order demand information to drive their production schedules and the procurement of components or raw materials, as illustrated in Figure 4. Walmart's continuous replenishment system is an example of the pull-based model.

The Internet and Internet technology make it possible to move from sequential supply chains, where information and materials flow sequentially from company to company, to concurrent supply chains, where information flows in many directions simultaneously among members of a supply chain network. Complex supply networks of manufacturers, logistics suppliers, outsourced manufacturers, retailers, and distributors are able to adjust immediately to changes in schedules or orders. Ultimately, the Internet could create a "digital logistics nervous system" throughout the supply chain (see Figure 5).

BUSINESS VALUE OF SUPPLY CHAIN MANAGEMENT SYSTEMS

You have just seen how supply chain management systems enable firms to streamline both their internal and external supply chain processes and provide management with more accurate information about what to produce, store, and move. By implementing a networked and integrated supply chain management system, companies match supply to demand, reduce inventory levels, improve delivery service, speed product time to market, and use assets more effectively.

Total supply chain costs represent the majority of operating expenses for many businesses and in some industries approach 75 percent of the total operating budget. Reducing supply chain costs may have a major impact on firm profitability.

In addition to reducing costs, supply chain management systems help increase sales. If a product is not available when a customer wants it, customers often try to purchase it from someone else. More precise control of the supply chain enhances the firm's ability to have the right product available for customer purchases at the right time.

FIGURE 4   PUSH- VERSUS PULL-BASED SUPPLY CHAIN MODELS

Push-Based Model

Supplier		Manufacturer		Distributor		Retailer		Customer
Supply to forecast		Production based on forecasts		Inventory based on forecasts		Stock based on forecasts		Purchase what is on shelves

Pull-Based Model

Supplier		Manufacturer		Distributor		Retailer		Customer
Supply to order		Produce to order		Automatically replenish warehouse		Automatically replenish stock		Customer orders

The difference between push- and pull-based models is summarized by the slogan "Make what we sell, not sell what we make."

FIGURE 5   THE FUTURE INTERNET-DRIVEN SUPPLY CHAIN

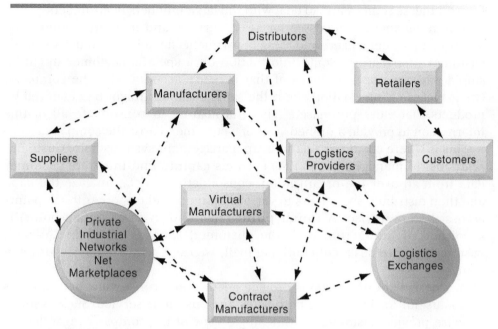

The future Internet-driven supply chain operates like a digital logistics nervous system. It provides multidirectional communication among firms, networks of firms, and e-marketplaces so that entire networks of supply chain partners can immediately adjust inventories, orders, and capacities.

3 CUSTOMER RELATIONSHIP MANAGEMENT SYSTEMS

You've probably heard phrases such as "the customer is always right" or "the customer comes first." Today these words ring more true than ever. Because competitive advantage based on an innovative new product or service is often very short lived, companies are realizing that their only enduring competitive strength may be their relationships with their customers. Some say that the basis of competition has switched from who sells the most products and services to who "owns" the customer, and that customer relationships represent a firm's most valuable asset.

WHAT IS CUSTOMER RELATIONSHIP MANAGEMENT?

What kinds of information would you need to build and nurture strong, long-lasting relationships with customers? You'd want to know exactly who your customers are, how to contact them, whether they are costly to service and sell to, what kinds of products and services they are interested in, and how much money they spend on your company. If you could, you'd want to make sure you knew each of your customers well, as if you were running a small-town store. And you'd want to make your good customers feel special.

In a small business operating in a neighborhood, it is possible for business owners and managers to really know their customers on a personal, face-to-face basis. But in a large business operating on a metropolitan, regional, national, or even global basis, it is impossible to "know your customer" in this intimate way. In these kinds of businesses there are too many customers and too many different ways that customers interact with the firm (over the Web, the phone, fax, and in person). It becomes especially difficult to integrate information from all theses sources and to deal with the large numbers of customers.

A large business's processes for sales, service, and marketing tend to be highly compartmentalized, and these departments do not share much essential customer information. Some information on a specific customer might be stored and organized in terms of that person's account with the company. Other pieces of information about the same customer might be organized by products that were purchased. There is no way to consolidate all of this information to provide a unified view of a customer across the company.

This is where customer relationship management systems help. Customer relationship management (CRM) systems capture and integrate customer data from all over the organization, consolidate the data, analyze the data, and then distribute the results to various systems and customer touch points across the enterprise. A **touch point** (also known as a contact point) is a method of interaction with the customer, such as telephone, e-mail, customer service desk, conventional mail, Web site, wireless device, or retail store.

Well-designed CRM systems provide a single enterprise view of customers that is useful for improving both sales and customer service. Such systems likewise provide customers with a single view of the company regardless of what touch point the customer uses (see Figure 6).

Good CRM systems provide data and analytical tools for answering questions such as these: "What is the value of a particular customer to the firm over his or her lifetime?" "Who are our most loyal customers?" (It can cost six times more to sell to a new customer than to an existing customer.) "Who are our most profitable customers?" and "What do these profitable customers want to buy?" Firms use the answers to these questions to acquire new customers, provide better service and support to existing customers, customize their offerings more precisely to customer preferences, and provide ongoing value to retain profitable customers.

FIGURE 6   CUSTOMER RELATIONSHIP MANAGEMENT (CRM)

CRM systems examine customers from a multifaceted perspective. These systems use a set of integrated applications to address all aspects of the customer relationship, including customer service, sales, and marketing.

CUSTOMER RELATIONSHIP MANAGEMENT SOFTWARE

Commercial CRM software packages range from niche tools that perform limited functions, such as personalizing Web sites for specific customers, to large-scale enterprise applications that capture myriad interactions with customers, analyze them with sophisticated reporting tools, and link to other major enterprise applications, such as supply chain management and enterprise systems. The more comprehensive CRM packages contain modules for **partner relationship management (PRM)** and **employee relationship management (ERM)**.

PRM uses many of the same data, tools, and systems as customer relationship management to enhance collaboration between a company and its selling partners. If a company does not sell directly to customers but rather works through distributors or retailers, PRM helps these channels sell to customers directly. It provides a company and its selling partners with the ability to trade information and distribute leads and data about customers, integrating lead generation, pricing, promotions, order configurations, and availability. It also provides a firm with tools to assess its partners' performances so it can make sure its best partners receive the support they need to close more business.

ERM software deals with employee issues that are closely related to CRM, such as setting objectives, employee performance management, performance-based compensation, and employee training. Major CRM application software vendors include Oracle-owned Siebel Systems and PeopleSoft, SAP, Salesforce.com, and Microsoft Dynamics CRM.

Customer relationship management systems typically provide software and online tools for sales, customer service, and marketing. We briefly describe some of these capabilities.

Sales Force Automation (SFA)

Sales force automation modules in CRM systems help sales staff increase their productivity by focusing sales efforts on the most profitable customers, those who are good candidates for sales and services. CRM systems provide sales prospect and contact information, product information, product configuration capabilities, and sales quote generation capabilities. Such software can assemble information about a particular customer's past purchases to help the salesperson make personalized recommendations. CRM software enables sales, marketing, and delivery departments to easily share customer and prospect information. It increases each salesperson's efficiency in reducing the cost per sale as well as the cost of acquiring new customers and retaining old ones. CRM software also has capabilities for sales forecasting, territory management, and team selling.

Customer Service

Customer service modules in CRM systems provide information and tools to increase the efficiency of call centers, help desks, and customer support staff. They have capabilities for assigning and managing customer service requests.

One such capability is an appointment or advice telephone line: When a customer calls a standard phone number, the system routes the call to the correct service person, who inputs information about that customer into the system only once. Once the customer's data are in the system, any service representative can handle the customer relationship. Improved access to consistent and accurate customer information help call centers handle more calls per day and decrease the duration of each call. Thus, call centers and customer service groups achieve greater productivity, reduced transaction time, and higher quality of service at lower cost. The customer is happier because he or she spends less time on the phone restating his or her problem to customer service representatives.

CRM systems may also include Web-based self-service capabilities: The company Web site can be set up to provide inquiring customers personalized support information as well as the option to contact customer service staff by phone for additional assistance.

Marketing

CRM systems support direct-marketing campaigns by providing capabilities for capturing prospect and customer data, for providing product and service information, for qualifying leads for targeted marketing, and for scheduling and tracking direct-marketing mailings or e-mail (see Figure 7). Marketing modules also include tools for analyzing marketing and customer data, identifying profitable and unprofitable customers, designing products and services to satisfy specific customer needs and interests, and identifying opportunities for cross-selling.

Cross-selling is the marketing of complementary products to customers. (For example, in financial services, a customer with a checking account might be sold a money market account or a home improvement loan.) CRM tools also help firms manage and execute marketing campaigns at all stages, from planning to determining the rate of success for each campaign.

Figure 8 illustrates the most important capabilities for sales, service, and marketing processes that would be found in major CRM software products. Like enterprise software, this software is business-process driven, incorporating hundreds of business processes thought to represent best practices in each of these areas. To achieve maximum benefit, companies need to revise and model their business processes to conform to the best-practice business processes in the CRM software.

Figure 9 illustrates how a best practice for increasing customer loyalty through customer service might be modeled by CRM software. Directly

FIGURE 7   HOW CRM SYSTEMS SUPPORT MARKETING

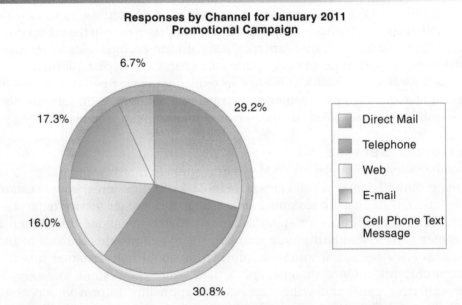

Customer relationship management software provides a single point for users to manage and evaluate marketing campaigns across multiple channels, including e-mail, direct mail, telephone, the Web, and wireless messages.

FIGURE 8   CRM SOFTWARE CAPABILITIES

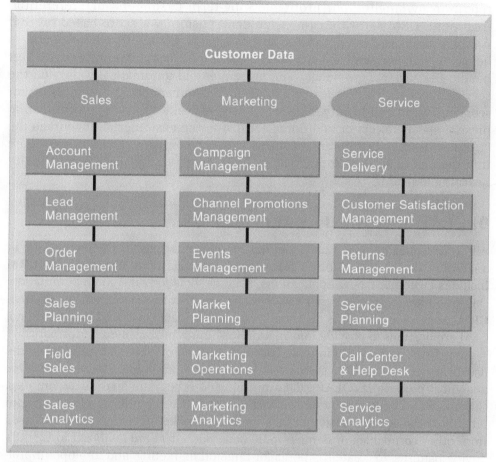

The major CRM software products support business processes in sales, service, and marketing, integrating customer information from many different sources. Included are support for both the operational and analytical aspects of CRM.

FIGURE 9   CUSTOMER LOYALTY MANAGEMENT PROCESS MAP

This process map shows how a best practice for promoting customer loyalty through customer service would be modeled by customer relationship management software. The CRM software helps firms identify high-value customers for preferential treatment.

servicing customers provides firms with opportunities to increase customer retention by singling out profitable long-term customers for preferential treatment. CRM software can assign each customer a score based on that person's value and loyalty to the company and provide that information to help call centers route each customer's service request to agents who can best handle that customer's needs. The system would automatically provide the service agent with a detailed profile of that customer that includes his or her score for value and loyalty. The service agent would use this information to present special offers or additional service to the customer to encourage the customer to keep transacting business with the company. You will find more information on other best-practice business processes in CRM systems in our Learning Tracks.

OPERATIONAL AND ANALYTICAL CRM

All of the applications we have just described support either the operational or analytical aspects of customer relationship management. **Operational CRM** includes customer-facing applications, such as tools for sales force automation, call center and customer service support, and marketing automation. **Analytical CRM** includes applications that analyze customer data generated by operational CRM applications to provide information for improving business performance.

Analytical CRM applications are based on data warehouses that consolidate the data from operational CRM systems and customer touch points for use with online analytical processing (OLAP), data mining, and other data analysis techniques. Customer data collected by the organization might be combined with data from other sources, such as customer lists for direct-marketing campaigns purchased from other companies or demographic data. Such data are analyzed to identify buying patterns, to create segments for targeted marketing, and to pinpoint profitable and unprofitable customers (see Figure 10).

FIGURE 10   ANALYTICAL CRM DATA WAREHOUSE

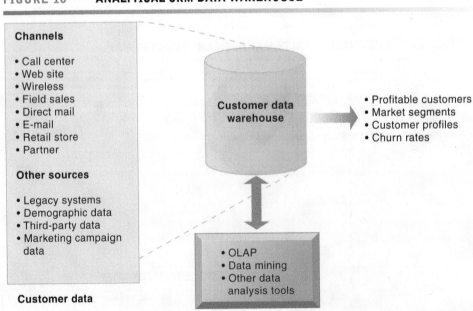

Analytical CRM uses a customer data warehouse and tools to analyze customer data collected from the firm's customer touch points and from other sources.

Another important output of analytical CRM is the customer's lifetime value to the firm. **Customer lifetime value (CLTV)** is based on the relationship between the revenue produced by a specific customer, the expenses incurred in acquiring and servicing that customer, and the expected life of the relationship between the customer and the company.

BUSINESS VALUE OF CUSTOMER RELATIONSHIP MANAGEMENT SYSTEMS

Companies with effective customer relationship management systems realize many benefits, including increased customer satisfaction, reduced direct-marketing costs, more effective marketing, and lower costs for customer acquisition and retention. Information from CRM systems increases sales revenue by identifying the most profitable customers and segments for focused marketing and cross-selling.

Customer churn is reduced as sales, service, and marketing better respond to customer needs. The **churn rate** measures the number of customers who stop using or purchasing products or services from a company. It is an important indicator of the growth or decline of a firm's customer base.

4 ENTERPRISE APPLICATIONS: NEW OPPORTUNITIES AND CHALLENGES

Many firms have implemented enterprise systems and systems for supply chain management and customer relationship because they are such powerful instruments for achieving operational excellence and enhancing decision making. But precisely because they are so powerful in changing the way the organization works, they are challenging to implement. Let's briefly examine some of these challenges, as well as new ways of obtaining value from these systems.

ENTERPRISE APPLICATION CHALLENGES

Promises of dramatic reductions in inventory costs, order-to-delivery time, as well as more efficient customer response and higher product and customer profitability make enterprise systems and systems for supply chain management and customer relationship management very alluring. But to obtain this value, you must clearly understand how your business has to change to use these systems effectively.

Enterprise applications involve complex pieces of software that are very expensive to purchase and implement. It might take a large Fortune 500 company several years to complete a large-scale implementation of an enterprise system or a system for SCM or CRM. The total cost for an average large system implementation based on SAP or Oracle software, including software, database tools, consulting fees, personnel costs, training, and perhaps hardware costs, runs over $12 million. The implementation cost of a enterprise system for a small or mid-sized company based on software from a "Tier II" vendor such as Epicor or Lawson averages $3.5 million. (Wailgum, 2009).

Enterprise applications require not only deep-seated technological changes but also fundamental changes in the way the business operates. Companies must make sweeping changes to their business processes to work with the software. Employees must accept new job functions and responsibilities. They must learn how to perform a new set of work activities and understand how the information they enter into the system can affect other parts of the company. This requires new organizational learning.

Supply chain management systems require multiple organizations to share information and business processes. Each participant in the system may have to change some of its processes and the way it uses information to create a system that best serves the supply chain as a whole.

Some firms experienced enormous operating problems and losses when they first implemented enterprise applications because they didn't understand how much organizational change was required. For example, Kmart had trouble getting products to store shelves when it first implemented i2 Technologies supply chain management software in July 2000. The i2 software did not work well with Kmart's promotion-driven business model, which created sharp spikes in drops in demand for products. Overstock.com's order tracking system went down for a full week in October 2005 when the company replaced a home-grown system with an Oracle enterprise system. The company rushed to implement the software, and did not properly synchronize the Oracle software's process for recording customer refunds with its accounts receivable system. These problems contributed to a third-quarter loss of $14.5 million that year.

Enterprise applications also introduce "switching costs." Once you adopt an enterprise application from a single vendor, such as SAP, Oracle, or others, it is very costly to switch vendors, and your firm becomes dependent on the vendor to upgrade its product and maintain your installation.

Enterprise applications are based on organization-wide definitions of data. You'll need to understand exactly how your business uses its data and how the data would be organized in a customer relationship management, supply chain management, or enterprise system. CRM systems typically require some data cleansing work.

Enterprise software vendors are addressing these problems by offering pared-down versions of their software and "fast-start" programs for small and medium-sized businesses and best-practice guidelines for larger companies. Our Interactive Session on Technology describes how on-demand and cloud-based tools deal with this problem as well.

Companies adopting enterprise applications can also save time and money by keeping customizations to the minimum. For example, Kennametal, a $2 billion metal-cutting tools company in Pennsylvania, had spent $10 million over 13 years maintaining an ERP system with over 6,400 customizations. The company is now replacing it with a "plain vanilla," non-customized-version of SAP enterprise software and changing its business processes to conform to the software (Johnson, 2010).

NEXT-GENERATION ENTERPRISE APPLICATIONS

Today, enterprise application vendors are delivering more value by becoming more flexible, Web-enabled, and capable of integration with other systems. Standalone enterprise systems, customer relationship systems, and supply chain management systems are becoming a thing of the past.

The major enterprise software vendors have created what they call *enterprise solutions*, *enterprise suites*, or *e-business suites* to make their customer relationship management, supply chain management, and enterprise systems work closely with each other, and link to systems of customers and suppliers. SAP Business Suite, Oracle's e-Business Suite, and Microsoft's Dynamics suite (aimed at mid-sized companies) are examples, and they now utilize Web services and service-oriented architecture.

SAP's next-generation enterprise applications are based on its enterprise service-oriented architecture. It incorporates service-oriented architecture (SOA) standards and uses its NetWeaver tool as an integration platform linking SAP's own applications and Web services developed by independent software vendors. The goal is to make enterprise applications easier to implement and manage.

For example, the current version of SAP enterprise software combines key applications in finance, logistics and procurement, and human resources administration into a core ERP component. Businesses then extend these applications by linking to function-specific Web services such as employee recruiting or collections management provided by SAP and other vendors. SAP provides over 500 Web services through its Web site.

Oracle also has included SOA and business process management capabilities into its Fusion middleware products. Businesses can use Oracle tools to customize Oracle's applications without breaking the entire application.

Next-generation enterprise applications also include open source and on-demand solutions. Compared to commercial enterprise application software, open source products such as Compiere, Apache Open for Business (OFBiz), and Openbravo are not as mature, nor do they include as much support. However, companies such as small manufacturers are choosing this option because there are no software licensing fees and fees are based on usage. (Support and customization for open source products cost extra.)

SAP now offers an on-demand enterprise software solution called Business ByDesign for small and medium-sized businesses in select countries. For large businesses, SAP's on-site software is the only version available. SAP is, however, hosting function-specific applications (such as e-sourcing and expense management) available by subscription that integrate with customers' on-site SAP Business Suite systems.

The most explosive growth in software as a service (SaaS) offerings has been for customer relationship management. Salesforce.com has been the leader in hosted CRM solutions, but Oracle and SAP have also developed SaaS capabilities. SaaS and cloud-based versions of enterprise systems are starting to be offered by vendors such as NetSuite and Plex Online. Compiere sells both cloud and on-premise versions of its ERP systems. Use of cloud-based enterprise applications is starting to take off, as discussed in the Interactive Session on Technology.

The major enterprise application vendors also offer portions of their products that work on mobile handhelds. You can find out more about this topic in our Learning Track on Wireless Applications for Customer Relationship Management, Supply Chain Management, and Healthcare.

Salesforce.com and Oracle have added Web 2.0 capabilities that enable organizations to identify new ideas more rapidly, improve team productivity, and deepen interactions with customers. For example, Salesforce Ideas enables subscribers to harness the "wisdom of crowds" by allowing their customers to submit and discuss new ideas. Dell Computer deployed this technology as Dell IdeaStorm (dellideastorm.com) to encourage its customers to suggest and vote on new concepts and feature changes in Dell products.

INTERACTIVE SESSION: TECHNOLOGY

ENTERPRISE APPLICATIONS MOVE TO THE CLOUD

You've already read about Salesforce.com in this text. It's the most successful enterprise-scale software as a service (SaaS). Until recently, there were few other SaaS enterprise software applications available on the Internet. Today, that's changed, as a growing number of cloud-based enterprise resource planning (ERP) and customer relationship management (CRM) application providers enter this marketspace. While traditional enterprise software vendors like Oracle are using their well-established position to grab a share of the cloud-based application market, newcomers like RightNow, Compiere, and SugarCRM have found success using some different tactics.

Most companies interested in cloud computing are small to midsize and lack the know-how or financial resources to successfully build and maintain ERP and CRM applications in-house. Others are simply looking to cut costs by moving their applications to the cloud. According to the International Data Corporation (IDC), about 3.2 percent of U.S. small businesses, or about 230,000 businesses, use cloud services. Small-business spending on cloud services increased by 36.2 percent in 2010 to $2.4 billion.

Even larger companies have made the switch to the cloud. For example, camera manufacturer Nikon decided to go with a cloud-based solution as it attempted to merge customer data from 25 disparate sources and applications into a single system. Company officials were hoping to eliminate maintenance and administrative costs, but not at the expense of a storage system that met their requirements, was never out of service, and worked perfectly.

Nikon found its solution with RightNow, a cloud-based CRM provider located in Bozeman, Montana. The company was founded in 1997 and has attracted firms intrigued by its customizable applications, impeccable customer service, and robust infrastructure. Prices start at $110 per user per month and the average deployment time is 45 days.

Nikon had been using several different systems to perform business functions, and was struggling to merge customer data located in a variety of legacy systems. While looking for vendors to help implement a Web-based FAQ system to answer customer questions and provide support on the basis of these data, the company came across RightNow. Nikon found that not only did RightNow have the capabil-

ity to implement that system, but it also had an array of other useful services. When Nikon discovered that it could combine outbound e-mail, contact management, and customer records into a single system in RightNow's cloud, it made the move, expecting to receive a solid return on the investment.

What Nikon got was far more than expected: an astonishing 3,200 percent return on investment (ROI), equivalent to a savings of $14 million after three years! The FAQ system reduced the number of incoming calls to Nikon's customer service staff. More customers found the information they needed on the Web, call response times dropped by 50 percent, and incoming e-mail dropped by 70 percent. While Nikon still hosts its SAP ERP system internally due to its complexity, Nikon switched its entire CRM system to RightNow.

Not all companies experience gains of that magnitude, and cloud computing does have drawbacks. Many companies are concerned about maintaining control of their data and security. Although cloud computing companies are prepared to handle these issues, availability assurances and service-level agreements are uncommon. Companies that manage their CRM apps with a cloud infrastructure have no guarantees that their data will be available at all times, or even that the provider will still exist in the future.

Many smaller companies have taken advantage of a new type of cloud computing known as open source cloud computing. Under this model, cloud vendors make the source code of their applications available to their customers and allow them to make any changes they want on their own. This differs from the traditional model, where cloud vendors offer applications which are customizable, but not at the source code level.

For example, Jerry Skaare, president of O-So-Pure (OSP), a manufacturer of ultraviolet water purification systems, selected the Compiere Cloud Edition versions of ERP software hosted on the Amazon EC2 Cloud virtual environment. OSP had long outgrown its existing ERP system and was held back by inefficient, outdated processes in accounting, inventory, manufacturing, and e-commerce. Compiere ERP provides a complete end-to-end ERP solution that automates processes from accounting to purchasing, order fulfillment, manufacturing, and warehousing.

Compiere uses a model-driven platform that stores business logic in an applications dictionary rather than being hard-coded into software programs. Firms using Compiere are able to customize their applications by creating, modifying, or deleting business logic in the applications dictionary without extensive programming. In contrast to traditional ERP systems that encourage subscribers to modify their business processes to conform to the software, Compiere encourages its subscribers to customize its system to match their unique business needs.

The fact that the Compiere software is open source also makes it easier for users to modify. OSP was attracted to this feature, along with the robust functionality, scalability, and low cost, of the Compiere ERP Cloud Edition. Skaare said that he was comfortable that "the little idiosyncrasies of my company" could be handled by the software. Though Skaare is unlikely to make any changes himself, it's important for him to know that his staff has the option to tweak OSP's ERP applications. Open source cloud computing provides companies that flexibility.

Not to be outdone, established CRM companies like Oracle have moved into SaaS. Pricing starts at $70 per month per user. Oracle may have an edge because its CRM system has so many capabilities and includes embedded tools for forecasting and analytics, including interactive dashboards. Subscribers are able to use these tools to answer questions such as "How efficient is your sales effort?" or "How much are your customers spending?"

Bryant & Stratton College, a pioneer in career education, used Oracle CRM On Demand to create more successful marketing campaigns. Bryant & Stratton analyzed past campaigns for tech-savvy recent high school graduates, as well as older, non-traditional students returning to school later in life. Oracle CRM On Demand tracked advertising to prospective students and determined accurate costs for each lead, admissions application, and registered attending student. This information helped the school determine the true value of each type of marketing program.

Sources: Marta Bright, "Know Who. Know How." *Oracle Magazine*, January/February 2010; Brad Stone, "Companies Slowly Join Cloud-Computing," *The New York Times*, April 28, 2010; and Esther Shein, "Open-source CRM and ERP: New Kids on the Cloud," *Computerworld*, October 30, 2009.

CASE STUDY QUESTIONS

1. What types of companies are most likely to adopt cloud-based ERP and CRM software services? Why? What companies might not be well-suited for this type of software?

2. What are the advantages and disadvantages of using cloud-based enterprise applications?

3. What management, organization, and technology issues should be addressed in deciding whether to use a conventional ERP or CRM system versus a cloud-based version?

MIS IN ACTION

Visit the Web site of RightNow, Compiere, or another competing company offering a cloud-based version of ERP or CRM. Then answer the following questions:

1. What kinds of open source offerings does the company have, if any? Describe some of the features.

2. Toward what types of companies is the company marketing its services?

3. What other services does the company offer?

Enterprise application vendors have also beefed up their business intelligence features to help managers obtain more meaningful information from the massive amounts of data generated by these systems. Rather than requiring users to leave an application and launch separate reporting and analytics tools, the vendors are starting to embed analytics within the context of the application itself. They are also offering complementary analytics products, such as SAP Business Objects and Oracle Business Intelligence Enterprise Edition.

Service Platforms

Another way of extending enterprise applications is to use them to create service platforms for new or improved business processes that integrate information from multiple functional areas. These enterprise-wide service platforms provide a greater degree of cross-functional integration than the traditional enterprise applications. A **service platform** integrates multiple applications from multiple business functions, business units, or business partners to deliver a seamless experience for the customer, employee, manager, or business partner.

For instance, the order-to-cash process involves receiving an order and seeing it all the way through obtaining payment for the order. This process begins with lead generation, marketing campaigns, and order entry, which are typically supported by CRM systems. Once the order is received, manufacturing is scheduled and parts availability is verified—processes that are usually supported by enterprise software. The order then is handled by processes for distribution planning, warehousing, order fulfillment, and shipping, which are usually supported by supply chain management systems. Finally, the order is billed to the customer, which is handled by either enterprise financial applications or accounts receivable. If the purchase at some point required customer service, customer relationship management systems would again be invoked.

A service such as order-to-cash requires data from enterprise applications and financial systems to be further integrated into an enterprise-wide composite process. To accomplish this, firms need software tools that use existing applications as building blocks for new cross-enterprise processes (see Figure 11). Enterprise application vendors provide middleware and tools that use XML and Web services for integrating enterprise applications with older legacy applications and systems from other vendors.

FIGURE 11   ORDER-TO-CASH SERVICE

Order-to-cash is a composite process that integrates data from individual enterprise systems and legacy financial applications. The process must be modeled and translated into a software system using application integration tools.

Increasingly, these new services will be delivered through portals. Portal software can integrate information from enterprise applications and disparate in-house legacy systems, presenting it to users through a Web interface so that the information appears to be coming from a single source. For example, Valero Energy, North America's largest refiner, used SAP NetWeaver Portal to create a service for wholesale clients to view their account information all at once. SAP NetWeaver Portal provides an interface to clients' invoice, price, electronic funds, and credit card transaction data stored in SAP's customer relationship management system data warehouse as well as in non-SAP systems.

5   HANDS-ON MIS PROJECTS

The projects in this section give you hands-on experience analyzing business process integration, suggesting supply chain management and customer relationship management applications, using database software to manage customer service requests, and evaluating supply chain management business services.

Management Decision Problems

1. Toronto-based Mercedes-Benz Canada, with a network of 55 dealers, did not know enough about its customers. Dealers provided customer data to the company on an ad hoc basis. Mercedes did not force dealers to report this information, and its process for tracking dealers that failed to report was cumbersome. There was no real incentive for dealers to share information with the company. How could CRM and partner relationship management (PRM) systems help solve this problem?

2. Office Depot sells a wide range of office products and services in the United States and internationally, including general office supplies, computer supplies, business machines (and related supplies), and office furniture. The company tries to offer a wider range of office supplies at lower cost than other retailers by using just-in-time replenishment and tight inventory control systems. It uses information from a demand forecasting system and point-of-sale data to replenish its inventory in its 1,600 retail stores. Explain how these systems help Office Depot minimize costs and any other benefits they provide. Identify and describe other supply chain management applications that would be especially helpful to Office Depot.

Improving Decision Making: Using Database Software to Manage Customer Service Requests

Software skills: Database design; querying and reporting
Business skills: Customer service analysis

In this exercise, you'll use database software to develop an application that tracks customer service requests and analyzes customer data to identify customers meriting priority treatment.

Prime Service is a large service company that provides maintenance and repair services for close to 1,200 commercial businesses in New York, New Jersey, and Connecticut. Its customers include businesses of all sizes. Customers with service needs call into its customer service department with requests for repairing heating ducts, broken windows, leaky roofs, broken water pipes, and other problems. The company assigns each request a number and

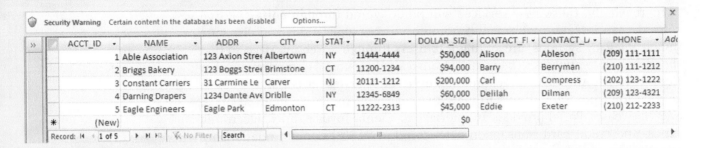

writes down the service request number, identification number of the customer account, the date of the request, the type of equipment requiring repair, and a brief description of the problem. The service requests are handled on a first-come-first-served basis. After the service work has been completed, Prime calculates the cost of the work, enters the price on the service request form, and bills the client.

Management is not happy with this arrangement because the most important and profitable clients—those with accounts of more than $70,000—are treated no differently from its clients with small accounts. It would like to find a way to provide its best customers with better service. Management would also like to know which types of service problems occur most frequently so that it can make sure it has adequate resources to address them.

Prime Service has a small database with client account information, which can be found in MyMISLab. A sample is shown above, but the Web site may have a more recent version of this database for this exercise. The database table includes fields for the account ID, company (account) name, street address, city, state, ZIP code, account size (in dollars), contact last name, contact first name, and contact telephone number. The contact is the name of the person in each company who is responsible for contacting Prime about maintenance and repair work.

Use your database software to design a solution that would enable Prime's customer service representatives to identify the most important customers so that they could receive priority service. Your solution will require more than one table. Populate your database with at least 15 service requests. Create several reports that would be of interest to management, such as a list of the highest—and lowest—priority accounts or a report showing the most frequently occurring service problems. Create a report listing service calls that customer service representatives should respond to first on a specific date.

Achieving Operational Excellence: Evaluating Supply Chain Management Services

Software skills: Web browser and presentation software
Business skills: Evaluating supply chain management services

Trucking companies no longer merely carry goods from one place to another. Some also provide supply chain management services to their customers and help them manage their information. In this project, you'll use the Web to research and evaluate two of these business services.

Investigate the Web sites of two companies, UPS Logistics and Schneider Logistics, to see how these companies' services can be used for supply chain management. Then respond to the following questions:

- What supply chain processes can each of these companies support for their clients?

- How can customers use the Web sites of each company to help them with supply chain management?
- Compare the supply chain management services provided by these companies. Which company would you select to help your firm manage its supply chain? Why?

LEARNING TRACK MODULES

The following Learning Tracks provide content relevant to topics covered in this chapter:

1. SAP Business Process Map
2. Business Processes in Supply Chain Management and Supply Chain Metrics
3. Best-Practice Business Processes in CRM Software

Review Summary

1. *How do enterprise systems help businesses achieve operational excellence?*

   Enterprise software is based on a suite of integrated software modules and a common central database. The database collects data from and feeds the data into numerous applications that can support nearly all of an organization's internal business activities. When new information is entered by one process, the information is made available immediately to other business processes.

   Enterprise systems support organizational centralization by enforcing uniform data standards and business processes throughout the company and a single unified technology platform. The firmwide data generated by enterprise systems helps managers evaluate organizational performance.

2. *How do supply chain management systems coordinate planning, production, and logistics with suppliers?*

   Supply chain management systems automate the flow of information among members of the supply chain so they can use it to make better decisions about when and how much to purchase, produce, or ship. More accurate information from supply chain management systems reduces uncertainty and the impact of the bullwhip effect.

   Supply chain management software includes software for supply chain planning and for supply chain execution. Internet technology facilitates the management of global supply chains by providing the connectivity for organizations in different countries to share supply chain information. Improved communication among supply chain members also facilitates efficient customer response and movement toward a demand-driven model.

3. *How do customer relationship management systems help firms achieve customer intimacy?*

   Customer relationship management (CRM) systems integrate and automate customer-facing processes in sales, marketing, and customer service, providing an enterprise-wide view of customers. Companies can use this knowledge when they interact with customers to provide them with better service or to sell new products and services. These systems also identify profitable or nonprofitable customers or opportunities to reduce the churn rate.

The major customer relationship management software packages provide capabilities for both operational CRM and analytical CRM. They often include modules for managing relationships with selling partners (partner relationship management) and for employee relationship management.

4. *What are the challenges posed by enterprise applications?*

Enterprise applications are difficult to implement. They require extensive organizational change, large new software investments, and careful assessment of how these systems will enhance organizational performance. Enterprise applications cannot provide value if they are implemented atop flawed processes or if firms do not know how to use these systems to measure performance improvements. Employees require training to prepare for new procedures and roles. Attention to data management is essential.

5. *How are enterprise applications used in platforms for new cross-functional services?*

Service platforms integrate data and processes from the various enterprise applications (customer relationship management, supply chain management, and enterprise systems), as well as from disparate legacy applications to create new composite business processes. Web services tie various systems together. The new services are delivered through enterprise portals, which can integrate disparate applications so that information appears to be coming from a single source. Open source, mobile, and cloud versioins of some of these products are becoming available.

Key Terms

Analytical CRM	Operational CRM
Bullwhip effect	Partner relationship management (PRM)
Churn rate	Pull-based model
Cross-selling	Push-based model
Customer lifetime value (CLTV)	Service platform
Demand planning	Supply chain
Employee relationship management (ERM)	Supply chain execution systems
Enterprise software	Supply chain planning systems
Just-in-time strategy	Touch point

Review Questions

1. How do enterprise systems help businesses achieve operational excellence?

- Define an enterprise system and explain how enterprise software works.
- Describe how enterprise systems provide value for a business.

2. How do supply chain management systems coordinate planning, production, and logistics with suppliers?

- Define a supply chain and identify each of its components.
- Explain how supply chain management systems help reduce the bullwhip effect and how they provide value for a business.
- Define and compare supply chain planning systems and supply chain execution systems.
- Describe the challenges of global supply chains and how Internet technology can help companies manage them better.

- Distinguish between a push-based and pull-based model of supply chain management and explain how contemporary supply chain management systems facilitate a pull-based model.

3. How do customer relationship management systems help firms achieve customer intimacy?

- Define customer relationship management and explain why customer relationships are so important today.
- Describe how partner relationship management (PRM) and employee relationship management (ERM) are related to customer relationship management (CRM).
- Describe the tools and capabilities of customer relationship management software for sales, marketing, and customer service.

- Distinguish between operational and analytical CRM.

4. What are the challenges posed by enterprise applications?

- List and describe the challenges posed by enterprise applications.
- Explain how these challenges can be addressed.

5. How are enterprise applications used in platforms for new cross-functional services?

- Define a service platform and describe the tools for integrating data from enterprise applications.
- How are enterprise applications taking advantage of cloud computing, wireless technology, Web 2.0, and open source technology?

Discussion Questions

1. Supply chain management is less about managing the physical movement of goods and more about managing information. Discuss the implications of this statement.

2. If a company wants to implement an enterprise application, it had better do its homework. Discuss the implications of this statement.

3. Which enterprise application should a business install first: ERP, SCM, or CRM? Explain your answer.

Video Cases

Video Cases and Instructional Videos illustrating some of the concepts in this chapter are available. Contact your instructor to access these videos.

Collaboration and Teamwork: Analyzing Enterprise Application Vendors

With a group of three or four students, use the Web to research and evaluate the products of two vendors of enterprise application software. You could compare, for example, the SAP and Oracle enterprise systems, the supply chain management systems from i2 and SAP, or the customer relationship management systems of Oracle's Siebel CRM and Salesforce.com. Use what you have learned from these companies' Web sites to compare the software packages you have selected in terms of business functions supported, technology platforms, cost, and ease of use. Which vendor would you select? Why? Would you select the same vendor for a small business as well as a large one? If possible, use Google Sites to post links to Web pages, team communication announcements, and work assignments; to brainstorm; and to work collaboratively on project documents. Try to use Google Docs to develop a presentation of your findings for the class.

Border States Industries Fuels Rapid Growth with ERP
CASE STUDY

Border States Industries Inc., also known as Border States Electric (BSE), is a wholesale distributor for the construction, industrial, utility, and data communications markets. The company is headquartered in Fargo, North Dakota, and has 57 sales offices in states along the U.S. borders with Canada and Mexico as well as in South Dakota, Wisconsin, Iowa, and Missouri. BSE has 1,400 employees and is wholly employee-owned through its employee stock ownership plan. For the fiscal year ending March 31, 2008, BSE earned revenues of over US $880 million.

BSE's goal is to provide customers with what they need whenever they need it, including providing custom services beyond delivery of products. Thus, the company is not only a wholesale distributor but also a provider of supply chain solutions, with extensive service operations such as logistics, job-site trailers, and kitting (packaging individually separate but related items together as one unit). BSE has distribution agreements with more than 9,000 product vendors.

BSE had relied on its own legacy ERP system called Rigel since 1988 to support its core business processes. However, Rigel had been designed exclusively for electrical wholesalers, and by the mid-1990s, the system could not support BSE's new lines of business and extensive growth.

At that point, BSE's management decided to implement a new ERP system and selected the enterprise software from SAP AG. The ERP solution included SAP's modules for sales and distribution, materials management, financials and controlling, and human resources.

BSE initially budgeted $6 million for the new system, with a start date of November 1, 1998. Senior management worked with IBM and SAP consulting to implement the system. Although close involvement of management was one key ingredient in the systems' success, day-to-day operations suffered while managers were working on the project.

BSE also decided to customize the system extensively. It wrote its own software to enable the ERP system to interface automatically with systems from other vendors, including Taxware Systems, Inc., Innovis Inc., and TOPCALL International GmbH. The Taxware system enabled BSE to comply with the sales tax requirements of all the states and municipalities where it conducts business. The Innovis system supported electronic data interchange (EDI) so that BSE could electronically exchange purchase and payment transactions with its suppliers. The TOPCALL system enabled BSE to fax customers and vendors directly from the SAP system.

At the time of this implementation, BSE had no experience with SAP software, and few consultants familiar with the version of the SAP software that BSE was using. Instead of adopting the best-practice business processes embedded in the SAP software, BSE hired consultants to further customize the SAP software to make its new SAP system look like its old Rigel system in certain areas. For example, it tried to make customer invoices resemble the invoices produced by the old Rigel system.

Implementing these changes required so much customization of the SAP software that BSE had to delay the launch date for the new ERP system until February 1, 1999. By that time, continued customization and tuning raised total implementation costs to $9 million (an increase of 50 percent).

Converting and cleansing data from BSE's legacy system took far longer than management had anticipated. The first group of "expert users" were trained too early in the project and had to be retrained when the new system finally went live. BSE never fully tested the system as it would be used in a working production environment before the system actually went live.

For the next five years, BSE continued to use its SAP ERP system successfully as it acquired several small companies and expanded its branch office infrastructure to 24 states. As the business grew further, profits and inventory turns increased. However, the Internet brought about the need for additional changes, as customers sought to transact business with BSE through an e-commerce storefront. BSE automated online credit card processing and special pricing agreements (SPAs) with designated customers. Unfortunately, the existing SAP software did not support these changes, so the company had to process thousands of SPAs manually.

To process a credit card transaction in a branch office, BSE employees had to leave their desks, walk over to a dedicated credit card processing system in the back office, manually enter the credit card numbers, wait for transaction approval, and then return to their workstations to continue processing sales transactions.

In 2004, BSE began upgrading its ERP system to a more recent version of the SAP software. The software included new support for bills of material and kitting, which were not available in the old system. This functionality enabled BSE to provide better support to utility customers because it could prepare kits that could be delivered directly to a site.

This time the company kept customization to a minimum and used the SAP best practices for wholesale distribution embedded in the software. It also replaced TOPCALL with software from Esker for faxing and e-mailing outbound invoices, order acknowledgments, and purchase orders and added capabilities from Vistex Inc. to automate SPA rebate claims processing. BSE processes over 360,000 SPA claims each year, and the Vistex software enabled BSE to reduce rebate fulfillment time to 72 hours and transaction processing time by 63 percent. In the past, it took 15 to 30 days for BSE to receive rebates from vendors.

BSE budgeted $1.6 million and 4.5 months for implementation, which management believed was sufficient for a project of this magnitude. This time there were no problems. The new system went live on its target date and cost only $1.4 million to implement—14 percent below budget.

In late 2006, BSE acquired a large company that was anticipated to increase sales volume by 20 percent each year. This acquisition added 19 new branches to BSE. These new branches were able to run BSE's SAP software within a day after the acquisition had been completed. BSE now tracks 1.5 million unique items with the software.

Since BSE first deployed SAP software in 1998, sales have increased 300 percent, profits have climbed more than 500 percent, 60 percent of accounts payable transactions take place electronically using EDI, and SPA processing has been reduced by 63 percent. The company turns over its inventory more than four times per year. Instead of waiting 15 to 20 days for monthly financial statements, monthly and year-to-date financial results are available within a day after closing the books. Manual work for handling incoming mail, preparing bank deposits, and taking checks physically to the bank has been significantly reduced. Over 60 percent of vendor invoices arrive electronically, which has reduced staff size in accounts payable and the number of transaction errors. Transaction costs are lower.

The number of full-time BSE employees did increase in the information systems area to support the SAP software. BSE had initially expected to have

3 IT staff supporting the system, but needed 8 people when the first ERP implementation went live in 1999 and 11 by 2006 to support additional SAP software and the new acquisition. BSE's information technology (IT) costs rose by approximately $3 million per year after the first SAP implementation. However, sales expanded during the same period, so the increased overhead for the system produced a cost increase of only .5 percent of total sales.

BSE management has pointed out that much of the work that was automated by the ERP systems has been in the accounting department and involved activities that were purely transactional. This has freed up resources for adding more employees who work directly with customers trying to reduce costs and increase sales.

In the past, BSE had maintained much of its data outside its major corporate systems using PC-based Microsoft Access database and Excel spreadsheet software. Management lacked a single company-wide version of corporate data because the data were fragmented into so many different systems. Now the company is standardized on one common platform and the information is always current and available to management. Management can obtain a picture of how the entire business is performing at any moment in time. Since the SAP system makes all of BSE's planning and budgeting data available online, management is able to make better and quicker decisions.

In 2006, Gartner Group Consultants performed an independent evaluation of BSE's ERP implementation. Gartner interviewed top executives and analyzed BSE data on the impact of the ERP system on BSE's business process costs, using costs as a percentage of sales as its final metric for assessing the financial impact of SAP software. Cost categories analyzed included costs of goods sold, overhead and administration, warehousing costs, IT support, and delivery.

Gartner's analysis validated that the SAP software implementation cost from 1998 to 2001 did indeed total $9 million and that this investment was paid back by savings from the new ERP system within 2.5 years. Between 1998 and 2006, the SAP software implemented by BSE produced total savings of $30 million, approximately one-third of BSE's cumulative earnings during the same period. As a percentage of sales, warehouse costs went down 1 percent, delivery costs decreased by .5 percent, and total overhead costs declined by 1.5 percent. Gartner calculated the total return on investment (ROI) for the project between 1998 and 2006 was $3.3 million per year, or 37 percent of the original investment.

BSE is now focusing on providing more support for Internet sales, including online ordering, inventory, order status, and invoice review, all within a SAP software environment. The company implemented SAP NetWeaver Master Data Management to provide tools to manage and maintain catalog data and prepare the data for publication online and in traditional print media. The company is using SAP's Web Dynpro development environment to enable wireless warehouse and inventory management activities to interact with the SAP software. And it is using SAP NetWeaver Business Intelligence software to learn more about customers, their buying habits, and opportunities to cross-sell and upsell products.

Sources: Border States Industries, "Operating System-SAP Software," 2010; Jim Shepherd and Aurelie Cordier, "Wholesale Distributor Uses ERP Solution to Fuel Rapid Growth," AMR Research, 2009; SAP AG, "Border States Industries: SAP Software Empowers Wholesale Distributor," 2008; www.borderstateselectric.com, accessed July 7, 2009; and "Border States (BSE)," 2008 ASUG Impact Award.

CASE STUDY QUESTIONS

1. What problems was Border States Industries encountering as it expanded? What management, organization, and technology factors were responsible for these problems?

2. How easy was it to develop a solution using SAP ERP software? Explain your answer.

3. List and describe the benefits from the SAP software.

4. How much did the new system solution transform the business? Explain your answer.

5. How successful was this solution for BSE? Identify and describe the metrics used to measure the success of the solution.

6. If you had been in charge of SAP's ERP implementations, what would you have done differently?

References

Aeppel, Timothy."'Bullwhip' Hits Firms as Growth Snaps Back." The Wall Street Journal (January 27, 2010).

Barrett, Joe. "Whirlpool Cleans Up Its Delivery Act." The Wall Street Journal (September 24, 2009).

Chickowski, Ericka. "5 ERP Disasters Explained."www.Baselinemag.com, accessed October 8, 2009.

D'Avanzo, Robert, Hans von Lewinski, and Luk N. Van Wassenhove. "The Link between Supply Chain and Financial Performance." Supply Chain Management Review (November 1, 2003).

Davenport, Thomas H. Mission Critical: Realizing the Promise of Enterprise Systems. Boston: Harvard Business School Press (2000).

Ferrer, Jaume, Johan Karlberg, and Jamie Hintlian."Integration: The Key to Global Success." Supply Chain Management Review (March 1, 2007).

Fleisch, Elgar, Hubert Oesterle, and Stephen Powell. "Rapid Implementation of Enterprise Resource Planning Systems." Journal of Organizational Computing and Electronic Commerce 14, no. 2 (2004).

Garber, Randy and Suman Sarkar. "Want a More Flexible Supply Chain?" Supply Chain Management Review (January 1, 2007).

Goodhue, Dale L., Barbara H. Wixom, and Hugh J. Watson. "Realizing Business Benefits through CRM: Hitting the Right Target in the Right Way." MIS Quarterly Executive 1, no. 2 (June 2002).

Greenbaum, Joshiua. "Is ERP Dead? Or Has It Just Gone Underground?" SAP NetWeaver Magazine 3 (2007).

Guinipero, Larry, Robert B. Handfield, and Douglas L. Johansen. "Beyond Buying." The Wall Street Journal (March 10, 2008).

Handfield, Robert B. and Ernest L. Nichols. Supply Chain Redesign: Transforming Supply Chains into Integrated Value Systems. Financial Times Press (2002).

Henschen, Doug. "Salesforce's Facebook Envy Goes Mobile." Information Week (September 13, 2010).

_____ "SAP Tries One Platform for Mobile Devices," Information Week (March 8, 2010).

Hitt, Lorin, D. J. Wu, and Xiaoge Zhou. "Investment in Enterprise Resource Planning: Business Impact and Productivity Measures." Journal of Management Information Systems 19, no. 1 (Summer 2002).

Johnson, Maryfran."What's Happening with ERP Today." CIO (January 27, 2010).

Kalakota, Ravi, and Marcia Robinson. E-Business 2.0. Boston: Addison-Wesley (2001).

_____. Services Blueprint: Roadmap for Execution. Boston: Addison-Wesley (2003).

Kanakamedala, Kishore, Glenn Ramsdell, and Vats Srivatsan. "Getting Supply Chain Software Right." McKinsey Quarterly No. 1 (2003).

Klein, Richard and Arun Rai. "Interfirm Strategic Information Flows in Logistics Supply Chain Relationships. MIS Quarterly 33, No. 4 (December 2009).

Kopczak, Laura Rock, and M. Eric Johnson. "The Supply-Chain Management Effect." MIT Sloan Management Review 44, no. 3 (Spring 2003).

Laudon, Kenneth C. "The Promise and Potential of Enterprise Systems and Industrial Networks." Working paper, The Concours Group. Copyright Kenneth C. Laudon (1999).

Lee, Hau, L., V. Padmanabhan, and Seugin Whang. "The Bullwhip Effect in Supply Chains." Sloan Management Review (Spring 1997).

Lee, Hau. "The Triple-A Supply Chain." Harvard Business Review (October 2004).

Li, Xinxin and Lorin M. Hitt. "Price Effects in Online Product Reviews: An Analytical Model and Empirical Analysis." MIS Quarterly 34, No. 4 (December 2010).

Liang, Huigang, Nilesh Sharaf, Quing Hu, and Yajiong Xue. "Assimilation of Enterprise Systems: The Effect of Institutional Pressures and the Mediating Role of Top Management." MIS Quarterly 31, no. 1 (March 2007).

Malhotra, Arvind, Sanjay Gosain, and Omar A. El Sawy. "Absorptive Capacity Configurations in Supply Chains: Gearing for Partner-Enabled Market Knowledge Creation." MIS Quarterly 29, no. 1 (March 2005).

Oracle Corporation. "Alcoa Implements Oracle Solution 20% below Projected Cost, Eliminates 43 Legacy Systems." www.oracle.com, accessed August 21, 2005.

Rai, Arun, Ravi Patnayakuni, and Nainika Seth. "Firm Performance Impacts of Digitally Enabled Supply Chain Integration Capabilities." MIS Quarterly 30 No. 2 (June 2006).

Ranganathan, C. and Carol V. Brown. "ERP Iinvestments and the Market Value of Firms: Toward an Understanding of Influential ERP Project Variables." Information Systems Research 17, No. 2 (June 2006).

Robey, Daniel, Jeanne W. Ross, and Marie-Claude Boudreau. "Learning to Implement Enterprise Systems: An Exploratory Study of the Dialectics of Change." Journal of Management Information Systems 19, no. 1 (Summer 2002).

Schwartz, Ephraim. "Does ERP Matter-Industry Stalwarts Speak Out." InfoWorld (April 10, 2007).

Scott, Judy E., and Iris Vessey. "Managing Risks in Enterprise Systems Implementations." Communications of the ACM 45, no. 4 (April 2002).

Seldon, Peter B., Cheryl Calvert, and Song Yang. "A Multi-Project Model of Key Factors Affecting Organizational Benefits from Enterprise Systems." MIS Quarterly 34, no. 2 (June 2010).

Strong, Diane M. and Olga Volkoff. "Understanding Organization-Enterprise System Fit: A Path to Theorizing the Information Technology Artifact." MIS Quarterly 34, No.4 (December 2010).

Wailgum, Thomas. "Why ERP Is Still So Hard." CIO (September 9. 2009).

Wailgum, Thomas. "The Future of ERP." Parts I and II. CIO (November 20, 2009).

Wing, George. "Unlocking the Value of ERP." Baseline (January/February 2010).

Chapter 10

E-commerce: Digital Markets, Digital Goods

From Chapter 10 of *Management Information Systems: Managing the Digital Firm*, 12/e. Kenneth C. Laudon, Jane P. Laudon. Copyright © 2012 by Pearson Education. Published by Prentice Hall. All rights reserved.

E-commerce: Digital Markets, Digital Goods

4Food, a new organic burger restaurant in Manhattan, opened its doors with a promise of delicious food. But what's equally delicious are its plans to drive the business using social networking. This restaurant wants to be much more than a place to dine. It wants to be a vast social networking experience.

Inside the restaurant, located at the corner of Madison Avenue and 40th Street, a 240-square-foot monitor constantly streams Twitter tweets, restaurant information, and Foursquare check-ins. Foursquare is a Web and mobile application that allows registered users to connect with friends and update their location information. Points are awarded for "checking in" at selected restaurants, bars, and other sites. Customers see tweets and status updates and reply to them or add their own messages with their cell phones or other mobile devices using 4Food's free Wi-Fi wireless Internet connection.

This restaurant has multiple options for placing an order. You can give your order to a restaurant employee using an iPad, or you can place the order online yourself. Naturally, 4Food has its own Facebook page, which it uses for social marketing. Tagging its Facebook wall makes you eligible to win an iPad. 4Food offered $20 worth of food to whoever was the first to tweet a picture of himself or herself in front of the restaurant's "tag wall"—a wall in the front of the restaurant inviting people to write "tweets" using a Magic Marker. 4Food also uses social networks for hiring and to promote it's "De-Junk NYC" campaign to promote innovative ideas for improving the city.

But what makes 4Food really stand out is its use of crowdsourcing for both marketing and menu development. This restaurant has an online tool for customers to invent their own sandwiches and other dishes and to give their inventions clever names. Every time someone orders an item invented by another customer, the inventor receives a $.25 in-store credit. With 4Food's list of ingredients, millions of combinations are possible.

Some customers will no doubt use their extensive social networks to promote the burgers they invented. Those with hundreds of thousands of followers on social networks could conceivably earn free burgers for the rest of their lives if they constantly promote 4Food. All of these measures create very low- cost incentives for large numbers of customers to actively promote the restaurant. They also generate word-of-mouth "buzz" with minimal expenditure. All it takes is establishing a presence on social networks and rolling out promotions.

Will 4Food be successful? Competing with 20,000 other New York City restaurants won't be easy. But by using social networking technology to forge ties with customers and giving those customers a stake in the success of products, 4Food hopes to have the recipe for a successful business.

Sources: Mike Elgan, "New York Burger Joint Goes Social, Mobile," *Computerworld,* May 31, 2010 and www.4food.com, accessed October 22, 2010.

4Food exemplifies the new face of e-commerce. Selling physical goods on the Internet is still important, but much of the excitement and interest now centers around services and social experiences-connecting with friends and family through social networking; sharing photos, video, and music, and ideas; and using social networking to attract customers and design new products and services. 4Food 's business model relies on mobile technology and social networking tools to attract customers, take orders, promote its brand, and use customer feedback to improve its menu offerings.

The chapter-opening diagram calls attention to important points raised by this case and this chapter. The business challenge facing 4Food is that it needs a way to stand out amid 20,000 other restaurants in New York City. E-commerce and social networking technology introduced new opportunities for linking to customers and for distinguishing products and services. 4Food's management decided to base its business model around social technology, and make social networking part of the dining experience. 4Food uses social networking and mobile technology—including Twitter, Foursquare, and Facebook—to attract customers, to process reservations, to promote its brand image, and to solicit customer feedback for improving its menu offerings. By taking advantage of social networking tools, 4Food is able to differentiate itself from other restaurants and promote the business at a very low cost.

1   E-COMMERCE AND THE INTERNET

Have you ever purchased music over the Web or streamed a movie? Have you ever used the Web to search for information about your sneakers before you bought them in a retail store? If so, you've participated in e-commerce. In 2010, 133 million adult Americans bought something online, as did millions of others worldwide. And although most purchases still take place through traditional channels, e-commerce continues to grow rapidly and to transform the way many companies do business. In 2010, e-commerce represents about 6 percent of all retail sales in the United States, and is growing at 12 percent annually (eMarketer, 2010a).

E-COMMERCE TODAY

E-commerce refers to the use of the Internet and the Web to transact business. More formally, e-commerce is about digitally enabled commercial transactions between and among organizations and individuals. For the most part, this means transactions that occur over the Internet and the Web. Commercial transactions involve the exchange of value (e.g., money) across organizational or individual boundaries in return for products and services.

E-commerce began in 1995 when one of the first Internet portals, Netscape.com, accepted the first ads from major corporations and popularized the idea that the Web could be used as a new medium for advertising and sales. No one envisioned at the time what would turn out to be an exponential growth curve for e-commerce retail sales, which doubled and tripled in the early years. E-commerce grew at double-digit rates until the recession of 2008–2009 when growth slowed to a crawl. In 2009, e-commerce revenues were flat (Figure 1), not bad considering that traditional retail sales were shrinking by 5 percent annually. In fact, e-commerce during the recession was the only stable segment in retail. Some online retailers forged ahead at a record pace: Amazon's 2009 revenues were up 25 percent over 2008 sales. Despite the recession, in 2010, the

FIGURE 1 **THE GROWTH OF E-COMMERCE**

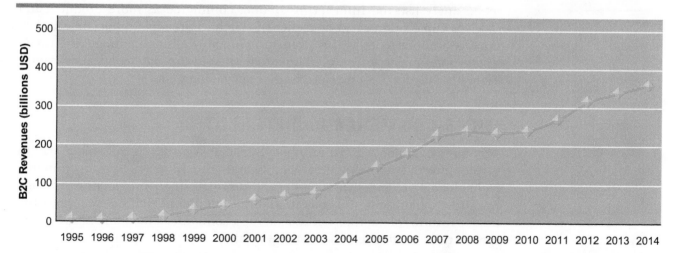

Retail e-commerce revenues grew 15–25 percent per year until the recession of 2008–2009, when they slowed measurably. In 2010, e-commerce revenues are growing again at an estimated 12 percent annually.

number of online buyers increased by 6 percent to 133 million, and the average annual purchase is up 5 percent to $1,139. Amazon's sales grew by 28 percent in the year.

Mirroring the history of many technological innovations, such as the telephone, radio, and television, the very rapid growth in e-commerce in the early years created a market bubble in e-commerce stocks. Like all bubbles, the "dot-com" bubble burst (in March 2001). A large number of e-commerce companies failed during this process. Yet for many others, such as Amazon, eBay, Expedia, and Google, the results have been more positive: soaring revenues, fine-tuned business models that produce profits, and rising stock prices. By 2006, e-commerce revenues returned to solid growth, and have continued to be the fastest growing form of retail trade in the United States, Europe, and Asia.

- Online consumer sales grew to an estimated $225 billion in 2010, an increase of more than 12 percent over 2009 (including travel services and digital downloads), with 133 million people purchasing online and 162 million shopping and gathering information but not necessarily purchasing (eMarketer, 2010a).

- The number of individuals of all ages online in the United States expanded to 221 million in 2010, up from 147 million in 2004. In the world, over 1.9 billion people are now connected to the Internet. Growth in the overall Internet population has spurred growth in e-commerce (eMarketer, 2010b).

- Approximately 80 million households have broadband access to the Internet in 2010, representing about 68 percent of all households.

- About 83 million Americans now access the Internet using a smartphone such as an iPhone, Droid, or BlackBerry. Mobile e-commerce has begun a rapid growth based on apps, ring tones, downloaded entertainment, and location-based services. In a few years, mobile phones will be the most common Internet access device.

- On an average day, an estimated 128 million adult U.S. Internet users go online. About 102 million send e-mail, 81 million use a search engine, and 71 million get news. Around 63 million use a social network, 43 million do online banking, 38 million watch an online video, and 28 million look for information on Wikipedia (Pew Internet & American Life Project, 2010).

- B2B e-commerce-use of the Internet for business-to-business commerce and collaboration among business partners expanded to more than $3.6 trillion.

The e-commerce revolution is still unfolding. Individuals and businesses will increasingly use the Internet to conduct commerce as more products and services come online and households switch to broadband telecommunications. More industries will be transformed by e-commerce, including travel reservations, music and entertainment, news, software, education, and finance. Table 1 highlights these new e-commerce developments.

WHY E-COMMERCE IS DIFFERENT

Why has e-commerce grown so rapidly? The answer lies in the unique nature of the Internet and the Web. Simply put, the Internet and e-commerce technologies are much more rich and powerful than previous technology revolutions like radio, television, and the telephone. Table 2 describes the unique features of the Internet and Web as a commercial medium. Let's explore each of these unique features in more detail.

Ubiquity

In traditional commerce, a marketplace is a physical place, such as a retail store, that you visit to transact business. E-commerce is ubiquitous, meaning

TABLE 1 THE GROWTH OF E-COMMERCE

BUSINESS TRANSFORMATION

- E-commerce remains the fastest growing form of commerce when compared to physical retail stores, services, and entertainment.

- The first wave of e-commerce transformed the business world of books, music, and air travel. In the second wave, nine new industries are facing a similar transformation scenario: marketing and advertising, telecommunications, movies, television, jewelry and luxury goods, real estate, online travel, bill payments, and software.

- The breadth of e-commerce offerings grows, especially in the services economy of social networking, travel, information clearinghouses, entertainment, retail apparel, appliances, and home furnishings.

- The online demographics of shoppers broaden to match that of ordinary shoppers.

- Pure e-commerce business models are refined further to achieve higher levels of profitability, whereas traditional retail brands, such as Sears, JCPenney, L.L.Bean, and Walmart, use e-commerce to retain their dominant retail positions.

- Small businesses and entrepreneurs continue to flood the e-commerce marketplace, often riding on the infrastructures created by industry giants, such as Amazon, Apple, and Google, and increasingly taking advantage of cloud-based computing resources.

- Mobile e-commerce begins to take off in the United States with location-based services and entertainment downloads including e-books.

TECHNOLOGY FOUNDATIONS

- Wireless Internet connections (Wi-Fi, WiMax, and 3G/4G smart phones) grow rapidly.

- Powerful handheld mobile devices support music, Web surfing, and entertainment as well as voice communication. Podcasting and streaming take off as mediums for distribution of video, radio, and user-generated content.

- The Internet broadband foundation becomes stronger in households and businesses as transmission prices fall. More than 80 million households had broadband cable or DSL access to the Internet in 2010 ,about 68 percent of all households in the United States (eMarketer, 2010a).

- Social networking software and sites such as Facebook, MySpace, Twitter, LinkedIn, and thousands of others become a major new platform for e-commerce, marketing, and advertising. Facebook hits 500 million users worldwide, and 180 million in the United States (comScore, 2010).

- New Internet-based models of computing, such as cloud computing, software as a service (SaaS), and Web 2.0 software greatly reduce the cost of e-commerce Web sites.

NEW BUSINESS MODELS EMERGE

- More than half the Internet user population have joined an online social network, contribute to social bookmarking sites, create blogs, and share photos. Together these sites create a massive online audience as large as television that is attractive to marketers.

- The traditional advertising business model is severely disrupted as Google and other technology players such as Microsoft and Yahoo! seek to dominate online advertising, and expand into offline ad brokerage for television and newspapers.

- Newspapers and other traditional media adopt online, interactive models but are losing advertising revenues to the online players despite gaining online readers.

- Online entertainment business models offering television, movies, music, sports, and e-books surge, with cooperation among the major copyright owners in Hollywood and New York with the Internet distributors like Google, YouTube, Facebook, and Microsoft.

that is it available just about everywhere, at all times. It makes it possible to shop from your desktop, at home, at work, or even from your car, using mobile commerce. The result is called a **marketspace**—a marketplace extended beyond traditional boundaries and removed from a temporal and geographic location.

TABLE 2   EIGHT UNIQUE FEATURES OF E-COMMERCE TECHNOLOGY

E-commerce Technology Dimension	Business Significance
Ubiquity. Internet/Web technology is available everywhere: at work, at home, and elsewhere via mobile devices.	The marketplace is extended beyond traditional boundaries and is removed from a temporal and geographic location. "Marketspace" is created; shopping can take place anytime, anywhere. Customer convenience is enhanced, and shopping costs are reduced.
Global reach. The technology reaches across national boundaries, around the Earth.	Commerce is enabled across cultural and national boundaries seamlessly and without modification. The marketspace includes, potentially, billions of consumers and millions of businesses worldwide.
Universal standards. There is one set of technology standards, namely Internet standards.	With one set of technical standards across the globe, disparate computer systems can easily communicate with each other.
Richness. Video, audio, and text messages are possible.	Video, audio, and text marketing messages are integrated into a single marketing message and consumer experience.
Interactivity. The technology works through interaction with the user.	Consumers are engaged in a dialog that dynamically adjusts the experience to the individual, and makes the consumer a co-participant in the process of delivering goods to the market.
Information Density. The technology reduces information costs and raises quality.	Information processing, storage, and communication costs drop dramatically, whereas currency, accuracy, and timeliness improve greatly. Information becomes plentiful, cheap, and more accurate.
Personalization/Customization. The technology allows personalized messages to be delivered to individuals as well as groups.	Personalization of marketing messages and customization of products and services are based on individual characteristics.
Social technology. User content generation and social networking.	New Internet social and business models enable user content creation and distribution, and support social networks.

From a consumer point of view, ubiquity reduces **transaction costs**—the costs of participating in a market. To transact business, it is no longer necessary that you spend time or money traveling to a market, and much less mental effort is required to make a purchase.

Global Reach

E-commerce technology permits commercial transactions to cross cultural and national boundaries far more conveniently and cost effectively than is true in traditional commerce. As a result, the potential market size for e-commerce merchants is roughly equal to the size of the world's online population (estimated to be more than 1.9 billion, and growing rapidly) (Internetworldstats.com, 2010).

In contrast, most traditional commerce is local or regional—it involves local merchants or national merchants with local outlets. Television and radio stations and newspapers, for instance, are primarily local and regional institutions with limited, but powerful, national networks that can attract a national audience but not easily cross national boundaries to a global audience.

Universal Standards

One strikingly unusual feature of e-commerce technologies is that the technical standards of the Internet and, therefore, the technical standards for conducting e-commerce are universal standards. They are shared by all nations around the world and enable any computer to link with any other computer regardless of the technology platform each is using. In contrast, most traditional commerce technologies differ from one nation to the next. For instance, television and radio standards differ around the world, as does cell telephone technology.

The universal technical standards of the Internet and e-commerce greatly lower **market entry costs**—the cost merchants must pay simply to bring their goods to market. At the same time, for consumers, universal standards reduce **search costs**—the effort required to find suitable products.

Richness

Information **richness** refers to the complexity and content of a message. Traditional markets, national sales forces, and small retail stores have great richness: They are able to provide personal, face-to-face service using aural and visual cues when making a sale. The richness of traditional markets makes them powerful selling or commercial environments. Prior to the development of the Web, there was a trade-off between richness and reach: The larger the audience reached, the less rich the message. The Web makes it possible to deliver rich messages with text, audio, and video simultaneously to large numbers of people.

Interactivity

Unlike any of the commercial technologies of the twentieth century, with the possible exception of the telephone, e-commerce technologies are interactive, meaning they allow for two-way communication between merchant and consumer. Television, for instance, cannot ask viewers any questions or enter into conversations with them, and it cannot request that customer information be entered into a form. In contrast, all of these activities are possible on an e-commerce Web site. Interactivity allows an online merchant to engage a consumer in ways similar to a face-to-face experience but on a massive, global scale.

Information Density

The Internet and the Web vastly increase **information density**—the total amount and quality of information available to all market participants, consumers, and merchants alike. E-commerce technologies reduce information collection, storage, processing, and communication costs while greatly increasing the currency, accuracy, and timeliness of information.

Information density in e-commerce markets make prices and costs more transparent. **Price transparency** refers to the ease with which consumers can find out the variety of prices in a market; **cost transparency** refers to the ability of consumers to discover the actual costs merchants pay for products.

There are advantages for merchants as well. Online merchants can discover much more about consumers than in the past. This allows merchants to segment the market into groups that are willing to pay different prices and permits the merchants to engage in **price discrimination**—selling the same goods, or nearly the same goods, to different targeted groups at different prices. For instance, an online merchant can discover a consumer's avid interest in expensive, exotic vacations and then pitch high-end vacation plans to that consumer at a premium price, knowing this person is willing to pay extra for such a vacation. At the same time, the online merchant can pitch the same vacation plan at a lower price to a more price-sensitive consumer. Information density also helps merchants differentiate their products in terms of cost, brand, and quality.

Personalization/Customization

E-commerce technologies permit **personalization**: Merchants can target their marketing messages to specific individuals by adjusting the message to a person's name, interests, and past purchases. The technology also permits **customization**—changing the delivered product or service based on a user's preferences or prior behavior. Given the interactive nature of e-commerce technology, much information about the consumer can be gathered in the marketplace at the moment of purchase. With the increase in information density, a great deal of information about the consumer's past purchases and behavior can be stored and used by online merchants.

The result is a level of personalization and customization unthinkable with traditional commerce technologies. For instance, you may be able to shape what you see on television by selecting a channel, but you cannot change the content of the channel you have chosen. In contrast, the *Wall Street Journal Online* allows you to select the type of news stories you want to see first and gives you the opportunity to be alerted when certain events happen.

Social Technology: User Content Generation and Social Networking

In contrast to previous technologies, the Internet and e-commerce technologies have evolved to be much more social by allowing users to create and share with their personal friends (and a larger worldwide community) content in the form of text, videos, music, or photos. Using these forms of communication, users are able to create new social networks and strengthen existing ones.

All previous mass media in modern history, including the printing press, use a broadcast model (one-to-many) where content is created in a central location by experts (professional writers, editors, directors, and producers) and audiences are concentrated in huge numbers to consume a standardized product. The new Internet and e-commerce empower users to create and distribute content on a large scale, and permit users to program their own content consumption. The Internet provides a unique many-to-many model of mass communications.

KEY CONCEPTS IN E-COMMERCE: DIGITAL MARKETS AND DIGITAL GOODS IN A GLOBAL MARKETPLACE

The location, timing, and revenue models of business are based in some part on the cost and distribution of information. The Internet has created a digital marketplace where millions of people all over the world are able to exchange massive amounts of information directly, instantly, and for free. As a result, the Internet has changed the way companies conduct business and increased their global reach.

The Internet reduces information asymmetry. An **information asymmetry** exists when one party in a transaction has more information that is important for the transaction than the other party. That information helps determine their relative bargaining power. In digital markets, consumers and suppliers can "see" the prices being charged for goods, and in that sense digital markets are said to be more "transparent" than traditional markets.

For example, before auto retailing sites appeared on the Web, there was a significant information asymmetry between auto dealers and customers. Only the auto dealers knew the manufacturers' prices, and it was difficult for consumers to shop around for the best price. Auto dealers' profit margins depended on this asymmetry of information. Today's consumers have access to a legion of Web sites providing competitive pricing information, and three-fourths of U.S. auto buyers use the Internet to shop around for the best deal. Thus, the Web has reduced the information asymmetry surrounding an auto purchase. The Internet has also helped businesses seeking to purchase from other businesses reduce information asymmetries and locate better prices and terms.

Digital markets are very flexible and efficient because they operate with reduced search and transaction costs, lower **menu costs** (merchants' costs of changing prices), greater price discrimination, and the ability to change prices dynamically based on market conditions. In **dynamic pricing**, the price of a product varies depending on the demand characteristics of the customer or the supply situation of the seller.

These new digital markets may either reduce or increase switching costs, depending on the nature of the product or service being sold, and they may cause some extra delay in gratification. Unlike a physical market, you can't immediately consume a product such as clothing purchased over the Web (although immediate consumption is possible with digital music downloads and other digital products.)

Digital markets provide many opportunities to sell directly to the consumer, bypassing intermediaries, such as distributors or retail outlets. Eliminating intermediaries in the distribution channel can significantly lower purchase transaction costs. To pay for all the steps in a traditional distribution channel, a product may have to be priced as high as 135 percent of its original cost to manufacture.

Figure 2 illustrates how much savings result from eliminating each of these layers in the distribution process. By selling directly to consumers or reducing the number of intermediaries, companies are able to raise profits while charging lower prices. The removal of organizations or business process layers responsible for intermediary steps in a value chain is called **disintermediation**.

FIGURE 2   THE BENEFITS OF DISINTERMEDIATION TO THE CONSUMER

The typical distribution channel has several intermediary layers, each of which adds to the final cost of a product, such as a sweater. Removing layers lowers the final cost to the consumer.

Disintermediation is affecting the market for services. Airlines and hotels operating their own reservation sites online earn more per ticket because they have eliminated travel agents as intermediaries. Table 3 summarizes the differences between digital markets and traditional markets.

Digital Goods

The Internet digital marketplace has greatly expanded sales of digital goods. **Digital goods** are goods that can be delivered over a digital network. Music tracks, video, Hollywood movies, software, newspapers, magazines, and books can all be expressed, stored, delivered, and sold as purely digital products. Currently, most of these products are sold as physical goods, for example, CDs, DVDs, newspapers, and hard-copy books. But the Internet offers the possibility of delivering all these products on demand as digital products.

In general, for digital goods, the marginal cost of producing another unit is about zero (it costs nothing to make a copy of a music file). However, the cost of producing the original first unit is relatively high—in fact, it is nearly the total cost of the product because there are few other costs of inventory and distribution. Costs of delivery over the Internet are very low, marketing costs remain the same, and pricing can be highly variable. (On the Internet, the merchant can change prices as often as desired because of low menu costs.)

The impact of the Internet on the market for these kinds of digital goods is nothing short of revolutionary, and we see the results around us every day. Businesses dependent on physical products for sales—such as bookstores, book publishers, music labels, and film studios—face the possibility of declining sales and even destruction of their businesses. Newspapers and magazines are losing readers to the Internet, and losing advertisers even as online newspaper readership soars. Record label companies are losing sales to music download sites and Internet piracy, and music stores are going out of business. Video rental firms, such as Blockbuster (now in bankruptcy), based on a physical DVD market and physical stores, lost sales to Netflix using an Internet catalog and streaming video model. Hollywood studios as well face the prospect that Internet pirates will distribute their product as a digital stream, bypassing Hollywood's monopoly on DVD rentals and sales, which

TABLE 3 DIGITAL MARKETS COMPARED TO TRADITIONAL MARKETS

	DIGITAL MARKETS	TRADITIONAL MARKETS
Information asymmetry	Asymmetry reduced	Asymmetry high
Search costs	Low	High
Transaction costs	Low (sometimes virtually nothing)	High (time, travel)
Delayed gratification	High (or lower in the case of a digital good)	Lower: purchase now
Menu costs	Low	High
Dynamic pricing	Low cost, instant	High cost, delayed
Price discrimination	Low cost, instant	High cost, delayed
Market segmentation	Low cost, moderate precision	High cost, less precision
Switching costs	Higher/lower (depending on product characteristics)	High
Network effects	Strong	Weaker
Disintermediation	More possible/likely	Less possible/unlikely

now accounts for more than half of industry film revenues. To date, pirated movies have not seriously threatened Hollywood revenues in part because the major film studios and Internet distributors like YouTube, Amazon, and Apple are learning how to cooperate. Table 4 describes digital goods and how they differ from traditional physical goods.

2 | E-COMMERCE: BUSINESS AND TECHNOLOGY

E-commerce has grown from a few advertisements on early Web portals in 1995, to over 6 percent of all retail sales in 2010 (an estimated $255 billion), surpassing the mail order catalog business. E-commerce is a fascinating combination of business models and new information technologies. Let's start with a basic understanding of the types of e-commerce, and then describe e-commerce business and revenue models. We'll also cover new technologies that help companies reach over 221 million online consumers in the United States, and an estimated 800 million more worldwide.

TYPES OF E-COMMERCE

There are many ways to classify electronic commerce transactions. One is by looking at the nature of the participants in the electronic commerce transaction. The three major electronic commerce categories are business-to-consumer (B2C) e-commerce, business-to-business (B2B) e-commerce, and consumer-to-consumer (C2C) e-commerce.

- **Business-to-consumer (B2C)** electronic commerce involves retailing products and services to individual shoppers. BarnesandNoble.com, which sells books, software, and music to individual consumers, is an example of B2C e-commerce.

- **Business-to-business (B2B)** electronic commerce involves sales of goods and services among businesses. ChemConnect's Web site for buying and selling chemicals and plastics is an example of B2B e-commerce.

- **Consumer-to-consumer (C2C)** electronic commerce involves consumers selling directly to consumers. For example, eBay, the giant Web auction site, enables people to sell their goods to other consumers by auctioning their merchandise off to the highest bidder, or for a fixed price. Craigslist is the most widely used platform used by consumers to buy from and sell directly to others.

TABLE 4 HOW THE INTERNET CHANGES THE MARKETS FOR DIGITAL GOODS

	DIGITAL GOODS	TRADITIONAL GOODS
Marginal cost/unit	Zero	Greater than zero , high
Cost of production	High (most of the cost)	Variable
Copying cost	Approximately 0	Greater than zero, high
Distributed delivery cost	Low	High
Inventory cost	Low	High
Marketing cost	Variable	Variable
Pricing	More variable (bundling, random pricing games)	Fixed, based on unit costs

Another way of classifying electronic commerce transactions is in terms of the platforms used by participants in a transaction. Until recently, most e-commerce transactions took place using a personal computer connected to the Internet over wired networks. Two wireless mobile alternatives have emerged: smartphones and dedicated e-readers like the Kindle using cellular networks, and smartphones and small tablet computers using Wi-Fi wireless networks. The use of handheld wireless devices for purchasing goods and services from any location is termed **mobile commerce** or **m-commerce**. Both business-to-business and business-to-consumer e-commerce transactions can take place using m-commerce technology, which we discuss in detail in Section 3.

E-COMMERCE BUSINESS MODELS

Changes in the economics of information described earlier have created the conditions for entirely new business models to appear, while destroying older business models. Table 5 describes some of the most important Internet business models that have emerged. All, in one way or another, use the Internet to add extra value to existing products and services or to provide the foundation for new products and services.

Portal

Portals such as Google, Bing, Yahoo, MSN, and AOL offer powerful Web search tools as well as an integrated package of content and services, such as news, e-mail, instant messaging, maps, calendars, shopping, music downloads, video streaming, and more, all in one place. Initially, portals were primarily "gateways" to the Internet. Today, however, the portal business model provides a destination site where users start their Web searching and linger to read news, find entertainment, and meet other people, and be exposed to advertising. Portals generate revenue primarily by attracting very large audiences, charging advertisers for ad placement, collecting referral fees for steering customers to other sites, and charging for premium services. In 2010, portals generated an estimated $13.5 billion in revenues. Although there are hundreds of portal/search engine sites, the top five sites (Google, Yahoo, MSN/Bing, AOL, and Ask.com) gather more than 95 percent of the Internet traffic because of their superior brand recognition (eMarketer, 2010e).

E-tailer

Online retail stores, often called **e-tailers**, come in all sizes, from giant Amazon with 2010 revenues of more than $24 billion, to tiny local stores that have Web sites. An e-tailer is similar to the typical bricks-and-mortar storefront, except that customers only need to connect to the Internet to check their inventory and place an order. Altogether, online retail generated about $152 billion in revenues for 2010. The value proposition of e-tailers is to provide convenient, low-cost shopping 24/7, offering large selections and consumer choice. Some e-tailers, such as Walmart.com or Staples.com, referred to as "bricks-and-clicks," are subsidiaries or divisions of existing physical stores and carry the same products. Others, however, operate only in the virtual world, without any ties to physical locations. Amazon, BlueNile.com, and Drugstore.com are examples of this type of e-tailer. Several other variations of e-tailers—such as online versions of direct mail catalogs, online malls, and manufacturer-direct online sales—also exist.

TABLE 5   INTERNET BUSINESS MODELS

CATEGORY	DESCRIPTION	EXAMPLES
E-tailer	Sells physical products directly to consumers or to individual businesses.	Amazon RedEnvelope.com
Transaction broker	Saves users money and time by processing online sales transactions and generating a fee each time a transaction occurs.	ETrade.com Expedia
Market creator	Provides a digital environment where buyers and sellers can meet, search for products, display products, and establish prices for those products. Can serve consumers or B2B e-commerce, generating revenue from transaction fees.	eBay Priceline.com ChemConnect.com
Content provider	Creates revenue by providing digital content, such as news, music, photos, or video, over the Web. The customer may pay to access the content, or revenue may be generated by selling advertising space.	WSJ.com GettyImages.com iTunes.com Games.com
Community provider	Provides an online meeting place where people with similar interests can communicate and find useful information.	Facebook MySpace iVillage , Twitter
Portal	Provides initial point of entry to the Web along with specialized content and other services.	Yahoo Bing Google
Service provider	Provides Web 2.0 applications such as photo sharing, video sharing, and user-generated content as services. Provides other services such as online data storage and backup.	Google Apps Photobucket.com Xdrive.com

Content Provider

While e-commerce began as a retail product channel, it has increasingly turned into a global content channel. "Content" is defined broadly to include all forms of intellectual property. **Intellectual property** refers to all forms of human expression that can be put into a tangible medium such as text, CDs, DVDs, or stored on any digital (or other) media, including the Web. Content providers distribute information content, such as digital video, music, photos, text, and artwork, over the Web. The value proposition of online content providers is that consumers can find a wide range of content online, conveniently, and purchase this content inexpensively, to be played, or viewed, on multiple computer devices or smartphones.

Providers do not have to be the creators of the content (although sometimes they are, like Disney.com), and are more likely to be Internet-based distributors of content produced and created by others. For example, Apple sells music tracks at its iTunes Store, but it does not create or commission new music.

The phenomenal popularity of the iTunes Store, and Apple's Internet-connected devices like the iPhone, iPod, and iPad, have enabled new forms of digital content delivery from podcasting to mobile streaming. **Podcasting** is a method of publishing audio or video broadcasts via the Internet, allowing subscribing users to download audio or video files onto their personal computers or portable music players. **Streaming** is a publishing method for music and video files that flows a continuous stream of content to a user's device without being stored locally on the device.

Estimates vary, but total download and subscription media revenues for 2010 are somewhere between $8 billion and $10 billion annually. They are the fastest growing segment within e-commerce, growing at an estimated 20 percent annual rate (eMarketer, 2010b).

Transaction Broker

Sites that process transactions for consumers normally handled in person, by phone, or by mail are transaction brokers. The largest industries using this model are financial services and travel services. The online transaction broker's primary value propositions are savings of money and time, as well as providing an extraordinary inventory of financial products and travel packages, in a single location. Online stock brokers and travel booking services charge fees that are considerably less than traditional versions of these services.

Market Creator

Market creators build a digital environment in which buyers and sellers can meet, display products, search for products, and establish prices. The value proposition of online market creators is that they provide a platform where sellers can easily display their wares and where purchasers can buy directly from sellers. Online auction markets like eBay and Priceline are good examples of the market creator business model. Another example is Amazon's Merchants platform (and similar programs at eBay) where merchants are allowed to set up stores on Amazon's Web site and sell goods at fixed prices to consumers. This is reminiscent of open air markets where the market creator operates a facility (a town square) where merchants and consumers meet. Online market creators will generate about $12 billion in revenues for 2010.

Service Provider

While e-tailers sell products online, service providers offer services online. There's been an explosion in online services. Web 2.0 applications, photo sharing, and online sites for data backup and storage all use a service provider business model. Software is no longer a physical product with a CD in a box, but increasingly software as a service (SaaS) that you subscribe to online rather than purchase from a retailer. Google has led the way in developing online software service applications such as Google Apps, Gmail, and online data storage services.

Community Provider

Community providers are sites that create a digital online environment where people with similar interests can transact (buy and sell goods); share interests, photos, videos; communicate with like-minded people; receive interest-related information; and even play out fantasies by adopting online personalities called avatars. The social networking sites Facebook, MySpace, LinkedIn, and Twitter; online communities such as iVillage; and hundreds of other smaller, niche sites such as Doostang and Sportsvite all offer users community-building tools and services. Social networking sites have been the fastest growing Web sites in recent years, often doubling their audience size in a year. However, they are struggling to achieve profitability. The Interactive Session on Organizations explores this topic.

INTERACTIVE SESSION: ORGANIZATIONS

TWITTER SEARCHES FOR A BUSINESS MODEL

Twitter, the social networking site based on 140-character text messages, is the buzz social networking phenomenon of the year. Like all social networking sites, such as Facebook, MySpace, YouTube, Flickr, and others, Twitter provides a platform for users to express themselves by creating content and sharing it with their "followers," who sign up to receive someone's "tweets." And like most social networking sites, Twitter faces the problem of how to make money. As of October 2010, Twitter has failed to generate earnings as its management ponders how best to exploit the buzz and user base it has created.

Twitter began as a Web-based version of popular text messaging services provided by cell phone carriers. Executives in a podcasting company called Odeo were searching for a new revenue-producing product or service. In March 2006, they created a stand-alone, private company called Twitter.

The basic idea was to marry short text messaging on cell phones with the Web and its ability to create social groups. You start by establishing a Twitter account online, and identifying the friends that you would like to receive your messages. By sending a text message called a "tweet" to a short code on your cell phone (40404), you can tell your friends what you are doing, your location, and whatever else you might want to say. You are limited to 140 characters, but there is no installation and no charge. This social network messaging service to keep buddies informed is a smash success.

Coming up with solid numbers for Twitter is not easy because the firm is not releasing any "official" figures. By September 2010, Twitter, according to comScore, had around 30 million unique monthly users in the United States, and perhaps 96 million worldwide, displacing MySpace as the number three global social network (behind Facebook and Microsoft's Live Profile).

The number of individual tweets is also known only by the company. According to the company, by early 2007, Twitter had transmitted 20,000 tweets, which jumped to 60,000 tweets in a few months. During the Iranian rebellion in June 2009, there were reported to be over 200,000 tweets per hour worldwide. In October 2010, Twitter was recording over 1.2 million tweets a month. On the other hand, experts believe that 80 percent of tweets are

generated by only 10 percent of users, and that the median number of tweet readers per tweet is 1 (most tweeters tweet to one follower). Even more disturbing is that Twittter has a 60 percent churn rate: only 40 percent of users remain more than one month. Obviously, many users lose interest in learning about their friends' breakfast menu, and many feel "too connected" to their "friends," who in fact may only be distant acquaintances, if that. On the other hand, celebrities such as Britney Spears have hundreds of thousands of "friends" who follow their activities, making Twitter a marvelous, free public relations tool. Twitter unfortunately does not make a cent on these activities.

The answer to these questions about unique users, numbers of tweets, and churn rate are critical to understanding the business value of Twitter as a firm. To date, Twitter has generated losses and has unknown revenues, but in February 2009, it raised $35 million in a deal that valued the company at $255 million. The following September, Twitter announced it had raised $100 million in additional funding, from private equity firms, previous investors, and mutual fund giant T. Rowe Price, based on a company valuation of a staggering $1 billion!

So how can Twitter make money from its users and their tweets? What's its business model and how might it evolve over time? To start, consider the company's assets and customer value proposition. The main asset is user attention and audience size (eyeballs per day). The value proposition is "get it now" or real-time news on just about anything from the mundane to the monumental. An equally important asset is the database of tweets that contains the comments, observations, and opinions of the audience, and the search engine that mines those tweets for patterns. These are real-time and spontaneous observations.

Yet another asset has emerged in the last year: Twitter is a powerful alternative media platform for the distribution of news, videos, and pictures. Once again, no one predicted that Twitter would be the first to report on terrorist attacks in Mumbai, the landing of a passenger jet in the Hudson River, the Iranian rebellion in June 2009, or the political violence in Bangkok and Kenya in May 2010.

How can these assets be monetized? Advertising, what else! In April 2010, Twitter announced it s first foray into the big-time ad marketplace with Promoted Tweets. Think Twitter search engine: in response to a user's query to Twitter's search function for, say netbooks, a Best Buy ad for netbooks will be displayed. The company claims Promoted Tweets are not really ads because they look like all other tweets, just a part of the tweet stream of messages. These so-called "organic tweets" differ therefore from traditional search engine text ads, or social network ads which are far from organic. So far, Best Buy, Bravo, Red Bull, Sony, Starbucks, and Virgin American have signed up. If this actually works, thousands of companies might sign up to blast messages to millions of subscribers in response to related queries.

A second Twitter monetization effort announced in June 2010 is called Promoted Trends. Trends is a section of the Twitter home page that lets users know what's hot, what a lot of people are talking about. The company claims this is "organic," and a true reflection of what people are tweeting about. Promoted Trends are trends that companies would like to initiate. A company can place a Promoted Trends banner on the bottom of the page and when users click on the banner, they are taken to the follower page for that movie or product. Disney bought Promoted Trends for its film *Toy Story 3*, according to Twitter.

In July 2010, Twitter announced its third initiative of the year: @earlybird accounts, which users can follow to receive special offers. Walt Disney Pictures has used the service to promote *The Sorcerer's Apprentice* by offering twofers (buy one ticket, get another one free). The service could work nicely with so-called real-time or "flash" marketing campaigns in entertainment, fashion, luxury goods, technology, and beauty products. So far, Twitter has over 50,000 @earlybird followers and hopes to reach "influentials," people who shape the purchasing decisions of many others.

Another monetizing service is temporal real-time search. If there's one thing Twitter has uniquely among all the social network sites, it's real-time information. In 2010, Twitter entered into agreements with Google, Microsoft, and Yahoo to permit these search engines to index tweets and make them available to the entire Internet. This service will give free real-time content to the search engines as opposed to archival content. It is unclear who's doing who a service here, and the financial arrangements are not public.

Other large players are experimenting. Dell created a Twitter outlet account, @DellOutlet, and is using it to sell open-box and discontinued computers.

Dell also maintains several customer service accounts. Twitter could charge such accounts a commission on sales because Twitter is acting like an e-commerce sales platform similar to Amazon. Other firms have used their Twitter followers' fan base to market discount air tickets (Jet Blue) and greeting cards (Somecards).

Freemium is another possibility: ask users to pay a subscription fee for premium services such as videos and music downloads. However, it may be too late for this idea because users have come to expect the service to be free. Twitter could charge service providers such as doctors, dentists, lawyers, and hair salons for providing their customers with unexpected appointment availabilities. But Twitter's most likely steady revenue source might be its database of hundreds of millions of real-time tweets. Major firms such as Starbucks, Amazon, Intuit (QuickBooks and Mint.com), and Dell have used Twitter to understand how their customers are reacting to products, services, and Web sites, and then making corrections or changes in those services and products. Twitter is a fabulous listening post on the Internet frontier.

The possibilities are endless, and just about any of the above scenarios offers some solution to the company's problem, which is a lack of revenue (forget about profits). The company is coy about announcing its business model, what one pundit described as hiding behind a "Silicon Valley Mona Lisa smile." These Wall Street pundits are thought to be party poopers in the Valley. In a nod to Apple's iTunes and Amazon's merchant services, Twitter has turned over its messaging capabilities and software platform to others, one of which is CoTweet.com, a company that organizes multiple Twitter exchanges for customers so they can be tracked more easily. Google is selling ad units based around a company's last five tweets (ads are displayed to users who have created or viewed tweets about a company). Twitter is not charging for this service. In the meantime, observers wonder if Twitter is twittering away its assets and may not ever show a profit for its $160 million investment.

Sources: Matthew Shaer, "Twitter Hits 145 Million User Mark, Sees Rise in Mobile Use," Christian Science Monitor, September 3, 2010; Jason Lipshutz, "Lady Gaga to Steal Britney Spears' Twitter Crown," Reuters, August 19, 2010; Emir Afrati, "Twitter's Early Bird Ad Ploy Takes Flight," *Wall Street Journal*, July 14, 2010; Jessica Guynn, "Twitter Tests New Promoted Trends Feature with 'Toy Story 3' from Disney's Pixar," *Los Angeles Times*, June 16, 2010; Erica Naone, "Will Twitter's Ad Strategy Work," *Technology Review*, April 15, 2010; Jessica Vascellaro and Emily Steel, "Twitter Rolls Out Ads," *Wall Street Journal*, April 14, 2010; Brad Stone, "Twitter's Latest Valuation: $1 Billion," *New York Times*, September 24, 2009; Jon Fine, "Twitter Makes a Racket. But Revenues?" *Business Week*, April 9, 2009.

CASE STUDY QUESTIONS

1. Based on your reading in this chapter, how would you characterize Twitter's business model?

2. If Twitter is to have a revenue model, which of the revenue models described in this chapter would work?

3. What is the most important asset that Twitter has, and how could it monetize this asset?

4. What impact will a high customer churn rate have on Twitter's potential advertising revenue?

MIS IN ACTION

1. Go to Twitter.com and enter a search on your favorite (or least favorite) car. Can you find the company's official site? What else do you find? Describe the results and characterize the potential risks and rewards for companies that would like to advertise to Twitter's audience.

2. How would you improve Twitter's Web site to make it more friendly for large advertisers?

3. Teenagers are infrequent users of Twitter because they use their cell phones for texting, and most users are adults 18–34 years of age. Find five users of Twitter and ask them how long they have used the service, are they likely to continue using the service, and how would they feel about banner ads appearing on their Twitter Web screen and phone screens. Are loyal users of Twitter less likely (or more likely) to tolerate advertising on Twitter?

E-COMMERCE REVENUE MODELS

A firm's **revenue model** describes how the firm will earn revenue, generate profits, and produce a superior return on investment. Although there are many different e-commerce revenue models that have been developed, most companies rely on one, or some combination, of the following six revenue models: advertising, sales, subscription, free/freemium, transaction fee, and affiliate.

Advertising Revenue Model

In the **advertising revenue model**, a Web site generates revenue by attracting a large audience of visitors who can then be exposed to advertisements. The advertising model is the most widely used revenue model in e-commerce, and arguably, without advertising revenues, the Web would be a vastly different experience from what it is now. Content on the Web—everything from news to videos and opinions—is "free" to visitors because advertisers pay the production and distribution costs in return for the right to expose visitors to ads. Companies will spend an estimated $240 billion on advertising in 2010, and an estimated $25 billion of that amount on online advertising (in the form of a paid message on a Web site, paid search listing, video, widget, game, or other online medium, such as instant messaging). In the last five years, advertisers have increased online spending and cut outlays on traditional channels such as radio and newspapers. Television advertising has expanded along with online advertising revenues.

Web sites with the largest viewership or that attract a highly specialized, differentiated viewership and are able to retain user attention ("stickiness") are able to charge higher advertising rates. Yahoo, for instance, derives nearly all its revenue from display ads (banner ads) and to a lesser extent search engine text ads. Ninety-eight percent of Google's revenue derives from selling keywords to advertisers in an auction-like market (the AdSense program). The average Facebook user spends over five hours a week on the site, far longer than other portal sites.

Sales Revenue Model

In the **sales revenue model**, companies derive revenue by selling goods, information, or services to customers. Companies such as Amazon (which sells books, music, and other products), LLBean.com, and Gap.com, all have sales revenue models. Content providers make money by charging for downloads of entire files such as music tracks (iTunes Store) or books or for downloading music and/or video streams (Hulu.com TV shows). Apple has pioneered and strengthened the acceptance of micropayments. **Micropayment systems** provide content providers with a cost-effective method for processing high volumes of very small monetary transactions (anywhere from $.25 to $5.00 per transaction). MyMISlab has a Learning Track with more detail on micropayment and other e-commerce payment systems.

Subscription Revenue Model

In the **subscription revenue model**, a Web site offering content or services charges a subscription fee for access to some or all of its offerings on an ongoing basis. Content providers often use this revenue model. For instance, the online version of *Consumer Reports* provides access to premium content, such as detailed ratings, reviews, and recommendations, only to subscribers, who have a choice of paying a $5.95 monthly subscription fee or a $26.00 annual fee. Netflix is one of the most successful subscriber sites with more that 15 million subscribers in September 2010. The Wall Street Journal has the largest online subscription newspaper with more than 1 million online subscribers. To be successful, the subscription model requires that the content be perceived as a having high added value, differentiated, and not readily available elsewhere nor easily replicated. Companies successfully offering content or services online on a subscription basis include Match.com and eHarmony (dating services), Ancestry.com and Genealogy.com (genealogy research), Microsoft's Xboxlive.com (video games), and Rhapsody.com (music).

Free/Freemium Revenue Model

In the **free/freemium revenue model**, firms offer basic services or content for free, while charging a premium for advanced or special features. For example, Google offers free applications, but charges for premium services. Pandora, the subscription radio service, offers a free service with limited play time, and a premium service with unlimited play. The Flickr photo-sharing service offers free basic services for sharing photos with friends and family, and also sells a $24.95 "premium" package that provides users unlimited storage, high-definition video storage and playback, and freedom from display advertising. The idea is to attract very large audiences with free services, and then to convert some of this audience to pay a subscription for premium services. One problem with this model is converting people from being "free loaders" into paying customers. "Free" can be a powerful model for losing money.

Transaction Fee Revenue Model

In the **transaction fee revenue model**, a company receives a fee for enabling or executing a transaction. For example, eBay provides an online auction marketplace and receives a small transaction fee from a seller if the seller is successful in selling an item. E*Trade, an online stockbroker, receives transaction fees each time it executes a stock transaction on behalf of a customer. The transaction revenue model enjoys wide acceptance in part because the true cost of using the platform is not immediately apparent to the user.

Affiliate Revenue Model

In the **affiliate revenue model**, Web sites (called "affiliate Web sites") send visitors to other Web sites in return for a referral fee or percentage of the revenue from any resulting sales. For example, MyPoints makes money by connecting companies to potential customers by offering special deals to its members. When members take advantage of an offer and make a purchase, they earn "points" they can redeem for free products and services, and MyPoints receives a referral fee. Community feedback sites such as Epinions and Yelp receive much of their revenue from steering potential customers to Web sites where they make a purchase. Amazon uses affiliates who steer business to the Amazon Web site by placing the Amazon logo on their blogs. Personal blogs may be involved in affiliate marketing. Some bloggers are paid directly by manufacturers, or receive free products, for speaking highly of products and providing links to sales channels.

WEB 2.0: SOCIAL NETWORKING AND THE WISDOM OF CROWDS

One of the fastest growing areas of e-commerce revenues are Web 2.0 online services. The most popular Web 2.0 service is social networking, online meeting places where people can meet their friends and their friends' friends. Every day over 60 million Internet users in the United States visit a social networking site like Facebook, MySpace, LinkedIn, and hundreds of others.

Social networking sites link people through their mutual business or personal connections, enabling them to mine their friends (and their friends' friends) for sales leads, job-hunting tips, or new friends. MySpace, Facebook, and Friendster appeal to people who are primarily interested in extending their friendships, while LinkedIn focuses on job networking for professionals.

Social networking sites and online communities offer new possibilities for e-commerce. Networking sites like Facebook and MySpace sell banner, video, and text ads; sell user preference information to marketers; and sell products such as music, videos, and e-books. Corporations set up their own Facebook and MySpace profiles to interact with potential customers. For example, Procter & Gamble set up a MySpace profile page for Crest toothpaste soliciting "friends" for a fictional character called "Miss Irresistable." Business firms can also "listen" to what social networkers are saying about their products, and obtain valuable feedback from consumers. At user-generated content sites like YouTube, high-quality video content is used to display advertising, and Hollywood studios have set up their own channels to market their products. The Interactive Session on Management looks more closely at social networking on Facebook, focusing on its impact on privacy.

At **social shopping** sites like Kaboodle, ThisNext, and Stylehive you can swap shopping ideas with friends. Facebook offers this same service on a voluntary basis. Online communities are also ideal venues to employ viral marketing techniques. Online viral marketing is like traditional word-of-mouth marketing except that the word can spread across an online commu-

INTERACTIVE SESSION: MANAGEMENT

FACEBOOK: MANAGING YOUR PRIVACY FOR THEIR PROFIT

Facebook is the largest social networking site in the world. Founded in 2004 by Mark Zuckerberg, the site had over 500 million worldwide users as of October 2010, and has long since surpassed all of its social networking peers. Facebook allows users to create a profile and join various types of self-contained networks, including college-wide, workplace, and regional networks. The site includes a wide array of tools that allow users to connect and interact with other users, including messaging, groups, photo-sharing, and user-created applications.

Although the site is the leader in social networking, it has waged a constant struggle to develop viable methods of generating revenue. Though many investors are still optimistic regarding Facebook's future profitability, it still needs to adjust its business model to monetize the site traffic and personal information it has accumulated.

Like many businesses of its kind, Facebook makes its money through advertising. Facebook represents a unique opportunity for advertisers to reach highly targeted audiences based on their demographic information, hobbies and personal preferences, geographical regions, and other narrowly specified criteria in a comfortable and engaging environment. Businesses both large and small can place advertisements that are fully integrated into primary features of the site or create Facebook pages where users can learn more about and interact with them.

However, many individuals on Facebook aren't interested in sharing their personal information with anyone other than a select group of their friends on the site. This is a difficult issue for Facebook. The company needs to provide a level of privacy that makes their users comfortable, but it's that very privacy that prevents it from gathering as much information as it would like, and the more information Facebook has, the more money it earns. Facebook's goal is to persuade its users to be comfortable sharing information willingly by providing an environment that becomes richer and more entertaining as the amount of information shared increases. In trying to achieve this goal, the site has made a number of missteps, but is improving its handling of users' privacy rights.

The launch of Facebook's Beacon advertising service in 2007 was a lightning rod for criticism of Facebook's handling of its private information.

Beacon was intended to inform users about what their friends were purchasing and what sites they were visiting away from Facebook. Users were angry that Beacon continued to communicate private information even after a user opted out of the service. After significant public backlash and the threat of a class-action lawsuit, Facebook shut down Beacon in September 2009.

Facebook has also drawn criticism for preserving the personal information of people who attempted to remove their profiles from the site. In early 2009, it adjusted its terms of service to assign it ownership rights over the information contained in deleted profiles. In many countries, this practice is illegal, and the user backlash against the move was swift.

In response, Facebook's chief privacy officer, Chris Kelly, presided over a total overhaul of Facebook's privacy policy, which took the form of an open collaboration with some of the most vocal critics of the old policies, including the previously mentioned protest group's founders. In February, Facebook went forward with the new terms after holding a vote open to all Facebook users, 75 percent of whom approved. The site now allows users either to deactivate or to delete their account entirely, and only saves information after deactivation.

In late 2009, tensions between Facebook and its users came to a head when the site rolled out new privacy controls for users, but had adjusted those settings to be public by default. Even users that had previously set their privacy to be "friends-only" for photos and profile information had their content exposed, including the profile of Zuckerberg himself. When asked about the change, Zuckerberg explained that the moves were in response to a shift in social norms towards openness and away from privacy, saying "we decided that these would be the social norms now and we just went for it."

The fallout from the change and is still ongoing, and more privacy problems keep cropping up. In October 2010, Facebook unveiled new features giving users more control over how they share personal information on the site with other users and third-party applications. These include a groups feature allowing users to distinguish specific circles of "friends" and choose what information they want to share with each group and whether the groups are public or private.

Shortly thereafter, a Wall Street Journal investigation found that some of the most popular Facebook applications (apps) had been transmitting user IDs—identifying information which could provide access to people's names and, in some cases, their friends' names—to dozens of advertising and Internet tracking companies. Sharing user IDs is in violation of Facebook's privacy policies.

All these privacy flaps have not diminished advertiser interest. Facebook serves ads on each user's home page and on the sidebars of user profiles. In addition to an image and headline from the advertiser, Facebook ads include the names of any user's friends who have clicked on a button indicating they like the brand or ad. A Nielsen Co. study found that including information about individuals a person knows in an ad boosted recall of the ad by 68 percent and doubled awareness of a brand's message. To determine what ads to serve to particular people, Facebook abstracts profile information into keywords, and advertisers match ads to those keywords. No individual data is shared with any advertiser.

However, it's still unclear how much money is there to be made from advertising on Facebook. The site insists that it doesn't plan to charge its users any kind of fee for site access. Facebook's 2010 revenue was expected to approach $1 billion, which is a far cry from a $33 billion private market valuation. But the site has already become a critical component of the Web's social fabric, and Facebook management insists that it's unworried about profitability in 2010 or the immediate future.

Sources: Emily Steel and Geoffrey A. Fowler, "Facebook in Privacy Breach," *The Wall Street Journal*, October 18, 2010; Jessica E. Vascellaro, "Facebook Makes Gains in Web Ads," *The Wall Street Journal*, May 12, 2010 and "Facebook Grapples with Privacy Issues," *The Wall Street Journal*, May 19, 2010; Geoffrey A. Fowler, "Facebook Fights Privacy Concerns," *The Wall Street Journal*, August 21, 2010 and "Facebook Tweaks Allow Friends to Sort Who They Really 'Like,'" *The Wall Street Journal*, October 5, 2010; Emily Steel and Geoffrey A. Fowler, "Facebook Touts Selling Power of Friendship," *The Wall Street Journal*, July 7, 2010; Brad Stone, "Is Facebook Growing Up Too Fast?" *The New York Times*, March 29, 2009; and CG Lynch, "Facebook's Chief Privacy Officer: Balancing Needs of Users with the Business of Social Networks", *CIO.com*, April 1 2009.

CASE STUDY QUESTIONS

1. What concepts in the chapter are illustrated in this case?

2. Describe the weaknesses of Facebook's privacy policies and features. What management, organization, and technology factors have contributed to those weaknesses?

3. List and describe some of the options that Facebook managers have in balancing privacy and profitability. How can Facebook better safeguard user privacy? What would be the impact on its profitability and business model?

4. Do you anticipate that Facebook will be successful in developing a business model that monetizes their site traffic? Why or why not?

MIS IN ACTION

Visit Facebook's Web site and review the site's privacy policy. Then answer the following questions:

1. To what user information does Facebook retain the rights?

2. What is Facebook's stance regarding information shared via third-party applications developed for the Facebook platform?

3. Did you find the privacy policy to be clear and reasonable? What would you change, if anything?

nity at the speed of light, and go much further geographically than a small network of friends.

The Wisdom of Crowds

Creating sites where thousands, even millions, of people can interact offers business firms new ways to market and advertise, to discover who likes (or hates) their products. In a phenomenon called "**the wisdom of crowds**," some argue that large numbers of people can make better decisions about a wide range of topics or products than a single person or even a small committee of experts (Surowiecki, 2004).

Obviously this is not always the case, but it can happen in interesting ways. In marketing, the wisdom of crowds concept suggests that firms should consult with thousands of their customers first as a way of establishing a relationship with them, and second, to better understand how their products and services are used and appreciated (or rejected). Actively soliciting the comments of your customers builds trust and sends the message to your customers that you care what they are thinking, and that you need their advice.

Beyond merely soliciting advice, firms can be actively helped in solving some business problems using what is called **crowdsourcing**. For instance, in 2006, Netflix announced a contest in which it offered to pay $1 million to the person or team who comes up with a method for improving by 10 percent Netflix's prediction of what movies customers would like as measured against their actual choices. By 2009, Netflix received 44,014 entries from 5,169 teams in 186 countries. The winning team improved a key part of Netflix's business: a recommender system that recommends to its customers what new movies to order based on their personal past movie choices and the choices of millions of other customers who are like them (Howe, 2008; Resnick and Varian, 1997).

Firms can also use the wisdom of crowds in the form of prediction markets. **Prediction markets** are established as peer-to-peer betting markets where participants make bets on specific outcomes of, say, quarterly sales of a new product, designs for new products, or political elections. The world's largest commercial prediction market is Betfair, founded in 2000, where you bet for or against specific outcomes on football games, horse races, and whether or not the Dow Jones will go up or down in a single day. Iowa Electronic Markets (IEM) is an academic market focused on elections. You can place bets on the outcome of local and national elections.

E-COMMERCE MARKETING

While e-commerce and the Internet have changed entire industries and enable new business models, no industry has been more affected than marketing and marketing communications. The Internet provides marketers with new ways of identifying and communicating with millions of potential customers at costs far lower than traditional media, including search engine marketing, data mining, recommender systems, and targeted e-mail. The Internet enables **long tail marketing**. Before the Internet, reaching a large audience was very expensive, and marketers had to focus on attracting the largest number of consumers with popular hit products, whether music, Hollywood movies, books, or cars. In contrast, the Internet allows marketers to inexpensively find potential customers for which demand is very low, people on the far ends of the bell (normal) curve. For instance, the Internet makes it possible to sell independent music profitably to very small audiences. There's always some demand for almost any product. Put a string of such long tail sales together and you have a profitable business.

The Internet also provides new ways—often instantaneous and spontaneous—to gather information from customers, adjust product offerings, and increase customer value. Table 6 describes the leading marketing and advertising formats used in e-commerce.

Many e-commerce marketing firms use behavioral targeting techniques to increase the effectiveness of banner, rich media, and video ads. **Behavioral**

TABLE 6   ONLINE MARKETING AND ADVERTISING FORMATS (BILLIONS)

MARKETING FORMAT	2010 REVENUE	DESCRIPTION
Search engine	$12.3	Text ads targeted at precisely what the customer is looking for at the moment of shopping and purchasing. Sales oriented.
Display ads	$5.8	Banner ads (pop-ups and leave-behinds) with interactive features; increasingly behaviorally targeted to individual Web activity. Brand development and sales.
Classified	$1.9	Job, real estate, and services ads; interactive, rich media, and personalized to user searches. Sales and branding.
Rich media	$1.57	Animations, games, and puzzles. Interactive, targeted, and entertaining. Branding orientation.
Affiliate and blog marketing	$1.5	Blog and Web site marketing steers customers to parent sites; interactive, personal, and often with video. Sales orientation.
Video	$1.5	Fastest growing format, engaging and entertaining; behaviorally targeted, interactive. Branding and sales.
Sponsorships	$.4	Online games, puzzle, contests, and coupon sites sponsored by firms to promote products. Sales orientation.
E-mail	$.27	Effective, targeted marketing tool with interactive and rich media potential. Sales oriented.

targeting refers to tracking the click-streams (history of clicking behavior) of individuals on thousands of Web sites for the purpose of understanding their interests and intentions, and exposing them to advertisements that are uniquely suited to their behavior. Proponents believe this more precise understanding of the customer leads to more efficient marketing (the firm pays for ads only to those shoppers who are most interested in their products) and larger sales and revenues. Unfortunately, behavioral targeting of millions of Web users also leads to the invasion of personal privacy without user consent. When consumers lose trust in their Web experience, they tend not to purchase anything.

Behavioral targeting takes place at two levels: at individual Web sites and on various advertising networks that track users across thousands of Web sites. All Web sites collect data on visitor browser activity and store it in a database. They have tools to record the site that users visited prior to coming to the Web site, where these users go when they leave that site, the type of operating system they use, browser information, and even some location data. They also record the specific pages visited on the particular site, the time spent on each page of the site, the types of pages visited, and what the visitors purchased (see Figure 3). Firms analyze this information about customer interests and behavior to develop precise profiles of existing and potential customers.

This information enables firms to understand how well their Web site is working, create unique personalized Web pages that display content or ads for products or services of special interest to each user, improve the customer's experience, and create additional value through a better understanding of the shopper (see Figure 4). By using personalization technology to modify the Web pages presented to each customer, marketers achieve some of the benefits of using individual salespeople at dramatically lower costs. For instance,

FIGURE 3   WEB SITE VISITOR TRACKING

Click 1	The shopper clicks on the home page. The store can tell that the shopper arrived from the Yahoo! portal at 2:30 PM (which might help determine staffing for customer service centers) and how long she lingered on the home page (which might indicate trouble navigating the site).
Click 2	
Click 3	The shopper clicks on blouses, clicks to select a woman's white blouse, then clicks to view the same item in pink. The shopper clicks to select this item in a size 10 in pink and clicks to place it in her shopping cart. This information can help the store determine which sizes and colors are most popular.
Click 4	
Click 5	
Click 6	From the shopping cart page, the shopper clicks to close the browser to leave the Web site without purchasing the blouse. This action could indicate the shopper changed her mind or that she had a problem with the Web site's checkout and payment process. Such behavior might signal that the Web site was not well designed.

E-commerce Web sites have tools to track a shopper's every step through an online store. Close examination of customer behavior at a Web site selling women's clothing shows what the store might learn at each step and what actions it could take to increase sales.

General Motors will show a Chevrolet banner ad to women emphasizing safety and utility, while men will receive different ads emphasizing power and ruggedness.

FIGURE 4   WEB SITE PERSONALIZATION

Firms can create unique personalized Web pages that display content or ads for products or services of special interest to individual users, improving the customer experience and creating additional value.

What if you are a large national advertising company with many different clients trying to reach millions of consumers? What if you were a large global manufacturer trying to reach potential consumers for your products? With millions of Web sites, working with each one would be impractical. Advertising networks solve this problem by creating a network of several thousand of the most popular Web sites visited by millions of people, tracking the behavior of these users across the entire network, building profiles of each user, and then selling these profiles to advertisers. Popular Web sites download dozens of Web tracking cookies, bugs, and beacons, which report user online behavior to remote servers without the users' knowledge. Looking for young, single consumers, with college degrees, living in the Northeast, in the 18–34 age range who are interested purchasing a European car? Not a problem. Advertising networks can identify and deliver hundreds of thousands of people who fit this profile and expose them to ads for European cars as they move from one Web site to another. Estimates vary, but behaviorally targeted ads are 10 times more likely to produce a consumer response than a randomly chosen banner or video ad (see Figure 5). So-called advertising exchanges use this same technology to auction access to people with very specific profiles to advertisers in a few milliseconds.

B2B E-COMMERCE: NEW EFFICIENCIES AND RELATIONSHIPS

The trade between business firms (business-to-business commerce or B2B) represents a huge marketplace. The total amount of B2B trade in the United States in 2009 was about $12.2 trillion, with B2B e-commerce (online B2B) contributing about $3.6 trillion of that amount (U.S. Census Bureau, 2010; authors' estimates). By 2014, B2B e-commerce should grow to about $5.1 trillion in the United States, assuming an average growth rate of about 7 percent. The process of conducting trade among business firms is complex and requires significant human interven-

FIGURE 5   HOW AN ADVERTISING NETWORK SUCH AS DOUBLECLICK WORKS

Advertising networks have become controversial among privacy advocates because of their ability to track individual consumers across the Internet.

tion, and therefore, it consumes significant resources. Some firms estimate that each corporate purchase order for support products costs them, on average, at least $100 in administrative overhead. Administrative overhead includes processing paper, approving purchase decisions, spending time using the telephone and fax machines to search for products and arrange for purchases, arranging for shipping, and receiving the goods. Across the economy, this adds up to trillions of dollars annually being spent for procurement processes that could potentially be automated. If even just a portion of inter-firm trade were automated, and parts of the entire procurement process assisted by the Internet, literally trillions of dollars might be released for more productive uses, consumer prices potentially would fall, productivity would increase, and the economic wealth of the nation would expand. This is the promise of B2B e-commerce. The challenge of B2B e-commerce is changing existing patterns and systems of procurement, and designing and implementing new Internet-based B2B solutions.

Business-to-business e-commerce refers to the commercial transactions that occur among business firms. Increasingly, these transactions are flowing through a variety of different Internet-enabled mechanisms. About 80 percent of online B2B e-commerce is still based on proprietary systems for **electronic data interchange (EDI)**. Electronic data interchange enables the computer-to-computer exchange between two organizations of standard transactions such as invoices, bills of lading, shipment schedules, or purchase orders. Transactions are automatically transmitted from one information system to another through a network, eliminating the printing and handling of paper at one end and the inputting of data at the other. Each major industry in the United States and much of the rest of the world has EDI standards that define the structure and information fields of electronic documents for that industry.

EDI originally automated the exchange of documents such as purchase orders, invoices, and shipping notices. Although some companies still use EDI for document automation, firms engaged in just-in-time inventory replenishment and continuous production use EDI as a system for continuous replenishment. Suppliers have online access to selected parts of the purchasing firm's production and delivery schedules and automatically ship materials and goods to meet prespecified targets without intervention by firm purchasing agents (see Figure 6).

Although many organizations still use private networks for EDI, they are increasingly Web-enabled because Internet technology provides a much more flexible and low-cost platform for linking to other firms. Businesses are able to extend digital technology to a wider range of activities and broaden their circle of trading partners.

FIGURE 6   ELECTRONIC DATA INTERCHANGE (EDI)

Companies use EDI to automate transactions for B2B e-commerce and continuous inventory replenishment. Suppliers can automatically send data about shipments to purchasing firms. The purchasing firms can use EDI to provide production and inventory requirements and payment data to suppliers.

Take procurement, for example. Procurement involves not only purchasing goods and materials but also sourcing, negotiating with suppliers, paying for goods, and making delivery arrangements. Businesses can now use the Internet to locate the lowest-cost supplier, search online catalogs of supplier products, negotiate with suppliers, place orders, make payments, and arrange transportation. They are not limited to partners linked by traditional EDI networks.

The Internet and Web technology enable businesses to create new electronic storefronts for selling to other businesses with multimedia graphic displays and interactive features similar to those for B2C commerce. Alternatively, businesses can use Internet technology to create extranets or electronic marketplaces for linking to other businesses for purchase and sale transactions.

Private industrial networks typically consist of a large firm using an extranet to link to its suppliers and other key business partners (see Figure 7). The network is owned by the buyer, and it permits the firm and designated suppliers, distributors, and other business partners to share product design and development, marketing, production scheduling, inventory management, and unstructured communication, including graphics and e-mail. Another term for a private industrial network is a **private exchange**.

An example is VW Group Supply, which links the Volkswagen Group and its suppliers. VW Group Supply handles 90 percent of all global purchasing for Volkswagen, including all automotive and parts components.

Net marketplaces, which are sometimes called e-hubs, provide a single, digital marketplace based on Internet technology for many different buyers and sellers (see Figure 8). They are industry owned or operate as independent intermediaries between buyers and sellers. Net marketplaces generate revenue from purchase and sale transactions and other services provided to clients. Participants in Net marketplaces can establish prices through online negotiations, auctions, or requests for quotations, or they can use fixed prices.

FIGURE 7   A PRIVATE INDUSTRIAL NETWORK

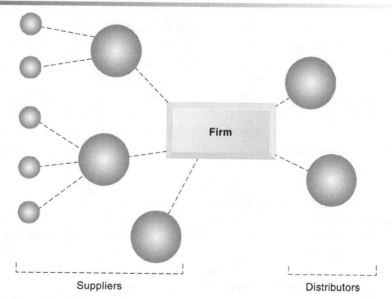

Suppliers   Distributors

A private industrial network, also known as a private exchange, links a firm to its suppliers, distributors, and other key business partners for efficient supply chain management and other collaborative commerce activities.

FIGURE 8 **A NET MARKETPLACE**

- Catalogs
- Sourcing
- Automated purchasing
- Processing and fulfillment

Suppliers   Buyers

Net marketplaces are online marketplaces where multiple buyers can purchase from multiple sellers.

There are many different types of Net marketplaces and ways of classifying them. Some Net marketplaces sell direct goods and some sell indirect goods. *Direct goods* are goods used in a production process, such as sheet steel for auto body production. *Indirect goods* are all other goods not directly involved in the production process, such as office supplies or products for maintenance and repair. Some Net marketplaces support contractual purchasing based on long-term relationships with designated suppliers, and others support short-term spot purchasing, where goods are purchased based on immediate needs, often from many different suppliers.

Some Net marketplaces serve vertical markets for specific industries, such as automobiles, telecommunications, or machine tools, whereas others serve horizontal markets for goods and services that can be found in many different industries, such as office equipment or transportation.

Exostar is an example of an industry-owned Net marketplace, focusing on long-term contract purchasing relationships and on providing common networks and computing platforms for reducing supply chain inefficiencies. This aerospace and defense industry-sponsored Net marketplace was founded jointly by BAE Systems, Boeing, Lockheed Martin, Raytheon, and Rolls-Royce plc to connect these companies to their suppliers and facilitate collaboration. More than 16,000 trading partners in the commercial, military, and government sectors use Exostar's sourcing, e-procurement, and collaboration tools for both direct and indirect goods. Elemica is another example of a Net marketplace serving the chemical industry.

Exchanges are independently owned third-party Net marketplaces that connect thousands of suppliers and buyers for spot purchasing. Many exchanges provide vertical markets for a single industry, such as food, electronics, or industrial equipment, and they primarily deal with direct inputs. For example, Go2paper enables a spot market for paper, board, and kraft among buyers and sellers in the paper industries from over 75 countries.

Exchanges proliferated during the early years of e-commerce but many have failed. Suppliers were reluctant to participate because the exchanges encouraged competitive bidding that drove prices down and did not offer any long-term relationships with buyers or services to make lowering prices worthwhile. Many essential direct purchases are not conducted on a spot basis because they require contracts and consideration of issues such as delivery timing, customization, and quality of products.

3 THE MOBILE DIGITAL PLATFORM AND MOBILE E-COMMERCE

Walk down the street in any major metropolitan area and count how many people are pecking away at their iPhones or BlackBerrys. Ride the trains, fly the planes, and you'll see your fellow travelers reading an online newspaper, watching a video on their phone, or reading a novel on their Kindle. In five years, the majority of Internet users in the United States will rely on mobile devices as their primary device for accessing the Internet. M-commerce has taken off.

In 2010, m-commerce represented less than 10 percent of all e-commerce, with about $5 billion in annual revenues generated by selling music, videos, ring tones, applications, movies, television, and location-based services like local restaurant locators and traffic updates. However, m-commerce is the fastest growing form of e-commerce, with some areas expanding at a rate of 50 percent or more per year, and is estimated to grow to $19 billion in 2014 (see Figure 9). In 2010, there were an estimated 5 billion cell phone subscribers worldwide, with over 855 million in China and 300 million in the United States (eMarketer, 2010d).

M-COMMERCE SERVICES AND APPLICATIONS

The main areas of growth in mobile e-commerce are location-based services, about $215 million in revenue in 2010; software application sales at stores such as iTunes (about $1.8 billion); entertainment downloads of ring tones, music, video, and TV shows (about $1 billion); mobile display advertising ($784 million); direct shopping services such as Slifter ($200 million); and e-book sales ($338 million).

FIGURE 9   CONSOLIDATED MOBILE COMMERCE REVENUES

Mobile e-commerce is the fastest growing type of B2C e-commerce although it represents only a small part of all e-commerce in 2010.

M-commerce applications have taken off for services that are time-critical, that appeal to people on the move, or that accomplish a task more efficiently than other methods. They are especially popular in Europe, Japan, South Korea, and other countries with strong wireless broadband infrastructures. The following sections describe some examples.

Location-Based Services

Wikitude.me provides a special kind of browser for smart phones equipped with a built-in global positioning system (GPS) and compass that can identify your precise location and where the phone is pointed. Using information from over 800,000 points of interest available on Wikipedia, plus thousands of other local sites, the browser overlays information about points of interest you are viewing, and displays that information on your smartphone screen, superimposed on a map or photograph that you just snapped. For example, users can point their smart phone cameras towards mountains from a tour bus and see the names and heights of the mountains displayed on the screen. Lost in a European medieval city, or downtown Los Angeles? Open up the Wikitude browser, point your camera at a building, and then find the address and other interesting details. Wikitude.me also allows users to geo-tag the world around them, and then submit the tags to Wikitude in order to share content with other users. In 2010, both Facebook and Twitter launched a Places feature that allows users to let their friends know where they are. These services compete with Foursquare and Gowalla, which allow users to check in at places and broadcast their location to friends.

Loopt is a free social networking application that allows you to share your status and track the location of friends via smartphones such as the iPhone, BlackBerry, and over 100 other mobile devices. Users also have the ability to integrate Loopt with other social networks, including Facebook and Twitter. Loopt has 4 million users. The service doesn't sell information to advertisers, but does post ads based on user location. Loopt's target is to deal with advertisers at the walking level (within 200 to 250 meters).

Foursquare provides a similar service to 4 million registered users, who are able to connect with friends and update their location. Points are awarded for "checking in" at designated venues. Users choose to have their check-ins posted on their accounts on Twitter, Facebook, or both. Users also earn badges by checking in at locations with certain tags, for check-in frequency, or for the time of check-in. More than 3,000 restaurants, bars, and other businesses (including 4Food, described in the chapter-opening case) use Foursquare to attract customers with promotions.

Banking and Financial Services

Banks and credit card companies are rolling out services that let customers manage their accounts from their mobile devices. JPMorgan Chase and Bank of America customers can use their cell phones to check account balances, transfer funds, and pay bills.

Wireless Advertising and Retailing

Although the mobile advertising market is currently small ($784 million), it is rapidly growing (up 17 percent from last year and expected to grow to over $6.2 billion by 2014), as more and more companies seek ways to exploit new databases of location-specific information. Alcatel-Lucent offers a new service to be managed by 1020 Placecast that will identify cell phone users within a specified distance of an advertiser's nearest outlet and notify them about the outlet's address and phone number, perhaps including a link to a coupon or other promotion. 1020 Placecast's clients include Hyatt, FedEx, and Avis Rent A Car.

Yahoo displays ads on its mobile home page for companies such as Pepsi, Procter & Gamble, Hilton, Nissan, and Intel. Google is displaying ads linked to cell phone searches by users of the mobile version of its search engine, while Microsoft offers banner and text advertising on its MSN Mobile portal in the United States. Ads are embedded in games, videos, and other mobile applications.

Shopkick is a mobile application that enables retailers such as Best Buy, Sports Authority, and Macy's to offer coupons to people when they walk into their stores. The shopkick app automatically recognizes when the user has entered a partner retail store, and offers a new virtual currency called "kickbucks," which can be redeemed for Facebook credits, iTunes Gift Cards, travel vouchers, DVD's, or immediate cash-back rewards at any of the partner stores.

In 2010, shoppers ordered about $2.2 billion in physical goods from Web sites via smartphones (over 1 billion of that at Amazon alone). Thirty percent of retailers have m-commerce Web sites—simplified versions of their Web sites that make it possible for shoppers to use cell phones to place orders. Clothing retailers Lilly Pulitzer and Armani Exchange, Home Depot, and 1–800 Flowers are among those companies with specialized apps for m-commerce sales.

Games and Entertainment

Cell phones have developed into portable entertainment platforms. Smartphones like the iPhone and Droid offer downloadable and streaming digital games, movies, TV shows, music, and ringtones.

Users of broadband services from the major wireless vendors can stream on-demand video clips, news clips, and weather reports. MobiTV, offered by Sprint and AT&T Wireless, features live TV programs, including MSNBC and Fox Sports. Film companies are starting to produce short films explicitly designed to play on mobile phones. User-generated content is also appearing in mobile form. Facebook, MySpace, YouTube, and other social networking sites have versions for mobile devices. In 2010, the top 10 most popular apps on Facebook are games, led by Farmville with over 16 million daily users.

4   BUILDING AN E-COMMERCE WEB SITE

Building a successful e-commerce site requires a keen understanding of business, technology, and social issues, as well as a systematic approach. A complete treatment of the topic is beyond the scope of this text, and students should consult books devoted to just this topic (Laudon and Traver, 2011). The two most important management challenges in building a successful e-commerce site are (1) developing a clear understanding of your business objectives and (2) knowing how to choose the right technology to achieve those objectives.

PIECES OF THE SITE-BUILDING PUZZLE

Let's assume you are a manager for a medium-sized, industrial parts firm of around 10,000 employees worldwide, operating in eight countries in Europe, Asia, and North America. Senior management has given you a budget of $1 million to build an e-commerce site within one year. The purpose of this site will be to sell and service the firm's 20,000 customers, who are mostly small machine and metal fabricating shops around the world. Where do you start?

First, you must be aware of the main areas where you will need to make decisions. On the organizational and human resources fronts, you will have to bring together a team of individuals who possess the skill sets needed to build and manage a successful e-commerce site. This team will make the key decisions about technology, site design, and social and information policies that will be applied at your site. The entire site development effort must be closely managed if you hope to avoid the disasters that have occurred at some firms.

You will also need to make decisions about your site's hardware, software, and telecommunications infrastructure. The demands of your customers should drive your choices of technology. Your customers will want technology that enables them to find what they want easily, view the product, purchase the product, and then receive the product from your warehouses quickly. You will also have to carefully consider your site's design. Once you have identified the key decision areas, you will need to think about a plan for the project.

BUSINESS OBJECTIVES, SYSTEM FUNCTIONALITY, AND INFORMATION REQUIREMENTS

In planning your Web site you need to answer the question, "What do we want the e-commerce site to do for our business?" The key lesson to be learned here is to let the business decisions drive the technology, not the reverse. This will ensure that your technology platform is aligned with your business. We will assume here that you have identified a business strategy and chosen a business model to achieve your strategic objectives. But how do you translate your strategies, business models, and ideas into a working e-commerce site?

Your planning should identify the specific business objectives for your site, and then develop a list of system functionalities and information requirements. Business objectives are simply capabilities you want your site to have. System functionalities are types of information systems capabilities you will need to achieve your business objectives. The information requirements for a system are the information elements that the system must produce in order to achieve the business objectives.

Table 7 describes some basic business objectives, system functionalities, and information requirements for a typical e-commerce site. The objectives must be translated into a description of system functionalities and ultimately into a set of precise information requirements. The specific information requirements for a system typically are defined in much greater detail than Table 7 indicates. The business objectives of an e-commerce site are similar to those of a physical retail store, but they must be provided entirely in digital form, 24 hours a day, 7 days a week.

BUILDING THE WEB SITE: IN-HOUSE VERSUS OUTSOURCING

There are many choices for building and maintaining Web sites. Much depends on how much money you are willing to spend. Choices range from outsourcing the entire Web site development to an external vendor to building everything yourself (in-house). You also have a second decision to make: will you host

TABLE 7 **SYSTEM ANALYSIS: BUSINESS OBJECTIVES, SYSTEM FUNCTIONALITY, AND INFORMATION REQUIREMENTS FOR A TYPICAL E-COMMERCE SITE**

BUSINESS OBJECTIVE	SYSTEM FUNCTIONALITY	INFORMATION REQUIREMENTS
Display goods	Digital catalog	Dynamic text and graphics catalog
Provide product information (content)	Product database	Product description, stocking numbers, inventory levels
Personalize/customize product	Customer on-site tracking	Site log for every customer visit; data mining capability to identify common customer paths and appropriate responses
Execute a transaction payment	Shopping cart/payment system	Secure credit card clearing; multiple options
Accumulate customer information	Customer database	Name, address, phone, and e-mail for all customers; online customer registration
Provide after-sale customer support	Sales database and customer relationship management system (CRM)	Customer ID, product, date, payment, shipment date
Coordinate marketing/advertising	Ad server, e-mail server, e-mail, campaign manager, ad banner manager	Site behavior log of prospects and customers linked to e-mail and banner ad campaigns
Understand marketing effectiveness	Site tracking and reporting system	Number of unique visitors, pages visited, products purchased, identified by marketing campaign
Provide production and supplier links	Inventory management system	Product and inventory levels, supplier ID and contact, order quantity data by product

(operate) the site on your firm's own servers or will you outsource the hosting to a Web host provider? There are some vendors who will design, build, and host your site, while others will either build or host (but not both). Figure 10 illustrates the alternatives.

FIGURE 10 **CHOICES IN BUILDING AND HOSTING WEB SITES**

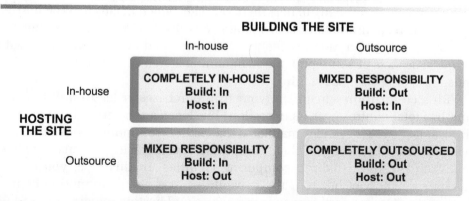

You have a number of alternatives to consider when building and hosting an e-commerce site.

The Building Decision

If you elect to build your own site, there are a range of options. Unless you are fairly skilled, you should use a pre-built template to create the Web site. For example, Yahoo Merchant Solutions, Amazon Stores, and eBay all provide templates that merely require you to input text, graphics, and other data, as well as the infrastructure to run the Web site once it has been created. This is the least costly and simplest solution, but you will be limited to the "look and feel" and functionality provided by the template and infrastructure.

If you have some experience with computers, you might decide to build the site yourself. There is a broad variety of tools, ranging from those that help you build everything truly "from scratch," such as Adobe Dreamweaver, Adobe InDesign, and Microsoft Expression, to top-of-the-line prepackaged site-building tools that can create sophisticated sites customized to your needs.

The decision to build a Web site on your own has a number of risks. Given the complexity of features such as shopping carts, credit card authentication and processing, inventory management, and order processing, development costs are high, as are the risks of doing a poor job. You will be reinventing what other specialized firms have already built, and your staff may face a long, difficult learning curve, delaying your entry to market. Your efforts could fail. On the positive side, you may able to build a site that does exactly what you want, and develop the in-house knowledge to revise the site rapidly if necessitated by a changing business environment.

If you choose more expensive site-building packages, you will be purchasing state-of-the-art software that is well tested. You could get to market sooner. However, to make a sound decision, you will have to evaluate many different software packages and this can take a long time. You may have to modify the packages to fit your business needs and perhaps hire additional outside consultants to do the modifications. Costs rise rapidly as modifications mount. A $4,000 package can easily become a $40,000 to $60,000 development project.

In the past, bricks-and-mortar retailers typically designed their e-commerce sites themselves (because they already had the skilled staff and IT infrastructure in place to do this). Today, however, larger retailers rely heavily on external vendors to provide sophisticated Web site capabilities, while also maintaining a substantial internal staff. Medium-size start-ups will often purchase a sophisticated package and then modify it to suit their needs. Very small mom-and-pop firms seeking simple storefronts will use templates.

The Hosting Decision

Now let's look at the hosting decision. Most businesses choose to outsource hosting and pay a company to host their Web site, which means that the hosting company is responsible for ensuring the site is "live" or accessible, 24 hours a day. By agreeing to a monthly fee, the business need not concern itself with technical aspects of setting up and maintaining a Web server, telecommunications links, or specialized staffing.

With a **co-location** agreement, your firm purchases or leases a Web server (and has total control over its operation) but locates the server in a vendor's physical facility. The vendor maintains the facility, communications lines, and the machinery. In the age of cloud computing, it is much less expensive to host your Web site in virtualized computing facilities. In this case, you do not purchase the server, but rent the capabilities of a cloud computing center. There is an extraordinary range of prices for cloud hosting, ranging from $4.95 a month, to several hundred thousands of dollars per month depending on the size of the Web site, bandwidth, storage, and support requirements. Very large providers (such as IBM, HP, and Oracle) achieve large economies of scale by establishing huge "server farms" located strategically around the country and the globe. What this means is that the cost of pure hosting has fallen as fast as the fall in server prices, dropping about 50 percent every year.

Web Site Budgets

Simple Web sites can be built and hosted with a first-year cost of $5,000 or less. The Web sites of large firms with high levels of interactivity and linkage to corporate systems cost several million dollars a year to create and operate. For instance, in September 2006, Bluefly, which sells discounted women's and men's designer clothes online, embarked on the process of developing an improved version of its Web site based on software from Art Technology Group (ATG). It launched the new site in August 2008. To date, it has invested over $5.3 million in connection with the redevelopment of the Web site. In 2010, Bluefly had online sales of $81 million, and is growing at 7.5 percent a year. It's e-commerce technology budget is over $8 million a year, roughly 10 percent of its total revenues (Bluefly, Inc., 2010).

Figure 11 provides some idea of the relative size of various Web site cost components. In general, the cost of hardware, software, and telecommunications for building and operating a Web site has fallen dramatically (by over 50 percent) since 2000, making it possible for very small entrepreneurs to create fairly sophisticated sites. At the same time, the costs of system maintenance and content creation have risen to make up more than half of typical Web site budgets. Providing content and smooth 24/7 operations are both very labor-intensive.

FIGURE 11   COMPONENTS OF A WEB SITE BUDGET

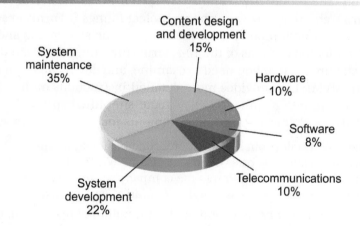

5   HANDS-ON MIS PROJECTS

The projects in this section give you hands-on experience developing e-commerce strategies for businesses, using spreadsheet software to research the profitability of an e-commerce company, and using Web tools to research and evaluate e-commerce hosting services.

Management Decision Problems

1. Columbiana is a small, independent island in the Caribbean. It wants to develop its tourist industry and attract more visitors. The island has many

historical buildings, forts, and other sites, along with rain forests and striking mountains. A few first-class hotels and several dozen less-expensive accommodations can be found along its beautiful white sand beaches. The major airlines have regular flights to Columbiana, as do several small airlines. Columbiana's government wants to increase tourism and develop new markets for the country's tropical agricultural products. How can a Web presence help? What Internet business model would be appropriate? What functions should the Web site perform?

2. Explore the Web sites of the following companies: Blue Nile, J.Crew, Circuit City, Black&Decker, Peet's Coffee & Tea, and Priceline. Determine which of these Web sites would benefit most from adding a company-sponsored blog to the Web site. List the business benefits of the blog. Specify the intended audience for the blog. Decide who in the company should author the blog, and select some topics for the blog.

Improving Decision Making: Using Spreadsheet Software to Analyze a Dot-Com Business

Software skills: Spreadsheet downloading, formatting, and formulas
Business skills: Financial statement analysis

Publicly traded companies, including those specializing in e-commerce, are required to file financial data with the U.S. Securities and Exchange Commission. By analyzing this information, you can determine the profitability of an e-commerce company and the viability of its business model.

Pick one e-commerce company on the Internet, for example, Ashford, Buy.com, Yahoo, or Priceline. Study the Web pages that describe the company and explain its purpose and structure. Use the Web to find articles that comment on the company. Then visit the Securities and Exchange Commission's Web site at www.sec.gov and select Filings & Forms to access the company's 10-K (annual report) form showing income statements and balance sheets. Select only the sections of the 10-K form containing the desired portions of financial statements that you need to examine, and download them into your spreadsheet. (MyMISLab provides more detailed instructions on how to download this 10-K data into a spreadsheet.) Create simplified spreadsheets of the company's balance sheets and income statements for the past three years.

- Is the company a dot-com success, borderline business, or failure? What information dictates the basis of your decision? Why? When answering these questions, pay special attention to the company's three-year trends in revenues, costs of sales, gross margins, operating expenses, and net margins.

- Prepare an overhead presentation (with a minimum of five slides), including appropriate spreadsheets or charts, and present your work to your professor and classmates.

Achieving Operational Excellence: Evaluating E-Commerce Hosting Services

Software skills: Web browser software
Business skills: Evaluating e-commerce hosting services

This project will help develop your Internet skills in commercial services for hosting an e-commerce site for a small start-up company.

You would like to set up a Web site to sell towels, linens, pottery, and tableware from Portugal and are examining services for hosting small business

Internet storefronts. Your Web site should be able to take secure credit card payments and to calculate shipping costs and taxes. Initially, you would like to display photos and descriptions of 40 different products. Visit Yahoo! Small Business, GoDaddy, and Volusion and compare the range of e-commerce hosting services they offer to small businesses, their capabilities, and costs. Also examine the tools they provide for creating an e-commerce site. Compare these services and decide which you would use if you were actually establishing a Web store. Write a brief report indicating your choice and explaining the strengths and weaknesses of each.

LEARNING TRACK MODULES

The following Learning Tracks provide content relevant to topics covered in this chapter:

1. Building a Web Page
2. E-commerce Challenges: The Story of Online Groceries
3. Build an E-commerce Business Plan
4. Hot New Careers in E-commerce

Review Summary

1. *What are the unique features of e-commerce, digital markets, and digital goods?*

   E-commerce involves digitally enabled commercial transactions between and among organizations and individuals. Unique features of e-commerce technology include ubiquity, global reach, universal technology standards, richness, interactivity, information density, capabilities for personalization and customization, and social technology.

   Digital markets are said to be more "transparent" than traditional markets, with reduced information asymmetry, search costs, transaction costs, and menu costs, along with the ability to change prices dynamically based on market conditions. Digital goods, such as music, video, software, and books, can be delivered over a digital network. Once a digital product has been produced, the cost of delivering that product digitally is extremely low.

2. *What are the principal e-commerce business and revenue models?*

   E-commerce business models are e-tailers, transaction brokers, market creators, content providers, community providers, service providers, and portals. The principal e-commerce revenue models are advertising, sales, subscription, free/freemium, transaction fee, and affiliate.

3. *How has e-commerce transformed marketing?*

   The Internet provides marketers with new ways of identifying and communicating with millions of potential customers at costs far lower than traditional media. Crowdsourcing utilizing the "wisdom of crowds" helps companies learn from customers in order to improve product offerings and increase customer value. Behavioral targeting techniques increase the effectiveness of banner, rich media, and video ads.

4. *How has e-commerce affected business-to-business transactions?*

   B2B e-commerce generates efficiencies by enabling companies to locate suppliers, solicit bids, place orders, and track shipments in transit electronically. Net marketplaces provide a single, digital marketplace for many buyers and sellers. Private industrial networks link a firm with its suppliers and other strategic business partners to develop highly efficient and responsive supply chains.

5. *What is the role of m-commerce in business, and what are the most important m-commerce applications?*

M-commerce is especially well-suited for location-based applications, such as finding local hotels and restaurants, monitoring local traffic and weather, and providing personalized location-based marketing. Mobile phones and handhelds are being used for mobile bill payment, banking, securities trading, transportation schedule updates, and downloads of digital content, such as music, games, and video clips. M-commerce requires wireless portals and special digital payment systems that can handle micropayments.

6. *What issues must be addressed when building an e-commerce Web site?*

Building a successful e-commerce site requires a clear understanding of the business objectives to be achieved by the site and selection of the right technology to achieve those objectives. E-commerce sites can be built and hosted in-house or partially or fully outsourced to external service providers.

Key Terms

Advertising revenue model
Affiliate revenue model
Behavioral marketing
Business-to-business (B2B) electronic commerce
Business-to-consumer (B2C) electronic commerce
Co-location
Community providers
Consumer-to-consumer (C2C) electronic commerce
Cost Transparency
Crowdsourcing
Customization
Digital goods
Disintermediation
Dynamic pricing
Electronic data interchange (EDI)
E-tailer
Exchanges
Free/freemium revenue model
Information asymmetry
Information density
Intellectual property
Long tail marketing
Market creator

Market entry costs
Marketspace
Menu costs
Micropayment systems
Mobile commerce (m-commerce)
Net marketplaces
Personalization
Podcasting
Prediction market
Price discrimination
Price transparency
Private exchange
Private industrial networks
Revenue model
Richness
Sales revenue model
Search costs
Social shopping
Streaming
Subscription revenue model
Transaction costs
Transaction fee revenue model
Wisdom of crowds

Review Questions

1. What are the unique features of e-commerce, digital markets, and digital goods?

   - Name and describe four business trends and three technology trends shaping e-commerce today.

   - List and describe the eight unique features of e-commerce.

   - Define a digital market and digital goods and describe their distinguishing features.

2. What are the principal e-commerce business and revenue models?

   - Name and describe the principal e-commerce business models.

   - Name and describe the e-commerce revenue models.

3. How has e-commerce transformed marketing?

   - Explain how social networking and the "wisdom of crowds" help companies improve their marketing.

   - Define behavioral targeting and explain how it works at individual Web sites and on advertising networks.

4. How has e-commerce affected business-to-business transactions?

   - Explain how Internet technology supports business-to-business electronic commerce.

- Define and describe Net marketplaces and explain how they differ from private industrial networks (private exchanges).

5. What is the role of m-commerce in business, and what are the most important m-commerce applications?

- List and describe important types of m-commerce services and applications.

- Describe some of the barriers to m-commerce.

6. What issues must be addressed when building an e-commerce Web site?

- List and describe each of the factors that go into the building of an e-commerce Web site.

- List and describe four business objectives, four system functionalities, and four information requirements of a typical e-commerce Web site.

- List and describe each of the options for building and hosting e-commerce Web sites.

Discussion Questions

1. How does the Internet change consumer and supplier relationships?

2. The Internet may not make corporations obsolete, but the corporations will have to change their business models. Do you agree? Why or why not?

3. How have social technologies changed e-commerce?

Video Cases

Video Cases and Instructional Videos illustrating some of the concepts in this chapter are available. Contact your instructor to access these videos.

Collaboration and Teamwork: Performing a Competitive Analysis of E-commerce Sites

Form a group with three or four of your classmates. Select two businesses that are competitors in the same industry and that use their Web sites for electronic commerce. Visit these Web sites. You might compare, for example, the Web sites for iTunes and Napster, Amazon and BarnesandNoble.com, or E*Trade and Scottrade. Prepare an evaluation of each business's Web site in terms of its functions, user friendliness, and ability to support the company's business strategy. Which Web site does a better job? Why? Can you make some recommendations to improve these Web sites? If possible, use Google Sites to post links to Web pages, team communication announcements, and work assignments; to brainstorm; and to work collaboratively on project documents. Try to use Google Docs to develop a presentation of your findings for the class.

Amazon vs. Walmart: Which Giant Will Dominate E-commerce?
CASE STUDY

Since arriving on the dot-com scene in 1995, Amazon.com has grown from a small online bookseller to one of the largest retailing companies in the world, and easily the largest e-commerce retailer. The company has come a long way from its roots as a small Internet start-up selling books online. In addition to books, Amazon now sells millions of new, used, and collectible items in categories such as apparel and accessories, electronics, computers, kitchen and housewares, music, DVDs, videos, cameras, office products, toys and baby items, computers, software, travel services, sporting goods, jewelry, and watches. In 2010, sales of electronics and general merchandise comprised the majority of Amazon's sales for the first time.

Amazon.com would like to be "The Walmart of the Web," and it is indeed the Internet's top retailer. But in 2010, another firm emerged as a serious challenger for the title of 'Walmart of the Web': Walmart. Though Walmart is a latecomer to the world of e-commerce, the world's largest retailer appears to have its sights set on Amazon and is ready to battle it out for online e-tailing supremacy.

In contrast with Amazon, Walmart was founded as a traditional, off-line, physical store in 1962, and has grown from a single general store managed by founder Sam Walton to the largest retailer in the world with nearly 8,000 stores worldwide.

Based in Bentonville, Arkansas, Walmart made $405 billion in sales last year, which is about 20 times as much as Amazon. In fact, based on current size alone, the battle between Walmart and Amazon is far from a clash of two similarly powerful titans. Walmart is clearly the bigger and stronger of the two, and for the time being, Amazon is not a big threat to Walmart as a whole.

Amazon, however, is not an easy target. The company has created a recognizable and highly successful brand in online retailing as a mass-market, low-price, high-volume online superstore. It has developed extensive warehousing facilities and an extremely efficient distribution network specifically designed for Web shopping. Its premium shipping service, Amazon Prime, provides "free" two-day shipping at an affordable price (currently only $79 per year), often considered to be a weak point for online retailers. Even without Amazon Prime, designated Super Saver items totaling at least $25.00 ship for free.

Amazon's technology platform is massive and powerful enough to support not only sales of its own items but also those of third-party small and large businesses, which integrate their products into Amazon's Web site and use its order entry and payment systems to process their own sales. (Amazon does not own these products, and shipping is handled by the third party, with Amazon collecting 10-20 percent on the sale). This enables Amazon to offer an even wider array of products than it could carry on its own while keeping inventory costs low and increasing revenue. Amazon has further expanded its product selection via acquisitions such as the 2009 purchase of online shoe shopping site Zappos.com, which earned $1 billion in retail sales in 2008 and gave the company an edge in footwear.

In the third quarter of 2009, when retail sales dipped 4 percent across the board, Amazon's sales increased by 24 percent. Its sales of electronics and general merchandise, which is the most prominent area of competition between Amazon and Walmart, were up 44 percent. And e-commerce is expected to become an increasingly large portion of total retail sales. Some estimates indicate that e-commerce could account for 15 to 20 percent of total retail in the United States within the next decade, as more and more shoppers opt to avoid the hassle of shopping at a physical location in favor of shopping online. If this happens, Amazon is in the best position to benefit. In the meantime, e-commerce has not suffered as much from the recession and is recovering more quickly than traditional retail, giving Walmart more reason for concern.

However, Walmart also brings a strong hand to the table. It is an even larger and more recognizable brand than Amazon. Consumers associate Walmart with the lowest price, which Walmart has the flexibility to offer on any given item because of its size and ability to keep overhead costs to a minimum. Walmart can lose money selling a hot product at extremely low margins and expect to make money on the strength of the large quantities of other items it sells. It also has a legendary continuous inventory replenishment system that starts restocking merchandise as soon as an item reaches the checkout counter. Walmart's efficiency, flexibility, and ability to fine-tune its inventory to carry exactly what customers want have been enduring sources of competitive advantage. Walmart also has a significant physical presence, with stores all across the United States and in many other countries, and its stores provide the instant gratification of shopping, buying an item, and taking it home immediately, as opposed to waiting when ordering from Amazon.

Walmart believes Amazon's Achilles' heel is the costs and delays of shipping online purchases to buyers. Customers who buy some of the more than 1.5 million products on Walmart.com can have them shipped free to a local Walmart, and pick up their purchases at these stores. Internet shoppers may be tempted to pick up other items once they are inside the store. New service desks at the front of some stores make it even easier for shoppers to retrieve their purchases. A Walmart on the outskirts of Chicago is testing a drive-through window, similar to those found at pharmacies and fast-food restaurants, where shoppers can pick up their Internet orders.

In late 2009, Walmart.com began aggressively lowering prices on a wide variety of popular items, making sure in each instance to undercut Amazon's price. The types of items Walmart discounted included books, DVDs, other electronics, and toys. The message was clear: Walmart is not going down without a fight in e-commerce. And Walmart.com executive Raul Vazquez echoed the same thought, saying that Walmart will adjust its prices "as low as we need to" to be the "low-cost leader" on the Web. In other words, the two companies are now locked in a price war, and both sites are determined to win.

The most high profile area where the two companies have done battle is in online book sales. Amazon's Kindle e-book reader may have started the conflict by offering the most popular books in e-book format for just $9.99. Though many publishers have since balked at allowing their books to be sold in the e-book format for that price, the battle has raged on in traditional formats. Several high-profile book releases, such as Stephen King's newest novel, *Under the Dome*, illustrated just how low both companies are willing to go. Walmart lowered its price for the novel to just $10, claiming that it wasn't in response to the $9.99 e-book price. Amazon matched that price shortly thereafter. In response, Walmart dropped the price to $9.00 a few days later. The book's retail cover price is $35 dollars, and its wholesale price is about $17. This means that both retailers are losing at least $7 on every copy of *Under the Dome* that they sell at that price.

Walmart sees its massive price cuts as a way to gain market share quickly as they enter the online bookselling marketplace at a time when e-book readers and Apple iPhones and iPads make the e-book format popular. Amazon has demonstrated that in the short term it is more than capable of competing with Walmart on price. As of this case's writing, Amazon had raised its price on the *Under the Dome* back up to $17. Walmart's price, of course, was $16.99. The two sites have had similar clashes over many high-profile books, like J.K. Rowling's *Harry Potter and the Half-Blood Prince* and James Patterson's *I, Alex Cross*, the latter selling for $13.00 on Amazon and $12.99 on Walmart.com as of this writing.

The feud between the two sites has spilled over into other types of merchandise. Amazon and Walmart.com have competed over Xbox 360 consoles, popular DVD releases, and other big-ticket electronics. Even popular toys like the perennial top seller Easy-Bake Oven have been caught up in the fray. With the 2009 holiday shopping season in full swing, Walmart dropped its price for the toy from $28 to just $17. Amazon slashed its price to $18 on the very same day.

Amazon claims it doesn't see shipping as a weakness. According to Amazon spokesperson Craig Berman, "Shopping on Amazon means you don't have to fight the crowds. We bring the items to your doorstep. You don't have to fight through traffic or find a parking space." Moreover, Amazon has taken steps recently to speed delivery times. In October, it began offering same-day delivery in seven U.S. cities, at an extra cost to shoppers. By working with carriers and improving its own internal systems, Amazon also started offering second-day deliveries on Saturdays, shaving two days off some orders. And Amazon continues to expand its selection of goods to be as exhaustive as Walmart's. In November 2010, Walmart introduced free shipping for all online orders.

Amazon founder and CEO Jeff Bezos is fond of describing the U.S. retail market as having "room for many winners." Will this hold true for Walmart and Amazon going forward? Walmart remains unchallenged among traditional physical retailers, but will it topple Amazon on the Web? Or will Amazon continue to be the "Walmart" of online retailers? Alternatively, will Walmart end up enlarging the online retail market space, helping Amazon grow in the process?

Sources: Kelly Evans, "How America Now Shops: Online Stores, Dollar Retailers (Watch Out Walmart)," *The Wall Street Journal*, March 23, 2010; Brad Stone, "The Fight Over Who Sets Prices at the Online Mall," *The New York Times*, February 8, 2010; Paul Sharma, "The Music Battle, Replayed with Books," *The Wall Street Journal*, November 24, 2009; Martin Peers, "Rivals Explore Amazon's Territory," *The Wall Street Journal*, January 7, 2010; "Is Wal-Mart Gaining on Amazon.com?" *The Wall Street Journal*, reprinted on MSN Money, December 18, 2009; "Amazon Steps Into Zappos' Shoes," *eMarketer*, July 24, 2009; Brad Stone, "Can Amazon Be the Wal-Mart of the Web?" *The New York Times*, September 20, 2009; and Brad Stone and Stephanie Rosenbloom, "Price War Brews Between Amazon and Wal-Mart," *The New York Times*, November 24, 2009.

CASE STUDY QUESTIONS

1. What concepts in the chapter are illustrated in this case?

2. Analyze Amazon and Walmart.com using the value chain and competitive forces models.

3. What are the management, organization, and technology factors that have contributed to the success of both Wal-Mart and Amazon?

4. Compare Wal-Mart's and Amazon's e-commerce business models. Which is stronger? Explain your answer.

5. Where would you prefer to make your Internet purchases? Amazon or Walmart.com? Why?

References

Adomavicius, Gediminas and Alexander Tuzhilin. "Personalization Technologies: A Process-Oriented Perspective." Communications of the ACM 48, no. 10 (October 2005).

Bakos, Yannis. "The Emerging Role of Electronic Marketplaces and the Internet." Communications of the ACM 41, no. 8 (August 1998).

Bluefly, Inc. Form 10K Report for Fiscal Year Ended December 31, 2009, filed with the Securities and Exchange Commission (February 19, 2010).

Bluefly, Inc. "Form 10K Report for Fiscal Year Ended December 31, 2009." Filed with the Securities and Exchange Commission (February 19, 2010).

Bo, Xiao and Izak Benbasat. "E-Commerce Product Recommendation Agents: Use, Characteristics, and Impact." MIS Quarterly 31, no. 1 (March 2007).

Brynjolfsson, Erik, Yu Hu, and Michael D. Smith. "Consumer Surplus in the Digital Economy: Estimating the Value of Increased Product Variety at Online Booksellers." Management Science 49, no. 11 (November 2003).

Cain Miller, Claire and Jenna Wortham. "Technology Aside, Most People Still Decline to be Located." The New York Times (August 29, 2010).

Cain Miller, Claire. "Take a Step Closer for an Invitation to Shop." The New York Times (February 23, 2010).

Clemons, Eric K. "Business Models for Monetizing Internet Applications and Web Sites: Experience, Theory, and Predictions." Journal of Management Information Systems 26, No. 2 (Fall 2009).

Clifford, Stephanie. "Aisle by Aisle, an App that Pushes Bargains." The New York Times (August 17, 2010).

Clifford, Stephanie. "Web Coupons Know Lots About You, and They Tell." The New York Times (April 16, 2010).

ComScore. "Facebook Takes Lead In Time Spent. comScore Media Metrix. Press Release. (September 9, 2010).

ComScore. "Facebook Takes Lead In Time Spent." comScore Media Metrix Press Release (September 9, 2010).

Dou, Wenyu, Kai H. Lim, Chenting Su, Nan Zhou, and Nan Cui. "Brand Positioning Strategy Using Search Engine Marketing." MIS Quarterly 34, no.2 (June 2010).

EMarketer, "US Mobile Subscribers." eMarketer Chart (March 2010d)

EMarketer. "Paid Music Content." eMarketer Report (January 2010c).

EMarketer. "US Internet Users, 2010." eMarketer Report (April 2010b).

EMarketer. "US Portal Advertising Revenues." Report. April 2010e

EMarketer. "US Retail E-commerce Forecast." eMarketer Report (March 2010a).

Evans, Philip and Thomas S. Wurster. Blown to Bits: How the New Economics of Information Transforms Strategy. Boston, MA: Harvard Business School Press (2000).

Fuller, Johann, Hans Muhlbacher, Kurt Matzler, and Gregor Jawecki. "Customer Empowerment Through Internet-Based Co-Creation." Journal of Management Information Systems 26, No. 3 (Winter 2010).

Hallerman, David. "US Advertising Spending: The New Reality." EMarketer (April 2009a).

Helft, Miguel. "Data, Not Design, Is King in the Age of Google." The New York Times (May 10, 2009).

Howe, Heff. Crowdsourcing: Why the Power of the Crowd Is Driving the Future of Business. New York: Random House (2008).

Internetworldstats.com. "Internet Usage Statistics: The Big Picture." Internetworldstats.com, (June 2010).

Jiang, Zhengrui and Sumit Sarkar. "Speed Matters: The Role of Free Software Offer in Software Diffusion." Journal of Management Information Systems 26, No. 3 (Winter 2010).

Kaplan, Steven and Mohanbir Sawhney. "E-Hubs: the New B2B Marketplaces." Harvard Business Review (May-June 2000).

Kauffman, Robert J. and Bin Wang. "New Buyers' Arrival Under Dynamic Pricing Market Microstructure: The Case of Group-Buying Discounts on the Internet, Journal of Management Information Systems 18, no. 2 (Fall 2001).

Laseter, Timothy M., Elliott Rabinovich, Kenneth K. Boyer, and M. Johnny Rungtusanatham. "Critical Issues in Internet Retailing." MIT Sloan Management Review 48, no. 3 (Spring 2007).

Laudon, Kenneth C. and Carol Guercio Traver. E-Commerce: Business, Technology, Society, 7th edition. Upper Saddle River, NJ: Prentice-Hall (2011).

Leimeister, Jan Marco, Michael Huber, Ulrich Bretschneider, and Helmut Krcmar." Leveraging Crowdsourcing: Activation-Supporting Components for IT-Based Ideas Competition." Journal of Management Information Systems 26, No. 1 (Summer 2009).

Magretta, Joan. "Why Business Models Matter." Harvard Business Review (May 2002).

Markoff, John. "The Cellphone, Navigating Our Lives." The New York Times (February 17, 2009).

Mattioli, Dana. "Retailers Answer Call of Smartphones." The Wall Street Journal (June 11, 2010).

Michael D. Smith and Rahul Telang. "Competing with Free: The Impact of Movie Broadcasts on DVD Sales and Internet Piracy." MIS Quarterly 33, No. 2 (June 2009).

Miller, Claire Cain. "Google Campaign to Build Up Its Display Ads." The New York Times (September 21, 2010).

Pavlou, Paul A., Huigang Liang, and Yajiong Xue. "Understanding and Mitigating Uncertainty in Online Exchange Relationships: A Principal-Agent Perspective." MIS Quarterly 31, no. 1 (March 2007).

Pew Internet & American Life Project. "US Daily Internet Activities." (2010).

Pew Internet & American Life Project. "US Daily Internet Activities." Pew Internet & American Life Project, 2010.

Philips, Jeremy. "To Rake It In, Give It Away." The Wall Street Journal (July 8, 2009).

Rayport, Jeffrey. "Demand-Side Innovation: Where IT Meets Marketing." Optimize Magazine (February 2007).

Resnick, Paul and Hal Varian. "Recommender Systems." Communications of the ACM (March 2007).

Rosenbloom, Stephanie. "Cellphones Let Shoppers Point, Click, and Purchase." The New York Times (February 26, 2010).

Schoder, Detlef and Alex Talalavesky. "The Price Isn't Right." MIT Sloan Management Review (August 22, 2010).

Schultze, Ulrike and Wanda J. Orlikowski. "A Practice Perspective on Technology-Mediated Network Relations: The Use of Internet-Based Self-Serve Technologies." Information Systems Research 15, no. 1 (March 2004).

Smith, Michael D., Joseph Bailey and Erik Brynjolfsson."Understanding Digital Markets: Review and Assessment" in Erik Brynjolfsson and Brian Kahin, ed. Understanding the Digital Economy. Cambridge, MA: MIT Press (1999).

Steel, Emily, "Exploring Ways to Build a Better Consumer Profile." The Wall Street Journal (March 15, 2010).

Steel, Emily."Marketers Watch Friends Interact Online." The Wall Street Journal (April 15, 2010).

Story, Louise. "To Aim Ads, Web Is Keeping Closer Eye on You. " The New York Times (March 10, 2008).

Stross, Randall. "Just Browsing? A Web Store May Follow You Out the Door." The New York Times (May 17, 2009).

Surowiecki, James. The Wisdom of Crowds: Why the Many Are Smarter Than the Few and How Collective Wisdom Shapes Business, Economies, Societies and Nations. Boston: Little, Brown (2004).

Tsai, Jessica. "Social Media: The Five-Year Forecast." destinationcrm.com (April 27, 2009).

United States Census Bureau. "E-Stats Report. Measuring the Electronic Economy." (May 27, 2010).

United States Census Bureau. "E-Stats Report. Measuring the Electronic Economy." (May 27, 2010). www.census.gov.

Worthen, Ben. "Branching Out: Mobile Banking Finds New Users." The Wall Street Journal (February 3, 2009).

Chapter 13

Building Information Systems

From Chapter 13 of *Management Information Systems: Managing the Digital Firm*, 12/e. Kenneth C. Laudon, Jane P. Laudon. Copyright © 2012 by Pearson Education. Published by Prentice Hall. All rights reserved.

Building Information Systems

Interactive Sessions:

Can Business Process
   Management Make a
   Difference?

Zimbra Zooms Ahead with
   OneView

CIMB GROUP REDESIGNS ITS ACCOUNT OPENING PROCESS

CIMB Group, headquartered in Kuala Lumpur, is Malaysia's second largest financial services provider and the third largest company on the Malaysian stock exchange. It offers a full range of financial products and services, including consumer banking, corporate and investment banking, insurance, and asset management, and its retail banking network of over 1,100 branches is the largest in Southeast Asia.

What's wrong with this? Not much, except management wants to do even better. The company launched a five-year information technology transformation initiative in January 2008 to align its information technology investments more closely with its resources. It used the ARIS business process management (BPM) tool from IDS Scheer to identify 25 different areas for improving technology, people, and processes. The ARIS software helped identify gaps and inefficiencies in existing processes.

The process of opening an account at a retail branch was singled out as needing improvement. Improving this process was given high priority because it provided customers with their first impression of CIMB Group's service and customer experience.

The old account-opening process was cumbersome and time-consuming, requiring filling out four separate data entry screens for customer information, account details, name and address details, and details concerning the automated teller machine (ATM) card. New technology created opportunities for a short-cut. Malaysia has a compulsory identity card for its citizens and permanent residents known as the Government Multipurpose Card, or MyKad. It is the world's first smart identity card, incorporating a microchip with identification data (such as name, address, gender, and religion) and capabilities for user authentication, government services, electronic payments, education, loyalty programs, mobile applications, and other conveniences.

CIMB Group's systems-building team modified the front end of the customer account system to reduce the number of data entry screens and to accept customer data obtained from scanning a MyKad card. By automatically extracting most of the identification data required to open an account from a MyKad card, CIMB only needs to use a single data entry screen to set up a new account. CIMB Group was thus able to streamline the account-opening process, reducing the time required to open a bank account by 56 percent. The experience became more personal and engaging for both the bank officer and the customer. Productivity has increased, lowering CIMB Group's cost by 8 to 9 percent annually.

Sources: Avanti Kumar, "Reaching for the Skies," MIS Asia, April 16, 2010; www.ids-scheer.com, accessed October 5, 2010; and www.cimb.com, accessed October 5, 2010.

Corbis 2010

The experience of CIMB Group illustrates some of the steps required to design and build new information systems. Building the new system entailed analyzing the organization's problems with existing information systems, assessing people's information requirements, selecting appropriate technology, and redesigning business processes and jobs. Management had to monitor the system-building effort and evaluate its benefits and costs. The new information system represented a process of planned organizational change.

The chapter-opening diagram calls attention to important points raised by this case and this chapter. CIMB Group's process for setting up a new account was excessively manual and inefficient, dragging down business operations and raising costs. It also detracted from the brand image the company wanted to project as a company with high-quality customer service. Management had an opportunity to use information technology and the information stored in MyKad smart cards to streamline and redesign this process.

CIMB's system-building team evaluated alternative system solutions. It selected a solution that replaces the process of entering customer and account data manually into a series of four data entry screens with one that obtains most of the same data by swiping a MyKad smart card. This solution did not replace CIMB's existing banking system entirely, but enhanced it with a more efficient and streamlined user interface. These enhancements improved business operations by reducing the amount of time to open a new account with CIMB Group and making the customer experience more pleasant.

1 SYSTEMS AS PLANNED ORGANIZATIONAL CHANGE

Building a new information system is one kind of planned organizational change. The introduction of a new information system involves much more than new hardware and software. It also includes changes in jobs, skills, management, and organization. When we design a new information system, we are redesigning the organization. System builders must understand how a system will affect specific business processes and the organization as a whole.

SYSTEMS DEVELOPMENT AND ORGANIZATIONAL CHANGE

Information technology can promote various degrees of organizational change, ranging from incremental to far-reaching. Figure 1 shows four kinds of structural organizational change that are enabled by information technology: (1) automation, (2) rationalization, (3) business process redesign, and (4) paradigm shifts. Each carries different risks and rewards.

The most common form of IT-enabled organizational change is **automation**. The first applications of information technology involved assisting employees with performing their tasks more efficiently and effectively. Calculating paychecks and payroll registers, giving bank tellers instant access to customer deposit records, and developing a nationwide reservation network for airline ticket agents are all examples of early automation.

FIGURE 1   **ORGANIZATIONAL CHANGE CARRIES RISKS AND REWARDS**

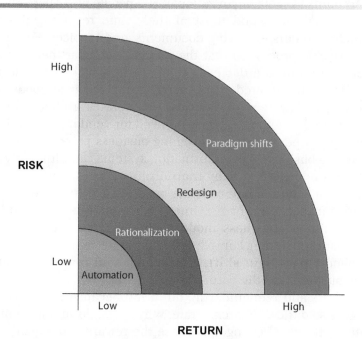

The most common forms of organizational change are automation and rationalization. These relatively slow-moving and slow-changing strategies present modest returns but little risk. Faster and more comprehensive change—such as redesign and paradigm shifts—carries high rewards but offers substantial chances of failure.

A deeper form of organizational change—one that follows quickly from early automation—is **rationalization of procedures**. Automation frequently reveals new bottlenecks in production and makes the existing arrangement of procedures and structures painfully cumbersome. Rationalization of procedures is the streamlining of standard operating procedures. For example, CIMB Bank's system for handling retail banking accounts is effective not only because it uses computer technology but also because the company simplified the business process for opening a customer account. CIMB streamlined its workflow to take advantage of the system's new user interface and software for importing personal data from MyKad.

Rationalization of procedures is often found in programs for making a series of continuous quality improvements in products, services, and operations, such as total quality management (TQM) and six sigma. **Total quality management (TQM)** makes achieving quality an end in itself and the responsibility of all people and functions within an organization. TQM derives from concepts developed by American quality experts such as W. Edwards Deming and Joseph Juran, but it was popularized by the Japanese. **Six sigma** is a specific measure of quality, representing 3.4 defects per million opportunities. Most companies cannot achieve this level of quality, but use six sigma as a goal for driving ongoing quality improvement programs.

A more powerful type of organizational change is **business process redesign**, in which business processes are analyzed, simplified, and redesigned. Business process redesign reorganizes workflows, combining steps to cut waste and eliminate repetitive, paper-intensive tasks. (Sometimes the new design eliminates jobs as well.) It is much more ambitious than rationalization of procedures, requiring a new vision of how the process is to be organized.

A widely cited example of business process redesign is Ford Motor Company's invoiceless processing, which reduced headcount in Ford's North American Accounts Payable organization of 500 people by 75 percent. Accounts payable clerks used to spend most of their time resolving discrepancies between purchase orders, receiving documents, and invoices. Ford redesigned its accounts payable process so that the purchasing department enters a purchase order into an online database that can be checked by the receiving department when the ordered items arrive. If the received goods match the purchase order, the system automatically generates a check for accounts payable to send to the vendor. There is no need for vendors to send invoices.

Rationalizing procedures and redesigning business processes are limited to specific parts of a business. New information systems can ultimately affect the design of the entire organization by transforming how the organization carries out its business or even the nature of the business. For instance, the long-haul trucking and transportation firm Schneider National used new information systems to change its business model. Schneider created a new business managing logistics for other companies. This more radical form of business change is called a **paradigm shift**. A paradigm shift involves rethinking the nature of the business and the nature of the organization.

Paradigm shifts and reengineering often fail because extensive organizational change is so difficult to orchestrate. Why, then, do so many corporations contemplate such radical change? Because the rewards are equally high (see Figure 1). In many instances, firms seeking paradigm shifts and pursuing reengineering strategies achieve stunning, order-of-magnitude increases in their returns on investment (or productivity).

BUSINESS PROCESS REDESIGN

Like CIMB Group, described in the chapter-opening case, many businesses today are trying to use information technology to improve their business processes. Some of these systems entail incremental process change, but others require more far-reaching redesign of business processes. To deal with these changes, organizations are turning to business process management. **Business process management** provides a variety of tools and methodologies to analyze existing processes, design new processes, and optimize those processes. BPM is never concluded because process improvement requires continual change. Companies practicing business process management go through the following steps:

1. **Identify processes for change:** One of the most important strategic decisions that a firm can make is not deciding how to use computers to improve business processes, but understanding what business processes need improvement. When systems are used to strengthen the wrong business model or business processes, the business can become more efficient at doing what it should not do. As a result, the firm becomes vulnerable to competitors who may have discovered the right business model. Considerable time and cost may also be spent improving business processes that have little impact on overall firm performance and revenue. Managers need to determine what business processes are the most important and how improving these processes will help business performance.

2. **Analyze existing processes:** Existing business processes should be modeled and documented, noting inputs, outputs, resources, and the sequence of activities. The process design team identifies redundant steps, paper-intensive tasks, bottlenecks, and other inefficiencies.

Figure 2 illustrates the "as-is" process for purchasing a book from a physical bookstore. Consider what happens when a customer visits a physical book-

FIGURE 2   AS-IS BUSINESS PROCESS FOR PURCHASING A BOOK FROM A PHYSICAL BOOKSTORE

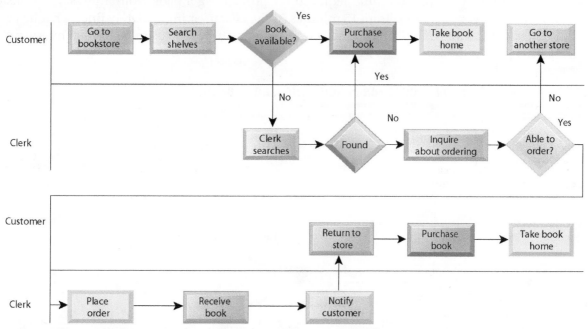

Purchasing a book from a physical bookstore requires many steps to be performed by both the seller and the customer.

store and searches its shelves for a book. If he or she finds the book, that person takes it to the checkout counter and pays for it via credit card, cash, or check. If the customer is unable to locate the book, he or she must ask a bookstore clerk to search the shelves or check the bookstore's inventory records to see if it is in stock. If the clerk finds the book, the customer purchases it and leaves. If the book is not available locally, the clerk inquires about ordering it for the customer, from the bookstore's warehouse or from the book's distributor or publisher. Once the ordered book arrives at the bookstore, a bookstore employee telephones the customer with this information. The customer would have to go to the bookstore again to pick up the book and pay for it. If the bookstore is unable to order the book for the customer, the customer would have to try another bookstore. You can see that this process has many steps and might require the customer to make multiple trips to the bookstore.

3. **Design the new process:** Once the existing process is mapped and measured in terms of time and cost, the process design team will try to improve the process by designing a new one. A new streamlined "to-be" process will be documented and modeled for comparison with the old process.

Figure 3 illustrates how the book-purchasing process can be redesigned by taking advantage of the Internet. The customer accesses an online bookstore over the Internet from his or her computer. He or she searches the bookstore's online catalog for the book he or she wants. If the book is available, the customer orders the book online, supplying credit card and shipping address information, and the book is delivered to the customer's home. If the online bookstore does not carry the book, the customer selects another online bookstore and searches for the book again. This process has far fewer steps than that for purchasing the book in a physical bookstore, requires much less effort on the part of the customer, and requires less sales staff for customer service. The new process is therefore much more efficient and time-saving.

The new process design needs to be justified by showing how much it reduces time and cost or enhances customer service and value. Management first measures the time and cost of the existing process as a baseline. In our example, the time required for purchasing a book from a physical bookstore might range from 15 minutes (if the customer immediately finds what he or she wants) to 30 minutes if the book is in stock but has to be located by sales staff.

FIGURE 3   REDESIGNED PROCESS FOR PURCHASING A BOOK ONLINE

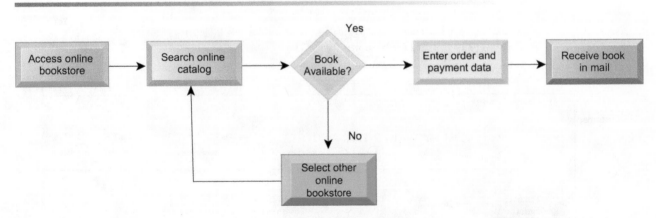

Using Internet technology makes it possible to redesign the process for purchasing a book so that it requires fewer steps and consumes fewer resources.

If the book has to be ordered from another source, the process might take one or two weeks and another trip to the bookstore for the customer. If the customer lives far away from the bookstore, the time to travel to the bookstore would have to be factored in. The bookstore will have to pay the costs for maintaining a physical store and keeping the book in stock, for sales staff on site, and for shipment costs if the book has to be obtained from another location.

The new process for purchasing a book online might only take several minutes, although the customer might have to wait several days or a week to receive the book in the mail and will have to pay a shipping charge. But the customer saves time and money by not having to travel to the bookstore or make additional visits to pick up the book. Booksellers' costs are lower because they do not have to pay for a physical store location or for local inventory.

4. **Implement the new process:** Once the new process has been thoroughly modeled and analyzed, it must be translated into a new set of procedures and work rules. New information systems or enhancements to existing systems may have to be implemented to support the redesigned process. The new process and supporting systems are rolled out into the business organization. As the business starts using this process, problems are uncovered and addressed. Employees working with the process may recommend improvements.

5. **Continuous measurement:** Once a process has been implemented and optimized, it needs to be continually measured. Why? Processes may deteriorate over time as employees fall back on old methods, or they may lose their effectiveness if the business experiences other changes.

Although many business process improvements are incremental and ongoing, there are occasions when more radical change must take place. Our example of a physical bookstore redesigning the book-purchasing process so that it can be carried out online is an example of this type of radical, far-reaching change. When properly implemented, business process redesign produces dramatic gains in productivity and efficiency, and may even change the way the business is run. In some instances, it drives a "paradigm shift" that transforms the nature of the business itself.

This actually happened in book retailing when Amazon challenged traditional physical bookstores with its online retail model. By radically rethinking the way a book can be purchased and sold, Amazon and other online bookstores have achieved remarkable efficiencies, cost reductions, and a whole new way of doing business.

BPM poses challenges. Executives report that the largest single barrier to successful business process change is organizational culture. Employees do not like unfamiliar routines and often try to resist change. This is especially true of projects where organizational changes are very ambitious and far-reaching. Managing change is neither simple nor intuitive, and companies committed to extensive process improvement need a good change management strategy.

Tools for Business Process Management

Over 100 software firms provide tools for various aspects of BPM, including IBM, Oracle, and TIBCO. These tools help businesses identify and document processes requiring improvement, create models of improved processes, capture and enforce business rules for performing processes, and integrate existing systems to support new or redesigned processes. BPM software tools also provide analytics for verifying that process performance has been improved and for measuring the impact of process changes on key business performance indicators.

Some BPM tools document and monitor business processes to help firms identify inefficiencies, using software to connect with each of the systems a company uses for a particular process to identify trouble spots. Canadian mutual fund company AIC used Sajus BPM monitoring software to check inconsistencies in its process for updating accounts after each client transaction. Sajus specializes in "goal-based" process management, which focuses on finding the causes of organizational problems through process monitoring before applying tools to address those problems.

Another category of tools automate some parts of a business process and enforce business rules so that employees perform that process more consistently and efficiently.

For example, American National Insurance Company (ANCO), which offers life insurance, medical insurance, property casualty insurance, and investment services, used Pegasystems BPM workflow software to streamline customer service processes across four business groups. The software built rules to guide customer service representatives through a single view of a customer's information that was maintained in multiple systems. By eliminating the need to juggle multiple applications simultaneously to handle customer and agent requests, the improved process increased customer service representative workload capacity by 192 percent.

A third category of tools helps businesses integrate their existing systems to support process improvements. They automatically manage processes across the business, extract data from various sources and databases, and generate transactions in multiple related systems. For example, the Star Alliance of 15 airlines, including United and Lufthansa, used BPM to create common processes shared by all of its members by integrating their existing systems. One project created a new service for frequent fliers on member airlines by consolidating 90 separate business processes across nine airlines and 27 legacy systems. The BPM software documented how each airline processed frequent flier information to help airline managers model a new business process that showed how to share data among the various systems.

The Interactive Session on Organizations describes how several companies used similar tools for their business process management programs. As you read this case, think about the kinds of changes the companies using these BPM tools were able to make in the way they ran their businesses.

2   OVERVIEW OF SYSTEMS DEVELOPMENT

New information systems are an outgrowth of a process of organizational problem solving. A new information system is built as a solution to some type of problem or set of problems the organization perceives it is facing. The problem may be one in which managers and employees realize that the organization is not performing as well as expected, or that the organization should take advantage of new opportunities to perform more successfully.

The activities that go into producing an information system solution to an organizational problem or opportunity are called **systems development**. Systems development is a structured kind of problem solved with distinct activities. These activities consist of systems analysis, systems design, programming, testing, conversion, and production and maintenance.

INTERACTIVE SESSION: ORGANIZATIONS

CAN BUSINESS PROCESS MANAGEMENT MAKE A DIFFERENCE?

If you're a large successful company, business process management might be just what you're looking for. AmerisourceBergen and Diebold Inc. are two examples. AmerisourceBergen is one of the world's largest pharmaceutical services companies and a member of the Fortune 25, with $70 billion in revenue in 2009. It provides drug distribution and related services designed to reduce costs and improve patient outcomes, servicing both pharmaceutical manufacturers and healthcare providers.

Because it is so large, AmerisourceBergen has numerous and complicated relationships with manufacturers, pharmacies, and hospitals. Frequently changing business conditions cause contract prices to fluctuate. When they do, both the distributor and manufacturer need to analyze these changes and make sure they comply with their business rules and federal regulations. Managing these contract and pricing details associated with each of these relationships had been very time-consuming and paper-intensive, relying heavily on e-mail, telephone, fax, and postal mail. Many of these processes were redundant.

AmerisourceBergen's management believed the company had many old and inefficient business processes. After an extensive BPM vendor analysis, the company selected Metastorm BPM software. Metastorm BPM provides a complete set of tools for analyzing, managing, and redesigning business processes. Business professionals, managers, and information systems specialists are able to create rich graphical models of business processes as well as new user interfaces and business rules. Metastorm has an engine for deploying redesigned processes along with capabilities for integrating the processes it manages with external systems.

For its first BPM project, AmerisourceBergen decided to automate and implement an online collaborative contract and chargeback process, which is responsible for a $10 billion annual cash flow. This process drives the establishment of pricing and terms with each of the company's manufacturers and also controls compliance with pricing terms and the payment of rebates from the manufacturer if the company is forced to sell at a lower price to compete. Any disputes or inaccurate pricing data create costly delays in obtaining the refunds the company is owed.

Metasource BPM makes it possible for all contract changes to be recorded into the system and validated against internal business rules, and also enables AmerisourceBergen to link with its trading partners for collaborative BPM. All contract information is housed in a single repository, making it much easier to investigate chargebacks and communicate contract and pricing information with trading partners and among internal departments.

The BPM project was successful and resulted in lower headcount, fewer disputes, more accurate pricing information, and a high return on investment. This early success encouraged the company to expand BPM to other areas of the business and use it to support a broader business transformation program. AmerisourceBergen used Metastorm BPM to create six new specialized processes for managing and automating high-volume, highly specialized supplier credits which interface with its SAP enterprise system.

To meet federal and industry-specific regulations, AmerisourceBergen must carefully track and match all direct, indirect, and third-party credits with the appropriate product inflows and outflows. The company used Metastorm BPM to create specialized processes that interface with SAP, including the ability to receive, track, reconcile, and expedite all credit variances, such as discrepancies in invoices and purchase orders. After the SAP system identifies the variances, it passes credits to Metastorm BPM for exception handling, resolution, and reconciliation with master credit data. Reconciled credits are then returned to the SAP system. More than 1.2 million credit/debit adjustment documents and paper-based credits are seamlessly passed between Metastorm and SAP this way.

To date, AmerisourceBergen has automated nearly 300 processes, benefiting from more efficient and accurate record tracking, faster turnaround times, greater management into key performance indicators, and an online audit trail of all activities. AmerisourceBergen's BPM projects had such positive outcomes that the company won a Global Excellence in BPM and Workflow award in 2009.

Diebold, Inc. is another recent convert to business process management. Diebold is a global leader in integrated self-service delivery and security systems and services, with 17,000 associates across 90 countries. The company makes, installs, and services ATMs, vaults, currency-processing systems, and other security equipment used in financial, retail, and government markets. Diebold hoped to use business process management to understand and improve its order fulfillment process. The company selected Progress Savvion's BusinessManager BPM solution for this task.

BusinessManager provides a platform for defining an organization's business processes and deploying those processes as Web-accessible applications. The platform gives managers real-time visibility to monitor, analyze, control, and improve the execution of those processes and can integrate these processes with existing operational systems. BusinessManager receives and organizes data from multiple sources to provide a more complete view of the Diebold order process. Diebold managers are able to track orders in real time at any step in the process and also predict future performance based on past data. Since the tool enables managers to learn how long each step of the process usually takes, they can forecast where orders ought to be and compare that with where the system says the orders actually are. BusinessManager can detect whether production of an item is complete and where specific items are located.

Pleased with these capabilities, Diebold immediately used BusinessManager for other processes, such as issue resolution. The system aggregates input from various sources, such as workers in the field and in factories. Diebold is now able to quickly identify issues raised by employees and customers and determine how long it takes to resolve them.

Sources: Judith Lamont, "BPM, Enterprisewide and Beyond," *KMWorld*, February 1, 2010; "Customer Success Story:

CASE STUDY QUESTIONS

AmerisourceBergen," www.metastorm.com, accessed November 4, 2010; and www.progress.com, accessed November 4, 2010.

1. Why are large companies such as AmerisourceBergen and Diebold good candidates for business process management?

2. What were the business benefits for each company from redesigning and managing their business processes?

3. How did BPM change the way these companies ran their businesses?

4. What might be some of the problems with extending BPM software across a large number of business processes?

MIS IN ACTION

5. What companies stand to gain the most by implementing BPM?

Search online for "BPM software provider" or "enterprise-wide BPM" and visit the Web site of a major BPM vendor not mentioned in this case. Then answer the following questions:

1. What types of companies have benefited from this software?

2. What are some of the important functionalities of the BPM products offered?

3. Would this company have been a better fit than Savvion or Metastorm for Diebold or AmerisourceBergen, respectively? Why or why not?

Figure 4 illustrates the systems development process. The systems development activities depicted usually take place in sequential order. But some of the activities may need to be repeated or some may take place simultaneously, depending on the approach to system building that is being employed (see Section 4).

SYSTEMS ANALYSIS

Systems analysis is the analysis of a problem that a firm tries to solve with an information system. It consists of defining the problem, identifying its causes,

FIGURE 4   **THE SYSTEMS DEVELOPMENT PROCESS**

Building a system can be broken down into six core activities.

specifying the solution, and identifying the information requirements that must be met by a system solution.

The systems analyst creates a road map of the existing organization and systems, identifying the primary owners and users of data along with existing hardware and software. The systems analyst then details the problems of existing systems. By examining documents, work papers, and procedures; observing system operations; and interviewing key users of the systems, the analyst can identify the problem areas and objectives a solution would achieve. Often the solution requires building a new information system or improving an existing one.

The systems analysis also includes a **feasibility study** to determine whether that solution is feasible, or achievable, from a financial, technical, and organizational standpoint. The feasibility study determines whether the proposed system is expected to be a good investment, whether the technology needed for the system is available and can be handled by the firm's information systems specialists, and whether the organization can handle the changes introduced by the system.

Normally, the systems analysis process identifies several alternative solutions that the organization can pursue and assess the feasibility of each. A written systems proposal report describes the costs and benefits, and the advantages and disadvantages, of each alternative. It is up to management to determine which mix of costs, benefits, technical features, and organizational impacts represents the most desirable alternative.

Establishing Information Requirements

Perhaps the most challenging task of the systems analyst is to define the specific information requirements that must be met by the chosen system solution. At the most basic level, the **information requirements** of a new system involve identifying who needs what information, where, when, and how. Requirements analysis carefully defines the objectives of the new or modified system and develops a detailed description of the functions that the new system must perform. Faulty requirements analysis is a leading cause of systems failure and high systems development costs. A system designed around the wrong set of requirements will either have to be discarded because of poor performance or will need to undergo major modifications. Section 3 describes alternative approaches to eliciting requirements that help minimize this problem.

Some problems do not require an information system solution but instead need an adjustment in management, additional training, or refinement of existing organizational procedures. If the problem is information related, systems analysis still may be required to diagnose the problem and arrive at the proper solution.

SYSTEMS DESIGN

Systems analysis describes what a system should do to meet information requirements, and **systems design** shows how the system will fulfill this objective. The design of an information system is the overall plan or model for that system. Like the blueprint of a building or house, it consists of all the specifications that give the system its form and structure.

The systems designer details the system specifications that will deliver the functions identified during systems analysis. These specifications should address all of the managerial, organizational, and technological components of the system solution. Table 1 lists the types of specifications that would be produced during systems design.

Like houses or buildings, information systems may have many possible designs. Each design represents a unique blend of all technical and organizational components. What makes one design superior to others is the ease and efficiency with which it fulfills user requirements within a specific set of technical, organizational, financial, and time constraints.

TABLE 1   DESIGN SPECIFICATIONS

OUTPUT	PROCESSING	DOCUMENTATION
Medium	Computations	Operations documentation
Content	Program modules	Systems documentation
Timing	Required reports	User documentation
	Timing of outputs	
INPUT		CONVERSION
Origins	MANUAL PROCEDURES	Transfer files
Flow	What activities	Initiate new procedures
Data entry	Who performs them	Select testing method
	When	Cut over to new system
USER INTERFACE	How	
Simplicity	Where	TRAINING
Efficiency		Select training techniques
Logic	CONTROLS	Develop training modules
Feedback	Input controls (characters, limit,	Identify training facilities
Errors	reasonableness)	
	Processing controls (consistency, record counts)	ORGANIZATIONAL CHANGES
DATABASE DESIGN	Output controls (totals, samples of output)	Task redesign
Logical data model	Procedural controls (passwords, special forms)	Job design
Volume and speed requirements		Process design
File organization and design	SECURITY	Organization structure design
Record specifications	Access controls	Reporting relationships
	Catastrophe plans	
	Audit trails	

The Role of End Users

User information requirements drive the entire system-building effort. Users must have sufficient control over the design process to ensure that the system reflects their business priorities and information needs, not the biases of the technical staff. Working on design increases users' understanding and acceptance of the system. Insufficient user involvement in the design effort is a major cause of system failure. However, some systems require more user participation in design than others, and Section 3 shows how alternative systems development methods address the user participation issue.

COMPLETING THE SYSTEMS DEVELOPMENT PROCESS

The remaining steps in the systems development process translate the solution specifications established during systems analysis and design into a fully operational information system. These concluding steps consist of programming, testing, conversion, production, and maintenance.

Programming

During the **programming** stage, system specifications that were prepared during the design stage are translated into software program code. Today, many organizations no longer do their own programming for new systems. Instead, they purchase the software that meets the requirements for a new system from external sources such as software packages from a commercial software vendor, software services from an application service provider, or outsourcing firms that develop custom application software for their clients (see Section 3).

Testing

Exhaustive and thorough **testing** must be conducted to ascertain whether the system produces the right results. Testing answers the question, "Will the system produce the desired results under known conditions?" Some companies are starting to use cloud computing services for this work.

The amount of time needed to answer this question has been traditionally underrated in systems project planning. Testing is time- consuming: Test data must be carefully prepared, results reviewed, and corrections made in the system. In some instances, parts of the system may have to be redesigned. The risks resulting from glossing over this step are enormous.

Testing an information system can be broken down into three types of activities: unit testing, system testing, and acceptance testing. **Unit testing**, or program testing, consists of testing each program separately in the system. It is widely believed that the purpose of such testing is to guarantee that programs are error-free, but this goal is realistically impossible. Testing should be viewed instead as a means of locating errors in programs, focusing on finding all the ways to make a program fail. Once they are pinpointed, problems can be corrected.

System testing tests the functioning of the information system as a whole. It tries to determine whether discrete modules will function together as planned and whether discrepancies exist between the way the system actually works and the way it was conceived. Among the areas examined are performance time, capacity for file storage and handling peak loads, recovery and restart capabilities, and manual procedures.

Acceptance testing provides the final certification that the system is ready to be used in a production setting. Systems tests are evaluated by users and reviewed by management. When all parties are satisfied that the new system meets their standards, the system is formally accepted for installation.

The systems development team works with users to devise a systematic test plan. The **test plan** includes all of the preparations for the series of tests we have just described.

Figure 5 shows an example of a test plan. The general condition being tested is a record change. The documentation consists of a series of test plan screens maintained on a database (perhaps a PC database) that is ideally suited to this kind of application.

Conversion is the process of changing from the old system to the new system. Four main conversion strategies can be employed: the parallel strategy, the direct cutover strategy, the pilot study strategy, and the phased approach strategy.

In a **parallel strategy,** both the old system and its potential replacement are run together for a time until everyone is assured that the new one functions correctly. This is the safest conversion approach because, in the event of errors or processing disruptions, the old system can still be used as a backup. However, this approach is very expensive, and additional staff or resources may be required to run the extra system.

The **direct cutover strategy** replaces the old system entirely with the new system on an appointed day. It is a very risky approach that can potentially be more costly than running two systems in parallel if serious problems with the new system are found. There is no other system to fall back on. Dislocations, disruptions, and the cost of corrections may be enormous.

The **pilot study strategy** introduces the new system to only a limited area of the organization, such as a single department or operating unit. When this pilot version is complete and working smoothly, it is installed throughout the rest of the organization, either simultaneously or in stages.

The **phased approach strategy** introduces the new system in stages, either by functions or by organizational units. If, for example, the system is

FIGURE 5   A SAMPLE TEST PLAN TO TEST A RECORD CHANGE

Procedure	Address and Maintenance "Record Change Series"		Test Series 2		
	Prepared By:		Date:	Version:	
Test Ref.	Condition Tested	Special Requirements	Expected Results	Output On	Next Screen
2.0	Change records				
2.1	Change existing record	Key field	Not allowed		
2.2	Change nonexistent record	Other fields	"Invalid key" message		
2.3	Change deleted record	Deleted record must be available	"Deleted" message		
2.4	Make second record	Change 2.1 above	OK if valid	Transaction file	V45
2.5	Insert record		OK if valid	Transaction file	V45
2.6	Abort during change	Abort 2.5	No change	Transaction file	V45

When developing a test plan, it is imperative to include the various conditions to be tested, the requirements for each condition tested, and the expected results. Test plans require input from both end users and information systems specialists.

introduced by function, a new payroll system might begin with hourly workers who are paid weekly, followed six months later by adding salaried employees (who are paid monthly) to the system. If the system is introduced by organizational unit, corporate headquarters might be converted first, followed by outlying operating units four months later.

Moving from an old system to a new one requires that end users be trained to use the new system. Detailed **documentation** showing how the system works from both a technical and end-user standpoint is finalized during conversion time for use in training and everyday operations. Lack of proper training and documentation contributes to system failure, so this portion of the systems development process is very important.

Production and Maintenance

After the new system is installed and conversion is complete, the system is said to be in **production**. During this stage, the system will be reviewed by both users and technical specialists to determine how well it has met its original objectives and to decide whether any revisions or modifications are in order. In some instances, a formal **postimplementation audit** document is prepared. After the system has been fine-tuned, it must be maintained while it is in production to correct errors, meet requirements, or improve processing efficiency. Changes in hardware, software, documentation, or procedures to a production system to correct errors, meet new requirements, or improve processing efficiency are termed **maintenance**.

Approximately 20 percent of the time devoted to maintenance is used for debugging or correcting emergency production problems. Another 20 percent is concerned with changes in data, files, reports, hardware, or system software. But 60 percent of all maintenance work consists of making user enhancements, improving documentation, and recoding system components for greater processing efficiency. The amount of work in the third category of maintenance problems could be reduced significantly through better systems analysis and design practices. Table 2 summarizes the systems development activities.

TABLE 2 SYSTEMS DEVELOPMENT

CORE ACTIVITY	DESCRIPTION
Systems analysis	Identify problem(s) Specify solutions Establish information requirements
Systems design	Create design specifications
Programming	Translate design specifications into program code
Testing	Perform unit testing Perform systems testing Perform testing
Conversion	Plan conversion Prepare documentation Train users and technical staff
Production and maintenance	Operate the system Evaluate the system Modify the system

MODELING AND DESIGNING SYSTEMS: STRUCTURED AND OBJECT-ORIENTED METHODOLOGIES

There are alternative methodologies for modeling and designing systems. Structured methodologies and object-oriented development are the most prominent.

Structured Methodologies

Structured methodologies have been used to document, analyze, and design information systems since the 1970s. **Structured** refers to the fact that the techniques are step by step, with each step building on the previous one. Structured methodologies are top-down, progressing from the highest, most abstract level to the lowest level of detail—from the general to the specific.

Structured development methods are process-oriented, focusing primarily on modeling the processes, or actions that capture, store, manipulate, and distribute data as the data flow through a system. These methods separate data from processes. A separate programming procedure must be written every time someone wants to take an action on a particular piece of data. The procedures act on data that the program passes to them.

The primary tool for representing a system's component processes and the flow of data between them is the **data flow diagram (DFD)**. The data flow diagram offers a logical graphic model of information flow, partitioning a system into modules that show manageable levels of detail. It rigorously specifies the processes or transformations that occur within each module and the interfaces that exist between them.

Figure 6 shows a simple data flow diagram for a mail-in university course registration system. The rounded boxes represent processes, which portray the

FIGURE 6 **DATA FLOW DIAGRAM FOR MAIL-IN UNIVERSITY REGISTRATION SYSTEM**

The system has three processes: Verify availability (1.0), Enroll student (2.0), and Confirm registration (3.0). The name and content of each of the data flows appear adjacent to each arrow. There is one external entity in this system: the student. There are two data stores: the student master file and the course file.

transformation of data. The square box represents an external entity, which is an originator or receiver of information located outside the boundaries of the system being modeled. The open rectangles represent data stores, which are either manual or automated inventories of data. The arrows represent data flows, which show the movement between processes, external entities, and data stores. They contain packets of data with the name or content of each data flow listed beside the arrow.

This data flow diagram shows that students submit registration forms with their name, identification number, and the numbers of the courses they wish to take. In process 1.0, the system verifies that each course selected is still open by referencing the university's course file. The file distinguishes courses that are open from those that have been canceled or filled. Process 1.0 then determines which of the student's selections can be accepted or rejected. Process 2.0 enrolls the student in the courses for which he or she has been accepted. It updates the university's course file with the student's name and identification number and recalculates the class size. If maximum enrollment has been reached, the course number is flagged as closed. Process 2.0 also updates the university's student master file with information about new students or changes in address. Process 3.0 then sends each student applicant a confirmation-of-registration letter listing the courses for which he or she is registered and noting the course selections that could not be fulfilled.

The diagrams can be used to depict higher-level processes as well as lower-level details. Through leveled data flow diagrams, a complex process can be broken down into successive levels of detail. An entire system can be divided into subsystems with a high-level data flow diagram. Each subsystem, in turn, can be divided into additional subsystems with second-level data flow diagrams, and the lower-level subsystems can be broken down again until the lowest level of detail has been reached.

Another tool for structured analysis is a data dictionary, which contains information about individual pieces of data and data groupings within a system. The data dictionary defines the contents of data flows and data stores so that systems builders understand exactly what pieces of data they contain. **Process specifications** describe the transformation occurring within the lowest level of the data flow diagrams. They express the logic for each process.

In structured methodology, software design is modeled using hierarchical structure charts. The **structure chart** is a top-down chart, showing each level of design, its relationship to other levels, and its place in the overall design structure. The design first considers the main function of a program or system, then breaks this function into subfunctions, and decomposes each subfunction until the lowest level of detail has been reached. Figure 7 shows a high-level structure chart for a payroll system. If a design has too many levels to fit onto one structure chart, it can be broken down further on more detailed structure charts. A structure chart may document one program, one system (a set of programs), or part of one program.

Object-Oriented Development

Structured methods are useful for modeling processes, but do not handle the modeling of data well. They also treat data and processes as logically separate entities, whereas in the real world such separation seems unnatural. Different modeling conventions are used for analysis (the data flow diagram) and for design (the structure chart).

FIGURE 7   **HIGH-LEVEL STRUCTURE CHART FOR A PAYROLL SYSTEM**

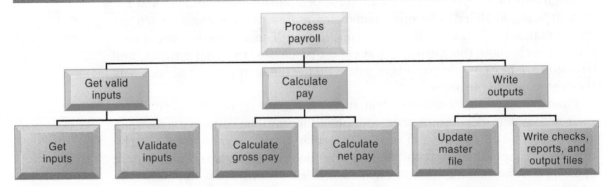

This structure chart shows the highest or most abstract level of design for a payroll system, providing an overview of the entire system.

Object-oriented development addresses these issues. Object-oriented development uses the **object** as the basic unit of systems analysis and design. An object combines data and the specific processes that operate on those data. Data encapsulated in an object can be accessed and modified only by the operations, or methods, associated with that object. Instead of passing data to procedures, programs send a message for an object to perform an operation that is already embedded in it. The system is modeled as a collection of objects and the relationships among them. Because processing logic resides within objects rather that in separate software programs, objects must collaborate with each other to make the system work.

Object-oriented modeling is based on the concepts of *class* and *inheritance*. Objects belonging to a certain class, or general categories of similar objects, have the features of that class. Classes of objects in turn can inherit all the structure and behaviors of a more general class and then add variables and behaviors unique to each object. New classes of objects are created by choosing an existing class and specifying how the new class differs from the existing class, instead of starting from scratch each time.

We can see how class and inheritance work in Figure 8, which illustrates the relationships among classes concerning employees and how they are paid. Employee is the common ancestor, or superclass, for the other three classes. Salaried, Hourly, and Temporary are subclasses of Employee. The class name is in the top compartment, the attributes for each class are in the middle portion of each box, and the list of operations is in the bottom portion of each box. The features that are shared by all employees (id, name, address, date hired, position, and pay) are stored in the Employee superclass, whereas each subclass stores features that are specific to that particular type of employee. Specific to hourly employees, for example, are their hourly rates and overtime rates. A solid line from the subclass to the superclass is a generalization path showing that the subclasses Salaried, Hourly, and Temporary have common features that can be generalized into the superclass Employee.

Object-oriented development is more iterative and incremental than traditional structured development. During analysis, systems builders document the functional requirements of the system, specifying its most important properties and what the proposed system must do. Interactions between the system and its users are analyzed to identify objects, which include both data and processes. The object-oriented design phase describes how the objects will

FIGURE 8   **CLASS AND INHERITANCE**

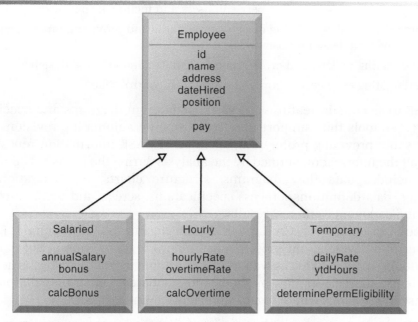

This figure illustrates how classes inherit the common features of their superclass.

behave and how they will interact with one other. Similar objects are grouped together to form a class, and classes are grouped into hierarchies in which a subclass inherits the attributes and methods from its superclass.

The information system is implemented by translating the design into program code, reusing classes that are already available in a library of reusable software objects and adding new ones created during the object-oriented design phase. Implementation may also involve the creation of an object-oriented database. The resulting system must be thoroughly tested and evaluated.

Because objects are reusable, object-oriented development could potentially reduce the time and cost of writing software because organizations can reuse software objects that have already been created as building blocks for other applications. New systems can be created by using some existing objects, changing others, and adding a few new objects. Object-oriented frameworks have been developed to provide reusable, semicomplete applications that the organization can further customize into finished applications.

Computer-Aided Software Engineering

Computer-aided software engineering (CASE)—sometimes called *computer-aided systems engineering*—provides software tools to automate the methodologies we have just described to reduce the amount of repetitive work the developer needs to do. CASE tools also facilitate the creation of clear documentation and the coordination of team development efforts. Team members can share their work easily by accessing each other's files to review or modify what has been done. Modest productivity benefits can also be achieved if the tools are used properly.

CASE tools provide automated graphics facilities for producing charts and diagrams, screen and report generators, data dictionaries, extensive reporting facilities, analysis and checking tools, code generators, and documentation generators. In general, CASE tools try to increase productivity and quality by :

- Enforcing a standard development methodology and design discipline
- Improving communication between users and technical specialists
- Organizing and correlating design components and providing rapid access to them using a design repository
- Automating tedious and error-prone portions of analysis and design
- Automating code generation and testing and control rollout

CASE tools contain features for validating design diagrams and specifications. CASE tools thus support iterative design by automating revisions and changes and providing prototyping facilities. A CASE information repository stores all the information defined by the analysts during the project. The repository includes data flow diagrams, structure charts, entity-relationship diagrams, data definitions, process specifications, screen and report formats, notes and comments, and test results.

To be used effectively, CASE tools require organizational discipline. Every member of a development project must adhere to a common set of naming conventions and standards as well as to a development methodology. The best CASE tools enforce common methods and standards, which may discourage their use in situations where organizational discipline is lacking.

3   ALTERNATIVE SYSTEMS-BUILDING APPROACHES

Systems differ in terms of their size and technological complexity and in terms of the organizational problems they are meant to solve. A number of systems-building approaches have been developed to deal with these differences. This section describes these alternative methods: the traditional systems life cycle, prototyping, application software packages, end-user development, and outsourcing.

TRADITIONAL SYSTEMS LIFE CYCLE

The **systems life cycle** is the oldest method for building information systems. The life cycle methodology is a phased approach to building a system, dividing systems development into formal stages. Systems development specialists have different opinions on how to partition the systems-building stages, but they roughly correspond to the stages of systems development that we have just described.

The systems life cycle methodology maintains a very formal division of labor between end users and information systems specialists. Technical specialists, such as system analysts and programmers, are responsible for much of the systems analysis, design, and implementation work; end users are limited to providing information requirements and reviewing the technical staff's work. The life cycle also emphasizes formal specifications and paperwork, so many documents are generated during the course of a systems project.

The systems life cycle is still used for building large complex systems that require a rigorous and formal requirements analysis, predefined specifications, and tight controls over the system-building process. However, the systems life cycle approach can be costly, time-consuming, and inflexible. Although systems builders can go back and forth among stages in the life cycle, the systems life cycle is predominantly a "waterfall" approach in which tasks in one stage are completed before work for the next stage begins. Activities can be repeated, but volumes of new documents must be generated and steps retraced if requirements and specifications need to be revised. This encourages freezing of specifications relatively early in the development process. The life cycle approach is also not suitable for many small desktop systems, which tend to be less structured and more individualized.

PROTOTYPING

Prototyping consists of building an experimental system rapidly and inexpensively for end users to evaluate. By interacting with the prototype, users can get a better idea of their information requirements. The prototype endorsed by the users can be used as a template to create the final system.

The **prototype** is a working version of an information system or part of the system, but it is meant to be only a preliminary model. Once operational, the prototype will be further refined until it conforms precisely to users' requirements. Once the design has been finalized, the prototype can be converted to a polished production system.

The process of building a preliminary design, trying it out, refining it, and trying again has been called an **iterative** process of systems development because the steps required to build a system can be repeated over and over again. Prototyping is more explicitly iterative than the conventional life cycle, and it actively promotes system design changes. It has been said that prototyping replaces unplanned rework with planned iteration, with each version more accurately reflecting users' requirements.

Steps in Prototyping

Figure 9 shows a four-step model of the prototyping process, which consists of the following:

Step 1: *Identify the user's basic requirements.* The system designer (usually an information systems specialist) works with the user only long enough to capture the user's basic information needs.

Step 2: *Develop an initial prototype.* The system designer creates a working prototype quickly, using tools for rapidly generating software.

Step 3: *Use the prototype.* The user is encouraged to work with the system to determine how well the prototype meets his or her needs and to make suggestions for improving the prototype.

Step 4: *Revise and enhance the prototype.* The system builder notes all changes the user requests and refines the prototype accordingly. After the prototype has been revised, the cycle returns to Step 3. Steps 3 and 4 are repeated until the user is satisfied.

When no more iterations are required, the approved prototype then becomes an operational prototype that furnishes the final specifications for the application. Sometimes the prototype is adopted as the production version of the system.

Advantages and Disadvantages of Prototyping

Prototyping is most useful when there is some uncertainty about requirements or design solutions and often used for designing an information system's **end-user interface** (the part of the system with which end users interact, such as online display and data entry screens, reports, or Web pages). Because prototyping encourages intense end-user involvement throughout the systems

FIGURE 9   THE PROTOTYPING PROCESS

The process of developing a prototype can be broken down into four steps. Because a prototype can be developed quickly and inexpensively, systems builders can go through several iterations, repeating steps 3 and 4, to refine and enhance the prototype before arriving at the final operational one.

development life cycle, it is more likely to produce systems that fulfill user requirements.

However, rapid prototyping can gloss over essential steps in systems development. If the completed prototype works reasonably well, management may not see the need for reprogramming, redesign, or full documentation and testing to build a polished production system. Some of these hastily constructed systems may not easily accommodate large quantities of data or a large number of users in a production environment.

END-USER DEVELOPMENT

Some types of information systems can be developed by end users with little or no formal assistance from technical specialists. This phenomenon is called **end-user development**. A series of software tools categorized as fourth-generation languages makes this possible. **Fourth-generation languages** are software tools that enable end users to create reports or develop software applications with minimal or no technical assistance. Some of these fourth-generation tools also enhance professional programmers' productivity.

Fourth-generation languages tend to be nonprocedural, or less procedural, than conventional programming languages. Procedural languages require specification of the sequence of steps, or procedures, that tell the computer what to do and how to do it. Nonprocedural languages need only specify what has to be accomplished rather than provide details about how to carry out the task.

Table 3 shows that there are seven categories of fourth-generation languages: PC software tools, query languages, report generators, graphics languages, application generators, application software packages, and very high-level programming languages. The table shows the tools ordered in terms of ease of use by nonprogramming end users. End users are most likely to work with PC software tools and query languages. **Query languages** are software tools that provide immediate online answers to requests for information that are not predefined, such as "Who are the highest-performing sales representatives?" Query languages are often tied to data management software and to database management systems.

On the whole, end-user-developed systems can be completed more rapidly than those developed through the conventional systems life cycle. Allowing users to specify their own business needs improves requirements gathering and often leads to a higher level of user involvement and satisfaction with the system. However, fourth-generation tools still cannot replace conventional tools for some business applications because they cannot easily handle the processing of large numbers of transactions or applications with extensive procedural logic and updating requirements.

TABLE 3 CATEGORIES OF FOURTH-GENERATION LANGUAGES

FOURTH-GENERATION TOOL	DESCRIPTION	EXAMPLE	
PC software tools	General-purpose application software packages for PCs.	WordPerfect Microsoft Access	**Oriented toward end users**
Query language	Languages for retrieving data stored in databases or files. Capable of supporting requests for information that are not predefined.	SQL	↑
Report generator	Extract data from files or databases to create customized reports in a wide range of formats not routinely produced by an information system. Generally provide more control over the way data are formatted, organized, and displayed than query languages.	Crystal Reports	
Graphics language	Retrieve data from files or databases and display them in graphic format. Some graphics software can perform arithmetic or logical operations on data as well.	SAS/GRAPH Systat	
Application generator	Contain preprogrammed modules that can generate entire applications, including Web sites, greatly speeding development. A user can specify what needs to be done, and the application generator will create the appropriate program code for input, validation, update, processing, and reporting.	WebFOCUS QuickBase	
Application software package	Software programs sold or leased by commercial vendors that eliminate the need for custom-written, in-house software.	Oracle PeopleSoft HCM mySAP ERP	
Very high-level programming language	Generate program code with fewer instructions than conventional languages, such as COBOL or FORTRAN. Designed primarily as productivity tools for professional programmers.	APL Nomad2	↓ **Oriented toward IS professionals**

End-user computing also poses organizational risks because it occurs outside of traditional mechanisms for information systems management and control. When systems are created rapidly, without a formal development methodology, testing and documentation may be inadequate. Control over data can be lost in systems outside the traditional information systems department. To help organizations maximize the benefits of end-user applications development, management should control the development of end-user applications by requiring cost justification of end-user information system projects and by establishing hardware, software, and quality standards for user-developed applications.

APPLICATION SOFTWARE PACKAGES AND OUTSOURCING

Much of today's software is not developed in-house but is purchased from external sources. Firms can rent the software from a software service provider, they can purchase a software package from a commercial vendor, or they can have a custom application developed by an outside outsourcing firm.

Application Software Packages

During the past several decades, many systems have been built on an application software package foundation. Many applications are common to all business organizations—for example, payroll, accounts receivable, general ledger, or inventory control. For such universal functions with standard processes that do not change a great deal over time, a generalized system will fulfill the requirements of many organizations.

If a software package can fulfill most of an organization's requirements, the company does not have to write its own software. The company can save time and money by using the prewritten, predesigned, pretested software programs from the package. Package vendors supply much of the ongoing maintenance and support for the system, including enhancements to keep the system in line with ongoing technical and business developments.

If an organization has unique requirements that the package does not address, many packages include capabilities for customization. **Customization** features allow a software package to be modified to meet an organization's unique requirements without destroying the integrity of the packaged software. If a great deal of customization is required, additional programming and customization work may become so expensive and time-consuming that they negate many of the advantages of software packages.

When a system is developed using an application software package, systems analysis will include a package evaluation effort. The most important evaluation criteria are the functions provided by the package, flexibility, user friendliness, hardware and software resources, database requirements, installation and maintenance efforts, documentation, vendor quality, and cost. The package evaluation process often is based on a **Request for Proposal (RFP)**, which is a detailed list of questions submitted to packaged-software vendors.

When a software package is selected, the organization no longer has total control over the system design process. Instead of tailoring the system design specifications directly to user requirements, the design effort will consist of trying to mold user requirements to conform to the features of the package. If the organization's requirements conflict with the way the package works and the package cannot be customized, the organization will have to adapt to the package and change its procedures.

The Interactive Session on Technology describes the experience of Zimbra, a software company that selected a software package solution for its new marketing automation system. As you read this case, be aware of the management, technology, and organization issues that had to be addressed when the company selected a new software package solution.

Outsourcing

If a firm does not want to use its internal resources to build or operate information systems, it can outsource the work to an external organization that specializes in providing these services. Cloud computing and SaaS providers are one form of outsourcing. Subscribing companies would use the software and computer hardware provided by the service as the technical platform for their systems. In another form of outsourcing, a company could hire an external vendor to design and create the software for its system, but that company would operate the system on its own computers. The outsourcing vendor might be domestic or in another country.

Domestic outsourcing is driven primarily by the fact that outsourcing firms possess skills, resources, and assets that their clients do not have. Installing a new supply chain management system in a very large company might require hiring an additional 30 to 50 people with specific expertise in supply chain management software, licensed from a vendor. Rather than hire permanent new employees, most of whom would need extensive training in the software package, and then release them after the new system is built, it makes more sense, and is often less expensive, to outsource this work for a 12-month period.

In the case of **offshore outsourcing**, the decision tends to be much more cost-driven. A skilled programmer in India or Russia earns about USD $9,000 per year, compared to $65,000 per year for a comparable programmer in the United States. The Internet and low-cost communications technology have drastically reduced the expense and difficulty of coordinating the work of global teams in faraway locations. In addition to cost savings, many offshore outsourcing firms offer world-class technology assets and skills. Wage inflation outside the United States has recently eroded some of these advantages, and some jobs have moved back to the United States.

Nevertheless, there is a very strong chance that at some point in your career, you'll be working with offshore outsourcers or global teams. Your firm is most likely to benefit from outsourcing if it takes the time to evaluate all the risks and to make sure outsourcing is appropriate for its particular needs. Any company that outsources its applications must thoroughly understand the project, including its requirements, method of implementation, anticipated benefits, cost components, and metrics for measuring performance.

Many firms underestimate costs for identifying and evaluating vendors of information technology services, for transitioning to a new vendor, for improving internal software development methods to match those of outsourcing vendors, and for monitoring vendors to make sure they are fulfilling their contractual obligations. Companies will need to allocate resources for documenting requirements, sending out RFPs, travel expenses, negotiating contracts, and project management. Experts claim it takes from three months to a full year to fully transfer work to an offshore partner and make sure the vendor thoroughly understands your business.

INTERACTIVE SESSION: TECHNOLOGY

ZIMBRA ZOOMS AHEAD WITH ONEVIEW

Zimbra is a software company whose flagship product is its Zimbra Collaboration Suite (ZCS), an open source messaging and communications software package, that relies heavily on Ajax to provide a variety of business functions. Purchased by Yahoo in 2007, the company now has accumulated 50 million paid mailboxes. In addition to e-mail, ZCS combines contact lists, a shared calendar, instant messaging, hosted documents, search, and VoIP into one package, and can be used from any mobile Web browser.

As an open source software company, Zimbra uses viral marketing models, word-of-mouth marketing, and open standards to grow its business. Customers are as free to criticize Zimbra and ZCS as they are to praise the company and its flagship offering. For the most part, this strategy has proven very successful for the company thus far.

Zimbra makes sales via its Web site and offers both free and commercial versions. Zimbra's business model hinges on driving large numbers of visitors to its Web site, allowing them to try the most basic version of the software for free, and then persuading them to purchase one of its more full-featured commercial versions. Zimbra has over 200,000 visitors to its Web site each week.

Zimbra's sales process begins when one of these 200,000 weekly visitors downloads a 60-day trial version. Salespeople try to identify which people using the trial version are most likely to upgrade to one of its commercial versions and then contact them via e-mail and telephone to try to close the sale. To make this work, Zimbra's sales team needs to be able to weed out the interested buyers from its huge volume of Web visitors. As Greg Armanini, Zimbra's director of marketing, pointed out, the sales team will be overwhelmed with a large number of unqualified leads unless sales and marketing automation tools are able to focus sales reps only on the leads that will generate revenue.

Zimbra uses its Web site to track visitor activity and tie it to sales lead information in its Salesforce.com customer relationship management (CRM) system. Identifying sales prospects that visit the Web site regularly and alerting sales reps when those prospects are visiting the site helps the sales team select which prospects to contact by telephone and when to call them.

Zimbra initially used marketing automation software from Eloqua, which had a large number of features but was too complicated for both marketing and sales staff to use. For example, the Eloqua system required salespeople to code conditional logic for any data field containing data they wanted to collect. Though doable, this task was a poor use of Zimbra's sales staff time. Eloqua only worked with the Microsoft Internet Explorer Web browser, while two-thirds of Zimbra's sales department used Mozilla Firefox. And Eloqua was expensive. Zimbra could only afford its entry-level package, which provided access to only five salespeople and one marketing person.

Zimbra did not need many of Eloqua's features, but it did need a more streamlined solution that focused on the core areas of its marketing strategy: lead generation, e-mail marketing, and Web analytics. The new marketing automation system had to be easy to install and maintain. Many available options required several well-trained administrators, and Zimbra could not afford to allocate even one employee for this purpose.

After examining several software products, Zimbra choose OneView, an on-demand marketing automation solution from LoopFuse, a Georgia-based software company that specializes in sales and marketing automation. OneView was more highly targeted than the Eloqua software. Not only that, but much of OneView consists of automated processes that allowed Zimbra to quickly implement the solution and to maintain it without dedicating someone to the task full-time. The core functions of OneView include Web site visitor tracking, automated marketing program communication, customer activity alerts, and CRM integration.

Zimbra was also pleased with LoopFuse's convenient pricing options, including its "unlimited seating" and "pay-per-use" options, which allowed Zimbra to pay for only the services it needed for as many users as it required. Because of these options, Zimbra was able to deploy LoopFuse across almost its entire 30-person sales force.

Other benefits of OneView include easy integration with Salesforce.com, Zimbra's preferred CRM solution, simplified reporting processes, and the ability to manage a larger number of leads thanks to having more salespeople and time to devote to demand generation. OneView works with multiple Web browsers, including Firefox. The old solution offered so many ways to handle and organize data that generating data reports could take a long time. With OneView's simplified reporting processes, the sales staff can generate reports in a fraction of the time.

Has OneView improved Zimbra's bottom line? OneView reduced the amount of time Zimbra spent using and maintaining its marketing system by 50 percent. Zimbra reports that since changing vendors, it has witnessed a jump in its close rate on qualified sales leads from 10 to 15 percent, a huge increase. The answer appears to be a resounding "yes."

Sources: Jessica Tsai, "Less is More," *Customer Relationship Management,* August 2009, www.destinationCRM.com; and "LoopFuse OneView helps Zimbra Raise Sales and Marketing Efficiency by 50 Percent," www.loopfuse.com, May 2009.

CASE STUDY QUESTIONS

1. Describe the steps in Zimbra's sales process. How well did its old marketing automation system support that process? What problems did it create? What was the business impact of these problems?

2. List and describe Zimbra's requirements for a new marketing software package. If you were preparing the RFP for Zimbra's new system, what questions would you ask?

3. How did the new marketing system change the way Zimbra ran its business? How successful was it?

MIS IN ACTION

Visit the LoopFuse Web site and then answer the following questions:

1. List and describe each of the major features of LoopFuse OneView.

2. Select two of these features and describe how they would help Zimbra's sales team.

Outsourcing offshore incurs additional costs for coping with cultural differences that drain productivity and dealing with human resources issues, such as terminating or relocating domestic employees. All of these hidden costs undercut some of the anticipated benefits from outsourcing. Firms should be especially cautious when using an outsourcer to develop or to operate applications that give it some type of competitive advantage.

Figure 10 shows best- and worst-case scenarios for the total cost of an offshore outsourcing project. It shows how much hidden costs affect the total project cost. The best case reflects the lowest estimates for additional costs, and the worst case reflects the highest estimates for these costs. As you can see, hidden costs increase the total cost of an offshore outsourcing project by an extra 15 to 57 percent. Even with these extra costs, many firms will benefit from offshore outsourcing if they manage the work well. Under the worst-case scenario, a firm would still save about 15 percent.

4   APPLICATION DEVELOPMENT FOR THE DIGITAL FIRM

In the digital firm environment, organizations need to be able to add, change, and retire their technology capabilities very rapidly to respond to new opportu-

FIGURE 10   TOTAL COST OF OFFSHORE OUTSOURCING

TOTAL COST OF OFFSHORE OUTSOURCING				
Cost of outsourcing contract			$10,000,000	
Hidden Costs	Best Case	Additional Cost ($)	Worst Case	Additional Cost ($)
1. Vendor selection	0%	20,000	2%	200,000
2. Transition costs	2%	200,000	3%	300,000
3. Layoffs & retention	3%	300,000	5%	500,000
4. Lost productivity/cultural issues	3%	300,000	27%	2,700,000
5. Improving development processes	1%	100,000	10%	1,000,000
6. Managing the contract	6%	600,000	10%	1,000,000
Total additional costs		1,520,000		5,700,000
	Outstanding Contract ($)	Additional Cost ($)	Total Cost ($)	Additional Cost
Total cost of outsourcing (TCO) best case	10,000,000	1,520,000	11,520,000	15.2%
Total cost of outsourcing (TCO) worst case	10,000,000	5,700,000	15,700,000	57.0%

If a firm spends $10 million on offshore outsourcing contracts, that company will actually spend 15.2 percent in extra costs even under the best-case scenario. In the worst-case scenario, where there is a dramatic drop in productivity along with exceptionally high transition and layoff costs, a firm can expect to pay up to 57 percent in extra costs on top of the $10 million outlay for an offshore contract.

nities. Companies are starting to use shorter, more informal development processes that provide fast solutions. In addition to using software packages and external service providers, businesses are relying more heavily on fast-cycle techniques such as rapid application development, joint application design, agile development, and reusable standardized software components that can be assembled into a complete set of services for e-commerce and e-business.

RAPID APPLICATION DEVELOPMENT (RAD)

Object-oriented software tools, reusable software, prototyping, and fourth-generation language tools are helping systems builders create working systems much more rapidly than they could using traditional systems-building methods and software tools. The term **rapid application development (RAD)** is used to describe this process of creating workable systems in a very short period of time. RAD can include the use of visual programming and other tools for building graphical user interfaces, iterative prototyping of key system elements, the automation of program code generation, and close teamwork among end users and information systems specialists. Simple systems often can be assembled from prebuilt components. The process does not have to be sequential, and key parts of development can occur simultaneously.

Sometimes a technique called **joint application design (JAD)** is used to accelerate the generation of information requirements and to develop the initial systems design. JAD brings end users and information systems specialists together in an interactive session to discuss the system's design. Properly prepared and facilitated, JAD sessions can significantly speed up the design phase and involve users at an intense level.

Agile development focuses on rapid delivery of working software by breaking a large project into a series of small subprojects that are completed in short periods of time using iteration and continuous feedback. Each mini-project is worked on by a team as if it were a complete project, including planning, requirements analysis, design, coding, testing, and documentation. Improvement or addition of new functionality takes place within the next iteration as developers clarify requirements. This helps to minimize the overall risk, and allows the project to adapt to changes more quickly. Agile methods emphasize face-to-face communication over written documents, encouraging people to collaborate and make decisions quickly and effectively.

COMPONENT-BASED DEVELOPMENT AND WEB SERVICES

We have already described some of the benefits of object-oriented development for building systems that can respond to rapidly changing business environments, including Web applications. To further expedite software creation, groups of objects have been assembled to provide software components for common functions such as a graphical user interface or online ordering capability that can be combined to create large-scale business applications. This approach to software development is called **component-based development**, and it enables a system to be built by assembling and integrating existing software components. Increasingly, these software components are coming from cloud services. Businesses are using component-based development to create their e-commerce applications by combining commercially available components for shopping carts, user authentication, search engines, and catalogs with pieces of software for their own unique business requirements.

Web Services and Service-Oriented Computing

Web services are loosely coupled, reusable software components delivered using Extensible Markup Language (XML) and other open protocols and standards that enable one application to communicate with another with no custom programming required to share data and services. In addition to supporting internal and external integration of systems, Web services can be used as tools for building new information system applications or enhancing existing systems. Because these software services use a universal set of standards, they promise to be less expensive and less difficult to weave together than proprietary components.

Web services can perform certain functions on their own, and they can also engage other Web services to complete more complex transactions, such as checking credit, procurement, or ordering products. By creating software components that can communicate and share data regardless of the operating system, programming language, or client device, Web services can provide significant cost savings in systems building while opening up new opportunities for collaboration with other companies.

5   HANDS-ON MIS PROJECTS

The projects in this section give you hands-on experience analyzing business process problems, designing and building a customer system for auto sales, and redesigning business processes for a company that wants to purchase goods over the Web.

Management Decision Problems

1. A customer purchasing a Sears Roebuck appliance, such as a washing machine, can also purchase a three-year service contract for an additional fee. The contract provides free repair service and parts for the specified appliance using an authorized Sears service provider. When a person with a Sears service contract needs an appliance repaired, such as a washing machine, he or she calls the Sears Repairs & Parts department to schedule an appointment. The department makes the appointment and gives the caller the date and approximate time of the appointment. The repair technician arrives during the designated time frame and diagnoses the problem. If the problem is caused by a faulty part, the technician either replaces the part if he is carrying the part with him or orders the replacement part from Sears. If the part is not in stock at Sears, Sears orders the part and gives the customer an approximate time when the part will arrive. The part is shipped directly to the customer. After the part has arrived, the customer must call Sears to schedule a second appointment for a repair technician to replace the ordered part. This process is very lengthy.

   It may take two weeks for the first repair visit to occur, another two weeks to receive the ordered part, and another week for the second repair visit to occur in which the ordered part is installed.

   - Diagram the existing process.
   - What is the impact of the existing process on Sears' operational efficiency and customer relationships?
   - What changes could be made to make this process more efficient? How could information systems support these changes? Diagram the new improved process.

2. Management at your agricultural chemicals corporation has been dissatisfied with production planning. Production plans are created using best guesses of demand for each product, which are based on how much of each product has been ordered in the past. If a customer places an unexpected order or requests a change to an existing order after it has been placed, there is no way to adjust production plans. The company may have to tell customers it can't fill their orders, or it may run up extra costs maintaining additional inventory to prevent stock-outs.

   At the end of each month, orders are totaled and manually keyed into the company's production planning system. Data from the past month's production and inventory systems are manually entered into the firm's order management system. Analysts from the sales department and from the production department analyze the data from their respective systems to determine what the sales targets and production targets should be for the next month. These estimates are usually different. The analysts then get together at a high-level planning meeting to revise the production and sales targets to take into account senior management's goals for market share, revenues, and profits. The outcome of the meeting is a finalized production master schedule.

   The entire production planning process takes 17 business days to complete. Nine of these days are required to enter and validate the data. The remaining days are spent developing and reconciling the production and sales targets and finalizing the production master schedule.

- Draw a diagram of the existing production planning process.
- Analyze the problems this process creates for the company.
- How could an enterprise system solve these problems? In what ways could it lower costs? Diagram what the production planning process might look like if the company implemented enterprise software.

Improving Decision Making: Using Database Software to Design a Customer System for Auto Sales

Software skills: Database design, querying, reporting, and forms
Business skills: Sales lead and customer analysis

This project requires you to perform a systems analysis and then design a system solution using database software.

Ace Auto Dealers specializes in selling new vehicles from Subaru. The company advertises in local newspapers and is also listed as an authorized dealer on the Subaru Web site and other major auto-buyer Web sites. The company benefits from a good local word-of-mouth reputation and name recognition and is a leading source of information for Subaru vehicles in the Portland, Oregon, area.

When a prospective customer enters the showroom, he or she is greeted by an Ace sales representative. The sales representative manually fills out a form with information such as the prospective customer's name, address, telephone number, date of visit, and make and model of the vehicle in which the customer is interested. The representative also asks where the prospect heard about Ace—whether it was from a newspaper ad, the Web, or word of mouth—and this information is noted on the form also. If the customer decides to purchase an auto, the dealer fills out a bill of sale form.

Ace does not believe it has enough information about its customers. It cannot easily determine which prospects have made auto purchases, nor can it identify which customer touch points have produced the greatest number of sales leads or actual sales so it can focus advertising and marketing more on the channels that generate the most revenue. Are purchasers discovering Ace from newspaper ads, from word of mouth, or from the Web?

Prepare a systems analysis report detailing Ace's problem and a system solution that can be implemented using PC database management software. The company has a PC with Internet access and the full suite of Microsoft Office desktop productivity tools. Then use database software to develop a simple system solution. Your systems analysis report should include the following:

- Description of the problem and its organizational and business impact
- Proposed solution, solution objectives, and solution feasibility
- Costs and benefits of the solution you have selected
- Information requirements to be addressed by the solution
- Management, organization, and technology issues to be addressed by the solution, including changes in business processes

On the basis of the requirements you have identified, design the database and populate it with at least 10 records per table. Consider whether you can use or modify Ace's existing customer database in your design. You can find this database on the myMISlab. Print out the database design. Then use the system you have created to generate queries and reports that would be most useful to management. Create several prototype data input forms for the system and review them with your instructor. Then revise the prototypes.

Achieving Operational Excellence: Redesigning Business Processes for Web Procurement

Software skills: Web browser software
Business skills: Procurement

This project requires you to rethink how a business should be redesigned when it moves to the Web.

You are in charge of purchasing for your firm and would like to use the Grainger (www.grainger.com) B2B e-commerce site for this purpose. Find out how to place an order for painting supplies by exploring the Catalog, Order Form, and Repair Parts Order capabilities of this site. Do not register at the site. Describe all the steps your firm would need to take to use this system to place orders online for 30 gallons of paint thinner. Include a diagram of what you think your firm's business process for purchasing should be and the pieces of information required by this process.

In a traditional purchase process, whoever is responsible for making the purchase fills out a requisition form and submits it for approval based on the company's business rules. When the requisition is approved, a purchase order with a unique purchase order identification number is sent to the supplier. The purchaser might want to browse supplier catalogs to compare prices and features before placing the order. The purchaser might also want to determine whether the items to be purchased are available. If the purchasing firm were an approved customer, that company would be granted credit to make the purchase and would be billed for the total cost of the items purchased and shipped after the order was shipped. Alternatively, the purchasing company might have to pay for the order in advance or pay for the order using a credit card. Multiple payment options might be possible. How might this process have to change to make purchases electronically from the Grainger site?

LEARNING TRACK MODULES

The following Learning Tracks provide content relevant to topics covered in this chapter:

1. Unified Modeling Language (UML)
2. A Primer on Business Process Design and Documentation
3. A Primer on Business Process Management

Review Summary

1. *How does building new systems produce organizational change?*

   Building a new information system is a form of planned organizational change. Four kinds of technology-enabled change are (a) automation, (b) rationalization of procedures, (c) business process redesign, and (d) paradigm shift, with far-reaching changes carrying the greatest risks and rewards. Many organizations are using business process management to redesign work flows and business processes in the hope of achieving dramatic productivity breakthroughs. Business process management is also useful for promoting, total quality management (TQM), six sigma, and other initiatives for incremental process improvement.

2. *What are the core activities in the systems development process?*

   The core activities in systems development are systems analysis, systems design, programming, testing, conversion, production, and maintenance. Systems analysis is the study and analysis of problems of existing systems and the identification of requirements for their solutions. Systems design provides the specifications for an information system solution, showing how its technical and organizational components fit together.

3. *What are the principal methodologies for modeling and designing systems?*

   The two principal methodologies for modeling and designing information systems are structured methodologies and object-oriented development. Structured methodologies focus on modeling processes and data separately. The data flow diagram is the principal tool for structured analysis, and the structure chart is the principal tool for representing structured software design. Object-oriented development models a system as a collection of objects that combine processes and data. Object-oriented modeling is based on the concepts of class and inheritance.

4. *What are the alternative methods for building information systems?*

   The oldest method for building systems is the systems life cycle, which requires that information systems be developed in formal stages. The stages must proceed sequentially and have defined outputs; each requires formal approval before the next stage can commence. The systems life cycle is useful for large projects that need formal specifications and tight management control over each stage of systems building, but it is very rigid and costly.

   Prototyping consists of building an experimental system rapidly and inexpensively for end users to interact with and evaluate. Prototyping encourages end-user involvement in systems development and iteration of design until specifications are captured accurately. The rapid creation of prototypes can result in systems that have not been completely tested or documented or that are technically inadequate for a production environment.

   Using a software package reduces the amount of design, programming, testing, installation, and maintenance work required to build a system. Application software packages are helpful if a firm does not have the internal information systems staff or financial resources to custom develop a system. To meet an organization's unique requirements, packages may require extensive modifications that can substantially raise development costs.

   End-user development is the development of information systems by end users, either alone or with minimal assistance from information systems specialists. End-user-developed systems can be created rapidly and informally using fourth-generation software tools. However, end-user development may create information systems that do not necessarily meet quality assurance standards and that are not easily controlled by traditional means.

Outsourcing consists of using an external vendor to build (or operate) a firm's information systems instead of the organization's internal information systems staff. Outsourcing can save application development costs or enable firms to develop applications without an internal information systems staff. However, firms risk losing control over their information systems and becoming too dependent on external vendors. Outsourcing also entails "hidden" costs, especially when the work is sent offshore.

5. *What are new approaches for system building in the digital firm era?*

Companies are turning to rapid application design, joint application design (JAD), agile development, and reusable software components to accelerate the systems development process. Rapid application development (RAD) uses object-oriented software, visual programming, prototyping, and fourth-generation tools for very rapid creation of systems. Agile development breaks a large project into a series of small subprojects that are completed in short periods of time using iteration and continuous feedback. Component-based development expedites application development by grouping objects into suites of software components that can be combined to create large-scale business applications. Web services provide a common set of standards that enable organizations to link their systems regardless of their technology platform through standard plug- and-play architecture

Key Terms

Acceptance testing

Agile development

Automation

Business process management

Business process redesign

Component-based development

Computer-aided software engineering (CASE)

Conversion

Customization

Data flow diagram (DFD)

Direct cutover strategy

Documentation

End-user development

End-user interface

Feasibility study

Fourth-generation languages

Information requirements

Iterative

Joint application design (JAD)

Maintenance

Object

Object-oriented development

Offshore outsourcing

Paradigm shift

Parallel strategy

Phased approach strategy

Pilot study strategy

Postimplementation audit

Process specifications

Production

Programming

Prototype

Prototyping

Query languages

Rapid application development (RAD)

Rationalization of procedures

Request for Proposal (RFP)

Six sigma

Structure chart

Structured

Systems analysis

Systems design

Systems development

Systems life cycle

System testing

Test plan

Testing

Total quality management (TQM)

Unit testing

Review Questions

1. How does building new systems produce organizational change?

- Describe each of the four kinds of organizational change that can be promoted with information technology.

- Define business process management and describe the steps required to carry it out.

- Explain how information systems support process changes that promote quality in an organization.

2. What are the core activities in the systems development process?

- Distinguish between systems analysis and systems design. Describe the activities for each.
- Define information requirements and explain why they are difficult to determine correctly.
- Explain why the testing stage of systems development is so important. Name and describe the three stages of testing for an information system.
- Describe the role of programming, conversion, production, and maintenance in systems development.

3. What are the principal methodologies for modeling and designing systems?

- Compare object-oriented and traditional structured approaches for modeling and designing systems.

4. What are the alternative methods for building information systems?

- Define the traditional systems life cycle. Describe each of its steps and its advantages and disadvantages for systems building.

- Define information system prototyping. Describe its benefits and limitations. List and describe the steps in the prototyping process.
- Define an application software package. Explain the advantages and disadvantages of developing information systems based on software packages.
- Define end-user development and describe its advantages and disadvantages. Name some policies and procedures for managing end-user development.
- Describe the advantages and disadvantages of using outsourcing for building information systems.

5. What are new approaches for system building in the digital firm era?

- Define rapid application development (RAD) and agile development and explain how they can speed up system-building.
- Explain how component-based development and Web services help firms build and enhance their information systems.

Discussion Questions

1. Why is selecting a systems development approach an important business decision? Who should participate in the selection process?

2. Some have said that the best way to reduce systems development costs is to use application software packages or fourth-generation tools. Do you agree? Why or why not?

3. Why is is so important to understand how a business process works when trying to develop a new information system?

Video Cases

Video Cases and Instructional Videos illustrating some of the concepts in this chapter are available. Contact your instructor to access these videos.

Collaboration and Teamwork: Preparing Web Site Design Specifications

With three or four of your classmates, select a system described in this text that uses the Web. Review the Web site for the system you select. Use what you have learned from the Web site and the description in this text to prepare a report describing some of the design specifications for the system you select.

If possible, use Google Sites to post links to Web pages, team communication announcements, and work assignments; to brainstorm; and to work collaboratively on project documents. Try to use Google Docs to develop a presentation of your findings for the class.

Are Electronic Medical Records a Cure for Health Care?
CASE STUDY

Creating more efficient health care systems in the United States has been a pressing medical, social, and political issue for decades. Despite the fact that 15 percent of Americans are uninsured and another 20 percent on top of that are underinsured, or unable to pay for necessary health care, the U.S. spends more money per person on health care than any other country in the world. In 2009, the United States spent $2.5 trillion on health care, which was 17.6 percent of its gross domestic product (GDP). Approximately 12 percent of that figure was spent on administrative costs, most of which involve the upkeep of medical records.

The astronomical health care spending figures in the United States are inflated by inefficiency, errors, and fraud. The good news is that information technology may present an opportunity for health care providers to save money and provide better care. Health care providers have begun to create electronic medical record (EMR) systems at the urging of the government in an effort to eliminate much of the inefficiency inherent in paper-based record-keeping. Many insurance companies are also lending their support to the development of EMR systems.

An electronic medical record system contains all of a person's vital medical data, including personal information, a full medical history, test results, diagnoses, treatments, prescription medications, and the effect of those treatments. A physician would be able to immediately and directly access needed information from the EMR without having to pore through paper files. If the record holder went to the hospital, the records and results of any tests performed at that point would be immediately available online.

Many experts believe that electronic records will reduce medical errors and improve care, create less paperwork, and provide quicker service, all of which will lead to dramatic savings in the future: an estimated $77.8 billion per year. The government's short-term goal is for all health care providers in the United States to have functional EMR systems in place that meet a set of basic functional criteria by the year 2015. Its long-term goal is to have a fully functional nationwide electronic medical record-keeping network.

Evidence of EMR systems in use today suggests that these benefits are possible for doctors and hospitals, but the challenges of setting up individual systems, let alone a nationwide system, are daunting. Even with stimulus money, many smaller practices are finding it difficult to afford the costs and time commitment for upgrading their recordkeeping systems. In 2010, 80 percent of physicians and 90 percent of hospitals in the United States are still using paper medical records.

It's also unclear whether the systems being developed and implemented in 2010 will be compatible with one another in 2015 and beyond, jeopardizing the goal of a national system where all health care providers can share information. And there are many other smaller obstacles that health care providers, health IT developers, and insurance companies need to overcome for electronic health records to catch on nationally, including patients' privacy concerns, data quality issues, and resistance from health care workers.

The government plans to pay out the stimulus money provided by the American Recovery and Reinvestment Act to health care providers in two ways. First, $2 billion will be provided up front to hospitals and physicians to help set up electronic records. Another $17 billion will also be available as a reward for providers that successfully implement electronic records by 2015. The stimulus specifies that to qualify for these rewards, providers must demonstrate "meaningful use" of electronic health record systems. The bill defines this as the successful implementation of certified e-record products, the ability to write at least 40 percent of their total prescriptions electronically, and the ability to exchange and report data to government health agencies. Individual practices can receive up to $64,000 for successful implementations, and hospitals can make as much as $11.5 million.

But in addition to the reward of stimulus money, the government will also assess penalties on practices that fail to comply with the new electronic recordkeeping standards. Providers that cannot meet the standards by 2015 will have their Medicare and Medicaid reimbursements reduced by 1 percent per year until 2018, with further, more stringent penalties coming beyond that time if a sufficiently low number of providers are using electronic health records.

Electronic medical recordkeeping systems typically cost around $30,000 to $50,000 per doctor. While the stimulus money should eventually be enough to cover that cost, only a small amount of it is available up front. For many providers, especially medical practices with fewer than four doctors and hospitals with fewer than 50 beds, this creates a significant problem. The expenditure of overhauling recordkeeping systems represents a significant increase in the short-term budgets and workloads of smaller health care providers. Smaller providers are also less likely to have started digitizing their records compared to their larger counterparts.

Many smaller practices and hospitals have balked at the transition to EMR systems for these reasons, but the evidence of these systems in action suggests that the move may be well worth the effort. The most prominent example of electronic medical records in use today is the Veterans Affairs (VA) system of doctors and hospitals. The VA system switched to digital records years ago, and far exceeds the private sector and Medicare in quality of preventive services and chronic care. The 1,400 VA facilities use VistA, record-sharing software developed by the government that allows doctors and nurses to share patient histories. A typical VistA record lists a patient's health problems, weight and blood pressure since beginning treatment at the VA, images of the patient's X-rays, lab results, and other test results, lists of medications, and reminders about upcoming appointments.

But VistA is more than a database; it also has many features that improve quality of care. For example, nurses scan tags for patients and medications to ensure that the correct dosages of medicines are going to the correct patients. This feature reduces medication errors, which is one of the most common and costly types of medical errors, and speeds up treatment as well. The system also generates automatic warnings based on specified criteria. It can notify providers if a patient's blood pressure goes over a certain level or if a patient is overdue for a regularly scheduled procedure like a flu shot or a cancer screening. Devices that measure patients' vital signs can automatically transmit their results into the VistA system, which automatically updates doctors at the first sign of trouble.

The results suggest that electronic records offer significant advantages to hospitals and patients alike. The 40,000 patients in the VA's in-home monitoring program reduced their hospital admissions by 25 percent and the length of their hospital stays by 20 percent. More patients receive necessary periodic treatments under VistA (from 27 percent to 83 percent for flu vaccines and from 34 percent to 84 percent for colon cancer screenings).

Patients also report that the process of being treated at the VA is effortless compared to paper-based providers. That's because instant processing of claims and payments are among the benefits of EMR systems. Insurance companies traditionally pay claims about two weeks after receiving them, despite quickly processing them soon after they are received. Additionally, today's paper-based health care providers must assign the appropriate diagnostic codes and procedure codes to claims. Because there are thousands of these codes, the process is even slower, and most providers employ someone solely to perform this task. Electronic systems hold the promise of immediate processing, or real-time claims adjudication, just like when you pay using a credit card—claim data would be sent immediately, and diagnostic and procedure code information are automatically entered.

VistA is far from the only option for doctors and hospitals starting the process of updating their records. Many health IT companies are eagerly awaiting the coming spike in demand for their EMR products and have developed a variety of different health record structures. Humana, Aetna, and other health insurance companies are helping to defray the cost of setting up EMR systems for some doctors and hospitals. Humana has teamed up with health IT company Athenahealth to subsidize EMR systems for approximately 100 primary care practices within Humana's network. Humana pays most of the bill and offers further rewards to practices that meet governmental performance standards. Aetna and IBM, on the other hand, have launched a cloud-based system that pools patient records and is licensed to doctors both inside and outside of Aetna.

There are two problems with the plethora of options available to health care providers. First, there are likely to be many issues with the sharing of medical data between different systems. While the majority of EMR systems are likely to satisfy the specified criteria of reporting data electronically to governmental agencies, they may not be able to report the same data to one another, a key requirement for a nation-wide system. Many fledgling systems are designed using VistA as a guide, but many are not. Even if medical data are easily shared, it's another problem altogether for doctors to actually locate the information they need quickly and easily.

Many EMR systems have no capacity to drill down for more specific data, forcing doctors to wade through large repositories of information to find the one piece of data they need. EMR vendors are developing search engine technology intended for use in medical records. Only after EMR systems become more widespread will the extent of the problems with data sharing and accessibility become clearer.

The second problem is that there is a potential conflict of interest for the insurance companies involved in the creation of health record systems. Insurers are often accused of seeking ways to avoid providing care for sick people. While most insurers are adamant that only doctors and patients will be able to access data in these systems, many prospective patients are skeptical. In 2009, a poll conducted for National Public Radio found that 59 percent of respondents said they doubted the confidentiality of online medical records; even if the systems are secure, the perception of poor privacy

could affect the success of the system and quality of care provided. One in eight Americans have skipped doctor visits or regular tests, asked a doctor to change a test result, or paid privately for a test, motivated mostly by privacy concerns. A poorly designed EMR network would amplify these concerns.

Sources: Katherine Gammon, "Connecting Electronic Medical Records," *Technology Review*, August 9, 2010; Avery Johnson, "Doctors Get Dose of Technology From Insurers," *The Wall Street Journal*, August 8, 2010; David Talbot, "The Doctor Will Record Your Data Now," *Technology Review*, July 23, 2010; Tony Fisher and Joyce Norris-Montanari, "The Current State of Data in Health Care," Information-Management.com, June 15, 2010; Laura Landro, "Breaking Down the Barriers," *The Wall Street Journal*, April 13, 2010; Jacob Goldstein, "Can Technology Cure Health Care?", *The Wall Street Journal*, April 13, 2010; Deborah C. Peel, "Your Medical Records Aren't Secure," *The Wall Street Journal*, March 23, 2010; Jane E. Brody, "Medical Paper Trail Takes Electronic Turn," *The New York Times*, February 23, 2010; and Laura Landro, "An Affordable Fix for Modernizing Medical Records," *The Wall Street Journal*, April 30, 2009.

CASE STUDY QUESTIONS

1. What management, organization, and technology factors are responsible for the difficulties in building electronic medical record systems? Explain your answer.

2. What stages of system building will be the most difficult when creating electronic medical record systems? Explain your answer.

3. What is the business and social impact of not digitizing medical records (to individual physicians, hospitals, insurers, patients)?

4. What are the business and social benefits of digitizing medical recordkeeping?

5. Name two important information requirements for physicians, two for patients, and two for hospitals that should be addressed by electronic medical records systems.

6. Diagram the "as-is" and "to-be" processes for prescribing a medication for a patient before and after an EMR system is implemented.

References

Albert, Terri C., Paulo B. Goes, and Alok Gupta. "GIST: A Model for Design and Management of Content and Interactivity of Customer-Centric Web Sites." MIS Quarterly 28, no. 2 (June 2004).

Alter, Allan E. "I.T. Outsourcing: Expect the Unexpected." CIO Insight (March 7, 2007).

Armstrong, Deborah J. and Bill C. Hardgrove. "Understanding Mindshift Learning: The Transition to Object-Oriented Development." MIS Quarterly 31, no. 3 (September 2007).

Aron, Ravi, Eric K. Clemons, and Sashi Reddi. "Just Right Outsourcing: Understanding and Managing Risk." Journal of Management Information Systems 22, no. 1 (Summer 2005).

Ashrafi, Noushin and Hessam Ashrafi. Object-Oriented Systems Analysis and Design. Upper Saddle River, NY: Prentice-Hall (2009).

Avison, David E. and Guy Fitzgerald. "Where Now for Development Methodologies?" Communications of the ACM 41, no. 1 (January 2003).

Babcock, Charles. "Platform as a Service: What Vendors Offer." Information Week (October 3, 2009).

Baily, Martin N. and Diana Farrell. "Exploding the Myths of Offshoring." The McKinsey Quarterly (July 2004).

Barthelemy, Jerome. "The Hidden Costs of IT Outsourcing." Sloan Management Review (Spring 2001).

Broadbent, Marianne, Peter Weill, and Don St. Clair. "The Implications of Information Technology Infrastructure for Business Process Redesign." MIS Quarterly 23, no. 2 (June 1999).

Brown, Susan A., Norman L. Chervany, and Bryan A. Reinicke. "What Matters When Introducing New Technology." Communications of the ACM 50, No. 9 (September 2007).

Cha, Hoon S., David E. Pingry, and Matt E. Thatcher. "A Learning Model of Information Technology Outsourcing: Normative Implications. "Journal of Management Information Systems 26, No. 2 (Fall 2009).

Champy, James A. X-Engineering the Corporation: Reinventing Your Business in the Digital Age. New York: Warner Books (2002).

Curbera, Francisco, Rania Khalaf, Nirmal Mukhi, Stefan Tai, and Sanjiva Weerawarana. "The Next Step in Web Services." Communications of the ACM 46, no 10 (October 2003).

Davidson, Elisabeth J. "Technology Frames and Framing: A Socio-Cognitive Investigation of Requirements Determination. MIS Quarterly 26, no. 4 (December 2002).

DeMarco, Tom. Structured Analysis and System Specification. New York: Yourdon Press (1978).

Den Hengst, Marielle and Gert-Jan DeVreede. "Collaborative Business Engineering: A Decade of Lessons from the Field." Journal of Management Information Systems 20, no. 4 (Spring 2004).

Dibbern, Jess, Jessica Winkler, and Armin Heinzl. "Explaining Variations in Client Extra Costs between Software Projects Offshored to India." MIS Quarterly 32, no. 2 (June 2008).

El Sawy, Omar A.Redesigning Enterprise Processes for E-Business. McGraw-Hill (2001).

Erickson, Jonathan. "Dr Dobb's Report: Agile Development." Information Week (April 27, 2009).

Feeny, David, Mary Lacity, and Leslie P. Willcocks. "Taking the Measure of Outsourcing Providers." MIT Sloan Management Review 46, No. 3 (Spring 2005).

Fischer, G., E. Giaccardi. Y.Ye, A.G. Sutcliffe, and N. Mehandjiev. " Meta-Design: A Manifesto for End-User Development." Communications of the ACM 47, no. 9 (September 2004).

Gefen, David and Catherine M. Ridings. "Implementation Team Responsiveness and User Evaluation of Customer Relationship Management: A Quasi-Experimental Design Study of Social Exchange Theory." Journal of Management Information Systems 19, no. 1 (Summer 2002).

Gefen, David and Erran Carmel. "Is the World Really Flat? A Look at Offshoring in an Online Programming Marketplace." MIS Quarterly 32, no. 2 (June 2008).

Gemino, Andrew and Yair Wand." Evaluating Modeling Techniques Based on Models of Learning." Communications of the ACM 46, no. 10 (October 2003).

George, Joey, Dinesh Batra, Joseph S. Valacich, and Jeffrey A. Hoffer. Object Oriented System Analysis and Design, 2nd ed. Upper Saddle River, NJ: Prentice Hall (2007).

Goo, Jahyun, Rajive Kishore, H. R. Rao, and Kichan Nam. The Role of Service Level Agreements in Relational Management of Information Technology Outsourcing: An Empirical Study." MIS Quarterly 33, No. 1 (March 2009).

Grunbacher, Paul, Michael Halling, Stefan Biffl, Hasan Kitapci, and Barry W. Boehm. "Integrating Collaborative Processes and Quality Assurance Techniques: Experiences from Requirements Negotiation." Journal of Management Information Systems 20, no. 4 (Spring 2004).

Hahn, Eugene D., Jonathan P. Doh, and Kraiwinee Bunyaratavej. "The Evolution of Risk in Information Systems Offshoring: The Impact of Home Country Risk, Firm Learning, and Competitive Dynamics. MIS Quarterly 33, No. 3 (September 2009).

Hammer, Michael, and James Champy. Reengineering the Corporation. New York: HarperCollins (1993).

Hammer, Michael."Process Management and the Future of Six Sigma." "Sloan Management Review 43, no.2 (Winter 2002)

Hickey, Ann M., and Alan M. Davis. "A Unified Model of Requirements Elicitation." Journal of Management Information Systems 20, no. 4 (Spring 2004).

Hirscheim, Rudy and Mary Lacity."The Myths and Realities of Information Technology Insourcing." Communications of the ACM 43, no. 2 (February 2000).

Hoffer, Jeffrey, Joey George, and Joseph Valacich. Modern Systems Analysis and Design, 5th ed. Upper Saddle River, NJ: Prentice Hall (2008).

Hopkins, Jon. "Component Primer." Communications of the ACM 43, no. 10 (October 2000).

Irwin, Gretchen. "The Role of Similarity in the Reuse of Object-Oriented Analysis Models." Journal of Management Information Systems 19, no. 2 (Fall 2002).

Ivari, Juhani, Rudy Hirscheim, and Heinz K. Klein. "A Dynamic Framework for Classifying Information Systems Development Methodologies and Approaches." Journal of Management Information Systems 17, no. 3 (Winter 2000-2001).

Iyer, Bala, Jim Freedman, Mark Gaynor, and George Wyner. "Web Services: Enabling Dynamic Business Networks." Communications of the Association for Information Systems 11 (2003).

Johnson, Richard A. The Ups and Downs of Object-Oriented Systems Development." Communications of the ACM 43, no.10 (October 2000).

Kendall, Kenneth E., and Julie E. Kendall. Systems Analysis and Design, 9th ed. Upper Saddle River, NJ: Prentice Hall (2011).

Kettinger, William J., and Choong C. Lee. "Understanding the IS-User Divide in IT Innovation." Communications of the ACM 45, no.2 (February 2002).

Kindler, Noah B., Vasantha Krishnakanthan, and Ranjit Tinaikar. "Applying Lean to Application Development and Maintenance." The McKinsey Quarterly (May 2007).

Koh, Christine, Song Ang, and Detmar W. Straub. "IT Outsourcing Success: A Psychological Contract Perspective." Information Systems Research 15 no. 4 (December 2004).

Krishna, S., Sundeep Sahay, and Geoff Walsham. "Managing Cross-Cultural Issues in Global Software Outsourcing." Communications of the ACM 47, No. 4 (April 2004).

Lee, Gwanhoo and Weidong Xia. "Toward Agile: An Integrated Analysis of Quantitative and Qualitative Field Data." MIS Quarterly 34, no. 1 (March 2010).

Lee, Jae Nam, Shaila M. Miranda, and Yong-Mi Kim."IT Outsourcing Strategies: Universalistic, Contingency, and Configurational Explanations of Success." Information Systems Research 15, no. 2 (June 2004).

Levina, Natalia, and Jeanne W. Ross. "From the Vendor's Perspective: Exploring the Value Proposition in Information Technology Outsourcing." MIS Quarterly 27, no. 3 (September 2003).

Limayem, Moez, Mohamed Khalifa, and Wynne W. Chin. "Case Tools Usage and Impact on System Development Performance." Journal of Organizational Computing and Electronic Commerce 14, no. 3 (2004).

Majchrzak, Ann, Cynthia M. Beath, and Ricardo A. Lim. "Managing Client Dialogues during Information Systems Design to Facilitate Client Learning." MIS Quarterly 29, no. 4 (December 2005).

Mani, Deepa, Anitesh Barua, and Andrew Whinston. "An Empirical Analysis of the Impact of Information Capabilities Design on Business Process Outsourcing Performance." MIS Quarterly 34, no. 1 (March 2010).

Nelson, H. James, Deborah J. Armstrong, and Kay M. Nelson. Patterns of Transition: The Shift from Traditional to Object-Oriented Development." Journal of Management Information Systems 25, No. 4 (Spring 2009).

Nidumolu, Sarma R. and Mani Subramani."The Matrix of Control: Combining Process and Structure Approaches to Managing Software Development." Journal of Management Information Systems 20, no. 4 (Winter 2004).

O'Donnell, Anthony. "BPM: Insuring Business Success." Optimize Magazine (April 2007).

Overby, Stephanie, "The Hidden Costs of Offshore Outsourcing," CIO Magazine (Sept.1, 2003).

Palmer, Jonathan W. "Web Site Usability, Design and Performance Metrics." Information Systems Research 13, no.3 (September 2002).

Phillips, James and Dan Foody. "Building a Foundation for Web Services." EAI Journal (March 2002).

Pitts, Mitzi G. and Glenn J. Browne."Stopping Behavior of Systems Analysts During Information Requirements Elicitation." Journal of Management Information Systems 21, no. 1 (Summer 2004).

Prahalad, C. K. and M.S.. Krishnan."Synchronizing Strategy and Information Technology." Sloan Management Review 43, no. 4 (Summer 2002).

Ravichandran, T. and Marcus A. Rothenberger."Software Reuse Strategies and Component Markets." Communications of the ACM 46, no. 8 (August 2003).

Silva, Leiser and Rudy Hirschheim. "Fighting Against Windmills: Strategic Information Systems and Organizational Deep Structures." MIS Quarterly 31, no. 2 (June 2007).

Sircar, Sumit, Sridhar P. Nerur, and Radhakanta Mahapatra. "Revolution or Evolution? A Comparison of Object-Oriented and Structured Systems Development Methods." MIS Quarterly 25, no. 4 (December 2001).

Smith, Howard and Peter Fingar. Business Process Management: The Third Wave Tampa, Florida: Meghan-Kiffer Press (2002).

Swanson, E. Burton and Enrique Dans. "System Life Expectancy and the Maintenance Effort: Exploring their Equilibration." MIS Quarterly 24, no. 2 (June 2000).

Turetken, Ozgur, David Schuff, Ramesh Sharda, and Terence T. Ow. "Supporting Systems Analysis and Design through Fisheye Views." Communications of the ACM 47, no. 9 (September 2004).

Van Den Heuvel, Willem-Jan and Zakaria Maamar. "Moving Toward a Framework to Compose Intelligent Web Services." Communications of the ACM 46, no. 10 (October 2003).

Vitharana, Padmal."Risks and Challenges of Component-Based Software Development." Communications of the ACM 46, no. 8 (August 2003).

Watad, Mahmoud M. and Frank J. DiSanzo. "Case Study: The Synergism of Telecommuting and Office Automation." Sloan Management Review 41, no. 2 (Winter 2000).

Wulf, Volker, and Matthias Jarke. "The Economics of End-User Development." Communications of the ACM 47, no. 9 (September 2004).

Yourdon, Edward, and L. L. Constantine. Structured Design. New York: Yourdon Press (1978).

Glossary

3G networks Cellular networks based on packet-switched technology with speeds ranging from 144 Kbps for mobile users to over 2 Mbps for stationary users, enabling users to transmit video, graphics, and other rich media, in addition to voice.

4G networks The next evolution in wireless communication is entirely packet switched and capable of providing between 1 Mbps and 1 Gbps speeds; up to ten times faster than 3G networks. Not widely deployed in 2010.

acceptable use policy (AUP) Defines acceptable uses of the firm's information resources and computing equipment, including desktop and laptop computers, wireless devices, telephones, and the Internet, and specifies consequences for noncompliance.

acceptance testing Provides the final certification that the system is ready to be used in a production setting.

accountability The mechanisms for assessing responsibility for decisions made and actions taken.

accumulated balance digital payment systems Systems enabling users to make micropayments and purchases on the Web, accumulating a debit balance on their credit card or telephone bills.

affiliate revenue model an e-commerce revenue model in which Web sites are paid as "affiliates" for sending their visitors to other sites in return for a referral fee.

agent-based modeling Modeling complex phenomena as systems of autonomous agents that follow relatively simple rules for interaction.

agency theory Economic theory that views the firm as a nexus of contracts among self-interested individuals who must be supervised and managed.

agile development Rapid delivery of working software by breaking a large project into a series of small sub-projects that are completed in short periods of time using iteration and continuous feedback.

Ajax Development technique for creating interactive Web applications capable of updating the user interface without reloading the entire browser page.

analog signal A continuous waveform that passes through a communications medium; used for voice communications.

analytical CRM Customer relationship management applications dealing with the analysis of customer data to provide information for improving business performance.

Android A mobile operating system developed by Android, Inc. (purchased by Google) and later the Open Handset Alliance as a flexible, upgradeable mobile device platform.

antivirus software Software designed to detect, and often eliminate, computer viruses from an information system.

application controls: Specific controls unique to each computerized application that ensure that only authorized data are completely and accurately processed by that application.

application server Software that handles all application operations between browser-based computers and a company's back-end business applications or databases.

application software package A set of prewritten, precoded application software programs that are commercially available for sale or lease.

application software Programs written for a specific application to perform functions specified by end users.

apps Small pieces of software that run on the Internet, on your computer, or on your cell phone and are generally delivered over the Internet.

artificial intelligence (AI) The effort to develop computer-based systems that can behave like humans, with the ability to learn languages, accomplish physical tasks, use a perceptual apparatus, and emulate human expertise and decision making.

attribute A piece of information describing a particular entity.

augmented reality A technology for enhancing visualization. Provides a live direct or indirect view of a physical real-world environment whose elements are augmented by virtual computer-generated imagery.

authentication The ability of each party in a transaction to ascertain the identity of the other party.

authorization management systems Systems for allowing each user access only to those portions of a system or the Web that person is permitted to enter, based on information established by a set of access rules.

authorization policies Determine differing levels of access to information assets for different levels of users in an organization.

automation Using the computer to speed up the performance of existing tasks.

autonomic computing Effort to develop systems that can manage themselves without user intervention.

backward chaining A strategy for searching the rule base in an expert system that acts like a problem solver by beginning with a hypothesis and seeking out more information until the hypothesis is either proved or disproved.

balanced scorecard method Framework for operationalizing a firms strategic plan by focusing on measurable financial, business process, customer, and learning and growth outcomes of firm performance.

bandwidth The capacity of a communications channel as measured by the difference between the highest and lowest frequencies that can be transmitted by that channel.

banner ad A graphic display on a Web page used for advertising. The banner is linked to the advertiser's Web site so that a person clicking on it will be transported to the advertiser's Web site.

batch processing A method of collecting and processing data in which transactions are accumulated and stored until a specified time when it is convenient or necessary to process them as a group.

baud A change in signal from positive to negative or vice versa that is used as a measure of transmission speed.

behavioral models Descriptions of management based on behavioral scientists' observations of what managers actually do in their jobs.

behavioral targeting Tracking the click-streams (history of clicking behavior) of individuals across multiple Web sites for the purpose of understanding their interests and intentions, and exposing them to advertisements which are uniquely suited to their interests.

benchmarking Setting strict standards for products, services, or activities and measuring organizational performance against those standards.

best practices The most successful solutions or problem-solving methods that have been developed by a specific organization or industry.

biometric authentication Technology for authenticating system users that compares a person's unique characteristics such as fingerprints, face, or retinal image, against a stored set profile of these characteristics.

bit A binary digit representing the smallest unit of data in a computer system. It can only have one of two states, representing 0 or 1.

blade server Entire computer that fits on a single, thin card (or blade) and that is plugged into a single chassis to save space, power and complexity.

blog Popular term for Weblog, designating an informal yet structured Web site where individuals can publish stories, opinions, and links to other Web sites of interest.

blogosphere Totality of blog-related Web sites.

Bluetooth Standard for wireless personal area networks that can transmit up to 722 Kbps within a 10-meter area.

botnet A group of computers that have been infected with bot malware without users' knowledge, enabling a hacker to use the amassed resources of the computers to launch distributed denial-of-service attacks, phishing campaigns or spam.

broadband High-speed transmission technology. Also designates a single communications medium that can transmit multiple channels of data simultaneously.

bugs Software program code defects.

bullwhip effect Distortion of information about the demand for a product as it passes from one entity to the next across the supply chain.

bus topology Network topology linking a number of computers by a single circuit with all messages broadcast to the entire network.

business continuity planning Planning that focuses on how the company can restore business operations after a disaster strikes.

business driver A force in the environment to which businesses must respond and that influences the direction of business.

business ecosystem Loosely coupled but interdependent networks of suppliers, distributors, outsourcing firms, transportation service firms, and technology manufacturers

business functions Specialized tasks performed in a business organization, including manufacturing and production, sales and marketing, finance and accounting, and human resources.

business intelligence Applications and technologies to help users make better business decisions.

business model An abstraction of what an enterprise is and how the enterprise delivers a product or service, showing how the enterprise creates wealth.

business performance management Attempts to systematically translate a firm's strategies (e.g., differentiation, low-cost producer, market share growth, and scope of operation) into operational targets.

business process management Business process management (BPM) is an approach to business which aims to continuously improve and manage business processes.

business process redesign Type of organizational change in which business processes are analyzed, simplified, and redesigned.

business processes The unique ways in which organizations coordinate and organize work activities, information, and knowledge to produce a product or service.

business-to-business (B2B) electronic commerce Electronic sales of goods and services among businesses.

business-to-consumer (B2C) electronic commerce Electronic retailing of products and services directly to individual consumers.

byte A string of bits, usually eight, used to store one number or character in a computer system.

cable Internet connections Internet connections that use digital cable lines to deliver high-speed Internet access to homes and businesses.

call center An organizational department responsible for handling customer service issues by telephone and other channels.

capacity planning The process of predicting when a computer hardware system becomes saturated to ensure that adequate computing resources are available for work of different priorities and that the firm has enough computing power for its current and future needs.

capital budgeting The process of analyzing and selecting various proposals for capital expenditures.

carpal tunnel syndrome (CTS) Type of RSI in which pressure on the median nerve through the wrist's bony carpal tunnel structure produces pain.

case-based reasoning (CBR) Artificial intelligence technology that represents knowledge as a database of cases and solutions.

cell phone A device that transmits voice or data, using radio waves to communicate with radio antennas placed within adjacent geographic areas called cells.

centralized processing Processing that is accomplished by one large central computer.

change agent In the context of implementation, the individual acting as the catalyst during the change process to ensure successful organizational adaptation to a new system or innovation.

change management Managing the impact of organizational change associated with an innovation, such as a new information system.

channel conflict Competition between two or more different distribution chains used to sell the products or services of the same company.

channel The link by which data or voice are transmitted between sending and receiving devices in a network.

chat Live, interactive conversations over a public network.

chief information officer (CIO) Senior manager in charge of the information systems function in the firm.

chief knowledge officer (CKO) Senior executive in charge of the organization's knowledge management program.

chief privacy officer (CPO) Responsible for ensuring the company complies with existing data privacy laws.

chief security officer (CSO) Heads a formal security function for the organization and is responsible for enforcing the firm's security policy.

choice Simon's third stage of decision making, when the individual selects among the various solution alternatives.

Chrome OS Google's lightweight computer operating system for users who do most of their computing on the Internet; runs on computers ranging from netbooks to desktop computers.

churn rate Measurement of the number of customers who stop using or purchasing products or services from a company. Used as an indicator of the growth or decline of a firm's customer base.

classical model of management Traditional description of management that focused on its formal functions of planning, organizing, coordinating, deciding, and controlling.

click fraud Fraudulently clicking on an online ad in pay per click advertising to generate an improper charge per click.

clicks-and-mortar Business model where the Web site is an extension of a traditional bricks-and-mortar business.

clickstream tracking Tracking data about customer activities at Web sites and storing them in a log.

client The user point-of-entry for the required function in client/server computing. Normally a desktop computer, workstation, or laptop computer.

client/server computing A model for computing that splits processing between clients and servers on a network, assigning functions to the machine most able to perform the function.

cloud computing Web-based applications that are stored on remote servers and accessed via the "cloud" of the Internet using a standard Web browser.

coaxial cable A transmission medium consisting of thickly insulated copper wire; can transmit large volumes of data quickly.

Code Division Multiple Access (CDMA) Major cellular transmission standard in the United States that transmits over several frequencies, occupies the entire spectrum, and randomly assigns users to a range of frequencies over time.

collaboration Working with others to achieve shared and explicit goals.

collaborative commerce The use of digital technologies to enable multiple organizations to collaboratively design, develop, build and manage products through their life cycles.

collaborative filtering Tracking users' movements on a Web site, comparing the information gleaned about a user's behavior against data about other customers with similar interests to predict what the user would like to see next.

collaborative planning, forecasting, and replenishment (CPFR) Firms collaborating with their suppliers and buyers to formulate demand forecasts, develop production plans, and coordinate shipping, warehousing, and stocking activities.

co-location a kind of Web site hosting in which firm purchase or rent a physical server computer at a hosting company's location in order to operate a Web site.

community provider a Web site business model that creates a digital online environment where people with similar interests can transact (buy and sell goods); share interests, photos, videos; communicate with like-minded people; receive interest-related information; and even play out fantasies by adopting online personalities called avatars.

competitive forces model Model used to describe the interaction of external influences, specifically threats and opportunities, that affect an organization's strategy and ability to compete.

complementary assets Additional assets required to derive value from a primary investment.

component-based development Building large software systems by combining pre-existing software components.

computer Physical device that takes data as an input, transforms the data by executing stored instructions, and outputs information to a number of devices.

computer abuse The commission of acts involving a computer that may not be illegal but are considered unethical.

computer crime The commission of illegal acts through the use of a computer or against a computer system.

computer forensics The scientific collection, examination, authentication, preservation, and analysis of data held on or retrieved from computer storage media in such a way that the information can be used as evidence in a court of law.

computer hardware Physical equipment used for input, processing, and output activities in an information system.

computer literacy Knowledge about information technology, focusing on understanding of how computer-based technologies work.

computer software Detailed, preprogrammed instructions that control and coordinate the work of computer hardware components in an information system.

computer virus Rogue software program that attaches itself to other software programs or data files in order to be executed, often causing hardware and software malfunctions.

computer vision syndrome (CVS) Eyestrain condition related to computer display screen use; symptoms include headaches, blurred vision, and dry and irritated eyes.

computer-aided design (CAD) Information system that automates the creation and revision of designs using sophisticated graphics software.

computer-aided software engineering (CASE) Automation of step-by-step methodologies for software and systems development to reduce the amounts of repetitive work the developer needs to do.

computer-based information systems (CBIS) Information systems that rely on computer hardware and software for processing and disseminating information.

connectivity The ability of computers and computer-based devices to communicate with each other and share information in a meaningful way without human intervention..

consumer-to-consumer (C2C) electronic commerce Consumers selling goods and services electronically to other consumers.

controls All of the methods, policies, and procedures that ensure protection of the organization's assets, accuracy and reliability of its records, and operational adherence to management standards.

conversion The process of changing from the old system to the new system.

cookies Tiny file deposited on a computer hard drive when an individual visits certain Web sites. Used to identify the visitor and track visits to the Web site.

cooptation Bringing the opposition into the process of designing and implementing a solution without giving up control of the direction and nature of the change.

copyright A statutory grant that protects creators of intellectual property against copying by others for any purpose for a minimum of 70 years.

core competency Activity at which a firm excels as a world-class leader.

core systems Systems that support functions that are absolutely critical to the organization.

cost transparency the ability of consumers to discover the actual costs merchants pay for products.

counterimplementation A deliberate strategy to thwart the implementation of an information system or an innovation in an organization.

critical success factors (CSFs) A small number of easily identifiable operational goals shaped by the industry, the firm, the manager, and the broader environment that are believed to assure the success of an organization. Used to determine the information requirements of an organization.

cross-selling Marketing complementary products to customers.

crowdsourcing Using large Internet audiences for advice, market feedback, new ideas and solutions to business problems. Related to the 'wisdom of crowds' theory.

culture The set of fundamental assumptions about what products the organization should produce, how and where it should produce them, and for whom they should be produced.

customer lifetime value (CLTV) Difference between revenues produced by a specific customer and the expenses for acquiring and servicing that customer minus the cost of promotional marketing over the lifetime of the customer relationship, expressed in today's dollars.

customer relationship management (CRM) Business and technology discipline that uses information systems to coordinate all of the business processes surrounding the firm's interactions with its customers in sales, marketing, and service.

customer relationship management systems Information systems that track all the ways in which a company interacts with its customers and analyze these interactions to optimize revenue, profitability, customer satisfaction, and customer retention.

customization The modification of a software package to meet an organization's unique requirements without destroying the package software's integrity.

cybervandalism Intentional disruption, defacement, or destruction of a Web site or corporate information system.

data Streams of raw facts representing events occurring in organizations or the physical environment before they have been organized and arranged into a form that people can understand and use.

data administration A special organizational function for managing the organization's data resources, concerned with information policy, data planning, maintenance of data dictionaries, and data quality standards.

data cleansing Activities for detecting and correcting data in a database or file that are incorrect, incomplete, improperly formatted, or redundant. Also known as data scrubbing.

data definition DBMS capability that specifies the structure and content of the database.

data dictionary An automated or manual tool for storing and organizing information about the data maintained in a database.

data-driven DSS A system that supports decision making by allowing users to extract and analyze useful information that was previously buried in large databases.

data element A field.

data flow diagram (DFD) Primary tool for structured analysis that graphically illustrates a system's component process and the flow of data between them.

data governance Policies and processes for managing the availability, usability, integrity, and security of the firm's data.

data inconsistency The presence of different values for same attribute when the same data are stored in multiple locations.

data management software Software used for creating and manipulating lists, creating files and databases to store data, and combining information for reports.

data manipulation language A language associated with a database management system that end users and programmers use to manipulate data in the database.

data mart A small data warehouse containing only a portion of the organization's data for a specified function or population of users.

data mining Analysis of large pools of data to find patterns and rules that can be used to guide decision making and predict future behavior.

data quality audit A survey and/or sample of files to determine accuracy and completeness of data in an information system.

data redundancy The presence of duplicate data in multiple data files.

data visualization Technology for helping users see patterns and relationships in large amounts of data by presenting the data in graphical form.

data warehouse A database, with reporting and query tools, that stores current and historical data extracted from various operational systems and consolidated for management reporting and analysis.

data workers People such as secretaries or bookkeepers who process the organization's paperwork.

database A group of related files.

database (rigorous definition) A collection of data organized to service many applications at the same time by storing and managing data so that they appear to be in one location.

database administration Refers to the more technical and operational aspects of managing data, including physical database design and maintenance.

database management system (DBMS) Special software to create and maintain a database and enable individual business applications to extract the data they need without having to create separate files or data definitions in their computer programs.

database server A computer in a client/server environment that is responsible for running a DBMS to process SQL statements and perform database management tasks.

dataconferencing Teleconferencing in which two or more users are able to edit and modify data files simultaneously.

decisional roles Mintzberg's classification for managerial roles where managers initiate activities, handle disturbances, allocate resources, and negotiate conflicts.

decision-support systems (DSS) Information systems at the organization's management level that combine data and sophisticated analytical models or data analysis tools to support semistructured and unstructured decision making.

dedicated lines Telephone lines that are continuously available for transmission by a lessee. Typically conditioned to transmit data at high speeds for high-volume applications.

deep packet inspection (DPI) Technology for managing network traffic by examining data packets, sorting out low-priority data from higher priority business-critical data, and sending packets in order of priority.

demand planning Determining how much product a business needs to make to satisfy all its customers' demands.

denial of service (DoS) attack Flooding a network server or Web server with false communications or requests for services in order to crash the network.

Descartes' rule of change A principle that states that if an action cannot be taken repeatedly, then it is not right to be taken at any time.

design Simon's second stage of decision making, when the individual conceives of possible alternative solutions to a problem.

digital asset management systems Classify, store, and distribute digital objects such as photographs, graphic images, video, and audio content.

digital certificate An attachment to an electronic message to verify the identity of the sender and to provide the receiver with the means to encode a reply.

digital checking Systems that extend the functionality of existing checking accounts so they can be used for online shopping payments.

digital credit card payment system Secure services for credit card payments on the Internet that protect information transmitted among users, merchant sites, and processing banks.

digital dashboard Displays all of a firm's key performance indicators as graphs and charts on a single screen to provide one-page overview of all the critical measurements necessary to make key executive decisions.

digital divide Large disparities in access to computers and the Internet among different social groups and different locations.

digital firm Organization where nearly all significant business processes and relationships with customers, suppliers, and employees are digitally enabled, and key corporate assets are managed through digital means.

digital goods Goods that can be delivered over a digital network.

digital market A marketplace that is created by computer and communication technologies that link many buyers and sellers.

Digital Millennium Copyright Act (DMCA) Adjusts copyright laws to the Internet Age by making it illegal to make, distribute, or use devices that circumvent technology-based protections of copyrighted materials.

digital signal A discrete waveform that transmits data coded into two discrete states as 1-bits and 0-bits, which are represented as on-off electrical pulses; used for data communications.

digital subscriber line (DSL) A group of technologies providing high-capacity transmission over existing copper telephone lines.

digital wallet Software that stores credit card, electronic cash, owner identification, and address information and provides this data automatically during electronic commerce purchase transactions.

direct cutover A risky conversion approach where the new system completely replaces the old one on an appointed day.

disaster recovery planning Planning for the restoration of computing and communications services after they have been disrupted.

disintermediation The removal of organizations or business process layers responsible for certain intermediary steps in a value chain.

disruptive technologies Technologies with disruptive impact on industries and businesses, rendering existing products, services and business models obsolete.

distance learning Education or training delivered over a distance to individuals in one or more locations.

distributed database A database that is stored in more than one physical location. Parts or copies of the database are physically stored in one location, and other parts or copies are stored and maintained in other locations.

distributed denial-of-service (DDoS) attack Numerous computers inundating and overwhelming a network from numerous launch points.

distributed processing The distribution of computer processing work among multiple computers linked by a communications network.

documentation Descriptions of how an information system works from either a technical or end-user standpoint.

domain name English-like name that corresponds to the unique 32-bit numeric Internet Protocol (IP) address for each computer connected to the Internet

Domain Name System (DNS) A hierarchical system of servers maintaining a database enabling the conversion of domain names to their numeric IP addresses.

domestic exporter Form of business organization characterized by heavy centralization of corporate activities in the home county of origin.

downsizing The process of transferring applications from large computers to smaller ones.

downtime Period of time in which an information system is not operational.

drill down The ability to move from summary data to lower and lower levels of detail.

due process A process in which laws are well-known and understood and there is an ability to appeal to higher authorities to ensure that laws are applied correctly.

dynamic pricing Pricing of items based on real-time interactions between buyers and sellers that determine what a item is worth at any particular moment.

e-government Use of the Internet and related technologies to digitally enable government and public sector agencies' relationships with citizens, businesses, and other arms of government.

e-learning Instruction delivered through purely digital technology, such as CD-ROMs, the Internet, or private networks.

efficient customer response system System that directly links consumer behavior back to distribution, production, and supply chains.

electronic billing and payment presentation system Systems used for paying routine monthly bills that allow users to view their bills electronically and pay them through electronic funds transfers from banks or credit card accounts.

electronic business (e-business) The use of the Internet and digital technology to execute all the business processes in the enterprise. Includes e-commerce as well as processes for the internal management of the firm and for coordination with suppliers and other business partners.

electronic commerce The process of buying and selling goods and services electronically involving transactions using the Internet, networks, and other digital technologies.

electronic data interchange (EDI) The direct computer-to-computer exchange between two organizations of standard business transactions, such as orders, shipment instructions, or payments.

electronic payment system The use of digital technologies, such as credit cards, smart cards and Internet-based payment systems, to pay for products and services electronically.

e-mail The computer-to-computer exchange of messages.

employee relationship management (ERM) Software dealing with employee issues that are closely related to CRM, such as setting objectives, employee performance management, performance-based compensation, and employee training.

encryption The coding and scrambling of messages to prevent their being read or accessed without authorization.

end-user development The development of information systems by end users with little or no formal assistance from technical specialists.

end-user interface The part of an information system through which the end user interacts with the system, such as on-line screens and commands.

end users Representatives of departments outside the information systems group for whom applications are developed.

enterprise applications Systems that can coordinate activities, decisions, and knowledge across many different functions, levels, and business units in a firm. Include enterprise systems, supply chain management systems, and knowledge management systems.

enterprise content management systems Help organizations manage structured and semistructured knowledge, providing corporate repositories of documents, reports, presentations, and best practices and capabilities for collecting and organizing e-mail and graphic objects.

enterprise portal Web interface providing a single entry point for accessing organizational information and services, including information from various enterprise applications and in-house legacy systems so that information appears to be coming from a single source.

enterprise software Set of integrated modules for applications such as sales and distribution, financial accounting, investment management, materials management, production planning, plant maintenance, and human resources that allow data to be used by multiple functions and business processes.

enterprise systems Integrated enterprise-wide information systems that coordinate key internal processes of the firm.

enterprise-wide knowledge management systems General-purpose, firmwide systems that collect, store, distribute, and apply digital content and knowledge.

entity A person, place, thing, or event about which information must be kept.

entity-relationship diagram A methodology for documenting databases illustrating the relationship between various entities in the database.

ergonomics The interaction of people and machines in the work environment, including the design of jobs, health issues, and the end-user interface of information systems.

e-tailer Online retail stores from the giant Amazon to tiny local stores that have Web sites where retail goods are sold.

ethical "no free lunch" rule Assumption that all tangible and intangible objects are owned by someone else, unless there is a specific declaration otherwise, and that the creator wants compensation for this work.

ethics Principles of right and wrong that can be used by individuals acting as free moral agents to make choices to guide their behavior.

evil twins Wireless networks that pretend to be legitimate to entice participants to log on and reveal passwords or credit card numbers.

exchange Third-party Net marketplace that is primarily transaction oriented and that connects many buyers and suppliers for spot purchasing.

executive support systems (ESS) Information systems at the organization's strategic level designed to address unstructured decision making through advanced graphics and communications.

expert system Knowledge-intensive computer program that captures the expertise of a human in limited domains of knowledge.

explicit knowledge Knowledge that has been documented.

external integration tools Project management technique that links the work of the implementation team to that of users at all organizational levels.

extranet Private intranet that is accessible to authorized outsiders.

Fair Information Practices (FIP) A set of principles originally set forth in 1973 that governs the collection and use of information about individuals and forms the basis of most U.S. and European privacy laws.

fault-tolerant computer systems Systems that contain extra hardware, software, and power supply components that can back a system up and keep it running to prevent system failure.

feasibility study As part of the systems analysis process, the way to determine whether the solution is achievable, given the organization's resources and constraints.

feedback Output that is returned to the appropriate members of the organization to help them evaluate or correct input.

fiber-optic cable A fast, light, and durable transmission medium consisting of thin strands of clear glass fiber bound into cables. Data are transmitted as light pulses.

field A grouping of characters into a word, a group of words, or a complete number, such as a person's name or age.

file transfer protocol (FTP) Tool for retrieving and transferring files from a remote computer.

file A group of records of the same type.

firewall Hardware and software placed between an organization's internal network and an external network to prevent outsiders from invading private networks.

focused differentiation Competitive strategy for developing new market niches for specialized products or services where a business can compete in the target area better than its competitors.

folksonomies User-created taxonomies for classifying and sharing information.

foreign key Field in a database table that enables users find related information in another database table.

formal control tools Project management technique that helps monitor the progress toward completion of a task and fulfillment of goals.

formal planning tools Project management technique that structures and sequences tasks, budgeting time, money, and technical resources required to complete the tasks.

forward chaining A strategy for searching the rule base in an expert system that begins with the information entered by the user and searches the rule base to arrive at a conclusion.

fourth-generation language A programming language that can be employed directly by end users or less-skilled programmers to develop computer applications more rapidly than conventional programming languages.

franchiser Form of business organization in which a product is created, designed, financed, and initially produced in the home country, but for product-specific reasons relies heavily on foreign personnel for further production, marketing, and human resources.

free/fremium revenue model an e-commerce revenue model in which a firm offers basic services or content for free, while charging a premium for advanced or high value features.

fuzzy logic Rule-based AI that tolerates imprecision by using nonspecific terms called membership functions to solve problems.

Gantt chart Visually representats the timing, duration, and resource requirements of project tasks.

general controls Overall control environment governing the design, security, and use of computer programs and the security of data files in general throughout the organization's information technology infrastructure.

genetic algorithms Problem-solving methods that promote the evolution of solutions to specified problems using the model of living organisms adapting to their environment.

geographic information system (GIS) System with software that can analyze and display data using digitized maps to enhance planning and decision-making.

global culture The development of common expectations, shared artifacts, and social norms among different cultures and peoples

global positioning system (GPS) Worldwide satellite navigational system.

graphical user interface (GUI) The part of an operating system users interact with that uses graphic icons and the computer mouse to issue commands and make selections.

Gramm-Leach-Bliley Act Requires financial institutions to ensure the security and confidentiality of customer data.

green computing Refers to practices and technologies for designing, manufacturing, using, and disposing of computers, servers, and associated devices such as monitors, printers, storage devices, and networking and communications systems to minimize impact on the environment.

grid computing Applying the resources of many computers in a network to a single problem.

group decision-support system (GDSS) An interactive computer-based system to facilitate the solution to unstructured problems by a set of decision makers working together as a group.

hacker A person who gains unauthorized access to a computer network for profit, criminal mischief, or personal pleasure.

hertz Measure of frequency of electrical impulses per second, with 1 Hertz equivalent to 1 cycle per second.

high-availability computing Tools and technologies ,including backup hardware resources, to enable a system to recover quickly from a crash.

HIPAA Law outlining rules for medical security, privacy, and the management of health care records.

hotspot A specific geographic location in which an access point provides public Wi-Fi network service.

hubs Very simple devices that connect network components, sending a packet of data to all other connected devices.

hybrid AI systems Integration of multiple AI technologies into a single application to take advantage of the best features of these technologies.

hypertext markup language (HTML) Page description language for creating Web pages and other hypermedia documents.

hypertext transfer protocol (HTTP) The communications standard used to transfer pages on the Web. Defines how messages are formatted and transmitted.

identity management Business processes and software tools for identifying the valid users of a system and controlling their access to system resources.

identity theft Theft of key pieces of personal information, such as credit card or Social Security numbers, in order to obtain merchandise and services in the name of the victim or to obtain false credentials.

Immanuel Kant's Categorical Imperative A principle that states that if an action is not right for everyone to take it is not right for anyone.

implementation Simon's final stage of decision-making, when the individual puts the decision into effect and reports on the progress of the solution.

industry structure The nature of participants in an industry and their relative bargaining power. Derives from the competitive forces and establishes the general business environment in an industry and the overall profitability of doing business in that environment.

inference engine The strategy used to search through the rule base in an expert system; can be forward or backward chaining.

information Data that have been shaped into a form that is meaningful and useful to human beings.

information asymmetry Situation where the relative bargaining power of two parties in a transaction is determined by one party in the transaction possessing more information essential to the transaction than the other party.

information density The total amount and quality of information available to all market participants, consumers, and merchants.

information policy Formal rules governing the maintenance, distribution, and use of information in an organization.

information requirements A detailed statement of the information needs that a new system must satisfy; identifies who needs what information, and when, where, and how the information is needed.

information rights The rights that individuals and organizations have with respect to information that pertains to themselves.

information system Interrelated components working together to collect, process, store, and disseminate information to support decision making, coordination, control, analysis, and visualization in an organization.

information systems department The formal organizational unit that is responsible for the information systems function in the organization.

information systems literacy Broad-based understanding of information systems that includes behavioral knowledge about organizations and individuals using information systems as well as technical knowledge about computers.

information systems managers Leaders of the various specialists in the information systems department.

information systems plan A road map indicating the direction of systems development: the rationale, the current situation, the management strategy, the implementation plan, and the budget.

information technology (IT) All the hardware and software technologies a firm needs to achieve its business objectives.

information technology (IT) infrastructure Computer hardware, software, data, storage technology, and networks providing a portfolio of shared IT resources for the organization.

informational roles Mintzberg's classification for managerial roles where managers act as the nerve centers of their organizations, receiving and disseminating critical information.

informed consent Consent given with knowledge of all the facts needed to make a rational decision.

input The capture or collection of raw data from within the organization or from its external environment for processing in an information system.

instant messaging Chat service that allows participants to create their own private chat channels so that a person can be alerted whenever someone on his or her private list is on-line to initiate a chat session with that particular individual.

intangible benefits Benefits that are not easily quantified; they include more efficient customer service or enhanced decision making.

intellectual property Intangible property created by individuals or corporations that is subject to protections under trade secret, copyright, and patent law.

intelligence The first of Simon's four stages of decision making, when the individual collects information to identify problems occurring in the organization.

intelligent agent Software program that uses a built-in or learned knowledge base to carry out specific, repetitive, and predictable tasks for an individual user, business process, or software application.

internal integration tools Project management technique that ensures that the implementation team operates as a cohesive unit.

international information systems architecture The basic information systems required by organizations to coordinate worldwide trade and other activities.

Internet Global network of networks using universal standards to connect millions of different networks.

Internet Protocol (IP) address Four-part numeric address indicating a unique computer location on the Internet.

Internet Service Provider (ISP) A commercial organization with a permanent connection to the Internet that sells temporary connections to subscribers.

Internet telephony Technologies that use the Internet Protocol's packet-switched connections for voice service.

Internet2 Research network with new protocols and transmission speeds that provides an infrastructure for supporting high-bandwidth Internet applications.

interorganizational systems Information systems that automate the flow of information across organizational boundaries and link a company to its customers, distributors, or suppliers.

interpersonal roles Mintzberg's classification for managerial roles where managers act as figureheads and leaders for the organization.

intranet An internal network based on Internet and World Wide Web technology and standards.

intrusion detection system Tools to monitor the most vulnerable points in a network to detect and deter unauthorized intruders.

investment workstation Powerful desktop computer for financial specialists, which is optimized to access and manipulate massive amounts of financial data.

IT governance Strategy and policies for using information technology within an organization, specifying the decision rights and accountabilities to ensure that information technology supports the organization's strategies and objectives.

iterative A process of repeating over and over again the steps to build a system.

Java Programming language that can deliver only the software functionality needed for a particular task, such as a small applet downloaded from a network; can run on any computer and operating system.

Joint Application Design (JAD) Process to accelerate the generation of information requirements by having end users and information systems specialists work together in intensive interactive design sessions.

just-in-time Scheduling system for minimizing inventory by having components arrive exactly at the moment they are needed and finished goods shipped as soon as they leave the assembly line.

key field A field in a record that uniquely identifies instances of that record so that it can be retrieved, updated, or sorted.

key performance indicators Measures proposed by senior management for understanding how well the firm is performing along specified dimensions.

keylogger Spyware that records every keystroke made on a computer to steal personal information or passwords or to launch Internet attacks.

knowledge Concepts, experience, and insight that provide a framework for creating, evaluating, and using information.

knowledge—and information-intense products Products that require a great deal of learning and knowledge to produce.

knowledge base Model of human knowledge that is used by expert systems.

knowledge discovery Identification of novel and valuable patterns in large databases.

knowledge management The set of processes developed in an organization to create, gather, store, maintain, and disseminate the firm's knowledge.

knowledge management systems Systems that support the creation, capture, storage, and dissemination of firm expertise and knowledge.

knowledge network system Online directory for locating corporate experts in well-defined knowledge domains.

knowledge workers People such as engineers or architects who design products or services and create knowledge for the organization.

learning management system (LMS) Tools for the management, delivery, tracking, and assessment of various types of employee learning.

legacy system A system that has been in existence for a long time and that continues to be used to avoid the high cost of replacing or redesigning it.

legitimacy The extent to which one's authority is accepted on grounds of competence, vision, or other qualities. Making judgments and taking actions on the basis of narrow or personal characteristics.

liability The existence of laws that permit individuals to recover the damages done to them by other actors, systems, or organizations.

Linux Reliable and compactly designed operating system that is an offshoot of UNIX and that can run on many different hardware platforms and is available free or at very low cost. Used as alternative to UNIX and Windows NT.

local area network (LAN) A telecommunications network that requires its own dedicated channels and that encompasses a limited distance, usually one building or several buildings in close proximity.

long tail marketing Refers to the ability of firms to profitably market goods to very small online audiences, largely because of the lower costs of reaching very small market segments (people who fall into the long tail ends of a Bell curve).

mainframe Largest category of computer, used for major business processing.

maintenance Changes in hardware, software, documentation, or procedures to a production system to correct errors, meet new requirements, or improve processing efficiency.

malware Malicious software programs such as computer viruses, worms, and Trojan horses.

managed security service provider (MSSP) Company that provides security management services for subscribing clients.

management information systems (MIS) The study of information systems focusing on their use in business and management..

management-level systems Information systems that support the monitoring, controlling, decision-making, and administrative activities of middle managers.

managerial roles Expectations of the activities that managers should perform in an organization.

man-month The traditional unit of measurement used by systems designers to estimate the length of time to complete a project. Refers to the amount of work a person can be expected to complete in a month.

market creator An e-commerce business model in which firms provide a digital online environment where buyers and sellers can meet, search for products, and engage in transactions.

marketspace A marketplace extended beyond traditional boundaries and removed from a temporal and geographic location.

mashups Composite software applications that depend on high-speed networks, universal communication standards, and open-source code.

mass customization The capacity to offer individually tailored products or services using mass production resources..

megahertz A measure of cycle speed, or the pacing of events in a computer; one megahertz equals one million cycles per second.

menu costs Merchants' costs of changing prices.

metric A standard measurement of performance.

metropolitan area network (MAN) Network that spans a metropolitan area, usually a city and its major suburbs. Its geographic scope falls between a WAN and a LAN.

microbrowser Web browser software with a small file size that can work with low-memory constraints, tiny screens of handheld wireless devices, and low bandwidth of wireless networks.

micropayment Payment for a very small sum of money, often less than $10.

microprocessor Very large scale integrated circuit technology that integrates the computer's memory, logic, and control on a single chip.

microwave A high-volume, long-distance, point-to-point transmission in which high-frequency radio signals are transmitted through the atmosphere from one terrestrial transmission station to another.

middle management People in the middle of the organizational hierarchy who are responsible for carrying out the plans and goals of senior management.

midrange computer Middle-size computer that is capable of supporting the computing needs of smaller organizations or of managing networks of other computers.

minicomputer Middle-range computer used in systems for universities, factories, or research laboratories.

MIS audit Identifies all the controls that govern individual information systems and assesses their effectiveness.

mobile commerce (m-commerce) The use of wireless devices, such as cell phones or handheld digital information appliances, to conduct both business-to-consumer and business-to-business e-commerce transactions over the Internet.

mobile wallets (m-wallets) Store m-commerce shoppers' personal information and credit card numbers to expedite the purchase process.

moblog Specialized blog featuring photos with captions posted from mobile phones.

model An abstract representation that illustrates the components or relationships of a phenomenon.

model-driven DSS Primarily stand-alone system that uses some type of model to perform "what-if" and other kinds of analyses.

modem A device for translating a computer's digital signals into analog form for transmission over ordinary telephone lines, or for translating analog signals back into digital form for reception by a computer.

module A logical unit of a program that performs one or several functions.

Moore's Law Assertion that the number of components on a chip doubles each year

MP3 (MPEG3) Compression standard that can compress audio files for transfer over the Internet with virtually no loss in quality.

multicore processor Integrated circuit to which two or more processors have been attached for enhanced performance, reduced power consumption and more efficient simultaneous processing of multiple tasks.

multimedia The integration of two or more types of media such as text, graphics, sound, voice, full-motion video, or animation into a computer-based application.

multinational Form of business organization that concentrates financial management and control out of a central home base while decentralizing

multiplexing Ability of a single communications channel to carry data transmissions from multiple sources simultaneously.

multitiered (N-tier) client/server architecture Client/server network which the work of the entire network is balanced over several different levels of servers.

nanotechnology Technology that builds structures and processes based on the manipulation of individual atoms and molecules.

natural language Nonprocedural language that enables users to communicate with the computer using conversational commands resembling human speech.

net marketplace A single digital marketplace based on Internet technology linking many buyers to many sellers.

netbook Small low-cost, lightweight subnotebook optimized for wireless communication and Internet access.

network The linking of two or more computers to share data or resources, such as a printer.

network economics Model of strategic systems at the industry level based on the concept of a network where adding another participant entails zero marginal costs but can create much larger marginal gains.

network interface card (NIC) Expansion card inserted into a computer to enable it to connect to a network.

network operating system (NOS) Special software that routes and manages communications on the network and coordinates network resources.

networking and telecommunications technology Physical devices and software that link various computer hardware components and transfer data from one physical location to another.

neural network Hardware or software that attempts to emulate the processing patterns of the biological brain.

nonobvious relationship awareness (NORA) Technology that can find obscure hidden connections between people or other entities by analyzing information from many different sources to correlate relationships.

normalization The process of creating small stable data structures from complex groups of data when designing a relational database.

object Software building block that combines data and the procedures acting on the data.

object-oriented DBMS An approach to data management that stores both data and the procedures acting on the data as objects that can be automatically retrieved and shared; the objects can contain multimedia.

object-oriented development Approach to systems development that uses the object as the basic unit of systems analysis and design. The system is modeled as a collection o objects and the relationship between them.

object-oriented programming An approach to software development that combines data and procedures into a single object.

object-relational DBMS A database management system that combines the capabilities of a relational DBMS for storing traditional information and the capabilities of an object-oriented DBMS for storing graphics and multimedia.

Office 2010 The latest version of Microsoft desktop software suite with capabilities for supporting collaborative work on the Web or incorporating information from the Web into documents.

offshore outsourcing Outsourcing systems development work or maintenance of existing systems to external vendors in another country.

on-demand computing Firms off-loading peak demand for computing power to remote, large-scale data processing centers, investing just enough to handle average processing loads and paying for only as much additional computing power as the market demands. Also called utility computing.

on-line analytical processing (OLAP) Capability for manipulating and analyzing large volumes of data from multiple perspectives.

online processing A method of collecting and processing data in which transactions are entered directly into the computer system and processed immediately.

online transaction processing Transaction processing mode in which transactions entered on-line are immediately processed by the computer.

open-source software Software that provides free access to its program code, allowing users to modify the program code to make improvements or fix errors.

operating system Software that manages the resources and activities of the computer.

operational CRM Customer-facing applications, such as sales force automation, call center and customer service support, and marketing automation.

operational management People who monitor the day-to-day activities of the organization.

operational-level systems Information systems that monitor the elementary activities and transactions of the organization.

opt-in Model of informed consent permitting prohibiting an organization from collecting any personal information unless the individual specifically takes action to approve information collection and use.

opt-out Model of informed consent permitting the collection of personal information until the consumer specifically requests that the data not be collected.

organization (behavioral definition) A collection of rights, privileges, obligations, and responsibilities that are delicately balanced over a period of time through conflict and conflict resolution.

organization (technical definition) A stable, formal, social structure that takes resources from the environment and processes them to produce outputs.

organizational and management capital Investments in organization and management such as new business processes, management behavior, organizational culture, or training.

organizational impact analysis Study of the way a proposed system will affect organizational structure, attitudes, decision making, and operations.

organizational learning Creation of new standard operating procedures and business processes that reflect organizations' experience.

output The distribution of processed information to the people who will use it or to the activities for which it will be used.

outsourcing The practice of contracting computer center operations, telecommunications networks, or applications development to external vendors.

P3P Industry standard designed to give users more control over personal information gathered on Web sites they visit. Stands for Platform for Privacy Preferences Project.

packet switching Technology that breaks messages into small, fixed bundles of data and routes them in the most economical way through any available communications channel..

paradigm shift Radical reconceptualization of the nature of the business and the nature of the organization.

parallel strategy A safe and conservative conversion approach where both the old system and its potential replacement are run together for a time until everyone is assured that the new one functions correctly.

particularism Making judgments and taking action on the basis of narrow or personal characteristics, in all its forms (religious, nationalistic, ethnic, regionalism, geopolitical position).

partner relationship management (PRM) Automation of the firm's relationships with its selling partners using customer data and analytical tools to improve coordination and customer sales.

patch Small pieces of software to repair the software flaws without disturbing the proper operation of the software.

patent A legal document that grants the owner an exclusive monopoly on the ideas behind an invention for 17 years; designed to ensure that inventors of new machines or methods are rewarded for their labor while making widespread use of their inventions.

peer-to-peer Network architecture that gives equal power to all computers on the network; used primarily in small networks.

personal area network (PAN) Computer network used for communication among digital devices (including telephones and PDAs) that are close to one person.

personal digital assistant (PDA) Small, pen-based, handheld computer with built-in wireless telecommunications capable of entirely digital communications transmission.

personalization Ability of merchants to target marketing messages to specific individuals by adjusting the message for a person's name, interests, and past purchases.

PERT chart Network diagram depicting project tasks and their interrelationships.

pharming Phishing technique that redirects users to a bogus Web page, even when an individual enters the correct Web page address.

phased approach Introduces the new system in stages either by functions or by organizational units.

phishing Form of spoofing involving setting up fake Web sites or sending e-mail messages that resemble those of legitimate businesses that ask users for confidential personal data.

pilot study A strategy to introduce the new system to a limited area of the organization until it is proven to be fully functional; only then can the conversion to the new system across the entire organization take place.

pivot table Spreadsheet tool for reorganizing and summarizing two or more dimensions of data in a tabular format.

podcasting Publishing audio broadcasts via the Internet so that subscribing users can download audio files onto their personal computers or portable music players.

pop-up ad Ad that opens automatically and does not disappear until the user clicks on it.

portal Web interface for presenting integrated personalized content from a variety of sources. Also refers to a Web site service that provides an initial point of entry to the Web.

portfolio analysis An analysis of the portfolio of potential applications within a firm to determine the risks and benefits, and to select among alternatives for information systems.

post-implementation audit Formal review process conducted after a system has been placed in production to determine how well the system has met its original objectives.

prediction markets An analysis of the portfolio of potential applications within a firm to determine the risks and benefits, and to select among alternatives for information systems.

predictive analytics The use of data mining techniques, historical data, and assumptions about future conditions to predict outcomes of events, such as the probability a customer will respond to an offer or purchase a specific product.

price discrimination Selling the same goods, or nearly the same goods, to different targeted groups at different prices.

price transparency The ease with which consumers can find out the variety of prices in a market.

primary activities Activities most directly related to the production and distribution of a firm's products or services.

primary key Unique identifier for all the information in any row of a database table.

privacy The claim of individuals to be left alone, free from surveillance or interference from other individuals, organizations, or the state.

private cloud A proprietary network or a data center that ties together servers, storage, networks, data, and applications as a set of virtualized services that are shared by users inside a company.

private exchange Another term for a private industrial network.

private industrial networks Web-enabled networks linking systems of multiple firms in an industry for the coordination of trans-organizational business processes.

process specifications Describe the logic of the processes occurring within the lowest levels of a data flow diagram.

processing The conversion, manipulation, and analysis of raw input into a form that is more meaningful to humans.

procurement Sourcing goods and materials, negotiating with suppliers, paying for goods, and making delivery arrangements.

product differentiation Competitive strategy for creating brand loyalty by developing new and unique products and services that are not easily duplicated by competitors.

production The stage after the new system is installed and the conversion is complete; during this time the system is reviewed by users and technical specialists to determine how well it has met its original goals.

production or service workers People who actually produce the products or services of the organization.

profiling The use of computers to combine data from multiple sources and create electronic dossiers of detailed information on individuals.

program-data dependence The close relationship between data stored in files and the software programs that update and maintain those files. Any change in data organization or format requires a change in all the programs associated with those files.

programmers Highly trained technical specialists who write computer software instructions.

programming The process of translating the system specifications prepared during the design stage into program code.

project Planned series of related activities for achieving a specific business objective.

project management Application of knowledge, tools, and techniques to achieve specific targets within a specified budget and time period.

protocol A set of rules and procedures that govern transmission between the components in a network.

prototype The preliminary working version of an information system for demonstration and evaluation purposes.

prototyping The process of building an experimental system quickly and inexpensively for demonstration and evaluation so that users can better determine information requirements.

public cloud A cloud maintained by an external service provider, accessed through the Internet, and available to the general public.

public key encryption Uses two keys: one shared (or public) and one private.

public key infrastructure(PKI) System for creating public and private keys using a certificate authority (CA) and digital certificates for authentication.

pull-based model Supply chain driven by actual customer orders or purchases so that members of the supply chain produce and deliver only what customers have ordered.

pure-play Business models based purely on the Internet.

push-based model Supply chain driven by production master schedules based on forecasts or best guesses of demand for products, and products are "pushed" to customers.

query language Software tool that provides immediate online answers to requests for information that are not predefined.

radio-frequency identification (RFID) Technology using tiny tags with embedded microchips containing data about an item and its location to transmit short-distance radio signals to special RFID readers that then pass the data on to a computer for processing.

Rapid Application Development (RAD) Process for developing systems in a very short time period by using prototyping, fourth-generation tools, and close teamwork among users and systems specialists.

rational model Model of human behavior based on the belief that people, organizations, and nations engage in basically consistent, value-maximizing calculations.

rationalization of procedures The streamlining of standard operating procedures, eliminating obvious bottlenecks, so that automation makes operating procedures more efficient.

real options pricing models Models for evaluating information technology investments with uncertain returns by using techniques for valuing financial options.

record A group of related fields.

recovery-oriented computing Computer systems designed to recover rapidly when mishaps occur.

referential integrity Rules to ensure that relationships between coupled database tables remain consistent.

relational DBMS A type of logical database model that treats data as if they were stored in two-dimensional tables. It can relate data stored in one table to data in another as long as the two tables share a common data element.

Repetitive Stress Injury (RSI) Occupational disease that occurs when muscle groups are forced through repetitive actions with high-impact loads or thousands of repetitions with low-impact loads.

Request for Proposal (RFP) A detailed list of questions submitted to vendors of software or other services to determine how well the vendor's product can meet the organization's specific requirements.

resource allocation The determination of how costs, time, and personnel are assigned to different phases of a systems development project.

responsibility Accepting the potential costs, duties, and obligations for the decisions one makes.

revenue model A description of how a firm will earn revenue, generate profits, and produce a return on investment.

richness Measurement of the depth and detail of information that a business can supply to the customer as well as information the business collects about the customer.

ring topology A network topology in which all computers are linked by a closed loop in a manner that passes data in one direction from one computer to another.

risk assessment Determining the potential frequency of the occurrence of a problem and the potential damage if the problem were to occur. Used to determine the cost/benefit of a control.

Risk Aversion Principle Principle that one should take the action that produces the least harm or incurs the least cost.

router Specialized communications processor that forwards packets of data from one network to another network.

routines Precise rules, procedures and practices that have been developed to cope with expected situations.

RSS Technology using aggregator software to pull content from Web sites and feed it automatically to subscribers' computers.

SaaS (Software as a Service) Services for delivering and providing access to software remotely as a Web-based service.

safe harbor Private self-regulating policy and enforcement mechanism that meets the objectives of government regulations but does not involve government regulation or enforcement.

Sarbanes-Oxley Act Law passed in 2002 that imposes responsibility on companies and their management to protect investors by safeguarding the accuracy and integrity of financial information that is used internally and released externally.

scalability The ability of a computer, product, or system to expand to serve a larger number of users without breaking down.

scope Defines what work is and is not included in a project.

scoring model A quick method for deciding among alternative systems based on a system of ratings for selected objectives.

search costs The time and money spent locating a suitable product and determining the best price for that product.

search engine A tool for locating specific sites or information on the Internet.

search engine marketing Use of search engines to deliver in their results sponsored links, for which advertisers have paid.

search engine optimization (SEO) the process of changing a Web site's content, layout, and format in order to increase the ranking of the site on popular search engines, and to generate more site visitors.

Secure Hypertext Transfer Protocol (S-HTTP) Protocol used for encrypting data flowing over the Internet; limited to individual messages.

Secure Sockets Layer (SSL) Enables client and server computers to manage encryption and decryption activities as they communicate with each other during a secure Web session.

security Policies, procedures, and technical measures used to prevent unauthorized access, alteration, theft, or physical damage to information systems.

security policy Statements ranking information risks, identifying acceptable security goals, and identifying the mechanisms for achieving these goals.

Semantic Web Ways of making the Web more "intelligent," with machine-facilitated understanding of information so that searches can be more intuitive, effective, and executed using intelligent software agents.

semistructured decisions Decisions in which only part of the problem has a clear-cut answer provided by an accepted procedure.

senior management People occupying the topmost hierarchy in an organization who are responsible for making long-range decisions.

sensitivity analysis Models that ask "what-if" questions repeatedly to determine the impact of changes in one or more factors on the outcomes.

server Computer specifically optimized to provide software and other resources to other computers over a network.

server farm Large group of servers maintained by a commercial vendor and made available to subscribers for electronic commerce and other activities requiring heavy use of servers.

service level agreement (SLA) Formal contract between customers and their service providers that defines the specific responsibilities of the service provider and the level of service expected by the customer.

service platform Integration of multiple applications from multiple business functions, business units, or business partners to deliver a seamless experience for the customer, employee, manager, or business partner.

service-oriented architecture Software architecture of a firm built on a collection of software programs that communicate with each other to perform assigned tasks to create a working software application

shopping bot Software with varying levels of built-in intelligence to help electronic commerce shoppers locate and evaluate products or service they might wish to purchase.

Simple Object Access Protocol (SOAP) Set of rules that allows Web services applications to pass data and instructions to one another.

six sigma A specific measure of quality, representing 3.4 defects per million opportunities; used to designate a set of methodologies and techniques for improving quality and reducing costs.

smart card A credit-card-size plastic card that stores digital information and that can be used for electronic payments in place of cash.

smartphone Wireless phone with voice, text, and Internet capabilities.

sniffer Type of eavesdropping program that monitors information traveling over a network.

social bookmarking Capability for users to save their bookmarks to Web pages on a public Web site and tag these bookmarks with keywords to organize documents and share information with others.

social engineering Tricking people into revealing their passwords by pretending to rrbe legitimate users or members of a company in need of information.

social networking sites Online community for expanding users' business or social contacts by making connections through their mutual business or personal connections.

social shopping Use of Web sites featuring user-created Web pages to share knowledge about items of interest to other shoppers.

sociotechnical design Design to produce information systems that blend technical efficiency with sensitivity to organizational and human needs.

sociotechnical view Seeing systems as composed of both technical and social elements.

software localization Process of converting software to operate in a second language.

Glossary

software package A prewritten, precoded, commercially available set of programs that eliminates the need to write software programs for certain functions.

spam Unsolicited commercial e-mail.

spamming Form of abuse in which thousands and even hundreds of thousands of unsolicited e-mail and electronic messages are sent out, creating a nuisance for both businesses and individual users.

spyware Technology that aids in gathering information about a person or organization without their knowledge.

SQL injection attack Attacks against a Web site that take advantage of vulnerabilities in poorly coded SQL (a standard and common database software application) applications in order to introduce malicious program code into a company's systems and networks.

star topology A network topology in which all computers and other devices are connected to a central host computer. All communications between network devices must pass through the host computer.

storage area network (SAN) A high-speed network dedicated to storage that connects different kinds of storage devices, such as tape libraries and disk arrays so they can be shared by multiple servers.

storage technology Physical media and software governing the storage and organization of data for use in an information system.

stored value payment systems Systems enabling consumers to make instant on-line payments to merchants and other individuals based on value stored in a digital account.

strategic information systems Computer systems at any level of the organization that change goals, operations, products, services, or environmental relationships to help the organization gain a competitive advantage.

strategic transitions A movement from one level of sociotechnical system to another. Often required when adopting strategic systems that demand changes in the social and technical elements of an organization.

streaming A publishing method for music and video files that flows a continuous stream of content to a user's device without being stored locally on the device.

structure chart System documentation showing each level of design, the relationship among the levels, and the overall place in the design structure; can document one program, one system, or part of one program.

structured Refers to the fact that techniques are carefully drawn up, step by step, with each step building on a previous one.

structured decisions Decisions that are repetitive, routine, and have a definite procedure for handling them.

structured knowledge Knowledge in the form of structured documents and reports.

Structured Query Language (SQL) The standard data manipulation language for relational database management systems.

supply chain Network of organizations and business processes for procuring materials, transforming raw materials into intermediate and finished products, and distributing the finished products to customers.

supply chain execution systems Systems to manage the flow of products through distribution centers and warehouses to ensure that products are delivered to the right locations in the most efficient manner.

supply chain management Integration of supplier, distributor, and customer logistics requirements into one cohesive process.

supply chain management systems Information systems that automate the flow of information between a firm and its suppliers in order to optimize the planning, sourcing, manufacturing, and delivery of products and services.

supply chain planning systems Systems that enable a firm to generate demand forecasts for a product and to develop sourcing and manufacturing plans for that product.

support activities Activities that make the delivery of a firm's primary activities possible. Consist of the organization's infrastructure, human resources, technology, and procurement.

switch Device to connect network components that has more intelligence than a hub and can filter and forward data to a specified destination.

switching costs The expense a customer or company incurs in lost time and expenditure of resources when changing from one supplier or system to a competing supplier or system.

syndicator Business aggregating content or applications from multiple sources, packaging them for distribution, and reselling them to third-party Web sites.

system testing Tests the functioning of the information system as a whole in order to determine if discrete modules will function together as planned.

systems analysis The analysis of a problem that the organization will try to solve with an information system.

systems analysts Specialists who translate business problems and requirements into information requirements and systems, acting as liaison between the information systems department and the rest of the organization.

systems design Details how a system will meet the information requirements as determined by the systems analysis.

systems development The activities that go into producing an information systems solution to an organizational problem or opportunity.

systems life cycle A traditional methodology for developing an information system that partitions the systems development process into formal stages that must be completed sequentially with a very formal division of labor between end users and information systems specialists.

T lines High-speed data lines leased from communications providers, such as T-1 lines (with a transmission capacity of 1.544 Mbps).

tacit knowledge Expertise and experience of organizational members that has not been formally documented.

tangible benefits Benefits that can be quantified and assigned a monetary value; they include lower operational costs and increased cash flows.

taxonomy Method of classifying things according to a predetermined system.

teams Teams are formal groups whose members collaborate to achieve specific goals.

teamware Group collaboration software that is customized for teamwork.

technology standards Specifications that establish the compatibility of products and the ability to communicate in a network.

technostress Stress induced by computer use; symptoms include aggravation, hostility toward humans, impatience, and enervation.

telecommunications system A collection of compatible hardware and software arranged to communicate information from one location to another.

teleconferencing The ability to confer with a group of people simultaneously using the telephone or electronic-mail group communication software.

telepresence Telepresence is a technology that allows a person to give the appearance of being present at a location other than his or her true physical location.

Telnet Network tool that allows someone to log on to one computer system while doing work on another.

test plan Prepared by the development team in conjunction with the users; it includes all of the preparations for the series of tests to be performed on the system.

testing The exhaustive and thorough process that determines whether the system produces the desired results under known conditions.

text mining Discovery of patterns and relationships from large sets of unstructured data.

token Physical device similar to an identification card that is designed to prove the identity of a single user.

touch point Method of firm interaction with a customer, such as telephone, e-mail, customer service desk, conventional mail, or point-of-purchase.

topology The way in which the components of a network are connected.

Total Cost of Ownership (TCO) Designates the total cost of owning technology resources, including initial purchase costs, the cost of hardware and software upgrades, maintenance, technical support, and training.

Total Quality Management (TQM) A concept that makes quality control a responsibility to be shared by all people in an organization.

trade secret Any intellectual work or product used for a business purpose that can be classified as belonging to that business, provided it is not based on information in the public domain.

transaction costs Costs incurred when a firm buys on the marketplace what it cannot make itself.

transaction cost theory Economic theory stating that firms grow larger because they can conduct marketplace transactions internally more cheaply than they can with external firms in the marketplace.

transaction fee revenue model An online e-commerce revenue model where the firm receives a fee for enabling or executing transactions.

transaction processing systems (TPS) Computerized systems that perform and record the daily routine transactions necessary to conduct the business; they serve the organization's operational level.

transborder data flow The movement of information across international boundaries in any form.

Transmission Control Protocol/Internet Protocol (TCP/IP) Dominant model for achieving connectivity among different networks. Provides a universally agree-on method for breaking up digital messages into packets, routing them to the proper addresses, and then reassembling them into coherent messages.

transnational Truly global form of business organization with no national headquarters; value-added activities are managed from a global perspective without reference to national borders, optimizing sources of supply and demand and local competitive advantage.

Trojan horse A software program that appears legitimate but contains a second hidden function that may cause damage.

tuple A row or record in a relational database.

twisted wire A transmission medium consisting of pairs of twisted copper wires; used to transmit analog phone conversations but can be used for data transmission.

Unified communications Integrates disparate channels for voice communications, data communications, instant messaging, e-mail, and electronic conferencing into a single experience where users can seamlessly switch back and forth between different communication modes.

Unified Modeling Language (UML) Industry standard methodology for analysis and design of an object-oriented software system.

unified threat management (UTM) Comprehensive security management tool that combines multiple security tools, including firewalls, virtual private networks, intrusion detection systems, and Web content filtering and anti-spam software.

uniform resource locator (URL) The address of a specific resource on the Internet.

unit testing The process of testing each program separately in the system. Sometimes called program testing.

UNIX Operating system for all types of computers, which is machine independent and supports multiuser processing, multitasking, and networking. Used in high-end workstations and servers.

unstructured decisions Nonroutine decisions in which the decision maker must provide judgment, evaluation, and insights into the problem definition; there is no agreed-upon procedure for making such decisions.

Usenet Forums in which people share information and ideas on a defined topic through large electronic bulletin boards where anyone can post messages on the topic for others to see and to which others can respond.

user interface The part of the information system through which the end user interacts with the system; type of hardware and the series of on-screen commands and responses required for a user to work with the system.

user-designer communications gap The difference in backgrounds, interests, and priorities that impede communication and problem solving among end users and information systems specialists.

Utilitarian Principle Principle that assumes one can put values in rank order and understand the consequences of various courses of action.

utility computing Model of computing in which companies pay only for the information technology resources they actually use during a specified time period. Also called on-demand computing or usage-based pricing.

value chain model Model that highlights the primary or support activities that add a margin of value to a firm's products or services where information systems can best be applied to achieve a competitive advantage.

value web Customer-driven network of independent firms who use information technology to coordinate their value chains to collectively produce a product or service for a market.

Value-Added Network (VAN) Private, multipath, data-only, third-party-managed network that multiple organizations use on a subscription basis.

videoconferencing Teleconferencing in which participants see each other over video screens.

virtual company Organization using networks to link people, assets and ideas to create and distribute products and services without being limited to traditional organizational boundaries or physical location.

Virtual Private Network (VPN) A secure connection between two points across the Internet to transmit corporate data. Provides a low-cost alternative to a private network.

Virtual Reality Modeling Language (VRML) A set of specifications for interactive three-dimensional modeling on the World Wide Web.

virtual reality systems Interactive graphics software and hardware that create computer-generated simulations that provide sensations that emulate real-world activities.

virtual world Computer-based simulated environment intended for its users to inhabit and interact via graphical representations called avatars.

virtualization Presenting a set of computing resources so that they can all be accessed in ways that are not restricted by physical configuration or geographic location.

Voice over IP (VoIP) Facilities for managing the delivery of voice information using the Internet Protocol (IP).

war driving Technique in which eavesdroppers drive by buildings or park outside and try to intercept wireless network traffic.

Web 2.0 Second-generation, interactive Internet-based services that enable people to collaborate, share information, and create new services online, including mashups, blogs, RSS, and wikis.

Web 3.0 Future vision of the Web where all digital information is woven together with intelligent search capabilities.

Web beacons Tiny objects invisibly embedded in e-mail messages and Web pages that are designed to monitor the behavior of the user visiting a Web site or sending e-mail.

Web browser An easy-to-use software tool for accessing the World Wide Web and the Internet.

Web bugs Tiny graphic files embedded in e-mail messages and Web pages that are designed to monitor online Internet user behavior.

Web hosting service Company with large Web server computers to maintain the Web sites of fee-paying subscribers.

Web mining Discovery and analysis of useful patterns and information from the World Wide Web.

Web server Software that manages requests for Web pages on the computer where they are stored and that delivers the page to the user's computer.

Web services Set of universal standards using Internet technology for integrating different applications from different sources without time-consuming custom coding. Used for linking systems of different organizations or for linking disparate systems within the same organization.

Web site All of the World Wide Web pages maintained by an organization or an individual.

Wi-Fi Standards for Wireless Fidelity and refers to the 802.11 family of wireless networking standards.

Wide Area Network (WAN) Telecommunications network that spans a large geographical distance. May consist of a variety of cable, satellite, and microwave technologies.

wiki Collaborative Web site where visitors can add, delete, or modify content, including the work of previous authors.

WiMax Popular term for IEEE Standard 802.16 for wireless networking over a range of up to 31 miles with a data transfer rate of up to 75 Mbps. Stands for Worldwide Interoperability for Microwave Access.

Windows Microsoft family of operating systems for both network servers and client computers. The most recent version is Windows Vista.

Windows 7 The successor to Microsoft Windows Vista operating system released in 2009.

Wintel PC Any computer that uses Intel microprocessors (or compatible processors) and a Windows operating system.

wireless portals Portals with content and services optimized for mobile devices to steer users to the information they are most likely to need.

wireless sensor networks (WSNs) Networks of interconnected wireless devices with built-in processing, storage, and radio frequency sensors and antennas that are embedded into the physical environment to provide measurements of many points over large spaces.

wisdom The collective and individual experience of applying knowledge to the solution of problems.

wisdom of crowds The belief that large numbers of people can make better decisions about a wide range of topics or products than a single person or even a small committee of experts (first proposed in a book by James Surowiecki).

WML (Wireless Markup Language) Markup language for Wireless Web sites; based on XML and optimized for tiny displays.

workflow management The process of streamlining business procedures so that documents can be moved easily and efficiently from one location to another.

World Wide Web A system with universally accepted standards for storing, retrieving, formatting, and displaying information in a networked environment.

worms Independent software programs that propagate themselves to disrupt the operation of computer networks or destroy data and other programs.

XML (eXtensible Markup Language) General-purpose language that describes the structure of a document and supports links to multiple documents, allowing data to be manipulated by the computer. Used for both Web and non-Web applications.

Case 1

Milligan's Backyard Storage Kits

Spreadsheet Case   **Difficulty Rating:** ★

CASE BACKGROUND

Milligan's Backyard Storage Kits, a mail order company, sells a variety of backyard storage unit kits and landscaping decorations to its customers. Although the company makes a profit, David Milligan, the company's owner, realizes that he can improve his company's operations if he better manages his inventory. Mr. Milligan requests your help in preparing an Inventory Analysis worksheet. The Inventory Analysis worksheet provides Mr. Milligan with information about his annual sales, cost of goods sold, gross profit, markup, inventory turnover, and days in inventory for his products. Preparing the worksheet for Mr. Milligan requires you to insert columns, use several functions, and apply proper formatting to the worksheet and cells.

CASE SCENARIO

Ten years ago, David Milligan was short on storage space. After shopping around for a backyard storage unit and not finding one that met his specifications, Mr. Milligan built his own storage unit for his backyard. Realizing that many homeowners had similar storage needs, Mr. Milligan began selling a backyard storage unit kit via mail order. He felt that given good instructions, precut lumber, and the necessary hardware, just about anyone could assemble a storage unit. His idea proved popular, and he now stocks and sells 35 different items, including storage barn, gazebo, and landscaping decoration kits.

From Chapter 1 of *MIS Cases: Decision Making with Application Software*, 4/e. Lisa Miller. Copyright © 2009 by Pearson Prentice Hall. All rights reserved.

Milligan's Backyard Storage Kits

Mr. Milligan does not use a formal, consistent inventory tracking system. Periodically, Mr. Milligan or his staff visually checks to see which kits are in stock. Although he does try to keep a certain level of each kit in stock, the lack of a formal inventory tracking system has led to the overstocking of some items and understocking of still other items. In fact, on occasion, a customer will request a particular kit, and it is only then that Mr. Milligan realizes that the kit is out of stock. If a kit is not available, Mr. Milligan must tell the customer that he is currently out of stock, and then hope that the customer will wait for a kit to become available.

Lately, Mr. Milligan has become concerned with his inventory management methods. He now wants to better manage his inventory. As a starting point, he wants to examine costs, sales, markup percentages, gross profits, inventory levels, inventory turnover, and days in inventory for his products. He asks you to review his inventory and make suggestions for improvement. He provides you with the data contained in Figure 1 and asks you to prepare an Inventory Analysis worksheet.

Figure 1: Inventory Data

Milligan's Backyard Storage Units					
Inventory Data					
Item No.	Description	Unit Cost	Unit Sales Price	Average on Hand	Average Unit Sales/Year
A00100	8' x 6' Aluminum Shed	$148.14	$199.99	48	475
A00110	10' x 8' Aluminum Shed	$185.17	$249.99	50	400
A00120	12' x 20' Aluminum Shed	$1,393.56	$1,950.99	32	65
A00130	6' x 4' Aluminum Shed	$346.36	$519.59	50	241
A00140	8' x 4' Aluminum Shed	$424.58	$620.75	50	215
A00150	10' x 14' Aluminum Shed	$650.99	$1,200.00	20	250
A00210	8' x 10' Aluminum Barn	$840.47	$1,050.59	75	202
A00310	12' x 8' Double Door Aluminum Shed	$1,043.57	$1,304.47	80	302
A00320	16' x 10' Double Door Aluminum Shed	$1,141.84	$1,507.24	12	50
A00410	8' x 10' Wood Barn	$541.33	$804.49	50	700
A00420	8' x 12' Wood Barn	$751.87	$999.99	48	140
A00430	10' x 16' Wood Barn	$808.26	$1,074.99	10	67
A00510	8' x 10' Picnic Table	$269.28	$399.99	26	299
A00520	3' x 7' Picnic Table	$207.42	$299.99	77	850
A00530	8' Child's Picnic Table	$210.59	$350.99	44	157
A00610	10' Octagon Cedar Gazebo	$2,499.99	$2,999.99	71	144
A00620	12' Cedar Octagon Gazebo	$2,963.99	$3,430.99	15	39
A00710	4' x 6' Cedar Shed	$333.33	$500.00	80	200
A00720	8' x 10' Cedar Shed	$1,135.32	$1,702.99	72	75
A00730	6' x 10' Cedar Garden Hut	$1,135.00	$1,350.00	80	175
A00740	8' x 10' Cedar Cabana Shed	$1,148.56	$1,607.99	75	136
A00750	6' x 6' Cedar Garden Hut	$879.99	$950.78	114	325
A00810	6' x 20' Covered Bridge	$1,250.00	$1,400.99	42	75
A00820	8' x 40' Covered Bridge	$2,509.72	$4,700.00	2	2
A00910	Wagon Planter	$11.42	$15.99	237	702

A00920	Mailbox Planter	$21.02	$27.99	230	845
A00930	4' Windmill	$30.66	$45.99	275	201
A00940	6' Windmill	$43.99	$65.99	300	278
A00950	6' Wishing Well	$53.32	$79.99	300	780
A00960	12' Wishing Well	$130.66	$195.99	25	147
A01100	Monroe Wooden Trellis	202.30	$252.87	10	25
A01110	Majesty Copper Trellis	379.29	$505.72	14	35
A01120	Boston Folding Trellis	145.92	$207.56	12	42
A01130	Miniature Folding Trellis	48.00	$54.87	20	100
A01140	Milligan's Superior Trellis	764.81	$899.78	1	7

Design Specifications

Mr. Milligan asks you to determine the cost of average inventory, annual sales, cost of goods sold, annual gross profit, gross margin ratio, markup percentage, inventory turnover, and days in inventory for each inventory item. The determination of these values requires you to add columns to the Inventory Analysis worksheet. Mr. Milligan asks you to use the formulas shown in Figure 2.

As Mr. Milligan will use the Inventory Analysis worksheet during a presentation, he wants the worksheet to have a professional appearance. To enhance the worksheet's appearance, you include an appropriate header and format to the worksheet, column, and row labels. The header should display the name of the business, the name of the worksheet, and the current date. As you construct the worksheet, you use the currency format for all columns containing dollar values. Also, for any column that contains a percentage, you use the percentage format and format the data to two decimal places.

Figure 2: Inventory Analysis Worksheet Formulas

Inventory Analysis Worksheet Formulas	
Annual Gross Profit	Annual Sales - Cost of Goods Sold
Annual Sales	Unit Sales Price * Average Unit Sales Per Year
Cost of Average Inventory	Unit Cost * Average Units on Hand
Cost of Goods Sold	Unit Cost * Average Unit Sales Per Year
Gross Margin Ratio	$\dfrac{\text{Annual Gross Profit}}{\text{Annual Sales Per Unit}}$
Markup Based on Cost	$\dfrac{\text{Unit Sales Price - Unit Cost}}{\text{Unit Cost}}$

Inventory Turnover	$\dfrac{\text{Cost of Goods Sold}}{\text{Cost of Average Inventory}}$
Days in Inventory	$\dfrac{365}{\text{Inventory Turnover}}$

Information Specifications

For the cost of average inventory, annual sales, cost of goods sold, annual gross profit, gross margin ratio, and markup percentage values, Mr. Milligan wants the average, minimum, and maximum value for each. Mr. Milligan wants to know the maximum unit cost, unit sales price, inventory turnover, and days in inventory values, as well as the minimum unit cost, unit sales price, inventory turnover, and days in inventory values. He also wants to know the total cost of average inventory, total annual gross profit, total cost of goods sold, and the total annual sales.

Mr. Milligan also needs answers to the following questions. Using your newly designed Inventory Analysis worksheet, provide Mr. Milligan with answers to his questions.

1. Mr. Milligan wants a markup of at least 30 percent on all items. Which items have markups less than 30 percent?

2. In terms of annual sales, which item has the lowest annual sales?

3. In terms of annual sales, what were Mr. Milligan's biggest selling items last year? Identify the top five.

4. What are the company's total annual sales?

5. What is the company's annual gross profit?

6. Based on average unit sales, which five items had the lowest sales? Based on average unit sales, which five items had the highest sales?

7. Mr. Milligan wants a column chart that compares the top five selling items. Based on annual sales, prepare the column chart for Mr. Milligan.

8. Which items have an inventory turnover greater than 12?

9. Which items have days in inventory values greater than 150 days?

Implementation Concerns

Although you are free to work with the design of your worksheet, the worksheet should have a consistent, professional appearance. Also, you should use appropriate formatting for the cells and worksheet. For instance, dollar values should display a dollar sign and be formatted to two decimal places.

Test Your Design

After creating the Inventory Analysis worksheet, you should test your design. Perform the following steps. Keep in mind that you may need to insert additional rows and columns to provide Mr. Milligan with this information.

1. Add the following six items to the Inventory Analysis worksheet.

Item No.	Description	Unit Cost	Unit Sales Price	Average on Hand	Average Unit Sales/Year
A01020	10' x 20' Aluminum Carport	$999.99	$1,789.95	27	45
A01030	12' x 24' Aluminum Carport	$1,199.99	$1,888.72	25	50
A01040	14' x 20' Aluminum Carport	$1,307.84	$2,500.99	15	27
A02010	8' x 12' Arbor Roof	$1,326.42	$1,550.42	4	10
A02020	12' x 20' Arbor Roof	$2,787.96	$4,100.00	10	12
A00160	6' x 6' Aluminum Shed	$370.11	$458.93	75	150

2. For each inventory item, Mr. Milligan wants to know what percentage of the company's total annual sales the item generated.

3. What is the gross margin per unit for each inventory item? Which inventory item(s) has (have) the largest gross margin per unit? Least?

4. Prepare a bar chart that compares the age of inventory for the trellis items.

5. Based on inventory turnover, which five items are held the longest in inventory?

6. Mr. Milligan wants to reduce his inventory by $200,000. Which items would you recommend that he remove from his inventory? Why?

CASE DELIVERABLES

In order to satisfactorily complete this case, you should build the worksheet(s) as described in the case scenario and then prepare both written and oral presentations. Unless otherwise specified, submit the following deliverables to your professor.

1. A written report discussing any assumptions you have made about the case and the key elements of the case. Additionally, what features did you add to make the worksheet(s) more functional? User friendly? (Please note that these assumptions cannot violate any of the requirements specified above and must be approved by your professor.)

2. A printout of the worksheet(s).
3. A printout of each worksheet's formulas.

4. An electronic, working copy of your worksheet(s) that meet the criteria mentioned in the case scenario and specifications sections.

5. Results for each question posed above. (A memo to your instructor discussing these results should also be provided.)

6. As mentioned above, you should prepare an oral presentation. (Your instructor will establish the time allocated for your presentation.) You should use a presentation package and discuss the key features of your worksheet(s). Also, discuss how the worksheet(s) is(are) beneficial for Mr. Milligan. What additional information should be included in the worksheet(s) to make it more useful?

Case 2

Piedmont Trailer Manufacturing Company

Spreadsheet Case   **Difficulty Rating:** ★

SKILLS CHECK

You should review the following areas:

SPREADSHEET SKILLS

- ✓ Cell Formatting
- ✓ Cell Reference
- ✓ Chart
- ✓ Consolidating Worksheets
- ✓ Formula

- ✓ IRR Function
- ✓ Protecting Cells
- ✓ Range Name
- ✓ SUM Function
- ✓ Worksheet Formatting

CASE BACKGROUND

Piedmont Trailer Manufacturing Company, a nationally recognized trailer manufacturer, produces a wide range of quality standard and custom-built trailers, ranging from gooseneck to bumper pull trailers. Although the Piedmont Trailer Manufacturing Company uses state-of-the-art information systems for most of its business processes, its custom order-tracking process is primarily manual-based and requires major renovations. In an effort to improve the custom order-tracking process, a systems analysis and design project is currently underway. As part of the systems development team, one of your responsibilities is to prepare an economic feasibility analysis for an upcoming presentation to management.

Ms. Geraldine Pablo, the project manager, asks you to construct an Economic Feasibility workbook. The purpose of this workbook is to summarize and analyze the benefits and costs associated with the proposed custom order-tracking project. The preparation of an Economic Feasibility workbook requires you to design five worksheets, use several formulas and functions, use basic cell and worksheet formatting, and consolidate data from multiple worksheets into a summary worksheet.

CASE SCENARIO

Quality trailers and excellent customer service are the two primary reasons why the Piedmont Trailer Manufacturing Company is the nation's largest manufacturer of standard and custom-built trailers. Although the majority of the company's income is derived from the sale of standard trailers, the number of custom orders is on the rise. When a custom order is placed, the request is captured on several paper forms and then routed to the production department. Often it takes three months before a custom order is released to production. This is due in part to the careful attention given to the customer by helping him select the right finishes, fixtures, trailer size, and other amenities. Management has decided that the custom ordering process is inefficient, time-consuming, and costly. In an effort to improve the custom order-tracking process, your project team is assigned the task of developing a custom order-tracking system.

During the planning phase, your project team identified several tangible benefits and costs. The new custom order-tracking system will save the company money by decreasing storage, staff, and order rework expenses. Additionally, the proposed system should increase sales, improve order processing speed, provide better data management, and streamline activities. Table 1 summarizes these benefits and their respective savings.

The proposed custom order-tracking system will incur both one-time and recurring costs. From one of your business courses, you recall that one-time costs often occur during the start up and development of a project, and recurring costs occur throughout the useful life of the new system. The one-time costs for this project currently include development personnel, training, project-related technology purchases, site-preparation, and miscellaneous costs. Table 2 lists the one-time costs and their estimated dollar values. Recurring costs include software maintenance, hardware, supplies, new information technology positions, and site rental costs. Table 3 summarizes these recurring costs.

Table 1: Yearly Recurring Benefits

Benefit	Approximate Dollar Value
Storage Savings	$30,000
Staff Reduction (2 people)	$45,000
Reduced Order Rework	$14,000
Increased Sales	$100,000
Faster Order Processing	$40,000
Better Data Management	$125,000
Streamline Activities	$80,000

Table 2: One-Time Costs

One-Time Cost	Approximate Dollar Value
Development Personnel	$142,000
Training	$45,000
Project-Related Technology Purchases	$65,000
Site Preparation	$105,250
Miscellaneous	
Conference-Related	$7,500
Supplies	$2,704
Duplication	$3,249

Table 3: Yearly Recurring Costs

Cost	Approximate Dollar Value
Software Maintenance	$55,000
Hardware	$30,000
Supplies	$35,000
IT Positions (3 people)	$160,000
Site Rental	$38,000

Design Specifications

Since the project is in the early stages of development, you want your workbook to be as flexible as possible, so that additional costs and benefits, when identified, are easily added to the Economic Feasibility workbook. You decide that the Economic Feasibility workbook should contain at least five worksheets: Documentation, One-Time Cost, Recurring Cost, Tangible Benefit, and Economic Feasibility Summary. The Documentation worksheet provides information about the creator, each individual worksheet, and the date created. (Your professor will provide additional guidelines for the Documentation worksheet.)

You decide to construct the One-Time Cost, Recurring Cost, and Tangible Benefit worksheets first, because these worksheets have a simple design. These worksheets each contain two columns, with the first column identifying the items in the category, and the second column containing the dollar values associated with the items. Each worksheet totals the dollar values; these totals are then used in the Economic Feasibility Summary worksheet.

Piedmont Trailer Manufacturing Company

As Figure 1 shows, the Economic Feasibility Summary worksheet has a more complex design. Since the Economic Feasibility Summary worksheet is a summary worksheet, it consolidates data from the One-Time Cost, Recurring Cost, and Tangible Benefit worksheets, requiring you to reference specific cells on these worksheets.

As part of the Economic Feasibility Summary worksheet design, you must discount the recurring benefits and costs to their present values. Although several ways exist to determine the present value of the benefits, you decide to multiply the recurring benefit (or cost) by a present value factor. Since each year requires a different present value factor, the worksheet must compute the present value factor for each year. You decide to use the formula provided below to determine each year's present value factor. (In the following formula, "i" refers to the discount rate, and "n" refers to the year. The worksheet shown in Figure 1 assumes that the project's useful life is five years.) To determine the present value of a benefit or cost for a particular year, you multiply the recurring value of the benefit or cost for that year by the present value factor for that year. The net present value of all benefits (or costs) is a summation of the benefits (or costs) up to and including the current year. The overall net present value is the difference between the net present value of all benefits and the net present value of all costs. The cash flow section provides a summary of the cash flows on a yearly basis, as well as a summation of the overall cash flows.

$$PVF = 1/(1+i)^n$$

Figure 1: Economic Feasibility Summary Worksheet*

Piedmont Trailer Manufacturing Company Custom Order-Tracking Project (Current Date)							
Discount Rate	.14						Totals
Year	0	1	2	3	4	5	
Benefits							
Recurring Value of Benefits	$0.00	$434,000.00	$434,000.00	$434,000.00	$434,000.00	$434,000.00	
Present Value Factor	1.000000	.877193	.769468	.674972	.592080	.519369	
Present Value of Benefits	$0.00	$380,701.75	$333,948.91	$292,937.64	$256,962.84	$225,406.00	
Net Present Value of All Benefits	$0.00	$380,701.75	$714,650.66	$1,007,588.30	$1,264,551.14	$1,489,957.14	$1,489,957.14
Costs							
One-Time Costs	($370,703.00)						
Recurring Costs		($318,000.00)	($318,000.00)	($318,000.00)	($318,000.00)	($318,000.00)	
Present Value Factor		.877193	.769468	.674972	.592080	.519369	
Present Value of Recurring Costs		($278,947.37)	($244,690.67)	($214,640.94)	($188,281.53)	($165,159.24)	
Net Present Value of All Costs	($370,703.00)	($649,650.37)	($894,341.04)	($1,108,981.98)	($1,297,263.51)	($1,462,422.75)	($1,462,422.75)
Overall Net Present Value							$27,534.39

Cash Flow Analysis							
Yearly NPV Cash Flow	($370,703.00)	$101,754.39	$89,258.23	$78,296.70	$68,681.31	$60,246.77	
Overall NPV Cash Flow	($370,703.00)	($268,948.61)	($179,690.38)	($101,393.68)	($32,712.37)	$27,534.39	

*Adapted from Modern Systems Analysis and Design, fifth edition, Jeffrey A. Hoffer, Joey F. George, and Joseph S. Valacich

Although Ms. Pablo is the primary user of the Economic Feasibility workbook, other project team members will have access to this workbook. Therefore, you decide that all cells, other than input cells, should be protected. (You may wish to use your system's online help feature to review worksheet protection.)

Information Specifications

Ms. Pablo wants to generate optimistic, realistic, and pessimistic views of the data, so she requests the ability to quickly change the discount rate. To satisfy this requirement, you include a cell on your Economic Feasibility Summary worksheet to hold the discount rate. Figure 1 shows that the discount rate is placed at the top of the worksheet. The discount rate is used in several formulas, so referencing this cell in a formula facilitates the economic feasibility analysis.

The Economic Feasibility Summary worksheet summarizes the costs and benefits, shows the present values of the costs and benefits, calculates the overall net present value, and shows the yearly and overall cash flows for the project. Although not shown in Figure 1, Ms. Pablo requests that the project's breakeven point and internal rate of return be determined. During her presentation to management, Ms. Pablo will use the breakeven point to help justify the project's viability and show how quickly management will recover its investment in the project. Since the internal rate of return provides an indication of the project's profitability, Ms. Pablo will use the internal rate of return to help justify management's investment in the project.

Ms. Pablo needs answers to the following questions. Using your newly designed Economic Feasibility workbook, provide Ms. Pablo with answers to her questions.

1. How will discount rates of 8, 10, 12, 14, and 16 percent affect the project's feasibility?

2. Reset the discount rate to 14 percent. Prepare a breakeven chart that compares the net present value of all benefits to the net present value of all costs.

3. If management stipulates that the internal rate of return must be equal to or greater than the discount rate, is this project still justifiable?

4. Assuming the discount rate is 14 percent, how will eliminating an additional staff position of $32,500 affect the economic feasibility assessment?

5. Assume that the staff position mentioned in Step 3 is eliminated, the site preparation cost increases to $120,000, and the discount rate is 14 percent. What impact will these changes have on the project's feasibility?

6. Assume that management has enough money to fund two development projects. After you determine this project's internal rate of return, compare its internal rate of return to the internal rate of returns for the proposed development projects listed in the following table. Based on the projects' internal rate of returns, do you think management will fund the custom order-tracking system?

Proposed Project	IRR
Delivery System	15.7 percent
Human Resources System	27.8 percent
Inventory Tracking System	18.9 percent
Forecasting System	23.7 percent

Implementation Concerns

To design the Economic Feasibility workbook described in the case scenario, you will create a workbook consisting of five worksheets. You should create separate worksheets for the documentation, one-time costs, recurring costs, recurring benefits, and economic feasibility summary. Since the Economic Feasibility Summary worksheet consolidates data from three of the worksheets, you should create this worksheet last.

Although you are free to work with the design of your worksheets, each worksheet should have a consistent, professional appearance. You should also use proper formatting for the cells. For instance, dollar values should display with a dollar sign and be formatted to two decimal places.

Test Your Design

After creating the Economic Feasibility workbook described in the case scenario, you should test the design of your worksheets. Perform the following operations.

1. What recommendations would you make if the useful life of the project is three years instead of five years? Six years? (Use the original case values and assume a discount rate of 14 percent.)

2. Identify at least three additional benefits that might be derived from this project. Estimate their value and include the values in your analysis. What impact do these new benefits have on your economic feasibility?

3. Identify at least one additional one-time cost and at least three additional recurring costs. Estimate their values and include these values in your analysis. What impact do these new costs have on your economic feasibility? Is the project still justifiable? Why or why not?

CASE DELIVERABLES

In order to satisfactorily complete this case, you should build the workbook as described in the case scenario and then prepare both written and oral presentations. Unless otherwise specified, submit the following deliverables to your professor.

1. A written report discussing any assumptions you have made about the case and the key elements of the case. Additionally, what features did you add to make the worksheets more functional? User friendly? (Please note that these assumptions cannot violate any of the requirements specified above and must be approved by your professor.)

2. A printout of each worksheet.

3. A printout of each worksheet's formulas.

4. An electronic, working copy of your workbook that meets the criteria mentioned in the case scenario and specifications sections.

5. Results for each question posed above. (A memo to your instructor discussing these results should also be provided.)

6. As mentioned above, you should prepare an oral presentation. (Your instructor will establish the time allocated for your presentation.) You should use a presentation package and discuss the key features of your worksheets. Also, discuss how the workbook is beneficial for Ms. Pablo. What additional information should be included in the workbook to make it more useful?

Case 3

Francisco's Lawn Care

From Chapter 3 of *MIS Cases: Decision Making with Application Software*, 4/e. Lisa Miller. Copyright © 2009 by Pearson Prentice Hall. All rights reserved.

Francisco's Lawn Care

Spreadsheet Case   **Difficulty Rating:** ★

CASE BACKGROUND

Fernando Francisco owns and operates a small, growing lawn care business called Francisco's Lawn Care. Record keeping for the business has reached a point where Mr. Francisco needs a better system for tracking his customers, service dates, customer payments, and revenue. After considering several options for improving his record keeping system, Mr. Fernando decided that a Microsoft Excel workbook will be beneficial for him. The Lawn Care workbook contains several worksheets, including Customer, Payment, and Amortization worksheets. The preparation of this workbook requires you to create and format multiple worksheets, create several formulas, use several functions, and prepare charts.

CASE SCENARIO

As Mr. Francisco's client base continues to grow, he does not want to rely on his memory for price quotes, service dates, payments, and business revenue. Instead he will use Microsoft Excel to track this information. As you are familiar with Microsoft Excel, you agree to develop Mr. Francisco's Lawn Care workbook.

Currently, Mr. Francisco keeps basic information about his lawn care customers in a spiral notebook. In the notebook, he records the customer's first and last names, standard fee, additional weekly charges, total weekly charges, service day, lawn size, and start date. When a customer requests an estimate, Mr. Francisco provides an initial price quote based on the standard fees shown in Figure 1. The standard fee is the minimum price charged for a certain lawn size. Before giving a final quote, Mr. Francisco visits the customer's site and may adjust the initial quote based on his site visit. Any additional weekly charges are determined after Mr. Francisco visits the customer's site. Additional charges include such things as extra weed eating, yard fertilization, or cleaning a flower bed. For each customer, the total weekly charges include the standard fee plus additional weekly charges.

Figure 1: Pricing Guide

Francisco's Lawn Care Standard Pricing Guide	
Lawn Size	Standard Price
Small	$25.00
Medium	$35.00
Large	$50.00
Commercial	$75.00

After Mr. Francisco's site visit, the customer is given a final quote for the total weekly charges. If the customer agrees to the final quote, a weekly lawn maintenance schedule is arranged. Mr. Francisco wants a quote sheet developed, summing the weekly charges. After he returns to his office, he will prepare the quote sheet and mail it to the customer.

In one of your conversations with Mr. Francisco, he mentions that he needs to purchase new lawn care equipment, and he will purchase the lawn care equipment on credit. Before purchasing the lawn care equipment, he will evaluate different payment scenarios. As part of the workbook's design, he asks you to build an amortization schedule for him.

Design Specifications

The Lawn Care workbook will store the customer, service, and payment information that is currently kept in the spiral notebook. In the Lawn Care workbook, a worksheet should be created and named Customers. The Customers worksheet will store customer information. The Customers worksheet should have columns for customer first and last names, standard fee, additional weekly charges, total weekly charges, service day, lawn size, start date, and comments. Mr. Francisco will use the Comments column to record relevant comments about the customer's service, such as why additional charges were applied. When viewing the Customers worksheet, Mr. Francisco wants to see a total count of his customers, anticipated total revenue by day, anticipated total weekly revenue, and anticipated total monthly revenue. As the standard fee is based on lawn size, Mr. Francisco recommends that you recreate the standard pricing guide in the Customers worksheet, and then use the VLOOKUP function to retrieve the standard lawn size price. (If you are unfamiliar with the

VLOOKUP function, consider using your system's online help feature to learn more about it.) The customer entries should be sorted alphabetically by last name.

Mr. Francisco asks you to create a Payment worksheet for him. The Payment worksheet enables Mr. Francisco to track customer payments. The Payment worksheet should include the payment date, customer's first and last name, total weekly charges, one-time fees, this week's total charges, amount paid, remaining balance, and comments columns.

Periodically, a customer will ask Mr. Francisco if he can remove a tree limb or trim a hedge. As this one-time fee is not reflected in the established total weekly charges, Mr. Francisco wants a one-time fee column included in the Payment worksheet. Sometimes a customer does not pay the correct amount, so Mr. Francisco wants a column to track the remaining balance. The Comments column enables Mr. Francisco to enter any comments about the transaction for later reference. For the total weekly charges column, Mr. Francisco recommends that you look up this value from the Customer worksheet.

Mr. Francisco asks you to prepare a quote sheet for him. After the initial site visit, Mr. Francisco will use the quote sheet to prepare a summary of the quoted charges. The quote sheet should show the standard fee, any additional weekly charges and the total weekly charges. Mr. Francisco wants the business name, current date and start date provided on the quote sheet.

Mr. Francisco will purchase new lawn care equipment on credit. To help him manage his payments, he asks you to create an amortization schedule. For each month, the schedule shows how much of the payment applies to interest, how much of the payment applies to the principle, and the remaining loan balance. Mr. Francisco will periodically make additional monthly payments of differing amounts, so he wants this capability built into the schedule.

Information Specifications

In addition to the information requirements specified above, Mr. Francisco requests answers to the following questions.

1. Mr. Francisco wants a list of his customers based on service day. Provide Mr. Francisco with this list.

2. Mr. Francisco wants to compare the business's anticipated revenue by week day. Prepare a chart that compares the anticipated revenue by week day. (You select the chart.)

3. Mr. Francisco wants to compare the business's weekly revenue by lawn size. Prepare a chart that compares weekly revenue by lawn size. (You select the chart.)

4. A local hardware store is advertising zero percent interest on all purchases, as long as the balance is paid within one year of the purchase date. If Mr. Francisco takes advantage of this offer, what will his monthly payments be? (Assume he spends $12,000 on new equipment and makes monthly payments.)

5. If the interest rate is 5 percent and the loan period is for two years, what are Mr. Francisco's monthly payments?

Implementation Concerns

Although you are free to work with the design of your workbook, it should have a consistent, professional appearance. You should apply appropriate formatting to the cells and worksheets. For instance, all cells containing dollar values should use a currency format and be formatted to two decimal places. Your worksheets should have appropriate headers, as well as appropriate column and row headings.

To prepare the Lawn Care workbook according to the specifications provided above, you will design several worksheets, construct formulas, may use the IF, COUNTIF, COUNTA, SUM, SUMIF, and VLOOKUP functions, and create charts. If you are not familiar with any of these skills, use your system's online help feature to learn more about the skill.)

Test Your Design

After creating your workbook, you should test your design. Perform the following steps.

1. If the lawn care business operates seven months out of the year, what is the projected revenue for the year? (Assume no new clients are added.)

2. Mr. Francisco has five new clients. Add the following new clients to your Lawn Care workbook. (Make any additional assumptions that you feel are necessary.)

Last Name	First Name	Additional Weekly Charges	Scheduled Day	Lawn Size	Start Date
Your Last Name	Your First Name	$10.00	Tuesday	Small	5/6/2008
Malcom	Loretta	$15.00	Tuesday	Large	5/6/2008
Orosco	Amilso		Tuesday	Commercial	5/6/2008
Popoola	Rajesh		Wednesday	Medium	5/7/2008
Rishel	Ravi	$25.00	Wednesday	Medium	5/7/2008

3. Mr. Francisco may raise his prices for next year. Using his current customer data for analysis, what impact will these prices have on next year's revenue?

New Lawn Care Prices	
Commercial	$90.00
Large	$60.00
Medium	$45.00
Small	$35.00

CASE DELIVERABLES

In order to satisfactorily complete this case, you should build the worksheet as described in the case scenario and then prepare both written and oral presentations. Unless otherwise specified, submit the following deliverables to your professor.

1. A written report discussing any assumptions you have made about the case and the key elements of the case. Additionally, what features did you add to make the worksheet(s) more functional? User friendly? (Please note that these assumptions cannot violate any of the requirements specified above and must be approved by your professor.)

2. A printout of each worksheet and chart.

3. A printout of each worksheet's formulas.

4. An electronic, working copy of your workbook that meets the criteria mentioned in the case scenario and specifications sections.

5. Results for each question posed above. (A memo to your instructor discussing these results should also be provided.)

6. As mentioned above, you should prepare an oral presentation. (Your instructor will establish the time allocated for your presentation.) You should use a presentation package and discuss the key features of your workbook. Also, discuss how the workbook is beneficial for Mr. Francisco. What additional information should be included in the workbook to make it more useful?

Case 4

Maxi's Grocery Mart

Spreadsheet Case   **Difficulty Rating:** ★★

SKILLS CHECK
You should review the following areas:

SPREADSHEET SKILLS

- ✓ Absolute Cell Reference
- ✓ Cell Formatting
- ✓ Chart
- ✓ Formula
- ✓ IF Function
- ✓ Page Break
- ✓ Protecting Cells
- ✓ Relative Cell Reference
- ✓ SUM Function
- ✓ Worksheet Formatting

CASE BACKGROUND

Since its opening almost 50 years ago, Maxi's Grocery Mart has continued to grow and evolve with the times. The family-owned business has survived many ups and downs and is currently experiencing a modest growth in business. Leroy Feronti, the current owner, wants to expand his family's business by renovating the grocery mart building. While Mr. Feronti has some personal funds available, he will need to procure a loan from the local bank. Before approaching the local bank, he would like to prepare and review several pro forma financial statements. If Mr. Feronti decides to go forward with the renovation, he will use the pro forma financial statements as part of his loan application. Mr. Feronti wants the pro forma income statement prepared first, and he asks you to prepare it for him. Preparation of the pro forma income statement requires you to design a worksheet with input and information sections, properly format the worksheet, construct simple formulas, perform what-if analysis, and generate a chart.

CASE SCENARIO

Maxi's Grocery Mart is a family-owned business that has been in operation since the 1950s. Although Leroy Feronti is very active with his business, he does employ a store manager, assistant manager, and 17 full-time employees. The store manager and assistant manager are paid a salary, and the employees are paid an hourly wage. Each employee works 40 hours a week, 50 weeks a year.

Figure 1: Maxi's Food Mart Income Statement Outline

Maxi's Food Mart
Pro Forma Income Statement

	2008	2009	2010	2011
Sales				
Deli	Assume 5 percent of total sales each year.			
Dairy	Assume 19 percent of total sales each year.			
Canned Goods	Assume 10 percent of total sales each year.			
Frozen Foods	Assume 22 percent of total sales each year.			
Meats	Assume 21 percent of total sales each year.			
Produce	Assume 12.5 percent of total sales each year.			
Dry Goods	Assume 9 percent of total sales each year.			
Video Sales	Assume 1.5 percent of total sales each year.			
Total Sales	Assume $3,750,000.00 in total sales for 2008.			
Cost of Goods Sold				
Deli	Assume 50 percent of deli sales each year.			
Dairy	Assume 50 percent of dairy sales each year.			
Canned Goods	Assume 75 percent of canned good sales each year.			
Frozen Foods	Assume 65 percent of frozen food sales each year.			
Meats	Assume 50 percent of meat sales each year.			
Produce	Assume 65 percent of produce sales each year.			
Dry Goods	Assume 66 percent of dry good sales each year.			
Video Sales	Assume 30 percent of video sales each year.			
Total Cost of Goods Sold				
Gross Profit				
Operating Expenses				
Sales and Marketing	Assume 5.5 percent of total sales each year.			
General and Administrative	Assume 8.75 percent of total sales each year.			
Depreciation	Assume $20,000 per year.			
Wages	Includes the employees' wages, store manager's salary, and assistant manager's salary.			
Common Costs	Mr. Feronti's salary.			
Total Operating Expenses				
Income Before Taxes				
Income Taxes				
Net Income				

Figure 2: Assumptions and Additional Information

Maxi's Food Mart Assumptions and Additional Information	
Growth and Tax Rates	**Salary**
2009 Growth: 6.25 percent	Mr. Feronti: 12 percent of gross profit
2010 Growth: 7.75 percent	Store Manager: $57,000
2011 Growth: 8.25 percent	Assistant Manager: $42,000
Tax Rate: 35 percent	Employee Hourly Wage: $13.00

Having recently assumed ownership of the business from his parents, Mr. Feronti feels that one of the keys to the business's continued success is the renovation of the grocery mart building. Renovating the existing building will cost approximately $450,000. Mr. Feronti must borrow $300,000 from the local bank and will use income generated from the grocery mart to repay the loan. Mr. Feronti asks you to prepare a set of pro forma financial statements for him. He will use these statements to analyze his business. If he decides to pursue the renovation project, he will use the pro forma statements as part of his loan application.

Mr. Feronti asks you to use the income statement outline shown in Figure 1 and use the grocery mart's 2008 sales as the base period. You will use the 2008 sales to estimate Mr. Feronti's sales, cost of goods sold, expenses, taxes, and net income for the next three years. When preparing the pro forma income statement, several assumptions and additional information are necessary. Figure 2 provides these assumptions and additional information.

Design Specifications

As Mr. Feronti will use the pro forma income statement as part of his loan application, he requests that it have a consistent, professional, and well-organized appearance. Mr. Feronti specifically requests that you include an appropriate header and apply proper formatting to the cells and worksheet.

Using Figures 1 and 2 as guides, you decide that the worksheet requires both input and information sections. Figure 1 provides an outline and guidelines for constructing the information section and Figure 2 provides the necessary data for the input section. By creating separate sections, it is easy for Mr. Feronti to not only view the input data to his income statement, but also, if necessary, change the parameters, thus facilitating his decision-making activities.

The information section contains the pro forma income statement, and this section provides Mr. Feronti with information about his projected sales, cost of goods sold, operating expenses, and net income for years 2009 - 2011. The information section uses the grocery mart's 2008 sales as the basis for these projections. You make sure that, where appropriate, the information section formulas reference the cell values contained in the input section.

As you study Figure 1, you realize that Mr. Feronti wants his store item sales, cost of goods sold, and operating expenses expressed as a percentage of total sales. To facilitate Mr. Feronti's analysis, you place the total sales value in the input section, along with the other assumptions. By doing this, your formulas in the information section can reference the actual total sales figure. As you study Figure 2, you notice that Mr. Feronti's salary is 12 percent of gross profit. Since Mr. Feronti only draws his salary if the grocery mart makes a profit, you must build this logic into the income statement. You do so by using the IF function. To keep the information section's formulas from accidentally being updated, you protect the cells in the information section.

Mr. Feronti wants the input and information sections printed on separate pages. For each section's printout, he wants the results printed on a single page. The printouts should utilize a portrait orientation and be centered horizontally and vertically.

Information Specifications

Mr. Feronti needs information to support his decision making about the upcoming renovation to Maxi's Grocery Mart. Using the newly constructed pro forma income statement, provide Mr. Feronti with the information that he needs. (Before answering each of the following questions, reset your worksheet to its original values.)

1. What impact will sales growths of 9 percent in 2009, 9.5 percent in 2010, and 10 percent in 2011 have on the grocery mart's net income?

2. What impact will sales growths of 4 percent in 2009, 5 percent in 2010, and 5.5 in 2011 have on Mr. Feronti's net income?

3. Mr. Feronti wants a chart that compares the store items based on their 2008 sales. He asks you to select an appropriate chart type and then prepare the chart.

4. If Mr. Feronti decreases his salary to 8 percent and increases the employees' hourly wages to $15, what impact will this have on the grocery mart's net income?

5. Assume Mr. Feronti has 19 employees instead of 17. What impact will two additional employees have on the business's net income?

Implementation Concerns

The preparation of this case requires you to apply basic spreadsheet construction concepts. Since Mr. Feronti will change the input values during his decision-making activities, you should have a separate input section for the input values. Keep in mind that the formulas in the information section will reference the input cells. You should use absolute and relative cell references, as opposed to constant values.

Test Your Design

After creating the pro forma income statement worksheet, you should test your design. Perform the following steps.

1. Assume sales in 2008 were $2.5 million, instead of $3.75 million. Now, assume sales in 2008 were $7 million. What impact, if any, do these changes have? Are there any significant changes in the sales, expenses, or net income? (Other than the changes specified in this question, use the original case values.)

2. Make the following changes to the percent of sales for the following items. The deli accounts for 4 percent of sales; dairy items account for 18 percent of sales; canned goods account for 18 percent; frozen food items account for 20 percent; and meats account for 17 percent.

3. Make the following salary changes. Mr. Feronti takes home 16 percent of the gross profit, the store manager makes $60,000, and the assistant manager makes $48,000. How will these changes impact the grocery mart's net income?

4. Reset your sales percentages and salaries back to their original values and then make the following changes. Assume a discount chain is opening a grocery store in a neighboring town. Mr. Feronti thinks this may cause his sales to decrease. He thinks his growth may decrease in 2009 by 12 percent, 2010 by 10 percent and 2011 by 5 percent. Would you still recommend renovating the grocery mart? Why or why not?

CASE DELIVERABLES

In order to satisfactorily complete this case, you should build the worksheet as described in the case scenario and then prepare both written and oral presentations. Unless otherwise specified, submit the following deliverables to your professor.

1. A written report discussing any assumptions you have made about the case and the key elements of the case. Additionally, what features did you add to make the worksheet more functional? User friendly? (Please note that these assumptions cannot violate any of the requirements specified above and must be approved by your professor.)

2. A printout of each worksheet and chart.

3. A printout of the worksheet's formulas.

4. An electronic, working copy of your worksheet that meets the criteria mentioned in the case scenario and specifications sections.

5. Results for each question posed above. (A memo to your instructor discussing these results should also be provided.)

6. As mentioned above, you should prepare an oral presentation. (Your instructor will establish the time allocated for your presentation.) You should use a presentation package and discuss the key features of your worksheet. Also, discuss how the worksheet is beneficial for Mr. Feronti. What additional information should be included in the worksheet to make it more useful?

Case 5

Klein Technology Seminars

Worksheet Case   Difficulty Rating: ★★

CASE BACKGROUND

Klein Technology Seminars provides information technology seminars to local corporations and continuously strives to provide its corporate clients with quality, timely instruction. As part of its quality-first strategy, seminar students are asked to complete customer satisfaction surveys. These satisfaction surveys are then reviewed by Dr. Klein, the company's founder. Based on the survey results, Dr. Klein makes adjustments to the company's courses.

To facilitate his analysis of the customer satisfaction surveys, Dr. Klein asks you to develop a Survey Results workbook. The preparation of this workbook requires you to design worksheets, use formulas, use several functions, use basic cell and worksheet formatting techniques, and prepare PivotTable and PivotChart reports.

CASE SCENARIO

Dr. Earl Klein is the founder and president of Klein Technology Seminars. As a former university vice president, Dr. Klein came into contact with many corporate executives. Frequently, the corporate executives would remark about the necessity of keeping their employees up-to-date in their field. Dr. Klein took this message to heart, and when he retired a few years ago, he formed Klein Technology Seminars.

From Chapter 5 of *MIS Cases: Decision Making with Application Software*, 4/e. Lisa Miller. Copyright © 2009 by Pearson Prentice Hall. All rights reserved.

Klein Technology Seminars

Since its beginning, Klein Technology Seminars has seen a steady growth in its business and has a reputation for providing quality instruction to its clients. The company's reputation is due in part to its 10 full-time, highly qualified instructors. The instructors teach a variety of courses, ranging from productivity to certification courses. The courses are one-week courses, last from 8 a.m. to 5 p.m. each day, and are limited to 24 students. The company offers its courses on its campus, at the client's site, and at other off-site locations.

Once seminar attendees finish a course, they complete satisfaction surveys. The surveys help Dr. Klein judge the quality of the courses, as well as the instructors. Figure 1 shows a copy of the survey.

Until now, Dr. Klein has just read through the surveys and has not had time to analyze the survey data. Dr. Klein realizes the surveys contain a wealth of information, and he wants to analyze the data with a spreadsheet application. Dr. Klein assigns you the task of developing a Survey Results workbook that will enable him to enter and track the results of the satisfaction surveys.

Once the surveys are collected, Dr. Klein or his secretary will code each survey respondent's answers. For each question, the possible responses are given a unique number. For instance, if a respondent answers "no" for Question 1, then Dr. Klein will record "1" in the worksheet cell. If the respondent answers "yes" for Question 1, then Dr. Klein will record "2" in the worksheet cell. Figure 2 shows how the questionnaire responses are coded.

Figure 1: Customer Satisfaction Survey

Klein Technology Seminars
Satisfaction Survey

1. **Have you previously attended a technology seminar offered   by Klein Technology Seminars?**

    a. No
    b. Yes

2. **Have you attended a technology seminar offered by another company?**

    a. No
    b. Yes

3. **Overall, I am satisfied with the course.**

    Strongly Agree   Agree   Neutral   Disagree   Strongly Disagree

4. **I will take another course with Klein Technology Seminars.**

    Strongly Agree   Agree   Neutral   Disagree   Strongly Disagree

5. **The information presented will be useful on   my job.**

    Strongly Agree   Agree   Neutral   Disagree   Strongly Disagree

6. **The instructor was knowledgeable about the subject matter.**

    Strongly Agree   Agree   Neutral   Disagree   Strongly Disagree

7. **The seminar's content is timely.**

    Strongly Agree   Agree   Neutral   Disagree   Strongly Disagree

8. **The instructor met the stated course objectives.**

    Strongly Agree   Agree   Neutral   Disagree   Strongly Disagree

---

Figure 2: Customer Satisfaction Survey Codes

If Response Is:	Code
No	1
Yes	2
Strongly Agree	5
Agree	4
Neutral	3
Disagree	2
Strongly Disagree	1

Design Specifications

Dr. Klein hands you a copy of an incomplete workbook called Klein Survey. The Klein Survey workbook currently contains sample survey data in the Response worksheet. Dr. Klein asks you to use the data from the Response worksheet when designing the Survey Results workbook. Figures 3 and 4 show how the survey data are currently organized in the Response worksheet. Columns A through E provide general information about the course. As the general information is readily available, it is not necessary to collect this information from the survey respondent. Instead, Dr. Klein will enter the general course information as he enters the respondent's answers into the worksheet. Figure 5 explains the codes for Columns A through E.

Columns F - M display data that have been captured on the survey forms. The data displayed in these columns have been coded, meaning the survey responses have been coded using the codes displayed in Figure 2. For instance, if a student circled "no" as her answer for Question 1 on the survey form, then a "1" is displayed in Column F. Likewise, if a student circled "yes" as her answer for Question 1, then a "2" is displayed in Column F. (The codes help facilitate the analysis of the data.)

Figure 3: Survey Results Sample Data

Columns A - E

	A	B	C	D	E
1	Course No.	Location	Instructor ID	Class Size	Seminar Start Date
2	RTS1	2	2	10	10/6/2008
3	RTS1	2	2	10	10/6/2008
4	RTS1	2	2	10	10/6/2008
5	RTS1	2	2	10	10/6/2008
6	RTS3	3	5	12	10/6/2008
7	RTS3	3	5	12	10/6/2008
8	RTS3	3	5	12	10/6/2008

Figure 4: Survey Results Sample Data
Columns F - M

	F	G	H	I	J	K	L	M
1	Question 1	Question 2	Question 3	Question 4	Question 5	Question 6	Question 7	Question 8
2	1	2	4	3	4	4	4	4
3	2	2	5	4	4	5	4	5
4	1	2	1	2	5	1	2	5
5	2	1	1	2	4	4	4	4
6	2	2	4	4	2	5	4	5
7	2	1	4	2	1	5	5	2
8	2	1	5	5	5	4	5	2

The Response worksheet contains survey responses for a two-week period. Dr. Klein wants you to add a Summary worksheet to the Klein Survey workbook and then save the workbook as Survey Results. The purpose of the Summary worksheet is to summarize the survey response data contained in the Response worksheet. For each worksheet, you should include a worksheet title. Dr. Klein wants the title to reflect the contents of the worksheet, as well as the date range for the data the worksheet covers. Dr. Klein wants descriptive names for the column headings.

Figure 5: General Course Information Codes

Column	Codes	Explanation
A	Uses the actual course number.	Contains the course number.
B	1 = Client's Site 2 = Klein Technology Seminars 3 = Another Location	Indicates where the course was offered. The course can be offered at the client's site, at Klein Technology Seminars or at another location.
C	Uses the instructor's identification number.	Contains the instructor's identification number.
D	Uses the number of students enrolled in the class.	Indicates the number of students enrolled in the class. (Not all students submit a survey.)
E	Uses the start date of the seminar.	Indicates the starting date of the seminar.

When the survey forms are returned, Dr. Klein or his assistant will code and then enter the individual survey results into the Response worksheet. When entering survey data into the Response worksheet, Dr. Klein wants the results for each survey assigned a respondent number. This request requires the insertion of a new column. This column should be the leftmost column in the worksheet, and should include a unique number for each row that contains survey results. So, if you have 20 surveys, the surveys would be numbered 1 through 20, respectively.

As previously mentioned, the purpose of the Summary worksheet is to summarize the data contained in the Response worksheet. For each question, the Summary worksheet should provide a count for each possible response. The count should reflect the number of times a particular response for the question was given. For instance, the Summary worksheet should show how many "1" entries, "2" entries, and "3" entries appear in the Location column for the Response worksheet. For Questions 3 - 8, Dr. Klein wants to see their averages, modes, and medians displayed in the Summary worksheet. The Summary worksheet should also provide the average, mode, and median class size.

Where possible, Dr. Klein wants the Summary worksheet information displayed in a graphic format. Specifically, he asks you to prepare several charts, including a column chart comparing the user satisfaction ratings for each course, a column chart comparing the satisfaction ratings by instructor, and a bar chart showing the number of respondents who strongly agreed that the courses were useful.

Information Specifications

Dr. Klein will analyze the survey data at varying levels of detail. As mentioned above, Dr. Klein wants the survey results entered into a Response worksheet, and in the Summary worksheet he wants to see summarized results. Dr. Klein also wants to view data based on multiple conditions (such as satisfaction ratings for instructors by course). You suggest to Dr. Klein that the PivotTable and PivotChart reports are excellent tools for this type of analysis. Dr. Klein will use these tools to view the overall satisfaction ratings for each of his instructors by course, as well as the objectives met ratings for each course by instructor.

In addition to the information requests specified above, Dr. Klein wants answers for the following questions.

1. For each course, what is its average class size?

2. What percentage of respondents has attended a seminar before? Use a pie chart to summarize the results.

3. How many respondents who have taken a seminar course with another company agreed or strongly agreed that they would take another course with Klein Technology Seminars?

4. How many students strongly agreed that their instructor was knowledgeable about the subject matter? Display this information on a separate page for each course.

5. How did the students rate their instructor on the instructor's ability to meet course objectives? For each instructor, provide a count for each response. If possible, Dr. Klein wants this information summarized in a chart. (You select the chart.)

6. Which instructor had the highest percent of strongly agreed responses for Question 6?

Implementation Concerns

Although you are free to work with the design of your workbook, the worksheets should have a consistent, professional appearance. Also, you should use appropriate formatting for the cells and worksheets.

This case requires you to insert columns into worksheets, consolidate information into a summary worksheet, use formulas, use several functions, and use the PivotTable and PivotChart report tools. Although it depends on how you design the Summary worksheet, the COUNTIF function can be used in a formula to determine the response counts.

Test Your Design

After creating the Survey Results workbook, you should test your design. Perform the following steps.

1. Copy the survey results from the TYD Data worksheet located in the Klein Survey workbook and then paste these results immediately below the row containing the last October 13, 2008 entry.

2. Figures 6, 7, and 8 provide the results for three surveys. Enter the results for each survey into the Response worksheet. (You will need to code the response data.) For the survey results shown in Figure 6, the course was offered during the week of October 13th; the course number is RTS4; the location is 3; the Instructor ID is 2, and the course was conducted with 15 students. For the survey results shown in Figure 7, the course was offered during the week of October 20th; the course number is RTS4; the location is 2; the Instructor ID is 3, and the course was conducted with 23 students. For the survey results shown in Figure 8, the course was offered during the week of October 27th; the course number is RTS2; the location is 1; the Instructor ID is 4, and the course was conducted with 10 students.

3. Provide counts of the satisfaction ratings by class size for each instructor. Summarize this information in a PivotTable.

4. Which instructor had the highest percent of strongly disagree responses for Question 8?

5. Of those students who attended a seminar provided by another company, how did they rate Klein Technology Seminars? How do these results compare to students who have not attended a seminar offered by another company? Use a PivotTable to summarize this information. Also, prepare a chart that summarizes this information. (You select the chart.)

6. By class, how many students strongly agreed that the class provided useful information for their jobs? Summarize your results in a bar chart.

Figure 6: Survey Results

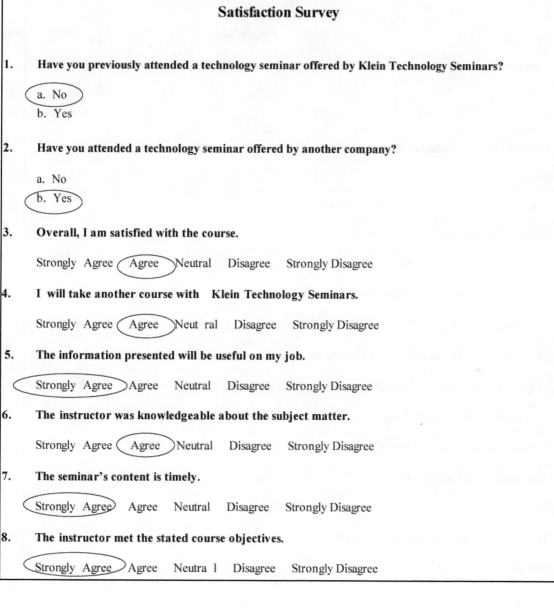

Klein Technology Seminars
Satisfaction Survey

1. Have you previously attended a technology seminar offered by Klein Technology Seminars?

    (a. No)
    b. Yes

2. Have you attended a technology seminar offered by another company?

    a. No
    (b. Yes)

3. Overall, I am satisfied with the course.

    Strongly Agree   (Agree)   Neutral   Disagree   Strongly Disagree

4. I will take another course with   Klein Technology Seminars.

    Strongly Agree   (Agree)   Neut ral   Disagree   Strongly Disagree

5. The information presented will be useful on my job.

    (Strongly Agree)   Agree   Neutral   Disagree   Strongly Disagree

6. The instructor was knowledgeable about the subject matter.

    Strongly Agree   (Agree)   Neutral   Disagree   Strongly Disagree

7. The seminar's content is timely.

    (Strongly Agree)   Agree   Neutral   Disagree   Strongly Disagree

8. The instructor met the stated course objectives.

    (Strongly Agree)   Agree   Neutra l   Disagree   Strongly Disagree

Figure 7: Second Survey Results

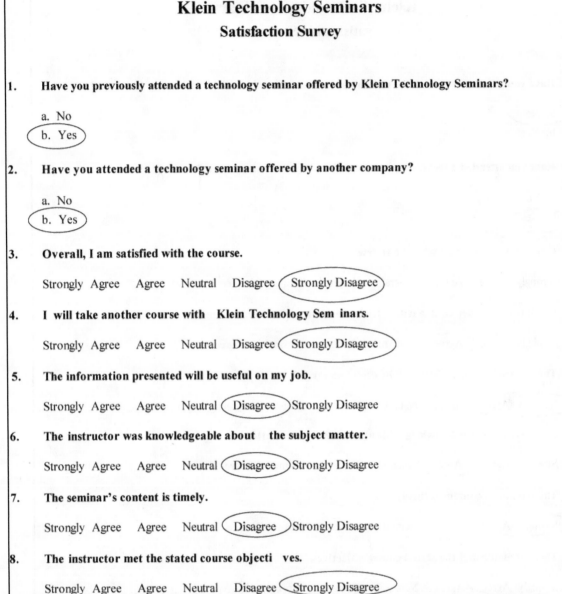

Klein Technology Seminars
Satisfaction Survey

1. Have you previously attended a technology seminar offered by Klein Technology Seminars?

   a. No
   b. Yes

2. Have you attended a technology seminar offered by another company?

   a. No
   b. Yes

3. Overall, I am satisfied with the course.

   Strongly Agree   Agree   Neutral   Disagree   Strongly Disagree

4. I will take another course with Klein Technology Sem inars.

   Strongly Agree   Agree   Neutral   Disagree   Strongly Disagree

5. The information presented will be useful on my job.

   Strongly Agree   Agree   Neutral   Disagree   Strongly Disagree

6. The instructor was knowledgeable about the subject matter.

   Strongly Agree   Agree   Neutral   Disagree   Strongly Disagree

7. The seminar's content is timely.

   Strongly Agree   Agree   Neutral   Disagree   Strongly Disagree

8. The instructor met the stated course objecti ves.

   Strongly Agree   Agree   Neutral   Disagree   Strongly Disagree

Figure 8: Third Survey Results

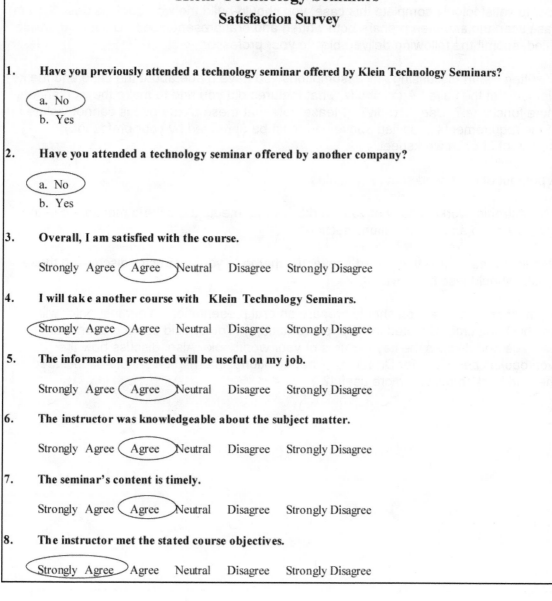

CASE DELIVERABLES

In order to satisfactorily complete this case, you should build the workbook as described in the case scenario and then prepare both written and oral presentations. Unless otherwise specified, submit the following deliverables to your professor.

1. A written report discussing any assumptions you have made about the case and the key elements of the case. Additionally, what features did you add to make the worksheets more functional? User friendly? (Please note that these assumptions cannot violate any of the requirements specified above and must be approved by your professor.)

2. A printout of each worksheet.

3. A printout of each worksheet's formulas.

4. An electronic, working copy of your workbook that meets the criteria mentioned in the case scenario and specifications sections.

5. Results for each question posed above. (A memo to your instructor discussing these results should also be provided.)

6. As mentioned above, you should prepare an oral presentation. (Your instructor will establish the time allocated for your presentation.) You should use a presentation package and discuss the key features of your workbook. Also, discuss how the workbook is beneficial for Dr. Klein. What additional information should be included in the workbook to make it more useful?

Case 6

Terrell & Terrell Property Management, Inc.

Spreadsheet Case   **Difficulty Rating:** ★★

CASE BACKGROUND

Reyna and Rupert Terrell own a small property management business, consisting of four duplex units, three rent houses, and three commercial buildings. As part of their property management business, the Terrells track each unit's income and expenses, as well as the overall income and expenses for their business. Although their existing file management system is adequate, the Terrells want a more flexible property management system that will enable them to monitor and analyze their business's cash flows at varying levels of detail.

The Terrells ask you to prepare a standard cash flow worksheet template that summarizes each rental property's income and expenses, a summary worksheet that summarizes the business's income and expenses from all the rental properties, and several workbooks that will be used to organize the cash flow worksheets. Designing the cash flow worksheets requires you to format cells and worksheets appropriately, use several functions, use external workbook references, and work with multiple workbooks.

Terrell & Terrell Property Management, Inc.

CASE SCENARIO

Last year Reyna and Rupert Terrell were looking for ways to earn additional retirement income. After locating, purchasing, and renovating several properties in the Crater Lake area, they began renting their properties to the public. The Terrells currently own four duplex units, three rent houses, and three commercial buildings. Although the rental properties generate a modest income for the Terrells, maintaining the properties can be expensive at times, because all units have appliance, property tax, insurance, advertisement, routine maintenance, materials, cable, utility, labor, and miscellaneous expenses.

The duplexes, rent houses, and commercial buildings are equipped with major appliances, such as dishwashers, washers, dryers, and refrigerators. When an appliance is no longer repairable, the Terrells replace the appliance and charge the expense to the unit. The Terrells must also pay property tax and insurance for each unit. The property tax is paid once a year, usually in December, and insurance is paid twice a year, generally in June and December. Routine maintenance includes such things as mowing, general landscaping, replacing air filters, cleaning empty rental units, and hauling off trash. When a rental unit requires repairs or routine maintenance, the Terrells record the labor charges, as well as the cost of the materials. Materials include any necessary items used to repair or clean a unit. As an enticement for potential renters, the Terrells pay for basic cable, even for the commercial buildings. When a unit is vacant, the Terrells place an advertisement in the local newspaper and run the advertisement until the unit is rented.

The Terrells use a simple filing system to track each rental unit's income and expenses. Although the filing system provides the Terrells with the necessary income and expense data, analyzing the income and expense data is cumbersome at best. The Terrells realize that using a spreadsheet application will make their property management activities much easier, more efficient, and more accurate. The Terrells ask you to organize their income and expense data into electronic workbooks, so that they can better manage their rental properties.

Design Specifications

The Terrells ask you to create a cash flow worksheet for each rental unit and a summary cash flow worksheet. As the Terrells want each cash flow worksheet to have a similar look and feel and will use the cash flow worksheet for future properties that they purchase, you decide that a standard cash flow template is necessary. Once you create the standard cash flow template, the Terrells can use the template to enter income and expense data for each rental unit. Figure 1 provides a sketch of a partially completed cash flow worksheet. (Figure 1 shows a cash flow worksheet for six months. Your cash flow worksheet should accommodate 12 months.)

As Figure 1 shows, the cash flow worksheet records the monthly income and expenses for a particular rental unit. Although not shown in Figure 1, the Terrells want to know each month's total expenses, monthly cash flow, overall cash flow, year-to-date total for each expense, and year-to-date total income. The monthly cash flow is the difference between the monthly income and total monthly expenses, and the overall cash flow is a summation of the monthly cash flow up to and including the current month. The year-to-date total for each expense sums the expenses incurred so far that year. The year-to-date total income displays the total income received so far in a given year.

Figure 1: Cash Flow Worksheet

Terrell and Terrell Property Management, Inc.
Cash Flow Worksheet
(Current Date)

	1/1/08	2/1/08	3/1/08	4/1/08	5/1/08	6/1/08
Rent						
Expenses						
Advertising						
Appliances						
Cable						
Insurance						
Labor						
Material						
Miscellaneous						
Property						
Routine Maintenance						
Utilities						

The Terrells want the individual cash flow worksheets grouped according to property type. Since they have three main types of rental properties, you create Duplex, House, and Commercial workbooks. After the cash flow worksheets and workbooks are created, you prepare a Summary worksheet and place the Summary worksheet in its own Summary workbook. The Summary worksheet summarizes the income and expense data contained in the other workbooks. The Summary worksheet should show the name of the rental unit, as well as the rental unit's year-to-date income and year-to-date total for each expense category. The Summary worksheet should also show the total expenses and overall cash flow for each property type (commercial, duplex, and house). As the Summary worksheet must reference data contained in multiple workbooks, you use external cell references in the Summary worksheet to retrieve the necessary data from the other workbooks. (At this point, you may wish to review your system's online help feature to review external cell references.) The Terrells also request that the Summary worksheet resemble the individual cash flow worksheets.

Information Specifications

The Terrells will use the cash flow worksheets to better manage the income and expenses for their rental units. Each individual cash flow worksheet provides information specific to a particular rental unit's monthly income and expenses, year-to-date income and expenses, monthly cash flow, and overall cash flow. In addition to this information, the Terrells request average, minimum, and maximum values for each expense category in the individual cash flow worksheets, as well as the summary worksheet. The Terrells ask you to use data from the Summary worksheet to prepare two charts. The first chart compares the income for each unit, and the second chart compares the overall expenses for each unit. (You may select the chart types.)

In addition to the information requirements specified above, Mr. and Mrs. Terrell request answers to the following questions. Using the newly designed worksheets, provide Mr. and Mrs. Terrell with answers to these questions.

1. What was the rental income from all units last year?

2. On average, how much was spent in each expense category this past year?

3. Based on data contained in the Summary worksheet, where did the Terrells incur the largest expense?

4. What are the total revenues by property type?

5. What are the total expenses by property type?

6. What is the operating income by property type?

7. Should the Terrells raise the rent on any of their properties? Why?

Implementation Concerns

Although you are free to work with the design of your worksheets, each worksheet should have a consistent, professional appearance. Also, you should use appropriate formatting for the cells and worksheets. For instance, dollar values should display a dollar sign and be formatted to two decimal places. Since the worksheets have similar categories and contain similar data, you should strive to keep the worksheets' appearances similar.

The Terrells will use the individual cash flow worksheets to maintain the income and expense data for their individual rental property units. The Summary worksheet summarizes the data contained in the individual cash flow worksheets. As the Summary worksheet references external data, you will use external workbook references. Although you can manually enter an external workbook reference into a Summary worksheet cell, it is easier and less error-prone, if you use the point-and-click method. (For more information about external workbook references, use your system's online help feature.)

Test Your Design

After creating the Commercial, Duplex, House, and Summary workbooks, you should test your design. Perform the following steps.

1. Prepare a cash flow worksheet and update the Summary worksheet for the following property.

   The Terrells purchased a third duplex and currently rent one of the duplex units. (The second unit is undergoing renovations.) The duplex unit is located at 1412 Mockingbird and rents for $1,950.00 a month. The duplex unit was rented in November and December. October expenses include $2,500.00 in labor, $705.00 in materials, $25.00 in advertising, $98.00 in utilities, $1,050.72 in appliances, and $50.00 in routine maintenance. November expenses include $84.48 in cable, $98.00 in utilities, and $50.00 in routine maintenance. December expenses include $84.48 in cable, $98.00 in utilities, and $50.00 in routine maintenance. Property taxes and an insurance premium are paid in December. The property taxes are $1,050.00, and the insurance premium is $600.00.

2. The Terrells want a chart comparing the year-to-date income for each rental unit category. (You may choose which chart type to use.)

3. What is the overall cash flow for the rental properties?

CASE DELIVERABLES

In order to satisfactorily complete this case, you should build the workbooks as described in the case scenario and then prepare both written and oral presentations. Unless otherwise specified, submit the following deliverables to your professor.

1. A written report discussing any assumptions you have made about the case and the key elements of the case. Additionally, what features did you add to make the worksheets and workbooks more functional? User friendly? (Please note that these assumptions cannot violate any of the requirements specified above and must be approved by your professor.)

2. A printout of each worksheet and chart.

3. A printout of each worksheet's formulas.

4. Electronic, working copies of your workbooks that meet the criteria mentioned in the case scenario and specifications sections.

5. Results for each question posed above. (A memo to your instructor discussing these results should also be provided.)

6. As mentioned above, you should prepare an oral presentation. (Your instructor will establish the time allocated for your presentation.) You should use a presentation package and discuss the key features of your worksheets and workbooks. Also, discuss how the worksheets and workbooks are beneficial for Mr. and Mrs. Terrell. What additional information should be included in the worksheets and workbooks to make them more useful?

Case 7

Mark's Collectibles, Inc.

Spreadsheet Case   **Difficulty Rating:** ★ ★ ★

CASE BACKGROUND

Mark's Collectibles is a newly established online reseller of the very popular Tree Point Babies stuffed animals. Periodically, Mark Allan, the owner of the small, online business, downloads his Web site's traffic statistics from his Web hosting service. As the downloaded data are not in a useful format, Mr. Allan hires you to prepare a Site Statistics Analysis worksheet. The Site Statistics Analysis worksheet provides Mr. Allan with information about his Web site's visitors, including the number of visited pages, types of operating systems, browsers, visit durations, and used bandwidth. Preparing the worksheet requires you to properly format and design the Site Statistics Analysis worksheet, determine the visit duration for each visitor, the most popular operating systems, most popular browsers, most popular site connections, and amount of used bandwidth.

CASE SCENARIO

A few years ago, small, stuffed animals called Tree Point Babies became very popular with collectors, and demand for retired Tree Point Babies has continued to grow. Each month

Mark's Collectibles, Inc.

Tree Point Babies issues several new stuffed animals. Collectors, like Mark Allan, purchase many of these stuffed animals in the hopes that the stuffed animals can be resold at a later date for a profit.

Mark's Collectibles is a newly formed, small, online reseller of the popular Tree Point Babies. In an effort to widen his market, Mr. Allan has built a small Web site, showing high-quality images of his available Tree Point Babies. Mr. Allan pays a nominal fee to a Web hosting service to host his Web site. As part of its service, the Web hosting service provides Mr. Allan with a text file containing traffic statistics for his Web site. Figure 1 shows a sample of this data. (The bandwidth is shown in kilobytes.) Currently, Mr. Allan purchases 10GB of bandwidth each month from the Web hosting service. If he uses more than his allotted amount, he is charged for the extra bandwidth.

Figure 1: Sample Data from Web Site Statistics Text File

IP Address	Operating System	Browser	Site Connection	Add To Favorites	Entry	Exit	Bandwidth	Viewed Page
999.010.210.133	Windows	Internet Explorer	HotBot	Yes	39731.47638	39731.49344	400	4
999.250.150.140	Linux	Firefox	Yahoo	No	39724.47352	39724.48189	1	3
999.111.233.190	Windows	Netscape	Lycos	Yes	39724.58203	39724.60697	250	2
999.140.152.160	Windows	Internet Explorer	AltaVista	No	39726.4299	39726.44541	750	15
999.180.007.222	Macintosh	Internet Explorer	Dogpile	No	39726.61228	39726.62361	255	4

Design Specifications

As previously mentioned, Mr. Allan periodically downloads a text file that contains the Web site's traffic data. As Figure 1 shows, the text file is not in a useful format, and the data must be formatted in order to provide useful information to Mr. Allan.

Mr. Allan gives you the most recent text file containing his Web site's traffic data and asks you to import the data into a worksheet. To improve the appearance of the data, Mr. Allan asks you to properly format the data. For instance, you can apply a time format that will more easily display the dates and times of visitor entries and exits. He also asks you to include a header in the worksheet. He specifically requests that a worksheet title and date range indicating the time series for the data be placed at the top of the worksheet.

Mr. Allan wants each row of data to be assigned a visitor number. The visitor number is intended to help him quickly determine the number of visits his Web site has received and is not intended to uniquely identify each visitor. Including a visitor number for each record requires the addition of a new column. Mr. Allan wants the Visitor Number column to be the leftmost column in the worksheet.

For each visit, Mr. Allan wants to know the visit duration. As you study the imported data, you notice that the entry and exit times for each visit are included. You decide to insert a Visit Duration column. You determine the visit duration values for this column by taking the difference between the exit and entry times.

Information Specifications

For the Visit Duration, Bandwidth, and Viewed Pages columns, Mr. Allan wants the worksheet to display the median and mean for each of these columns. Mr. Allan wants the worksheet to display the mode for the Bandwidth and Viewed Pages columns. The median identifies the middle numbers from the visit duration, bandwidth, and viewed pages values. The mode indicates the most frequently occurring bandwidth and number of viewed pages values. The mean provides averages for the visit duration, bandwidth, and viewed pages columns. Mr. Allan also wants the worksheet to show the maximum and minimum values for the Visit Duration, Bandwidth, and Viewed Pages columns.

Mr. Allan needs answers to the following questions. Using your newly designed Site Statistics Analysis worksheet, provide Mr. Allan with answers to his questions.

1. What is the average daily bandwidth used?

2. How many pages were viewed in October? November? December? Assume Mr. Allan wants a chart that compares the number of viewed pages for each month. What type of chart would be appropriate? Prepare the chart.

3. What is the average stay for each visitor? What is the longest time a visitor stayed at the Web site? What is the shortest visit?

4. Mr. Allan wants a chart that compares the site connections used to link to his Web site and the number of times the site connection was used. The chart should display the site connection data by month.

5. What percentage of visitors added the Web site to their list of favorite links? The chart should compare the visitor percentages by month.

6. Mr. Allan wants to know the average stay by operating system, connection, and browser. Mr. Allan wants this information displayed in pivot tables. Based on the results, what conclusions might you draw?

Implementation Concerns

Although you are free to work with the design of your worksheet, the worksheet should have a consistent, professional appearance. Also, you should use appropriate formatting for the cells and worksheet. Your instructor will provide you with either the text file containing the Web site statistics data referenced in the case scenario or with instructions on how to obtain the necessary Web site statistics data.

Test Your Design

After creating the Site Statistics Analysis worksheet, you should test your design. Perform the following steps.

1. Add the following data for January 2009 to your worksheet.

IP Address	Operating System	Browser	Site Connection	Add To Favorites	Entry	Exit	Bandwidth	Viewed Pages
999.010.210.133	Windows	Internet Explorer	Google	Yes	39814.48	39814.5	420	4
999.244.150.140	Windows	Firefox	Yahoo	No	39815.59	39815.63	100	3
999.107.233.190	Windows	Firefox	Lycos	Yes	39816.92139	39817.02	250	2
999.144.152.163	Windows	Firefox	AltaVista	No	39814.05	39814.12	950	15
999.182.007.219	Macintosh	Internet Explorer	HotBot	No	39818.48	39818.5	450	7

2. Which operating system is most popular? Prepare a chart comparing the operating systems and their percentages. The chart should display the operating system percentages by month.

3. Which browser is most popular? Prepare a chart comparing the browsers and their percentages. Prepare a chart comparing the browsers and their overall counts by month.

4. How much bandwidth was used for each month? Prepare a chart that compares the bandwidth usages by month. Should Mr. Allan consider raising or lowering his bandwidth?

5. Mr. Allan wants to know the average bandwidth by operating system, connection, and browser. Mr. Allan wants this information displayed in pivot tables. Based on the results, what conclusions might you draw?

6. Mr. Allan performs daily maintenance on his Web site, including backups and updates. The maintenance process usually takes between 30 minutes to 1 hour to complete. Using the site visit data, how can he determine the best time to maintain his Web site with the least disruption to his visitors? What is the best time?

CASE DELIVERABLES

In order to satisfactorily complete this case, you should build the worksheet as described in the case scenario and then prepare both written and oral presentations. Unless otherwise specified, submit the following deliverables to your professor.

1. A written report discussing any assumptions you have made about the case and the key elements of the case. Additionally, what features did you add to make the worksheet more functional? User friendly? (Please note that these assumptions cannot violate any of the requirements specified above and must be approved by your professor.)

2. A printout of the worksheet.

3. A printout of the worksheet formulas.

4. An electronic, working copy of your worksheet that meets the criteria mentioned in the case scenario and specifications sections.

5. Results for each question posed above. (A memo to your instructor discussing these results should also be provided.)

6. As mentioned above, you should prepare an oral presentation. (Your instructor will establish the time allocated for your presentation.) You should use a presentation package and discuss the key features of your worksheet. Also, discuss how the worksheet is beneficial for Mr. Allan. What additional information should be included in the worksheet to make it more useful?

Case 8

Megan Davis Convention Center

From Chapter 8 of *MIS Cases: Decision Making with Application Software*, 4/e. Lisa Miller. Copyright © 2009 by Pearson Prentice Hall. All rights reserved.

Megan Davis Convention Center

Spreadsheet Case   Difficulty Rating: ★ ★ ★

CASE BACKGROUND

The Megan Davis Convention Center, located on the outskirts of a metropolitan area, is a popular attraction for corporate meetings, special events, and educational seminars. The convention center's location, view, facilities, and outstanding reputation attract individuals and corporations from all over the United States. To ensure a reservation, the convention center's clients will often book rooms a year or more in advance.

Mavis Billingsley, the convention center's events coordinator, is responsible for scheduling the meeting rooms and helping the center's clients plan their special events. Ms. Billingsley currently uses the MDCC Reservations database to track the convention center's meeting room reservations. She would like to import the reservation data into a spreadsheet application for analysis. She asks you to import the reservation data into a worksheet, enhance the worksheet by inserting columns, and use the Subtotal, Chart, PivotTable, and Filter tools to analyze the reservation data.

CASE SCENARIO

As the events coordinator for the Megan Davis Convention Center, Ms. Billingsley is responsible for managing the meeting room reservations. The Megan Davis Convention

Center currently has five standard meeting rooms, a conference center, a boardroom, and an auditorium. A client may book one or all of the rooms. Although the conference center is primarily used for larger meetings, the center can be converted into four smaller meeting rooms, thus providing the convention center with extra meeting rooms. When booking a meeting room, the client may request a particular seating arrangement, such as circular, classroom, lecture, or U-shape. The number of available seats within a given meeting room is dependent upon the seating arrangement. Figure 1 shows the types of seating arrangements and their codes.

Figure 1: Available Seating Arrangements

Megan Davis Convention Center
Available Seating Arrangements

Seating Arrangement	Code
Circular	CI
Classroom	CL
Lecture	LE
U-Shape	US

Each day, Ms. Billingsley fields calls from potential clients, requesting information about room availability, room capacity, and charges. Convention center clients are quoted either a standard, advanced, or special rate. The standard rate applies to all bookings that are made less than six months in advance. The advanced rate applies to clients who book six months or more in advance, and the special rate is a negotiating tool used to attract large, highly recognizable companies or organizations to the Megan Davis Convention Center. Figure 2 summarizes the meeting room rates.

Figure 2: Meeting Room Rates

Megan Davis Convention Center
Daily Meeting Room Rates

Room Code	Meeting Room	Advance Rate	Standard Rate	Special Rate
AU	Auditorium	$2,418.75	$2,925.00	$1,735.00
BD	Boardroom	$1,912.50	$2,550.00	$1,330.00
CF	Conference Center	$2,475.00	$3,200.00	$1,900.00
AL	Alabama	$1,950.00	$2,300.00	$1,390.00
CA	California	$1,987.50	$2,350.00	$1,422.50
CO	Colorado	$1,968.75	$2,325.00	$1,375.00
FL	Florida	$1,950.00	$2,300.00	$1,390.00
GA	Georgia	$1,931.12	$2,275.00	$1,431.25

Design Specifications

The reservation data that Ms. Billingsley needs are currently stored in the Reservation Details table in the MDCC Reservations database. As Ms. Billingsley will use a spreadsheet application to analyze the reservation data, you import the data into a worksheet for her. As you recall, importing data into a worksheet is easily accomplished by using either Microsoft Query or Get External Data From Access.

Ms. Billingsley requests that you retrieve all fields from the Reservation Details table. Once you import the reservation data into the worksheet, you realize that the imported reservation data do not include the daily room charge, number of reserved days, or total charges for the clients. Ms. Billingsley explains that these data are not stored in the database because these values can be looked up or derived from the contents of other database fields. Therefore, it is not necessary for the database to store the daily room charges, number of reserved days, and total charges for each record. As Ms. Billingsley needs this information for her analysis, you insert the necessary columns into your worksheet.

The Daily Room Charge column specifies the daily meeting room rate that the customer is charged for a particular meeting room. To determine the daily room charge, you must use the room code and assigned rate code to look up how much a client is charged. Determining the value for this column requires using the imported room code and rate code to look up the appropriate rate in a lookup table. As a lookup table is necessary, you use Figure 2's data to construct your lookup table. You decide that the lookup table may need to be modified in the future, so you decide to place the lookup table in its own worksheet.

The Number of Reserved Days column specifies the number of days that the client reserved the meeting room. Determining the values for this column requires a formula that works with dates. Subtracting the reservation start date from the reservation end date does not give you the correct number of days that the client reserved the room, so you must modify your formula to implement the necessary logic to determine the correct number of reserved days.

The Total Charges column shows the total charges for the meeting room, based on the number of days that the room is reserved by the client. For instance, if a room is rented at $1,735.00 per day and the client rents the room for 2 days, then the total charges amount is $3,470.00.

Information Specifications

When a client books a meeting room, Ms. Billingsley enters the reservation data into the MDCC Reservations database for processing. Ms. Billingsley knows that the MDCC Reservations database contains important details about her clients' reservations, and she now wants to use a spreadsheet application to analyze the reservation data. Specifically, Ms. Billingsley wants to know how frequently the standard rate is charged, as opposed to the advanced or special rates. She wants a pivot table and chart that compares the count for each rate. (You should select an appropriate chart type.) She wants a count of the seating styles used in each room. She also wants to see the total charges by room.

Ms. Billingsley wants to review the booking habits of the convention center's clients. For instance, she wants to know how far in advance, on average, the center's clients book the meeting rooms. She also wants to know the number of rooms her clients book, as well as the total charges for each client. Additionally, Ms. Billingsley requests that you prepare a chart comparing the revenue by room.

In addition to the information requirements specified above, Ms. Billingsley requests answers to the following questions. Where appropriate, use the PivotTable, Subtotal, Chart, and Filter tools to provide Ms. Billingsley with answers to her questions.

1. On average, what is the length of time that a client books a room?

2. Using a reservation start date of August 5, 2008, what are the total charges for each client?

3. Overall, what is the average daily room charge?

4. Which seating arrangement is most popular?

5. Which reservations were made on February 15, 2008? What are the total charges for the reservations?

6. Based on the total charges for each customer, identify the five customers with the highest total charges.

7. Display each room's total charges as a percentage of the total charges for all rooms.

Implementation Concerns

Although you are free to work with the design of your worksheet, it should have a consistent, professional appearance. You should also apply appropriate formatting to the cells and worksheet. For instance, all cells containing dollar values should use a currency format and be formatted to two decimal places. Also, your worksheet should have an appropriate header, as well as appropriate column and row headings.

To prepare your worksheet according to the specifications provided above, you will import external data, insert columns, construct formulas that may include the IF and VLOOKUP functions, work with dates, and use several tools, such as PivotTable, Filter, Chart, Microsoft Query, and Subtotal.

You can use the Get External Data from Access command or Microsoft Query to import reservation data. The Microsoft Query Wizard guides you through the process of retrieving external data from the Reservation Details table in the MDCC Reservations database. Keep in mind the Test Your Design section requires you to retrieve external data that meet specific criteria. (You may wish to use your system's online help feature to review how to use Microsoft Query and the Microsoft Query Wizard.)

Test Your Design

After creating your worksheet, you should test your design. Perform the following steps.

1. Ms. Billingsley requests that you retrieve **only** the reservation data with a start date of August 12, 2008, from the Reservation Details table.

2. When retrieving data from the Reservation Details table, Ms. Billingsley wants the query to prompt her for a reservation start date. Create a new query that prompts Ms. Billingsley for a specific reservation date. Run the query several times and enter different reservation start dates.

3. When retrieving data from the Reservations Details table, Ms. Billingsley wants to retrieve reservation information for a given customer. Create a query that will prompt Ms. Billingsley for a given customer number. Run the query several times and enter different customer numbers.

CASE DELIVERABLES

In order to satisfactorily complete this case, you should build the worksheet as described in the case scenario and then prepare both written and oral presentations. Unless otherwise specified, submit the following deliverables to your professor. When preparing the following documentation, use all of the data contained in the Reservation Details table.

1. A written report discussing any assumptions you have made about the case and the key elements of the case. Additionally, what features did you add to make the worksheet(s) more functional? User friendly? (Please note that these assumptions cannot violate any of the requirements specified above and must be approved by your professor.)

2. A printout of each worksheet. (This includes your charts and pivot tables.)

3. A printout of each worksheet's formulas.

4. An electronic, working copy of your workbook that meets the criteria mentioned in the case scenario and specifications sections.

5. Results for each question posed above. (A memo to your instructor discussing these results should also be provided.)

6. As mentioned above, you should prepare an oral presentation. (Your instructor will establish the time allocated for your presentation.) You should use a presentation package and discuss the key features of your workbook. Also, discuss how the workbook is beneficial for Ms. Billingsley. What additional information should be included in the workbook to make it more useful?

Case 9

BJR Investments, Inc.

Spreadsheet Case   Difficulty Rating: ★★★

SKILLS CHECK

You should review the following areas:

SPREADSHEET SKILLS

- ✓ Advanced Filter
- ✓ DAVERAGE Function
- ✓ DMAX Function
- ✓ DMIN Function
- ✓ DSUM Function
- ✓ Excel Table
- ✓ Filter

- ✓ IF Function
- ✓ PivotChart
- ✓ PivotTable
- ✓ Range Name
- ✓ Web Query
- ✓ Worksheet Formatting

CASE BACKGROUND

BJR Investments, Inc., is a full-service brokerage firm, providing a variety of financial planning services to its current and prospective clients. Bradley J. Reynolds, the owner of BJR Investments, Inc., and his staff provide investment advice in such areas as tax advantage planning, retirement and estate planning, mutual funds, pensions, stocks, and risk management. Mr. Reynolds enjoys helping his clients manage their portfolios, which range in size from $1,000 to well over $3,000,000. His clients appreciate his advice, personal touch, and 15 years of investment experience. However, it is his attention to detail that keeps the business growing.

Mr. Reynolds wants to develop a Portfolio worksheet for each client. He feels that the Portfolio worksheet can provide him with current data about his client's investments, thus helping him keep better track of the client's investments. The Portfolio worksheet organizes the client's stock information into an Excel table and requires the retrieval of up-to-date stock information from the Web. Once current stock information is retrieved, Mr. Reynolds will analyze the information by using the Filter, Advanced Filter, PivotChart, and PivotTable tools.

CASE SCENARIO

Mr. Reynolds asks you to develop a Portfolio worksheet that he will use for each client. For each stock, the Portfolio worksheet provides Mr. Reynolds with the stock symbol, company name, industry, market capitalization, and capitalization level, as well as the number of shares, purchase date, purchase price, commission, total cost, portfolio percentage, current value of the shares, last price, previous close, return, and price-earning (P/E) and earnings-per-share (EPS) ratios for the stock. As the Portfolio worksheet is organized around the client's investments, Mr. Reynolds can carefully monitor a client's investment activity and provide timely, more accurate advice to the client. Mr. Reynolds thinks his clients will appreciate this special attention to detail.

Once the Portfolio worksheet is developed, Mr. Reynolds will use the PivotChart, PivotTable, Filter and Advanced Filter tools to analyze the client's portfolio and provide the best possible advice to the client. Mr. Reynolds will also print a copy of the worksheet, charts and pivot tables for the client.

Mr. Reynolds is anxious to begin using the worksheet at his firm, and he provides you with a partially completed worksheet for one of his clients. He asks you to complete the Portfolio worksheet for him.

Design Specifications

The partially completed Portfolio worksheet includes symbol, company, industry, number of shares, purchase date, and purchase price columns. The worksheet needs a descriptive title, appropriate column headings, and proper formatting for the cells. You supply a descriptive worksheet title and column headings for the worksheet. As this worksheet deals with stock information, you decide that the header should show the date, as well as the current time. For cells involving dollar values, you specify a currency format with two decimal places.

For each stock, Mr. Reynolds wants to see the symbol, company name, industry, market capitalization, market capitalization level, exchange, number of shares, purchase date, purchase price, commission, total cost, portfolio percentage, current value of the shares, last price, previous close, return, P/E ratio, and EPS ratio. Figure 1 provides a sketch of the proposed worksheet. As you study the worksheet, you realize that Mr. Reynolds must enter values for the symbol, industry, number of shares, purchase date, and purchase price. The values for the remaining columns are retrieved or computed based on the contents of the entered values. The company name, market capitalization, exchange, last price, previous close, and EPS values are retrieved from the Web.

BJR Investments, Inc.

Figure 1: Current Portfolio Worksheet

BJR Investments, Inc. Portfolio Worksheet (Current Date and Time)																	
Symbol	Company	Industry	Capitalization Level	Market Capitalization	Exchange	No. of Shares	Purchase Date	Purchase Price	Commission	Total Cost	Portfolio Percentage	Current Share Value	Last Price	Previous Close	Return	PE Ratio	EPS

The total cost, portfolio percentage, current share value, return, commission, and P/E ratio are computed, thus requiring formulas. Figure 2 provides formulas for computing the total cost, portfolio percentage, current value, P/E ratio, and return. You ask Mr. Reynolds to explain how to derive the commission. Mr. Reynolds explains that he charges either 2 percent of the purchase price or a $25 flat fee, whichever is greater. Based on this explanation, you decide that the commission cells must determine what fee to charge. The determination of what commission to charge requires the use of the IF function. Although the P/E ratio is retrievable from the Web, Mr. Reynolds wants this value computed based on data contained in the worksheet. The P/E ratio computation is easy to make, because a stock's P/E ratio is determined by dividing the stock's last price by the stock's EPS.

Figure 1 includes a capitalization level column. As Mr. Reynolds explains, this column specifies whether the stock's market capitalization is large-cap, mid-cap, small-cap, or micro-cap. Figure 3 shows the capitalization classifications. The IF function can be used to determine the company's capitalization level.

Figure 2: Required Portfolio Worksheet Formulas

Portfolio Worksheet Formulas	
Current Value	Last Price * Number of Shares
P/E Ratio	$\dfrac{\text{Last Price}}{\text{EPS}}$
Portfolio Percentage	$\dfrac{\text{Current Value of the Stock}}{\text{Total Current Value of All Stock}}$
Return	$\dfrac{\text{(Current Value of the Stock - Cost of the Stock)}}{\text{Cost of the Stock}}$
Total Cost	(Purchase Price * Number of Shares) + Commission

Figure 3: Capitalization Classifications

Portfolio Worksheet Formulas	
Large-Cap	Greater than $5 billion
Mid-Cap	Between $500 million and $5 billion
Small-Cap	Between $150 million and $500 million
Micro-Cap	Below $150 million

As you study the requirements for the new worksheet, you realize that the capitalization, last price, previous close, and EPS ratio require current stock market information. Luckily, you recall that the MSNStockQuote function makes retrieval of this information easy. When the MSNStockQuote function is refreshed, it returns the latest available stock market information to the cell. You decide to use the MSNStockQuote function to retrieve the company name, capitalization, last price, previous close, and EPS values. Once you obtain the most recent stock market information, you can use formulas to calculate the current value and return. (In addition to the MSNStockQuote function, the MSN MoneyCentral Investor Stock Quotes Web query retrieves current stock information. Your instructor will specify which feature to use. At this point, you may wish to use your system's online help function to review Web queries.)

Mr. Reynolds requests the averages, minimums, and maximums for the commission, purchase price, current share value, return, and P/E ratio columns. Mr. Reynolds wants the minimums and maximums for the portfolio percentages, previous close, and EPS columns. As he will work with this data as a table, he requests that you use database functions, where applicable, to determine the values for these columns.

Information Specifications

Mr. Reynolds will analyze the stock data at varying levels of detail. For instance, he wants to see the return by industry, and he wants a chart comparing the return by industry. Next, he wants to see the return, P/E, and EPS for each stock. He wants this information categorized by industry, and he does not wish to see grand totals. You suggest that he use the PivotTable and PivotChart tools for this purpose.

In addition to the information requirements specified above, Mr. Reynolds requests that you perform the following operations. Where appropriate, you should use the Advanced Filter, Filter, and PivotTable tools.

1. Identify the most expensive stock.

2. Identify which stock has the highest return. Lowest return.

3. Identify which stock has the largest P/E ratio. Lowest P/E ratio.

4. Identify which stock had the highest previous close. Lowest.

5. Identify which trades the client pays a $25 flat fee. Identify which trades the client pays a 2 percent commission.

6. Identify which stocks have a purchase price greater than $50 and a negative return.

7. Identify which stocks have a purchase price less than $50 and a positive return.

8. Identify the purchase price, last price and previous close for each stock. Mr. Reynolds wants to view this information on a separate "page" for each industry.

9. Identify which stocks are traded on NASDAQ. Identify which stocks are traded on NYSE.

Implementation Concerns

Although you are free to work with the design of your worksheet, the worksheet should have a consistent, professional appearance. You should also use proper formatting for the cells. For instance, dollar values should display with a dollar sign and be formatted to two decimal places.

To complete the case scenario, your worksheet must retrieve current stock information. Although the case scenario suggests using the MSNStockQuote function, you can also use the MSN MoneyCentral Investor Stock Quotes Web query. As the MSNStockQuote function provides more control over the information that is returned, it is the preferred method. However, the MSNStockQuote function requires the MSN MoneyCentral Stock Quotes add-in. Although this add-in is available on Microsoft's Web site, you may, for a variety of reasons, not have immediate access to the add-in. (Your professor will specify which method to use.) If you elect to use the MoneyCentral Investor Stock Quotes Web query, you will need to modify your worksheet to accommodate the information that the Web query returns.

The case scenario mentions that the commission fee is based on the purchase price. For each trade, Mr. Reynolds wants to charge either a 2 percent commission or a $25 flat fee, depending on which rate results in a higher commission. Building this logic into the commission cells requires using the IF function. (At this point, you may wish to use your system's online help feature to review the IF function.)

You will need to use the Advanced Filter tool to provide Mr. Reynolds with the information that he needs. The Advanced Filter tool requires a criteria range. As a general rule the criteria range should be placed above or below the Excel table. When filtering data in a table, you should use the DAVERAGE, DMIN, DMAX, and DSUM functions, as opposed to the AVERAGE, MINIMUM, MAXIMUM, and SUM functions. The database functions will accurately reflect the correct average, minimum, maximum, and total values for a filtered table. However, other Microsoft Excel functions may not. In order for your database functions to work properly, you should create your criteria range before using the database functions.

Test Your Design

After creating the Portfolio worksheet described in the case scenario, you should test your worksheet design. Perform the following operations.

1. Add the following stocks to the Portfolio worksheet. For the purchase date, use today's date. For the purchase price, use the stock's Previous Close value.

New Stocks			
Symbol	**Company**	**Industry**	**Number of Shares**
HOG	Harley-Davidson, Inc.	Leisure Time	100
HNZ	H. J. Heinz Company	Foods	200
NBR	Nabors Industries Ltd.	Oil & Gas	50
NCR	NCR Corporation	Computers	200
HSY	The Hershey Company	Foods	100
HES	Hess Corporation	Oil	50
BBT	BB&T Corporation	Banks	50
BMS	Bemis Company, Inc.	Containers and Packaging	50
CCU	Clear Channel Communications Inc.	Broadcasting	50

2. What is the average commission for all stocks? Average P/E ratio for all stocks?

3. For the new stocks that were just purchased, which has the highest return? Lowest? For the new stocks, provide averages for the commission, current value, and P/E ratio. Now, provide the minimums and maximums for the new stocks.

4. Of the large capitalization firms, which has the highest return? P/E ratio? EPS?

5. Which mid-capitalization firm has the highest current value for its stock? Lowest?

6. Based on portfolio percentage, identify the top five firms with which the client is invested.

7. Based on the information provided in the Portfolio worksheet, which stock(s) would you recommended eliminating from the portfolio?

8. Mr. Reynolds wants a count of the companies by capitalization size. He also wants to view this information on a separate "page" for each industry.

CASE DELIVERABLES

In order to satisfactorily complete this case, you should build the worksheet(s) as described in the case scenario and then prepare both written and oral presentations. Unless otherwise specified, submit the following deliverables to your professor.

1. A written report discussing any assumptions you have made about the case and the key elements of the case. Additionally, what features did you add to make the worksheet(s) more functional? User friendly? (Please note that these assumptions cannot violate any of the requirements specified above and must be approved by your professor.)

2. A printout of each worksheet. (This includes your chart and pivot tables.)

3. A printout of each worksheet's formulas.

4. An electronic, working copy of your workbook that meets the criteria mentioned in the case scenario and specifications sections.

5. Results for each question posed above. (A memo to your instructor discussing these results should also be provided.)

6. As mentioned above, you should prepare an oral presentation. (Your instructor will establish the time allocated for your presentation.) You should use a presentation package and discuss the key features of your workbook. Also, discuss how the workbook is beneficial for Mr. Reynolds. What additional information should be included in the workbook to make it more useful?

Case 10

Madison's Department Store

From Chapter 10 of *MIS Cases: Decision Making with Application Software*, 4/e. Lisa Miller. Copyright © 2009 by Pearson Prentice Hall. All rights reserved.

Madison's Department Store

Spreadsheet Case   **Difficulty Rating:** ★★★★

CASE BACKGROUND

Sylvester Tarkio understands the importance of a department store's sales force, especially when it comes to the sales force of a premiere, upscale department store like Madison's. Customers have long enjoyed the expert knowledge, attention to detail, and service that Madison's sales staff provides. Maintaining the quality sales force is a daily job for Mr. Tarkio. He carefully evaluates the performance of his sales staff and makes adjustments when needed. Currently, Mr. Tarkio monitors the performance of his sales staff by reading daily and weekly sales productivity reports. The problem is that these reports are prepared on a word processor. Mr. Tarkio has no efficient way of analyzing the data in detail. As a new intern at Madison's, you have impressed Mr. Tarkio with your work. Mr. Tarkio asks you to prepare a Productivity workbook for him. You will prepare seven daily productivity worksheets and a weekly productivity summary worksheet, analyze the sales data by using the PivotTable, Advanced Filter and Filter tools, and generate several charts.

CASE SCENARIO

Madison's Department Store is a prestigious, upscale department store located in one of the metropolitan area malls. The store has specialty departments for women, men, children, cosmetics, cologne, linen, furniture, and housewares. One of the reasons why Madison's has such a fine reputation is because of its highly trained sales staff. Madison's management believes in rewarding its sales staff for its hard work, so in addition to an hourly wage, sales representatives are paid a commission on sales above an established quota.

Sales representatives are classified as either part-time or full-time. Part-time representatives are then subcategorized as sales assistants or sales partners. Full-time representatives are subcategorized as assistant managers, sales consultants, or sales associates. Part-time representatives work 20 hours a week, while full-time representatives work 40 hours a week.   Sales representatives have input into how many hours a day they work; however, they cannot work overtime. Within the company, sales representatives are ranked and paid according to their experience and tenure with the company. Sales representatives are paid a commission on all sales exceeding their established quota. As members of the sales staff may work a different number of hours on a given day, the sales quota is based on the hours worked. For instance, if a sales representative has an hourly quota of $100 in sales and he works 5 hours, then his daily sales quota is $500. For any sales above the $500 quota, the sales representative receives a commission. Figure 1 summarizes the hourly wages and established quotas.

Figure 1: Hourly Wages and Quotas

Sales Code	Sales Title	Hourly Wage	Quota	Commission Rate
AM	Assistant Manager	$23.50	$200.00	.030
PT1	Sales Assistant	$10.50	$100.00	.010
PT2	Sales Partner	$11.75	$125.00	.015
S1	Sales Associate	$13.50	$150.00	.020
S2	Sales Consultant	$15.00	$175.00	.025

At the end of each business day, Mr. Tarkio prepares a Daily Productivity Report. As Figure 2 shows, the Daily Productivity Report summarizes each employee's sales activity for the day. (The data shown in Figure 2 are for illustrative purposes only. Your report format and data may vary.) This report specifies the employee's name, rank, assigned department, daily sales, hours, base pay, commission, and gross pay. At the end of each week, Mr. Tarkio uses the Daily Productivity Reports to prepare a Weekly Productivity Report. The Weekly Productivity Report summarizes the Daily Productivity Reports. Mr. Tarkio currently uses a word processor to prepare the reports. However, he realizes that a spreadsheet application is a much better tool for the summarization and analysis work that he needs. Mr.

Tarkio asks you to develop a Productivity workbook for him.

Figure 2: Daily Productivity Report

Madison's Department Store
Daily Productivity Report
(Current Date)

Employee	Rank	Department	Sales	Hours Worked	Base Pay	Commission	Gross Pay
Allbaugh, Joshua	AM	Men's	$4,000.00	8.0	$188.00	$72.00	$260.00
Blake, Barney	S2	Cosmetics	$456.76	2.5	$37.50	$0.48	$37.98
Bolyard, Pat	S2	Housewares	$450.98	3.0	$45.00	$0	$45.00
Stanton, Catrina	S1	Women's	$821.36	7.0	$94.50	$0.00	$94.50

Design Specifications

Each day, Mr. Tarkio will enter each salesperson's sales and hours into a Daily Productivity worksheet. He then expects the worksheet to determine each salesperson's base pay, commission, and gross pay. While the gross pay involves adding the base pay to the commission, calculating the base pay and commission requires referencing values in a lookup table. As you want the lookup table to be easily accessible and updateable, you place the lookup table in its own worksheet.

The base pay and commission are dependent upon the salesperson's rank in the company. For instance, an assistant manager is paid $23.50 per hour and receives a 3 percent commission. In contrast, a sales associate is paid $13.50 per hour and receives a 2 percent commission. You use the VLOOKUP function to build this logic into the base pay, and you use the IF and VLOOKUP functions to build the logic into the commission cells. The base pay formula uses the salesperson's rank to retrieve the correct hourly wage and then multiplies the hourly wage by the number of hours. The determination of the appropriate commission requires more complicated logic than the base pay. For instance, the commission formula must determine if a commission is to be paid, the applicable commission rate, and the portion of sales on which to base the commission. As the commission formula involves several lookups and decisions, you realize that nesting the IF and VLOOKUP functions is required. (At this point, you may wish to review your system's online help feature to review the IF and VLOOKUP functions, as well as how to nest functions.)

As previously mentioned, Mr. Tarkio wants the Daily Productivity Reports summarized into a Weekly Productivity Report. The Weekly Productivity Report provides weekly sales, hours, base pay, commission, and gross pay totals for each salesperson. For instance, the sales column will reference and sum the individual sales for Sunday through Saturday.

After showing Mr. Tarkio the workbook prototype, he asks if you can determine the number of times each salesperson made his quota that week. You assure him that the worksheet can be modified to provide this information. On each worksheet, Mr. Tarkio requires grand totals, averages, minimums and maximums for the sales, base pay, commission, and gross pay columns. Also on each worksheet Mr. Tarkio wants to see the total quotas met and the percentage of quotas met.

Information Specifications

Mr. Tarkio wants to use the Productivity workbook to analyze the performance of his sales staff. He specifically requests that you show him how to use the PivotTable to analyze the sales data. Mr. Tarkio wants to compare the commissions and sales by department, view the commissions by individuals within each department, prepare a pie chart showing the commissions by department, and prepare pie charts for each department, comparing the department's sales representatives' sales.

In addition to the information requirements specified above, Mr. Tarkio wants answers to the following questions. Using the PivotTable, Advanced Filter and Filter tools, provide Mr. Tarkio with answers to these questions.

1. Which five sales representatives received the highest commissions last week?

2. Which sales representatives received commissions above average last week?

3. Excluding the Furniture Department and its employees, which sales representatives received commissions above average last week?

4. If sales staff must make their quotas at least 60 percent of the time, which sales staff did not achieve this goal?

5. For each department, which salesperson had the highest sales?

6. On average, how frequently will the sales staff make their quota?

7. What are the commissions and total sales for each sales position by department?

8. What are the base pay, commission, and gross pay categorized by sales position?

9. What are the total salaries and hours worked by department?

10. Which department's staff met their quotas more often than other departments? Least?

Implementation Concerns

Although you are free to work with the design of your workbook, each worksheet should have a consistent, professional appearance. You should use appropriate formatting for the cells and worksheets.

This case requires you to group worksheets, insert columns into worksheets, consolidate information into a summary worksheet, nest functions, use several functions, reference a lookup table, and use the retrieved value in a formula, work with an Excel table, prepare charts, and use several analytical tools to analyze the sales data.

In several instances, you can use the Advanced Filter tool to filter data contained in the summary worksheet. To provide Mr. Tarkio with correct answers, you should use the DAVERAGE, DMIN, and DMAX functions in the summary worksheet, as opposed to the AVERAGE, MIN, and MAX functions. When the Advanced Filter is used, the DAVERAGE, DMIN, and DMAX functions adjust their values based on the filtered data. The AVERAGE, MIN, and MAX functions do not.

The determination of each salesperson's commission requires nesting the VLOOKUP function within the IF function. The commission formula must look up the hourly sales quota, determine the daily sales quota, take the difference between the daily sales quota and the daily sales, and then multiply the applicable commission rate by the amount of sales above the quota.

Test Your Design

After creating the Productivity workbook described in the case scenario, you should test your design. Perform the following steps.

1. Mr. Tarkio hired four new sales personnel. Enter their data into the worksheets.

   Leandra Shekel is classified as a PT1 and works in the Men's Clothing Department. She worked 4 hours each day, Sunday through Thursday. Her sales Sunday through Thursday were $1,400.98, $1,500.42, $750.32, $550.08, and $900.78, respectively.

   Darise Ferrer was hired as an S1 and works in the Linen Department. She worked 8-hour shifts, Tuesday through Saturday. Her sales were $2,500.98, $878.23, $1,503.28, $602.98, and $1,304.17, respectively.

   Paulina Renfro is classified as an S1 and works in the Children's Department. She worked 8-hour shifts, Tuesday through Saturday. Her sales were $1,500.56, $402.22, $1,090.80, $908.43, and $350.98.
   Sethana Aynes is classified as a PT1 and works in the Women's Clothing Department. She worked 8 hours on Monday and her sales were $502.88. She worked 6 hours on

Tuesday, and her sales were $608.12.

2. Which salespersons received more than $1,500 in commissions last week? Which salespersons did not receive a commission last week?

3. Based on past performance, what would happen if Mr. Tarkio increased the sales quota for each position by $75 per hour? What would happen if Mr. Tarkio decreased the sales quota for each position by $75 per hour?

4. What would happen if Mr. Tarkio increased each sales position's commission by a half of a percent?

5. For the week, what are the average sales for the S1 employees working in the Children's Department? For the Children's Department S1 employees, which employee had the lowest sales for the week? For the Children's Department S1 employees, which employee had the maximum sales for the week?

6. For the week, what are the average sales for the PT1 employees working in the Women's Department? For the Women's Department PT1 employees, which employee had the lowest sales for the week? For the Women's Department PT1 employees, which employee had the most sales for the week?

7. For the week, Mr. Tarkio wants to see the total commissions paid by each department, each department's percentage of the total commissions paid for all departments, and the total sales for each department.

8. Based on your observations of the sales, sales quotas, and commissions, how might the sales quota system be improved?

CASE DELIVERABLES

In order to satisfactorily complete this case, you should build the workbook as described in the case scenario and then prepare both written and oral presentations. Unless otherwise specified, submit the following deliverables to your professor.

1. A written report discussing any assumptions you have made about the case and the key elements of the case. Additionally, what features did you add to make the worksheet(s) more functional? User friendly? (Please note that these assumptions cannot violate any of the requirements specified above and must be approved by your professor.)

2. A printout of each worksheet. (This includes your charts and PivotTables.)

3. A printout of each worksheet's formulas.

4. An electronic, working copy of your workbook that meets the criteria mentioned in the case scenario and specifications sections.

5. Results for each question posed above. (A memo to your instructor discussing these results should also be provided.)

6. As mentioned above, you should prepare an oral presentation. (Your instructor will establish the time allocated for your presentation.) You should use a presentation package and discuss the key features of your workbook. Also, discuss how the workbook is beneficial for Mr. Tarkio. What additional information should be included in the workbook to make it more useful?

Case 11

Lake West University

Worksheet Case　　　**Difficulty Rating:** ★★★★

SKILLS CHECK
You should review the following areas:

WORKSHEET SKILLS

- ✓ Chart
- ✓ Conditional Formatting
- ✓ COUNTA Function
- ✓ COUNTIF Function
- ✓ COUNTIFS Function
- ✓ Filter (Optional)

- ✓ IF Function
- ✓ Nesting Functions
- ✓ PivotChart
- ✓ PivotTable
- ✓ Template
- ✓ Worksheet Formatting

CASE BACKGROUND

Lake West University places a major emphasis on helping its students learn. To accomplish this mission, departments are strongly encouraged to assess their programs, majors, and courses. To better assess their courses, the Lake West University's Economics faculty include standard questions on final exams given in core Economics courses. Once exams are graded, Dr. Hash Haddock, the Economics Department chairperson, reviews student responses to the standard exam questions to determine how well course objectives are met.

Dr. Haddock asks you to finish designing a Lake West Assessment workbook for him. The workbook should provide a convenient way to analyze student responses for the ECON 2103 final exam's standard questions. This workbook will eventually serve as a template for other economics courses. When designing the workbook, the COUNTA, COUNTIF, COUNTIFS, and IF functions will prove useful. Conditional formatting should be used to highlight all questions with responses below a set minimum. To facilitate his analysis, Dr. Haddock will use the Filter command, PivotTable, PivotChart, and charting tools.

From Chapter 11 of *MIS Cases: Decision Making with Application Software*, 4/e. Lisa Miller. Copyright © 2009 by Pearson Prentice Hall. All rights reserved.

CASE SCENARIO

Lake West University is a four-year university located in the Midwestern United States. As part of a campus-wide initiative, Lake West University's Economics Department recently updated its assessment plan. As part of its updated assessment plan, the Economics Department includes a standard set of questions on all ECON 2103 final exams. ECON 2103 is an introductory economics course, and all business majors take this course as part of their degree plan. As the ECON 2103 course does not have prerequisite courses, freshmen, sophomores, juniors, and seniors enroll in the course. Each semester several ECON 2103 sections are offered.

Dr. Haddock needs a system that enables him to analyze results for the standard questions across all ECON 2103 sections, as well as the individual sections of the course. Dr. Haddock envisions using this system to compare responses between various semesters as well. He wants a standard template developed, so he can use the same format for other Economics Department course offerings. As you are Dr. Haddock's assistant, you are tasked with developing a Microsoft Excel workbook to track student responses for the ECON 2103 final exam standard questions.

Design Specifications

At the end of the semester, all ECON 2103 section instructors give Dr. Haddock their student responses for the final exams. No standardized reporting format has been implemented, so Dr. Haddock wants a standard workbook developed so all instructors will use the same reporting format. He feels that a standard workbook format enables him to easily consolidate section data into the Lake View Assessment workbook, allowing him to analyze results across all sections.

Dr. Haddock hands you a copy of an incomplete workbook called Lake West Assessment. Although Dr. Haddock has begun incorporating each section's student responses into the workbook, he has not had time to format the workbook or complete its design. Figure 1 shows how data are currently organized for one of the sections.

Figure 1: Sample Worksheet

Section 1: Instructor Jones			Q1	Q2	Q3	Q4	Q5	Q6	Q7	Q8	Q9	Q10
Student	Major	Classification	Q1	Q2	Q3	Q4	Q5	Q6	Q7	Q8	Q9	Q10
1	ACCT	Freshman	b	b	d	b	b	d	c	b	e	a
2	MIS	Senior	a	c	d	b	a	d	c	c	d	a
3	ACCT	Sophomore	a	c	d	b	a	b	c	c	e	a
4	ECON	Junior	a	c	e	b	a	b	c	c	e	a
5	MRKT	Sophomore	a	c	c	e	a	b	c	c	e	a
Correct Answer			a	c	d	b	a	b	c	c	e	a

As you study the workbook, you notice that the workbook contains several worksheets. Although Dr. Haddock initially created a separate worksheet for each section, he mentions that he would now like all student responses included on a single worksheet called Response. In the Response worksheet, Dr. Haddock wants counts of the correct and incorrect responses for each question. He also wants to see correct and incorrect counts by major and by classification.

As you study the student response data, you notice that student names are not included. Dr. Haddock indicates that he wants a number assigned to each student and does not want to include student names. He does want the student's major, classification, and response to each of the 10 standard questions included.

Dr. Haddock asks you to create a summary worksheet. For each section, the summary worksheet should show the correct response counts, incorrect response counts, and correct response percentages for each question by section. He also would like to see a correct response percentage for each question for all sections.

Dr. Haddock considers a correct response rate of 70 percent as acceptable. Response percentages lower than 70 percent are unacceptable and are marked for further analysis. Correct response percentages lower than 70 percent should display with a light red fill and dark red text. Dr. Haddock wants to see a count for correct responses, a count for incorrect responses, and the percentage of correct responses for each major. He also would like the same information organized by classification.

To facilitate his analysis, Dr. Haddock asks you to prepare Correct Response, Major Comparison, and Classification charts. You are free to select the chart format. The Correct Response chart compares each major's correct response percentages for each question. Dr. Haddock wants to know the majors of the students enrolled in the ECON 2103 sections. He will use the Major Comparison chart to view a breakdown by major. He asks that the Major Comparison chart provide both a count and a percentage for each major. Dr. Haddock wants to know how many seniors, juniors, sophomores, and freshmen took the ECON 2103 course. The Classification chart provides counts and percentages for the freshmen, sophomores, juniors, and seniors taking ECON 2103.

As Dr. Haddock is the department chairperson, he manages several economics classes. He wants to use this workbook for other classes, and requests that you create a template based on your newly created workbook.

Information Specifications

In addition to the information requests specified above, Dr. Haddock requests answers for the following questions.

1. Overall, which major's students answered the most questions correctly?

2. Which major's students answered the least number of questions correctly?

3. Which student(s) answered the most questions correctly?

4. Which section's students answered the most questions correctly?

5. Overall, which classification answered the most questions correctly?

6. How do freshmen economics majors compare to freshmen MIS majors?

7. For final exam Question 10, prepare a chart that compares the correct responses given by the different classifications across all sections. (You select the chart.)

Implementation Concerns

Although you are free to work with the design of your workbook, the worksheets should have a consistent, professional appearance. When designing the worksheets, you should apply basic cell and worksheet formatting principles.

Depending on how you choose to design the workbook, this case may require you to create new worksheets, modify existing worksheets, and consolidate information into a summary worksheet. To prepare this workbook according to Dr. Haddock's specifications, you will create formulas, use several functions, and use the PivotTable and PivotChart report tools. Your worksheet's design may require you to use the COUNTIFS function to determine response counts. The COUNTIFS function allows you to use multiple criteria to evaluate multiple cell ranges and count when the multiple criteria are met. You should use your system's online help feature to learn more about the COUNTIFS function.

When designing the workbook, cells containing a correct response percentage less than 70 percent use a light red fill with dark text. The conditional formatting command can accomplish this task. If you are unfamiliar with conditional formatting, use your system's online help feature to learn more about conditional formatting.

Flexibility is one of the key aspects of this case. Dr. Haddock will use this workbook as a template for other classes. When designing the workbook, you should design a workbook that is easily adaptable as Dr. Haddock's information needs change. For instance, the Test Your Design section asks you to modify the workbook's design to match the standard questions to their objective.

Test Your Design

After creating the Lake View Assessment workbook, you should test your design. Perform the following steps.

1. Professor Jones submitted responses for two addition students from Section 1. Please enter the following information into the appropriate worksheet(s).

Section 1: Instructor Jones												
Student	Student Major	Classification	Q1	Q2	Q3	Q4	Q5	Q6	Q7	Q8	Q9	Q10
Assign Next Available Number	MIS	Junior	c	e	d	e	e	d	c	d	e	c
Assign Next Available Number	FIN	Sophomore	c	d	d	b	b	d	c	d	c	c

2. Based on the following table, identify the sections achieving course objectives.

Objectives and Matching Questions	
Objective 1	Questions 1, 4, and 10
Objective 2	Questions 2, 5, and 7
Objective 3	Questions 3 and 8
Objective 4	Questions 6 and 9

3. Based on the acceptable percentage rate, which section did not meet at least 4 of its objectives?

4. Based on the acceptable percentage rate, did any section meet all of its objectives?

CASE DELIVERABLES

In order to satisfactorily complete this case, you should build the workbook as described in the case scenario and then prepare both written and oral presentations. Unless otherwise specified, submit the following deliverables to your professor.

1. A written report discussing any assumptions you have made about the case and the key elements of the case. Additionally, what features did you add to make the worksheets more functional? User friendly? (Please note that these assumptions cannot violate any of the requirements specified above and must be approved by your professor.)

2. A printout of each worksheet. (This includes your charts and PivotTables.)

3. A printout of each worksheet's formulas.

4. An electronic, working copy of your workbook that meets the criteria mentioned in the case scenario and specifications sections.

5. Results for each question posed above. (A memo to your instructor discussing these results should also be provided.)

6. As mentioned above, you should prepare an oral presentation. (Your instructor will establish the time allocated for your presentation.) You should use a presentation package and discuss the key features of your workbook. Also, discuss how the workbook is beneficial for Dr. Haddock. What additional information should be included in the workbook to make it more useful?

Case 12

Baylee Byrd Playsets, Inc.

From Chapter 12 of *MIS Cases: Decision Making with Application Software*, 4/e. Lisa Miller. Copyright © 2009 by Pearson Prentice Hall. All rights reserved.

Baylee Byrd Playsets, Inc.

Spreadsheet Case   **Difficulty Rating:** ★★★★★

CASE BACKGROUND

A weekend, backyard project that began two years ago has now become a thriving, growing business for Jacob Byrd. Jacob Byrd is the owner and operator of Baylee Byrd Playsets, Inc., a small, part-time business, specializing in the production of quality, custom-built playsets. After friends and neighbors convinced him that he should custom build playsets for their children, Mr. Byrd began his part-time business. Although Mr. Byrd realizes a modest profit from his business, he wants to evaluate the business's operating performance, so that he can determine the best pricing and marketing strategies for his playsets.

Although last year's sales were good, the net income for the business was only $4,183.50. Mr. Byrd feels that his net income should be much higher and has requested your help in evaluating his business's operating performance. To assist Mr. Byrd with the analysis of his business, you will create an income statement, perform breakeven analysis, use several financial ratios, prepare one-variable data tables, use Goal Seek and Solver to perform what-if analysis, prepare a chart, and use the Scenario Manager to prepare different scenarios.

Baylee Byrd Playsets, Inc.

CASE SCENARIO

Two years ago, Jacob Byrd searched for a playset for his four-year-old daughter, Baylee. After spending several months visiting toy and discount stores looking for just the right playset and not finding the perfect one, he decided to custom build a playset for Baylee. The custom-built playset soon became the talk of the town, and Mr. Byrd found himself building playsets for friends and neighbors.

The custom-built playsets are widely recognized throughout the community and in neighboring towns and are an impressive sight. The playsets are made of redwood and equipped with a wave slide, fort, fireman's pole, chin-up bar, safety step ladder, tube slide, bridge, 6' by 6' platform, and two swings.

Last year, Baylee Byrd Playsets, Inc., sold 85 units at $999.99 per unit and generated $84,999.15 in revenue. However, after expenses and taxes were deducted, the business's net income was only $4,183.50. Mr. Byrd would like to improve his net income, and he wonders what he needs to do to achieve this objective. Mr. Byrd needs to evaluate his cash flow to determine areas for improvement and has requested your help.

Design Specifications

After speaking with Mr. Byrd and evaluating his information needs, you decide that an Income Analysis worksheet will help him with his decision-making activities. The Income Analysis worksheet provides Mr. Byrd with several tools for analyzing his business's operating performance. The Income Analysis worksheet enables Mr. Byrd to input the number of units sold, revenue per unit, desired target income, and costs. Once the data are entered, the Income Analysis worksheet provides Mr. Byrd with an income statement, computes financial ratios, performs breakeven analysis, and updates the one-variable data tables.

You determine that the Income Analysis worksheet needs both input and results sections. Figure 1 shows a tentative sketch for the input section. The input section enables Mr. Byrd to input data about the number of units sold, revenue per unit, desired target income, and costs. Table 1 summarizes the company's sales and costs for the previous year. As you study Table 1's contents, you notice that the costs are separated into two categories: fixed and variable. From a previous business course, you recall that fixed costs remain constant and do not vary with sales volume. Fixed costs for Baylee Byrd Playsets, Inc., include such items as fixed overhead, selling expenses, administrative expenses, and depreciation. In contrast, variable costs change in direct proportion to the sales volume. Variable costs include such items as marketing and sales, labor, variable overhead, variable selling, and variable administrative.

Baylee Byrd Playsets, Inc.

Figure 1: Input Section Sketch

Input Section For Income Analysis Worksheet	
Sales and Cost Summary	
Number of Units Sold	
Revenue Per Unit	
Desired Target Income	
Variable Costs (per unit)	
Marketing and Sales	
Labor	
Variable Overhead	
Variable Selling	
Variable Administrative	
Fixed Costs	
Fixed Overhead	
Selling Expenses	
Administrative Expenses	
Depreciation	

Table 1: Sales and Costs for Previous Year

Income		Fixed Costs	
Units Sold	85	Fixed Overhead	$4,652.11
Price Per Unit	$999.99	Selling Expenses	$2,500.00
Desired Target Income	$30,000.00	Administrative Expenses	$2,399.99
		Depreciation	$7,000.00
Variable Costs (Per Unit)			
Marketing and Sales	$15.24		
Labor	$150.00		
Variable Overhead	$514.72		
Variable Selling	$25.83		
Variable Administrative	$23.75		

The results section uses the data from the input section to produce an income statement, compute financial ratios, and perform breakeven analysis. The results section will also display your one-variable data tables. (Descriptions for the one-variable data tables are provided in subsequent sections.) Figures 2 and 3 provide sketches for the income statement and ratios.

Baylee Byrd Playsets, Inc.

Figure 2: Income Statement

Baylee Byrd Playsets, Inc. Income Statement (Current Date)	
Sales	
Variable Expenses	
Marketing and Sales	
Labor	
Variable Overhead	
Variable Selling	
Variable Administrative	
Total Variable Expenses	
Contribution Margin	
Fixed Expenses	
Fixed Overhead	
Selling Expenses	
Administrative Expenses	
Depreciation	
Total Fixed Expenses	
Operating Income	
Income Taxes	
Net Income	

Figure 3: Ratios

Ratios	
BEP	
BEP with Target Income	
Contribution Margin Ratio	
Operating Margin Ratio	
Net Margin Ratio	

Information Specifications

The Income Analysis worksheet provides Mr. Byrd with information about his business's income, calculates several financial ratios, performs breakeven analysis, and displays one-variable data tables. Therefore, the Results section of the Income Analysis worksheet will have income statement, ratio, and data table result areas.

As Figure 2 shows, the income statement section of the worksheet summarizes the business's revenues and expenses, allowing Mr. Byrd to examine the company's overall operating performance. As you study the income statement outline, you realize that many of your calculations will reference the data contained in the Input section of the worksheet, requiring Mr. Byrd to input the data only once. Mr. Byrd provides you with the formulas shown in Figure 4.

Baylee Byrd Playsets, Inc.

Mr. Byrd wants to examine the impact that various target income levels have on the breakeven point. For instance, Mr. Byrd knows that a target income of $15,000 requires 117 playsets in order to break even. He would like to see what impact $20,000, $25,000, $30,000, $35,000, and $40,000 target incomes have on the breakeven point. Although he can change the target income cell value for each of the desired target income levels, you recommend that he use a one-variable data table. By creating a one-variable data table, the target income values and their associated breakeven points are arranged in a table, enabling Mr. Byrd to view and compare all the target income values and their associated breakeven points at the same time. (You may wish to use your system's online help feature to review one-variable data tables at this point.)

Figure 4: Required Formulas

Income Analysis Worksheet Formulas	
Breakeven Point	$$\frac{\text{Fixed Costs}}{\text{Revenue Per Unit} - \text{Variable Cost Per Unit}}$$
Breakeven Point with Target Income	$$\frac{\text{Fixed Costs} + \text{Target Income}}{\text{Revenue Per Unit} - \text{Variable Cost Per Unit}}$$
Contribution Margin	Sales – Total Variable Expenses
Contribution Margin Ratio	$$\frac{\text{Sales} - \text{Variable Cost}}{\text{Sales}}$$
Income Taxes (Assume a 35 percent tax rate)	Operating Income * Income Tax Rate
Net Income	Operating Income – Income Taxes
Net Margin	$$\frac{\text{Net Income}}{\text{Net Sales}}$$
Operating Income	Contribution Margin – Total Fixed Expenses
Operating Margin	$$\frac{\text{Operating Income}}{\text{Net Sales}}$$
Variable Cost Per Unit	$$\frac{\text{Total Variable Costs}}{\text{Number of Units Sold}}$$

Mr. Byrd wants to see how different scenarios impact the business's net income. In addition to the current scenario, Mr. Byrd wants to evaluate two other possible scenarios. In the first scenario, he wants to increase the number of units sold to 150, decrease revenue per unit to $950, and decrease variable costs per unit by $20. (You can choose which variable cost to reduce.) In the second scenario, he wants to increase the number of units sold to 100, increase revenue to $1,650 per unit, and increase labor by $50. Using Scenario Manager, you prepare the three scenarios. The first scenario uses the original values, and the remaining two scenarios use the data that Mr. Byrd has just given you. After you create the three scenarios, you generate a scenario summary report based on the three scenarios.

Mr. Byrd needs answers to the following questions. Using your newly designed Income Analysis worksheet, provide Mr. Byrd with answers to his questions.

1. Mr. Byrd wants a net margin ratio of 15 percent. Using Solver, adjust the values for the revenue and number of units sold. Revenue per unit cannot exceed $1,100, the number of units sold cannot exceed 250, and total variable expenses cannot exceed $110,000. In order to have a net margin of 15 percent, how many playsets will Mr. Byrd need to sell? What price should he charge? Generate an answer report. (As a starting point for this answer, reset your worksheet's values back to the original values in Table 1, and then make the changes requested in this question.)

2. Assume that fixed overhead costs are $7,500, variable overhead is $375, labor is $200, and depreciation is $8,500. If Mr. Byrd wants a net income of $30,000, what price should Mr. Byrd charge for his playsets?   How many playsets should Mr. Byrd sell? (As a starting point for this answer, reset your worksheet's values back to the original values in Table 1, and then make the changes requested in this question.)

3. Mr. Byrd wants a net income of $55,000. How many playsets should Mr. Byrd sell? What price should he charge? (As a starting point for this answer, reset your worksheet's values back to the original values in Table 1, and then make the changes requested in this question.)

4.   Mr. Byrd needs a 3-D pie chart that compares the business's fixed costs.

Implementation Concerns

For this case, you will design a worksheet to facilitate Mr. Byrd's analysis of his business. When designing the worksheet, you will apply basic cell and worksheet formatting principles, create formulas, perform what-if analysis by using Goal Seek and Solver, create several scenarios, generate a chart, and create two one-variable data tables.   Based on your what-if analysis, you will prepare several reports, including an answer report and a scenario summary report.

Although you are free to work with the design of your worksheet, the worksheet should have a consistent, professional appearance. You should use proper formatting for the cells. For instance, dollar values should display with a dollar sign and be formatted to two decimal places.

In several locations, the case references target income. Keep in mind that the target income does not reflect income taxes. Therefore, as it is used in this case, the target income is a better reflection of operating income, as opposed to net income.

Baylee Byrd Playsets, Inc.

Test Your Design

1. Assume that fixed overhead is $5,000, selling expenses are $4,500, administrative expenses are $3,000, and labor costs are $250. What is Mr. Byrd's net income? (As a starting point for this answer, reset your worksheet's values back to the original values in Table 1, and then make the changes requested in this question.)

2. In order to have a net income of $50,000, how many playsets must Mr. Byrd sell? What price should he charge for the playsets? (As a starting point for this answer, reset your worksheet's values back to the original values in Table 1, and then make the changes requested in this question.)

3. Mr. Byrd wants to identify the breakeven point and breakeven point with target income for varying pricing levels. Prepare a one-variable data table that shows this information. The pricing levels range from $1,000 to $2,500 in $50 increments. If Mr. Byrd does not want to sell more than 120 playsets and wants to have a $60,000 target income, how many units must he sell? What price should he charge? (As a starting point for this answer, reset your worksheet's values back to the original values in Table 1, and then make the changes requested in this question.)

CASE DELIVERABLES

In order to satisfactorily complete this case, you should build the workbook as described in the case scenario and then prepare both written and oral presentations. Unless otherwise specified, submit the following deliverables to your professor.

1. A written report discussing any assumptions you have made about the case and the key elements of the case. Additionally, what features did you add to make the worksheet more functional? User friendly? (Please note that these assumptions cannot violate any of the requirements specified above and must be approved by your professor.)

2. A printout of each worksheet and report.

3. An electronic, working copy of your workbook that meets the criteria mentioned in the case scenario and specifications sections.

4. Results for each question posed above. (A memo to your instructor discussing these results should also be provided.)

5. As mentioned above, you should prepare an oral presentation. (Your instructor will establish the time allocated for your presentation.) You should use a presentation package and discuss the key features of your worksheet. Also, discuss how the worksheet is beneficial for Mr. Byrd. What additional information should be included in the worksheet to make it more useful?

Case 13

Edmund Grant Pharmaceutical Company

Spreadsheet Case   **Difficulty Rating:** ★★★★★

CASE BACKGROUND

Keiko Lapeer is a district sales manager for the Edmund Grant Pharmaceutical Company. Ms. Lapeer has many responsibilities, including traveling, visiting with current and potential customers, supervising a growing sales staff, preparing numerous reports, and tracking her sales region's expenses. Each week, members of Ms. Lapeer's sales staff submit weekly expense claim forms. Currently, she scans through the expense forms, checks for anything out of the ordinary, and then authorizes reimbursement checks. Ms. Lapeer needs to become more organized about tracking her sales staff's expenses, and asks you to design an Expense worksheet for her. Specifically, she requests you to organize the expense data into an Excel table. To design the worksheet according to Ms. Lapeer's specifications, you are required to use database functions, other Microsoft Excel functions, and nest functions. You will then use the Filter, Advanced Filter, PivotTable, and PivotChart tools to analyze the data.

From Chapter 13 of *MIS Cases: Decision Making with Application Software*, 4/e. Lisa Miller. Copyright © 2009 by Pearson Prentice Hall. All rights reserved.

CASE SCENARIO

The Edmund Grant Pharmaceutical Company (EGPC) is a multinational company, well known in the United States for its anti-infective, wound care, and pain management products. The Edmund Grant Pharmaceutical Company's sales force is responsible for promoting EGPC products to doctors, pharmacists, and opticians around the globe. Keiko Lapeer is one of EGPC's many district sales managers and is responsible for supervising four sales areas.

As a district sales manager, Ms. Lapeer stays very busy. She often travels, attends several meetings a month, visits with customers, supervises a 23-member sales force, and performs managerial duties. As a manager, Ms. Lapeer's paperwork is often overwhelming, and she is looking for avenues of improvement. One area for improvement is the expense tracking of her sales force. She can easily spend an entire day just processing budget and expense reports. By using a spreadsheet application to analyze her sales force's expenses, she feels that she will save time and make better decisions.

Sales representatives are reimbursed for business meals and calls, gas, hotel, airfare, and other miscellaneous expenses. Each week, sales representatives complete expense claim forms and submit these forms to Ms. Lapeer. Figure 1 provides an example of the expense claim form. Ms. Lapeer summarizes the expense data contained on these forms and prepares several weekly reports. Report preparation is a tedious, time-consuming task, often requiring her to wade through the expense claim forms numerous times.

Figure 1: Expense Claim Form

Edmund Grant Pharmaceutical Company
Expense Claim Form

Employee Name: _____   For Week Ending:_____
Division Number:_____

Expense   **Mileage**

Meals: _____   Beginning Mileage: _____
Phone:_____   Ending Mileage: _____
Gas:_____
Hotel:_____
Airfare:_____
Miscellaneous: _____   Comments: _____
_____   _____
_____   _____
_____   _____
Total Expenses Claimed: _____   _____

Notice: All expense claims must be accompanied by receipts.

Edmund Grant Pharmaceutical Company

When a sales representative is hired, he is issued a company car. The sales representative may use his car for both business and personal travel, and he is given a weekly mileage limit. Each week, the sales representative reports the number of miles that he has driven that week. For any miles over the mileage limit, the employee is charged an overage fee. The allowable mileage and charge rate vary by sales position within the company. Table 1 summarizes the allowable mileage and charge rates. Ms. Lapeer wants the new Expense worksheet to determine the mileage overage amount and applicable charges for each sales representative.

Table 1: Allowable Mileage and Rates

Edmund Grant Pharmaceutical Company Allowable Mileage and Rates		
Position	Allowable Miles	Rate
MN	700	0.20
SU	600	0.22
S2	550	0.25
S1	500	0.32

When a car has 60,000 miles, the sales representative can request a new car. Ms. Lapeer wonders if there is some way that she can quickly determine when a car is reaching its end-of-service date. You recommend using conditional formatting to highlight ending mileage readings that are greater than 55,000 miles. If a sales representative has a car that is approaching its end-of-service date, Ms. Lapeer can remind the sales representative that it is time to request a new car.

Ms. Lapeer has used a spreadsheet application before and would like to organize the weekly expense data into a worksheet. She asks you to create an Expense worksheet for her. She specifically requests that you prepare an Excel table, establish a criteria range to support Advanced Filtering, include several database functions, insert four new columns, prepare pivot tables, and prepare several charts. Ms. Lapeer also requests that the new worksheet be saved as a template, so she can reuse it each week.

Design Specifications

As you examine the Expense worksheet, you realize that the worksheet columns need formatting. After formatting the columns, you decide that a mileage lookup table and four additional columns are necessary. Before inserting the four columns, you build the mileage lookup table. As you want to keep the mileage lookup table separate from the expense data, you place the table in its own worksheet. After creating the mileage lookup table, you insert the actual mileage, overage, overage charge, and total expense columns into the Expense worksheet. The actual mileage column calculates the actual miles that each employee drove during the week. Actual mileage is the difference between the week's ending mileage and the week's beginning mileage. You want the overage column to reference the mileage lookup table and then determine how many miles over the limit, if any, the employee has driven. (Performing this operation requires nesting IF and VLOOKUP functions. At this point, you may wish to use your system's online help feature to review how to nest functions.) The overage charge column uses the VLOOKUP function as well. This column multiplies the overage by the rate specified in the mileage table. The total expenses column is a summation of the expenses for that week.

Ms. Lapeer will use the Advanced Filter capability. Using the Advanced Filter requires the inclusion of a criteria range. For Ms. Lapeer's purposes, you decide the best place for the criteria range is above the Excel table. (At this point, you may wish to use your system's online help feature to review the Advanced Filter topic.) As Ms. Lapeer uses the criteria range, she needs to clear the range of the current conditions and enter new conditions in the criteria range. You decide to create a macro that will clear the criteria range and position the pointer in the upper left-hand cell of the criteria range. Once you have created the macro, you then assign it to a button named "Clear Criteria."

As you study the contents of the Expense worksheet, you realize that the contents are in a format suitable for creating an Excel table. You recall from one of your business courses that an Excel table is a collection of data, similar in concept to a database table. The data in this Excel table can be filtered, sorted, and manipulated in a variety of ways, thus facilitating Ms. Lapeer's decision-making activities. In fact, several database functions are available for usage with an Excel table, and you decide to use these functions in the Expense worksheet. Ms. Lapeer wants average, minimum, maximum, and total values for the meal, actual mileage, phone, gas, hotel, miscellaneous, airfare, overage, overage charge, and total expense columns in the table. Since Ms. Lapeer will manipulate the data in the Excel table, you use the DAVERAGE, DMIN, DMAX, and DSUM functions. (At this point, you may wish to use your system's online help feature to review list creation and usage.)

After you design the worksheet, Ms. Lapeer wants a template created. Then each week, she can use the template to create a worksheet for that week.

Information Specifications

Ms. Lapeer asks if it is possible to view the expense data at varying levels of detail and from different perspectives. She specifically requests a summary of all expenses categorized by division, the total expenses displayed by sales position and the total expenses for the meals, phone and gas expense categories by division and position. As the PivotTable tool can quickly change the way data are displayed and the level of summarization, you recommend that Ms. Lapeer use a pivot table.

As mentioned previously, Ms. Lapeer wants to know when a salesperson's car is approaching 60,000 miles. For any vehicle that has more than 55,000 miles, the spreadsheet application should highlight the ending mileage for that vehicle.

In addition to the information requirements specified above, Ms. Lapeer requests that you perform the following operations.

1. Identify which managers claimed airfare expenses totaling more than $1,700 and which supervisors claimed airfare expenses totaling more than $750.

2. Identify which sales representative(s) did not submit an expense claim form.

3. Identify hotel and airfare expenses by position.
4. Identify which managers traveled via airplane during the week.

5. Identify sales positions by division.

6. Identify which division had the lowest expenses for the week.

7. Identify which S1 sales representative(s) submitted hotel and airfare expenses this past week.

8. Identify which individuals went over their mileage limits.

Implementation Concerns

Although you are free to work with the design of your worksheet, it should have a consistent, professional appearance. You should also use proper formatting for the cells. For instance, dollar values should display with a dollar sign and be formatted to two decimal places.

This case scenario requires you to use an Excel table. Extracting the data requires you to prepare charts; use the DAVERAGE, DSUM, DMIN, DMAX, IF, and VLOOKUP functions; nest functions; establish a criteria range; prepare PivotTables and charts; and use the Filter and Advanced Filter tools. (You may wish to use your system's online help feature to review each of these areas.)

The determination of the overage amount for each salesperson requires the spreadsheet application to look up the mileage allowance, determine if the mileage is greater than the allowance, and then compute the actual overage amount, if any. Performance of this task requires nesting the VLOOKUP function inside the IF function. (At this point, you may wish to use your system's online help feature to review nesting functions.) Keep in mind that Ms. Lapeer wants the mileage overage amount to display in one column.

You should carefully consider the placement of the criteria range and the mileage table. It is generally recommended that the criteria range be placed above or below the Excel table. Placement of the criteria range in either of these locations facilitates the viewing of the criteria and filter results. Although your mileage lookup table may be placed in the Expense worksheet, consider placing the lookup table in its own worksheet. Using a separate worksheet for the mileage lookup table facilitates table maintenance and accessibility.

Test Your Design

After creating the Expense worksheet described in the case scenario, you should test your worksheet design. Perform the following operations.

1. Add the following three new employees to your Excel table.

Employee 1	Employee 2	Employee 3
Last Name: Ruokangas **First Name**: Leota **Division**: 1 **Position**: MN **Meals**: $376.89 **Phone**: $79.86 **Hotel**: $478.78 **Miscellaneous**: $2,987.42 **Airfare**: $894.87 **Beginning Mileage**: 101 **Ending Mileage**: 372	**Last Name**: Saghafi **First Name**: Abduellah **Division**: 3 **Position**: S1 **Meals**: $102.78 **Phone**: $10.07 **Hotel**: $0.00 **Miscellaneous**: $0.00 **Airfare**: $0.00 **Beginning Mileage**: 904 **Ending Mileage**: 1,150	**Last Name**: Omari **First Name**: Kyleena **Division**: 4 **Position**: S2 **Meals**: $257.88 **Phone**: $58.77 **Hotel**: $509.78 **Miscellaneous**: $877.89 **Airfare**: $250.75 **Beginning Mileage**: 67 **Ending Mileage**: 803

2. Make the following changes to your mileage table.

Allowable Mileage Table		
Position	**Allowable Miles**	**Rate**
MN	700	0.25
SU	600	0.28
S2	550	0.30
S1	500	0.32

3. Within each division, Ms. Lapeer wants to examine the expenses incurred by each employee. She would like to view the divisions one "page" at a time.

4. Prepare a column chart that compares the gas, hotel, airfare, and meal expenses for each division.

5. For each division, Ms. Lapeer wants to see the person's last name and the number of miles she/he drove last week. She would like to see a grand total for each division. Prepare a pivot table and also prepare a chart for Division 1. (Choose an appropriate chart.)

CASE DELIVERABLES

In order to satisfactorily complete this case, you should build the workbook as described in the case scenario and then prepare both written and oral presentations. Unless otherwise specified, submit the following deliverables to your professor.

1. A written report discussing any assumptions you have made about the case and the key elements of the case. Additionally, what features did you add to make the worksheets more functional? User friendly? (Please note that these assumptions cannot violate any of the requirements specified above and must be approved by your professor.)

2. A printout of each worksheet. (This includes your charts and pivot tables.)

3. A printout of each worksheet's formulas.

4. An electronic, working copy of your workbook that meets the criteria mentioned in the case scenario and specifications sections.

5. Results for each question posed above. (A memo to your instructor discussing these results should also be provided.)

6. As mentioned above, you should prepare an oral presentation. (Your instructor will establish the time allocated for your presentation.) You should use a presentation package and discuss the key features of your workbook. Also, discuss how the workbook is beneficial for Ms. Lapeer. What additional information should be included in the workbook to make it more useful?

Case 14

Molly Mackenzie Boat Marina

From Chapter 14 of *MIS Cases: Decision Making with Application Software*, 4/e. Lisa Miller. Copyright © 2009 by Pearson Prentice Hall. All rights reserved.

Molly Mackenzie Boat Marina

Integration Case   **Difficulty Rating:** ★ ★ ★ ★ ★

CASE BACKGROUND

Marvin and Dena Mackenzie own and operate the Molly Mackenzie Marina. Currently, data about the marina's daily operating activities are manually captured and processed. When necessary, reports are created using a word processing package. As the marina continues to grow, Mr. and Mrs. Mackenzie recognize the necessity of using information technology to capture details about the marina's daily operations, as well as facilitate decision-making activities. Mr. and Mrs. Mackenzie need a database to track information about customer reservations, customer payments, and the marina's rental properties. Mr. and Mrs. Mackenzie hire you to build the database. Building the database requires you to develop forms and subforms, reports, queries, and a switchboard. The forms will utilize buttons to facilitate data navigation. Once the database is developed, Mr. Mackenzie will export selected data from the marina database to a spreadsheet for further analysis. Mr. Mackenzie will use the Subtotals function, PivotTable, Solver, and charting tools to analyze the data.

CASE SCENARIO

The Molly Mackenzie Marina and its surrounding property are located on Lake Merewether in the Midwest. Lake Merewether is a popular tourist spot, attracting visitors year round. The lake's notoriety is due to its beautiful surroundings, camping facilities, excellent fishing, and ability to handle large boats. Lake visitors are primarily local, but many visitors come from across the nation. Lake Merewether is situated between two large cities, serving as a weekend getaway for many of its visitors.

Mr. Mackenzie uses a manual-based information system to manage the marina's rental property. However, he realizes that automating the marina's daily operations will make his management activities more efficient. Mr. and Mrs. Mackenzie spend numerous hours keeping the marina's paperwork up to date. The marina's popularity continues to grow, and Mr. Mackenzie is quickly realizing the necessity of using information technology to ease the marina's paperwork burden. In an effort to run the office in a more efficient manner, Mr. Mackenzie hires you to design a marina database and worksheet for him. Since you have worked as a part-time marina employee, you are familiar with the marina's daily operations and are eager to help.

The Molly Mackenzie Marina rents cabins, a variety of watercraft, and boat slips to its customers. When a customer requests a watercraft or a cabin, a price quote is given. The price quote is based on a daily rate. If a customer wants to rent a jet ski for a half day, then the daily rate is adjusted. Likewise, if a customer rents a cabin or boat slip for more than a day, Mr. Mackenzie will discount the daily rate, making a longer stay more attractive. Cabins can be rented for a weekend, week, or month at a reduced rate. Table 1 shows the discount codes and their associated percentage discounts. If a customer rents a jet ski for a half day, Mr. Mackenzie will charge the person 65 percent of the daily rate. If a person rents a boat slip for 180 days, Mr. Mackenzie will reduce the daily rate by 15 percent.

Table 1: Rate Codes and Discounts

Rate Code	Rate Description	Percentage
D	Daily	100.00%
HD	Half Day	65.00%
SD	Special Discount	25.00%
SM	Six Months	85.00%
Y	12 Months	80.00%
W	Weekend	90.00%

When a property is reserved, the customer places a deposit on the rental property. The deposit is applied to the rental fees for the property or is forfeited if the customer cancels the reservation. Mr. Mackenzie is flexible on the deposit amount. Mr. Mackenzie requires a minimum deposit from frequent customers, but does charge a hefty deposit for new customers. When a customer picks up the watercraft or checks into a cabin, he is required to pay the entire balance for the property, minus any deposit. If an advanced reservation was not made, the customer pays the entire balance when he rents the property.

When a customer requests a particular property, Mr. Mackenzie or an employee checks to see if the property is available for the dates requested by the customer. If the requested dates are available, reservation data are captured on a reservation form. Based on the length of stay, Mr. Mackenzie determines which rate is applicable. For a typical reservation, customer contact information (name, phone number, and mailing address), reservation dates, and property information (rental property number and rate), are recorded. When a reservation is made, the customer is given a reservation number. The customer uses the reservation number if he needs to cancel the reservation or when he checks in. When a payment is made, the payment date, payment amount, and any comments are recorded. When the customer returns the watercraft or checks out of the cabin, he stops by the office and is given an invoice showing his rental transactions.

Storage Specifications

To build the marina database, you decide Customer, Rate, Property, Payment, and Reservation tables are necessary. The Customer table stores basic customer information, such as customer identification number (CID), last name, first name, street address, city, state, zip, and phone number. As the customer identification number is unique for each customer, it serves as the primary key for the Customer table. Table 2 shows the Customer table structure.

The Rate table stores information about the rate codes, rate descriptions, and discount percentages. As the rate code value is unique for each rate code, the Rate Code field serves as the primary key. The rate description provides additional information about the rate code, such as daily, weekend, six-month, special discount, half price, or twelve-month. Where applicable, the discount percentage is multiplied by the daily rate to provide a reduced rate for the customer for a given rental property. Table 3 shows the Rate table structure.

The Property table stores information about each of the marina's rental properties. The property identification number (PID) is unique for each property. Therefore, the PID serves as the primary key. The Property table also includes rental price, description, and property category fields. The rental price field stores the daily rental price for the property. The description field further clarifies the type of property. The PCategory field classifies the type of property, such as cabin, jet ski, powerboat, boat slip, or fishing boat. Table 4 shows the Property table structure.

The Payment table stores information about each payment made by a marina customer. The Payment table includes PaymentID, customer identification number (CID), PaymentDate, PaymentAmount, Comment, and Deposit? fields. The PaymentID field stores a unique value for each payment record; therefore, it serves as the primary key for the Payment table. The CID field associates a given payment record with the customer making the payment. The PaymentDate stores the date the payment was made. The PaymentAmount field stores the amount paid. The Comment field stores any necessary comments about the payment. The Deposit? field indicates whether this payment is a deposit. Table 5 shows the Payment table structure.

The Reservation table stores information about each of the marina's rental property reservations. The Reservation table's fields include ResID, customer identification number (CID), ResDate, BookingDate, EndDate, PickUpTime, RateCode, and property identification number (PID). The ResID field contains a unique value for each reservation and serves as the table's primary key. The CID value associates a given customer with the reservation. The ResDate field indicates the starting date of the reservation. The BookingDate indicates when the reservation was made. The EndDate indicates the last day of the reservation. The PickUpTime field indicates the time that the rental property will be picked up. The RateCode field identifies the applicable rate code for the reservation. The PID field identifies the property associated with this reservation. Table 6 shows the Reservation table structure.

As part of the design process, relationships among tables are necessary. Where applicable, you should enforce referential integrity.

Table 2: Customer Table Structure

Field Name	Data Type	Field Description	Field Size	Comments
CID	AutoNumber	Uniquely identifies the customer. Serves as the primary key.	Long Integer	Is required.
Last Name	Text	Stores the customer's last name.	50	Is required.
First Name	Text	Stores the customer's first name.	25	Is required.
Street Address	Text	Stores the customer's street address.	50	
City	Text	Stores the name of the customer's city.	25	
State	Text	Stores the name of the customer's state.	2	
Zip	Text	Stores the customer's zip code. Use an input mask.	10	
Phone	Text	Stores the customer's phone number. Use an input mask.	10	

Table 3: Rate Table Structure

Field Name	Data Type	Field Description	Field Size	Comments
Rate Code	Text	Stores a unique identification number for each rate code. Serves as the primary key.	10	Is required.
Rate Description	Text	Stores the description for the rate code.	25	Is required.
Percentage	Number	Stores the discount percentage. Multiply this amount times the daily rate to get the adjusted price. Use percent format. Display 2 digits to the right of the decimal separator.	Single	Is required.

Table 4: Property Table Structure

Field Name	Data Type	Field Description	Field Size	Comments
PID	Text	Uniquely identifies the property. Serves as the primary key.	10	Is required.
RentalPrice	Number	Identifies the daily rental rate. Use currency format.	Long Integer	Is required.
Description	Text	Describes the rental property.	50	
PCategory	Text	Classifies the property.	2	

Table 5: Payment Table Structure

Field Name	Data Type	Field Description	Field Size	Comments
PaymentID	AutoNumber	Stores a unique value. Serves as primary key.	Long Integer	Is required.
CID	Number	Stores the customer's identification number. Consider using the Lookup Wizard.	Long Integer	Is required.
PaymentDate	Date/Time	Stores the date that the payment was made.		
PaymentAmount	Currency	Stores the amount paid.		Is required.
Deposit?	Yes/No	Indicates if this is a deposit.		
Comment	Text	Stores a comment about the transaction.	50	

Table 6: Reservation Table Structure

Field Name	Data Type	Field Description	Field Size	Comments
ResID	AutoNumber	Uniquely identifies each reservation. Serves as the primary key.	Long Integer	Is required.
CID	Number	Uniquely identifies the customer.	Long Integer	Is required.
ResDate	Date/Time	Identifies the start date of the reservation for the rental property.		Is required.
BookingDate	Date/Time	Identifies the date the reservation was made.		Is required.
EndDate	Date/Time	Identifies the final day of the reservation.		Is required.
PickUpTime	Date/Time	Identifies the time the property will be picked up or the check in time.		
RateCode	Text	Identifies the applied rate code. Use the Lookup Wizard.	50	Is required.
PID	Text	Identifies the rental property. Use the Lookup Wizard.	10	Is required.

Input Specifications

From your conversations with Mr. Mackenzie, you realize that the database must capture and store information about the marina's customers, rental property, rental reservations, and rental payments. Capturing this information requires you to build several forms and subforms. For instance, a customer form with reservation and payment history subforms is necessary. A sketch of the customer form is provided below.

The customer form captures and displays the customer's name, address, and phone number. Additionally, the customer form shows the customer identification number, total charges, the amount he has paid, and the balance due. The total charges field shows the total amount owed for the customer's current reservations. Likewise, the Amount Paid field shows the total paid toward the current reservations, and the Remaining Balance field indicates how much is still due.

When using the customer form, Mr. Mackenzie would like to view or enter information about the customer's current reservations and payments. You decide to use a tab control to organize each customer's reservation and payment information, as well as make the information easily accessible to Mr. Mackenzie as he views a customer's record.

On the reservation subform, Mr. Mackenzie wants to see, at a minimum, the reservation dates, booking date, property identification number, rate code, discount percentage, daily rental rate, discounted daily rental rate, total usage cost, and comments. When using the Reservation subform, Mr. Mackenzie wants to select the rental property number from a list of his rental properties and have the rental property's description and rental fee displayed. On the payment subform, Mr. Mackenzie wants to see the payment date, payment amount, and comments.

Figure 1: Customer Form

Customer Form

Customer Identification Number:	**Total Charges:**
Customer First Name:	**Paid on Account:**
Customer Last Name:	**Remaining Balance:**
Phone Number:	
Street Address:	
City: **State:** **Zip:**	

Reservations Tab   Payment Tab

Although Mr. Mackenzie encourages you to be creative with your form design, he requests that the forms have a consistent, professional appearance, be easy to use, and show the business name and logo. Additionally, each form must include buttons that allow Mr. Mackenzie to add, delete, find, and print records. To facilitate data entry, Mr. Mackenzie would like to use AutoLookup, combo boxes, and control tips for fields where these features can (or should) be used. Where possible, you should use validation rules, default values, input masks, and proper formatting.

When the Molly Mackenzie Marina database is first opened, Mr. Mackenzie wants a switchboard to automatically display. The switchboard allows Mr. Mackenzie to access his forms, reports, and queries from a common location. When Mr. Mackenzie finishes with the database, he wants the option of exiting the application from the main menu.

Information Specifications

Mr. Mackenzie requires a Daily Rental Property Reservation Report, a Rental Availability Report, and a customer invoice. He asks you to design and build these reports for him. Each evening a Daily Rental Property Reservation Report is printed. This report shows which properties are reserved for the next day. This report sorts the properties by rental property category, then by rental property number within each category. Employees use this reservation report to make sure that the reserved watercraft and cabins are in working order.

Often customers will ask when a rental property is available. Mr. Mackenzie requires the ability to locate a rental property's record and check its availability. The Rental Property Availability Report should be organized by rental category, showing which rental properties are available for rent the next day and the rental property should be sorted within each category.

Mr. Mackenzie asks you to prepare a customer invoice. The invoice will serve as a receipt for the customer's rental transactions.

Mr. Mackenzie wants answers to the following questions. Prepare queries to retrieve the information for Mr. Mackenzie. If you choose, you may generate reports based on your queries.

1. For cabin rental customers, what is the average length of stay?

2. How frequently are watercrafts rented? On average, what is the length of rental time?

3. Which boat slip rental option is the most popular? What is the rental revenue by rate code?

4. How much revenue did Mr. Mackenzie receive on fishing boat rental fees last week? Last month? Jet skis? (Use the last week in July for the weekly analysis.)

5. On average, how much does a customer spend on each visit?

6. If customers rent a cabin from the marina, are they also likely to rent a watercraft from us? What is the percentage?

Mr. Mackenzie wants to export data from the marina database to Microsoft Excel for further analysis. He would like answers to the following questions. Using Microsoft Excel, provide answers to his questions.

7. For the month of June, what are the average sales for each product category and product within each category? For the month of June, what are the total sales for each product category and product within each category?

8. For the first seven days of June, prepare a bar chart comparing rental revenues by category by day.

9. For the month of June, prepare a pie chart comparing the revenue by property category.

10. What is the average revenue for each cabin? Which cabin is rented most often?

11. Which rate code is used most often?

12. Mr. Mackenzie has $75,000 to spend on new jet skis. He is evaluating one-person, two-person, and four-person jet skis. The one-person jet ski costs $8,700; the two-person jet ski costs $11,000, and the four-person jet ski costs $15,000. For each jet ski, maintenance costs are $150 per hour. Mr. Mackenzie estimates that each one-person jet ski requires 1 hour of weekly maintenance; each two-person jet ski requires 1.5 hours of weekly maintenance, and each four-person jet ski requires 2 hours of weekly maintenance. Mr. Mackenzie does not want the total number of weekly maintenance hours for the new jet skis to total more than 40 hours. He wants to purchase a maximum of 3 four-person jet skis. The rental season lasts for 100 days.

If Mr. Mackenzie's main goal is to maximize his seasonal jet ski rental profit, how many jet skis should he purchase? Which jet skis should he purchase? Use Solver to help Mr. Mackenzie figure out how many one-person, two-person, and four-person jet skis he should buy. (You are free to make assumptions; however, these assumptions must be clearly stated in your analysis.)

Implementation Concerns

In order to build the Molly Mackenzie Marina database, you will construct several queries; design forms and subforms; design reports; construct tables; and establish relationships among tables. You are encouraged to be creative; however, your database should function properly and have a professional appearance.

To satisfy the spreadsheet requirements, you will export selected data from the marina database into a worksheet. To perform the required analysis, you will use several spreadsheet features, including Filter, PivotTable, Solver, Subtotal, and Microsoft Query.

As mentioned above, you are free to work with the design of the forms, reports, and worksheets. You are also free to make additional assumptions about this case. However, the assumptions should not violate any of the requirements and should be approved by your professor. To satisfy your assumptions, you may need to create additional forms or collect information that has not been previously specified.

Test Your Design

After creating your database and workbook, you should test your design. Perform the following steps.

1. Enter the following information into the marina database.

   Randall Petra rented a jet ski and cabin for July 4, 2008 – July 7, 2008. He made his reservations on May 1, 2008. He paid a 20 percent deposit and was given a weekend discount for the cabin. He was not given a discount for his jet ski rental. (You select the jet ski and the cabin. Make any other necessary assumptions).

Pauline Bishop rented two cabins for July 4, 2008 – July 6, 2008. She made her reservations on May 12, 2008. She paid a 30 percent deposit and was given a weekend discount for the cabins. (You select the cabins. Make any other necessary assumptions).

Frances Thomas rented a ski boat for July 4, 2008 – July 9, 2008. She made her reservations on June 25, 2008. She paid a 30 percent deposit and was not given a discount on the ski boat rental. (You select the ski boat. Make any other necessary assumptions).

2. On average, how far in advance do customers book their rentals?

3. Using Microsoft Excel's Subtotal function, identify the total discount in dollars given by rate code category.

4. On average, what is the daily, weekly, and monthly revenue by rental property category?

CASE DELIVERABLES

In order to satisfactorily complete this case, you should build the database and workbook as described in the case scenario and then prepare both written and oral presentations. Unless otherwise specified, submit the following deliverables to your professor.

1. A written report discussing any assumptions you have made about the case and the key elements of the case. Additionally, what features did you add to make the database and workbook more functional? User friendly? (Please note that these assumptions cannot violate any of the requirements specified above and must be approved by your professor.)

2. A printout of each worksheet.

3. A printout of the worksheet's formulas.

4. An electronic, working copy of your database that meets the criteria mentioned in the case scenario and specifications sections.

5. An electronic, working copy of your workbook that meets the criteria mentioned in the case scenario and specifications sections.

6. Results for each question posed above. (A memo to your instructor discussing these results should also be provided.)

7. As mentioned above, you should prepare an oral presentation. (Your instructor will establish the time allocated for your presentation.) You should use a presentation package and discuss the key features of your database and workbook. Also, discuss how the database and workbook are beneficial for Mr. Mackenzie. What additional information should be included in the database and workbook to make it more useful?

Index